Christmas 1993 —
For two of the best
cooks I know... Their
kitchen is always full of
love!

All our love,
Julie &
William

The Victory Garden Fish and Vegetable Cookbook

Also by Marian Morash

The Victory Garden Cookbook

Victory Garden Recipes: From the Garden to the Table (*Videobook*)

The Victory Garden Fish and Vegetable Cookbook

by

MARIAN MORASH

ALFRED A. KNOPF   NEW YORK   1993

THIS IS A BORZOI BOOK

PUBLISHED BY ALFRED A. KNOPF, INC.

A few recipes in this work were originally published

in Marian Morash's The Victory Garden Cookbook.

The Victory Garden™ is a trademark of the WGBH Educational Foundation.

Library of Congress Cataloging-in-Publication Data
Morash, Marian.
The victory garden fish and vegetable cookbook / by Marian
Morash. — 1st ed.
p.   cm.
Includes index.
ISBN 0-679-42362-1
1. Cookery (Vegetables)   2. Cookery (Fish)   I. Victory garden
(Television program)   II. Title.
TX801.M673   1993
641.6'5—dc20   92-44397
CIP

Manufactured in the United States of America

First Edition

Contents

ACKNOWLEDGMENTS   vii

INTRODUCTION   ix

BASIC INFORMATION ABOUT FISH AND SHELLFISH   xii

Appetizers and First Courses   2

Soups   52

Salads   78

Main Courses   110

Main Course Pasta and Rice Dishes   302

Vegetable Dishes   318

APPENDIXES:

    Basic Recipes   349

    Safety Guidelines   366

INDEX   369

Acknowledgments

PEOPLE OFTEN ASK ME where recipes come from—how are they created? They come from many sources, some from nothing more than notions and experimentation, some from recollections. I think of bowls of steaming clams fixed by my mother when I was a child . . . a luncheon of fiery red ripe tomatoes and lobster tail in an olive grove on the island of Corfu . . . a delicate sautéed fish at a waterfront restaurant on Lake Lucerne. Some recipes develop from ideas gleaned from dishes sampled in restaurants, some as adaptations of recipes in cookbooks past and present. As a cookbook author one can acknowledge the people who have helped with the actual work, but how does one acknowledge the network of inspiration that makes one want to cook? I think of those whose excitement about good food encourages me and who set standards of excellence for all of us—chefs like Jacques Pépin, Pierre Franey, Alice Waters, Wolfgang Puck, Jasper White, and Chris Schlesinger; authors like Julia Child, James Beard, Richard Olney, Evan Jones, Nina Simonds, and Barbara Kafka; and journalists such as Nancy Jenkins, Molly O'Neill, Sheryl Julian, Phyllis Hanes, and Phyllis Richmond, to mention just a few. My thanks for their knowledge.

I began my cooking career because of one person, Julia Child. Her investigative curiosity and enthusiasm about ingredients and techniques turned cooking into a stimulating experience rather than must-do drudgery. Working with her has been a challenge, an education, and always a total delight.

Chef Joe Hyde gave indispensable hands-on assistance and creative vision the first season of cooking at the Straight Wharf Restaurant. I worked with a wonderful kitchen staff at the restaurant. Finding time in a hectic restaurant schedule to devise new recipes was difficult, but we did it, thanks to my partner Susan Mayer and gifted cooks such as Linda Schwartz, Leslie Mackie, Sue Fisher, Liz Holland, Sara O'Neill, Gloria Paulsen, Meg DeGive, Alice Fleer, and Matt Lewis, among others. I thank Jock and Laine Gifford for having the faith that Susan and I could help them create a good restaurant, and Susan for being a true colleague in a venture I would never have undertaken alone. Life with our restaurant staff reminded me of the camaraderie and artistry I treasured backstage in the theater; the show never would go on without each person doing his or her job—people like Judy Janelli, a great waitress who could also cook, wash dishes, take reservations, or manage the front house, and maintain her joyous spirit at the same time.

The information in the boxes about fish and shellfish comes from my restaurant cooking experience, from talking to people in the field, and from reading. Among those who freely shared their knowledge with me were my friends Jon Rowley, of Fish Works in Seattle; Paul Zuccaro, of North Coast Seafoods in Boston; "clam man" Oscar Bunting, of Nantucket; Ed Schrauth, who ran the Straight Wharf Fish Store next to the restaurant; Walter Glidden, of historic Glidden's Seafood in Nantucket; charter boat captain Tom Mleczko; and marine biologist and writer Ken Kelly. Among my reading references were several government publications, including *Fishes of the Gulf of Maine*, by Henry B. Bigelow and William C. Schroeder; *Seafood Business* magazine and its Seafood Handbook series; Ian Dore's *Fresh Seafood: The Commercial Buyer's Guide; Seafood Nutrition,* by Joyce Nettleton; all the publications of the New England Fisheries Development Association; and *Fish: The Truth,* by Kenelm W. Coons. Ken Coons, the knowledgeable executive director of the association, kindly read the fish and shellfish information boxes in the book and gave me helpful notes about several points.

Part of our happy TV production crew: (left to right) Dick Holden, Hugh Kelly, Russ Morash, Marian, Kate Cohen, and Sue Fine.

I salute all the fishermen, farmers, purveyors, and culinary professionals who work so hard behind the scenes to bring such an abundance of good food to our restaurants and markets. My special thanks to those who so ably fulfilled my orders for this book and for our television shows: Carl Hutchins, of Wilson Farm; Marty Hagerty, of Fresh Pond Seafood; Walter Sadowski, of Straight Wharf Fish Store; Cheryl Williams, who presides over a tiny, impeccable fish market called The Fishmonger, adjacent to Alan Warner's Le Jardin, an oasis of fresh produce in Cambridge.

WGBH, the Boston public television station that produces "The Victory Garden," has always allowed me complete freedom of choice over recipes to demonstrate to viewers; I am grateful to the station and to viewers for their continued support for our cooking segments, and to our exceptionally talented production team.

Friends, both home cooks and professional cooks, have contributed some of their favorite recipes to this collection, and are gratefully acknowledged in recipe titles and headnotes. They are Acacio Afonseca, Marilyn Benson and Debbie Goodman, Jim Burke, Helen Cohen, Ruth Daniels, Sue Fine, K. Dun Gifford, Gladys Gifford, Pam Gilpatrick, Olga Hamwey, Bess Hopkins, Johanne Killeen and George Germon, Michael McSweeny, Ann Marotto, Leah and Willie Mason, Judy Miller, Naomi Morash, Gladys Porter, Michael Reddington, Holly Safford, Thekla and Richard Sanford, Kep Sweeney, Eugenie Voorhees, Helga Westphal, Claude Williams.

It is essential to me to have a very patient and experienced editor. Judith Jones was always accessible for advice, countenanced many delays, and yet tactfully reminded me, with gentle persuasion, that I must find time to finish the project. I am grateful for her encouragement and conviction about the book. Donald Cutler, along with his assistant Marion Hellthaler, helped me finish. As a literary agent, Don negotiated the arrangements for the book; as a minister, he officiated at my daughter Vicki's wedding (just one of the events that interrupted the writing of the book); and as a friend, he helped me pull the manuscript together in the final stage. His own passion for good food allowed him to ask thoughtful questions and helped me to be more specific in recipe instructions. Richard Howard, assisted by John Thompson, took the photographs in unflappable good spirits on a tight schedule, arriving at my kitchen early every morning and managing to shoot twelve to fourteen illustrations a day, for which all of the food had to be cooked to order. Sue Fine, a professional cook who has joined our family cooking team for the television segments, and whose sunny temperament eases our work and makes it fun, helped to compose the photographs. Judy Cannon added her professional cooking talents for the photography sessions.

Indeed, my work as a cook is part of what is truly a family venture and therefore all the more satisfying. My daughters, Vicki Evarts and Kate Cohen, never fail me when I need their assistance in shopping, cooking, washing up, or food styling, whether for shooting a television segment or doing photography for this book. I thank Vicki, her husband Tom, and my dear grandchildren Sophie and Allie; Kate and her husband Adam, who waited to have their first child, Russell Jack, just long enough for me to finish the manuscript; and, saving the greatest debt and thanks for last, my husband Russ, who is also my producer, my director, and my most faithful supporter.

Introduction

MOST AMERICANS ARE COOKING very differently from the way they usually did even a generation ago. Meat is no longer the inevitable centerpiece of the dinner plate. We are all seeking lighter fare, but we want it to have just as good or maybe even more intense flavor than the diet it has replaced. More vegetables, more salads, more pasta and rice dishes, and more fish are the order of the day. We want meals that are fresh, quick to prepare, satisfying to eat, and good for our health and well-being.

Although many are turning to the bounty of the sea to provide protein as well as delectable flavor, I find that home cooks are sometimes puzzled about how to prepare fish, beyond simple poaching, broiling, or pan-frying; or they may be uncertain as to which cooking techniques are best for specific species of fish and shellfish. More often than not, they don't know much about which vegetables, herbs, and aromatics best enhance fish.

In both my professional and home cooking I have always paired seasonal fish and vegetables whenever possible. In the spring I combine baked shad and boiled asparagus. Summer's striped bass joins cucumber and dill in a main course salad. And a fall supper of Nantucket bay scallops with a purée of squash and apples is worth anticipating the rest of the year. The combinations that please me often feature contrasts such as the crunchiness of broccoli against the silky smoothness of perfectly cooked shrimp, or the bright green of fresh peas setting off the pale pink of salmon. We all watch our food budgets, and it is worth noting that while fresh fish and shellfish can be expensive, vegetables stretch seafood a little and moderate the cost.

Since I began to cook professionally in the 1970s, the range of fresh produce available to most home cooks has expanded dramatically. Home vegetable gardens have sprung up everywhere. Tiny roadside stands have grown into mega-markets with vast parking lots. Today, a walk through almost any supermarket reveals a giant fresh-produce section featuring everything from storage onions to edible cactus and lemongrass stalks. Clearly there is a new emphasis on preparing fresh vegetables, fruits, and herbs.

As this trend was developing in the early 1970s, vegetables entered my life in a dramatic way when my husband, Russell, a television director and producer, was bitten by the vegetable-garden bug. Before long our garden was encroaching on the lawn, and I was preparing mounds of fresh vegetables every night of the gardening season. Russ translated his new passion into the television series "Crockett's Victory Garden," with James Underwood Crockett, and Jim quickly inspired a whole generation into soil preparation and successful vegetable gardening. (Some years later the name changed to "The Victory Garden.") In 1977 I began to do cooking segments on the show, featuring recipes to demonstrate to viewer gardeners how to cook their harvest. The response was very positive, and demand for the recipes led to my first cookbook, *The Victory Garden Cookbook,* which was published in 1982.

I think I should say a word about how I became a devoted cook in the first place, since that seemed less than inevitable while I was growing up and yet has everything to do with the origins of this book. Although my father was a professional chef who could make puff pastry blindfolded, and my mother was a marvelous home cook, I studied to become a theatrical set designer and had little time for, or interest in, cooking. Then, following the convention of those days, when I married I gave up my short-lived career in theater to stay home and raise a family.

In the early 1960s, just as I was adjusting to the role of homemaker and mother, Russell began a cooking series, "The French Chef," with a new talent—Julia Child. Most weeks Russ would bring home food left over from the shoot. Imagine your spouse arriving home with a whole uncooked goose, stuffed with prunes that are in turn stuffed with *foie gras,* along with written cooking instructions from Julia. . . . Tuna casseroles began to give way at our house to dishes like rolled fillet of sole with a mousseline topping. Everyone we knew began to buy copper pans and balloon whisks, as the kitchens of the sixties turned into small laboratories for *coq au vin* and cheese soufflé. Cooking with friends became our favorite form of entertainment.

My enthusiasm for cooking had been inspired by Julia Child and by the abundant produce from our garden, but in 1975 it broadened in a most unexpected way, to include seafood dishes. Friends Jock and Laine Gifford asked Susan Mayer and me to join them in opening a summer restaurant on Nantucket Island. Susan and I had spent many weekends cooking together, but our first reaction was that Jock and Laine must have lost their senses: neither of us had had any restaurant experience. However, the Giffords said the kind of cooking they wanted for the restaurant was exactly the kind Susan and I were already doing at home. The restaurant would specialize in fresh fish and shellfish dishes—something no other restaurant on Nantucket was doing in those days—and fresh vegetables: impeccably fresh ingredients simply and lovingly prepared. Before we realized the magnitude of what we had taken on, Susan and I were meeting with Nantucket fishermen and visiting the island's three farms to reserve what we would need of the island's limited harvest of fresh vegetables and herbs.

When the Straight Wharf Restaurant opened in 1976 with its fish and shellfish menu (well, one beef entrée, for the patron who just wouldn't eat seafood), people thought that we were crazy, that there wouldn't be enough interest in such fare to keep the kitchen staff busy. A meal I had had in Paris made me reasonably confident that the prophets of failure were wrong. We had lunched at a tiny storefront restaurant across the Seine from the Île Saint-Louis. The owner

and chef, Gilbert Le Coze, a handsome young man from Brittany, did all the cooking, and his beautiful sister, Maguy, managed the dining room. The luncheon was a revelation. The first course, a delicate mound of embryonic eels that looked like small gray earthworms, took a bit of courage to try, but turned out to be delicious. It was followed by creamy white scallops served with their coral roe still attached, a dish suggesting to me that our standard baked-cod dinner had some formidable competition. Seven courses of seafood convinced me that the chef was a genius and that he had created the entire meal from ingredients much neglected in America. Some years later, Le Coze would move to New York City and open Le Bernardin, a restaurant devoted exclusively to fish and shellfish, and tough New York critics would give it lavish praise and their highest ratings. But back in 1976 the Straight Wharf Restaurant proved to be a success too, and patrons kept the dining room full and the waiting list long. Our combination of fresh fish and vegetables had struck a positive chord.

The story of the Straight Wharf Restaurant, where I cooked for eleven summers, is a single reflection of a nationwide trend. Fresh seafood has substantially increased its place in our diet. The days of the fish dinner on Friday—and even then as a kind of penance—are long gone. An astonishing array of fish and shellfish, both wild and commercially "farmed," has become available to every cook.

This book attempts to take the fear out of fish cookery. Cooking becomes a pleasure when you are at ease with your ingredients. Throughout the book you will find boxed information on the fish and shellfish used most extensively in the recipes. I think you will be delighted to discover how easy it is to expand your repertoire. The more you use fish, the more you will realize how adaptable it is. A delicate-looking fillet of flounder can be rolled, folded, or molded. A piece of salmon can be butterflied, sliced, or pounded. Still, fish and shellfish need to be cooked with care—not fussily, but attentively—to bring out their subtle tastes. Cooking time, especially, requires close attention. The pallid fish we remember from the past was frequently overcooked, but fish cooked to perfection always has an attractive appearance and texture as well as taste.

The fish I emphasize in this book are those readily available to me in New England markets and featured on menus I did at the Straight Wharf Restaurant. Viewers of "The Victory Garden" will recognize some of those fish and even some of the recipes, for

Marian showing a salmon to her granddaughters Alexandra and Sophie.

over the years I have frequently combined fish or shellfish and vegetables in my cooking segments, and viewer response has welcomed these dishes enthusiastically. I have suggested alternative fish or shellfish in most recipes, including "rediscovered" fish such as ocean perch and recent entries such as orange roughy, to enable you to make substitutions based on market availability, price, and personal preference.

The vegetables I emphasize are those we grow in the Victory Garden. I have tried not to repeat recipes from *The Victory Garden Cookbook,* but there are a few basic ones that I have carried over because they go so well with fish and you may not have access to my earlier book. However, if you do have a copy, by all means consult it for the vegetable information

boxes—much like the fish information boxes in this book—and for more vegetable recipe ideas to mix and match as you please.

This book is arranged by courses: appetizers, soups, salads, main course fish and vegetable dishes, main course pasta and rice dishes, and vegetable accompaniments. Many of the recipes can easily cross from one course to another. You might use an appetizer dish as a light supper; a hearty soup or salad as a main course; or small portions of a main course as the first course of an elegant dinner party.

I hope this book will give you the guidance and courage to plunge into fish and vegetable cookery, if you have not yet done so. Happy cooking, and to your good health.

Basic Information About Fish and Shellfish

I REMEMBER THAT WHEN we opened the Straight Wharf Restaurant in the mid-1970s, my local fish markets had only a narrow range of seafood: swordfish, cod, haddock, flounder, perhaps mackerel, occasionally salmon, oysters, clams, shrimp, and lobster—if there was a tank. As one went into the interior of the country, there was even less fresh fish or shellfish available than what I could find living on the Atlantic Coast. Now there are about 500 species of fish and shellfish commercially available in this country, and they come in a variety of forms: fresh, frozen, smoked, salted, marinated, breaded, and canned. As the range of seafood has expanded, so have the sources. Each of us is less dependent on wild fish caught in local waters than we used to be. In fact, much of the fish we eat is not wild at all, but has been raised using intensive growing techniques in ponds, raceways, and net pens. Farmed fish is fed a controlled diet just as cattle and poultry are fed to speed weight gain. Fish farming yields a marketable product of somewhat greater uniformity than wild fish does, but sometimes it has a blander flavor.

Regardless of where the fish you purchase in a market has been "harvested" (caught in the wild or taken from a farm), there is a long chain through which the fish must pass. Seafood, to be truly delicious, must be carefully handled each step of the way: it must be quickly bled and gutted, properly refrigerated or frozen, always carefully handled to prevent bruising, kept uniformly at the right temperature, defrosted properly if frozen, and, with some exceptions, never refrozen once defrosted. If you were to study the odyssey of a fish from its original source to your table, you would marvel at how frequently we do get high-quality fish and shellfish, given the number of opportunities for something to go awry.

In my effort to find the best fish I have gone to some of the fishermen noted for setting high standards for their products—for example, Bruce Gore of Seattle for his salmon or Jerry Knecht of Portland, Maine, for his "boxed" haddock and cod—and I can testify to the high quality of fish their careful attention has guaranteed; similarly, I have sought out exemplary wholesalers, such as Paul Zuccaro of North Coast Seafoods, whose fish has never disappointed me in all my years of dealing with him, and retailers such as the Berkowitz family in Boston whose establishments are immaculate and whose fish and shellfish are impeccable. The best advice I have to offer is to search for the most knowledgeable and well-run fish market you can find: it might be a department in a supermarket, or it might be an independent fish market. You may have to pay more for superior-quality fish because everyone along the line has taken more time and care, but the difference is small compared with the advantage in quality gained. I remember asking once where some scallops had come from, and the girl behind the counter said they were "fish that swim in the ocean"; and when I recently asked a supermarket fish manager why small striped bass displayed in the middle of the winter were labeled "fresh wild" when the local bass season was long over and the bass were obviously small farmed fish, he said it was an old sign. My advice to you is to avoid such markets. I want my fish market to love its product and to be very knowledgeable about it, and you should demand the same.

For cooking purposes, there are two kinds of fish: roundfish and flatfish, more or less distinguished by shape or configuration. Bass and cod are examples of roundfish; flatfish include sole, flounder, and halibut. Except for some ethnic markets, you will rarely find whole flatfish for sale in American fish markets; unlike many other fish markets around the world, our markets sell flatfish as fillets or, in the case of the larger flatfish such as halibut, as fillets or steaks. If you find that you can buy whole flatfish and wish to prepare it yourself, I recommend consulting *Fish: The Basics,* by Shirley King, a professional chef. Her book provides text and illustrations for preparing flatfish and all kinds of seafood.

A roundfish has a backbone that runs midway down the center of the fish, with a thick strip of flesh on each side. A line of bones extends upward from the backbone, and two rows of bones fan out from the bottom of the backbone forming a bone cage that encloses and protects the internal organs of the fish. Other small support bones extend into the flesh from the dorsal (the fin on top of the fish) and anal fins. You will find roundfish sold whole or as fillets and steaks in most American fish markets. See pages xiv–xv for instructions on preparing whole roundfish.

Buying: A whole roundfish is usually sold scaled and gutted with head, fins, and tail left on. The market term for a gutted whole fish is a "drawn" fish, and it may either be scaled or the scales may still be on. If the fish hasn't been gutted by the time it gets to the market, reject it, for it is those internal organs that deteriorate first and cause bacterial contamination and the breakdown of the flesh. If the scales remain on a drawn fish at the market, you might want to save yourself a messy job and ask the market to scale the fish before you take it home. Another market term for a whole fish is "dressed," meaning that it has been gutted and scaled, and that the head, tail, and fins have also been removed. About 50 percent of a drawn whole fish will be edible flesh, and about 65 percent of a dressed whole fish will be edible flesh. Smaller gutted and scaled fish with their heads and tails on may be marketed as already boned "pan dressed" fish; these fish are very handy for stuffing, since they have already been boned.

Whole Fish. Look at the fish. The skin should shine as if it had just been splashed with water; the sheen on

fish is a sign of freshness. The gills, when opened, should be meat-red in color, not gray or brown or white. The eyes should be bright and clear, not cloudy or sunken. Holes in the membrane of the belly flaps indicate "belly burn," which might mean the fish wasn't gutted quickly enough or properly cleaned out. *Touch* the fish. The flesh should be firm and resilient, springing back when you press it. Softness, or lack of resilience, indicates that the fish is old. Lift up the dorsal (top) fin; the membranes between the spinelike rays should be attached, not collapsed. *Smell* the fish *and* the market. The smell of fresh fish should be sweet and moist like a cucumber or like the moist sea air at the shore. The whole fish market should smell the same way. If the fish or the market smell "fishy," move on.

Steaks and Fillets. Steaks are cross-sectional slices, including skin and backbone, of roundfish and the thicker flatfish. Ordinarily steaks are cut ¾-inch to 1-inch thick, but you can ask to have a fish steaked thicker or thinner than that. About 85 percent of the steak will be edible flesh. Steaks of the largest roundfish, such as tuna and swordfish, are sold with the backbone removed, and everything but the skin is edible. The *center cut* is a giant steak, a large chunk of the thickest part of the fish, starting just behind the pectoral fin and ending where the body of the fish begins to narrow. Steaking a fish is the way the retailer gets the most possible sellable product from the fish. After dressing (scaling, gutting, and removing the head and tail of) a cod, for example, a fish retailer can steak out the rest of the fish and get a 68–75 percent yield. If he fillets the same fish, the yield will be 33–37 percent, depending on the cut of the fillets. Therefore, as a general rule, steaks should cost less per pound than fillets of the same fish.

Fillets are flesh cut lengthwise away from the backbone on either side of the fish. They can be marketed skinless or skin-on; fillets cut from roundfish such as haddock are often sold skin-on, but cusk fillets are often skinned because the skin of cusk is very tough. Roundfish fillets are cut in two ways: as a whole fillet with the pin bones in it, which you will have to remove, or as a "J" cut with the pin bones removed. A skinless "J"-cut fillet is 100 percent edible flesh. Flatfish can be filleted into two wide, flat fillets, one from the top and one from the bottom of the fish; or they can be filleted into four pieces, two narrow lengths from the top and two more from the bottom.

Be as careful buying steaks and fillets as in buying

whole fish, perhaps even more so, because you don't have the whole fish to evaluate—for which reason many fish lovers buy whole fish whenever they can. The flesh should be shiny (the wet look again) and translucent; you should have the sense of looking "into" the flesh. Flesh that is opaque may be edible, but it won't be top quality. Red areas, or splotching, indicate bruising, and the flesh may still be edible, but it will soften and "turn" more quickly than unbruised flesh. Avoid any pieces of fish that are lackluster and yellowing. The flesh should feel firm and look cohesive; separations in the flesh are a sign of aging. Once again, smell for freshness. You should be able to close your eyes and not know you are smelling fish. I avoid buying fish in markets where the fish sits on cardboard trays tightly sealed in plastic wrap. I've had some bad experiences when I unwrapped such fish at home and found it to be smelly and yellow with age. I'm not saying that all such fish is bad, but I don't think the tight wrapping helps the fish, and the customer has no way to smell for freshness. If you have no other options, try the packaged fish, but by all means take it right back if it is not of top quality and complain fiercely. Your voice could bring change and better-quality fish to that market.

Frames. Fish frames (heads and backbones, or sometimes backbones without heads) are essential for good fish stock. Be sure that the frames you buy to make stock are just as fresh as a fillet or whole fish you would buy to cook; if not, your fish stock will taste "fishy." Cod and haddock frames are my favorites for fish stock. Make sure the gills are bright-colored to indicate freshness, but also make sure you remove the gills before cooking the frames; the gills of even very fresh fish frames will give stock a bitter, off flavor.

Storage: Once you accept a purchase of fish from your fish market, you must take the very best care of it so that it does not lose quality between the market and your table. If I set out to pick up fish or shellfish at a local market and know that I will have other stops before coming home to refrigerate it, I take a cooler of ice with me in the car to store the seafood in during transit. There is nothing that can harm your catch faster than lack of, or improper, refrigeration. Once home, I immediately store the fresh seafood in the refrigerator. I store whole fish and fish fillets and steaks wrapped loosely in butcher's paper or waxed paper, or loosely covered in a nonaluminum-lined pan, so that air can circulate around the flesh. The package sits on bags or packs of ice and is also topped with bags or packs of ice. Be sure that no water from the melting ice comes in contact with the fish, because it will cause the flesh to soften quickly. You will find more specific storage suggestions scattered throughout this book in the specific boxes of information about various shellfish and fish, including some guidelines concerning how long you can store fish at home before cooking it; but my rule is to try to cook it the very same day I bring it home. Storage will never make it taste any better. Fresh fish is fresh fish.

Frozen Fish. As a rule, I buy and cook fresh fish, keeping in mind what is available from local waters at any given time of year and thus what is apt to be exceptionally fresh in the local markets. But there are some exceptions to this rule. Bruce Gore's West Coast salmon, for example, has been quickly gutted and flash-frozen at sea, and its quality can be higher than the quality of a fresh salmon that spent a long time on the boat or in the wholesale market before being offered to the customer.

"Freeze a fish as fast as you can, defrost it as slowly as you can" is the rule to follow in order to minimize cell damage in fish from the freezing and thawing processes. When I use frozen fish, I thaw it in the refrigerator over a period of 8–10 hours or more, but then I cook it promptly once it is thawed.

Freezing fresh fish in a home refrigerator has its drawbacks. Because home refrigerators lack the capacity to freeze quickly, cell damage is a likely result of slow freezing, and this, in turn, tends to ruin texture and increase "drip loss"—loss of the juices in which the flavor is concentrated. Freezing a prepared dish can work well in home refrigerators.

Shellfish. Each species of shellfish has its own characteristics that influence how you buy, store, and prepare it; consult the boxes of information scattered throughout this book that deal with specific kinds of shellfish.

Fish Preparation: To scale a whole roundfish: This is a messy job, best done outdoors on several layers of newspaper or on a large cutting board. Wetting down the fish makes the scaling easier. If you are dealing with a very large fish, place it on a large board and nail its tail to the board to keep the fish in the right position as you work. Holding the fish firmly by its tail and starting at the tail end, scrape against the scales with a dull knife blade or the back of a heavy knife or a fish scaler. Work with short, firm strokes from tail to head; turn the fish, nailing again if necessary, to give you access to all the scales. Don't neglect the belly and fin areas. Run your hand from the tail up to the head when you've finished; the skin should be smooth, with no sharp edges. Rinse the scaled fish well in cold water.

To gut a whole roundfish: The easiest method is to slice open the belly of the fish from just behind the gill openings at the head all the way to the vent, or anal, opening. Save the roe (two sacs of eggs) of female fish, if you wish, by cutting them carefully out of the body cavity. Pull out all of the internal organs and viscera, and discard. With a sharp knife, slit the blood pockets (membranes) that run down both sides of the backbone inside the fish. Rinse the cleaned cavity well with cold water. If you wish to remove the head, cut it off just behind the gills. You can gut a fish without slitting open the belly, but it's a little more complicated and there is probably no reason not to slit the belly unless you wish to stuff the fish whole or are planning a presentation in which the fish will look best without a belly slit. The alternative method is to cut out the gills and make the cut around the gills large enough to enable you to remove the guts of the fish through the gill openings. Using cold water, flush out the cavity thoroughly to make sure you have removed all of the internal organs.

To remove the gills from a whole roundfish: These accordionlike filters on each side of the back of the head should *always* be removed before the fish is cooked. In a smaller fish, you can just pull them out; in a larger fish, you will have to open the gill cover, cut the gill at the top and bottom with strong kitchen scissors, and pull out the gill. Rinse the area well to remove any bits of gill tissue.

To remove the fins from a whole roundfish: When I poach or bake a whole fish, I often leave the fins on both to make the fish look like a fish for presentation and to help hold the fish together during cooking. (The fins pull off very easily once the fish is cooked.) Some preparations, such as baking a whole fish in pastry, require a de-finned fish, however. To remove the dorsal fin on the back, or top, of the fish, cut down and under each side of the fin to make a "V"-shaped wedge, freeing the short bones that hold the fin to the fish. Get a good grip on the end of the fin toward the tail—use pliers, if you wish—and pull the fin out toward the fish's head. Follow the same procedure with the anal fin. Snip off the pectoral, or side, fins and the pelvic fins with kitchen scissors.

To skin a whole roundfish: Since the skin of a fish helps to hold the flesh together during cooking, about the only time you would want to skin a whole fish would be preliminary to wrapping the fish in pastry or vegetable leaves before cooking. Make a shallow cut just through the skin—not into the flesh—around the narrow body of the fish, just in front of the tail. Make a similar cut through the skin around the body of the fish at the head end, just behind the gills. Make a third shallow cut down the length of the center of the back to join the first two cuts. Slip your knife under the skin where the cut along the back meets the cut around the gills and gently work the knife along between the skin and flesh, cutting with one hand and pulling the skin away from the flesh with the other; continue until you have freed the skin on one side from the center of the back around to the belly of the fish. Cut the large piece of skin off along the belly line, turn the fish on its other side, and repeat the procedure to remove the other half of the skin.

To remove the head and tail of a whole fish: Place the fish on its side on a flat work surface. Cut straight down through the backbone just behind the gills with a heavy, sharp knife. If the bone is thick, use a rubber mallet—a plumber's mallet is perfect—to whack the back of the knife and drive the blade through the bone. To remove the tail, cut straight down through the fish and backbone at the base of the tail.

To steak a whole fish: Place the cleaned fish on its side on a flat work surface. With a heavy, sharp knife, begin slicing straight down through the fish at the end where the head was removed, making the slices as thick as you prefer but generally about ¾–1 inch thick, and using a rubber mallet, if necessary, to strike the back of the knife and drive the blade through the backbone. Continue the slicing of steaks down the body of the fish from the head end to the tail.

To fillet a whole fish: Place the fish on a flat work surface with its back toward you and the head end of the fish angled slightly away from you to the right. With a boning or filleting knife held at a slight diagonal, make a cut just behind the gills and the pectoral, or side, fin, cutting down through the skin and flesh until you reach the backbone; then turn the blade so that it is flat against the backbone, and with smooth, slicing motions, cut down the length of the fish to the tail, keeping the knife as close as you can to the backbone. You will cut through the thinner rib bones, which surround the belly cavity, and through the pin bones if the fish has any. When the knife reaches the base of the tail, cut through the skin to separate the fillet from the body of the fish. Lift the fillet off and set it aside. (If you are filleting a large fish, it is easier to make two separate cuts from the head to the tail end. After making the cut behind the gills and pectoral fin down to the backbone, withdraw the knife enough so that the tip of the knife extends into the fish just far enough to rest on the backbone. Cut down the length of the fish with the knife at that depth, just freeing the flesh from the backbone. Return the knife to the head end and make a second cut the length of the fish to separate the meat between the backbone and the belly, pulling the whole side, or fillet, up and away from the fish as you make the second cut.) Turn the fish over, still with its back toward you and with the head now angled slightly away to the left. Repeat the process to sever the whole fillet on the second side from the skeleton of the fish. Discard the skeleton frame (or keep the frame to make fish stock) and place the two fillets skin side down on the work surface. Remove the belly bones by slipping the knife under the edge of the layer of bones at the thicker end of the fillet and cutting under them until they lift off. Check the fillets for other small bones and remove any with tweezers or pliers or cut them out carefully with a knife.

To skin a fillet: Place the fish fillet skin side down on a flat work surface. Using a sharp, 8-inch knife, cut a small slit between the skin and flesh about 1 inch deep at the tail or narrower end of the fillet. This cut will enable you to grip the end of the skin. Holding the skin firmly, work the knife along away from you with the other hand, using a gentle sawing motion and angling the blade so that it is turned slightly into the flesh and doesn't cut through the skin. Work your way down the length of the fish, pulling the loosened skin toward you

as the knife moves in the opposite direction away from you. (See illustration on page 227.)

To remove pin bones: Run your fingers along the inner light side of the fish fillet with gentle pressure; you will feel any pin bones beneath the surface. Remove them by plucking them out with tweezers or needle-nose pliers; if the pin bones are large, make a cut on each side, angling under the pin bones to create a "V"-shaped wedge, and lift them out.

Cooking Fish and Shellfish: There is relatively little useful advice of a general nature to give as to how long to cook fish and shellfish. Cooking time and "readiness" depend on the freshness of the flesh, the size, the thickness and density of the flesh, and the degree of leanness or fattiness of the flesh. I give specific information about cooking time in each recipe, and trust from my own experience that as you cook more fish, "doneness" will become apparent to you from watching, touching, and testing the flesh—and by the aroma of the cooked fish.

Microwaving Fish and Shellfish: I'm an old-fashioned cook, and I use my microwave oven in a limited way. However, seafood can be cooked very successfully in a microwave oven, and I recommend Barbara Kafka's books, *Microwave Gourmet* and *Microwave Gourmet Healthstyle Cookbook.*

Health and Seafood—Benefits and Concerns: One of the principal benefits of fish and shellfish is that seafood is nutritionally rich. I recommend your consulting *Seafood Nutrition,* by Joyce Nettleton, for her authoritative discussion of the many healthful consequences of eating fish and shellfish. At the same time, we encounter writings that question the safety of seafood. I recommend that you read the Appendix on pages 366–368 dealing with the safety factors you should be informed and cautious about when consuming seafood.

The Victory Garden Fish and Vegetable Cookbook

Appetizers and First Courses

Dips for Crudités and Crackers

Crudités have been in and out of fashion over the years, but general concern about nutrition and diet has them right back in style now. Anyone with a vegetable garden or access to a good vegetable market can make a memorable cocktail buffet by serving an assembly of raw vegetables, dips or spreads, and toasts and crackers. From my own garden I use small asparagus, scallions, cucumbers, cauliflower and broccoli flowerets, small white turnips, baby summer squash, slices of larger squash, sweet peppers in several colors, halved Brussels sprouts, tomatoes, wedges of cabbage, and sliced kohlrabi. What a range of color, shape, texture, and taste! Next to trays of several different vegetables I put bowls holding a variety of dips made from different vegetables and fish, and baskets of bread sticks, pita bread triangles, tortilla chips, crackers, and our favorite *Anchovy Toasts*. To the dips that follow, I might well add *Olive Salad* (page 50) or *Raw Bar Relish Al Forno* (page 14). All of these can be made ahead. With small plates stacked near this splendid array of food, each guest can make a selection. For a more complete cocktail buffet, I might add marinated shrimp, grilled seafood, and some *Swiss Chard and Cheese Squares* (page 49). Believe me, no one goes away hungry!

Opposite: An ice-filled Louisiana Cajun "boat" makes the perfect raw bar for clams, oysters, shrimp, and sauces.

Anchovy Toasts

Even people who dislike anchovies often like these toasts. The anchovy butter can be spread on the bread immediately or made well in advance and chilled; if made in advance, allow the butter to soften slightly before spreading on the bread. I prefer pita bread for the toasts, but you can use thin slices of any firm-textured bread. Control the salty anchovy flavor simply by using more or fewer anchovies. These are such great nibblers that guests are apt to become thirsty; have plenty of refreshing drinks on hand.

ANCHOVY BUTTER

4–8 flat anchovies, to taste
¼ lb softened unsalted butter
1 tsp fresh lemon juice

Pita bread pockets

Chop the anchovies, place in a mixing bowl, and mash into a purée with a fork or mortar. Add the butter and lemon juice, and beat all together until smooth. Put the mixture in a small bowl and chill until just before serving. Soften slightly before using.

MAKES ½ CUP

Before serving, open each pita bread pocket and separate it into 2 single rounds of bread. Spread the

Anchovy Toasts (continued)

anchovy butter on the insides of the pieces of pita bread and cut them into triangles or other shapes of your choosing. Place the buttered pieces of bread on a baking sheet and run them under a preheated broiler until they are toasty.

Smoked Bluefish Pâté

Using smoked fish for bluefish pâté saves the step and time of poaching fresh bluefish (as is done in the recipe that follows), and it provides a distinctive smoky taste. Diners at the Straight Wharf Restaurant never stopped asking for this spread, brightened with red onions and green parsley. Ask for fillets of younger, smaller smoked bluefish to avoid a large amount of dark meat.

Alternative smoked fish: Salmon, haddock, sable, or almost any smoked fish will do, but be prepared to adjust the amount of fish used, depending on the smokiness of the fish flavor.

⅓ lb smoked bluefish
1 lb cream cheese, at room temperature
1½ cups chopped parsley
½ cup chopped red onions
¼ cup fresh lemon juice
Salt and freshly ground pepper

Carefully remove the skin, bones, and any dark flesh from the fish and flake it into small pieces. Put the cream cheese in a mixer bowl and beat to soften. Add the bluefish and mix well. Add the parsley, onions, and lemon juice, and beat all together. Season with salt and freshly ground pepper to taste. Pack into a serving dish and refrigerate until ready to serve. Serve within a few days with melba rounds or toasted thin rounds of French bread or sourdough baguettes.

MAKES 3–3½ CUPS

❖Add a few tablespoons yogurt or sour cream to lighten the mixture.

❖Add horseradish, mustard, or drops of hot pepper sauce, to taste, if desired.

❖Multiply the recipe as many times as you like. This is a delicious and economical spread for a large party.

❖Line a bowl or fish mold with plastic wrap, letting the wrap overhang the edges. Pack the smoked bluefish into the container, cover, and chill until firm. When ready to serve, lift the pâté out of the container by the edges of the plastic wrap, and turn onto a serving plate. Remove the wrap and decorate the top of the pâté with chopped parsley and chopped red onions, if you like.

Fresh Bluefish Pâté

When the Straight Wharf Restaurant opened, we wanted to offer diners a complimentary snack as they looked over the menu. The creamy fresh salmon spread I made first was delicious but costly, and the search was on for an alternative. Bluefish was the solution. It is inexpensive and makes up into a unique spread. Loads of parsley masks the dull putty color of the fish.

Alternative fish: amberjack, salmon, and white fish, such as cod, hake, cusk

½-lb bluefish fillet
3 oz cream cheese, at room temperature
2 Tb sour cream
¼ cup chopped onions
⅓ cup chopped parsley
2 Tb fresh lemon juice
Salt and freshly ground pepper
Hot pepper sauce

Remove the skin from the bluefish and place the fillet in a large skillet. Add water to barely cover, and bring to a boil. Reduce the heat, cover, and poach gently for 8 minutes or until cooked through. Drain and cool the fish. If you don't like the dark meat, remove it. Break the fish into large flakes, making sure that all the bones have been removed.

In a mixer, beat the cream cheese until softened. Beat the bluefish into the cream cheese. (Do not purée to very smooth; there should be some texture.) Add the sour cream, onions, parsley, lemon juice, ½ teaspoon of salt, several grindings of pepper, and a few drops of hot pepper sauce. Mix well and add more lemon juice and seasonings to taste. Pack the pâté into a small serving dish and refrigerate. Serve within 24 hours with round melba toasts.

MAKES 1⅓ CUPS, OR SERVES 4 FOR COCKTAILS

❖Add horseradish or Dijon-style mustard.

❖Use leftover broiled, grilled, or baked bluefish, removing any tough cooked edges first because they will not soften and blend in the mixer.

❖Multiply the recipe as much as necessary. (We used to make it with 20 pounds of bluefish and 9 pounds of cream cheese!) Put the fish in a large baking pan. Cover with boiling water, cover the pan with aluminum foil, and poach in a 400-degree oven for 20 minutes or until the fish is opaque. Proceed as above, increasing the other ingredients proportionally.

Brandade

Brandade is a specialty of provincial France, with both the regions of Provence and Languedoc taking the original credit for it. Wherever it began, brandade, with its unique flavor of salt cod combined with fragrant garlic and warm potatoes, bound together in a silky liaison with olive oil and a bit of cream, is irresistible.

1 lb salt cod
1 lb potatoes
1–2 finely minced cloves garlic
Salt
⅔ cup olive oil
⅓–½ cup heavy cream
Freshly ground pepper
2–3 Tb fresh lemon juice

Soak and poach the salt cod, as in *To Prepare Salt Cod* (page 139).

Boil or bake the potatoes until tender; peel them and, with a fork, break the flesh up in a bowl; set aside and keep warm. Mash the garlic into a purée with a little salt. Heat the oil and cream in separate saucepans.

Drain the warm poached cod, pat it dry, and flake it into a mixing bowl. (If you have prepared the cod in advance and it is cold, flake it into a saucepan and warm it, stirring, with 1–2 tablespoons of the oil. Then turn the fish into a mixing bowl.) Add the warm potatoes to the mixing bowl, along with the puréed garlic. Beat the mixture with an electric mixer, adding the warm oil and warm cream alternately, a bit at a time, until the mixture resembles

Brandade (continued)

fluffy whipped potatoes. The consistency should be
smooth and spreadable, but not runny. Season to taste
with salt, freshly ground pepper, and lemon juice.
Serve with toasted triangles of Syrian bread or with
bread triangles sautéed in olive oil.

MAKES ABOUT 4 CUPS

❖Make brandade ahead and reheat slowly over a
low heat, adding more warm oil or cream if needed.

❖If you have a food processor, combine the cod,
potatoes, and minced garlic in the work bowl and
process. Then with the processor on, gradually add
the oil and cream.

❖There are many variations to brandade. You can
omit the potatoes completely. You will get a stronger
mixture that is not quite as light in texture. You can
also use less potato, or slightly more oil and less
cream. Experiment.

❖Spread on toasts, top with grated cheese, and
broil lightly.

❖Garnish with green and black olives and red
onion slices.

❖Serve as a whipped potato garnish to a grilled fish
plate like *Grilled Fillet of Haddock with Herbs* (page
148).

❖Leftover cold brandade can be shaped into patties and sautéed.

❖Pass brandade to add as a topping for fish chowder.

❖Spread on an English muffin, heat under the
broiler, and top with a poached egg.

Eggplant Dip

Two 1-lb eggplants
1 tsp minced garlic, puréed with ¼ tsp salt
Juice of 1 lemon (about ¼ cup)
½ cup chopped fresh parsley
Salt and freshly ground pepper
Slices red onion (optional)

Preheat the broiler. Place the eggplants on a baking
sheet and broil 8–10 inches below the heat, turning
once or twice, for 30 minutes or until the skin is
lightly charred and the flesh has softened. Remove

from the broiler and let stand until cool enough to
handle. Cut the eggplants in half lengthwise and
remove most of the seeds. Scrape the flesh off the
skins into a sieve, discarding the skins. When excess
liquid has drained, place the eggplant flesh into a food
processor. Add the garlic and lemon juice, and purée
until smooth. Remove the eggplant purée to a bowl,
stir in the parsley, season with salt and freshly ground
pepper, cover, and chill. Serve with slices of red
onion, if you like.

MAKES ABOUT 2½ CUPS

Mediterranean Eggplant
and Red Pepper Dip

1–1¼-lb eggplant
2 red peppers
2 cloves garlic
1 tsp salt
¼ cup fresh lemon juice
2 Tb tomato paste
¼ cup grated onions
2 Tb chopped parsley
1 Tb chopped fresh basil or 1 tsp dried
1 tsp Aleppo hot pepper★ or hot pepper sauce
⅓ cup fruity olive oil
Salt and freshly ground pepper

★Aleppo hot pepper is a ground hot pepper available in Middle Eastern grocery stores and in
some other specialty markets.

Place the whole eggplant and the red peppers on a
baking sheet in a preheated 350-degree oven.
Remove the peppers when they have softened
(20–30 minutes) and the eggplant when it has softened (about 50 minutes). Split the peppers in half as
soon as they are cool enough to handle; remove the
seeds and white membrane and any loose skin. Cut
the flesh and remaining skin into thin strips and then
cut the strips into small pieces. Set aside.

Mince the garlic and purée it with the salt; set
aside. Whisk the lemon juice and tomato paste
together in a small bowl; set aside.

When the eggplant has been baked to tender,
removed from the oven, and cooled enough to handle,

cut it lengthwise into quarters. Pull off and discard the skin and place the flesh in a food processor. Add the garlic-salt purée and process the mixture with an on-off motion so that it remains somewhat lumpy. (Alternatively, you can mash this mixture with a fork.)

Remove the eggplant purée to a bowl and stir in the lemon-tomato mixture, the peppers, onions, parsley, basil, Aleppo hot pepper or hot pepper sauce to taste, and olive oil, and mix all together. Season, if desired, with more hot pepper or lemon juice or salt and pepper. Cover and chill.   MAKES ABOUT 3 CUPS

Chopped Egg and Fresh Dill Spread

This spread is similar to the one my friend Pam always served in conjunction with her lobster appetizer (page 12), and this one goes well with lobster, too.

      6 large hard-boiled eggs, peeled
      ½ cup chopped fresh dill
      ¼ cup mayonnaise
      ¼ cup sour cream
      ½ tsp Dijon-style mustard
      Fresh lemon juice
      Salt and freshly ground pepper

Finely chop the eggs, place them in a bowl, add the dill, and mix. In a small bowl, mix the mayonnaise, sour cream, mustard, and a squeeze or two of fresh lemon juice. Stir the mixture into the eggs and dill, season with salt and freshly ground pepper, cover, and chill.   MAKES ABOUT 2 CUPS

❖Flavor the mayonnaise and sour cream with a bit of anchovy paste.

Guacamole

Among the many available versions of guacamole, mine is very simple to make, but delicious. If I have any fresh salsa in the house, I use it in place of the tomato pulp.

      3 very ripe avocados
      2 Tb fresh lemon juice, more if desired
      ⅓ cup chopped scallions or red onions
      1 generous Tb chopped cilantro
      1 Tb chopped hot chili peppers
      ⅓ cup peeled, seeded, and chopped tomatoes
      Salt and freshly ground pepper
      Hot pepper sauce

Slice the avocados in half lengthwise, cutting down to the pit; twist the halves of each avocado in opposite directions to separate the pit from the flesh. Remove the hard skins with a paring knife. Place the avocado flesh and 2 tablespoons lemon juice in a bowl, and mash the avocado with a fork into a slightly chunky purée. Add the scallions or red onions, cilantro, hot chili peppers, and tomatoes, stir, and season with salt, freshly ground pepper, hot pepper sauce, and more lemon juice, if desired. If not serving immediately, keep the mixture from darkening by sealing the surface with plastic wrap right against the surface or by spreading a thin layer of mayonnaise, sour cream, or vegetable or olive oil over the top. Serve with tortilla chips and crudités.

MAKES 2–3 CUPS, DEPENDING ON
THE SIZE OF THE AVOCADOS

❖Spread guacamole on a warm tortilla, roll it up, and garnish with sour cream.
❖Add garlic purée.

Salsa

The versatility of this raw tomato relish spiced with hot pepper makes it a special favorite around our house. Salsa can be a dip, part of a salad, an ingredient of egg dishes, or an excellent garnish for hot or cold fish dishes. One of my daughters mixes salsa with boiled rice—a very nice accompaniment to grilled fish.

      1 lb ripe tomatoes
      ½ cup finely chopped scallions or onions
      1 tsp minced garlic (optional)
      1–2 Tb finely chopped mild to medium-hot
          chili peppers★
      ¼ cup chopped cilantro, parsley, or
          a combination of both

Salsa (continued)

1 tsp salt
Fresh lime juice
Hot pepper sauce (optional)

★The "heat" of this sauce depends on how hot the peppers are and how much pepper you use.

Bring a pot of water to a boil and have a bowl of ice water off to one side. Core the tomatoes and drop them into the boiling water just until their skins begin to split—about 6–10 seconds if they are fully ripe, a little longer if they are less ripe. Remove the tomatoes from the pot and immediately plunge them into the ice water to stop the cooking action. Drain the tomatoes and remove their skins, which should slip right off. Cut the tomatoes in half and squeeze out the seeds and juice. Finely chop the pulp. (You will have about 2 cups pulp.)

In a bowl, combine the tomato pulp with the scallions or onion, garlic if you are using it, chili peppers, cilantro or parsley, and salt. Season with lime juice and a few drops of hot pepper sauce, if you like.

MAKES ABOUT 2½ CUPS

❖Add finely chopped cucumbers or avocados or tomatillos.

❖Substitute fresh lemon juice or red wine vinegar for the lime juice. Add a bit of oil, if you like.

❖Leave the tomato skins on, if you like. Cut ripe tomatoes in half, squeeze out the seeds and juice, chop the pulp, and proceed as above.

❖*Ruth's Salsa and Cheese Dip:* My sister-in-law grates equal parts Cheddar cheese and Monterey Jack cheese and mixes the cheese with salsa to a consistency that is soft enough to be "dipped" but not runny. She adds lots of hot pepper sauce. It's simple and delicious.

Tamara Dip

Tamara is the roe, or eggs, of carp; you can purchase it by the jar in many supermarkets and in stores specializing in Middle Eastern foods. The slightly salty, smooth-textured character of this spread appeals greatly to me.

3 slices fresh white bread
½ cup tamara
1–2 Tb chopped onions
Juice of 2 lemons
1–1½ cups olive oil
Freshly ground pepper
Chopped parsley

Trim the crusts off the bread. Moisten the bread slices with cool water, then squeeze them dry. Place the bread, tamara, onions, lemon juice, and ¼ cup of the oil in a blender or food processor. Blend or process until well mixed. Very gradually add the remaining oil until the mixture has the consistency of a thick mayonnaise. Season with freshly ground pepper and more lemon juice, if you like. Sprinkle with parsley.

MAKES ABOUT 2 CUPS

Tapenade

I agree with Elizabeth David's observation that while tapenade was created by a chef in Marseille less than a hundred years ago, "it has a kind of ancient, powerful flavor about it, as if it were something that might perhaps have been eaten by the Romans." The name is derived from *tapeno,* the word in Provençal for the capers that flavor it, but the base is black olives. I love every one of the ingredients and how they blend together. A food processor is almost a must for this recipe.

1-lb jar Mediterranean-style black olives with
   pits★
One 2-oz tin flat anchovies
2 heaping Tb drained capers
Juice of 1 lemon
6 Tb fruity olive oil
Chopped parsley (optional)
Finely chopped red onions (optional)

★A 1-lb jar of olives in brine will yield about ¾ lb drained olives, or about 54 olives. If you purchase the olives in bulk, you will only need ¾ pound.

Drain the olives and remove the pits. (You will have about 1½ cups pitted olives.) Pat them dry with paper towels and put them in the bowl of a food processor fitted with the steel blade. Drain the anchovies (you will have about 15 anchovy fillets) and add them to the bowl, along with the capers and the lemon juice. Process the mixture to a purée, stopping the machine and pushing down any mixture left on the sides of the bowl as necessary. With the machine running, slowly add the olive oil to make a smoother emulsion. Place the tapenade in a bowl, cover, and chill until ready to serve. Top with a sprinkling of parsley or red onions or both, if you like.   MAKES ABOUT 1½ CUPS

❖If you use standard canned pitted black olives, you will need only 12 ounces olives because their texture is firmer than the Mediterranean-style olives. The flavor of the tapenade will not be as intense.

❖Tapenade is nice as a filling for scooped-out cherry tomatoes, or as a topping for halved hard-boiled eggs or for halved boiled or baked new potatoes.

Shrimp Dip with Cloves

Ground or finely chopped shrimp minced with seasoned softened butter, chilled in a crock, and served with crackers or rounds of toasted bread is a familiar old staple of cocktail hours. This softer, lighter dip is an adaptation of a clove-flavored lobster-butter spread that my friends Thekla and Richard Sanford serve as the perfect flavor complement to their delicious Sanford Chardonnay wine. Instead of butter, I

use the new "light" cream cheese. Since the shellfish is ground into little pieces, small, less expensive shrimp suit this recipe well; the precooked tiny shrimp, now available fresh or frozen, are ideal. A food processor simplifies preparation, but you could finely dice the shrimp by hand if you prefer.

> ½ lb tiny precooked shrimp★
> 6 oz softened cream cheese
> Juice of ½ lemon (optional)
> ⅛–¼ tsp ground cloves
> Salt and freshly ground pepper

> ★To prepare and cook raw shrimp see directions in the Shrimp Box, page 265.

Pat the shrimp dry, put them into the bowl of a food processor fitted with a steel blade, and process into small pieces. Add the cream cheese and the lemon juice if you are using it, and process to mix thoroughly. Add ⅛ teaspoon of the ground cloves and process again. Taste for seasoning and continue to add the remaining cloves and salt and freshly ground pepper to taste. You want the clove to flavor but not overpower the shrimp. Place the mixture in a serving bowl, cover, and chill until ready to serve. Serve topped with a grinding of black pepper.   MAKES ABOUT 1⅓ CUPS

❖Substitute cooked lobster or crab for the shrimp.

❖Make a butter spread using equal parts softened unsalted butter and cooked and diced shellfish, season as above, and serve on lightly toasted bread rounds.

Cold Appetizers and First Courses

Bluefish Escabeche

Escabeche is a Spanish term for fish cooked quickly in oil, then steeped in a flavored marinade and served cold. Although we tend to think of this technique as Mediterranean and Latin American, cooked-and-then-marinated fish is prepared throughout the world;

Scandinavians, for example, have been treating herring this way for centuries. Spanish and Provençal recipes often call for small fresh fish, such as anchovies, sardines, smelts, or mullet, but here I am using fillets of our local Nantucket bluefish. The marinade can be laced with vegetables, fruits, herbs, and spices of your choice. I have deliberately added colorful vegetables to make this piquant dish as pretty as it is tasty.

Bluefish Escabeche (continued)

Alternative fish: Other dark-fleshed fish, such as herring, mackerel, amberjack, or tuna; or light-fleshed fish, such as swordfish, bass, cod, or halibut. Also cleaned small whole fish, such as smelts, sardines, anchovies, mullet, or whiting.

2 lb bluefish fillets
6 Tb light olive oil
2 cups thinly sliced onions
2 cups thinly sliced red peppers
1 cup thinly sliced carrots
2 tsp minced garlic
1 cup red wine vinegar or cider vinegar
1 cup dry vermouth or white wine
2 sprigs fresh thyme
2 sprigs parsley
Bay leaf
¼ tsp salt
Freshly ground pepper
¼ tsp crushed red pepper flakes (optional)
Flour for dredging★
Lemon wedges (optional)

★I use instant-blending flour (such as Wondra Quick-Mixing Flour) for this dish.

Skin the bluefish, remove any bones, trim off the dark meat, and cut the fillets into portions of 5–6 ounces each. Set aside.

To make the marinade: In a sauté pan, heat 2 tablespoons of the olive oil, add the onions, and cook for 4–5 minutes or until the onions are wilted and golden. Add the red peppers and carrots, and cook for 3–4 minutes until they are softened slightly. Stir in the garlic and cook for 30 seconds. Add the vinegar, vermouth, thyme, parsley, bay leaf, salt, a few grindings of pepper, and the pepper flakes, if desired. Bring the mixture to a boil, boil for 1 minute, then reduce the heat and cook gently for 5 minutes. Remove from the heat and set aside.

In a sauté pan large enough to hold the fish in one layer (use two pans or cook in batches, if necessary), heat the remaining 4 tablespoons of oil. Dredge the pieces of fish in flour and shake to remove excess flour. Fry the fish pieces on each side for 3–4 minutes, or until they are lightly colored and just opaque at the center.

Spoon a thin layer of marinade into a glass dish or an enamel or stainless pan large enough to hold the fish in one layer. Place the fish pieces in the dish or pan and spoon the remaining marinade over the top. Allow the marinated fish to cool to room temperature, cover, and refrigerate for 12–24 hours. Serve cold or at room temperature, with lemon wedges and more olive oil, if you like.　SERVES 6–8

❖Use small fillets like "snapper" bluefish, which are young bluefish 6–8 inches long, or other small whole fillets, such as herring or mackerel. Score these fillets on the skinned side to prevent them from curling in the pan. Cook them for 2–3 minutes on each side and marinate as above.

❖Instead of dredging the fish in flour, make a "dusting" mixture of herbs or spices. Live dangerously and dust the fish with *Blackened Seasoning Mixture* (page 141).

❖Add other vegetables, such as chopped tomato pulp or thinly sliced zucchini.

❖For a stronger marinade, use more vinegar and less wine.

❖Use white wine when marinating white-fleshed fish.

❖*Escabeche Citron:* Prepare and cook the fish as above. In place of the vegetable marinade, make a citrus marinade. In a sauté pan, heat ¼ cup olive oil, add 2 cups sliced onions, and cook for 4–5 minutes. Add 1 cup orange juice and ½ cup fresh lemon juice, bring the mixture to a boil, reduce the heat, and simmer for 5 minutes. Slice 1 lemon into thin rounds and add to the onion mixture. Add 2 tablespoons drained capers. Heat everything together for 1 minute and pour over the fish in a glass dish or an enamel or stainless pan. Cool, cover, and refrigerate for 12–24 hours.

Chervil Lobster in Lettuce

Two of my good friends, Thekla and Richard Sanford, like to recommend specific dishes to complement the distinctive, award-winning wines from their Sanford Winery. Shirley Sarvis, a food-and-wine consultant, devised this recipe to accompany a Sanford Chardonnay. The shellfish, dressing, and lettuce can be prepared well before serving and assembled at the last minute.

Alternative shellfish: lump crabmeat, small North Sea shrimp

WHITE PEPPER DRESSING

⅜ tsp salt
¼ tsp freshly ground white pepper
1 Tb fresh lemon juice
⅓ cup heavy cream
2 Tb light olive oil
4 tsp finely minced fresh chervil

½ lb cooked lobster meat, cut into ¼-inch
    chunks
24 inner leaves Boston lettuce or endive
Fresh chervil, for garnish

To make the dressing: In a small bowl, combine the salt, pepper, lemon juice, and heavy cream. Beat the mixture with a whisk until foamy, about 30 seconds. Gradually beat in the olive oil. Fold in the minced chervil. Taste and season with more salt and pepper, if desired.

To assemble: Form the lettuce leaves into 2–2½-inch cups. Pour some of the dressing over the lobster and mix gently until the lobster is well coated. Add more dressing as necessary. Pile the dressed lobster high into the lettuce cups or endive spears. Garnish each with a feather of chervil.   MAKES 24 APPETIZERS

Lobster Appetizer with Herb Mayonnaise

Good cooks are filed in my memory for their personalities and their signature dishes. Pam Gilpatric, a summer Nantucket friend, always served cocktails with a *Chopped Egg and Fresh Dill Spread* (page 7) and a beautiful plate of cold lobster, accompanied by mayonnaise flavored with fresh herbs from her garden. She laughed over the simplicity of these appetizers, but they were perfectly delicious.

HERB MAYONNAISE

3 Tb minced chives
3 Tb minced parsley
2 tsp minced fresh tarragon
1 sieved hard-boiled egg
2 Tb minced capers or dill pickles
1 tsp Dijon-style mustard
1 cup mayonnaise
Lemon juice
Salt and freshly ground pepper

To make the Herb Mayonnaise: Combine the chives, parsley, tarragon, egg, capers or dill pickles, mustard, and mayonnaise in a small bowl. Season to taste with lemon juice, salt, and freshly ground pepper. Cover and refrigerate until ready to serve.

MAKES ABOUT 1¼ CUPS

LOBSTER

Two 2-lb cooked lobsters (to steam lobsters, see page 186)
Sprigs of parsley
Lemon wedges

To prepare the lobster: Carefully remove the meat and roe, if any, from one of the lobsters, keeping the meat in big pieces and keeping the shell intact to decorate the serving plate.(Save the roe only if you wish to add it to the herb mayonnaise.) Use a strong pair of kitchen scissors to cut the underside of the claws, knuckles, tail, and body enough to remove the meat and roe. If you mar the upper side of the shell on the first attempt, you may try again on the second lobster; otherwise, remove the meat and any roe, if you wish, in large pieces from the second lobster without regard for the shell. Refrigerate the lobster meat in a covered dish, and wash and dry the lobster shell reserved for decoration. Push the lobster roe, if you wish to use it, through a fine sieve, add it to the herb mayonnaise, and refrigerate.

To serve: When ready, assemble the reserved lobster shell in the center of a large serving plate or tray. Put a jar of toothpicks at its head and a dish of herb mayonnaise at the end of each claw. Cut the lobster meat into generous bite-size pieces, and arrange them around the lobster shell. Garnish the plate with parsley and lemon wedges, and serve.

❖Inevitably there will be pieces of lobster too small to serve with toothpicks. Cut them into tiny pieces, mix with a bit of the herb mayonnaise (and some chopped celery, if you like), and serve on melba toast rounds on a separate tray.
❖Add more lobster meat, according to the size of the party.
❖Buy 1 pound cooked lobster-tail meat and serve the lobster appetizer without the shell decoration.
❖Slice the tops off 2 tomatoes, hollow them out, and use the tomatoes as dishes to hold the mayonnaise.
❖Lighten the herb mayonnaise with 1–2 tablespoons sour cream or yogurt; or use ½ cup mayonnaise and ½ cup sour cream or yogurt.
❖In the herb mayonnaise, substitute finely minced fresh basil leaves for the chives, parsley, and tarragon.

Lobster and Avocado Vinaigrette

For a special dinner party, this beautifully composed light starter salad sets the smoothness of green-and-yellow avocado against the crunchier texture of pink-and-white lobster, separated by a tart red tomato relish. Buy cooked whole lobster tails or prepare your own (see *To cook spiny lobster tails,* page 187).

2 cups peeled, seeded, and diced tomatoes
6 Tb finely chopped shallots
1 tsp red wine vinegar
Salt and freshly ground pepper
1 lb cooked lobster-tail meat
2 small ripe avocados
2 Tb fresh lemon juice
2 Tb chopped parsley
2 Tb chopped watercress
¾ cup *Lemon Vinaigrette* (page 365)
Sprigs of watercress, for garnish

In a small bowl, combine the tomatoes, 2 tablespoons of the shallots, the vinegar, ¼ teaspoon salt and a few grindings of pepper, and fold together. Marinate for 10 minutes, then put the mixture into a sieve, drain, discard the juice, and refrigerate the tomato mixture until ready to serve.

Slice the lobster-tail meat diagonally into medallions, cover, and refrigerate until ready to serve.

Just before serving, peel and seed the avocados and slice them lengthwise into thin slices or wedges. Dip each piece in lemon juice to prevent darkening. Combine the chopped parsley and watercress. Add half of this mixture and 2–3 tablespoons of lemon vinaigrette to the tomato mixture, and stir gently.

To serve, arrange the avocado slices in an overlapping pattern on one side of each of 4 serving plates. Arrange the lobster medallions opposite the avocados in an overlapping line. Spoon the tomato mixture into the center. Drizzle the remaining vinaigrette over the avocado slices and the lobster medallions. Sprinkle the avocados with the rest of the shallots. Sprinkle the lobster with the remaining chopped watercress and parsley. Decorate with watercress sprigs.   SERVES 4

Mussels Vinaigrette

Chef Joe Hyde once told me always to serve mussels in their shell. He thought the shells were beautiful and the mussel meats naked-looking without them. I agree. This appetizer was a favorite at the Straight Wharf Restaurant, and with good reason: the mussels are nicely dressed in their shiny black shells and are flavored with a tangy vinaigrette, colorful red onions, and fresh parsley from the garden.

4 lb mussels
1 cup dry vermouth or white wine
1 cup water
4 sprigs parsley
¾ cup *Vinaigrette* (page 365)
¾ cup chopped red onion
⅓ cup roughly chopped parsley

Just before serving, scrub off any muck and seaweed clinging to the mussel shells and pull the beards off the mussels. Give each mussel a twist between your fingers and thumb to identify any "false" mussel shells filled with sand or mud; discard these and any open shells that do not close when touched.

In a large, nonaluminum-lined pot, bring the vermouth, water, and parsley sprigs to a boil. Boil about 3 minutes to reduce slightly and evaporate the alcohol. Add the mussels, cover, bring to a boil, and steam the mussels over high heat. Shake the pot once or twice to distribute the mussels evenly. As soon as the shells open, in about 5 minutes, lift the mussels out of the pot with a large slotted spoon and place them in a wide, shallow bowl. Discard any mussels that have not opened.

Pour the broth slowly and carefully out of the pot into a bowl, leaving behind and discarding the last bit containing any sand from the mussels, or strain the mussel broth through cheesecloth into a bowl. Combine ½ cup of the broth with ½ cup of the vinaigrette. Pour this mixture over the mussels, add the chopped onions, and toss to coat. Refrigerate for 2 hours, tossing occasionally. Bring the mussels to room temperature, toss with the chopped parsley and the remaining vinaigrette, if you like, and serve.   SERVES 4–6

Oysters with Mignonette Sauce

At the Straight Wharf Restaurant on Nantucket, we served Cotuit oysters with mignonette sauce every night. Occasionally someone would order them with cocktail sauce, but if we could persuade the diner to try the mignonette, the cocktail sauce would come right back to the kitchen untouched. This classic sauce is good with clams, or try pouring it over hot poached fish. And keep in mind how easy it is to grow shallots in your own garden and how fresh and firm they taste when cultivated at home.

Oysters with Mignonette Sauce (continued)

MIGNONETTE SAUCE

¾ cup red wine vinegar★
¼ cup finely chopped shallots
¼ cup finely chopped parsley
2 Tb coarsely ground pepper
Dash of salt

★It is really essential to use the very
best red wine vinegar you can find.

To make the Mignonette Sauce: Combine
the ingredients in a small bowl and let
stand for 20–30 minutes before serving, or
refrigerate until ready to serve.

MAKES ABOUT I CUP

OYSTERS

Freshly shucked oysters, 6 per person (see *To
shuck an oyster,* page 16)
Cracked ice
Sprigs of parsley (optional)
Lemon wedges (optional)

Scrub the oysters and shuck just before serving. (A
good fish market will open them for you, place the
top shells back on to protect the meat, and pack them
in a bed of ice. The oysters will keep nicely in a
refrigerator for a few hours.)

To serve: Spread a bed of cracked ice across the bottom of each serving plate. Arrange the opened oysters
on the edge of the ice. Pour a little mignonette sauce
into a small ramekin or bowl, and place it in the center of each plate. Garnish with parsley and lemon
wedges, if you like. Provide a spoon to scoop the
sauce onto the oysters.

❖Replace the mignonette sauce with a dollop of
caviar or whitefish roe marketed as golden caviar on
each oyster.
❖Raw shellfish table: Prepare oysters and littleneck or topneck clams on the half shell and place
them on a bed of ice. Place bowls of mignonette

sauce, *Cocktail Sauce* (page 21), and *Raw Bar Relish Al
Forno* (below), around the shellfish. For added ele-
gance, serve a tin of caviar in a bed of ice to one side.
Provide lightly buttered toasts. Guests can spoon different sauces or the caviar onto the shellfish, or spread
the caviar on the toasts as an accompaniment to the
oysters and clams.

❖*Raw Bar Relish Al Forno:* I have trouble getting
my husband to take me out to dinner, but he will
actually drive the 2½-hour round-trip to Providence,
Rhode Island, for us to dine at Al Forno Restaurant.
The owner-chefs, Johanne Killeen and George Germon, make the best grilled pizzas in the world,
among many other original dishes. Here is the very
zippy relish they serve with raw clams and oysters. It
is delicious on smoked salmon and toast also, and I
serve it as a topping for grilled fish.

2 finely minced large stalks celery
4 finely minced large scallions (dark green tops
discarded)
2 seeded and finely chopped jalapeño peppers
1½ cups finely chopped cilantro
Juice of 2 lemons
Pinch of kosher salt (optional)

In a small bowl, combine the celery, scallions, peppers, cilantro, and lemon juice. (You may wish to add
the jalapeño peppers a little at a time to your own
taste.) Let the mixture sit for 15 minutes so the flavors
can blend, then spoon it on top of clams or oysters on
the half shell or serve on the side. The relish keeps
well, covered, for about 3 days in the refrigerator.
Since shellfish have ample natural saltiness, or brini-
ness, you may not need the optional salt.

MAKES ABOUT I½ CUPS

Gravlaks (Gravlax)

Marinating raw salmon in a brine of salt, sugar, and
fresh dill—a Scandinavian specialty—makes a delicious
appetizer that is a nice substitute for smoked salmon.
The curing method for gravlaks produces a lighter,
more delicate flavor than smoked salmon has. You can
easily cure salmon at home to make gravlaks. For
equipment you will need a glass or stainless baking pan
continued on page 17

SPECIAL INFORMATION ABOUT

OYSTERS

I TREASURE M.F.K. Fisher's line, "R is for Oyster." It conveys the rule I grew up with: that one could safely eat raw oysters only in months whose names contained an "r" (therefore, not in May, June, July, or August). I never knew the actual reason, only that if you ate a raw oyster in the wrong month, you would drop dead. There were, in fact, two reasons for the rule. One was that unless refrigerated very carefully oysters would quickly spoil in warm weather. The lesser known reason was that oysters spawn in the summer months and, filled with eggs and sperm, are not at their best for eating. Commercial oyster farmers, to fill the marketing gap in the calendar, have now ingeniously developed "triploid" varieties of oysters that do not spawn and can be eaten enjoyably year-round. Fisher's memorable line is a reminder of how things were when I was growing up.

There are five sources of oysters for the American market; they are distinguished by a combination of species and areas where they are gathered or commercially grown.

1. *American or Eastern oysters* harvested from Prince Edward Island down the Atlantic Coast to the Gulf of Mexico. They are usually named for the harvest area. Some of the better known are Malpeques from Prince Edward Island, Wellfleets, Cotuits, and Chathams from Cape Cod, Blue Points from Long Island Sound, Chincoteagues and Kent Islands from Chesapeake Bay, and Apalachicolas from the Gulf of Mexico. Both wild and farmed oysters are available in the marketplace. Connecticut, Louisiana, and Washington are the major wild oyster–producing states. Oyster farming is well developed in the Pacific Northwest.

2. *Native West Coast oysters*, commonly called Olympias, tiny, delicate sweet oysters once almost destroyed by the pollution of beds and now available from a few oyster farms, but expensive.

3. *Pacific oysters*, farmed from northern California to British Columbia, are named for location of harvesting: Wescott Bay, Shoalwater Bay, Willapa Bay, Quilcene from Puget Sound, etc. They are the most heavily farmed oysters in the world, first raised from Japanese seed oysters imported in 1905.

4. *European flat oysters*, commonly referred to as Belons for Belon, France, one of many locations where they are harvested in Europe. These oysters are now farmed in the United States on both coasts.

5. *Oysters imported from other countries*, including Pacific oysters farmed in New Zealand.

In a classic case of "you are what you eat," oysters vary in taste and color, depending on what algae and minerals are in the gallons of water each one siphons through itself each day. Taste ranges from sweet Cotuits (my favorite) to briny metallic Belons to slightly astringent Chincoteagues, and so on. Variations in taste make it delightful to have a tasting with different varieties. The color of oyster flesh is usually creamy, but it can range from pale tan to green-gray.

Buying: Check to make sure the oysters come from an approved and licensed source. Do not hesitate to ask the market to see the shipment tag, which will show the source and government approval. Always buy raw shellfish from the most reputable dealer. Live oysters in the shell should be tightly closed. Reject any that are open and do not close tightly when tapped. Discard any that sound hollow when tapped; they might be dead. The oysters should smell briny and fresh, without strong odor. Reject any with slimy shells

OYSTERS

Oysters (continued)

or that smell of sulfur. Buy single oysters; avoid clustered oysters that are harder to open and may be less plump than single oysters. Already shucked oysters packed in containers should look firm and plump, covered in their own juices that are clear, not cloudy.

Storage: Although some dealers say they will keep longer, especially in the winter, it is a safer average to say that oysters will keep 1–2 weeks after harvesting under perfect conditions—cool and damp. Refrigerate them at a temperature of 35–40 degrees, making sure that the flat side is up so that the oyster sits in its juices. If possible, keep oysters on a bed of ice, but not covered by ice; change the melting ice as necessary so that the oysters do not sit in water. Cover them with damp burlap or other loose cloth so that they have circulating air to breathe but have dampness to keep them from drying out.

Shucked oysters can be kept in their own juice in refrigerated containers sitting in ice, but make sure melting ice water cannot get into the container. I buy shucked oysters as close to the time of using them as I can, and don't keep them in the refrigerator longer than 2 days.

Preparation. To shuck an oyster: You can ask your fish market to open the oysters shortly before you will be using them, but you may have

to pay extra for the service. Opening them yourself is a skill worth mastering. Some open easily and others are frustrating, but practice makes perfect. Wear thick work gloves or protect the hand holding the oyster with a pot holder or folded towel. Use a short, stiff-bladed knife or an oyster knife. Scrub the oyster shells under cold running water. Plunge a few oysters at a time into a bowl of ice, which shocks them and makes them lose some grip on their shells. Hold a single oyster in the palm of the protected hand with the fat cup part of the shell down and the flat side up. Hold the hinged side of the shell facing away from your hand. Place the knife tip just to one side of the hinge, and forcibly wiggle it into the oyster between the top and bottom shells. Press down the knife, then twist it slightly to pop open the two shells. Slide the knife along the underside of the top shell to sever the adductor muscle, and remove the top shell. Now slide the knife under the oyster meat to loosen it from the bottom shell. If you are storing the

opened oysters for a short time before serving, set the oysters on the half shell on trays of rock salt to steady them, cover each oyster with a top shell, cover the trays loosely with plastic wrap, and refrigerate until serving time. (Hint: Julia Child likes to pry the oysters apart at the hinge with a "church key" bottle opener, then proceed as above.)

Yields: The grading system for live oysters is according to the number in a bushel. On the East Coast the minimum market size is 3 inches, and the classification is:
Standards, 200–250
Selects, 100–200
Extra large or extra selects, fewer than 100

❖The grading size for shucked oysters is according to the number of oyster meats per gallon:
Extra large, 160 or under
Large or extra selects,161–200
Mediums or selects, 201–300 (often used for frying)
Standards or small, 300–500
Very small, over 500

❖One pint shucked oysters will give you about 1 pound oyster meats. The count depends on the size of oyster and can vary considerably, but the equation still holds true: 1 pint = 1 pound. For serving raw oysters on the half shell, the standard serving is 6, but more if using very small oysters, such as Olympias. For oysters cooked with a topping or sauce, you might serve 4–5 per person.

Gravlaks (continued)

large enough to hold the fish, a board to place on top of the fish that will just fit inside the pan, and five pounds of weights; I use bricks, but heavy canned goods will do just as well. You will also need a little patience when making this dish because you have to let it cure for four days before serving. In the variations following the recipe, you will find how to make a smoky marinated salmon with Lapsang souchong tea leaves.

A word of caution: Since this is a curing technique and the salmon will not be cooked, the salmon should have been previously commercially frozen to avoid any risk of parasite infection.

Alternative fish: bluefish, thick striped bass fillets

Two 1½-lb boned salmon fillets, with skin on
5 Tb coarse salt
4 tsp sugar
2 bunches fresh dill
4 Tb cognac (optional)
Mustard-Dill Sauce (page 18)

Remove any bones from the fish with tweezers or needle-nose pliers. Combine the salt and sugar. Spread one-third of the fresh dill across the bottom of a glass or stainless baking dish large enough to hold the fish. Place the salmon fillets on the work surface, skin side down. Press two-thirds of the salt-sugar mixture evenly onto the flesh side of the fillets. Sprinkle with cognac, if desired. Spread half the remaining dill on 1 fillet, then place the second fillet, flesh side down, on top of the dill-covered fillet to make a sandwich. Rub the skin on the top fillet with half the remaining salt-sugar mixture, then turn the sandwich over and place the salted side down in the baking dish. Spread the remaining salt-sugar mixture across the skin of the top fillet and cover with the remaining dill.

Cover the salmon with plastic wrap, but do not seal the sides. Place a board or flat plate that will fit inside the pan on top of the fish, and place 5 pounds of weight—bricks or canned goods—on top of the board. Refrigerate for 4 days, turning the salmon over once each day and basting the fish with the accumulated juices in the pan.

To serve, remove the fillets from the pan, gently scrape off the dill with the dull side of a knife, and pat the fillets dry with paper towels. Set a fillet skin side down on a cutting board. Holding a long, flexible knife at a sharp diagonal, cut the salmon into thin slices. Serve with thin dark bread, lemon wedges, and Mustard-Dill Sauce. SERVES 8–10

❖The cured salmon with the marinade cleaned off and placed in a covered dish keeps for 7–10 days under refrigeration.

❖Cure just 1 fillet, if desired. Cut all amounts in half and treat as above, omitting the sandwiching instructions.

❖*Grilled Gravlaks:* Cut the gravlaks salmon into thick slices. Brush both sides of each side lightly with vegetable oil and grill over medium coals. Serve with *Mustard-Dill Sauce* (page 18) or *Horseradish Cream* (page 356).

❖*Lapsang Souchong Salmon:* The fragrance of smoky tea leaves offers a memorable alternative to the dill of the gravlaks. Omit the dill. Mix the coarse salt and sugar with 1 cup Lapsang souchong tea leaves. Rub the salmon with this mixture and proceed as above. Serve the tea leaf–marinated sliced salmon on toasts spread with *Ginger Butter* (page 353), and top with thinly sliced scallions. Decorate the serving plates with scallion flowers, if desired.

Garden Melon with Smoked Salmon, Smoked Ham, and Lime

When melons are ripe in our garden—be sure that the melon is very ripe—I make this appetizer, which is sweet, smoky, and tart all at the same time. Since you need only a little of each, treat yourself to the very best salmon and a good Vermont ham, or Black Forest or Westphalian ham, or a fine prosciutto.

Alternative fish: smoked sturgeon

1 medium-sized ripe cantaloupe or other ripe
    melon
8 paper-thin slices smoked salmon
8 paper-thin slices smoked ham
16 lime wedges

Cut the melon in half and scoop out the seeds. Cut each half into 4 equal crescent-shaped wedges and remove the rind from each piece. Put 1 piece of melon on its

Garden Melon with Smoked Salmon (continued)

side on each of 8 chilled serving plates. Artfully drape a slice of salmon and a slice of ham, slightly overlapping, over each piece of melon and garnish each serving with 2 lime wedges.   SERVES 8

❖Add a small fresh fig, cut through the center twice to form a star shape, to each serving.

Smoked Salmon with Toasts and Mustard-Dill Sauce

At the Four Seasons in New York on one memorable occasion, smoked salmon was brought to the table on a rolling cart, sliced before my eyes to gossamer thinness, and presented with warm toasts in a silver basket lined with white linen. What a treat!

Serve the salmon on large, flat plates, with the garnishes around the salmon; for the sauce, if possible, use tiny bowls—small Chinese sauce bowls would be perfect—that will also fit on the plates.

Alternative smoked fish: sturgeon

MUSTARD-DILL SAUCE

¼ cup Dijon-style mustard
1 tsp dry mustard
2 tsp sugar
2 Tb white or red wine vinegar
⅓ cup vegetable oil
¼ cup chopped fresh dill

To make the Mustard-Dill Sauce: In a bowl, whisk together the two mustards, the sugar, and vinegar. Gradually whisk in the oil in small amounts to make a thick emulsion. (Use a food processor or blender, if you like.) Stir in the chopped dill, cover, and refrigerate. Stir well again before using.

MAKES ¾ CUP

TOASTS, SALMON, AND GARNISH

9 slices thin, firm-textured white bread
½ lb very thinly sliced smoked salmon
12 lemon wedges
Sprigs of fresh dill
6 Tb drained capers
6 Tb chopped onions

Just before serving, trim the crusts off the bread and lightly toast it. Keep the toasts warm. Arrange equal portions of the salmon in the center of 6 large, flat serving plates. Decorate the salmon with 2 lemon wedges and a few sprigs of fresh dill. Place a small mound of capers and onions on each plate. Serve the mustard-dill sauce in small bowls that will fit on each plate or in a larger bowl to pass around the table. Slice the toasts in half diagonally and pass them in a napkin-lined basket, or serve 3 toasts on a small plate with each serving.   SERVES 6

❖*Smoked Salmon with Caviar:* Omit the mustard-dill sauce and the capers. Serve each plate of salmon with lemon wedges and toasts, and with a garnish of chopped onions and a generous dollop of caviar.

Poached Scallops with Celery

Poaching scallops takes just a few minutes and prepares them for a variety of recipes. In this dish I add crisp bits of celery to set off the incomparable smoothness of freshly poached scallops, and I dress the dish in a tart lemony vinaigrette as a way of accenting the sweetness of the scallops. Serve this appetizer at room temperature. It's a lovely way to begin a meal.

1 lb small sea or bay scallops
1 lemon
1 cup finely chopped celery and celery leaves
Lemon Vinaigrette (page 365)

Remove any tough bits of cartilage from the sides of the scallops, wipe off any bits of shell, and pat the scallops dry.

Bring a saucepan of water to a boil and squeeze the juice of ½ lemon into the boiling water. Drop the scallops into the water, reduce the heat, and simmer for 2–4 minutes, depending on the size of the scallops, or until the scallops have just turned opaque at the center. Drain the scallops immediately and pat off any excess water. Place the scallops in a bowl, squeeze the juice of the remaining ½ lemon over them, add the chopped celery and celery leaves, and toss. Dress the scallop mixture with the lemon vinaigrette to taste, toss again, and serve. SERVES 4 AS AN APPETIZER

❖Slice large sea scallops in half.

❖Poach the scallops, spoon into individual shells or au gratin dishes, coat them with a little cream sauce or tomato sauce, if you like, top with buttered bread crumbs or grated cheese, and run under the broiler just long enough to lightly brown the top.

❖*For salads:* Dress the poached scallops in a lemon or mustard vinaigrette or an herbal mayonnaise or rémoulade sauce. Serve dressed poached scallops, whole or sliced, on a bed of mixed greens. Use them in a combination fish salad or use them in place of tuna in *Salade Niçoise* (page 107).

❖*Main-Course Poached Scallops:* Use 1½ pounds scallops for 4 persons. Cook as above, toss in lemon juice, and spoon them over a favorite sauce. Try low-calorie *Tomato-Citrus Fondue* (page 364) or *Tomato Muffuletta Sauce* (page 212), or *Lemon Butter Sauce* (page 357) or *Mustard-Tarragon Butter Sauce* (page 235).

Scallops Ceviche

Ceviche is a classic Latin American marinated seafood dish in which raw shellfish or fish is "cooked," or "pickled," by marinating it in citrus juice until the seafood turns opaque. Do not be misled by the word "cooked," however; it is still raw seafood whose flesh has turned opaque by the action of the citrus marinade.

A traditional recipe in Peru is scallops ceviche—scallops marinated in lime juice, or lemon juice and lime juice, or a combination of other citrus juices. In certain areas fresh limes can be quite expensive, so by all means use a combination of lime and lemon juices or all lemon juice, if you wish. Ceviche can be as simple as just the marinated seafood with a dash of hot pepper sauce or flakes, or it can include all sorts of additional garnishes and seasonings, such as chopped

onions, peppers, tomatoes, hot chili peppers, coriander, or even coconut. See the variations that follow.

The amount of time to allow for marination depends on the size of the scallops or pieces of fish, the acidity of the marinade, and also your personal taste. A good rule of thumb is to marinate for at least 12 hours. The scallops are ready to eat when their flesh turns opaque all the way through. You can use a combination of scallops and sliced fish or all sliced fish. I use impeccably fresh scallops for ceviche, and to be safe, I use fish that has been previously commercially frozen, to avoid any problems with parasites. By the way, it is easier to slice the fish into thin strips when it is frozen.

Ceviche is an excellent cocktail food when accompanied by small toasts or toothpicks, or a refreshing first course or luncheon when served on a bed of salad greens.

Alternative shellfish: thinly sliced conch, abalone, poached shrimp, poached squid

Alternative fish: flounder, bass, halibut, snapper, Dover sole, orange roughy, ocean perch

1–1½ lb bay scallops or small sea scallops★
1 cup strained fresh lime juice, lemon juice, or
    a combination
Hot pepper sauce or hot pepper flakes
    (optional)
Salt and freshly ground pepper

★Large sea scallops can be cut into cross slices or smaller chunks.

In a glass or nonmetallic bowl or pan, combine the scallops, juice, and drops of hot pepper sauce or sprinkling of hot pepper flakes; mix well. Cover and refrigerate for 12 hours, turning once or twice for even marination. Drain the scallops, season with salt and freshly ground pepper, and serve.

❖*To add additional ingredients:* When the scallops have turned opaque, drain off the liquid and add any one or more of the following ingredients. Toss together, mix well, cover, and refrigerate for another 2 hours.
    Finely grated lime or lemon zest
    Finely chopped chives or scallions or thinly sliced
        red onions
    Finely chopped or julienned green or red peppers

Scallops Ceviche (continued)

Peeled, seeded, and chopped tomatoes
Finely chopped jalapeño chili peppers
Unsweetened grated coconut
Chopped fresh coriander
Thinly sliced sun-dried tomatoes softened in oil or
    water
Orange segments

❖Marinate the scallops in the citrus juice as above. Drain and combine with other shellfish, if desired, such as cooked mussels or squid, or poached shrimp, and toss with a *Lemon Vinaigrette* (page 365). Serve as part of a composed salad.

❖Drain the marinated scallops. Coat the scallops with *Herb Mayonnaise* (page 12) and serve as part of a composed salad.

❖Marinate the scallops in orange juice and lemon juice, drain, and garnish with finely chopped scallions and finely grated orange zest. Serve on shredded lettuce with mandarin orange sections.

❖Make a combination ceviche and use sliced scallops with fish cut into ¼-inch slices.

Celeriac "Rémoulade" with Shrimp

This is a delightful first course or luncheon dish with a mustard dressing that is lighter than a classic rémoulade. Since thin julienne or matchstick cut is essential for the somewhat tough raw flesh of celeriac, you will need the fine julienne disk of a food processor or a hand-operated julienne machine. You can serve the finished dish immediately, but the celeriac will become more tender if it marinates for a few hours in the refrigerator. It can be prepared up to two days in advance, and the shrimp can be cooked and refrigerated well before serving.

1½–2 lb whole celeriac
Fresh lemon juice or vinegar for acidulated
    water
2 Tb olive oil
2 Tb Dijon-style mustard
3 Tb mayonnaise
¾ cup sour cream

2–3 Tb milk or light cream
2 tsp chopped fresh tarragon (optional)
Salt and freshly ground pepper
4–5 jumbo (21–25 count) raw shrimp per person
Lemon Vinaigrette (page 365)
Crisp lettuce leaves
Sliced ripe tomatoes

To prepare the celeriac "rémoulade": With a sharp chef's knife, make a flat cut on both ends of the celeriac. Remove and discard the hairy outer dark skin, slicing down and around from top to bottom, as if removing the outer skin of an orange. Place the celeriac in a bowl and cover with water mixed with a little lemon juice or vinegar to prevent darkening. Set aside.

In a small bowl, beat the olive oil into the mustard with a whisk. Beat in the mayonnaise and the sour cream, and add enough milk or light cream so that the sauce is creamy. Stir in the tarragon, if you like.

Pat the reserved celeriac dry, cut it into chunks, and cut the chunks into very fine narrow strips—a julienne. You can attempt this by hand, but a julienne cutter is much easier. I like ⅛-inch square strips, but they can be larger. Immediately mix the celeriac with the mustard dressing, season with salt and freshly ground pepper, and marinate for 1 hour or longer.

MAKES 4–5 CUPS

Peel and devein the shrimp, leaving the last tail segment of shell on, if you prefer. Bring a large pot of water to a rolling boil, using enough water to cover the shrimp by at least 1 inch. Add 1 tablespoon salt for each 2 quarts water. Prepare a large bowl of ice water to one side to cool the shrimp immediately after they have cooked.

Drop the shrimp into the boiling water. Do not allow the water to return to a boil. Reduce the heat, if necessary, to keep the water at a gently simmer. The shrimp will be cooked in 1–2 minutes, or when the tails just curl and the shrimp turn pink. (To test, make an incision in 1 shrimp: the center should be white and turning opaque, no longer translucent.)

Lift the shrimp from the pot and immediately plunge them into the ice water to stop the cooking action. Drain well, place the shrimp in a large bowl, cover with bags of ice, and refrigerate.

When you are ready to serve, toss the shrimp with a bit of the lemon vinaigrette. Divide the celeriac and shrimp equally among the serving plates. Garnish with crisp lettuce leaves and slices of ripe tomato.

SERVES 6–8

❖Omit the vinaigrette and toss the shrimp with fresh lemon juice and chopped fresh tarragon.

❖*Celeriac Rémoulade:* Serve without the shrimp.

❖*Shrimp Rémoulade:* Omit the celeriac and toss the shrimp with the mustard–sour cream dressing. Add 1–2 tablespoons capers, chopped celery, or chopped sour pickle and chopped onions. Serve on a bed of lettuce, in an avocado half, or in a tomato shell.

Shrimp Cocktail

When you have impeccably fresh or fresh/frozen cooked shrimp, crisp lettuce, and a tasty cocktail sauce, shrimp cocktail is a winner. The prepared ingredients can wait in the refrigerator until a quick

assembly before serving. This is one recipe where I insist on using iceberg lettuce. I love its firm crunch with the smooth shrimp.

COCKTAIL SAUCE

1 cup chili sauce
2 Tb fresh lemon juice
2 tsp grated fresh horseradish or
   prepared horseradish
¼ tsp Worcestershire sauce
Dash of hot pepper sauce

To prepare the Cocktail Sauce: Combine the ingredients in a small bowl, adding more lemon juice or horseradish or hot pepper sauce to suit your taste. Cover and refrigerate until ready to use.

MAKES A GENEROUS CUP OF SAUCE

SHRIMP

1 lb jumbo (21–25 count) raw shrimp
Salt
Iceberg lettuce
Lemon wedges

To prepare the shrimp and lettuce: Peel and devein the shrimp, leaving the last tail-shell segment on, if you like. Bring a large pot of water to a rolling boil, using enough water to cover the shrimp by 1 inch. Add 1 tablespoon salt for each 2 quarts water. Prepare a large bowl of ice water and set aside. Drop the shrimp into the boiling water. The cold shrimp will cool the water slightly, so they will poach gently. Reduce heat, if necessary, to prevent the water from returning to a full boil. Leave the shrimp in the water for 1–2 minutes, or until the tails just curl and the shrimp turn pink. (To test, make an incision in 1 shrimp: raw shrimp are gray and translucent inside; cooked shrimp are white and opaque.) Lift the shrimp from the pot and immediately plunge them into the ice water to stop the cooking action. Drain the shrimp and store them in the refrigerator with bags of ice on top until ready to use.

Wash and dry the lettuce. Cut enough lettuce into ½-inch shreds to generously line the serving dishes. Refrigerate until ready to serve.

To assemble: Line chilled serving dishes (glass dishes

Shrimp Cocktail (continued)

are classic for shrimp cocktail) with shredded lettuce, making a small bed of lettuce in the center. Arrange 5–6 shrimp on the lettuce around the side of each dish. Spoon some cocktail sauce into the center and garnish with lemon wedges.　　　　　SERVES 4

❖For a simpler cocktail sauce, recommended by my friend Holly Safford, combine equal portions ketchup and prepared horseradish, and chill. Add lemon juice, if you like.

❖Individually frozen shrimp do not need to be thawed before cooking; adjust the time slightly. Bulk frozen shrimp should be thawed enough to separate before cooking.

❖Flavor the cooking water with sliced onions, lemon slices, and a bay leaf, or with prepared Shrimp Boil mix. Or poach the shrimp in beer. For 1–2 pounds shrimp use 4 cups light beer and enough added water to cover the shrimp. Flavor the beer broth with a bay leaf, ¼ teaspoon cayenne pepper, and 3 crushed cloves garlic. Bring the broth to a boil, and boil gently for 5 minutes. Drop in the shrimp and cook and chill as above.

Holly Safford's Guacamole Shrimp Tostadas

The advice from Holly's The Catered Affair in Boston is that every party has to have shrimp because everyone loves it. When clients wince at the cost of bowls of shrimp, Holly suggests these tostadas, which have such good flavor that no one notices that each serving uses only half a shrimp.

MARINADE

1 Tb chopped cilantro
2 Tb fresh lime juice
1 crushed clove garlic
1 tsp hot mustard
¼ tsp ground cumin
¼ tsp vegetable oil
½ tsp salt
¼ tsp freshly ground pepper

12 jumbo (21–25 count) raw shrimp

GUACAMOLE

2 ripe avocados
3 finely chopped serrano chili peppers or other fresh hot peppers
3 finely chopped sprigs cilantro (leaves only)
½ finely chopped medium onion
2 plum tomatoes, with skin on
Coarse salt

24 round corn tortilla chips
Salsa★
Sour cream
Cilantro leaves, for garnish (optional)

★Use a good prepared salsa or make *Salsa* (page 7).

To make the marinade: Combine all the ingredients in a large bowl and whisk until well mixed. Set aside.

Peel and devein the shrimp. Bring a pot of water sufficient to cover the shrimp by at least 1 inch to a rolling boil. Add 1 tablespoon of salt for each 2 quarts of water. Drop the shrimp into the boiling water. The cold shrimp will cool the water slightly, and they will poach in the hot water. If the water returns to a boil, reduce the heat until the water barely simmers. Cook the shrimp 1–2 minutes, or until the tails just curl and the flesh turns opaque. (To test, make an incision in 1 shrimp: raw shrimp will be gray and translucent; cooked shrimp will be white and opaque inside and pink on the outside.) Drain the shrimp and let them stand until cool enough to handle. Cut each shrimp in half lengthwise through its back. Combine the warm shrimp halves with the marinade and refrigerate for about 1 hour.

To make the guacamole: Peel and pit the avocados and mash them roughly with a fork or potato masher in a large bowl; they should not be perfectly smooth. Add the chili peppers, cilantro, and onion. Cut the tomatoes in small pieces and add them to the avocado mixture. Stir well and season with coarse salt. If not serving immediately, cover the surface of the mixture directly with plastic wrap.

To serve: On each tortilla chip place ½ teaspoon guacamole and ¼–½ teaspoon salsa; top with 1 marinated shrimp half and garnish with a small dollop of sour cream and cilantro leaf, if you like.

MAKES 24 APPETIZERS

Sue Fine's Marinated Shrimp

Good recipes circulate faster than proper credit can follow. Sue gave this recipe to me, but she said Tom Kantor gave it to her. Thank you, Tom. (Who gave it to Tom?) The shrimp should marinate for at least six hours before serving and should be turned occasionally in the marinade. This recipe can be doubled or tripled for a large crowd and can be prepared up to a day ahead.

    1 lb jumbo (21–25 count) raw shrimp
    1 thinly sliced medium-sized red onion
    2 lemons, cut into thin rounds
    ½ cup water

    ¼ cup white vinegar
    2 tsp salt
    2 tsp sugar
    1 tsp dry mustard
    1 Tb cracked peppercorns
    2 bay leaves
    ½ tsp minced fresh ginger
    ¼ cup fresh lemon juice
    ½ cup light vegetable or olive oil,
        or a combination

Bring a large pot of water to a rolling boil, using enough water to cover the shrimp by at least 1 inch. Add 1 tablespoon of salt for 2 quarts of water. Prepare a large bowl of ice water to one side to cool the shrimp immediately after they have cooked. Drop the shrimp

Sue Fine's Marinated Shrimp (continued)

into the boiling water. Do not allow the water to return to a boil. Reduce the heat, if necessary, to keep the water at a gentle simmer. The shrimp will be cooked in 1–3 minutes, or when the tails curl and the shrimp turn pink on the outside. (To test, make an incision in 1 shrimp: the center should be white and turning opaque, no longer translucent.) Lift the shrimp from the pot, immediately plunge them into the ice water to stop the cooking action and cool them, then drain. Peel and devein the shrimp, leaving the last tail segment on as a handle. Put the shrimp in a large bowl with the onion and lemon slices, cover, and refrigerate.

In a saucepan combine the water, vinegar, salt, sugar, mustard, peppercorns, bay leaves, and ginger, bring to a simmer, and cook gently for 5 minutes, then cool to room temperature. Whisk in the lemon juice and oil.

Pour the cooled marinade over the shrimp, onions, and lemon, toss well, cover, and refrigerate. Marinate for at least 6 hours. Serve with cocktail napkins to catch the drips.   MAKES APPROXIMATELY 24 SHRIMP

❖Add 1 tablespoon chopped cilantro and 1 finely minced small hot pepper.

Marinated Shrimp with Onions and Cilantro

In this and the preceding recipe you will find marinated shrimp with distinctively different flavors.

    2 lb peeled and deveined extra jumbo (21–25
        count) raw shrimp
    ¾–1 cup fresh lemon juice
    ¼ cup light olive oil
    1 halved and very thinly sliced large red onion
    1 thinly sliced lemon
    ¼ cup finely chopped cilantro or parsley
    1 Tb minced fresh oregano or 1 tsp dried
    Salt and freshly ground pepper

To poach the shrimp: Bring a large pot of water to a rolling boil, using enough water to cover the shrimp by at least 1 inch. Add 1 tablespoon salt for each 2 quarts water. Prepare a large bowl of ice water to one side.

Drop the shrimp into the boiling water. The cold shrimp will cool the water slightly, allowing the shrimp to poach. Let the water return to a simmer, but reduce the heat, if necessary, to keep the water from boiling again. Poach the shrimp until they turn pink on the outside and the tails just curl, about 1–2 minutes. (To test, cut into 1 shrimp. The flesh of raw shrimp is gray and translucent; that of cooked shrimp is white and opaque.) Lift the shrimp from the pot and immediately plunge them into the ice water to stop the cooking action, then drain.

Put the shrimp in a bowl, pour the lemon juice over them, toss, cover, and let them marinate for at least 1 hour, tossing occasionally. Then drain the shrimp, drizzle the olive oil over them, and add the onion, sliced lemon, cilantro or parsley, and oregano. Season with salt and freshly ground pepper, and toss to combine all the ingredients. Cover and refrigerate for 2–3 hours. Serve with toothpicks.

SERVES 15 IF EVERYONE EATS 3 SHRIMP,
BUT WHO STOPS AT 3?

❖Substitute fresh lime juice and lime slices for lemon, or use a combination.

Smoked Fish, Cucumber, and Caviar Canapés

Although I use smoked sturgeon, other smoked fish will serve just as well. This is a festive appetizer, and if you use American sturgeon caviar, you won't have to mortgage the house in order to afford this treat. You can prepare the canapés (minus the caviar) slightly ahead and chill them in the refrigerator. I cover them with plastic wrap or waxed paper and then lightly cover that with a wrung-out damp cloth to keep them fresh. Top the canapés with caviar just before serving.

Alternative smoked fish: salmon, sable, cod, bluefish

    8 slices square, thin black bread★
    Softened butter
    ½ lb thinly sliced smoked sturgeon
    1 pickling cucumber
    Small tin American sturgeon caviar (about ¼
        cup)

*I use imported square dark bread tightly packaged in cellophane found in the delicatessen section of the supermarket and often labeled Danish or German pumpernickel or rye bread. The loaf measures about 4 inches × 4 inches and contains about 15 thin slices.

Lightly butter the bread. Place a single layer of sturgeon on each slice, cutting and patching the slices of sturgeon as necessary to cover the bread evenly. Trim the edges of the bread with a sharp knife and then cut each slice into 4 squares.

Wash and dry the cucumber and trim off the ends. Remove the skin only if it is tough. Score the sides of the cucumber with a fork to make a decorative cut. Slice the cucumber into paper-thin slices and pat them dry. Place 1 cucumber slice on top of the smoked fish in the center of each bread square. Using a small fork, place about ⅓ teaspoon caviar on top of each slice of cucumber.　　MAKES 32 CANAPÉS

❖One pound of smoked fish will cover 15 slices of black bread and make 60 canapés.

❖Substitute peeled and chopped red peppers or chopped pimentos for the caviar. One 2½-ounce jar of pimentos will be enough for 60 canapés. Drain the pimentos, finely chop them, and gently squeeze or pat dry. Top each canapé with a small spoonful of pimento. The canapés can then be refrigerated a short while before serving.

❖Substitute thin slices of crisp and crunchy peeled raw kohlrabi for the cucumber.

❖Spread the bread with crème fraîche or sour cream in place of butter. If you make this substitution, assemble and serve the canapés immediately after spreading the bread.

Straight Wharf Fish Terrine

This terrine evolved through a number of versions and over the course of a few summers of restaurant cooking. Once I got it the way I wanted it, Julia Child honored the recipe by using it in her television series and book entitled *Julia Child and More Company*. The recipe reads long, but it is really quite simple, provided you have some essential equipment and good fresh fish and shell-fish for ingredients. You will need a nonaluminum-lined loaf pan; I use a 5 × 11-inch high-sided 3-quart enamel loaf pan. The extra height of the 3-quart pan allows for expansion of the terrine as it cooks; however, you can make this in a 2-quart enamel, glass, or stainless loaf pan, and the cooked terrine will rise slightly above the pan. Other essential equipment: a food processor, a high-sided roasting pan in which the terrine will sit to bake surrounded by a hot water bath, and a kettle of boiling water for the water bath. The terrine can be served hot or cold; it will keep for a few days in the refrigerator and is a lovely summer picnic dish. Remember to alert guests there is shellfish in the terrine in case they have allergies.

Alternative fish for the mousse: lean white-fleshed fish, such as halibut, tilefish, orange roughy, conger eel, monkfish

Alternative shellfish for the mousse: combination of scallops and shrimp

1 bunch watercress
2 Tb butter
⅓ cup finely chopped scallions or chives
¼ lb smoked salmon

FISH MOUSSE

1½ lb gray sole or other flounder
½ lb scallops
2 large eggs
2 cups lightly packed fresh bread crumbs
2–3 cups heavy cream
¼ cup fresh lemon juice
Salt and freshly ground pepper
Dash of nutmeg
2 Tb softened butter, to coat loaf pan

SOUR CREAM SAUCE

½ cup heavy cream
1 cup sour cream
1 tsp prepared horseradish
½ tsp Dijon-style mustard
Fresh lemon juice
Salt and freshly ground pepper
4 Tb cooking juices from terrine (optional)

Clean the watercress and remove any large tough stems. Finely chop the watercress. In a sauté pan, melt the butter, add the chopped watercress and scallions

Straight Wharf Fish Terrine (continued)

or chives, and stir together. Cook the mixture over medium heat for 1–2 minutes until it has wilted; remove the mixture to a bowl and set aside. Discard any bones from the smoked salmon, chop the fish into small pieces, and set aside.

To make the mousse: Remove any bones from the fish and cut the fish into 1–2-inch pieces. Cut any large scallops in half and combine the scallops and fish. Place half the combined fish and scallops into the bowl of a food processor fitted with a steel blade and purée the mixture. Remove the cover and add 1 of the eggs, 1 cup of the bread crumbs, 1 cup of the heavy cream, 2 tablespoons of the lemon juice, 1 teaspoon salt, a few grindings of pepper, and a dash of nutmeg. Purée for 30 seconds, remove the cover, scrape down the sides of the bowl with a rubber spatula, and process again until the mixture is smooth. Test a bit of the mousse with a spoon. It should hold its shape softly; if it seems too stiff, process in a bit more cream in a thin stream to get a smooth, soft-yet-firm consistency. Remove the purée to a bowl and repeat the procedure with the remaining half of the mousse ingredients. (If you have a processor with a very large bowl that will take the entire mixture at once, you can process the mousse in one batch.) Combine the two batches of mousse and season again with lemon juice and salt and freshly ground pepper, if desired. Since the seasonings will diminish as the fish mousse cooks and cools, the raw mousse should be slightly overseasoned. Take one-fifth of the mousse mixture, put it in a separate bowl, add the watercress mixture, and stir to make a green mousse. Take another fifth of the mousse mixture, place it in the food processor, add the chopped smoked salmon, process briefly to make a salmon-colored and salmon-flavored batch, and remove to another bowl.

To assemble the terrine: The terrine will have five layers of mousse. Using the softened butter, butter a 2–3-quart, nonaluminum-lined loaf pan. Cut pieces of waxed paper to fit the sides and bottom of the pan, butter the waxed paper, and line the pan to help in unmolding the cooked terrine later. Take one-third of the plain mousse mixture and spread it evenly on the bottom of the buttered-and-lined pan, smoothing it down with the back of a wet spoon. Then spread the green mixture in an even layer, smoothing it with a wet spoon. Take half the remaining plain mousse mixture to make the third layer. Use the salmon-colored mousse to make the fourth layer. The top layer will consist of the remaining plain mousse. Cut a piece of waxed paper to fit the top of the assembled terrine. Cut a piece of aluminum foil a little larger than the top of the loaf pan and tightly cover the pan with the foil, letting it come down over the edges but less than halfway down the outside of the pan. With a skewer, make a few small holes in the foil cover to enable steam to escape. Set the terrine in a high-sided roasting pan on a rack of a preheated 400-degree oven. Pull the rack out far enough to enable you to pour boiling water into the roasting pan. (The water should come about halfway up the sides of the loaf pan.) Carefully slide the rack back into the oven and bake for 1–1¼ hours. The terrine will be done when the top begins to rise above the pan and is springy to the light touch, and when the sides of the terrine shrink slightly from the sides of the pan and the terrine begins to smell good. If you want to be certain, use an instant thermometer and bake until the interior temperature reaches 160 degrees.

To make the sour cream sauce: Whip the heavy cream and fold it into a second bowl with sour cream in it. Mix in the horseradish and mustard, season with drops of lemon juice and salt and freshly ground pepper. Stir in the juices from the baked terrine, if desired.   MAKES ABOUT 2 CUPS

To serve the terrine hot: Leave the terrine in its water bath in a turned-off oven with the door ajar until ready to serve. Then remove the pan and wipe it down, remove the aluminum foil and waxed paper on top, and serve slices of the terrine directly from the loaf pan. Top with the sour cream sauce, which is a light and mild sauce that will not overpower the delicate flavor of the mousse, or with *White Butter Sauce* (page 114) or *Fresh Tomato Sauce* (page 364) or the *Roasted Red Pepper Purée* (page 360).

To serve cold: Remove the terrine from the water bath, remove the aluminum foil and waxed paper from the top, and let cool to room temperature. Drain off the accumulated juices and reserve for the sour cream sauce. Cover the cooled terrine again and refrigerate. Once the terrine is cold, it can be unmolded and either served immediately or wrapped and refrigerated again until ready to serve. To unmold, place a plate on top of the uncovered terrine and invert the pan. Remove the waxed paper and carefully pat the terrine dry with paper towels. Slice and serve with sour cream sauce, or wrap carefully in waxed paper, cover the waxed paper with aluminum foil, and store in the refrigerator.   SERVES 8–10

❖Add one or more minced fresh herbs, such as chives, chervil, tarragon, or parsley, to the sour cream sauce.

❖Add finely grated lemon rind to the sour cream sauce.

Swordfish Tonnato with Lemon Thyme

We needed to have some tasty appetizers at the restaurant that could be made ahead and served up without any fuss during our busy dinner hours. This one was inspired by the Italian *vitello tonnato*—cooked veal cloaked in a cold tuna sauce. Swordfish has just the right consistency for this dish. It is braised in the oven in liquid—not a usual treatment for swordfish, but this method of cooking keeps the fish moist and prevents it from drying out later, during its chill in the refrigerator.

The tonnato sauce can be made ahead and chilled, but better yet, prepare the entire dish ahead. It should chill for at least an hour before it is served, but because it keeps so beautifully in the refrigerator, you can make it up to two days before serving. Double or triple it, if you like; it's a perfect appetizer for a large crowd because you can set it up on individual plates, cover, refrigerate, and pull it out at serving time. The ideal plate is a small oblong, or use small, round plates. A food processor or blender is important in this preparation.

Alternative fish: tuna, shark, monkfish

2 lb swordfish steak, approximately ¾ inch thick
3–4 sprigs lemon thyme
1 bay leaf
1–1½ cups dry vermouth or white wine

Tonnato Sauce

2 Tb finely chopped lemon thyme leaves
1 Tb finely chopped parsley
4 Tb fresh lemon juice
1 Tb plus ¾ cup light olive oil or vegetable oil
1¼ cups mayonnaise
One 7-oz can tuna fish in oil

7 Tb drained capers
4 anchovies
Salt and freshly ground pepper

Place the swordfish, lemon thyme sprigs, and bay leaf in a glass or stainless baking pan. Pour in the vermouth or wine, cover the pan with aluminum foil, and bake in a preheated 400-degree oven for 15–20 minutes, or until the swordfish is just cooked through. Remove from the oven, uncover, and let the swordfish cool in the liquid.

To make the tonnato sauce: In a food processor or blender, purée the lemon thyme leaves, parsley, 1 tablespoon of the lemon juice, and 1 tablespoon of the olive oil. Mix this together with the mayonnaise in a large bowl and set aside. Drain the canned tuna and put it into the bowl of a food processor or blender. Add 3 tablespoons of the capers, the anchovies, and the remaining 3 tablespoons of lemon juice. Purée these together and gradually add the ¾ cup olive oil in a slow stream to make a smooth emulsion. Fold this tuna mixture into the mayonnaise and season to taste with salt and freshly ground pepper. Refrigerate, covered, until ready to use.   MAKES ABOUT 2½ CUPS

When the swordfish has cooled, remove it from its liquid to a cutting board. Cut the steak into strips about 2 inches wide. Then cut across and through each strip about every ⅜ of an inch to create pieces like dominoes.

On each of 8 serving plates, spoon 2–3 tablespoons of sauce to form a puddle. Distribute the swordfish dominoes evenly among the plates by arranging slightly overlapping slices, like a row of fallen dominoes, down the center of each plate. Spoon 1–2 tablespoons of the tonnato sauce down the center of the swordfish slices, forming a stripe of tonnato sauce on each serving. Cover each portion with plastic wrap, allowing enough wrap so that it does not press tightly on top of the sauce, and refrigerate.

When you are ready to serve, garnish each serving plate with a line of the remaining capers (4 tablespoons, or about ½ tablespoon per plate) down the stripe of sauce and decorate with additional sprigs of lemon thyme, if you like.   SERVES 8

❖If you don't have any lemon thyme, use thyme sprigs in the braising liquid to cook the swordfish and 1 tablespoon thyme in the tonnato sauce.

Tabbouleh: Plain or with Seafood

For a first course I serve scoops of tabbouleh in crisp lettuce-leaf "cups," accompanied by ripe sliced tomatoes. To make a main luncheon dish, I add seafood: tiny cooked North Sea shrimp or fresh crabmeat or smoked fish or *Mussels Vinaigrette* (page 13). All of them complement the distinctive taste and texture of the bulghur and its seasonings.

1 cup medium-grind bulghur
1½ cups water or enough to cover
1½ cups chopped parsley
¼ cup chopped mint
1 cup chopped scallions
½ cup olive oil
5 Tb fresh lemon juice, plus more to taste
Salt and freshly ground pepper
1 cup chopped pickling cucumbers, with skin on
1 cup chopped tomato pulp or chopped and seeded plum tomatoes
Crisp lettuce leaves

Cover the bulghur with water in a large bowl and let it soak for 30 minutes. Drain the bulghur and squeeze it in a towel until the kernels are fluffy and dry. Return the bulghur to the bowl and combine it with the parsley, mint, and scallions.

In a small bowl, beat the oil gradually into 5 tablespoons of the lemon juice and season to taste with salt and freshly ground pepper. Stir the dressing into the bulghur mixture and season to taste again, adding more lemon juice, if desired. Set aside to marinate for 30 minutes, then fold in the cucumbers and tomato pulp and set aside for 15 minutes.

Serve in lettuce-leaf cups.   SERVES 6–8

❖Substitute hollowed-out tomato shells for lettuce-leaf cups.

Hot Appetizers and First Courses

Artichokes with Oregano and Parsley

This artichoke dish comes from a friend, Marie Caratelli, who learned it from her grandmother. For a fancier version try the *Stuffed with Shrimp* variation.

4 large artichokes
1 lemon, cut in half
1–2 minced cloves garlic
¾ cup finely chopped parsley
3 Tb minced fresh oregano
½–1 tsp salt
¼ tsp freshly ground pepper, or more to taste
⅓ cup olive oil
1 cup dry vermouth or white wine
1 cup chicken broth
1 cup water

Trim the artichokes by cutting off their stems even with the bottom leaves so that the artichokes can stand upright. Place each artichoke on its side and, using a sharp knife, cut about ¾ inch off its top or crown. Pick off the bottom circle of very small leaves around the base of each artichoke. Using scissors, trim off the prickly tips of the leaves. Rub all the cut areas with a lemon half to prevent discoloration.

Place each artichoke on its side on a flat work surface, and pressing slightly with the palm of your hand, roll the artichoke enough to loosen and open its leaves, then stand it upright.

In a small bowl, mix together the garlic, parsley, oregano, salt, and pepper. Press the mixture down between the artichoke leaves, dividing it evenly among the artichokes.

Stand the artichokes close together in a nonaluminum pot that will just hold them, and drizzle the

Heat 3 tablespoons of olive oil in a sauté pan and sauté ¾ pound small peeled and deveined shrimp, tossing frequently, for 1–2 minutes until just pink and opaque. Season the shrimp with salt and freshly ground pepper and a sprinkling of lemon juice. Stuff the centers of the artichokes with the shrimp. Serve with the dipping juices, as above.   SERVES 4

Roasted Asparagus

For a perfect introduction to a fish dinner, try this light, refreshing appetizer. I always peel the asparagus because it makes the whole stalk as tender as the tips.

1½ lb asparagus
4 Tb melted butter
1 Tb fresh lemon juice
¼ cup freshly grated Parmesan cheese
Lemon wedges

Cut the very bottom end off each stalk of asparagus. Insert a small paring knife under the skin at the base and work it up toward the tip, making the cut shallower as the skin becomes thinner. About 2–3 inches from the tip, taper off the peel completely. (If you prefer, you may use a vegetable peeler.)

Take a saucepan or skillet wide enough to hold the spears lying down, fill it halfway with water, and bring to a boil. Plunge the spears into the water and boil for 1 minute; do not cook through. Immediately lift the asparagus spears from the pan and run them under cold water to stop the cooking action. Drain them and pat them dry. (If you wish to do this step in advance, spread the spears on a towel-lined tray, cover with waxed paper, and refrigerate until ready to roast.)

Place the asparagus in one layer in an ovenproof dish. Combine the melted butter and lemon juice, and pour over the asparagus. Sprinkle the grated cheese over all and bake in a preheated 500-degree oven for 8 minutes. Lift the asparagus with a wide spatula to serving plates and garnish each plate with a lemon wedge.   SERVES 4–6

oil over them. Add the vermouth, chicken broth, water, and half a lemon to the pot. Bring the liquid to a boil, reduce the heat, cover, and cook gently for 35–45 minutes, or until the artichokes are tender. (To test, pull out a leaf. It should detach easily, and the flesh at the base of the leaf should be tender.)

Lift the artichokes out of the liquid and place them on a warm plate. Cover them with a towel to keep them warm. Reduce the cooking juices to about 1 cup by boiling rapidly. Divide the reduced liquid into 4 sauce dishes to use as a dipping sauce. Serve with crusty bread to dunk into the sauce.   SERVES 4

❖ *Stuffed with Shrimp:* Cook the artichokes as above with the seasoning mixture pressed between the leaves. After lifting the artichokes out of the cooking liquid, pull out enough of the inner leaves of each so that you can scoop out the center fibrous choke with a tablespoon, being careful not to scoop out any of the tender heart meat underneath it. Set aside, covered with a cloth, to keep warm.

❖ You may omit the peeling of young asparagus, but unpeeled, larger asparagus can be a bit chewy.

❖ For a crunchy texture, do not boil the asparagus before baking it.

Roasted Asparagus (continued)

❖Brush the asparagus with olive oil and lemon juice instead of melted butter.

❖Omit the Parmesan cheese or substitute other grated cheeses.

Asparagus with a Yogurt Sauce

Nothing looks or tastes better to me at the beginning of a meal than asparagus. This appetizer is a version of the classic Asparagus with Hollandaise Sauce, but without using eggs or butter.

YOGURT SAUCE

1 clove garlic
¼ tsp salt
1 cup yogurt
1 Tb fresh lemon juice
1 Tb chopped lemon zest

ASPARAGUS

1½ lb asparagus
Fine strands of zest from 1 lemon
2 Tb finely chopped chives (optional)

To make the yogurt sauce: Finely chop the garlic and mash it in a small bowl with the salt to make a purée. Add the yogurt, lemon juice, and chopped lemon zest. Mix well, cover, and refrigerate until ready to serve.

To prepare the asparagus: Cut the very base end off each stalk. To peel off the tough outer skin, insert a small paring knife under the skin at the base and work it up toward the tip, making the cut shallower as the skin becomes thinner. About 2–3 inches below the tip, taper off the peel completely. (If you prefer, use a vegetable peeler.)

Take a saucepan or skillet wide enough to hold the spears lying down, fill it halfway with water, and bring the water to a boil. Drop in the asparagus spears and cook in gently boiling water until just tender, about 3–4 minutes. (To test, pierce 1 stalk with a sharp knife; the knife should slide in easily, but the spear should still be firm, not limp.) Lift the asparagus from the water and place on a flat rack to drain.

To serve, divide asparagus spears among the serving plates, with tips in the same direction, and spoon the yogurt sauce across the spears. Garnish the top of the sauce with strands of lemon zest and sprinkle with chives, if you like.   SERVES 4

❖*Asparagus Vinaigrette:* Prepare the asparagus as above. After lifting the spears from the cooking water, run them immediately under cold water, drain, and pat dry. Allow the asparagus to cool to room temperature, drizzle with *Lemon Vinaigrette* (page 365), and serve. Top with finely chopped hard-boiled eggs and chopped fresh herbs, if desired.

Smoked Cod Ramekins

Here is one way recipes get invented. My husband, Russell, returned from a "Victory Garden" filming trip to Ireland raving about a cod appetizer served him in a Dublin restaurant; he remembered that it was smoky and creamy and served in a crock. When I made up this recipe—inspired by nothing more than what I have recounted—he endorsed it heartily. You can prepare this dish well ahead of time, refrigerate it, and bake just before serving.

Alternative fish: finnan haddie, smoked bluefish, other smoked fish

¾ lb smoked cod
2–2½ cups milk
5 Tb butter
2 cups fresh bread crumbs
3 Tb flour
2 Tb dry sherry or dry vermouth
⅓ cup grated Swiss cheese
2 Tb freshly grated Parmesan cheese
¼ tsp Dijon-style mustard
2 Tb finely chopped parsley
Fresh lemon juice
Salt and freshly ground pepper

Rinse the cod under cold running water, drain or pat dry, and place in a skillet. Add enough milk to come at least halfway up the sides of the fish. Bring the milk to a simmer, turn the fish, cover, and remove from its liquid. When cool, remove the cod to a bowl, reserve 1½ cups of the poaching liquid, and break the cod into large flakes.

Wipe out the skillet and melt 2 tablespoons of the butter. Add the bread crumbs and cook, stirring, until they are golden brown. Set aside.

In a saucepan, heat the remaining 3 tablespoons of butter, stir in the flour, and cook, stirring, for 2–3 minutes. Remove from the heat, add the reserved poaching milk, and return to the heat, whisking the mixture until it is smooth. Bring the mixture to a boil, add the sherry or vermouth, reduce the heat, and simmer for about 8–10 minutes, stirring frequently, to thicken the sauce. Stir in the Swiss cheese, Parmesan cheese, mustard, and parsley. Season to taste with lemon juice, salt, and freshly ground pepper. Fold in the cod and cook for 2 minutes. Remove from the heat.

Butter six 6-ounce ramekins or small crocks and divide the cod mixture evenly among them. Top with the bread crumbs. Bake in a preheated 350-degree oven about 20 minutes or until hot and bubbly.   SERVES 6 AS AN APPETIZER

❖Pour the cod mixture into a single baking dish, top with the sautéed buttered bread crumbs, bake for 20 minutes, and serve as a main course.   SERVES 3–4

❖Add sliced sautéed mushrooms to the sauce.

❖Substitute fresh dill or other fresh herbs for the parsley.

❖Add sliced strips of ham or prosciutto.

Quahogs Stuffed with Aromatic Vegetables

When I was a kid, summer shore dinners always included stuffed quahogs, and they are still a great opener for a lobster feast. But I also serve them when we entertain more casually by offering a variety of small courses that guests sample throughout the evening. I like to serve the dishes one by one rather than putting everything out in a buffet at once, because I think each dish gets savored more when served by itself. The dishes always include some things that can be prepared ahead and then popped into the oven just before serving—such as these quahogs and perhaps *Roasted Asparagus* (page 29). I'll include one or two simple grilled or sautéed dishes,

such as *Grilled Zucchini Corfu* (page 50) or *White Beans with Shrimp and Basil* (page 48), and a salad or other cold dish.

The clams can be stuffed ahead of time and refrigerated, and the bread crumb topping can be prepared ahead and put on the clams just before baking. This recipe makes 16 stuffed quahogs. As part of a buffet or the kind of casual evening I have described, allow 1 per person; as an appetizer, allow 2 per person; and as a main course accompanied by a vegetable and salad, serve 3 or 4 per person. At my most expensive but very best fish market, 12 quahogs cost about $3.00, so this is an economical as well as a delicious recipe.

Twelve 3½–4-inch-wide quahog clams
1 loaf Italian bread
2 Tb olive oil
½ cup diced smoked ham
1 cup finely chopped onions
½ cup finely chopped celery
½ cup finely chopped red pepper
⅓ cup finely minced carrots
2–3 tsp chopped garlic
1 egg
¼ cup chopped parsley
1 Tb fresh thyme
1 Tb fresh tarragon
1 Tb fresh oregano (optional)
Hot pepper sauce
Freshly ground pepper
4 Tb butter
Lemon wedges

Scrub the clams well, discarding any open ones that do not close when handled; put them in a saucepan, add 1 cup water, cover, bring to a boil, and cook until the clams just open, about 8 minutes. Remove the clams with tongs to a colander to cool slightly, discarding any clams that have not opened when steamed. Pour the clam broth carefully into a bowl, leaving behind and discarding the last bit containing any sand from the clams; reserve the clear broth. When the clam meats are cool enough to handle, remove them from the shells, reserving the shells, and chop the meats into small dice. Cover and refrigerate. (You should have a generous 2 cups chopped clam meat.)

Twist the clam shells to separate the tops and bottoms. Select the 16 largest, most attractive half shells, remove any muscles attached to them, wash them

Quahogs Stuffed with Aromatic Vegetables (continued)

well or boil them to get them absolutely clean, and set aside; discard the remaining shells.

Cut off and discard the crust of the loaf of bread, and chop the loaf into big chunks. Put the bread into a food processor and process into chunky bread crumbs, or crumble by hand; you will need 5 cups of coarse bread crumbs. Spread the crumbs out on a baking sheet, place in a preheated 250-degree oven, and bake for 10–12 minutes to dry them out. Remove and set aside.

In a sauté pan, heat the olive oil, add the ham, and cook for 1–2 minutes. Stir in the onions, celery, peppers, and carrots, mix together, and cook for 4–5 minutes, stirring occasionally, until the vegetables are slightly tender. Stir in the garlic and cook for 30 seconds. Remove the pan from the heat and let cool slightly. (You will have 1¾–2 cups cooked ham and vegetables.)

In a large bowl, beat the egg and add the cooled vegetables, chopped clams, parsley, thyme, tarragon, and oregano (if you are using it). Mix all together, and gently fold in 4 cups of the bread crumbs and ¾ cup of the clam broth. Season the mixture with a few drops of hot pepper sauce and several grindings of black pepper. With a soupspoon, fill the 16 reserved shells with the stuffing, mounding it up in the center of the shells. Place the stuffed shells on a baking sheet. Cover with plastic wrap and refrigerate until ready to serve, if you wish.

Just before serving, crumble the remaining cup of bread crumbs to a medium texture either in a food processor or by hand. In a small sauté pan, heat 2 tablespoons of the butter, stir in the crumbs, and cook in the butter until they are lightly toasted. Place tiny bits of the remaining 2 tablespoons of butter on top of each stuffed clam. Divide the buttered bread crumbs over the clams and bake the clams in a preheated 400-degree oven for 15 minutes. Turn the oven to broil and place the clams under the broiler just long enough to lightly brown the bread crumbs. Serve immediately with lemon wedges.

SERVES 8 AS AN APPETIZER, 4 AS A MAIN COURSE

❖Top the clams with grated Parmesan or Jarlsberg cheese, either replacing the bread crumb topping or adding to it. Add the cheese just before broiling.

❖If larger quahog clams are not available, use 24–30 cherrystone clams to get the generous 2 cups of chopped clam meat needed for this recipe.

❖Experiment with other vegetable fillings. Try chopped summer squash, peppers, or tomatoes. Use diced linguiça sausage in place of smoked ham. Add Muenster cheese to the stuffing. Whatever you try, keep the cooked amount to about 2 cups, as above.

❖Experiment with other herbs. I love to use sage, but don't forget mint, basil, lovage, and cilantro. Or replace the herbs with spices such as curry.

❖Save any extra clam broth to freeze for use in fish soups and chowders. (You should get about 1⅓ cups broth from 12 quahogs and 2½ cups from 24 cherrystones.)

Chili Clams

The most challenging task of this zesty appetizer is opening the clams. See page 132 for instructions, or invite a guest who knows how, or get your fishmonger to open them. I prefer to open the clams just before cooking time, but you can open them a few hours earlier, put on the topping, cover them well, and refrigerate until ready to cook. The pickled peppers should be made a day or more in advance. If you don't have time to pickle peppers, use jarred pickled hot peppers from the market. The escargot butter needs to be chilled and can be made days ahead as well.

PICKLED PEPPERS

1 cup vinegar
2 cloves garlic
2 Tb sugar
1 tsp salt
6 small hot chili peppers, cut into small pieces

ESCARGOT BUTTER

½ lb softened butter
2 finely minced cloves garlic
2 Tb chopped shallots
2 Tb chopped parsley

CHILI CLAMS

3 strips bacon
24 littleneck clams (6 per person)
Lemon wedges (optional)

To make the pickled peppers: Combine the vinegar, garlic, sugar, and salt in a small pan, bring to a boil, and stir to dissolve the sugar. Pour this brine over the peppers in a small bowl, cool to room temperature, cover, and refrigerate for at least a day or longer until ready to use.

To make the escargot butter: Beat the ingredients together in a small bowl, cover, and refrigerate until ready to use.

To make the chili clams: Cut the bacon into ½-inch pieces. Open the clams, discarding the top shells, and place them in individual au gratin dishes or on pie pans or on baking sheets, spreading rock salt, if necessary, as a base to steady the clams and keep the juices from spilling out. Top each clam with a small spoonful of escargot butter, a piece of bacon, and a few pieces of hot chili peppers. Place under a preheated broiler until the bacon is crisp. Serve immediately with lemon wedges, if you like.   SERVES 4

❖Substitute topneck clams (6 per person) or cherrystone clams (4–5 per person).

❖Use prepared pickled hot peppers from the supermarket.

❖Use fresh hot chili peppers. Split the peppers, carefully remove the seeds and white membranes, chop the flesh into small pieces, and use as many pieces as you can stand!

Steamed Soft-Shell Clams (Steamers)

What childhood memories I have of sunny days along the Connecticut shore, jumping from one squirting hole in mucky sand to another, seeing who could dig up the most and the biggest soft-shell clams. After our haul we'd have to take a dip to wash off the salty mud, and after we had feasted on the clams, we had to take another dip to wash off the clam juice and melted butter.

If you have dug your own clams, make sure the area has been designated safe for clamming. You should soak them for 2 hours to allow them to release their sand. Always soak them in salt water (they will die in fresh water), either clean ocean water or fresh water with 3 tablespoons of salt for every 2 quarts of water. I have tried adding either cornmeal or vinegar to the water to encourage the clams to discharge their sand, and in my experience vinegar works better than cornmeal.

Soft-shell clams vary in size, but I allow a minimum of 12 per person. Russ usually brings home steamers that average 8 to a pound, so I plan on 1½ pounds per person, even more if the clams are to be a complete meal.

If you are buying clams, always buy them from a reputable merchant who knows exactly where his clams are coming from and that they have not been contaminated in any way. You can ask to see the shellfish tag that designates where they came from.

6 lb soft-shell clams
Salt
Vinegar
Melted butter with lemon juice (optional)

Gently scrub the clams. Discard any that do not close when handled.

If you have dug your own, cover them with natural salt water or a salt-water solution of 3 tablespoons salt and 1 tablespoon vinegar for every 2 quarts fresh water. Refrigerate the clams in this solution for 2 hours; then drain and rinse them, and discard any that do not close when handled.

In a pot large enough to hold the clams, put ½ inch to 1 inch of water, add the clams, cover, and bring the water to a boil. Steam the clams until they open, about 8-10 minutes. Discard any clams that do not open within 10-12 minutes.

Pile the clams into 4 big bowls. Carefully pour the broth left in the pot through cheesecloth into a container, leaving in the pot the last part of the broth that might contain sand. Pour some of the broth into 4 small bowls and serve the steamed clams with the broth, side bowls of melted butter with lemon juice, if you wish, and empty bowls in which to discard the shells.

There's a knack to eating steamed clams. Dislodge the clam from its shell by pulling the neck or loose siphon. Slip off and discard the black siphon skin; then hold the clam by the siphon, swirl it in the broth, dip it into melted butter, and enjoy.   SERVES 4

❖Some cooks swear that steamers are better with 2 cups beer added to the steaming water.

❖Gentrified cooks add dry vermouth or white wine to the steaming water.

❖Vegetarians add celery and/or onions to the steaming water.

Grilled Eggplant
with a Tapenade Topping

In the summertime we fire up the grill more evenings than not. When the main course is grilled fish and potato salad or steamed lobster and corn, I find this vegetable course is an excellent way to start the meal. Eggplant recipes often call for salting to draw out excess moisture, but I don't find it necessary for this recipe. The tapenade mixture is a chunkier version of the smooth black olive Provençal spread used on toasts or with crudités. All its ingredients can be chopped well ahead and quickly heated while the eggplant cooks.

GRILLED EGGPLANT

2 large eggplants
Olive oil

TAPENADE TOPPING

2 Tb olive oil
1 tsp finely chopped garlic
10 pitted and chopped Mediterranean-style
    black olives
2 Tb drained chopped capers
1 Tb chopped parsley
1–2 Tb chopped basil

To grill the eggplant: Partially or wholly peel the eggplants—I leave some very thin lengthwise strips of skin on for decoration—and cut them crosswise into ½-inch-thick slices or rounds. Brush both sides of the slices with oil and place them on a preheated medium-hot grill. Cook for 3–4 minutes or until lightly browned, keeping the grill covered with a lid or tent of aluminum foil. Turn the eggplant and grill the other side, covered, for 3–4 minutes or until lightly browned.

To prepare the tapenade topping: In a small saucepan, heat 2 tablespoons olive oil. Add the garlic and stir for 30 seconds. Add the olives and capers, cook gently until warmed through, then stir in the parsley and basil.

To serve: Arrange the eggplant slices on serving plates and top each slice with a spoonful of tapenade.

SERVES 4–6

❖ *To broil the eggplant:* Place the oiled eggplant slices on a baking sheet or broiler rack 6–8 inches below a preheated broiler. The distance is important to permit the eggplant to cook through as well as brown. Broil to brown on one side, then turn and broil until lightly browned on the other side.

❖ *Open-faced eggplant sandwiches:* Peel the eggplants and slice them *lengthwise* into ½-inch-thick slices. Brush the slices with oil, broil them until they're lightly browned on both sides, remove from the broiler, and spread 1 pound thinly sliced mozzarella cheese on top of the eggplant slices. Thinly slice 2 tomatoes, if you like, and spread the tomato slices over the cheese. Return the eggplant to the broiler close to the heat until the cheese is melted and browned. Remove to serving plates and top each sandwich with tapenade.

❖ Substitute *Salsa* (page 7) or *Olive Salad* (page 50) for the tapenade.

❖ Salt the eggplant to draw out excess liquid before cooking, if you like. Sprinkle the slices on both sides with salt and set aside to "weep" for 30 minutes. Wipe off the salt and pat the eggplant slices dry with paper towels before brushing with oil and cooking.

Leeks Vinaigrette
with a Mediterranean Topping

All I shall say about this dish is that it is a divine first course for virtually every meal I might prepare.

8 small to medium-sized leeks, about 1 inch
    thick
1 large or 2 medium-sized tomatoes
6 thin slices prosciutto, cut into thin strips
¼ cup pitted and chopped Mediterranean-style
    black olives
⅓ cup light olive oil
2 Tb fresh lemon juice
Grated zest of 2 lemons
1 tsp chopped fresh thyme
Salt and freshly ground pepper

Trim off the roots of the leeks. Remove any tough or withered outer leaves. Cut off and discard the green upper leaves, making the cut where the dark green begins to turn pale. Lay each leek on a cutting surface and cut a 1-inch slit down through the top end of the trimmed leek. Turn the leek a quarter turn and make a similar slit. Fold the cross-sectioned top leaves back a little and wash under running water to extract any sand.

Core the tomatoes and drop them into boiling water for 10 seconds, then lift them out with a slotted spoon and drop them into cold water to stop the cooking action. Remove their skins, slice them in half crosswise, squeeze out the seeds, and chop the pulp into ¼-inch dice. (You should have a generous ½ cup chopped tomato pulp.) Combine the tomato with the prosciutto strips and chopped olives, and set aside.

Bring 2 cups water to a boil in a skillet large enough to hold the leeks in one layer. Add the leeks, cover with a round of waxed paper, and then put on the lid. (The water should come halfway up the sides of the leeks.) Cook at a gentle boil for 10 minutes, or until the leeks are tender.

Drain the leeks, and when they are cool enough to handle, gently squeeze them to remove excess liquid. Place the leeks on a serving platter in a single-layer row, the root end of one next to the trimmed top end of the next one.

In a small bowl, gradually whisk the olive oil into the lemon juice, then stir in the lemon zest and thyme, and season to taste with salt and freshly ground pepper. Spoon the tomato topping across the center of the row of leeks. Drizzle the lemon vinaigrette over all and serve. SERVES 4

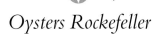

Mussels Marinière

This is the classic French recipe for mussels (see information about mussels, page 36). It is virtually a combination of appetizer and soup, so be sure to have plenty of crusty French bread at hand to soak up the juices.

    4 lb mussels
    4 Tb butter
    1–1½ cups chopped sweet onions (Spanish,
        Vidalia, Walla Walla, or Maui)
    1 cup dry vermouth or white wine
    4 sprigs parsley
    Juice of 1 lemon
    ½–1 cup heavy cream (optional)
    ⅓ cup chopped parsley

Just before cooking the mussels, scrub off any muck and seaweed clinging to their shells and pull off the beards. Give each mussel a twist between your fingers and thumb to identify any "false" mussels filled with sand; discard these and any open shells that do not close when handled.

In a nonaluminum-lined pot large enough to hold the mussels, melt the butter, add the onions, and stir them into the butter to cook for 1 minute. Add the vermouth, parsley sprigs, lemon juice, and the mussels. Shake the pot gently to mix all together. Cover, bring to a boil, and steam the mussels over high heat, shaking the pot occasionally. As soon as the shells have opened—in about 5 minutes—lift the mussels out of the pot with a slotted spoon, put them in a large bowl, then cover them with a towel to keep them warm. Discard any mussels that did not open during the steaming. Pour the broth slowly and carefully out of the pot into a saucepan, leaving behind and discarding the last bit containing the sand from the mussels. Bring the broth to a boil, reduce it slightly, add the cream (if you like), and cook just long enough to heat thoroughly.

Divide the mussels among warm serving bowls, ladle the broth over them, sprinkle with the chopped parsley, and serve with bread to soak up the juices.

SERVES 4–6

Oysters Rockefeller

The list of eighteen(!) ingredients in the original version of this famous dish created in Antoine's in New Orleans is still a secret, but it's no secret that oysters and spinach have a special affinity for each other. My version, with a mere twelve ingredients, is still darn good. This recipe is for six oysters, but you can multiply the ingredients as necessary to accommodate the number of diners and their passion for oysters. Consult page 16 for directions on shucking oysters or ask your fish market to shuck them, keeping the severed top shells in place to protect the oysters and keep them moist. Rock salt is handy to make a stable bed on a baking sheet for the oysters to sit on as they bake. Both the oysters and the spinach topping can be prepared in advance, so it takes only a few minutes to assemble and bake the dish just before serving.

continued on page 37

MUSSELS

I ate my first mussel in the early 1960s at a sidewalk café in Paris. Until then I had thought of mussels as fish bait, but my friend Gaston attacked his giant plate of steamed mussels with such gusto, using the shell of the one he had just eaten to scoop the meat out of the next one and nesting the pearly shells in neat rows around his plate, that I was quickly into the swing of eating the plump morsels. Returning home, we found mussels as unavailable in markets as they were popular throughout Europe. But shortly thereafter we were guests at chef Joe Hyde's beach house on Martha's Vineyard. Together we gathered buckets of mussels off nearby rocks. They were barnacle encrusted, and cleaning them looked to be a formidable task, but Joe dumped all the mussels into his power cement mixer, added some seawater, turned it on, and by the time we had toasted his ingenuity with some white wine and a few raw clams, the mussels were shiny clean. I've been a fan of mussels ever since; although there are many ways to serve them, they never taste better to me than when they are steamed in a bit of wine.

While there are other native species, such as the horse mussel, the domestic mussel we know and love is the Blue Mussel, 2–4 inches long, with a shell that is dark bluish-black on the outside

and pearl-colored on the inside. You may also find in your market imported farmed New Zealand Kiwis with emerald-green shells and meat distinguished in color by gender—orange for female, creamy for male; they may be marketed as mussels or as clams. Mussels live in clusters attached to rocks, pilings, and one another by a cluster of tough byssal threads coming out of the inner curve of the shell and commonly referred to as the beard. They are easy to gather wild simply by twisting and pulling them off their anchorage. Many areas do not require a license to gather mussels, but be sure to check with local shellfish authorities to learn what locations are designated as safe from pollution. I harvest wild mussels close to the water at low tide because the mussels that spend the most time in the water seem plumper to me. Wild mussels often harbor a live-in guest, the pea crab, a minute parasite-induced crab that is edible if you like the added

crunch but can be discarded once the mussel is cooked open; they also can harbor small rock pearls.

Buying: Wild mussels have a special flavor, but commercially farmed mussels are apt to be cleaner. You should feel free to ask your market where the mussels came from and when they were shipped. Farmed mussels have a thinner shell than wild mussels, and a higher ratio of meat to shell. Mussels are now sold in the shell, on the half shell, as mussel meats in containers, and as smoked meats. Depending on the environment in which they grew, the meat can range in color from pale cream to tan to orange.

Storage: Refrigerate mussels in a burlap bag or in a container that allows air circulation so that they can breathe; they can be stored in a vegetable drawer. Since mussels open and close and lose juices as they sit, serve as soon as possible after gathering or buying them. *Do not place them or store them in fresh water* where they will die. Mussel farmers suggest a shelf life of 7–10 days to their purveyors, but I never keep mussels at home more than 24 hours before cooking them.

Preparation: Check mussels for "mudders" filled with sandy mud instead of meat. They will feel heavier than the others. To test,

SPECIAL INFORMATION ABOUT

MUSSELS

hold the bottom shell of the mussel cupped in the fingers of one hand, and with your thumb try to slide the top shell off the bottom shell; a live mussel will tighten up, and a mudder will open to reveal its contents. Mussels will open naturally but should close tightly when handled or if tapped against a counter; discard mussels that do not respond appropriately. To purge mussels that have come from a sandy or muddy area of any sand or mud they have ingested, refrigerate them for at least 2 hours submersed in a salt-water mixture composed of 3 tablespoons salt and 1 tablespoon vinegar or 2 tablespoons cornmeal for each 2 quarts water. Change the water and additives once or twice during the purging so that the mussels do not exhaust the oxygen in the water and suffocate. Rinse the mussels under cold water and scrub the shells with a stiff brush to remove any muck or debris. Use a paring knife, if you wish, to scrape off barnacles. Just before cooking, grasp the beard of the mussel and pull hard to dislodge it and remove it entirely from the shell. The mussels store better with the beard intact, so I remove the beard only at the last minute before cooking. Mussels steam open in just a few minutes. They can be eaten immediately, or used in other cooked dishes, or chilled and eaten cold or in a salad.

Yields:

❖ A bushel of mussels 2¼–3 inches long = 1000 count
❖ A bushel of mussels 3–4 inches long = 650 count
❖ Depending on size, use about 20 mussels for a main course serving (about ¼ pound meat)
❖ A pound of live mussels = 15–20 mussels
❖ 4 pounds live mussels yield about 1 pound mussel meat

Oysters Rockefeller (continued)

6 large oysters, in the shell
2 Tb butter
⅓ cup minced scallions
⅓ cup minced celery
⅓ cup minced parsley
1–2 Tb minced fennel
1½ cups blanched chopped spinach
⅓ cup fresh bread crumbs
Hot pepper sauce
1 tsp Pernod
Salt and freshly ground pepper
¼ cup freshly grated Parmesan cheese

Shuck the oysters (see page 16). Place the top shells over the lower shells and set the oysters on a baking sheet lined with rock salt to stabilize the shells. Loosely cover the oysters with plastic wrap and refrigerate until ready to bake.

In a sauté pan, melt the butter, add the scallions, celery, parsley, and fennel, and stir and cook the vegetables until they are wilted. Add the spinach and cook the mixture for 4–5 minutes, or until the excess moisture in the pan has evaporated. Stir in the bread crumbs and mix well to bind the mixture together. Season with a few drops of hot pepper sauce, the Pernod, salt, and freshly ground pepper.

When you are ready to bake, remove and discard the top shells, distribute the cooked spinach mixture evenly over the oysters, sprinkle with the grated cheese, and bake in a preheated 450-degree oven for 8 minutes, or until the spinach topping is heated through.   SERVES 1 OR 2

❖ Add a bit of anchovy pâté or finely minced anchovies to the spinach mixture.

Onion and Anchovy Tart

Where there is any reasonable opportunity, I will add anchovies to a recipe—on pizza or in sandwiches or salads. Inspiration for this recipe comes from the French *pissaladière,* of which you will find dozens of

Onion and Anchovy Tart (continued)

versions in Europe. You can use the tart pastry I recommend or your favorite piecrust or, as my daughter does, spread the onion-and-anchovy filling on pizza dough. The onions should be cooked slowly and gently so that they braise down to a mellow color, with a silky perfume and delicious flavor. Salty anchovies and black olives will accent the virtues of the onions.

> *Tart Shell for a 10-Inch Tart* (page 362)
> 8 cups sliced Spanish onions
> ¼ cup olive oil
> 1 tsp chopped garlic
> ½ tsp sugar
> Salt and freshly ground pepper
> ½ cup grated Swiss cheese (optional)
> 1 can flat anchovies, drained
> 16 pitted Mediterranean-style black olives

Make a pastry shell for a 10-inch tart and partially bake it; see page 362.

In a large, heavy-bottomed pot, combine the onions, oil, and garlic. Cover, and braise slowly for 15 minutes, stirring occasionally. Uncover, stir in the sugar, re-cover, and continue cooking gently for 15 minutes. Uncover again, season with salt and freshly ground pepper, stir, and cook another 15 minutes. At the end of 45 minutes of braising, the onions should be tender and a beautiful golden-brown color, and they will have wilted considerably. (You should have about 4 cups.)

Lift the onions from the pot with a slotted spoon, letting their juices drain out, and spread them evenly in the tart shell. Sprinkle the grated cheese on top (if you are using it), and arrange the anchovies and olives in a decorative pattern on top of the filling. Bake in a preheated 400-degree oven for 20 minutes, or until the filling is hot and the pastry shell is baked through.

SERVES 8

❖Roll out your favorite homemade or store-bought pizza dough. Sprinkle freshly grated Parmesan cheese on the dough, spread on the cooked-onion mixture, decorate with anchovies and olives, and bake on a pizza stone or baking sheet in a 450-degree oven for 5–10 minutes.

Grilled Toasts with Smoked Salmon and Sorrel

From a ravishing display of tiers of open-faced sandwiches at Tivoli Gardens in Denmark, I sampled a delicious concoction—a morsel of toasted thinly sliced bread spread with a mustard butter and topped with thin slices of smoked salmon. It inspired me to create this open-faced sandwich, which I prepare in the summer when sorrel is available from my garden and the grill is in service to give the bread extra flavor. Sorrel's tart lemony taste is a good accompaniment to smoked salmon.

Alternative smoked fish: sable, haddock, bluefish, eel, thin slices of smoked scallops

> 4 cups sorrel leaves
> 1 Tb butter
> 2 Tb light cream
> 8 slices country-style bread
> 8–16 thin slices smoked salmon, or enough to cover the bread
> Lemon wedges (optional)

Wash the sorrel, and remove and discard any stems. Spin-dry the leaves and tear them into small pieces. In a nonstick frying pan, melt the butter and add the sorrel leaves, turning them in the butter over medium heat. The sorrel will wilt quickly and turn a dull green. Cook gently, stirring, until the sorrel is a soft purée and excess moisture has evaporated from the pan. Stir in the cream and blend well.

Grill the bread on both sides over hot coals to toast lightly. Spread the warm toast with 1–2 tablespoons of the sorrel purée per slice, depending on the size of the slices. Top with slices of salmon and serve with lemon wedges, if desired.

SERVES 8 AS A FIRST COURSE, 4 AS A LUNCHEON DISH

❖Broil or toast the bread instead of grilling.

❖Use olive oil instead of butter for the sorrel purée.

❖*Grilled Toasts with Fresh Salmon and Sorrel:* Cut thin slices of fresh salmon fillet. Sauté the slices briefly in 1–2 tablespoons butter or oil, or brush the slices with oil or melted butter and broil for 1–2 minutes. You may use fresh fish other than salmon.

Baked Scallops with Shallots

This is a simple dish that is nevertheless memorable. The shallots add a subtle perk to the silky smoothness of the scallops, and the garlic variation adds a heady fragrance that I relish. I serve French bread with this dish for dunking into the delicious juices from the scallops and the butter. If you are avoiding butter, you might try *Scallops Soffritto* (page 258). When I make this as a first course, I bake it in scallop shells that you can buy quite inexpensively. For a main course, I use individual au gratin dishes, although you could also use a larger baking dish.

1½ lb scallops
6 Tb unsalted butter
2 Tb minced shallots
⅔ cup *Buttered Bread Crumbs* (page 351)

Remove any tough pieces of cartilage on the sides of the scallops, wipe off any bits of shell, and pat them dry. If the scallops are very large, slice them across the grain into smaller pieces. Distribute the scallops evenly among 6-8 scallop shells or, if you are preparing a main course, into 4 au gratin dishes.

In a small skillet, melt the butter, add the shallots, and cook them about 1 minute, or until they have softened slightly. Spoon the butter and shallots evenly over the scallops. Distribute the buttered bread crumbs evenly over the scallops.

Bake in a preheated 400-degree oven for 12–15 minutes, or until the scallops have just turned opaque.

SERVES 6–8 AS A FIRST COURSE, 4 AS A MAIN COURSE

❖*Baked Scallops with Garlic:* Omit the shallots. Melt the butter and stir 1–2 tablespoons of minced garlic into it, being careful not to let the garlic turn brown.

Baked Scallops with Shallots (continued)

As soon as the garlic softens a little, spoon the garlic butter over the scallops, top with buttered bread crumbs, and bake as above.

Smoked Salmon with Vegetable Pancakes

There is no better way to begin a meal than with smoked salmon, which also makes a superb luncheon dish or light supper. I serve it in different ways, and it seems to take on a new life with every rendition. There are many brands of smoked salmon on the market. I think the best ones are the least salty. You don't need very much of it for a serving, so buy the very best quality you can afford. Smoked salmon should be served in very thin slices. In case you are concerned about your slicing skills, note that much of it is sold presliced. If you buy unsliced fillets, hold your knife almost parallel to the work surface and make very thin diagonal slices with a very sharp knife.

Broiled Scallops and Bacon Hors d'Oeuvres

This appetizer is as old as the hills, yet even when bacon was falling out of favor for its fat content, these morsels flew off the cocktail tray—perhaps because cooked bacon's crisp texture and saltiness complement the silky sweetness of scallops. I partially precook the bacon; otherwise the scallops are cooked before the bacon. By the way, if you have impeccably fresh bay scallops or small sea scallops, try one of my favorite cocktail preparations and sauté them au naturel as I do in *Sautéed Bay Scallops with Fall Purée of Squash and Apple* (page 247) and serve with toothpicks.

Alternative fish: small chunks of monkfish

Blini—buckwheat pancakes—are traditional with smoked salmon, but I prefer vegetable pancakes. If you are serving them as a first course, you might want to make small pancakes, 1–1½ inches in diameter, or make very large pancakes and then cut them into small rounds with a cookie cutter. Note that if the pan is too hot, the pancakes will brown on the outside before cooking completely on the inside. I recommend starting out at medium heat and then adjusting the heat to the thickness of the pancakes. Have wide spatulas to turn the pancakes, and watch for spattering oil. You can make these pancakes ahead and refrigerate or freeze them; they are never quite as good as freshly made, but they will come back to life by reheating them in a 400-degree oven.

1 lb sea scallops
⅓–½ lb bacon

Remove any tough cartilage from the sides of the scallops, wipe off any bits of shell, and pat them dry.

In a large frying pan, partially cook the bacon until it has released its fat but is still limp and flexible; remove it to brown paper or paper towels and drain it well. Cut the bacon pieces in halves or thirds so that they are just long enough to wrap around a scallop with a slight overlap. Wrap each scallop with a piece of bacon and secure the wrap with a toothpick. Place the wrapped scallops on a rack that is set in a baking pan and cook under a preheated broiler, turning once, just until the bacon is crisp and the scallops are opaque. Serve immediately.

❖ Roll the scallops in pancetta or prosciutto instead of bacon.

❖ Add something crunchy—a length of scallion or a thin slice of kohlrabi—next to the scallop before rolling it in the bacon.

❖ Substitute drained water chestnuts for one-third of the scallops.

½ lb very thinly sliced smoked salmon
Pancakes (recipes follow)
Lemon wedges
1–1½ cups *Crème Fraîche* (page 353) or sour cream
Freshly ground pepper

Arrange the salmon slices on large serving plates. Place the pancakes to one side of the salmon. Garnish the salmon with lemon wedges and pass crème fraîche or sour cream and a pepper mill.   SERVES 6

Grated Potato Pancakes

1 lb potatoes
¼ cup grated onions
2 eggs
1 tsp salt
⅛ tsp freshly ground pepper
2 Tb flour
½ tsp baking powder
1 Tb heavy cream (optional)
Vegetable oil

Peel the potatoes. Grate them with the large holes of a hand grater or with the grating disk of a food processor. Combine the grated potatoes and grated onions, and squeeze the mixture dry in a towel. Then put the grated vegetables in a bowl. Beat the eggs and add them to the grated vegetables along with the salt, pepper, flour, baking powder, and the cream (if you are using it); stir well.

Film the bottom of a frying pan with vegetable oil, heat the oil, and add a heaping spoonful of batter for each pancake, flattening the pancake lightly with the back of a spoon so that it is 2½–3 inches in diameter. Cook the pancakes at medium heat for 2–4 minutes, depending on their thickness, adjusting the heat as necessary so that each pancake is cooked in the center as it browns on the outside; turn and cook for 2–4 minutes on the other side until both sides are browned and crispy. Cook in batches as necessary, adding a little more vegetable oil to the pan as needed. Drain the pancakes on brown paper or paper towels, and keep them warm in a 200–250-degree oven, if necessary. MAKES 10–12 PANCAKES

❖Add chopped chives or scallions.

Corn Pancakes or Fritters

I scrape the kernels from the ears of corn in order to get both the flesh and the "milk," but you really need a corn scraper to keep the step from being too tedious. If you don't scrape the corn, follow the directions below for *Cut-Corn Kernels*. You can also use leftover cooked corn and follow the cut-corn treatment. If you are using market-bought corn, ask for one of the "sweet gene" varieties that holds its sugar in storage and does not convert it to starch quickly, thereby losing the special sweetness of corn.

6 ears fresh corn
2 eggs
½ tsp salt
2 Tb flour
Vegetable oil

Shuck the corn. Using a corn scraper, scrape the flesh and milk off the ears into a bowl. Lacking a corn scraper, you can run a sharp knife down the center of each row of kernels, then run the back of a heavy knife down the sides of the ear, pushing or scraping the flesh and milk into a shallow bowl. (You will have about 2 cups.)

Lightly beat the eggs and add them to the corn. Add the salt and flour to the corn mixture and stir them all together.

Film a sauté pan with enough oil to cover the bottom of the pan. Heat the oil, then drop the corn batter by large spoonfuls into the pan. Flatten each spoonful of batter in the pan slightly with the back of a spoon. Cook the pancakes over medium heat for about 3–4 minutes on each side, adjusting the heat as necessary to get pancakes cooked on the inside and golden brown on the outside. MAKES 12 PANCAKES

❖If the corn is very milky, add a bit more flour; if it is not milky at all, eliminate or reduce the amount of flour.

❖For a lighter batter, separate 3 eggs. Use 2 egg yolks in the batter. Beat 3 egg whites and fold into the batter just before frying.

❖*Cut-Corn Kernels:* Run a sharp knife straight down the sides of each ear from tip to stem, cutting the kernels off but leaving about ⅛–¼ inch of pulp on the cob so that the tough cob fibers don't get combined with the flesh of the corn. (You will have about 2½ cups of cut-corn kernels.) Purée one-third of the cut corn and add it back to the cut kernels to make the mixture milky.

Lacy Parsnip Pancakes

Originally I made these pancakes with grated Jerusalem artichokes, but the artichokes contain inulin—which causes physical distress for some people—so I switched to sweet parsnips, which make delicious pancakes. By all means try these pancakes with Jerusalem artichokes, but be cautious the first time in case you get a negative reaction.

Lacy Parsnip Pancakes (continued)

½ lb parsnips
2 eggs
Salt and freshly ground pepper
2 Tb butter
1 Tb vegetable oil

Peel and finely grate the parsnips. Beat together the eggs and ½ teaspoon salt, season with pepper, and stir the egg mixture into the parsnips. Heat the butter and oil in a wide, nonstick sauté pan and ladle out ¼ cup batter for each pancake; it will spread into a 3-inch pancake. Cook the pancakes over medium heat for 3–4 minutes on each side, adjusting the heat so that they do not brown before they cook through, or until they are nicely browned.   MAKES EIGHT 3-INCH PANCAKES

❖ Grate a bit of onion into the batter or add chopped chives.
❖ Use half parsnips and half carrots or salsify, or use all carrots.
❖ If you use Jerusalem artichokes or salsify, make the egg mixture first and grate the peeled vegetables directly into the egg mixture to prevent darkening.
❖ Add minced herbs.

Leek and Sorrel Pancakes

I love leeks enough to put them in practically everything. Here they are combined with sorrel, and both flavors go beautifully with smoked salmon. If sorrel is out of season, simply omit it from the recipe.

2 lb leeks
¼ lb sorrel
2 Tb butter, vegetable oil, or
    a combination
2 eggs
¼ cup flour
Salt and freshly ground pepper
Vegetable oil

Remove any withered outer leaves from the leeks, and cut off and discard the upper leaves down to the point where the dark green leaves begin to turn to pale green. Quarter the leeks lengthwise from the top down to within 1½ inches of the base and gently fan out the leaves. Fill the sink or a deep pot with lukewarm water and plunge the leeks upside down into the water several times to remove any soil; then drain them, pat dry, and chop into small pieces. (You will have about 4 cups chopped leeks.)

Wash the sorrel, and remove and discard any stems. Spin-dry the leaves and stack them in several piles. Thinly slice the piles of sorrel leaves into a chiffonade. (You will have 1½–2 cups sliced sorrel.) In a large sauté pan, heat the butter or oil or a combination, stir the leeks into the melted butter or oil, and cook, covered, over low heat, stirring occasionally, for about 7 minutes, or until the leeks are wilted and tender. Stir the sliced sorrel into the leeks and cook, covered, for 2 minutes, or until the sorrel has wilted and turned a khaki-green color. Remove the mixture to a bowl and stir to cool it down slightly. (You will have about 2 cups cooked leeks and sorrel.)

In another bowl, beat the eggs and whisk in the flour and ½ teaspoon salt to make a smooth batter. Add this batter to the leeks and sorrel and stir together, seasoning with more salt and pepper, if necessary.

Film the bottom of a large frying pan with just enough vegetable oil to cover, heat the oil, and drop the batter into the pan by spoonfuls, pressing each pancake down slightly with the back of a spoon to flatten it into a 2½–3-inch round. Cook the pancakes in batches as necessary and keep cooked pancakes warm in a 200–250-degree oven until ready to serve.

MAKES 12–15 PANCAKES

❖ *Zucchini variation:* Grate enough zucchini to make 6 cups. Toss the zucchini with ½ teaspoon salt and drain it in a colander for 20 minutes. Gently but firmly squeeze the moisture out of the zucchini. (You will have about 3 cups zucchini.) Use in place of the leeks and sorrel. Add ¼ cup grated onions and a bit of minced garlic, if you like.

Grilled Seafood with Sweet-and-Hot Grape Sauce

For a snappy beginning to a festive event, serve grilled bite-size pieces of silky shrimp and firm swordfish and shark steak accompanied by a delicious dipping sauce that begins sweet and ends hot. The sauce can be made days ahead. The seafood can marinate for a few hours before the swift and easy final preparation. The amount of marinade specified here will easily coat two pounds of seafood; adjust amounts to the size of your party. A food processor or blender is essential to make the purée for the dipping sauce. You will need skewers for the seafood.

Alternative seafood: scallops, monkfish, tuna

SWEET-AND-HOT GRAPE SAUCE

1 cup peeled, seeded, and chopped
  ripe tomatoes or canned plum
  tomatoes
½ cup chopped golden raisins
3 Tb fresh lemon or lime juice
1 Tb chopped and seeded green or
  red medium-hot chili peppers
1 Tb minced garlic (optional)
1 tsp minced fresh ginger
½ tsp soy sauce
Pinch of crushed red pepper flakes
1 cup grape jelly
⅔ cup orange juice

To make the Sweet-and-Hot Grape Sauce: Put the tomatoes, raisins, lemon or lime juice, chili pepper, garlic (if you are using it), ginger, soy sauce, and red pepper flakes into a food processor, and purée until smooth. In a saucepan, combine the purée, grape jelly, and orange juice, and whisk all together. Bring the mixture to a boil, reduce the heat, and simmer, stirring often, for 15–20 minutes, or until the sauce has thickened slightly. Remove from the heat, cool, and refrigerate until ready to use.

MAKES ABOUT 2 CUPS

MARINADE

1 cup *Lemon Vinaigrette* (page 365)
2 Tb tomato paste
¼ cup finely chopped parsley or cilantro
Dash of hot pepper sauce

Grilled Seafood with Sweet-and-Hot Grape Sauce (continued)

SEAFOOD GRILL

1 lb peeled and deveined raw shrimp
½ lb 1-inch-thick swordfish steak, cut into
     1-inch cubes
½ lb 1-inch-thick shark steak, cut into 1-inch
     cubes

To make the marinade: In a bowl large enough to hold
the seafood, whisk together the lemon vinaigrette,
tomato paste, parsley or cilantro, and hot pepper
sauce. Add the shrimp and fish, toss to coat the
seafood thoroughly, cover, and refrigerate for at least
1 hour and preferably 3–4 hours.

To prepare the seafood grill: Skewer the shrimp,
swordfish, and shark on separate long metal skewers.
Grill or broil them until each variety is just cooked
through. Timing will depend on the heat of the fire
but should not take longer than 4–5 minutes. Watch
carefully to avoid overcooking the seafood.

To serve: Remove the shrimp and fish from the grill
immediately to a serving platter and push them off the
skewers. Arrange the seafood around a center bowl of
sweet-and-hot grape sauce. Provide toothpicks.

❖For the grape jelly in the dipping sauce, I substitute beach plum jelly, which I make from beach
plums I gather in the late summer; or use store-
bought seedless plum preserves or other jelly.

❖For another marinade for the seafood, combine
equal parts soy sauce and sake (rice wine). Or make
the lemon vinaigrette with lime juice and cut down
the amount of oil. Or try the marinade in *Shrimp
Samurai with Sesame–Stir-Fried Spinach* (page 46).

❖For a dipping sauce, substitute refreshing *Cucumber-Dill Sauce* (page 354).

Deviled Seafood
and Artichoke Ramekins

In the kitchen, "deviled" means a dish whose ingredients are enrobed in a mustard-seasoned sauce. This
dish makes a great beginning to a winter meal, and it

can be prepared ahead and baked just before serving.
Here I use shrimp, but other cooked fish or shellfish
are easily substituted. Since the shrimp are cut into
small pieces, you can purchase whatever size shrimp
are the best buy at the time. The recipe is ideal for
tiny precooked shrimp. If you start with raw shrimp,
see the instructions on page 268 for poaching
shrimp. You can use fresh whole artichoke hearts, or
canned artichoke hearts refreshed under cold water
and drained. To prepare fresh artichoke hearts, see
page 350.

Alternative shellfish: cooked crabmeat, cooked lobster meat
Alternative fish: poached cod, haddock, salmon

4 Tb butter
2 Tb flour
2 cups milk
2 tsp Dijon-style mustard
½ lemon
1 tsp Worcestershire sauce
Salt
Cayenne pepper
½ cup heavy cream
1 egg yolk
1 cup fresh bread crumbs
1 lb tiny cooked shrimp or larger cooked
     shrimp, cut into small pieces
1½–2 cups cooked artichoke hearts, cut into
     small pieces (about 6 whole fresh hearts)

Heat 2 tablespoons of the butter in a saucepan, add the
flour, and cook with the butter for 1 minute. Remove
from the heat, add the milk all at once, and whisk
well. Return the saucepan to the heat, bring the mixture to a boil, whisking steadily, and then immediately
reduce the heat to a simmer and cook, stirring well,
until the mixture thickens, about 3–5 minutes. Stir in
the mustard, squeeze in the juice of half a lemon, and
season to taste with Worcestershire sauce, salt, and
cayenne pepper. Remove from the heat.

In a small bowl, whisk together the heavy cream
and egg yolk. Whisk this mixture gradually into the
hot sauce.

Melt the remaining 2 tablespoons of butter in a small
sauté pan, stir in the bread crumbs, and cook until the
crumbs are lightly colored. Remove from the heat.

Pat the shrimp and artichoke pieces dry with paper
towels and divide them evenly among 8 ramekins.
Spoon the sauce evenly over all. Top with the bread

crumbs and bake in a preheated 400-degree oven for about 30 minutes or until heated through and bubbly.

SERVES 8 AS AN APPETIZER

❖Add ¼ cup grated Parmesan or Swiss cheese, or a combination of both, into the sauce during final cooling.

❖Bake, as above, in buttered baking scallop shells.

Ann Marotto's Fresh Tomato Pie

My friend Ann Marotto says this is one dish she can't make enough of for her family when her garden is loaded with ripe red tomatoes. She serves it as a main luncheon dish or for a light supper, but this pretty quiche-like pie is also a great beginning for a simple fish dinner or a delicious accompaniment to a cup of soup. My family echoes the Marottos' acclaim for this happy marriage of pastry, cheese, and tomatoes.

PASTRY

½ cup cottage cheese
½ cup unsalted butter
1 cup flour
½ tsp salt

FILLING

Dijon-style mustard
2–3 sliced large beefsteak tomatoes
1 cup grated low-fat Swiss cheese
2 Tb sliced basil leaves
2 Tb chopped parsley
Salt and freshly ground pepper
½ cup grated mozzarella cheese
¼ cup freshly grated Parmesan cheese

To make the pastry: Combine all the ingredients in a mixing bowl, and cut together with a pastry blender. Use your hands to shape the mixture into a smooth dough. Form the dough into a ball, flatten it slightly, wrap in waxed paper, and chill in the refrigerator for 30 minutes or more. Roll the dough out slightly larger than a 9-inch pie pan, shape into the pie pan, and press the overhanging pastry into a fluted edge. Prick the pastry with a fork and refrigerate again for 30 minutes. Line the pastry with aluminum foil, and add dried beans or washed pebbles as weight to prevent the pie shell from warping as it bakes. Bake in a preheated 425-degree oven for 8 minutes, then remove the weighting material and the foil, and bake for 2 minutes more. Remove from the oven and set aside to cool.

To make the filling: Brush the bottom of the cooled pie shell with a thin coating of Dijon-style mustard. Layer the tomatoes, Swiss cheese, and herbs in the pie

Ann Marotto's Fresh Tomato Pie (continued)

shell. Season the top with salt and freshly ground pepper, and sprinkle the top with the mozzarella and Parmesan cheeses. Bake in a preheated 350-degree oven for 25–30 minutes. SERVES 6

Spring Salad with Warm Shrimp

This dish is a lovely way to bring the early spring garden to the dinner table. Spinach and radishes are among the first harvest, so this dish uses the first thinning of spinach greens and the first bright pink-red radishes. As the days warm and the harvest of spinach fades, substitute young mixed salad greens for the spinach.

6 cups small spinach leaves
12 medium radishes
¾ lb peeled and deveined extra jumbo (21–25 count) raw shrimp
1 Tb Dijon-style mustard
1 Tb minced shallots (optional)
3 Tb red wine vinegar or 2 Tb balsamic vinegar
⅓ cup orange juice
½ cup olive oil
Grated rind of 1 orange
Salt and freshly ground pepper

Remove any stems from the spinach; wash and spin-dry the leaves. Wash and dry the radishes, trim the ends, and cut them into very fine slices or fine julienne sticks. Cut the shrimp in half lengthwise so that you have about 36 halves.

In a small bowl, whisk together the mustard, shallots (if you are using them), vinegar, and orange juice. Gradually whisk in the olive oil. Stir in the orange rind and season the dressing with salt and freshly ground pepper.

Shortly before serving, bring water in a steamer to a boil. Toss the spinach with half the orange vinaigrette dressing and arrange the dressed spinach along one side of 4 serving plates. Steam the shrimp halves for about 1 minute, or until they are pink on the outside and just opaque on the inside. Remove them

immediately to a bowl, toss them with the remaining orange vinaigrette, and arrange the shrimp on the serving plates next to the spinach, allowing about 8–9 shrimp halves per person. Sprinkle the radishes evenly on top of the spinach and serve immediately.

SERVES 4 AS AN APPETIZER

❖Top the spinach with crumbled crisp bacon, chopped hard-boiled eggs, or a combination of both, in place of the radishes.
❖Mix tender early lettuces with the spinach.
❖For a rich but delicious variation on the orange vinaigrette, substitute *White Butter Sauce* (page 114) or *Ginger-Lime Butter Sauce* (page 220).

Shrimp Samurai with Sesame–Stir-Fried Spinach

Broiled, marinated shrimp are delicious by themselves, but the combination of flavors, colors, and textures in this dish as you go from the shrimp to the spinach to the ginger is spectacular. Much of the preparation is done well ahead, and final cooking and assembly goes quickly.

Pickled ginger (available by the jar in Oriental markets and many supermarkets)
1 lb jumbo (21–25 count) raw shrimp
Wooden skewers (soaked in water to prevent burning) or metal skewers

MARINADE

½ cup peanut oil
3 Tb fresh lemon juice
1 Tb tomato paste
2 tsp light soy sauce
2 tsp minced garlic
1 tsp grated fresh ginger
Few drops sesame oil

DIPPING SAUCE

⅓ cup sake (rice wine)
⅓ cup soy sauce

SESAME SPINACH

1½–2 lb spinach
2 Tb vegetable oil
Salt and freshly ground pepper
Sesame oil

Early preparation: Slice enough pickled ginger into small strips to allow a heaping tablespoon per serving. Set aside.

Peel and devein the shrimp, leaving the last tail segment on, if you like. Soak wooden skewers in a pan of water.

To make the marinade: Combine all the marinade ingredients in a large bowl, whisk them together, and add the shrimp. Turn the shrimp in the marinade to coat thoroughly, cover, and refrigerate for at least 2 hours.

To make the dipping sauce: Mix together the ingredients for the dipping sauce in a small bowl and set aside.

To prepare the spinach: Remove the spinach stems, wash the leaves, and spin them dry. Refrigerate the spinach in a plastic bag with a few air holes until ready to cook.

Final preparation: Thread 3 shrimp on each skewer and set aside. (The number of shrimp in a pound will vary slightly; adjust the number of shrimp on the skewers accordingly.) Preheat the broiler.

Heat the vegetable oil in a nonaluminum-lined skillet and drop in a handful of spinach. Stir the spinach, and as it wilts, add more handfuls until all the spinach turns bright green. Transfer the spinach to a colander to drain for a few seconds, wipe out the skillet, and return the spinach to the skillet. Stir quickly over medium heat, season with salt and freshly ground pepper and a few drops of sesame oil to taste. Remove from heat, but keep the spinach warm while the shrimp are cooking.

Cook the shrimp under the broiler, turning once, until pink and just opaque, about 3 minutes.

To serve as an appetizer: Arrange 1 skewer of shrimp on each serving plate, and divide the spinach equally among the plates. Garnish with a generous tablespoon of pickled ginger. Pour a little of the dipping sauce into small ramekins and serve with each plate.   SERVES 8

To serve as a luncheon or light supper: Arrange 2 skewers of shrimp on each plate. Or buy larger-sized extra jumbo (16-20 count) raw shrimp and cook them slightly longer, if necessary.   SERVES 4

❖ *To grill:* Place the shrimp on a preheated grill rack and cook for 3–4 minutes, turning once.

Broiled or Grilled Shrimp Skewers in a Cilantro-and-Lime Marinade

Lime juice and cilantro tenderize the shellfish and give it a very clean, refreshing taste. This is a sure hit for a cocktail party, and the pancetta variation is a winner, too.

Alternative shellfish: sea scallops

1½ lb jumbo (21–25 count) raw shrimp
½ cup fresh lime juice
¼ cup light olive oil or vegetable oil
⅓ cup chopped cilantro
Lime wedges

Broiled or Grilled Shrimp Skewers in a Cilantro-and-Lime Marinade (continued)

Peel and devein the shrimp, leaving the last tail-shell segment on for decoration, if you like, and put them in a large bowl. In a small bowl, whisk together the lime juice and oil, stir in the cilantro, and pour the mixture over the shrimp. Toss the shrimp in the marinade, cover, and refrigerate.

Preheat the broiler or grill. Thread the shrimp on long skewers for ease of cooking, pushing the skewer through the thick end of the shrimp and then through the tail section to form a "C" shape. Place the skewers 4–6 inches from the heat. Cook 2 minutes on one side, turn and cook the other side for 1–2 minutes, or until the shrimp are just opaque inside and springy to the touch. Adjust the cooking time, longer or shorter, to the heat of the broiler or grill.

Remove the shrimp from the skewers and serve with toothpicks and lime wedges.

3 SHRIMP PER PERSON WOULD MAKE THIS RECIPE ENOUGH FOR ABOUT 15 PEOPLE, BUT DON'T COUNT ON IT; THERE ARE NEVER ENOUGH SHRIMP

❖ *Shrimp and Pancetta Skewers:* Cut thinly sliced pancetta into 3-inch pieces. Wrap the raw shrimp with the pancetta pieces and skewer in the "C" shape as described above. Grill or broil as above. Remove to a serving plate and serve with toothpicks and lime wedges or a hot mustard sauce.

❖ An alternative but more time-consuming method is to thread the shrimp individually on small wooden skewers that have been soaked in water for 30 minutes; serve the shrimp on the skewer.

❖ For a main course, buy extra jumbo (16–20 count) raw shrimp and cook them slightly longer, if necessary. Allowing 5–6 shrimp per serving, 1½ pounds shrimp will serve 4.

White Beans with Shrimp and Basil

While traveling in Italy, I found one of my favorite appetizers was a warm plate of flavored cooked dried beans topped with shrimp. Here are two versions: one with poached shrimp, and one with sautéed shrimp. A good olive oil is very important. If you are starting from scratch with dried beans, allow time to soak and cook the beans. This can be done much earlier, even the day before. The shrimp and vegetables can be prepared ahead as well, and the final cooking goes very quickly.

1 cup dried cannellini beans or other dried
  white beans, such as Great Northern★
Salt
12 extra large (26–30 count) raw shrimp
¼ cup virgin olive oil, plus extra olive oil for
  flavoring
8 fresh sage leaves
¼ cup finely chopped red peppers
½ cup chopped tomato pulp
Freshly ground pepper
1 lemon, cut in half
6–8 finely sliced basil leaves

★You may substitute 3 cups canned cooked cannellini beans. Rinse and drain them.

Rinse the beans and pick them over. Put them in a pot, cover with 2 inches of water, and bring to a boil. Cook for 2 minutes, remove from heat, and let sit for 1 hour or overnight. Drain, rinse, return to the pot, and cover with 2 inches of water. Add 1 teaspoon salt, bring to a boil, reduce the heat, and cook according to package directions or until the beans are tender. Cooking time will depend on the size of the dried beans you use. Drain well. (You should have about 3 cups beans.)

Peel and devein the shrimp, leaving the tail section on as a "handle," if you like.

Heat ¼ cup of the olive oil in a large pan. Stir in the sage, red peppers, tomato pulp, and beans. Cook, stirring to coat well with the oil, until all the ingredients are heated through. Remove from the heat and cool very slightly. The mixture should be warm. Season to taste with salt and pepper and stir in more oil, if you like.

To poach the shrimp, bring a pot of water to a rolling boil; use enough water to cover the shrimp by at least 1 inch. Add 1 tablespoon salt for every 2 quarts water. When the water is rapidly boiling, drop in the shrimp. The cold shrimp will cool the water slightly, so they will poach in hot water rather than boil. If the water returns to the boil, turn down the heat so that the water is just simmering; you want the shrimp to cook gently, not boil. Cook 1–2 minutes, or until the tails just curl and the shrimp turn pink. (To test, make an incision in 1 shrimp: raw shrimp will be gray and translucent, and cooked shrimp will be white and turning opaque inside and pink on the outside.)

Drain the shrimp, toss immediately with the juice of the lemon, and season with salt and pepper.

Divide the bean mixture onto 4 individual plates and top each with 3 warm poached shrimp. Sprinkle with basil and serve. SERVES 4

❖*To sauté the shrimp:* Heat the sage, pepper, tomatoes, and beans as above. Remove to a warm bowl, wipe out the pan, and heat 1 tablespoon olive oil. Sauté the shrimp for 1–2 minutes on each side, or until they are just opaque. Remove the shrimp to a warm bowl or plate, toss with the juice of the lemon, and season with salt and pepper. Divide the bean mixture onto 4 plates and top with sautéed shrimp and basil.

❖Use fresh shelled beans in place of cooked dried beans.

❖Slice cooked lobster tails, sauté just to warm in olive oil, and use in place of shrimp.

Sautéed Squid

My introduction to fresh squid came from watching four-year-old Ben Mayer (now in college—this is not a recent event) squid fishing on the dock at Menemsha Harbor on Martha's Vineyard. Ben would pull one squid after another out of the water and rush home to spend endless hours cleaning the strange little creatures. The big payoff came when the squid were cut into rings, tossed with flour, and sautéed in a sizzling frying pan for 2–3 minutes. They remained on the plate only long enough for a sprinkling of lemon juice and then they were gone. Nearer to home, my daughter Kate always requests sautéed squid as an appetizer for her birthday dinner. Squid ranges in size from the tiny ones Ben caught to monsters of the deep. The most prevalent-sized squid in the markets have mantles or body sacs (the main meat) from 3–8 inches long.

2 lb cleaned squid
Butter or olive oil
Instant-blending flour (such as Wondra Quick-
  Mixing Flour)
Lemon wedges

Most markets now sell fresh cleaned squid or frozen cleaned squid. Still, it's a good idea to know how to clean squid yourself in case you catch some or decide to buy uncleaned squid at the market because the price is much better. For instructions on cleaning squid, see page 107.

You will probably purchase a mixture of the cleaned squid pieces, including the body sac, the arm-and-tentacle section, and two fin sections. Depending on how large the squid are, leave the arm-and-tentacle section in one piece, trimming the tentacles to the same length as the arms and making sure that the beak has been removed, or cut the arm-and-tentacle section into bite-size sections. Cut the fins into slices, and cut the body sac into ¼-inch rings. Pat dry. If you are preparing the squid in advance, which I advise, spread the pieces out in single layers on waxed paper, stack the waxed-paper layers, and refrigerate, covered, until ready to use.

To sauté the squid, heat 2–3 tablespoons butter or oil in a 10-inch sauté pan. Pat the pieces of squid as dry as possible with paper towels. Working with a small batch of squid at a time so as not to crowd the pan, toss the squid in the flour, then place it in a large but fine sieve and shake to remove excess flour. As soon as the butter or oil is sizzling, add the squid and cook for 2–3 minutes, tossing the pan to turn the squid on all sides. Remove the cooked squid to a brown-paper-lined baking sheet in a 200–250-degree oven to keep warm. Continue cooking in batches, but serve the squid as quickly as possible after it is cooked. Serve with lemon wedges. SERVES 4–6 AS AN APPETIZER

Swiss Chard and Cheese Squares

The versatility of this dish has made it a hit at our house for many years. My daughters use it for party buffets. It tastes equally good served warmed or cold, and the recipe can easily be doubled or tripled. Cut in small squares, it is finger food, and in larger squares it can grace a luncheon or supper plate.

Swiss Chard and Cheese Squares (continued)

1½ lb Swiss chard
2 Tb butter or vegetable oil
½ cup finely chopped onions
Salt and freshly ground pepper
4 large eggs
1 cup buttermilk
⅓ cup flour
Pinch of salt
Few drops of hot pepper sauce
2 cups shredded Cheddar cheese
2 cups shredded Monterey Jack cheese

Wash the Swiss chard and separate the stems from the leaves. Slice the stems into 1-inch diagonal pieces. Cut the leaves into large pieces. Bring a large pot of water to a boil and drop in the stems. Cook for 1 minute and add the leaves. Cook until the stems are tender, about 5 minutes. Drain the chard and run it under cold water to stop the cooking action; squeeze it gently to remove excess water and roughly chop it.

Heat the butter or oil in a sauté pan and add the onions. Cook until the onions are wilted and golden, about 4–5 minutes. Add the Swiss chard and cook, stirring gently, just long enough to evaporate any moisture in the chard. Season with salt and freshly ground pepper. Set aside to cool slightly.

Beat the eggs in a bowl, then whisk in the buttermilk, flour, salt, and hot pepper sauce. Set aside.

Combine the two cheeses.

Oil an 8 × 8-inch baking dish. Sprinkle one-third of the cheese evenly in the dish, then spoon half the Swiss chard mixture evenly on top of the cheese. Repeat with one-third of the cheese, then the other half of the chard. Top with the remaining third of the cheese. Pour the egg mixture over all and bake in a preheated 350-degree oven for 35–40 minutes, or until a knife inserted in the center comes out clean.

Let the dish sit for 15–20 minutes before cutting into squares. Serve warm, at room temperature, or chilled.   SERVES 12–16 AS AN APPETIZER,
6–8 AS A MAIN COURSE

❖Substitute spinach or kale or other greens for the Swiss chard. When I use spinach, I sauté it in olive oil and garlic before assembling the dish.

❖Substitute a combination of peeled sweet and hot peppers for the Swiss chard. Make it as hot as you can stand.

❖Add pieces of finnan haddie or other smoked fish to the greens or substitute them for the greens.

❖Serve with a fresh *Salsa* (page 7).

Grilled Zucchini Corfu

Grilled vegetables topped with a pungent olive salad remind me of a glorious luncheon in an olive grove on the Greek island of Corfu during my honeymoon. The squash needs only a brushing of oil before grilling, and the olive salad can be made well ahead. You can also use the olive salad as an excellent topping for grilled tuna or other grilled or broiled fish, or as a spread or dip. Try this dish as a vegetable accompaniment to a grilled fish dinner.

OLIVE SALAD

7–8-oz jar of green olives
    with pimento
1 cup walnuts
1 cup parsley leaves
6 plum tomatoes
1 tsp minced garlic
¼ cup virgin olive oil

To make the Olive Salad: Drain the olives and place them in a food processor. Pulse them into small, but not tiny, pieces and transfer to a bowl. Place the walnuts and parsley in the processor, pulse them into small pieces, and add them to the olives. Cut the plum tomatoes into chunks, place them in the processor, pulse them into small pieces (you should have about 1½ cups), and add them to the other ingredients. (All of the chopping can be done by hand, but a food processor is faster.) Stir in the garlic and the olive oil, mix well, cover, and refrigerate until ready to use.

MAKES ABOUT 3½ CUPS

ZUCCHINI

6 medium zucchini, yellow summer squash, or a
    combination of both
Vegetable oil

To grill the zucchini: Wash and dry the squash and
remove the ends. Cut each squash in half lengthwise.
Brush the squash on both sides with vegetable oil just
before grilling, and place on a preheated grill rack
about 4–5 inches from the heat. Cover the grill and
cook for 4 minutes, uncover, turn the squash, and
cook, covered, for another 4 minutes, or until the
squash are just tender. If you do not have a covered
grill, cover the squash loosely with aluminum foil or
allow a longer grilling time. Or it may be broiled.

Place the grilled squash, flat side up, on serving
dishes and top each piece with a spoonful of olive
salad.   SERVES 6 AS AN APPETIZER OR FIRST COURSE,

3–4 AS A MAIN LUNCHEON DISH

❖If you have great big squash, slice them into long
1-inch-thick diagonal slices.

❖Substitute eggplant or other vegetable for the
squash.

Soups

Vegetable Soups

Asparagus Soup

Pale green, elegantly smooth, flavored with one of my favorite vegetables, this is an easy soup to make. Although it would distinguish any meal, I think of it as an especially pleasing and smooth starter before serving *Chunky Salmon Hash* (page 230).

> 2 lb asparagus
> 2 Tb butter
> 1½ cups sliced leeks
> 5–6 cups chicken broth, or a combination of
>   broth and water
> ½ cup light cream
> Salt and freshly ground pepper
> Lemon juice (optional)

Peel the asparagus. Insert a sharp paring knife under the skin at the base and work it up toward the tip, making the cut shallower as the skin becomes thinner. Taper the cut off completely about 2–3 inches below the tip. You can also use a vegetable peeler.

Cut 1½ inches off the top of each asparagus stalk. Blanch these tip pieces in a pot of boiling water until they are just tender. Immediately drain them and run them under cold water to stop the cooking action.

Opposite: Marian serves Victory Garden Vegetable Soup
(page 61).

Cut the pieces in thin diagonal slices and set aside for garnish.

Chop the remaining raw asparagus into ½-inch pieces.

Heat the butter in a 4-quart pot and add the leeks. Cook, stirring, for 3–4 minutes, or until the leeks are slightly wilted. Stir the raw asparagus pieces into the leeks and add 5 cups of broth. Bring the mixture to a boil, reduce the heat, and cook gently, partially covered, for 20 minutes, or until the asparagus slices are completely tender and soft.

Transfer the mixture in batches to a food processor or food mill and purée. Return the purée to the pot, stir in the cream, and add more broth, if desired, to thin it a little. Add the asparagus slices and reheat. Season with salt and freshly ground pepper and a few drops of fresh lemon juice, if you like.   SERVES 6

Cuban Black Bean Soup

Black bean soup, considered a winter soup by some chefs, really works well in all seasons. Its spicy heat somehow warms in the winter and cools in the summer. It can be made well ahead and freezes nicely. Especially with the addition of shrimp, this soup is a meal in itself.

The version here is sharp and spicy. The *Corn and*

Cuban Black Bean Soup (continued)

Yellow Pepper Chowder (page 56) borders on the sweet, with a creamy texture. These two soups served side by side in the same soup plate (see *Side-by-Side Soup*, page 57) will delight your dinner guests.

  1 lb dried black beans
  3 Tb vegetable oil or bacon fat
  4 cups chopped onions
  1 Tb minced garlic
  5 cups chicken broth
  4 cups beef broth
  1 ham hock
  ¼ cup minced green chili peppers
  2 bay leaves
  2 Tb cumin
  2 Tb oregano
  2 tsp thyme
  ½ tsp salt
  ⅛ tsp allspice
  2 Tb red wine vinegar
  1 cup chopped red peppers
  1 cup chopped green peppers
  Sugar
  Salt and freshly ground pepper
  Hot pepper sauce (optional)
  Sour cream
  Chopped red onions
  Lime wedges

Place the beans in a saucepan and cover them with 2 inches of cold water. Bring the water to a boil, remove from the heat, cover, let the beans stand for 1 hour, then drain and set aside.

In a large, heavy-bottomed pot, heat the oil or bacon fat, add the onions, and cook them until they are wilted, about 8 minutes. Stir in the garlic and cook over low heat for 30 seconds. Add the drained beans, chicken broth and beef broth, ham hock, chili peppers, bay leaves, cumin, oregano, thyme, salt, and allspice. Bring the mixture to a boil, skim off any foam, reduce the heat to low, and cook, partially covered, for 1 hour, stirring occasionally. Add the vinegar and the red and green peppers, and cook gently, partially covered, for another hour, or until the beans are tender, stirring occasionally.

Discard the ham hock and the bay leaves. Stir a pinch of sugar into the soup. Remove about one-third of the soup (3–4 cups), put it in a food proces-sor, purée it, and return the puréed soup to the pot to provide a natural, creamy thickening. Stir well, reheat, season with salt and freshly ground pepper to taste, and with a few drops of hot pepper sauce, if you like.

Garnish each serving with a dollop of sour cream topped with chopped red onions. Serve lime wedges on the side.   MAKES 10–12 CUPS

❖ *Cuban Black Bean Soup with Shrimp:* After the soup has been thickened with the purée, add 1 pound peeled and deveined medium raw shrimp to the hot soup. Cook the soup until the shrimp are pink and opaque at the center, about 3–4 minutes. Remove from the heat and serve. To add more pieces of shrimp, slice each shrimp in half lengthwise before adding to the soup. Or use tiny cooked shrimp and heat just long enough to warm through.

❖Substitute cooked crabmeat for the shrimp and reheat just long enough to warm through.

❖When reheating leftover soup, add more chicken or beef broth, because the soup will thicken as it stands.

Broccoli de Rabe and Potato Soup

I can't remember just when it was that I fell in love with broccoli de rabe, but it's a real love affair. Every bit of this wonderful vegetable is edible: flowerets, leaves, and stems. In this earthy, peasant-style soup, you will be able to distinguish the flavors of all three main ingredients—the broccoli de rabe, the potatoes, and the olive oil—so use a top-quality fruity olive oil.

  1 lb broccoli de rabe
  2 lb potatoes
  6 cups liquid (half chicken broth and half water, or all water)
  ½ cup virgin olive oil, plus more to taste
  Salt and freshly ground pepper
  Freshly grated Parmesan cheese (optional)

Wash the broccoli de rabe, remove any tough stem ends, and peel any thick stalks. Cut the broccoli de rabe into 1½-inch pieces and set aside.

Peel and thinly slice the potatoes. Put them into a soup pot and add the 6 cups of liquid and ½ cup of the olive oil. Bring the mixture to a boil, reduce the heat, and boil gently until the potatoes are soft, about 30–40 minutes. Whisk the soup to completely break up the potatoes. Add the broccoli de rabe and cook for 3–4 minutes, or until the broccoli de rabe is tender.

Season with salt and freshly ground pepper, top with grated cheese, and serve with cruets of olive oil to add to the soup, if desired.   SERVES 6–8

Cauliflower Soup

A hearty cauliflower soup I tasted in Denmark almost thirty-five years ago convinced me of the suitability of this pale ivory vegetable for soup courses. This version is not as rich as the cauliflower soup in my first cookbook, *The Victory Garden Cookbook,* but I think it is just as delicious.

    1¾ lb trimmed cauliflower
    2–3 Tb fresh lemon juice
    Salt
    2 Tb butter
    1 cup chopped leeks
    ½ cup chopped celery
    5–6 cups chicken broth
    ½ cup light cream (optional)
    Freshly ground pepper
    2–3 Tb chopped chives

Separate the cauliflower flowerets from the stems and cut any thick skin off the stem pieces. Divide or cut about half the flowerets into ½-inch pieces, keeping their flower shape as much as possible. Chop the remaining flowerets and stem pieces.

Bring a large pot of water to a boil, add 2 tablespoons lemon juice and ½ teaspoon salt to the water, and drop only the cauliflower flowerets into the pot. (The chopped pieces will be used later.) Blanch the flowerets for 2–3 minutes, or until they are just tender. Drain them immediately and run them under cold water to stop the cooking action, or drop them into a bowl of ice water, drain them again, and set aside.

Heat the butter in the same pot, add the leeks and celery, and cook, stirring, for 3–4 minutes, or until

the vegetables have wilted. Add the chopped raw cauliflower and 5 cups of broth, bring the mixture to a boil, cover, and simmer for 10–15 minutes, or until the cauliflower is tender. Transfer the cooked cauliflower mixture to a food processor or blender and purée it, leaving the mixture slightly rough. Add more broth, if necessary, to get the consistency you like, and add the cream, if desired. Return the puréed mixture to the pot, season with salt and freshly ground pepper and more lemon juice, if desired. Add the reserved flowerets, stir gently, and reheat. Serve topped with chives.   SERVES 6–8

Chilled Cucumber-Yogurt Soup with Fresh Herbs

For the convenience of the cook, I often suggest how dishes can be prepared well ahead of serving. This is one of those dishes that need to be made well ahead so that the flavors can mingle. A cup of this refreshing soup, followed by *Shrimp Samurai with Sesame–Stir-Fried Spinach* (page 46), makes a lovely light supper on a hot summer night, and a bowl of this soup is sufficient to be a summer luncheon.

    4 cups yogurt
    2 finely minced cloves garlic
    2 cups finely minced, peeled, and seeded
        cucumbers
    4 tsp white vinegar
    4 tsp chopped fresh mint
    1 tsp chopped fresh dill
    Salt and freshly ground pepper
    Paper-thin slices cucumber, for garnish
        (optional)
    Small sprigs fresh dill, for garnish (optional)

Put the yogurt into a bowl and stir in the remaining ingredients except for the cucumber slices and dill sprigs. Cover and chill for at least 3 hours. If the soup is too thick, dilute it with a little cold water. Serve garnished with cucumber slices and sprigs of dill, if desired.   SERVES 4–6

❖Use only dill in place of the combination of mint and dill.

La Ribollita (Cabbage Soup)

I couldn't wait to get home from a trip to Tuscany to make my version of a soup I first tasted there for viewers of "The Victory Garden." Ribollita is a thick soup, almost a stew, made of humble ingredients—cabbage, beans, aromatic vegetables, bread—yet fit for a king. Here I use canned cannellini beans, but in the notes at the end of the recipe, I describe how to start from scratch with dried beans. Make sure you use good olive oil to drizzle on the soup before eating. The soup thickens as it sits, so add more broth when reheating leftovers. I think of this as a main course preceded by *Sautéed Squid* (page 49)—a perfect match—or grilled shrimp, followed by crisp *Mesclun Salad* (page 86), with lots of arugula.

3 Tb olive oil
2 chopped stalks celery
1 chopped onion
3 washed, trimmed, and chopped leeks
2 thinly sliced carrots
2 minced cloves garlic
6 peeled, seeded, and chopped tomatoes (about 3 cups)
1 lb sliced green cabbage (about 8 cups)
½ lb green beans, cut into 1-inch pieces
10 cups liquid (half chicken broth and half water, or all water)
3–4 cups canned cannellini beans
Salt and freshly ground pepper
1 loaf dry French or Italian bread, cut into ½-inch slices
Virgin olive oil
Freshly grated Parmesan cheese

Heat 3 tablespoons of oil in a large pot. Add the celery, onion, leeks, and carrots, and sauté for 3–4 minutes. Add the garlic, tomatoes, cabbage, and green beans, and stir well. Add the broth-and-water liquid to the vegetable mixture to cover. Bring the mixture to a boil, reduce the heat, and cook gently, partially covered, for 1 hour. Stir in the cannellini beans and cook for another 15–20 minutes. Season with salt and freshly ground pepper to taste.

To serve, place a slice of bread in the bottom of each soup dish and ladle the soup over the bread. Pass a cruet of virgin olive oil to drizzle over the top and

freshly grated Parmesan cheese to sprinkle on top of each serving.

MAKES 3 QUARTS, OR MORE
IF YOU THIN THE SOUP WITH MORE WATERED BROTH

❖ *To present in a baked soup terrine:* Line the bottom and sides of a deep ovenproof casserole with slices of bread. After the cannellini beans have been added to the recipe, as above, ladle the soup into the casserole and top with thinly sliced red onions. Top with a liberal grinding of black pepper, if you like, and sprinkle generously with freshly grated Parmesan cheese. Drizzle virgin olive oil over all, and bake in a preheated 375-degree oven for about 20 minutes or until heated through.

❖ *To use dried cannellini beans or Great Northern white beans:* Cover 1 cup of dried beans with 2 inches of water in a saucepan, bring to a boil, and cook for 2 minutes. Remove from the heat and let the beans soak in their liquid at least 1 hour. Drain the beans. Cook the celery, onion, leeks, and carrots as above, then add the garlic, tomatoes, and drained beans. Do not add the other vegetables at this time. Add 12 cups liquid (half chicken broth, half water) instead of 10 cups because the dried beans will absorb liquid as they cook. Bring the mixture to a boil, reduce the heat, and cook, partially covered, for 30 minutes. Add the cabbage and green beans, bring back to a boil, reduce the heat, and simmer for 45 minutes, or until the cannellini beans and other vegetables are tender.

❖This soup will accept with gratitude practically any kind of leftover vegetable

Corn and Yellow Pepper Chowder

2 Tb butter
½ cup chopped onions
3 cups diced yellow peppers
3 cups fresh corn kernels
3 cups chicken broth, plus extra if needed
Salt and freshly ground pepper

In a saucepan, melt the butter, add the onions, and cook until the onions are soft, about 3–4 minutes. Add the peppers and corn, and cook for 2 minutes to blend the flavors. Stir in the broth and bring the mix-

ture to a boil. Reduce the heat and cook the mixture, partially covered, for 25 minutes. Transfer the mixture to a food processor and purée it, leaving it in a somewhat rough consistency. (Depending on the amount of "milk" in the corn, you may want to thin the purée with a little more broth.) Return the purée to the cooking pan, reheat, and season with salt and freshly ground pepper.   SERVES 4

❖ Garnish with *Roasted Red Pepper Purée* (page 360).

❖ Add tiny cooked "salad" shrimp at the last minute just to heat through.

❖ Garnish with chopped fresh chives or with other fresh herbs.

❖ *Side-by-Side Soup:* Assemble a full recipe of *Corn and Yellow Pepper Chowder* and a half recipe of *Cuban Black Bean Soup* (page 53). Carefully ladle some black bean soup into one side of each shallow soup plate, and then ladle some corn chowder into the other side of the soup plate. Spoon a strip of *Roasted Red Pepper Purée* across the two soups roughly perpendicular to the line created by the meeting of the two soups. With a fork, make a light zigzagging pattern in the red pepper purée.   SERVES 8

Dandelion and Lentil Soup

This soup needs a special defense. Let's be frank. It has a dreary color, brown and dull green, definitely inelegant. Never mind, I love it. It's another of those "earthy" soups that gives me comfort, and it's very nutritious as well. The sharp taste of the dandelion greens cuts nicely against the smoothness of the lentils, which I like.

1 lb dandelion greens
3 Tb olive oil
1 cup chopped celery
1 cup thinly sliced carrots
1 cup chopped leeks or onions
½ cup chopped ham (optional)
2 peeled and crushed cloves garlic
1 tsp fresh oregano or 1 tsp dried
1 bay leaf
10 cups chicken broth, or half chicken and half
    beef broth
1¼ cups rinsed lentils
Salt and freshly ground pepper
Freshly grated Parmesan cheese (optional)
Fruity olive oil as a garnish (optional)

Dandelion and Lentil Soup (continued)

Wash the dandelion greens and remove any roots. Drain and chop into large pieces. (Makes about 16 cups)

In a large soup pot, heat the 3 tablespoons of olive oil. Add the celery, carrots, leeks or onions, and ham (if you are using it). Sauté over low heat, stirring occasionally, for 5 minutes. Add the garlic, oregano, bay leaf, chicken stock or combination chicken-and-beef stock, and lentils. Bring to a boil, reduce the heat, and cook gently, partially covered, for 30 minutes.

Add the dandelion greens, stirring them into the soup, and cook for another 20 minutes, or until the lentils are soft but not mushy. Season with salt and freshly ground pepper. Serve with Parmesan cheese and a cruet of fruity olive oil, if you like.

SERVES 6

❖Substitute collards, kale, or escarole for the dandelion greens.

❖Add slices of blanched linguiça or other smoked sausages.

Mushroom Soup

As a naïve bride in the early 1960s I decided to buy my husband, a dedicated gardener long before he created the "Victory Garden" public television series, something he did not have in his garden. I sent away for a homegrown mushroom kit. It arrived in due course with some mushroom spore and an instruction booklet, whose first direction was to "get one ton of manure, put it in a dark place, and *keep it warm!*" Any thought of growing mushrooms ended right there. This soup is the essence of mushroom because some of the mushrooms are stewed in the broth for flavor and because dried mushrooms are added to the fresh to intensify the flavor. You may be able to find exotic, strong-flavored fresh mushrooms in your market to add the intensity that the dried mushrooms provide. This soup can be made a day ahead, if you like, and any leftovers keep in the refrigerator for 2–3 days. You can add cream to the completed soup, or you can follow my example and serve the soup as is, accompanied by a pitcher of warm cream so that guests can add as much as they like.

1 oz dried shiitake, French cèpes, or other dried mushrooms
1 cup boiling water
2 lb large fresh mushrooms
3 Tb butter
1 cup finely chopped onions
2 Tb flour
8 cups chicken broth
2 Tb fresh lemon juice
Salt and freshly ground pepper
1–2 cups light cream
Chopped parsley

Brush or wash any sand or other debris off the dried mushrooms, place them in a small bowl, pour the boiling water over them, and let them soak for 30 minutes to plump up. Drain the soaked mushrooms, reserving the soaking liquid, thinly slice them, discarding any tough stem ends, and set aside. (You will have about 1½ cups sliced mushrooms.)

Wipe off the fresh mushrooms with paper towels or a mushroom brush, trim off any dirty or tough stem ends, and thinly slice them. (You will have about 16 cups sliced mushrooms.)

In a wide, heavy-bottomed soup pot, heat the butter, add the onions, and cook for 2–3 minutes to wilt. Add the sliced fresh mushrooms and stir to combine with the onions, reduce the heat to medium-low, cover the pot, and cook for 5 minutes, stirring occasionally, to wilt the mushrooms and release their juices. Uncover and cook for another 4–5 minutes to reduce the mushroom liquid; the mushrooms will have cooked down to about 4–5 cups. Remove the pot from the heat, lift out half (2–2½ cups) of the mushrooms and set them aside in a bowl. Return the pot to the heat, whisk the flour into the mixture, and cook for 2–3 minutes. Gradually add the chicken broth, whisking it into the mushroom mixture until smooth. Carefully add the reserved soaking liquid of the dried mushrooms, discarding the last bit that might contain debris from the mushrooms. Bring the pot of soup to a boil, reduce the heat, and simmer for 15 minutes. Add the reserved fresh mushrooms and the reserved dried mushrooms and the lemon juice. Bring the mixture to a boil again, reduce the heat, and simmer for 10 minutes. Season with salt and freshly ground pepper. When you are ready to serve, warm the cream and pour it into a warm pitcher to accompany the soup. Sprinkle the soup with parsley and serve.

MAKES 10–12 CUPS

❖Use only fresh mushrooms.

❖Substitute fresh Roman, shiitake, or French mushrooms or other strong-flavored fresh mushrooms for the dried mushrooms. Wipe them clean and slice them thin. Sauté them in butter, if you like, before adding them to the soup, or simmer them in a little chicken broth to wilt them.

❖Pass sour cream instead of warm light cream.

❖Stretch the soup easily by adding another 2 cups broth or water. Or expand the recipe as much as you wish for a large party.

❖Add ½ cup minced celery with the chopped onions.

Fiesta Soup (Pumpkin Soup)

I was set to make this soup and serve it dramatically in a pumpkin shell for "Good Morning America" one time, but no one could find a ten-pound field pumpkin in New York City. If you have such a pumpkin, try the variation that follows, *Fiesta Soup in a Pumpkin Shell*. If not, never mind—the soup is delicious served in a soup bowl. Accompany it with a green salad and crusty bread.

2 Tb vegetable oil
1 cup chopped onions
1 tsp minced garlic
2 cups peeled, seeded, and chopped tomatoes
1 cup fresh or canned tomato sauce
4 cups chicken broth
4 oz chopped mild fresh or canned chili peppers
1 tsp cumin
Dash of hot pepper sauce
1 cup diced winter squash or pumpkin
4 crisp cooked corn tortillas or packaged taco
    shells
1 chopped ripe avocado
2 cups peeled and deveined small raw shrimp
3 Tb chopped fresh cilantro
1 cup grated Cheddar cheese (optional)

Heat the oil in a large saucepan, add the onions, and cook until they are wilted, about 5 minutes. Stir in the garlic and cook for 30 seconds. Add the tomatoes, tomato sauce, broth, chili peppers, cumin, hot pepper sauce, and squash. Bring the mixture to a boil, reduce the heat, and cook gently for 8–10 minutes, or until the squash is just tender.

While the squash is cooking, break 2 of the tortillas into narrow strips and break the remaining 2 tortillas into small pieces. Set aside the small tortilla pieces in a bowl.

Add the tortilla strips, avocado, and the shrimp to the squash mixture. Reheat until the shrimp turn pink on the outside and opaque on the inside, about 4–5 minutes. Remove from the heat and serve. Garnish soup dishes with cilantro, the reserved tortilla pieces, and Cheddar cheese, if you like.

SERVES 4–6 AS A MAIN COURSE, 8 AS A FIRST COURSE

❖Substitute tiny cooked shrimp for larger raw shrimp and just heat through.

❖Omit the tortillas and add ¼ cup rice when the tomatoes and broth are added. Cook until the rice is tender.

❖Omit the shellfish and serve as a vegetable soup.

❖After Thanksgiving Day, replace the shrimp with 2 cups leftover turkey.

❖*Fiesta Soup in a Pumpkin Shell:* Cut a lid from a 10-pound pumpkin, leaving the stem on as a handle. (If it is impossible to find a 10-pound pumpkin, use 2 small sugar pumpkins; their flesh is even sweeter than that of a field pumpkin, and the cooking time remains the same.) Clean out the pumpkin. Set it in a baking dish that can come to the table. Surround the outside base of the pumpkin with crushed aluminum foil. (As the pumpkin cooks, it may lean in one direction; the foil keeps it upright.) Pour ½ inch of hot water into the bottom of the baking dish.

Use the ingredients and directions above, but *omit* the diced winter squash or pumpkin. Cook the onions and garlic, and add the tomatoes, tomato sauce, chicken broth, chili peppers, cumin, and hot pepper sauce. Bring the mixture to a boil and pour it into the pumpkin. Put on the pumpkin lid and cover the pumpkin top with a piece of aluminum foil to keep the lid from browning. Place the pumpkin in a preheated 400-degree oven and bake for 60 minutes. While the pumpkin is baking, prepare the tortillas as above.

Remove the pumpkin lid, add the tortilla strips, avocado, and shrimp, replace the lid and foil, and bake for 10–15 minutes, or until the shrimp are cooked through.

To serve, bring the soup in its pumpkin shell to the table. Remove the lid and ladle the soup into bowls.

Fiesta Soup (continued)

With a wide fork and spoon, scrape out a portion of pumpkin flesh to add to each serving. Garnish with the cilantro, reserved tortilla pieces, and grated Cheddar cheese.

Roasted Red Onion Soup

In my first cookbook I have a Victory Garden recipe for onion soup that requires long, slow braising of the onions to brown them and bring out their flavor. It is luscious, but the onions need constant stirring. Once when we had a surplus of red onions in the Victory Garden, I made this variation of onion soup for our viewers. Roasting them in the oven simplified the whole preparation. This soup can be made well ahead and reheated.

> 3 lb red onions
> 4 Tb light olive oil
> 1 tsp sugar
> 1 heaping Tb flour
> 8 cups beef broth
> 1 cup dry vermouth
> Salt and freshly ground pepper
> ¼ cup cognac (optional)
> *French Bread Croutons* (page 355) (optional)
> 1 cup grated Swiss cheese (optional)

Peel and slice the onions. Put them in a large, oven-proof pot, pour the olive oil over them, and toss to coat the onions lightly. Place the pot in a preheated 450-degree oven, uncovered, for 20 minutes. Stir in the sugar and flour, and continue roasting for another 15 minutes.

Using hot pads, transfer the pot to the stovetop, add the broth and vermouth, partially cover, and cook at a gentle simmer for 30 minutes. Season with salt and freshly ground pepper and add the cognac, if desired. Serve as is or top with croutons and sprinkle with Swiss cheese, if you like.   SERVES 6–8

❖*Gratinéed:* If you have tureens that will accept the direct heat of the broiler without cracking, pour the soup into them, top with croutons and grated cheese (adding some Parmesan to the Swiss, if you like), place under the broiler until nicely browned, and serve. Otherwise pour the soup into a large, ovenproof tureen or individual ovenproof tureens, top with croutons and grated cheese, and bake in a preheated 450-degree oven for 30 minutes before serving.

❖Sometimes I double the amount of onions and add a bit more olive oil in order to make a very thick soup.

Split Pea Soup with Celeriac

Adding a big, fat celeriac from the garden to old-fashioned split pea soup brings a wonderful new taste and texture to this popular cool-night supper dish. Elsewhere, as in *Celeriac "Rémoulade" with Shrimp* (page 20), I have incorporated the concentrated celery flavor of celeriac in cold dishes; here, cooked and puréed into a soup, it proves again its indispensability in my garden. If you wish, make this soup a day or two ahead; it will thicken considerably as it cools, but while reheating, you can thin it with water to the consistency you like. This may be more than traditionalists can bear, but instead of adding protein for a complete meal in the form of ham or cooked sausage, try adding slices of monkfish or chunks of cod to make a delicious main-course soup.

> 1 large celeriac, about 2 lb
> 3 cups chopped leeks
> 1 cup chopped onions
> 1-lb package dried green split peas
> Ham hock or ham bone (optional)
> 3 quarts water
> Salt and freshly ground pepper
> 1½ lb peeled potatoes
> 1 lb peeled carrots

Cut off the stems and leaves of the celeriac, trim a thin slice off the root end, and cut down and around all sides of the bulb to remove the gnarled outer skin. (You should have a 1½-pound bulb of creamy flesh.) Cut the celeriac bulb into ¾-inch slices, and the slices into chunks. Place the celeriac in an 8–10-quart heavy-bottomed pan, along with the leeks and onions. Rinse the dried peas and add them to the pot. For a slightly smoky flavor, add the ham hock or bone, if desired. Add 3 quarts of water and 1 tablespoon of the salt to the pot, and bring the mixture to a boil. Skim any foam from the surface, partially cover, and cook at a gentle boil for 1 hour, stirring occasionally to make sure the peas are not sticking to the bottom of the pan. While the split peas cook, slice the potatoes and carrots into ¼-inch slices, thicker if you like. Reserve the sliced potatoes until needed in a bowl of water to prevent them from darkening. After the soup has cooked for 1 hour, mash the celeriac with a wide, flat spoon or firm spatula against the sides of the pan to make a rough purée. Stir the soup, add the drained potatoes and the carrots, and cook, covered, at a gentle boil for another 30–40 minutes—or until the vegetables are tender, the peas have dissolved, and the soup has thickened. The celeriac makes the soup very thick; add water to thin the consistency, if you wish. Remove and discard any ham hock or bone, season the soup with salt and freshly ground pepper, and serve with crusty bread.

MAKES 2–3 QUARTS

❖ *Pea Soup with Monkfish:* The firm texture of monkfish is perfect for this soup. Remove and discard any outer membranes from 1 pound of monkfish tail and cut the fish into ⅜-inch-thick slices. When the soup is completely cooked, as above, add the monkfish, simmer for 4–5 minutes or until the fish just turns opaque, and serve.

❖ In place of the monkfish, use other firm-fleshed white fish, such as shark. Or use large chunks of white fish like cod, which will flake into the soup more readily than the firmer monkfish. Or use a combination of fish and sliced cooked sausage, such as kielbasa or linguiça, or cubes of a good smoked ham.

Victory Garden Vegetable Soup

This is my favorite vegetable soup, its distinctive flavor defined by a fragrant ripe tomato base and by the flavor of charred, peeled red peppers. Making the aromatic tomato purée and preparing the peppers take a little more time than a conventional vegetable soup would, but the taste is more than worth the time. I always make a large amount because it goes quickly and makes a delicious leftover. Almost every step of this recipe can be made ahead. You can broil and peel the peppers a day or two before; prepare the tomatoes and other vegetables as you can and refrigerate them. Make the soup in the morning or the day before, and reheat at serving time. It's just like having gold in the refrigerator.

2 lb red peppers
2 Tb olive oil
1 cup chopped onions
1 cup chopped leeks
2 cups sliced celery
4–5 cups peeled, seeded, and chopped ripe
    tomatoes★
1–2 tsp minced garlic
1 Tb red wine vinegar
1 tsp sugar
2 pieces dried orange peel or 2 tsp ground
10 cups chicken broth
2 cups sliced carrots
1½ cups sliced turnips
1½ cups sliced green cabbage
1½ cups green beans, cut into 1-inch lengths
1 cup sliced zucchini or yellow squash
¼ cup raw rice
Salt and freshly ground pepper
Hot pepper sauce (optional)
2–3 Tb chopped parsley, for garnish

★If you lack vine-ripened tomatoes, use half fresh tomatoes for texture and half drained canned Italian plum tomatoes for flavor.

To peel the peppers, follow the directions on page 360. Cut the peeled peppers lengthwise in halves or thirds, and peel off the charred skin with a paring knife. Cut the peeled flesh lengthwise into strips and set aside. (You should have 2–2½ cups sliced peeled peppers.)

In an 8–10-quart, nonaluminum-lined soup pot, heat the oil, add the onions, leeks, and ½ cup of the celery, and sauté about 4–5 minutes, or until the vegetables wilt. Add the tomatoes, garlic, vinegar, sugar, and orange peel, and stir all together. Cook the mixture, covered, for 5 minutes, then uncover and cook another 8–10 minutes to evaporate the juices and thicken the mixture. Transfer the tomato mixture in batches to a food processor and purée to a rough purée, or put the mixture through a large sieve, leaving it coarsely textured. Return the tomato purée to the soup pot, add the broth, and bring to a boil. Add

Victory Garden Vegetable Soup (continued)

the remaining 1½ cups of the celery, the carrots, and turnips, and cook at a gentle boil for 5 minutes. Stir in the cabbage, beans, zucchini or yellow squash, rice, and the reserved pepper strips, bring the mixture back to a boil, reduce the heat, and simmer, partially covered, for about 15 minutes, or until the vegetables are tender and the rice is cooked. Season with salt and freshly ground pepper and with drops of hot pepper sauce, if desired. Serve sprinkled with chopped parsley.   MAKES 4½ QUARTS

❖Substitute vegetables freely, using what you have. Replace turnips with thin slices of parsnips, rutabaga, kohlrabi, or potatoes. Use thinly sliced kale, collards, or spinach in place of cabbage. Substitute pieces of broccoli de rabe for beans. Add fresh peas or sugar snap peas. If you have only a few vegetables, simply use more of each. If you must make this soup without the broiled peppers, sacrificing the distinctive flavor they contribute, add some sliced pimento to the soup.

❖Substitute small pasta, such as orzo or tubettini, for the rice, adding the pasta to the pot when the broth comes to a boil.

❖For a richer flavor, substitute beef broth for part of the chicken broth.

❖This soup is easily reduced by half or by quarters.

❖*With Fish:* You can add fish directly to the soup, but the fish in any leftover portion will turn mushy and make the soup cloudy and less fresh-tasting. Or you can cook the fish separately, distribute it among serving bowls, ladle the hot soup over it, and refrigerate leftover soup to serve another day.

Method #1: Turn this soup into a seafood-vegetable stew by adding 2½ pounds firm, white-fleshed, nonoily fish such as cod, bass, monkfish, tilefish, etc., or shellfish such as scallops or peeled raw shrimp, or a combination of fish and shellfish. Cut the fish into 1–1½-inch chunks. Drop the fish or shellfish into the finished simmering soup, pushing the pieces down into the liquid. Simmer for 3–4 minutes or until the seafood is just opaque, watching it carefully to avoid overcooking. The fish will thicken the mixture; thin the soup, if you wish, by adding 2 or more cups chicken broth.

Method #2: In a wide saucepan, heat 2 cups chicken broth, add the fish or shellfish or combination, cover the surface of the fish with a round of waxed paper, then cover the pan with a lid and gently cook the seafood about 4 minutes or until just opaque. Evenly distribute the cooked seafood among the serving bowls and ladle the soup over it.

Puréed Butternut Squash and Chestnut Soup with Black Caviar

If you are looking for an earthy yet elegant soup, look no further. This silky, soft orange-colored, slightly sweet soup, garnished with a sprinkling of salty black caviar, should please the most discriminating dinner guest. You can make the soup without the chestnuts, but I love the unique sweet taste they contribute, and their mealy texture thickens the soup.

½ lb raw chestnuts
2–2½-lb butternut squash
2 Tb butter
1 chopped onion
1 chopped carrot
1 chopped stalk celery
5 cups chicken broth
Salt and freshly ground pepper
¼ tsp ground ginger (optional)
1½ cups light cream
Small tin Russian sevruga caviar or American
    sturgeon caviar

To peel the chestnuts: Use a sharp paring knife to make cross-shaped incisions through the shell and inner skin on the flat side of the chestnuts. Drop the chestnuts into a large pot of boiling salted water and boil for 5–10 minutes, drain, then re-cover the chestnuts in the pot with warm water while you peel them. Insert a knife into the opening made by the incisions and peel away the shell and the brown inner skin. Peel separately any inner skins that do not pull off with the shells. (You will have about 1½ cups peeled chestnuts.)

Halve, peel, and seed the squash, and cut the flesh into ½-inch cubes. In a 4-quart saucepan, melt the butter, add the onion, carrot, and celery, and cook gently until the vegetables are wilted. Stir in the squash, chestnuts, 4 cups of the broth, and ½ teaspoon salt. Bring the mixture to a boil, cover, reduce the heat, and cook for 30–40 minutes, or until the squash and chestnuts are very tender. Stir in the ginger, if desired. Transfer the mixture to a food processor or blender and purée it, adding the remaining cup of chicken broth as necessary to thin the mixture down. Return the puréed mixture to the saucepan, add the cream, season with salt and freshly ground pepper, and reheat. To serve, ladle the soup into warm bowls and, using a small fork, garnish the center of each serving with caviar.   MAKES 8 CUPS

❖Substitute toasted pecans for the caviar as a garnish.
❖Replace the cream with the same amount of chicken broth; add more chicken broth if you prefer a thinner soup.

Fish and Vegetable Soups

Bourride

Bourride is a thick fish soup from Provence distinguished by the addition of the highly flavored pungent garlic-mayonnaise, aïoli. In *The Victory Garden Cookbook* I had a bourride thickened with potatoes; here I have a lighter version which calls for fewer potatoes and more aromatic vegetables. This is a fine dish for using less expensive kinds of local fish. The puréed soup base can be prepared well in advance. Serve bourride with a crisp green salad.

Alternative fish: Use a combination of native white fish: grouper, wolffish, monkfish, ocean perch, bass, snapper.

   3–3½ lb hake, cod, cusk, and pollock fillets
   1 cup dry vermouth or white wine
   2 large pinches of saffron threads
   3 Tb olive oil
   3 cups chopped leeks, onions, or
      a combination of both
   1 cup chopped celery
   ½ cup chopped carrots
   2 minced cloves garlic
   1½ cups peeled, seeded, and chopped tomatoes
   1 bay leaf
   1 sprig fresh thyme or ½ tsp dried
   1 cup peeled and chopped potatoes
   2 quarts *Fish Stock* (page 355)
   Aïoli (page 349)
   Salt and freshly ground pepper
   French Bread Croutons with Garlic (page 355)
   Chopped parsley

Remove any skin or bones from the fish fillets, cut the fillets into 2–3-inch chunks, and refrigerate until ready to use.

Pour the wine into a small bowl, stir in the saffron, and set aside to steep.

In an 8-quart soup pot, heat the oil, add the leeks or onions, celery, and carrots, and sauté the vegetables for 8–10 minutes or until they are wilted, stirring occasionally. Add the garlic, tomatoes, bay leaf, thyme, potatoes, and the fish stock; bring the mixture to a boil, reduce the heat, and cook for 20 minutes. Remove the bay leaf and thyme sprig if you used fresh thyme, transfer the cooked soup in batches to a food processor, and purée it; or put the cooked soup through a food mill, then put the puréed soup in a large bowl. You can prepare the soup ahead to this point, cool, cover, and refrigerate. Reheat the soup before proceeding with the recipe. (Makes about 12 cups soup base)

Wipe out the soup pot, place the fish chunks in the pot, and pour the hot soup over the fish. Bring the soup to a boil, reduce the heat, and simmer for 4–5 minutes, or until the fish is just opaque.

Put 1 cup aïoli in a large bowl and slowly whisk a ladle (about 1 cup) of the hot soup liquid (without the fish) into the aïoli. Continue to whisk in 2–3 more ladles of soup, then pour the combined aïoli-soup mixture back into the soup pot. Stir the soup gently so you don't break up the fish, and season with salt and freshly ground pepper. Heat gently to thicken, but do not simmer or the soup may curdle.

Place 2 croutons in each soup bowl. Ladle the soup into the bowls, evenly distributing the fish into each

Bourride (continued)

bowl. Sprinkle with parsley and serve extra aïoli on the side, if desired.   SERVES 8 AS A MAIN COURSE

❖For a thicker soup, add ½–1 cup more potatoes.

❖While traditional bourride contains no shellfish, you might want to include some scallops with the fish.

Bluefish and Chinese Cabbage Soup

A quick, light, no-fat, no-fuss soup! While a concentrated fish stock would be ideal for the broth, a chicken stock will also make a fine soup. You will find it easier to slice the fish paper-thin if you partially freeze it first.

Alternative fish: paper-thin slices of tuna, cod, halibut, bass, shark, monkfish, salmon

¼ lb washed and trimmed raw Chinese
    cabbage leaves
1 lb skinned bluefish fillets
1–1½ oz Chinese rice noodles
6–8 cups concentrated fish stock or
    chicken stock
1 Tb soy sauce
Freshly ground pepper
2–3 chopped scallions

Slice the cabbage leaves diagonally into fine strips about ⅛ inch wide and 2–3 inches long.

Remove any bones and dark meat from the bluefish. Slice the fish fillets paper-thin.

In a large soup pot, place the cabbage, rice noodles, and fish in alternate layers. In a saucepan, bring the fish or chicken stock to a boil and pour it over the layered vegetable, pasta, and fish. Immediately put the soup pot over high heat, bring the soup mixture to a boil, reduce the heat, and cook over medium heat for 3–4 minutes. Add the soy sauce, stir all the ingredients together, and ladle the soup into warm soup bowls. Sprinkle with freshly ground pepper and chopped scallions.

   MAKES 2 QUARTS

❖Substitute other greens for the Chinese cabbage.

Manhattan Clam Chowder

As a New Englander it's hard to admit, but I have always loved Manhattan clam chowder. Its tangy tomato base is a welcome relief from milk- and cream-based soups. I like to make it in the summer and fall with ripe fresh tomatoes and other vegetables from my garden, but you can make it with canned tomatoes any time of the year. All the preparation for the clams can be done way ahead, even the day before you make the soup. I divide the clam meat into two parts: the soft bellies and the tougher muscle sections. The tough muscles, minced almost to a purée, thicken and flavor the soup.

24–30 large quahog clams
2 Tb butter
1 Tb olive oil
2 cups finely chopped onions
1½ cups finely chopped carrots
1 cup chopped celery
1 cup chopped sweet red peppers
2 tsp minced garlic (optional)
4 cups peeled, seeded, and diced tomatoes
1 tsp thyme
1 bay leaf
2 cups diced potatoes, cut into ¼-inch cubes
½ cup chopped fresh parsley
Salt and freshly ground pepper

Scrub the clams and squeeze each open one to make sure it closes up when handled. Discard any that do not close. Place the clams in a large stockpot. Add 4 cups water, cover, and bring to a boil. Cook just long enough to open the shells, about 5–7 minutes. Using tongs, immediately remove the clams from the pot to prevent overcooking. Cook any that have not opened a little longer, but discard any that have not opened after 10-12 minutes. Shake or spoon the clam meats out of their shells, taking care to save all the juices in the shells and return those juices to the pot. Discard the shells.

Carefully and slowly pour the clam broth from the stockpot into a large bowl. Sand from the clams will have settled to the bottom of the pot; be careful not to let any of the sandy broth get into the bowl. Discard the sandy broth and set aside the reserved broth. (You should have about 8 cups clam broth.)

Separate the soft clam bellies from the tougher muscle meat. Chop the soft belly meat into small chunks, place in a bowl, cover with a bit of the broth, and refrigerate until ready to use. (You will have about 2 cups chopped clams.)

Mince the clam muscles until they are almost a purée; this is most easily done in a food processor fitted with a steel blade. Put the minced clams in a bowl, cover with more of the broth, and refrigerate until ready to use. (Depending on the size of the clams, you will have 1–2 cups minced clam meat.)

In a 6–8-quart saucepan, heat the butter and the oil. Add the onions and cook, stirring, for 5–6 minutes, until they are wilted. Stir in the carrots, celery, red peppers, and garlic (if you like), and cook for about 2 minutes more.

Stir in the diced tomatoes, bring to a boil, cover, reduce the heat, and cook gently for 5 minutes. (This step will release the water in the tomatoes.) Uncover the pan and boil gently for 4–5 minutes to reduce the tomato liquid.

Add the minced clam meat in its liquid, the thyme, bay leaf, potatoes, and clam broth. Bring to a boil, reduce the heat, skim off any foam, and cook gently until the potatoes are tender, about 20 minutes.

Add the chopped clams and their liquid, and cook gently for another 2–3 minutes. Remove the bay leaf, stir in the parsley, season with salt and freshly ground pepper, and serve.　　　MAKES 3½–4 QUARTS

❖If you are using canned tomatoes, you can omit the cooking steps that release and reduce tomato juices. Drain and seed enough canned tomatoes to make 4 cups pulp; dice the pulp, stir it into the vegetable mixture, cook for 2–3 minutes, then add the herbs and potatoes and proceed as above.

❖A thicker version of Manhattan clam chowder uses canned crushed tomatoes. Use 3 cups tomatoes and omit the steps that release and reduce the fresh tomato juices.

❖Other vegetables are delicious in this soup. I'll add corn kernels, green beans, or even fresh peas. Add during the last 5–10 minutes of cooking.

❖Flavor with hot pepper sauce or add some minced fresh hot peppers.

❖Add other herbs, such as fresh oregano or fresh basil.

❖If you like the smoky, salty flavor of salt pork, prepare salt pork as in *New England Clam Chowder* and substitute it for the butter and oil used here.

New England Clam Chowder

The very first thing Russ does every spring as our car rolls off the ferry in Nantucket is to drive directly to the shellfish office and buy his clamming license. We have hardly unpacked when he appears equipped with clamming rake and floating clam basket. In a few hours I know I will be making the first New England clam chowder of the season, with many more to follow.

There are as many absolutes to a New England clam chowder as there are New Englanders. The carrot option here is for my friend Gladys, a Rhode Island traditionalist who must have them in her chowder, but it is not necessary to this cook who has lived in Connecticut and Massachusetts. It's all right to add your favorite ingredients, but I must make one restriction: *never* use flour or arrowroot in a New England clam chowder.

You can steam open the clams and prepare all the meats the day before you make the chowder. You can also complete the chowder and reheat it the next day; Russ thinks it gets better with age.

  ¼ lb salt pork
  24–30 large quahog clams
  2–3 Tb butter
  1–1½ cups diced onions
  2–3 cups finely diced carrots (optional)
  1½ lb peeled and diced potatoes (about 3 cups)
  4 cups half-and-half, or 3 cups milk and 1 cup
    heavy cream
  Freshly ground pepper
  Pilot crackers (optional)

Cut the salt pork into strips and blanch the strips in boiling water for 5 minutes to remove excess salt. Drain, cut into ¼-inch dice, and set aside.

Scrub the clams and squeeze each open one to make sure it closes up when handled. Discard any that do not close. Place the clams in a large stockpot, add 4 cups water, cover, and bring to a boil. Cook just long enough to open the shells, about 5–7 minutes. Using tongs, immediately remove the clams that have opened from the pot. Discard any clams that have not opened in 10–12 minutes. Remove the meats, taking care to save all the juices in the shells, and return those juices to the pot. Discard the shells.

Carefully and slowly pour the clam broth from the

New England Clam Chowder (continued)

stockpot into a large bowl. Sand from the clams will have settled in the bottom of the pot; be careful not to let any of the sandy broth get into the bowl. Discard the sandy broth and set the reserved broth aside. (You should have about 8 cups clam broth.)

Separate the soft clam bellies from the tougher muscle meat. Chop the soft belly meat into small chunks, place in a bowl, cover with a bit of the broth, and refrigerate until ready to use. (You will have approximately 2 cups chopped clams.)

Mince the clam muscles until they are almost a purée. This is most easily done in a food processor fitted with a steel blade. Put the minced clams in the same bowl that already holds the belly meat.

(Depending on the size of the clams, you will have 1–2 cups minced clam meat.)

Place the diced salt pork in a clean 4-quart pot. Cook over moderate heat, stirring often, until the pieces have rendered their fat and are browned and slightly crisp. Remove the crisped pieces and reserve.

Remove all but 2 tablespoons of the fat in the pan and add 1 tablespoon of the butter. Add the onions and carrots (if you are using them), and cook about 5 minutes, or until the onions are golden and wilted. Add the reserved clam broth and the potatoes, bring to a boil, reduce the heat, skim off any foam, and cook gently for 20 minutes, or until the potatoes are tender.

Stir in the half-and-half and bring to a simmer. Add the minced clams and the chopped clams in their liquid, and cook gently for another 2–3 minutes to just heat through. Season with pepper and swirl in the remaining butter. Top each serving with the crisped salt pork pieces and serve with pilot crackers, if desired.   MAKES 3½–4 QUARTS

❖If you like the chewy texture of the clam muscle meat, just chop the entire clam into small pieces and omit the mincing procedure.

❖Some folks like to leave some of the crisped salt pork in the pot and let it cook along with the potatoes. I find that the clam liquid usually is salty enough, so I add the salt pork as a final garnish.

❖If you prefer to omit the salt pork altogether, use 2 tablespoons butter and 1 tablespoon oil to cook the onions and carrots.

❖Use half evaporated and half regular milk in place of the half-and-half.

New England Fish Chowder

I have it on good authority that no decent New England chowder ever contains thickening agents; that's hard to believe after seeing gluey chowders served in restaurants across the nation under the menu designation "New England." What a New England fish chowder should contain is salt pork, milk, and one or more fishes from the cod family. If you want more body in your chowder and are willing to flout tradition, I recommend using a softened-butter-flour mixture called beurre manié. The base of this soup can be prepared and refrigerated well ahead; then it can be reheated and the fish swiftly cooked in it just before serving.

Alternative fish: Lesser-known white fish that might be bargains, such as pollock, monkfish, catfish, croaker, drumfish. Thick slices or fillets are best for this recipe.

   6 oz salt pork
   5 cups chopped onions or a combination of
      onions and white of leeks
   1 cup chopped celery
   5 cups sliced potatoes
   6 cups *Fish Stock* (page 355)
   1 bay leaf
   ½ tsp thyme
   Salt and freshly ground pepper

BEURRE MANIÉ (optional)

   3 Tb butter, at room temperature
   3 Tb flour

   3 cups milk or half-and-half
   2 Tb butter
   2½–3 lb skinless cod, haddock, cusk, or other
      firm-fleshed white fish, cut into 1½–2-inch
      chunks
   Chopped parsley
   Pilot crackers or chowder crackers

Cut off and discard the rind of the salt pork. Cut the piece of salt pork into ⅜-inch-thick slices, then cut the slices lengthwise into ⅜-inch-wide strips. Bring a pan of water to a boil, drop in the salt pork strips, blanch for 5 minutes, drain, let cool slightly, then cut the strips crosswise into ⅜-inch dice.

In a large 3–4-quart saucepan, cook the salt pork until lightly browned on all sides. Remove any pork bits, drain on paper towels, and set aside. Discard all but 2–3 tablespoons of the rendered fat in the pan. Add the onions and celery to the fat and cook, stirring, until the vegetables are wilted, about 8–10 minutes. Add the potatoes, fish stock, bay leaf, thyme, and a generous grinding of pepper. Bring the mixture to a boil, reduce the heat, and simmer until the potatoes are tender, about 15 minutes.

To make the beurre manié: If you like a thicker broth, work 3 tablespoons butter and 3 tablespoons flour together with your fingers to form a soft paste. Once the broth is simmering, gradually whisk in the beurre manié a bit at a time and cook to thicken slightly.

If you are preparing the chowder base ahead of time, remove the pan from the heat, let cool, then cover and refrigerate until just before serving.

When you are ready to serve, heat the milk or half-and-half and 2 tablespoons butter in a small saucepan.

Bring the chowder base to a simmer and season with salt and freshly ground pepper. Add the fish and the heated milk and butter, and cook gently until the fish just turns opaque, about 5–6 minutes. Serve in warmed soup bowls. Sprinkle with browned salt pork bits and parsley. Serve with pilot crackers or chowder crackers.   SERVES 6–8

❖For an even richer flavor, replace 1 cup milk with heavy cream.

Cod, Coconut, and Cilantro Soup, Thai-Style

The wonderful characteristic spices of Thai cooking give this delicate soup a memorable flavor. It contains ingredients you might not have in your pantry—nam pla (fish sauce), lemongrass, and coconut milk in particular—but you will find these items in all Oriental markets and in many supermarkets. Use chicken broth or a concentrated fish broth, depending on what is available to you. I prepare the ingredients well in advance but make the soup just before serving it.

Alternative fish: haddock, halibut, bass, snapper, sturgeon, wolffish, monkfish, any firm-fleshed white fish, salmon

Alternative shellfish: thin slices large sea scallops, sliced abalone

1 lb skinned cod fillet
1–2 stalks lemongrass (optional)
1 small bunch cilantro
3 chili peppers
5 cups chicken broth or concentrated fish stock
3 cups coconut milk
½ tsp ground ginger
⅛ tsp cardamom
1 cup thinly sliced mushrooms
2 Tb thinly sliced scallions
¼ cup fresh lemon juice
¼ cup fish sauce (nam pla)
½ tsp sugar
2 Tb lemon zest (optional)

Remove any bones from the fish and cut the fillet into very thin slices, cover, and refrigerate until ready to cook. "Bruise" the stalks of lemongrass, if you are using them, by hitting them with a rubber mallet or hard object to crush them slightly. Set aside. Wash the cilantro, separate the stems from the leaves, and chop the leaves to get 2 tablespoons chopped cilantro. Set aside. With kitchen string, tie the cilantro stems and the lemongrass (if you are using it) into a bundle. Set aside. Cut the chili peppers open and remove the stems, seeds, and inner membrane. Slice the pepper flesh into thin strips and set aside.

In a soup pot, place the chicken broth or fish stock, coconut milk, ginger, and cardamom, mix well, and

add the bundle of cilantro stems. Bring the mixture to a boil, add the mushrooms and sliced fish, reduce the heat, and simmer gently, uncovered, 3–5 minutes, or just until the fish turns opaque. Remove the cilantro-stem bundle, and stir in the peppers, scallions, lemon juice, fish sauce, and sugar. Stir well. Just before serving, sprinkle with chopped cilantro and garnish with lemon zest, if desired.   SERVES 4–6

Cod and Winter-Vegetable Soup

The codfish is a beloved year-round resident of New England waters. In the winter I like to combine chunks of cod with root and storage vegetables in a hearty soup that needs only the addition of a fresh green salad and a crusty bread to make a filling winter lunch or supper. For an added treat, top each serving with a spoonful of warmed spicy salsa.

Alternative fish: haddock, cusk, grouper, any chunky white fish

1½–2 lb cod fillets
2 Tb butter
3 chopped ribs celery
1 seeded and chopped green pepper
1 peeled and chopped onion
1 lb peeled winter squash, cut into ¾-inch chunks
3 peeled potatoes, cut into ¾-inch chunks
3 peeled large carrots, cut into ½-inch slices
8 cups chicken stock
Salt and freshly ground pepper
1½ cups *Salsa* (page 7) (optional)
3 Tb chopped parsley

Remove any skin and bones from the fish and cut the fillets into 2-inch chunks. Refrigerate until ready to use.

In a large soup pot, heat the butter; add the celery, chopped peppers, and onions, and cook for 8–10 minutes, or until the vegetables are wilted and tender. Stir in the squash, potatoes, carrots, and the chicken stock. Bring the mixture to a boil, reduce the heat, and cook gently for about 15 minutes, or until the vegetables are just tender. Add the fish chunks and cook at a simmer, or just below a simmer, about 5 minutes, or until the fish just turns opaque. Season the soup with salt and freshly ground pepper. While the fish is cooking, heat the salsa slightly in a small saucepan, if you wish to use it.

Serve the soup in warmed bowls, sprinkle with parsley, and pass the salsa, if desired.　　SERVES 4–6

Cod, Smoked Cod, and Parsnip Chowder

Parsnips, which were once a staple in New England chowders and are now used less frequently in cooking than they deserve to be, disappeared from chowders because their pithy texture required hours of boiling. New varieties of parsnips cook to tenderness in 15 minutes, and in this recipe parsnips release their sweet natural sugar and flavor into a smoky cod broth.

Alternative fish: haddock, pollock, cusk, whiting

Alternative smoked fish: smoked haddock or smoked pollock

1-lb thick cod fillet
½ lb lightly smoked cod★
½ lemon
Sprig thyme
1 lb parsnips
½ lb potatoes
3 Tb butter
1 chopped small onion
1 cup milk
1 cup whipping cream
Salt and freshly ground pepper
Chopped chives

★If the smoked cod has a strong smoky flavor, soak it in water for 30 minutes, drain, and rinse.

Remove any skin and bones from the cod and smoked cod. In a large saucepan, cover the cod and smoked cod with water and add the juice of half a lemon and the thyme. Bring the cooking liquid to a simmer and poach the fish for 8–10 minutes, or until the fish is just cooked and tender. Remove the fish to a bowl and reserve the poaching liquid. When the fish has cooled enough to handle, break it into large bite-size pieces and set aside.

While the cod is cooking, peel the parsnips and cut them into ¼-inch-thick slices. Peel the potatoes, cut them into ½-inch dice, and place them in a bowl of water to prevent discoloring.

Melt 2 tablespoons of the butter in a large saucepan or kettle. Add the onion and cook until wilted and golden. Add the parsnips, potatoes, and 3 cups of the reserved poaching liquid. Bring the mixture to a boil, reduce the heat, cover, and simmer for 15 minutes, or until the vegetables are tender.

Heat the milk and cream in a small saucepan and add them to the vegetable mixture. Add the cod and smoked cod and stir. Add salt and freshly ground pepper to taste.

Just before serving, stir in the remaining tablespoon of butter. Top each serving with freshly ground pepper and chives. Serve with hot French rolls or chowder crackers, if you like.　　SERVES 6–8

❖Use 1½ pounds fresh cod alone if no lightly smoked fish is available.

Gazpacho with Crabmeat

Gazpacho, a favorite summer soup of mine, is delicious all by itself, but it is even more elegant topped with fresh crabmeat. If you can, net your own blue crabs, steam them, and patiently pick out the meat.

I urge you, please, to hand-chop the vegetables; they really taste better than vegetables chopped by machine. Hand-chopping takes more time, but you can prepare this soup a day, even two, before you serve it.

Alternative shellfish: shrimp, lobster

5 large ripe tomatoes
2½ cucumbers
1 large green pepper
12 scallions
1–2 tsp minced garlic
Salt and freshly ground pepper
¼ cup red wine vinegar
⅓ cup olive oil
3 cups tomato juice
1–1½ cups beef, chicken, or vegetable broth
Hot pepper sauce
Worcestershire sauce
½ lb fresh crabmeat
Croutons (optional)

Gazpacho with Crabmeat (continued)

Peel and seed the tomatoes, chop the pulp into ¼-inch dice, and put it in a large bowl. Remove the ends of the cucumbers, peel them, score the flesh with a fork, and cut 2 cucumbers in half lengthwise. Seed the halved cucumbers with a teaspoon and chop them into ¼-inch dice, then add them to the tomatoes. Cut the remaining half cucumber into paper-thin slices; put the slices in a small bowl, cover, and refrigerate until ready to serve the soup. Wash and trim the green pepper and the scallions, chop them into ¼-inch dice, and add to the tomatoes and cucumbers.

In a small bowl, mash the garlic with 1 teaspoon salt. Whisk in the vinegar and the oil. Mix this dressing into the chopped vegetables, stir in the tomato juice, and add 1 cup of the broth or 1½ cups if you like a thinner consistency. Season the soup with a dash of hot pepper sauce, a few dashes of Worcestershire sauce, salt, and pepper. Chill.

When you are ready to serve, ladle the gazpacho into chilled bowls and top with the reserved sliced cucumbers and a generous sprinkling of flaked crabmeat. Serve croutons on the side, if you like.

SERVES 6

❖Fold the crabmeat into the soup instead of using it as a garnish on top.

❖Use ½–¾ pound cooked shrimp instead of crabmeat. Slice the shrimp in half lengthwise, and just before serving, fold them into the soup or use the shrimp to garnish the tops of individual servings.

❖Use cooked tail meat of lobster sliced into very thin medallions.

❖Double or triple this recipe.

❖I have a friend who likes to stir in 1 tablespoon honey.

❖Use red or yellow peppers, or add chopped celery or fennel.

❖Omit the crabmeat.

Lobster Bisque

There is no shortcut to a full-flavored lobster bisque, but this luxurious soup is worth the effort. "Bisque" has come to mean a thick puréed soup of shellfish. Both the shell and the body of the shellfish contribute to the

essence of the dish. I cut up live lobsters and then sauté them, guaranteeing that all of the juices of the lobsters will intensify the soup; you can, however, prepare the lobsters with the *Fast-Boil Method* (page 185), or make this dish with cooked lobster or with lobster shells alone. Two ingredients are absolutely essential to the quality of the dish: a good fish stock as a base and beautiful ripe tomatoes for color and flavor.

> Six 1½–lb live lobsters (culls, if available, are less expensive)
> 3 Tb olive oil
> 2 Tb butter (clarified, if possible)
> 2 chopped carrots
> 2 chopped leeks
> 1 chopped onion
> 2 chopped stalks celery
> ⅓ cup cognac
> 2 cups dry vermouth or white wine
> 4 chopped whole tomatoes
> ½ cup tomato paste
> 3 crushed cloves garlic
> 2 cups beef broth
> 10 cups or more *Fish Stock* (page 355), *Lobster Stock* (page 358), or a combination of both
> 2 Tb *glace de viande* (optional)★
> 2 Tb fresh tarragon or 2 tsp dried
> 1 Tb fresh thyme or 1 tsp dried
> Bay leaf
> ⅔ cup raw rice
> Salt and freshly ground pepper
> Cayenne pepper
> 2 cups peeled, seeded, and finely diced tomatoes (optional)
> 2 Tb butter
> ½–1 cup heavy cream

★ *Glace de viande* is a gelatinous meat glaze made by the slow reduction of a brown veal stock. If you are lucky enough to have some, use it here to add a rich character to the soup.

As described in *To cut an uncooked or partially cooked lobster in pieces* (page 186), cut up the lobsters on a board with grooves to catch the juices or on a board inside a larger container to catch the juices. Leave the tail sections whole, remove and discard the stomach sacs and intestinal veins, but leave any tomalley (if you wish to use it) and any roe in the body shells.

In a large, deep-sided sauté pan, heat the oil and butter, add the lobster pieces, and sauté, stirring and turning until the shells are red on all sides. Remove the claw and tail pieces to a platter and let them cool slightly. Add the carrots, leeks, onion, and celery to the body shells left in the pan and sauté, stirring, for 8–10 minutes. Pour in the cognac and ignite it, shaking the pan until the flames subside. Pour in the vermouth, bring to a boil, and deglaze the pan. Transfer the contents of the pan to a large stockpot.

Remove the lobster meat from the reserved claws and tails, catching and saving any juices. Cut the meat into bite-size pieces, place them in a bowl, cover, and refrigerate until just before serving.

Add the claw and tail shells and any lobster juices to the stockpot. Add the 4 chopped tomatoes, tomato paste, garlic, beef broth, and fish stock. If you need more liquid to cover the shells, use additional fish stock or tomato juice. Add the *glace de viande* (if you have it), the tarragon, thyme, and bay leaf. Bring the mixture to a boil, reduce the heat, and boil gently for 30 minutes. Remove and discard the lobster shells, and strain the soup through a fine sieve, pressing out the vegetable juices and pulp. Transfer 1½ cups of the soup to a small saucepan, return the remainder to the stockpot, and boil gently until the volume has reduced to 2 quarts.

Bring the 1½ cups soup to a boil, sprinkle in the raw rice, and simmer for 20 minutes. Transfer the rice mixture to a food processor or blender and purée it. (For additional flavor, cook ½ cup of the reserved lobster meat with the rice and purée the rice and lobster meat together.) Set the purée aside.

When the soup in the stockpot has reduced to 2 quarts, whisk in the puréed rice to thicken it, controlling the thickness of the bisque to your taste by the amount you add. Season the soup with salt, freshly ground pepper, and cayenne pepper; it should be slightly peppery. Add the finely diced tomatoes, if desired.

Just before serving, heat the butter in the sauté pan, add the reserved lobster meat, and cook just until warmed through. In a small saucepan, heat the cream and pour it into the hot soup. To serve, place a spoonful of lobster meat in each serving bowl and ladle the bisque over it.   SERVES 8–10

❖In place of cutting up live lobsters, use the *Fast-Boil Method* (page 185) or steam the lobsters, remove the meat, chop up the shells, and proceed as above.

❖To make a respectable bisque without the expense of whole lobsters, order 6–8 lobster bodies from your fish market and proceed as above without lobster meat, or buy ½ pound lobster meat in addition to the bodies.

❖To serve the bisque chilled, omit the finely diced tomatoes and the pieces of lobster meat. Substitute light cream for heavy cream. Heat the cream with 1 teaspoon curry powder, if desired; add it to the hot soup and then chill the soup before serving.

Lobster and Striped Bass Main-Course Soup

This dish makes a divine meal for people you most dearly love to cook for. It is a version of bouillabaisse using my two summer favorites—lobster, the king of shellfish, and striped bass, the cleanest-fleshed fish in our waters—instead of a wider variety of seafood. I make the fish broth that is the soup's base from bass frames, but you could use cod or haddock. The secret of this dish is to cook the lobsters in the fish broth, preserving all the flavorful juices. There are two natural stopping places along the way, so you can prepare this soup to fit your schedule.

Alternative fish: thick cod, haddock, halibut, snapper, sturgeon

¼ cup olive oil
6 cups chopped leeks
2 cups chopped celery
1 cup chopped onions
½ cup chopped carrots
6 cups peeled, seeded, and chopped tomatoes
2 tsp minced hot peppers
5 quarts *Fish Stock* (page 355)
5 chicken lobsters
Sprinkle of saffron threads
Zest of 1 orange
2 tsp tomato paste
Herb bouquet tied in washed cheesecloth: 1 tsp thyme, 4 sprigs parsley, 1 crushed clove garlic, 1 bay leaf, ¼ tsp fennel seeds
2–2½ lb striped bass fillets
Salt and freshly ground pepper
Pernod (optional)
Rouille (page 360) (optional)

Lobster and Striped Bass Main-Course Soup (continued)

In a stockpot with a nonaluminum interior large enough to hold the lobsters, heat the oil, add the leeks, celery, onions, and carrots, and sauté over medium heat until the vegetables are wilted and lightly colored. Add the tomatoes, hot peppers, and 2 quarts of the fish stock, and bring to a boil. Add the lobsters to the pot, reduce the heat to a gentle boil, and cook for 15 minutes.

Remove the lobsters from the pot and set them aside to cool. Add the remaining 3 quarts of fish stock, the saffron threads, orange zest, and tomato paste, and stir all together. Add the herb bouquet in cheesecloth and bring the mixture to a boil, reduce the heat, and simmer for 20 minutes. Remove the herb bouquet. (You can interrupt preparation at this point, cool the broth, and refrigerate the broth and lobsters separately.)

Dismantle the lobsters over a pot or bowl to catch any juices that come out of the shells, reserving the tail sections and the claw-and-knuckle sections. Discard the bodies, but reserve the tomalley (if you wish to use it). Crack the claws and, if you wish, cut each tail section in half. If you are using the tomalley, mix it with a little broth and then stir it into the pot. Put any lobster juices into the pot. (Dismantling the lobsters can also be done ahead, and the broth and lobster pieces can be refrigerated.)

Remove the skin and any bones from the bass fillets. Cut the flesh into 1–1½-inch chunks and refrigerate until ready to use.

About 30 minutes before serving, reheat the broth and season with salt and freshly ground pepper. Add the striped bass and cook at a gentle simmer for 8–10 minutes, or until the fish just turns opaque. Add the lobster pieces and reheat for a few minutes. Stir in a splash of Pernod, if you like. Serve in big soup bowls. Pass rouille, if desired, and crusty French bread.

SERVES 8–10

❖ When dismantling the lobsters, remove the lobster meat from the shells, if you wish. I think it's more fun to leave the meat in the shell and provide some lobster picks.

❖ Use larger lobsters and cut the tail sections into several pieces and separate the knuckles from the claws. Allow 18–20 minutes rather than 15 minutes of cooking time for 1½–2-pound lobsters.

❖ Steam a few mussels and garnish each serving with 2–3 mussels in their shells.

❖ If you use small bass fillets, reduce the cooking time for the bass. Thick bass fillets are best to use.

My Favorite Lobster Stew

A creamy lobster stew is not to be declined, but mostly I prefer this version in which the acidity of tomatoes tempers the rich flavor of lobster. This dish is worth every minute it takes to make. I like it equally with or without the optional cream. You could add a few potatoes and call it "chowder." If you make it the day before serving it, the stew only improves from sitting in the refrigerator overnight. The lobsters are killed with a knife, but you can use the optional *Fast-Boil Method* (page 185); if it's any consolation, I think the knife is kinder to the lobster.

Two 3-lb lobsters (culls, if available, are less
    expensive)
2 Tb butter
4 Tb vegetable oil
2 cups chopped celery
2 cups chopped carrots
2 cups chopped leeks
2 cups chopped onions
½ cup cognac
1 quart dry vermouth or white wine
¼ cup tomato paste
2 cups peeled, seeded, and chopped tomatoes
2 Tb softened butter

12 new potatoes (optional)
2 cups or more light cream (optional)

As described in *To cut an uncooked or partially cooked lobster in pieces* (page 186), cut up the lobsters on a board, catching and reserving any juices, leaving the tail sections whole, removing and discarding the stomach sacs and intestinal veins, reserving any tomalley (if you wish to use it) and roe.

In a large, deep-sided sauté pan, heat the butter and oil, add the lobster pieces, and sauté, turning frequently, until all sides of the shells are red. Add the celery, carrots, leeks, and onions, and cook, stirring, for 3–4 minutes, or until the vegetables are lightly colored. Add the cognac, ignite it, and shake the pan until the flames die down. Add the vermouth, tomato paste, tomatoes, and 1 quart water. Bring the mixture to a boil, reduce the heat, and cook gently for 8 minutes, turning the lobster pieces in the liquid occasionally.

Remove the lobster pieces to a cutting board, let them cool enough to handle, and remove the lobster meat from the shells. (You will have 1–1½ pounds lobster meat.)

Put the lobster shells and any lobster juices into a large stockpot, add the vegetables and liquid from the sauté pan, and cover the shells with up to 6 more cups water. Bring the mixture to a boil, reduce the heat, and cook gently for 1 hour to make the lobster-broth base for the stew. While the lobster broth is cooking, cut the lobster meat into bite-size pieces, cover, and refrigerate. Sieve any tomalley (if you wish to use it) and roe, and mix them with the softened butter and refrigerate. If you are using the potatoes, cook them in boiling water in a saucepan until just barely tender; drain them, let them cool enough to handle, and cut them into thick slices.

When the lobster broth has cooked for 1 hour, use a sieve or colander to strain it back into the deep-sided sauté pan or another large pot. Remove and discard the lobster shells from the sieve. Transfer the vegetables left in the sieve to a food processor or blender and roughly purée them; set aside. Reheat the lobster broth and cook it at a gentle boil to reduce the volume to 2 quarts. Heat the cream, if you are using it.

Beat 1 cup of lobster broth into the roe-butter mixture, then whisk that back into the pot of broth. Add the puréed vegetables, the potatoes (if you are using them), the pieces of lobster meat, and the warmed cream, if desired. Reheat and serve.

MAKES 2½–3 QUARTS

My Favorite Lobster Stew (continued)

❖Add chunks of cooked vegetables, such as thick slices of carrots or braised leeks.

❖Use only 2 cups dry vermouth or white wine, and add more water.

❖For more intense flavor, use *Lobster Stock* (page 358) or *Fish Stock* (page 355) in place of the water.

Salmon and Corn Chowder

Early corn ripens in our garden just about the time we are traditionally celebrating the Fourth of July with fresh salmon. This chowder, combining both, is just the ticket after a brisk sail. Now that fresh, farmed salmon and stay-sweet varieties of corn are frequently available all year, you can treat yourself to this warming soup on the darkest winter day.

1-lb boned, skinned salmon fillet
4 cups corn kernels
6 cups liquid (3 cups chicken broth and 3 cups
     water; or 6 cups *Salmon Stock,* page 361, or
     Fish Stock, page 355)
6 thick slices bacon
2 Tb butter
1 cup chopped leeks
1 cup chopped celery
½ cup finely chopped red peppers
1 lb peeled potatoes, cut into ½-inch dice
½–1 cup heavy cream
Salt and freshly ground pepper
Chopped chives (optional)

Remove any pin bones from the salmon and cut the fillet into 4 equal pieces. In a food processor or blender, purée 1 cup of the corn kernels and set aside.

Pour the 6 cups of liquid into a wide sauté pan and bring to a boil. Drop in the salmon pieces, reduce the heat to just under a simmer, and poach the salmon for 8 minutes. Remove the salmon to a plate to cool, and reserve the poaching liquid.

In a soup pot, brown the bacon. Remove the bacon to brown paper to drain, and discard all but 1 tablespoon of the bacon fat in the pot. Break the bacon into small pieces and return one-quarter of it to the pot. Add the butter to the pot and let it melt. Add the leeks and

celery, and cook for 2–3 minutes. Add the red peppers, potatoes, the remaining 3 cups of corn kernels, the puréed corn, and reserved poaching liquid, and stir. Bring the mixture to a boil, reduce the heat, and simmer, partially covered, for 15–20 minutes, or until the potatoes are tender.

Flake the salmon into 1-inch pieces. (You will have about 3 cups.) Add the salmon to the pot, along with the amount of heavy cream you prefer. Heat gently and season with salt and freshly ground pepper. Sprinkle with chopped fresh chives, if you like.

SERVES 6–8

❖If you prefer to omit the heavy cream, purée 2 of the 4 cups of corn rather than 1 cup as above. The additional purée will thicken the soup.

❖Omit the bacon.

Scallop Chowder

Without a doubt, this chowder belongs in the category of "comfort" foods. With potatoes and aromatic vegetables already in the soup, it is a meal in itself. Serve with a green salad and crusty bread for a perfect winter supper. Frozen scallops work very well in this dish. Just thaw the scallops and add them to the soup, along with all the defrosted juices.

1 lb potatoes
1–1½ lb scallops
2–3 Tb butter
2 cups diced leeks
1 cup diced celery
½ cup diced carrots
Salt and freshly ground pepper
2 cups half-and-half

Peel and dice the potatoes, cover them with water, and set aside.

Remove any tough bits of cartilage on the sides of the scallops and wipe off any bits of shell.

Heat the butter in a large saucepan. Add the leeks, celery, and carrots, and cook gently until they are wilted but not browned.

When the vegetables are softened, drain the potatoes and add them to the pan, along with 1 quart water and 1 teaspoon salt. Bring the mixture to a boil, reduce the heat, cover, and cook gently until the potatoes are tender, about 15 minutes.

In a small saucepan, heat but do not boil the half-and-half.

When the potatoes are tender, add the scallops and their juice to the large saucepan. Cook for 1 minute, add the warm half-and-half, and heat the chowder for 2–3 minutes. Serve at once with plenty of freshly ground pepper.　　　　　MAKES 10 CUPS

❖When the potatoes are just tender, remove the chowder base from the heat and let it cool. Reheat at serving time and proceed with the recipe.

❖Replace some of the half-and-half with heavy cream.

❖Cut down on the diced potatoes and add some diced parsnips for a sweet flavor.

❖Add fresh corn kernels with the scallops.

Scallop and Mussel Stew

My inspiration here is the famous old-fashioned oyster stew, for which you will also find a recipe below; the dish consists of shellfish simmered in milk or cream, enriched with a bit of butter. After such a silky smooth dish, I would serve a crisp *Chicory Salad* (page 85).

2 lb mussels
¾ cup dry white wine
1 qt half-and-half
1–2 tsp minced fresh thyme
1 lb scallops and their juices
Juice of ½ lemon
Salt and freshly ground pepper
Hot pepper sauce (optional)
2–3 Tb softened butter

Scrub off any muck and seaweed clinging to the mussel shells, and pull the beards off the mussels. Give each mussel a twist between your fingers and thumb to identify any "false" mussels that are filled with sand; discard these and any open shells that do not close when touched. In a large, nonaluminum-lined saucepan, heat the wine, add the mussels, and cook, covered, over medium heat just until the mussels open. With a slotted spoon, lift the mussels out of the pan and

put them into a large bowl. As soon as they are cool enough to handle, remove the meats in the bowl, saving any juices from the shells. Discard the shells and any mussels that did not open during the cooking. Carefully pour the cooking broth from the saucepan into a container (you should have about 1 cup), but discard the last bit of broth containing any sand.

Clean out the saucepan, then combine in it the cooking broth, the half-and-half, and the thyme. Bring the mixture to a boil, reduce the heat, and simmer for 5 minutes. Add the scallops and their juices and the mussels and their juices and simmer together for 1–2 minutes. Season with squeezes of fresh lemon juice, salt and freshly ground pepper, and a few drops of hot pepper sauce, if desired. Stir in the butter and serve immediately with pilot crackers.　　SERVES 4

❖Add cooked julienned or diced vegetables when you add the scallops. Or sauté 4 cups finely shredded raw spinach in 2 tablespoons butter until wilted (you should have about 1 cup cooked spinach) and add with the scallops.

❖For a richer stew, use light cream or replace some of the half-and-half with heavy cream. To lighten the stew, substitute milk for some or all of the half-and-half.

❖*Oyster Stew:* Replace the mussels and scallops with 1½ pints oyster meats and their liquor or shuck 3 dozen oysters for their meats and liquor. Substitute the oyster liquor for the mussel broth to combine with the half-and-half. In a large sauté pan, heat 2 tablespoons butter and poach the oysters in the butter for 3–4 minutes to plump. Add the oysters and butter to the heated half-and-half mixture and simmer as above. Add 1 cup sautéed spinach, if desired.

Scallop and Bok Choy Soup

About five years ago I began experimenting with bok choy grown in the Victory Garden. This soup uses every bit of that crisp Chinese green. Serve this soup as soon as it is made. You can prepare all the ingredients well in advance, assemble everything at serving time, and cook the soup in several minutes.

Alternative fish: monkfish or any thinly sliced, firm-fleshed, lean white fish

Scallop and Bok Choy Soup (continued)

8 cups chicken broth, *Fish Stock* (page 355), or a
    combination of broth or stock or water
4 cups thinly sliced stems bok choy
½ cup thinly sliced scallions
¼ cup rice wine, broth, or water
1½ cups thinly sliced sea scallops
4 oz rice noodles
4 cups thinly sliced leaves bok choy
1 Tb soy sauce
Red pepper flakes
Hot pepper sauce
½ cup sliced water chestnuts, for garnish
½ cup sliced radishes, for garnish

In a large saucepan, bring the broth to a boil, turn off
the heat, and keep covered and hot.

In another large saucepan, place the bok choy
stems, scallions, and rice wine, and cook, covered,
over gentle (or medium-low) heat for 2–3 minutes to
tenderize the stems. Uncover, and layer in the scallops, rice noodles, and bok choy leaves. Pour the hot
broth over the bok choy leaves, bring the broth to a
boil, reduce the heat, and cook gently for 3–4 minutes, or until the noodles are tender. Add the soy
sauce and season with a pinch of red pepper flakes and
a few drops of hot pepper sauce. Stir well. For a
crunchy texture, garnish with water chestnuts and
radishes.   SERVES 6–8

Straight Wharf Fish Soup

This simple country fish soup—you might call it a
simplified bouillabaisse—became a signature dish in
my cooking days at the Straight Wharf Restaurant. I
used readily available New England cod, but any
firm-fleshed white fish will do. There are several
options for advance preparation. You can make the
stock weeks ahead and freeze it or make it fresh the
day before you assemble the soup. The rouille can
also be made well ahead. You can even make a complete soup base a day ahead, refrigerate it, and then
just before serving, reheat it and add and cook the fish
in it. In the summer I use garden-ripened tomatoes,
and in other seasons I combine fresh tomatoes from
the market and canned, seeded plum tomatoes.

Alternative fish: halibut, tilefish, wolffish, monkfish,
or other firm-fleshed white fish or combinations of
fish and scallops

2 Tb olive oil
3–4 cups thinly sliced onions
6 cups peeled, seeded, and roughly chopped
    ripe tomatoes
Herb bouquet wrapped in washed cheesecloth:
    4 sprigs parsley, 1 peeled clove garlic, 1 tsp
    fresh thyme, 1 bay leaf, ¼ tsp fennel seed
3–4 strips dried orange peel
2 quarts *Fish Stock* (page 355)
Salt and freshly ground pepper
Hot pepper sauce
2½–3 lb skinned and boned 1½–2-inch chunks
    cod, haddock, cusk, or other firm-fleshed
    white fish
5–6 saffron threads
Pernod (optional)
Chopped parsley
Rouille (page 360)

In a nonaluminum-lined 8-quart soup pot, heat the
oil, add the onions, and cook, stirring occasionally,
over medium-high heat until they are wilted and
golden, about 10 minutes. Stir in the tomatoes, bring
the mixture to a boil, cover, reduce the heat, and
cook gently for 5 minutes to release the juice of the
tomatoes. Uncover the pan and boil gently for 4–5
minutes to reduce the liquid.

Add the herb bouquet in cheesecloth, orange peel,
and fish stock; bring the mixture to a boil, reduce the
heat, and simmer for 30 minutes. Season with salt and
freshly ground pepper and a few drops of hot pepper
sauce. Remove and discard the herb bouquet and the
orange peel. (Cool and refrigerate the soup base at
this point, if you like.)

Just before serving, bring the soup base to a boil.
Drop in the chunks of fish and the saffron threads.
Bring the soup to a gentle boil again and cook until
the fish turns opaque, about 4–5 minutes. Add a
splash of Pernod, if desired. Serve in warm soup
bowls, sprinkle with chopped parsley, and serve
rouille on the side to stir into the soup.

                      MAKES 3–4 QUARTS

❖If you use only canned tomatoes, drain them and
remove as many seeds as possible. Omit the steps to
release and reduce the juices of the fresh tomatoes.

❖Use half leeks and half onions.

❖Add 2 cups fresh clam broth or mussel broth for added flavor. Always inform your guests that the soup contains a shellfish stock in case of allergies.

❖Extend the soup with 2 more cups fish stock.

❖Spread toasted French bread rounds with rouille, place them in the bottom of the soup bowls, and ladle the soup over them or float them on top of the soup. Or serve the soup with crusty French bread rolls.

Garden Vegetable Chowder with Shrimp and Chicken

Chowders traditionally have potatoes in them; this one does not. I call it a chowder because it is heartier than a soup, but not as thick as a stew; and all the ingredients cook in one pot, harking back to the origin of "chowder" as a dish made in the French *chaudière,* or large pot. No reason, however, that one couldn't add a few chopped-up potatoes or other vegetables to this garden vegetable base. This makes a perfect supper for those cool rainy nights that interrupt a hot summer season. Much of it can be made in advance, and the final cooking takes just a few minutes.

Alternative shellfish: scallops, cooked lobster

Alternative fish to substitute for the shrimp: pieces of cod, haddock, bass, snapper, monkfish, salmon

2 Tb butter
1 Tb vegetable oil
1 cup chopped onions or leeks
1 cup chopped celery
¼ cup chopped mild green chili peppers
1 cup dry vermouth or white wine
2 cups peeled, seeded, and chopped tomatoes

4 cups chicken or shrimp broth, or a
    combination of both
4 ears corn, with kernels cut off the cob
    to make about 3 cups
2 cups zucchini, chopped into ½-inch pieces
1 lb chicken breasts, cut into ½-inch slices
1 lb peeled and deveined raw shrimp
Salt and freshly ground pepper
Hot pepper sauce (optional)
Chopped cilantro (optional)
Lime wedges (optional)

Heat the butter and oil in a large pot. Add the onions or leeks and celery, and cook them over low heat until they have wilted and turned golden, about 8 minutes. Stir in the chili peppers, add the vermouth or wine, and boil to reduce the liquid by one-third. Add the tomatoes and broth, and bring to a boil. Add the corn and zucchini, and cook gently for 3–4 minutes. (You can set the chowder aside at this point, cool, and refrigerate until just before serving, when it will need to be reheated.)

Add the chicken and simmer, covered, 3 minutes. Add the shrimp and simmer, covered, for another 2–3 minutes or longer, depending on the size of the shrimp—they should just turn pink on the outside. Season with salt and freshly ground pepper, and with hot pepper sauce, if desired. Serve in bowls, sprinkled with cilantro, if desired. Pass lime wedges, if you like, and serve with crusty bread.   SERVES 4

❖Add ¾ cup diced raw potato, or substitute the potato for the zucchini. Add the potatoes with the broth and cook until just tender. Add the tomatoes after the potatoes have cooked.

❖Add ¼ cup orzo with the broth and tomatoes, and cook about 8–10 minutes, or until almost tender, before adding the remaining vegetables.

Salads

Vegetable Salads

Green Bean and Seared Red Onion Salad

Searing the outer layer of the red onion gives it a smoky flavor which complements the flavor of the cooked beans. Use an iron frying pan, if you have one, to sear the onion. The onion should not be wilted; it should be dark and barely soft on the outside, crisp and crunchy on the inside. This dish works equally well served with a dish such as *Swordfish with Mushrooms and Cream* (page 296) to establish a contrast of colors and textures, or with any grilled fish, which will have texture similar to that of the smoky seared outside of the onions.

1 lb green beans
2 red onions
1 Tb vegetable oil or light olive oil
1 Tb red wine vinegar
¼–½ tsp Dijon-style mustard
Salt and freshly ground pepper
3 Tb virgin olive oil
2 Tb roughly chopped Italian parsley

Bring a large pot of water to a boil, and prepare a large bowl of ice water to one side. Wash and trim

Opposite: Marian puts the final touches on a Salade Niçoise *(page 107).*

the stem ends of the beans, cut the beans into 1½-inch pieces, and drop them into the pot of boiling water. Cook for 3–4 minutes, or until tender but still crisp. Drain the beans into a colander and then drop them immediately into the ice water to stop the cooking action. Drain them again and pat dry. Place the beans in a large salad bowl and set aside.

Remove the outer skins of the onions and cut each onion in half vertically from stem end to root. Put the onion halves cut side down on a work surface and cut a thin slice off the stem and root ends. Some red onions have a flattened shape, but if an onion is quite round, make an additional cut or cuts down through the halves to make slices about 1 inch thick.

Heat your heaviest, preferably iron, frying pan to very hot. Add the vegetable oil and swirl it around the bottom of the pan. The pan should be smoking.

Put the onion slices in the frying pan so that you see the semicircular rings like the rings of a tree. (Note that there may be spattering when the cool, moist onion touches the smoking hot oil. Protect your clothing with an apron and stand back to avoid hot oil.) Sear for about 1 minute or until charcoal brown, then, using two spatulas to hold the onion rings in place, carefully turn them over and sear the opposite side. Remove the onions to a cutting board and stand them with the unseared flat surface down (the surface made by cutting the onions in half at the beginning of the preparation). Starting at one side, cut down through the onion half crosswise every ½ inch. Add the onion pieces to the beans.

Composed Asparagus Salad

What a colorful dish to serve before a main course of grilled or broiled fish. You can prepare all of the components, including the cooked asparagus, ahead of time; pat the cooked asparagus dry, spread the spears out on a towel-covered baking sheet, cover with plastic wrap, and refrigerate. Bring everything back to room temperature before serving this salad.

1½ lb asparagus
3 hard-boiled eggs
12 radishes
¼ tsp Dijon-style mustard
2 Tb fresh lemon juice
½ cup virgin olive oil
Salt and freshly ground pepper
Black olives

Peel the asparagus by inserting a sharp paring knife under the thick skin at the base of the spear and working the blade up toward the tip, making the cut shallower as the skin becomes thinner and tapering the cut off completely about 2–3 inches from the tip. You can also use a vegetable peeler, if you like. Bring a pot of water wide enough to hold the asparagus lengthwise to a boil, and drop in the peeled asparagus. Once the water returns to a boil, cook the asparagus for 3–4 minutes, or until a sharp knife point can just pierce the stalk. Be careful to avoid overcooking. Drain the asparagus, run under cold water to stop the cooking action, and place the spears on a draining rack. As soon as the spears are cool enough to handle, pat them dry with a towel.

Grate the egg whites and yolks of the hard-boiled eggs through the small hole of a grater. Wash, dry, and thinly slice the radishes. In a small bowl, mix the mustard and lemon juice together, gradually beat in the oil, and season well with salt and freshly ground pepper.

To serve, arrange the asparagus on a serving platter or divide it among 4 individual plates. Spoon some of the vinaigrette over the asparagus, decorate with the grated eggs, radishes, and olives, and spoon a bit of the vinaigrette over the garnish.   SERVES 4

❖For a main luncheon dish, toss cooked shrimp with a little fresh lemon juice or vinaigrette and spread them over the asparagus, then add the garnish.

Green Bean and Seared Red Onion Salad (continued)

In a small bowl, whisk together the vinegar, mustard, and ¼ teaspoon salt. Gradually whisk the olive oil into the mixture. Pour this vinaigrette over the beans and onions, add the parsley, and toss all together. Season with salt and freshly ground pepper.

SERVES 4

❖Brush the onions with oil and sear on an uncovered grill.

❖Make the salad ahead, refrigerate, and then bring to room temperature before serving.

❖Sear the onions before cooking the beans. Then cook the beans, drain them, add the onions and vinaigrette, and serve as a warm salad.

❖Add a can of flat anchovies, chopped, with their oil.

❖Add tiny cooked shrimp.

❖Add seeded, chopped ripe tomatoes.

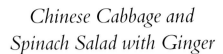

Chinese Cabbage and Spinach Salad with Ginger

I like the freshness and versatility of this salad. With the addition of shellfish for protein, it becomes a complete meal. The cabbage and spinach and all the other sliced or grated components can be prepared in advance.

1 lb Chinese cabbage
1 lb spinach
3 Tb red wine vinegar
2 Tb sweet ginger syrup★
1 Tb grated orange peel
1 tsp finely minced fresh ginger
Salt and freshly ground pepper
½ tsp chili paste or dash of hot pepper sauce
2 Tb vegetable oil
1 cored, seeded, and thinly sliced red pepper
1 roughly grated carrot
½ cup thinly sliced scallions
⅓–½ cup very thinly sliced stem ginger★
6–8 thinly sliced mushrooms
½ cup toasted pine nuts

★Ginger syrup is what jarred stem ginger is packed in. It can be found in Oriental markets and in some grocery stores.

Wash the Chinese cabbage, remove any withered leaves, and pat dry. Thinly slice it diagonally across the stems and leaves to make a chiffonade, or thin julienne slice. Put the sliced cabbage in a large salad bowl.

Wash the spinach, remove the large stems, and spin-dry the leaves. Fold or roll up the spinach leaves and thinly slice them to make a chiffonade. Add the spinach to the sliced cabbage.

In a small bowl, combine the vinegar, ginger syrup, orange peel, fresh ginger, ¼ teaspoon salt, and the chili paste or hot pepper sauce. Whisk in the oil and season with freshly ground pepper and more salt, if desired.

Add the sliced red peppers, grated carrots, scallions, stem ginger, and mushrooms to the combined cabbage and spinach. Pour the dressing over all and

toss. Sprinkle the top with pine nuts and serve immediately.   SERVES 4–6

❖Use all Chinese cabbage or all spinach.
❖ *With Shrimp:* Add 1½ cups cooked medium shrimp that have been sliced in half lengthwise.
❖ *With Smoked Scallops:* Add 1 cup thinly sliced smoked scallops.

Celery and Parmesan Salad

From a sublime food-and-wine excursion through Italy, I remember a simple salad made memorable by the superb quality of the Parmesan cheese and, of course, by the truffle. You probably won't have a truffle handy, but make sure you use very good fresh Parmesan. This is a wonderful beginning course for a fish dinner or salad course following the main course.

6 cups very thinly sliced celery
¼ lb freshly slivered Parmesan cheese, plus
    shavings for garnish
⅓ cup olive oil
2 Tb fresh lemon juice
Salt and freshly ground pepper
1 finely sliced truffle (optional)

In a large bowl, combine the celery and Parmesan slivers. In a small bowl, whisk the olive oil into the lemon juice, season the mixture with salt and freshly ground pepper, and pour it over the celery and cheese. Add the truffle slices, if available. Toss and serve, topping each serving with a decorative shaving of Parmesan.   SERVES 4–6

❖Substitute thinly sliced fennel for the celery.

Julienned Carrot Salad

Proper shredding can turn big storage or wintered-over carrots into airy long threads for a light and delicate salad. A hand grater will suffice; a food processor fitted with a fine shredding disk will do it better, and a Mouli julienne machine will do it perfectly. The

Julienned Carrot Salad (continued)

vivid color of shredded carrots will enhance any meal of flavorful but pale fish.

    ¾–1 lb carrots
    2 Tb chopped chives
    2 Tb chopped fresh thyme, tarragon, or chervil
    1 Tb chopped parsley
    1 Tb fresh lemon juice
    Salt and freshly ground pepper
    3 Tb olive oil

Peel the carrots and grate them into long, thin strands. In a large bowl, combine the carrots, chives, herbs, and parsley.

In a small bowl, whisk together the lemon juice and ½ teaspoon salt. Whisk the olive oil into the mixture. Pour the dressing over the carrot-and-herb mixture and toss well. Add freshly ground black pepper, taste for seasoning, and season again, if desired. Cover and refrigerate for at least 30 minutes before serving.

SERVES 6

❖Garnish other salads with julienned carrots.

Coleslaw

Fried fish with coleslaw is as American as apple pie with cheese or ice cream. You don't have to fry fish to justify making coleslaw; this crisp salad goes equally well with grilled, poached, baked, or sautéed fish, or as a snack by itself.

    8 cups finely sliced green cabbage
    1 cup grated carrots
    1 cup chopped red onions
    ¾–1 cup mayonnaise
    ½ cup red wine vinegar
    1 Tb Dijon-style mustard
    2 tsp sugar
    Salt and freshly ground pepper

In a large bowl, combine the cabbage, carrots, and red onions. In a small bowl, combine the mayonnaise, vinegar, mustard, and sugar; pour the mixture over the vegetables and toss thoroughly. Season with

salt and freshly ground pepper. Cover and refrigerate at least 1 hour; longer marination will tenderize the cabbage even more. Before serving, toss well again and season with more salt and pepper, if desired.

MAKES 8 CUPS

❖Add chopped red or green sweet peppers or celery.

❖Use a combination of red and green cabbage, but marinate longer to tenderize the red cabbage.

❖Substitute sour cream for the mayonnaise, or combine sour cream and mayonnaise; thin either with yogurt.

❖Omit the mayonnaise completely and marinate the vegetables in ½ cup white wine vinegar or cider vinegar.

❖Add caraway seeds or raisins.

Corn Salad

Leftover ears of corn from last night's dinner, spruced up with fresh garden vegetables, become a crisp and refreshing summer salad; if you try the shrimp variation, you will have a nutritionally balanced meal in one dish.

    6 large ears cooked corn
    1½ cups chopped green and red peppers
    1 cup peeled, seeded, and chopped cucumbers
    ½ cup chopped red onions
    2 Tb white wine vinegar
    3 Tb light olive oil
    ¼ cup chopped parsley
    2 tsp minced lovage, celery leaves, or cilantro
    Salt and freshly ground pepper
    Loose-leaf lettuce leaves

Cut the kernels off the ears of corn. (You should have about 4 cups.) In a serving bowl, combine the corn, peppers, cucumbers, and onions. In a small bowl, whisk the oil gradually into the vinegar, stir in the parsley and lovage or other herbs. Season with salt and freshly ground pepper. Pour the dressing over the vegetables, toss well, and marinate for 20 minutes. Serve on crisp lettuce leaves.

MAKES ABOUT 8 CUPS

❖*With Shrimp:* Add 1½ cups tiny cooked shrimp to the serving bowl before dressing the salad.

Green and White Summer Salad

Pickling cucumbers have green skins tender enough to leave on so as to give pleasant crunch to this salad and white flesh with seeds so small they need not be removed. For seasoning I use ingredients that are in full flavor in the midst of summer, like peppers, scallions, and basil. This salad is perfect to serve with a *Mixed Fish Grill with Arctic Char and a Warm Herb-and-Caper Vinaigrette* (page 111).

1 peeled clove garlic, split in half

3 Tb fruity olive oil

18 large basil leaves

1½ lb pickling cucumbers

2 green peppers

8–10 cleaned and trimmed scallions

¼ lb feta cheese

8 anchovies, rinsed, dried, and cut into small pieces (optional)

Mediterranean-style black olives (optional)

Rub a large, shallow bowl with garlic and add the oil. Tear the basil leaves into pieces and add to the oil; toss lightly and set aside to marinate.

Wash and pat the cucumbers dry. Remove the ends, score the skin with the tines of a fork, and slice into ¼-inch rounds. Cut the peppers in half lengthwise, remove the stems, seeds, and white membranes, and cut into pieces roughly 1 inch square. Slice the scallions. Break the feta cheese into small pieces.

To assemble the salad, add the cucumbers, peppers, and scallions to the basil and turn into the oil to coat well. Add the feta cheese and anchovies, if desired, and toss all together. Serve with side bowls of olives, if you like. SERVES 4

Lentil Salad

Lentils were a staple in my mother's kitchen, making regular appearances in soups and stews and as a side vegetable; they will always be, therefore, a nostalgic comfort food for me. In the summer I serve lentil salad as a companion to all sorts of fish and shellfish dishes. This salad tastes best at room temperature.

Lentil Salad (continued)

You can make it ahead, refrigerate it, then bring it to room temperature before serving.

> 2 cups lentils
> 8 cups water
> Salt and freshly ground pepper
> 1 tsp minced garlic
> 2 finely diced strips lemon peel
> 3 Tb fresh lemon juice
> ½ cup olive oil
> 1½ cups chopped scallions
> ¼ cup sliced green olives with pimentos
> 2 Tb chopped parsley

Wash and pick through the lentils, put them in a pot, cover with 2 inches of water, and soak for 1 hour. Drain, return the lentils to the pot, add 8 cups water and 2 teaspoons salt. Heat the water to just under a boil, and simmer the lentils about 15 minutes, skimming off any foam that rises, or until the lentils are tender but still hold their shape. Drain. (You should have about 6 cups.)

While the lentils are cooking, make the vinaigrette dressing. In a small bowl, mash the garlic and ½ teaspoon salt together until they make a purée. Add the lemon peel and lemon juice, and whisk in the olive oil.

Remove the warm lentils to a large bowl, pour the vinaigrette over them, toss, and season with salt and freshly ground pepper. Let the lentils cool slightly, then add the scallions, olives, and parsley. Serve on a bed of lettuce, if you like.   SERVES 6–8

❖Use chopped red onions in place of scallions.
❖Use chopped red peppers in place of olives.
❖The cooked lentils, dressed with the vinaigrette, make a delicious warm side vegetable.

Caesar Salad

Caesar Cardini invented this popular salad in his restaurant in Tijuana, Mexico. He used only small or medium whole interior leaves of romaine lettuce, and there were no anchovies in his salad. I use every scrap of romaine, breaking the larger leaves across their width into pieces. I no longer use raw egg in this salad, and I don't miss it. The anchovies added by others to Caesar salad are a separate garnish that people can accept or decline. For a complete meal I combine this salad with *Grilled Seafood with Sweet-and-Hot Grape Sauce* (page 43).

GARLIC CROUTONS

> 1 tsp minced garlic
> ¼ tsp salt
> 4 Tb olive oil
> 5–6 slices Italian bread, ½–¾ inch thick

CAESAR SALAD

> 1–1¼ lb romaine lettuce
> 2 tsp finely chopped garlic
> Salt and freshly ground pepper
> ½–¾ cup good-quality olive oil
> 6–8 flat anchovies (optional)
> Juice of 1 lemon
> ½ cup freshly grated Parmesan cheese
> Worcestershire sauce (optional)

To make the garlic croutons: Put the garlic on a flat work surface, sprinkle the salt over it, and mash the mixture into a purée. Place the garlic-salt purée in a small bowl and mix in the oil. Remove the crusts from the bread, if you like, brush the slices on both sides with the garlic oil, cut the slices into ½-inch cubes, put the cubes on a baking sheet, and toast until dry in a preheated 350-degree oven.

To prepare the salad: Immerse the lettuce in a sinkful of cold water. Remove the leaves and wash them thoroughly. Break the larger leaves crosswise into large pieces; the pieces can be larger than bite-size, and this salad should be served with knives as well as forks. Spin-dry the lettuce, layer it with paper towels to absorb moisture, and refrigerate in a large plastic bag pierced with some air holes until ready to serve. (You should have 16–20 cups loosely packed lettuce.) Mash the garlic with ½ teaspoon salt into a purée. Put the garlic-salt purée into a small bowl and gradually whisk the oil into it. Cut the anchovies in half and set aside.

Just before serving, place the romaine in a large salad bowl, pour the garlic oil over it, and toss to coat well. Squeeze the juice from the lemon, drizzle the juice over the salad, and toss again. Add the Parmesan cheese, a dash of Worcestershire sauce (if you are using it), salt and freshly ground pepper, and the croutons. Toss once again and serve with the anchovies as a garnish.   SERVES 4–6

❖Emulate Caesar and use only the interior leaves of romaine, reserving the larger outer leaves for a mixed salad. Make a dressing with the garlic, lemon juice, and oil. Arrange the romaine leaves on flat serving plates, drizzle the dressing over the salad, and sprinkle with grated Parmesan cheese. Top with anchovies, if desired. Omit the croutons.

❖Cut the olive oil to ⅓ cup, if you wish.

❖If you wish to use eggs in the dressing, add 2 tablespoons of a liquid pasteurized egg product, such as Simply Eggs, with the lemon juice.

Chicory (Curly Endive) Salad

The quality of the greens is critical for this salad. Use blanched curly chicory—those beautiful cream-colored heads, with just a few green outer leaves.

½ lb chicory
¼ lb ¼-inch-thick bacon slices
1–2 cups cubed French bread
2 Tb virgin olive oil
1–2 Tb chopped shallots (optional)
1–2 tsp minced garlic
2 Tb red wine vinegar
Salt and freshly ground pepper
Crumbled Gorgonzola cheese (optional)

Wash and spin-dry the chicory. Break it into bite-size pieces, place the pieces in a serving bowl, cover loosely with plastic wrap or damp paper towels, and refrigerate.

Cut the thick bacon slices crosswise every ¼ inch to make sticks called "lardons" that are ¼ inch on each side and about 1 inch (the width of the bacon slice) long. Place the lardons in a sauté pan and cook until crisp, then remove them to brown paper to drain. Remove and discard all but 2 tablespoons of fat from the pan, add the bread cubes and cook, stirring occasionally, until they are browned on all sides. Remove the croutons from the pan to brown paper to drain. Place the lardons and bread cubes in separate bowls and set aside.

When you are ready to serve, wipe out the sauté pan, add and heat the oil, add the shallots (if you are using them), and cook for 1 minute. Stir in the garlic, then immediately add the vinegar and bring to a boil, swirling the pan to deglaze it. Pour the hot-oil-and-vinegar mixture over the chicory, add half the bacon lardons, toss well, and season with salt and freshly ground pepper. Serve topped with the remaining bacon, the bread cubes, and some crumbled Gorgonzola cheese, if desired.   SERVES 4

❖*With Scallops:* Omit the bread cubes and Gorgonzola cheese. Remove and discard any tough cartilage on the sides of ½ pound bay scallops, and pat the scallops dry with paper towels. (If you are using larger sea scallops, slice them in half or in quarters.) Wipe out the sauté pan after you have cooked the oil, garlic, and vinegar, add and heat 1 tablespoon vegetable oil, add the scallops and cook, tossing frequently, for 2 minutes. Lift the scallops from the pan and arrange them on top of the dressed chicory salad.

Greek Salad

For a complete meal I serve this salad, which is one of my favorites, with *Pan-Fried Scrod Cod or Haddock in an Egg Coating* (page 136) and a glass of retsina.

12–14 cups mixed lettuces
2 cucumbers
3 large ripe tomatoes
4–5 scallions
8–10 radishes
1 minced clove garlic (optional)
2 Tb fresh lemon juice
½ cup light olive oil
2 Tb chopped fresh mint
Salt and freshly ground pepper
8–12 pepperoncini (pickled peppers)
16 Greek black olives
1½ cups feta cheese
Pita bread

Wash and spin-dry the lettuces, break them into bite-size pieces, put them in a large bowl, cover loosely with plastic wrap or damp paper towels, and refrigerate. Peel the cucumbers and score the sides length-

Greek Salad (continued)

wise with a fork; then halve, seed, and slice them. Cut the tomatoes into wedges. Trim and chop the scallions, and trim and quarter or slice the radishes.

If you are using the garlic, purée it with ¼ teaspoon salt. In a small bowl, combine the garlic purée with the lemon juice and gradually whisk in the olive oil. Add the mint and season with salt and freshly ground pepper.

Just before serving, toss the lettuces with half the vinaigrette. Arrange the cucumbers, tomatoes, scallions, radishes, pepperoncini, olives, and feta cheese decoratively on top of the lettuce. Drizzle the remaining vinaigrette over all. Serve with pita bread.

SERVES 4–6

❖Use cherry tomatoes cut in half.

Green Salad with Saga Blue Cheese

More often than not, I combine a salad and cheese course, accompanying it with a crusty French baguette. This salad offers an array of loose-leaf lettuces dressed in a mustard vinaigrette. Creamy Saga Blue cheese contrasts pleasantly with the crisp greens.

   1 head Boston or Bibb lettuce
   1 small head red-leaf lettuce or radicchio
   1 small bunch arugula
   1 Belgian endive (optional)
   1 clove garlic
   Salt and freshly ground pepper
   1 tsp Dijon-style mustard
   1½ Tb balsamic vinegar or red wine vinegar
   6–7 Tb light olive oil
   ⅓–½ lb Saga Blue cheese

Wash the lettuces and arugula well; drain and spin-dry in a salad spinner or pat dry with towels. Break the leaves into bite-size pieces and place them in a salad bowl. Wipe the endive (if you are using it) with a damp towel and cut out the core, separate the leaves, and add them to the salad bowl. To keep the greens crisp, put them in plastic bags, place a few paper towels

in each bag to absorb moisture, prick some air holes in the bags, and refrigerate until ready to serve.

Chop the garlic, place it in a small bowl, add ⅛ teaspoon salt, and mash the garlic and salt together to make a purée. Stir in the mustard and vinegar. Gradually whisk in the oil to make a smooth emulsion. Season with salt and freshly ground pepper.

Just before serving, cut the Saga Blue cheese into 4 equal wedges and slice the bread. Pour the vinaigrette over the salad greens, toss well, and divide among 4 salad plates. Place a wedge of cheese on each salad plate and serve, accompanied by a basket of bread.   SERVES 4

❖Substitute other lettuces and other creamy cheeses, such as Brie or Saint André.

Mesclun Salad

"Mesclun" signifies a mixture of young lettuces, each leaf no larger than three inches. The goal is to combine several different colors, textures, shapes, and flavors. If you grow your own, you can wander about the garden picking tender small leaves of different lettuces, or you can buy mesclun mixes in seed packets, grow them together, and keep harvesting them young. A good mesclun could include pale yellow French *chicorée frisée,* otherwise known as curly endive; lamb's lettuce or corn salad (*mâche* in French), with a small rosette-shaped dark green leaf; arugula or rocket, with dark green mustard-tasting leaves; radicchio, with slightly reddish leaves when young; dandelion or chicory, with pointed leaves and an almost bitter taste; cos, a type of romaine that is sweet and crisp when young; Bibb lettuce, with soft spreading leaves; red and green oak-leaf lettuce. Some of the following could be combined with the lettuces or used as a garnish: green or purple baby basil, flat-leaf parsley, nasturtium blossoms, summer savory, chive flowers, or garlic chives. Or add fresh herbs of your choice. The mesclun greens should be dressed with the finest-quality oil and vinegar.

   1 lb mesclun mixed lettuces

   ½ cup virgin olive oil
   2 Tb excellent red wine vinegar
   Salt and freshly ground pepper

inch-thick slices, or use individual baby goat cheeses. Brush each piece with olive oil and roll it in fine fresh bread crumbs. Bake in a preheated 400-degree oven until the cheese is slightly bubbly. Run under the broiler to brown lightly, if desired. Top each serving of dressed mesclun greens with a piece of baked cheese.

❖*Mesclun Salad with Warm Salmon:*
¾-lb salmon fillet
6–8 cups mesclun
Zest of 1 lemon
5 Tb light olive oil
1 Tb fresh lemon juice
Salt and freshly ground pepper
1 Tb butter
Nasturtium blossoms or long chives, for garnish

Alternative fish: any firm-fleshed fish that will hold together when cut into cubes

Remove any bones and skin from the salmon. Trim off any dark fat from the salmon. Cut the fillet crosswise into ½-inch-wide slices, and then cut the slices crosswise into ½-inch cubes. Set aside.

Wash and spin-dry the lettuces, and keep them crisp in the refrigerator until ready to serve.

Bring a small pan of water to a boil, drop in the lemon zest, and blanch for 30 seconds to soften; then run under cold water, drain, and pat dry. In a small bowl, gradually whisk 4 tablespoons of the oil into the lemon juice and season the dressing with salt and freshly ground pepper.

In a large, nonstick sauté pan, heat the butter and the remaining tablespoon of olive oil. Pat the salmon cubes as dry as possible with paper towels. Add the salmon to the sauté pan and cook, turning, for 3–4 minutes, or until the salmon is warmed through but still tender; do not overcook. Season the mixture with salt and freshly ground pepper.

Pour two-thirds of the vinaigrette dressing over the mesclun lettuces and toss well, adding more dressing if the leaves need more coating. Add the lemon zest, toss again, and arrange the lettuces on 4 serving plates. Divide the salmon evenly over the servings of lettuce, and garnish with nasturtium blossoms or chives.   SERVES 4

❖Poach the salmon, if you prefer, by dropping the salmon cubes into simmering water to poach for 3–4 minutes or until just cooked through.

Wash and spin-dry or pat the lettuces dry, and place them in a salad bowl.

In a small bowl, whisk the olive oil into the vinegar and season with salt and freshly ground pepper. (Makes about ⅔ cup)

Just before serving, drizzle half the vinaigrette on the mesclun greens and toss well. Add more dressing as desired.   SERVES 6

❖Mix 1–2 teaspoons Dijon-style mustard into the vinegar before adding the olive oil.
❖For a sharper vinaigrette, use 1 part vinegar to 3 parts oil.
❖Mash together 1–2 teaspoons minced garlic and ¼ teaspoon salt to make a paste; whisk the paste and the vinegar together before adding the oil.
❖Use fresh lemon juice in place of the vinegar.
❖*With Baked Cheese:* Cut a log of goat cheese (or other cheeses such as Saint André or Brie) into ¾-

Mesclun Salad (continued)

❖Cut thick bacon into ¼-inch cubes, fry, and add to the salad.

❖Make the same salad using baby spinach leaves in place of mesclun. Sprinkle with finely chopped whites of hard-boiled eggs instead of garnishing with nasturtiums or chives.

❖ *With Bay Scallops:* Replace the salmon cubes with tiny bay scallops. Remove any tough bits of cartilage from the sides of the scallops, pat them dry, and sauté or poach as you would the salmon above.

Parsley and Orzo Salad

Orzo, the rice-shaped pasta, delights me so much that I use it frequently in soups and stews, or cooked and tossed with olive oil and seasonings as a side dish, or, as here, in a salad.

This recipe can be made well ahead and can be doubled or tripled for a larger party. The salad is a nice side dish with cold poached salmon, bass, or haddock.

½ lb orzo
1 cup chopped parsley
2 Tb chopped mint
½ lb crumbled feta cheese (about 1½ cups)
1 cup chopped red onions
1 cup chopped red peppers
⅓ cup light olive oil
2 Tb fresh lemon juice
Salt and freshly ground pepper

Bring a pot of water to a boil, drop in the orzo, and cook according to the package directions until just firm, or al dente. Drain and remove to a serving bowl; set aside to cool. When the orzo is cool, add the parsley, mint, feta cheese, onions, and peppers, and toss.

In a small bowl, whisk the oil into the lemon juice. Pour the dressing over the orzo mixture, toss, season with salt and freshly ground pepper, toss again, and serve.   MAKES ABOUT 10 CUPS

❖Use 5-6 cups cooked brown rice instead of the orzo.

❖Replace peppers with chopped radishes.

Fresh Pea Salad

This is simple and simply wonderful with cold poached salmon.

3 cups shelled peas
1 Tb red wine vinegar
½ tsp salt
½ tsp freshly ground pepper
⅓ cup heavy cream
Crisp young lettuce leaves

Bring a pot of water to a boil, drop in the peas, and blanch them for 1½–2 minutes or until just tender. Drain them immediately and run them under cold water to stop the cooking action. Drain again and pat them gently with paper towels to absorb any excess moisture. Put the peas in a bowl.

In a small bowl, combine the vinegar, salt and freshly ground pepper, and slowly beat in the cream. Pour this dressing over the peas, toss gently, and serve in cups of lettuce leaves.   SERVES 3–4

Seared Red Pepper Salad

Searing red peppers gives them a wonderful smoky taste. This salad is delicious on its own, or as part of an antipasto platter, or as a colorful side dish for fish or shellfish kabobs.

4 large red sweet peppers
3 Tb virgin olive oil
2 tsp minced garlic
1 Tb chopped thyme leaves
3 Tb roughly chopped parsley
1 Tb balsamic vinegar

Remove the stems, cores, and white membranes of the peppers. Cut each pepper lengthwise into 1-inch-wide strips, then cut each strip diagonally into 1-inch pieces.

In a large sauté pan—preferably an iron one—heat the oil until it is smoking hot. Add the peppers, spreading them evenly in the pan. Turn the heat to medium-high and cook the peppers, tossing, for 5–6 minutes, or until the skin sears, or blackens, and the peppers wilt slightly.

When the peppers are just tender, add the garlic and quickly toss with the peppers; do not let the garlic brown. Turn the peppers, garlic, and oil into a bowl and toss with the thyme, parsley, and vinegar. Serve warm or at room temperature. SERVES 4

❖ Use red wine vinegar in place of balsamic vinegar.
❖ Use a combination of red, green, and yellow peppers.

Pinto Bean and Parsley Salad

For a *Cook's Magazine* article on fresh herbs, I devised this recipe several years ago. It reflects my inclination to use lots of parsley from my garden. Almost any dried bean can take the place of the pinto beans. This dish is a perfect addition to an outdoor feast of *Grilled Whole Small Bass with Fennel* (page 119) or any grilled shrimp dish.

½ crushed clove garlic, puréed with a pinch of
    salt
3 Tb olive oil
1⅓ cups picked-over, rinsed, and drained dried
    pinto beans
Salt and freshly ground pepper
1 cup chopped fresh parsley
3 Tb minced fresh cilantro leaves
2 chopped small red bell peppers
2 minced stalks celery
4 chopped scallions
2 tsp minced hot peppers
¼ cup fresh lemon juice
Few drops of hot pepper sauce

In a large bowl, combine the garlic and olive oil, and set aside. In a large saucepan, cover the beans with at least 2 inches of water. Bring the water to a boil, skim off any foam, and cook for 2 minutes. Remove the pan from the heat and set aside for 1 hour.

Drain the beans, cover again with 2 inches of water, and return to the heat. Add 2 teaspoons salt, bring to a boil, skim off any foam, reduce the heat, and simmer until the beans are just tender, about 30–40 minutes.

Drain the beans again, remove them to the serving bowl, combine with the garlic and oil, and mix well. Add the parsley, cilantro, red bell peppers, celery, scallions, hot peppers, lemon juice, and hot pepper sauce, and toss all together. Season with salt and freshly ground pepper. Marinate for 2 hours, tossing occasionally, before serving. SERVES 4–6

Grilled Potato Salad

An advantage of grilled fish for dinner is its quick preparation, and I like the rest of the meal to be just as simple. The potatoes in this recipe can be precooked, and both the potatoes and onions skewered in the morning. The vinaigrette can be made early in the day as well; all you have to do is come home from the beach and light the grill.

16 small new potatoes
2 large sweet Spanish, Vidalia, Maui, or Walla
    Walla onions
Vegetable oil
Salt and freshly ground pepper
¼ cup *Vinaigrette* (page 365)
¼ cup roughly chopped fresh dill
Crumbled bacon bits (optional)

Place the potatoes in a saucepan, cover them with water, bring the water to a boil, reduce the heat, and cook gently for 10 minutes, or until the potatoes are just cooked through. Drain the potatoes immediately, run cold water over them to stop the cooking action, put them in a colander, and let them cool. Peel the onions and cut them into wedges. Thread the onion wedges on skewers. Cut the potatoes in half and thread them on other skewers. Brush the potatoes and onions with the oil, and season them with salt and freshly ground pepper.

Place the skewers over the hot coals of a grill, cook for 1–2 minutes, then turn them and cook the other side. Cooking time will vary with the temperature of the coals. When the potatoes and onions are warmed through and nicely charred on the outside, push them off the skewers into a large bowl. Pour the vinaigrette over the vegetables, sprinkle them with the dill, toss, season with salt and freshly ground pepper, and sprinkle with crumbled bacon, if you like. SERVES 4–6

Potato Salad Vinaigrette

When my mother made potato salad, she boiled the potatoes, peeled them while they were hot, and marinated them immediately with very good vinegar and seasonings so that the potatoes would absorb those flavors as they slowly cooled. I follow her example in using the very best oil and vinegar I can find to dress the potatoes. I like a simple potato salad with just a few other vegetables added for crunchiness. You can refrigerate this salad, but bring it back to room temperature before serving. When we have lobster picnics at the beach, this dish always goes to accompany *Cold Lobster with Garden Tomatoes* (page 100).

> 3 lb new potatoes
> 3 Tb red wine vinegar
> ¼ cup chicken broth or reserved potato-
>   cooking water
> ½ cup finely chopped scallions
> ½ cup finely chopped red onions
> Salt and freshly ground pepper
> ½ tsp Dijon-style mustard
> ⅓ cup virgin olive oil
> 2–3 Tb chopped parsley (optional)

In a large pot, cover the potatoes with water, bring to a boil, and cook at a gentle boil until they are just tender, about 20 minutes. Drain (reserving ¼ cup of the cooking water, if desired) and allow to cool until you can handle them. Peel the warm potatoes and slice them into a large bowl. Add 2 tablespoons of the vinegar, the chicken broth or reserved cooking water, scallions, and onions. Season with salt and freshly ground pepper, and gently fold all together. Allow the mixture to marinate at room temperature for 10–15 minutes, then turn the mixture together one more time.

In a small bowl, whisk together the mustard and the remaining tablespoon of vinegar, and gradually beat in the oil. Season the vinaigrette with salt and pepper. Pour the vinaigrette over the potatoes, add the parsley (if you like), season again with salt and pepper as desired, then fold all together again and serve.   SERVES 6–8

❖Leave the potato skins on.
❖Add finely chopped celery or pickles.

❖Substitute chopped fresh chives for the onions.
❖Add crumbled bacon.

Seared Squash and Pepper Salad

For the pleasure of the variations in color and taste, I alternate vegetables in this salad, using green zucchini and red peppers one time, and green peppers and yellow summer squash the next time. This salad plus grilled or broiled fish makes a complete main course.

> 1½–2 lb zucchini
> 1½ lb red peppers
> ¼ cup olive oil
> 1 tsp minced garlic (optional)
> ⅓ cup red wine vinegar
> 1–2 tsp light soy sauce
> 1 Tb sugar
> ¼ cup toasted sesame seeds (optional)

Wash and trim the ends off the zucchini. Cut each zucchini into 4 long strips and "roll-cut" the strips into 1½-inch-long pieces. (To roll-cut, make a diagonal cut 1½ inches from one end, roll the strip over one-quarter turn and cut at the same angle as the first cut to make another 1½-inch piece, and continue turning and cutting the length of the strip, always keeping the knife at the same angle. See illustration on facing page.)

Wash the red peppers, cut them in half lengthwise, and remove the stems, seeds, and white membranes. Cut the pepper halves lengthwise into 1½-inch-wide strips and then cut the strips into triangular 1½-inch pieces.

In an iron frying pan (if you have it) or other large skillet, heat 2 tablespoons of the oil until the oil is very hot. Add the peppers, watching for spattering, and sear on all sides, turning, for 2–3 minutes. Remove the peppers to a large bowl and set aside. Add the remaining 2 tablespoons oil and, when it is very hot, add the zucchini pieces, sear them on all sides, and remove them to the bowl with the peppers. Stir the garlic, if you are using it, into the oil in the pan for 30 seconds and add to the bowl with the vegetables.

In a small saucepan, heat the vinegar, soy sauce, and sugar until the sugar dissolves. Pour the mixture over the seared vegetables and toss all together. Allow

the dressed vegetables to marinate for at least 30 minutes to absorb the flavor of the dressing. Serve topped with sesame seeds, if desired.   SERVES 4–6

❖To toast sesame seeds, spread them out in a nonstick sauté pan and cook them until lightly browned, stirring them or shaking the pan so that they toast evenly.

Summer Squash Salad

The appearance of summer squash is one of the most welcome sights in the garden to me. It is a refreshing and versatile vegetable, and in this recipe I combine it with five of its garden companions.

1 lb yellow summer squash
1 lb zucchini
1 lb cucumbers
Salt and freshly ground pepper
1½ lb ripe tomatoes
1 cup chopped red onions
¼ cup chopped parsley
2 Tb chopped mint
2 Tb red wine vinegar
6 Tb olive oil

Wash and dry the summer squash and zucchini, trim the ends, cut each one lengthwise into ½-inch-wide strips, and then cut the strips into ½-inch cubes. Place in a large bowl. (Makes 6–7 cups)

Peel, halve, and seed the cucumbers, cut the halves lengthwise into ½-inch-wide strips, and then cut the strips into ½-inch cubes. Put the cubes in a colander,

Summer Squash Salad (continued)

toss them with ¼ teaspoon salt, and let them drain. (Makes about 2 cups)

Wash and core the tomatoes, cut them in half crosswise, squeeze out the seeds, and cut them into ½-inch chunks. Add the tomatoes, red onions, parsley, and mint to the bowl of squash and zucchini cubes.

In a small bowl, whisk the oil into the vinegar. Pat the cucumbers lightly with paper towels to remove any excess salt and add them to the bowl of vegetables. Pour the oil-and-vinegar mixture over the vegetables and toss. Season with salt and freshly ground pepper.   SERVES 4–6

❖Add some finely chopped sun-dried tomatoes.

Vine-Ripened Tomato Salad

The biggest event in our garden every summer is the harvest of the first ripe tomato. Of the several varieties we grow, "Brandywine" deserves a special mention. It is quite an ugly duckling—often greenish rather than red on top, eccentrically shaped with odd depressions, subject to tomato blights and diseases and funny spots. Not a fruit you would ever pick up for beauty. Nevertheless, grow it or get it if you can; it is the very best tomato I've ever eaten. Aside from plucking a perfectly ripe tomato off the vine and eating it as you would pick and eat a ripe apple, the next best recipe is a fresh tomato salad.

    Ripe tomatoes, at room temperature
    Salt and freshly ground pepper
    Excellent olive oil

Prepare the tomatoes just before serving them. Remove the stems. To lose less of the jelly, slice them from top to bottom, parallel to the stem rather than crosswise. Sprinkle the slices with salt and freshly ground pepper, and drizzle olive oil over them.

❖Substitute balsamic vinegar or a good red wine vinegar for the olive oil, or use a combination of oil and vinegar.

❖Drizzle the tomato slices with a favorite vinaigrette.

❖Add sliced fresh basil, or chopped or sliced herbs, such as parsley, chives, oregano, mint, or thyme.

❖Alternate slices of tomato with slices of fresh buffalo mozzarella cheese, and top the tomatoes and cheese with oil and/or balsamic vinegar and with strips of fresh basil.

❖Alternate tomato slices with thinly sliced sweet onion rings and top with fresh herbs, salt and pepper, and olive oil.

❖Top the tomato slices with thin slices of feta cheese or crumbled feta cheese, and dress with salt and pepper and oil.

❖Serve the sliced tomatoes with Niçoise olives and flat anchovies; drizzle with olive oil.

❖*Chunky Tomato and Cucumber Salad:* Core 1½–2 pounds ripe tomatoes, peeling and seeding them, if desired, and cut them into small chunks. Peel and seed 1 pound cucumbers and cut them into small chunks. Chop 1 small red onion or prepare ¾ cup sliced scallions. In a large bowl, combine the tomatoes, cucumbers, and onion or scallions. Add 2 tablespoons chopped mint and 2 tablespoons chopped parsley. Add 1 tablespoon red wine vinegar or fresh lemon juice and 2 tablespoons light olive oil, and toss. Season with more vinegar and oil, if desired, and with salt and freshly ground pepper.   SERVES 4

Warm Tomato Salad with Grilled Bread and Goat Cheese

This delicious warm tomato-and-bread combination has become very popular; one of the best versions I've had is the signature dish at Stellina's Restaurant in Watertown, Massachusetts. This dish can be a complete luncheon. For a casual supper, combine it with a hearty fish appetizer such as *White Beans with Shrimp and Basil* (page 48) or *Grilled Seafood with Sweet-and-Hot Grape Sauce* (page 43). The better the flavor of the tomatoes, the better the result. I use several varieties of tomatoes from our garden for this dish, and out of season I buy fresh plum tomatoes.

    1 Tb chopped garlic
    ½ cup virgin olive oil
    2 lb plum, cherry, or standard tomatoes
    ½ cup or more fresh basil leaves

1 loaf sourdough baguette or
   French bread baguette
Salt and freshly ground pepper
¼-lb goat-cheese log

Combine the garlic and oil, and set aside so that the garlic perfumes the oil.

Wash and dry the tomatoes. Cut plum tomatoes or standard tomatoes in half lengthwise and then into bite-size pieces; cut cherry tomatoes in half. Set aside in a bowl.

Before serving, cut the basil leaves into strips with scissors or a sharp knife. Cut the bread into ½-inch slices and brush both sides of each slice with the garlic-flavored oil. Reserve the remaining oil. Grill both sides of the bread, or broil under a preheated broiler. Toss the tomatoes with the remaining oil and spread them out on a baking sheet. Warm the tomatoes in a preheated 400-degree oven until heated through but not softened. Put the warmed tomatoes in a large bowl, fold in the basil, and season with salt and freshly ground pepper.

Arrange 2–3 slices of bread on each serving plate and generously spoon the tomatoes over the bread. Slice the goat-cheese log into ½-inch rounds, divide them evenly among the plates, and serve.

SERVES 6 AS AN APPETIZER,
4 AS A LUNCHEON OR LIGHT SUPPER

❖In place of goat cheese sprinkle feta cheese over the tomatoes or serve a slice of feta cheese on the side of each plate.

❖Add strips of flat anchovies across the top of the tomatoes.

❖*With Warmed Cheese:* Cut the goat-cheese log into ½-inch-thick slices, place the slices on a cookie sheet, and brush them with garlic oil. Bake the cheese just long enough to warm it.

Spinach Salad
with a Cheese Dressing

Make sure that the spinach is young, tender, and impeccably clean. You can prepare the components well in advance and combine them at serving time.

½ lb spinach leaves (the smaller the better)
1 very thin French bread baguette
1 crushed clove garlic (optional)
4 oz blue cheese
¾ cup low-fat yogurt
1 tsp fresh lemon juice
1 tsp Dijon-style mustard
Salt and freshly ground pepper

Remove any large stems from the spinach, wash and spin-dry the leaves, and refrigerate until ready to serve.

Thinly slice the baguette. Arrange the slices on a baking sheet and bake in a preheated 300-degree oven for about 15 minutes or until light brown. Rub the toasted bread with garlic, if you wish, and set aside.

In a small bowl, mash together with a fork 1½ ounces of the cheese and 2–3 tablespoons of the yogurt. Cut the remaining cheese into small cubes and refrigerate until ready to serve.

Add the remaining yogurt, the lemon juice, and mustard to the mashed cheese and whisk all together, or beat all together with a wooden spoon, or combine in a food processor. When the mixture is smooth, pour it into a jar, cover, and refrigerate.

To serve, toss the spinach with the yogurt dressing in a large bowl. Season with salt and freshly ground pepper. Top with the toasted bread slices and cheese cubes and serve. SERVES 4

❖Use other cheeses, such as Saint André, Stilton, feta, or Brie, in place of the blue cheese.

Wilted Spinach Salad

This salad needs very fresh spinach to give its full effect; the warm dressing will wilt the spinach slightly, but it will still have a fresh-from-the-garden taste.

3 lb spinach
2 tsp sugar
½ tsp salt
½ tsp dried mustard
½ cup cider vinegar
2 Tb vegetable oil
Freshly ground pepper
½ cup crumbled feta cheese
French Bread Croutons (page 355)

Wash the spinach thoroughly, removing and discarding the stems of all but the small tender leaves, and spin-dry. Set it aside in a large bowl.

In a small saucepan, combine the sugar, salt, mustard, vinegar, and oil, and heat the mixture until the sugar has dissolved. Pour the dressing over the spinach and toss well. Season with freshly ground pepper. Garnish the salad with feta cheese and French bread croutons, and serve. SERVES 4–6

Fish and Vegetable Salads

Bluefish Salad

Cooked bluefish and cooked dried beans team up with crisp garden vegetables in this salad. The dish is an ideal fate for leftover fish, but the dish is also certainly delicious enough to merit cooking fish just to make the salad. It can be made well ahead and refrigerated until ready to serve.

Alternative fish: cooked or leftover fish of almost any kind; salmon or a combination of salmon and a white fish would be attractive.

1 lb cooked, skinned bluefish fillets
½ tsp minced garlic
Salt and freshly ground pepper
3 Tb light olive oil

3 cups cooked kidney or cannellini beans
2 cups chopped celery, fennel bulb, or a
    combination of both
1 cup chopped red peppers
½ cup chopped red onions
½ cup chopped scallions
½ cup chopped parsley
¼ cup fresh lemon juice
Hot pepper sauce (optional)

Remove any bones and dark meat from the fish, flake it into medium-sized pieces, and set aside. (You will have about 2 cups.)

In a small bowl, mash the garlic and ¼ teaspoon salt together to make a purée, and stir the oil into it. Place the beans in a large bowl, pour the garlic-oil mixture over them, and stir to coat the beans. Add the fish, celery or fennel, red peppers, red onions, scallions, parsley, and lemon juice. Fold the ingredients together gently so as not to break the fish into smaller pieces. Season with salt and freshly ground pepper and a few drops of hot pepper sauce, if desired. Refrigerate for 1 hour before serving. Remove the salad from the refrigerator a little before serving to take the chill off the dressing.

MAKES ABOUT 8 CUPS, OR

JUST ENOUGH FOR MY TWO SONS-IN-LAW

❖Add 1–2 tablespoons chopped cilantro or other fresh herbs to taste.

❖This is a versatile dish. Use other beans, such as pinto beans, and whatever chopped vegetables you have on hand.

Warm Salad of Spinach, Lettuce Greens, and Smoked Bluefish

This dish works well as a luncheon salad or as an appetizer for dinner.

Alternative fish: smoked sturgeon, cod, sable, or even freshened salt cod

    ½ lb smoked bluefish
    4 strips bacon
    ½ cup light olive oil
    2 Tb balsamic vinegar (or 2 Tb red wine vinegar
        plus ½ tsp sugar)

¼ tsp Dijon-style mustard
⅓ cup finely chopped red onions
12 cups mixed young lettuce greens and
    stemmed spinach, washed and dried
Salt and freshly ground pepper
French Bread Croutons with Garlic (page 355)

Remove the skin, any bones, and the dark flesh from the smoked bluefish, and flake it into medium-sized pieces.

In a sauté pan, fry the bacon until it is crisp and brown. Remove the strips to brown paper to drain, then crumble the bacon into bits and set aside.

Just before serving, in a small saucepan, whisk together 6 tablespoons of the oil, the vinegar, and mustard; warm this vinaigrette over low heat. In a sauté pan, heat 2 more tablespoons of the oil. Add the onions and sauté them until slightly wilted, about 1 minute. Add the bluefish and cook until heated through, about 2–3 minutes.

To serve, place the salad greens in a large bowl, pour the hot vinaigrette dressing over them, toss, and season with salt and freshly ground pepper. Divide the greens among 4 serving plates, and with a slotted spoon place the bluefish-onion mixture on top of each portion. Sprinkle with bacon bits and serve with 2 or 3 croutons on each plate.   SERVES 4

❖Use all spinach. Add some chopped hard-boiled eggs with the bacon bits.

❖Stir toasted nuts into the sautéed bluefish-and-onion mixture.

❖Sauté thin strips of red peppers with the bluefish.

Emerald Coast Amberjack Fish Salad

On location with a television crew of "The Victory Garden" in the panhandle of Florida, I met two of the world's friendliest people, Leah and Willie Mason. When Leah learned that I was working on a cookbook, she immediately volunteered a favorite recipe from her mother. The delicious amberjack I ate in Destin, Florida, reminded me a lot of New England bluefish. Any of this salad left over will taste equally good the next day.

Emerald Coast Amberjack Fish Salad (continued)

Alternative fish: cobia, bluefish, salmon, shark, or other firm-fleshed fish

1-lb cooked amberjack fillet
1 cup chopped celery
¼ cup drained capers
1 Tb fresh lemon juice
1 Tb fresh lime juice
Hot pepper sauce
Mayonnaise
Sour cream
Salt and white pepper
Lettuce leaves
Chopped parsley
Garnish: tomato wedges, hard-boiled eggs,
     sweet pickles

Remove the skin and any bones from the fish. Flake the fish into a large bowl; add the celery, capers, lemon and lime juices, a few drops of hot pepper sauce to taste, and fold all together. Toss with a dressing of equal parts mayonnaise and sour cream to moisten the salad to your liking. Season with salt and white pepper. Cover and chill in the refrigerator for several hours.

Serve on lettuce leaves, sprinkle with parsley, and garnish with tomato wedges, halved hard-boiled eggs, and sweet pickles.   SERVES 4–6

Striped Bass, Cucumber, and Dill Salad

Striped bass is plentiful in the summer on Nantucket, and I serve it frequently. For a fish salad using fresh fish, I prefer to poach the fish; poaching keeps the flesh moist, and it flakes easily into bite-size pieces. This salad is fine with almost any leftover fish— grilled, broiled, or baked, as well as poached.

Alternative fish: cod, halibut, salmon, snapper, sturgeon, wolffish

1½–2-lb striped bass fillets
3 cucumbers
2 cups loosely packed fresh dill

2 tsp fresh lemon juice
½ cup sour cream
Salt and freshly ground pepper
1 cup thinly sliced red onions
½ cup thinly sliced carrots
½ cup thinly sliced dill pickles (optional)

Remove any skin and bones from the fish. Cut the fish into 3–4 pieces. Using a 4-inch-high pan that is large enough to hold the fish in one layer, fill three-quarters of the pan with water and bring it to a boil. Reduce the heat to a gentle simmer, add the fish, and poach for 8 minutes or until the flesh is just opaque. Remove the fish to a plate, allow to cool, cover, and refrigerate.

Trim the ends of the cucumbers and peel them. Score the cucumbers, making grooves lengthwise with a fork for decoration. Slice each cucumber in half lengthwise and scoop out the seeds with a teaspoon. Thinly slice the cucumbers and place the slices in a sieve to drain.

Place 1 cup of the dill and 1 teaspoon of the lemon juice into a food processor or blender, and process to make a very fine mince or purée. Remove the minced dill to a bowl and fold in the sour cream. Season the mixture with the remaining teaspoon of lemon juice, salt and freshly ground pepper, and refrigerate. Roughly chop the remaining cup of dill and set it aside.

When ready to serve, flake the fish into bite-size pieces in a large bowl. Add the cucumbers, red onions, carrots, and dill pickles, if you are using them. Add the dill sauce to the bowl. It will be thick but will thin out from the juice of the cucumbers. Fold the dill sauce gently into the fish and vegetables. Add the roughly chopped dill, season with salt and freshly ground pepper, and fold gently again.   SERVES 6–8

Salt Cod Salad

Salt cod is more versatile than one might think. Its special flavor makes a unique and delicious salad, but you must allow at least 24 hours advance preparation time for the soaking of the fish; see *To Prepare Salt Cod* (page 139).

1 lb salt cod
1 tsp minced garlic
¼ tsp salt

¼ tsp Dijon-style mustard
2 Tb red wine vinegar
½ cup olive oil
Salt and freshly ground pepper
3–4 cups mixed green lettuce leaves
½ cup crumbled feta cheese (optional)
Garnish: 16 cherry tomatoes, Mediterranean-
    style black olives, lemon wedges

Soak the salt cod, cut it into 4 equal pieces, and poach following salt cod instructions on page 139.

To make the vinaigrette dressing, mash the garlic and salt together to make a purée, and place it in a small bowl. Stir in the mustard and vinegar, then gradually whisk in the oil.

Drain the poached salt cod, place it on a platter, and let it cool slightly, then dress it with the vinaigrette while the fish is still slightly warm. The fish should be served at room temperature. Divide the lettuce leaves among 4 serving plates and place equal portions of fish on each bed of greens. Sprinkle with feta cheese, if desired. Garnish each serving with tomatoes, olives, and lemon wedges.   SERVES 4

❖ *Salt Cod Salad with Potatoes:* Omit the feta cheese and salad greens. Wash 2 pounds small, red new potatoes, leaving their skins on, and drop them into a pot of boiling water; boil gently for 15–20 minutes or until just tender. Drain the potatoes and let them cool enough to handle. While they are still warm, cut the potatoes into ¼-inch-thick slices, and spread the potato slices on a serving platter. Sprinkle them with 2 tablespoons finely chopped red onions. Drizzle one-third of the vinaigrette over the potatoes. Distribute the flaked, poached salt cod evenly over the potato slices, drizzle on the remaining vinaigrette, and sprinkle with 2 tablespoons drained capers. Garnish as above.

Tomatoes with Crabmeat and Pesto Cream

When vine-ripened tomatoes make the summer garden red and basil is in full bloom, this dish makes a superb lunch. Peeling the tomatoes makes it all a bit more elegant, but you can omit that step if you like.

Crème fraîche is available in most markets, but you can make your own ahead of time (page 353) or use sour cream. A food processor is essential for this recipe.

Alternative shellfish and fish: cooked lobster, cooked tuna, shark, salmon, or other firm-fleshed white fish

4 large ripe tomatoes
3 cups packed basil leaves
1–2 tsp minced garlic
½ tsp salt
¼ cup parsley leaves
¼ cup light olive oil
⅓ cup freshly grated Parmesan cheese
1 cup *Crème Fraîche* (page 353) or sour cream
2 cups fresh lump crabmeat
4 Tb chopped pickled or roasted red peppers
    (optional)

Core the tomatoes. To peel them, bring a pot of water to a boil. Prepare a bowl of ice water. Drop the tomatoes into the boiling water for 10 seconds, or until the skins just begin to split. Lift the tomatoes with a slotted spoon and lower them quickly into the ice water to stop the cooking action. When they are cool enough to handle, peel off the skins. Set aside.

Reserve ⅓ cup of the basil leaves. Put the remaining basil into the bowl of a food processor fitted with a steel blade. Mash the garlic and salt together into a purée and add the mixture to the basil in the processor bowl. Process the mixture to a paste, then add the olive oil gradually in a thin stream. Add the Parmesan cheese and process until fairly smooth, scraping down the sides as necessary. Set aside. If you are not serving shortly, cover the pesto with a film of olive oil to prevent its darkening.

Stack the reserved basil leaves and cut them into very narrow slices to make a chiffonade. Set aside.

When ready to serve, combine the pesto and crème fraîche or sour cream in a small bowl. Remove any bones or cartilage from the crabmeat and put the crabmeat into a second bowl. Gently fold ½ cup of the pesto cream into the crabmeat. Place 2 or more spoonfuls of the remaining pesto cream sauce on each of 4 serving plates, spreading it lightly around the surface of the plates. Quarter each tomato, cutting only two-thirds of the way down through the tomato so that it opens like a flower but is still attached at the base. Put one tomato-flower in the center of the sauce on each plate and evenly divide the crabmeat mixture among the centers of the tomatoes. Sprinkle

Tomatoes with Crabmeat and Pesto Cream (continued)

the basil chiffonade over the top and place a spoonful of red peppers in the center of the crabmeat, if desired.   SERVES 4 AS A LUNCHEON DISH

❖Add other garnishes, such as black olives, halved hard-boiled eggs, or baby radishes.

Crab Louis

Crabmeat has always been something of a luxury. On a Boston Ritz-Carlton Hotel menu from July 1938, a main course of fried clams and tartar sauce cost seventy-five cents, less than a crabmeat-cocktail appetizer for eighty cents or a crabmeat salad for a dollar and ten cents. Crab Louis is thought to have been created by a San Francisco chef, so Dungeness crab would be regionally appropriate, but any impeccably fresh lump crabmeat will do nicely. For culinary purists, serve this succulent dish of fresh crabmeat and fresh garden vegetables only with lemon wedges; for culinary historians, serve it the way Louis served it, with homemade Russian dressing lightened with whipped cream.

RUSSIAN DRESSING

1⅓ cups mayonnaise
¼ cup finely chopped green peppers
¼ cup finely minced scallions
3 Tb chili sauce
1 Tb red wine vinegar or fresh lemon
    or lime juice
Salt and freshly ground pepper

To make the Russian Dressing: In a bowl, combine the mayonnaise, peppers, scallions, chili sauce, and vinegar. Season with salt and freshly ground pepper. Refrigerate until ready to use. The flavor intensifies if the dressing marinates for a few hours or more.   MAKES ABOUT 1¾ CUPS

❖*Crab Louis Dressing:* Whip ½ cup heavy cream and fold it into the Russian dressing.

Turn the Russian dressing into a Crab Louis dressing, cover, and refrigerate until ready to serve.

CRABMEAT SALAD

1½ lb fresh lump crabmeat
1 large head romaine lettuce
8 small pickling cucumbers
12 cherry tomatoes
4 hard-boiled eggs
24 green olives with pimentos
Lemon wedges

To prepare the salad: Pick over the crabmeat, removing any bits of shell or cartilage, and refrigerate until ready to serve. Wash and spin-dry the lettuce, discarding any tough outer or damaged leaves. Set aside 8 small inner leaves, each large enough to make a cup shape, and finely shred the remaining leaves. Wash and dry the cucumbers, trim the ends, and score the skins lengthwise with a fork for decoration. Thinly slice each cucumber, keeping the slices together in the form of the cucumber. Remove the stems of the cherry tomatoes and cut each in half. Peel and quarter or slice the eggs.

On each of 4 chilled serving plates, arrange a bed of about 1½ cups shredded lettuce. Evenly divide the crabmeat among the plates, mounding it up in the center. Place 2 cucumbers to one side of the crabmeat, fanning the slices out slightly. Arrange 6 cherry tomato halves on one side of the cucumbers and 1 quartered or sliced egg on the other side. On the opposite side of each plate from the cucumbers, arrange 2 of the reserved romaine leaves, cupped side up. Spoon some dressing into the lettuce cups, place 6 olives next to the lettuce cups, and garnish the plates with lemon wedges. Serve with a basket of thin white and rye bread toasts.   SERVES 4

❖Substitute 4 peeled whole tomatoes cut into wedges or slices for the cherry tomatoes; or substitute 2 large cucumbers, peeled, seeded, and sliced, for the small pickling cucumbers.
❖Substitute a tablespoon or more of drained large capers for the olives.
❖Forget tradition and use small leaves of young mixed lettuces in place of shredded romaine, or place the crabmeat in a ripe avocado half.
❖Substitute peeled slices of roasted red peppers for tomatoes or thin slices of raw kohlrabi for the cucumbers.

Helga Westphal's Herring Salad

My son-in-law Adam adores herring, and through him I acquired the recipe to a delicious herring salad that Helga Westphal, a neighbor, used to make for Adam's family. My few liberties with Helga's recipe include using pickled herring from my local fish market where Helga uses canned matjes herring. Although this dish is a perfect place for leftover cooked beets and potatoes, I cook the vegetables up just to have the salad, and I always serve it with black bread.

   1 lb pickled herring
   2 large Granny Smith apples
   2 cups cooked beets, cut into ½-inch cubes
   2 cups cooked potatoes, cut into ½-inch cubes
   2 cups dill pickles, cut into ½-inch cubes
   1 cup finely chopped onions
   1 cup ham, cut into ½-inch cubes (optional)
   ½ cup mayonnaise
   ½ cup sour cream
   ¼ cup red wine vinegar
   Salt and freshly ground pepper

Drain the herring from its brine, cut it into ½-inch cubes or slices, and place it in a large bowl. (Makes about 2 cups) Quarter the apples, remove the cores, and cut the apples into ½-inch cubes. (Makes about 1½–2 cups) Add the apples to the herring, along with the beets, potatoes, pickles, onions, and ham, if you are using it.

In a small bowl, whisk together the mayonnaise, sour cream, and vinegar. Pour the mixture over the herring and vegetables, and gently fold all together. Season with salt and freshly ground pepper.

MAKES 10 CUPS

Cherry Tomato and Lobster Salad

The salad combination of cherry tomatoes and shellfish first came to my attention in Italy at the home of the wine makers Walter and Patrizia Filiputti. In Patrizia's version, the shellfish was sweet langoustines seasoned with fresh oregano; the salad was simple but spectacular. Here is my version with American lobster.

Alternative shellfish: 3 cups mixed cooked shellfish, such as lump crabmeat, squid, scallops

   Three 1½-lb lobsters
   4–5 cups stemmed, halved cherry tomatoes
      (combination red and yellow, if desired)★
   ¼ cup chopped chives
   5 Tb mild olive oil
   2 Tb red wine vinegar
   Salt and freshly ground pepper

  ★Counting from the garden, about forty-five 1-inch cherry tomatoes make 4 cups.

In a large pot with a rack or an upside-down pie pan in the bottom, put 2 inches of water, bring the water to a rolling boil, add the lobsters, cover the pot, and steam the lobsters for 18 minutes. Remove the lobsters; when they are cool enough to handle, remove the meat (see *To remove meat from a cooked lobster,* page 188) and cut it into bite-size pieces; then place the lobster pieces in a bowl, cover, and refrigerate. (Makes about 3 cups)

Shortly before serving, combine the lobster meat, tomatoes, and chives in a large bowl. In a small bowl, gradually whisk the oil into the vinegar to make a vinaigrette. Season the dressing with salt and freshly ground pepper. Pour the dressing over the lobster and tomatoes, and gently mix all together. Marinate in the refrigerator for 20 minutes or more. Bring to room temperature before serving.

SERVES 6–8 AS A FIRST COURSE,
4–6 AS A LUNCHEON SALAD

❖Replace the chives with chopped shallots or ½ cup chopped red onions or chopped scallions.
❖Add 1 tablespoon fresh herbs, such as basil, mint, dill, or oregano.
❖Buy 1–1¼ pound cooked lobster meat instead of whole live lobsters.

Old-Fashioned Lobster Salad

If you start with whole live lobsters instead of cooked lobster meat, you can add the tomalley (if you wish to use it) to the mayonnaise that enrobes this salad, and you can sprinkle the roe over the finished salad as a

Old-Fashioned Lobster Salad (continued)

garnish. But you can also make a delicious salad starting with one pound of cooked lobster meat from your market.

> Two 2-lb lobsters
> ⅔ cup diced celery
> ½ cup diced scallions
> 1–2 Tb minced parsley
> 1 Tb fresh lemon juice
> Salt and freshly ground pepper
> Hot pepper sauce
> ¼ cup sour cream
> ¾ cup mayonnaise
> Garnish: sliced avocados and peeled roasted red
>   peppers (see page 360)

In a large pot with a rack or an upside-down pie pan in the bottom, put 2 inches of water, bring the water to a rolling boil, add the lobsters, cover the pot, and steam the lobsters for 20 minutes. Remove the lobsters; when they are cool enough to handle, remove the meat and any roe and tomalley. Push the roe through a fine sieve and set aside. Sieve the tomalley (if you are using it) and set it aside to add to the mayonnaise.

Cut the lobster meat into ½-inch pieces, place them in a bowl, add the celery, scallions, parsley, and lemon juice, and toss. Season with salt and freshly ground pepper and a few drops of hot pepper sauce. Cover the lobster mixture and marinate in the refrigerator for at least 30 minutes.

Just before serving, fold the sour cream and the tomalley (if you are using it) into the mayonnaise. Drain any liquid from the lobster mixture. Pour the sour-cream-and-mayonnaise dressing over the lobster and mix gently until the lobster is well coated. Season with salt and pepper. Serve on a lettuce leaf with a garnish of sliced avocados and peeled roasted red peppers. Sprinkle the salad with lobster roe.

SERVES 4

❖*Lobster Salad Roll:* Serve the lobster salad in buttered hot dog rolls that have been baked in a 375-degree oven for 10 minutes or toasted on a grill.

❖Serve the salad in a peeled and quartered ripe tomato.

❖Garnish the salad with blanched asparagus spears dressed with a light vinaigrette.

❖Extend the salad by adding more vegetables.

Cold Lobster
with Garden Tomatoes

When a clambake is just too much work, we cook lobsters at home and take them to the beach. Served chilled, with fresh tomatoes and an herb mayonnaise, they are all we need. The sea is a great place to wash off the lobster juices! For the beach, we would pack the lobsters, unsliced tomatoes, and mayonnaise in separate containers, all well chilled, and would prepare the tomato cups and assemble the dish just before serving. Of course, this luncheon dish is just as good served at home, especially if the tomatoes are picked right off the vine.

> Two 2-lb cold cooked lobsters (see *Cooking
>   Methods,* page 186)
> 4 ripe tomatoes
> *Herb Mayonnaise* (page 12)
> 2 Tb chopped chives
> Chive spears
> Lemon wedges

Split the lobsters in half lengthwise. Remove any roe and tomalley, and push the roe and the tomalley (if you wish to use it) through a fine sieve. Clean out the body cavities, removing the sand sacs, intestinal veins, and any loose cartilage. Pull the tail meat out, cut it into pieces, and return it, equally divided, to the 4 half-tail shells. Twist the claws off the bodies, remove the meat, cut it into pieces, and evenly distribute it among the 4 half-body cavities. Cover the stuffed half-lobster shells, and refrigerate.

When ready to serve, core the tomatoes and cut each into wedges from the top down, but do not cut all the way through to the base of the tomato. You want each tomato to open into a cup to hold the herb mayonnaise. Place the lobster halves on serving plates. Mix the sieved roe and tomalley (if you are using it) into the herb mayonnaise. Place a tomato next to each lobster half and spoon a generous dollop of herb mayonnaise into the tomato. Sprinkle the lobsters and tomatoes with chopped chives. Garnish each plate with chive spears and lemon wedges.   SERVES 4

❖Lighten the mayonnaise with 1–2 tablespoons sour cream or yogurt.

❖Substitute puréed fresh basil leaves for the chives, parsley, and tarragon in the mayonnaise.

Composed Lobster Salad and Dressings

What could make a more elegant luncheon on a fine summer day than a beautifully arranged lobster salad. All you need is cooked lobster meat cut into bite-size pieces, crisp salad greens, and a tasty dressing. (I offer three possibilities below, or use the vinaigrette recipes in the Appendix, page 365.) Decorate each plate with festive fresh vegetable garnishes. All the ingredients can be prepared ahead and refrigerated, and assembled just before serving.

Alternative seafood: big chunks of crabmeat or a combination of lobster meat and cooked scallops or chunks of monkfish

1½ cups loosely packed salad greens per person
Vinaigrette or olive oil
⅓ lb cooked lobster meat per person (see *Cooking Methods,* page 186)
Dressing for lobster (see below)
Garnish

Wash and spin-dry the salad greens. Try combining loose-leaf greens, such as Boston or Bibb lettuce, with a combination of arugula, young spinach, watercress, inner hearts of romaine, or spears of endive. Place the greens in a bowl and toss with just enough vinaigrette or olive oil to lightly coat the leaves.

Cut the lobster meat into bite-size pieces or slices. In a bowl, combine the lobster meat with just enough dressing to lightly coat.

To serve, arrange the dressed salad greens on serving plates and top with the dressed lobster meat. Garnish the servings with some of the following or with other fresh vegetables of your choice: fresh herbs, black olives, roasted red peppers, peeled tomato wedges, red or yellow cherry tomatoes, hard-boiled eggs, artichoke hearts, asparagus tips, or even slices of truffle.

CLASSIC RÉMOULADE DRESSING

3 Tb Dijon-style mustard
2 Tb red wine vinegar
½ cup olive oil
½ cup vegetable oil
Sieved roe or tomalley (optional)
1–2 Tb heavy cream (optional)
Salt and freshly ground pepper
1 Tb chopped fresh tarragon

Place the mustard and vinegar in a bowl and gradually whisk in the olive oil and vegetable oil. Whisk in lobster roe or tomalley, if desired. Whisk in the cream (if you are using it) to lighten the dressing. Season with salt and freshly ground pepper, and stir in the tarragon.

MAKES ABOUT I CUP

MAYONNAISE PLUS

1 cup mayonnaise

Fold into the mayonnaise one or more of the following: peeled, seeded, and finely diced tomatoes, a dash of tomato paste, sour cream, fresh lemon juice, fresh chopped herbs, chopped and drained capers and dill pickles, hot pepper sauce, and chopped, roasted, and peeled red peppers.

See *Herb Mayonnaise* (page 12).

MUSTARD–SOUR CREAM DRESSING

2 Tb olive oil
2 Tb Dijon-style mustard
3 Tb mayonnaise
¾ cup sour cream
Sieved roe or tomalley (optional)
Salt and freshly ground pepper
2–3 Tb light cream or milk

In a small bowl, whisk the oil into the mustard. Whisk in the mayonnaise and then the sour cream. Fold in the roe or tomalley, if you are using them. Season with salt and freshly ground pepper. If desired, thin the dressing by whisking in light cream or milk.

MAKES ABOUT I CUP

❖Add 1 tablespoon each minced fresh tarragon and chives.

Broiled Salmon
and Coleslaw Salad

In Finland I first tasted the combination of salmon and coleslaw; it was so refreshing that I've served it many times since, sometimes as an appetizer, other times as a luncheon dish, and again, perhaps combined with fresh green beans blanched and then dressed with a vinaigrette, as the main course for dinner. The coleslaw in this dish is made with a yogurt-based dressing that is lighter and slightly more acidic than the dressing on my more traditional *Coleslaw* (page 82)—an alternate version for this dish. I think the lighter dressing is just right with the delicate flavor of salmon. The recipe deliberately makes more coleslaw than four people will eat in one meal because this is one of the world's best leftovers, even better the day after, when it has marinated longer.

Alternative fish: striped bass, sturgeon, tuna, bluefish, halibut, firm-fleshed cod or haddock

COLESLAW SALAD

8 cups thinly sliced cabbage
1 thinly sliced red onion
4 grated carrots (about 1½ cups)

1 cup yogurt
½ cup mayonnaise
¼ cup sour cream
1 Tb fresh lemon juice
2 tsp Dijon-style mustard
1 tsp sugar (optional)
Salt and freshly ground pepper
⅓ cup chopped fresh dill

BROILED SALMON

1¼–1½-lb salmon fillet
Vegetable oil

Lettuce leaves
Sliced tomatoes
Lemon wedges

To make the coleslaw salad: In a large bowl, combine the cabbage, onion, and carrots. In a small bowl, combine the yogurt, mayonnaise, sour cream, lemon juice, mustard, and sugar, if desired. Pour the dressing over the vegetables and toss to coat the vegetables well. Season with salt and freshly ground pepper, cover, and refrigerate until ready to serve. Just before serving, mix in the dill.   MAKES ABOUT 10 CUPS

To prepare the salmon: Skin the fish and remove any bones. Slice the fillet on the diagonal into ¼-inch-thick slices and lightly brush the slices on both sides with oil. Place the slices on a nonstick baking sheet and refrigerate until ready to cook.

Just before serving, arrange lettuce leaves on 4 serving plates, spoon coleslaw onto the lettuce, and garnish each plate with tomato slices. Place the salmon 4 inches below a preheated broiler and cook for 1–2 minutes, or until the salmon is just lightly colored. Lift the salmon slices with a spatula and arrange them in a fan shape on the plates, to the side of and slightly overlapping the coleslaw. Serve with lemon wedges. SERVES 4

Salmon Salad in a Tomato Flower

This quickly made salad uses leftover cooked salmon and can be served in an avocado half or just by itself, or it can be used as filling for a sandwich; but I think it is especially beautiful sitting in the center of a ripe tomato. Crème fraîche gives a light taste to the dish, but you could use sour cream or mayonnaise (or a combination of the two) or yogurt. To my eye, the tomatoes look their best peeled, but you can omit that step, if you prefer. Both the tomatoes and the fish salad can be prepared ahead and refrigerated until ready to serve.

Alternative fish: any firm-fleshed cooked fish

4 large ripe tomatoes
2 cups flaked cooked salmon
1½ cups finely chopped celery
¼ cup finely chopped red onions
1 Tb minced chives
1–2 Tb chopped basil
½ cup *Crème Fraîche* (page 353) or sour cream
1 cup peeled, seeded, and chopped cucumbers
Salt and freshly ground pepper
Watercress (optional)

To prepare the tomatoes, bring a pot of water to a boil and place a bowl of ice water to one side. Core the tomatoes with a small paring knife and drop them into the boiling water. As soon as the skins begin to

split (about 6–10 seconds for ripe tomatoes), lift the tomatoes immediately with a slotted spoon and drop them into the ice water. In a few seconds, as they cool, remove the tomatoes from the ice water and peel or slip off the skins. Set the tomatoes aside.

To prepare the salmon salad, combine the salmon, celery, onions, chives, and basil in a bowl. Gently fold in the crème fraîche or sour cream. Just before serving, add the cucumbers and season with salt and freshly ground pepper. (Makes about 4 cups)

Just before serving, place a bed of watercress, if you like, on each of 4 serving plates. Take each tomato and make 3 cuts three-quarters of the way down through it so that it will open into 6 equal wedges, but be sure all of the wedges are still attached at the base. The tomato will look like a flower with 6 petals. Place a tomato "flower" on each plate and evenly divide the salmon salad among the centers of the tomatoes. SERVES 4

❖This salad can use whatever leftover fish you have and whatever vegetables are available. Substitute finely chopped red or green peppers for the cucumbers, add a bit of hot pepper, or try other fresh herbs.

Sweet-and-Tart Broiled Salmon Salad with Arugula

The sharp mustard taste of arugula contrasts in just the right way with the sweetness of crisp apples. Balsamic vinegar, with its sweet, oaky flavor, is important to the blend of this salad. When salmon is added to the greens and fruit, the result is a lovely appetizer course or a main course for a light luncheon.

Alternative fish: bass, snapper, swordfish, tuna, shark

1–1¼-lb skinned salmon fillet
¾ lb arugula
5 Tb virgin olive oil
2 Tb balsamic vinegar
Salt and freshly ground pepper
1 large green apple

Remove any bones from the salmon and cut the fillet into four 4-ounce portions. Set aside, covered, in the refrigerator.

Sweet-and-Tart Broiled Salmon Salad (continued)

Stem, wash, and spin-dry the arugula, and set it aside in a bowl. In a small saucepan, whisk 3 tablespoons of the oil into the vinegar to make a vinaigrette. Season with salt and freshly ground pepper.

Brush the salmon portions with the remaining 2 tablespoons of oil and season them with salt and pepper. Place the salmon on an oiled broiler pan, skinned side down, and cook under a preheated broiler for 6–8 minutes or until opaque at the center. Cooking time will depend on the thickness of the portions. When the salmon is almost done, warm the vinaigrette over low heat.

Peel and core the apple and cut it into paper-thin slices. (If you slice the apple ahead, keep the slices in cold water to prevent darkening, and then pat dry before using.)

When ready to serve, pour two-thirds of the warm vinaigrette over the arugula and toss. Divide the dressed arugula evenly on 4 serving plates and top each serving with a piece of salmon. Arrange the apple slices on top and slightly to one side of the fish. Drizzle the remaining vinaigrette over all and serve.   SERVES 4

❖Cook the salmon on a preheated well-oiled grill.

Shrimp Salad with a Mustard-Tarragon Dressing

Both mustard and fresh tarragon (which is very easy to grow in your garden) have a way of intensifying the flavor of shrimp. I serve this salad with a garnish of sliced ripe tomatoes, Greek olives, and slices of avocado that have been brushed with lemon juice.

  1 Tb Dijon-style mustard
  1½ Tb red wine vinegar or lemon juice
  1 Tb minced shallots (optional)
  2 Tb light olive oil
  2 Tb vegetable oil
  Salt and freshly ground pepper
  1 lb peeled and deveined extra jumbo (21–25
      count) or jumbo (26–30 count) raw shrimp
  1 Tb chopped fresh tarragon
  Bibb lettuce leaves

In a small bowl, beat together the mustard, vinegar or lemon juice, and shallots, if you like. Gradually whisk in the olive and vegetable oils to make a thick emulsion. Season with salt and freshly ground pepper, and set aside.

Bring a large pot with enough water to cover the shrimp by 1 inch to a rolling boil. Add 1 tablespoon salt for every 2 quarts water. Drop the shrimp into the boiling water. They will cool the water slightly below the boiling point. Reduce the heat, if necessary, to keep the water from returning to a boil. Let the shrimp poach in the hot water for about 2 minutes, until they have turned pink on the outside and opaque on the inside and the tails have curled. Lift the shrimp with a slotted spoon immediately from the water to a colander and run them under cold water to stop the cooking action. As soon as the shrimp are cool enough to handle, drain them, pat them dry, and slice them in half lengthwise.

Combine the shrimp and the mustard vinaigrette in a bowl, add the tarragon, and toss to mix. Cover and marinate in the refrigerator for at least 30 minutes, remove from the refrigerator long enough before serving to let the chill come off the vinaigrette, toss again, arrange on crisp Bibb lettuce leaves, and serve.   SERVES 4–6

❖Serve the dressed shrimp on cooked artichoke bottoms (see page 349 for artichoke preparation).
❖*Shrimp and Artichoke Salad:* Cut the shrimp into small pieces. Omit the tarragon. Combine the shrimp with 1½–2 cups chopped artichoke hearts. Mix with the vinaigrette dressing and serve at room temperature or chilled.

Green Bean and Shrimp Salad with a Sweet Ginger Dressing

What could be prettier than pink shrimp, green beans, and red peppers? Both chili paste and sweet stem ginger are available in Asian markets and gourmet shops.

Alternative shellfish: cooked sliced lobster meat, cooked lump crabmeat

SHRIMP AND VEGETABLES

1½ lb extra jumbo (16–20 count) raw shrimp
2 lb green beans
1 sweet red pepper

SWEET GINGER DRESSING

2 Tb stem ginger syrup
2 Tb vegetable oil
2 Tb rice vinegar or red wine vinegar
1 Tb orange juice
1 tsp grated orange zest
½–1 tsp chili paste, or to taste
1 Tb finely diced stem ginger

To prepare the shrimp and vegetables: Peel and devein the shrimp. Bring a large pot of water to a rolling boil, using enough water to cover the shrimp by at least 1 inch. Add 1 tablespoon salt for every 2 quarts water. Prepare a large bowl of ice water to one side to cool the shrimp immediately after they have cooked. Drop the shrimp into the boiling water. Do not allow the water to return to a boil, reducing the heat as necessary to maintain a gentle simmer. The shrimp will be cooked in 1–2 minutes or when the shrimp turn pink on the outside and the tails just curl. (To test, make an incision in 1 shrimp; the center should be white and opaque, no longer gray and translucent.) Drain the shrimp and plunge them into the ice water. Drain well, place in a large bowl, cover with bags of ice, and refrigerate until chilled.

Remove the stems of the green beans and drop the beans into a large pot of boiling water. Bring the water back to a boil and cook, uncovered, for 4–8 minutes, depending on the size of the beans; they should be tender but retain their crunchiness. Drain them, run them under cold water to stop the cooking action, and pat them dry with paper towels. Leave small beans whole, but cut large beans on a diagonal into 1½-inch-long pieces. Set aside.

Cut the red pepper in half lengthwise and remove the stem, seeds, and white membrane. Cut into thin lengthwise strips, then cut the strips down to about 1½-inch lengths.

To make the dressing: In a small bowl, whisk together the ginger syrup, oil, rice or red wine vinegar, orange juice and zest, and chili paste until well blended. Stir in the diced stem ginger.

Just before serving, pat the shrimp dry and slice them in half lengthwise.

To serve: Combine the beans and pepper in a large bowl, pour ⅓ cup of the dressing over them, toss well, fold in the shrimp, and add more dressing, if you wish. Serve at room temperature.   SERVES 6–8

❖ *With Pasta:* Try this salad as a topping on hot fresh Chinese noodles or other pasta of your choice.

Jim Burke's Warm Squid Salad with Arugula

Boston has been justifiably well known for its colleges and museums, and now also for its restaurants. Jim Burke was one of the first innovative chefs in Boston's culinary renaissance. His two restaurants in Waltham, a nearby suburb, The Tuscan Grill and The Iguana Café, draw crowds because of his creative Italian cooking in which squid has a prominent place.

8 oz fresh squid
3 bunches arugula
⅔ cup olive oil
1 tsp chopped garlic
½ cup peeled, seeded, and chopped tomatoes
¼ cup red wine vinegar
1 Tb fresh basil
1 Tb chopped fresh parsley
Pinch of crushed red pepper flakes
Salt

Clean the squid as necessary, following the directions on page 107. Cut the squid crosswise into rings about ¼ inch wide, pat dry, and set aside.

Wash and dry the arugula, and divide it among 4 serving plates.

In a medium-sized sauté pan, heat ⅓ cup of the oil until it is smoking; add the squid and sauté it quickly, tossing rapidly in the pan, for 1–2 minutes, or until the flesh turns opaque. Quickly add the garlic, tomatoes, vinegar, basil, parsley, red pepper flakes, and the remaining ⅓ cup olive oil, and cook, tossing, just until the mixture is heated through. Season with salt.

Lift the squid rings from the pan, place equal portions on top of the arugula, and spoon the pan juices over each serving.   SERVES 4

SPECIAL INFORMATION ABOUT
SQUID

WATCHING SQUID PROPEL themselves through salt water in jetlike bursts is as fascinating as watching a science fiction movie. These strange mollusks, which actually belong to the same family that includes clams and oysters, look like creatures from some other evolutionary time.

I have been captivated by the firm texture and sweet taste of squid since I first caught, cleaned, cooked, and ate it. It has long been a popular food in other countries but has only recently become widely available in American markets and restaurants, although in Italian markets and cooking, squid—often referred to as calamari—has long been a staple.

Four species of squid are marketed in the United States:

1. *California or Monterey squid*, a small squid harvested in the Pacific.
2. *Longfin*, also called winter squid or Boston squid, harvested in the Atlantic in winter months.
3. *Shortfin*, also harvested in the Atlantic, but in summer months.
4. *Giant squid*, imported and sold as tenderized steaks.

The squid we find in our markets range from about 4 inches to a foot in length. Their anatomy features a soft outer body, referred to as the mantle, with wings or fins on either side of the narrow tail end. The head is suspended in the center of the front of the open-ended body, with arms and tentacles growing out of the top

of the head and surrounding the parrotlike beak, or mouth, of the squid. The head is connected to the body and its attached sac of visceral organs and protective ink sac by a hard, plasticlike strip of bone called the cuttlebone. The squid dissuades attackers by clouding the water with a dark fluid from the ink sac. The cuttlebone is also called the quill, or pen, and one can actually write by dipping the point of the cuttlebone in ink from the ink sac. There is a grayish speckled membrane covering the flesh that needs to be removed before cooking. About 80 percent of the squid—including body, fins, arms, and tentacles—is edible.

Buying:

Fresh. You will find it in the market whole—cleaned or uncleaned; or as cleaned tubes (bodies) with arms and tentacles; or cleaned and cut up into strips and rings with separated arms and tentacles. The meat should look shiny, from white to translucent, and should have virtually no odor at all.

Frozen. You will find it whole and cleaned, or as cleaned steaks, as tubes with arms and tentacles, or as rings and strips. I've been very pleased with the frozen squid I have purchased. Once I bought a package of frozen squid rings in a Chicago supermarket. When I opened them and saw how large they were, I thought they would be tough; but they were as tender and sweet as the small squid I've caught and cleaned myself and cooked immediately.

SPECIAL INFORMATION ABOUT
SQUID

Storage: If I have caught squid or have bought uncleaned squid (often the price of uncleaned squid is a persuasive factor), I try to clean it as soon as I get home; if cleaning is delayed at all, I refrigerate the squid, covered with a lid or plastic wrap, in a glass or non-aluminum-lined dish or pan. I keep cleaned squid stacked in single layers between waxed paper and covered until I am ready to cook.

To clean squid: The procedure is not complicated after you have worked through it once or twice, but it can be time-consuming if you have a lot of squid to clean. Grasp the head of the squid and gently pull it out and away from the body, or mantle. The sac of visceral organs may come out of the open-ended body with the head. If not, you can remove it later. With a sharp knife, cut the arms and tentacles off the head just above the eyes, discarding the head, eyes, any attached viscera, and lumpy bits of white. Cut the two long tentacles to the same length as the arms, and pinch out and discard the "beak," located

near the base of the arms and tentacles. Rinse the arm and tentacle pieces and set aside. Pull or rub off the speckled outer membrane, or skin, covering the body and the two fins at the tail end. Discard the membrane, cut the fins off the body, and set aside. Feel inside the body for the internal thin-shell cuttlebone, grasp it, and remove it along with the sac of inklike fluid. At this point, if the sac of visceral organs did not come out with the head, pull it out. Discard the cuttlebone, ink sac, and any viscera. Turn the tubular body inside out by pushing the tail end of the body all the way through. Rinse the body well, pulling or rubbing off the very thin membrane on the inside of the body, then rinse again. Repeat these steps with each squid to be cleaned. Depending on how large the squid are, leave the arm-and-tentacle section as is or cut it into bite-size pieces. Depending on the recipe, leave the body section in one piece or cut into rings or strips. Pat all of the squid meat dry, spread the pieces in single layers between waxed paper, stack

the layers, place in a glass or non-aluminum-lined pan or dish, cover with a lid or plastic wrap, and refrigerate until ready to cook.

Cooking: You can sauté or poach squid rings for 1–2 minutes and they will stay very firm yet tender. You can stuff small squid bodies with a cooked stuffing, heat them for up to 15 minutes, and they will be tender; but if you cook them longer, they will begin to toughen. Strangely, if you let the squid cook for an hour or more, it will begin to get tender again. My favorite ways of cooking squid are simple and fast. For more elaborate ways with squid, see the wonderful cookbooks of Marcella Hazan, Giuliano Bugialli, and Margaret and Franco Romagnoli.

Yields:
❖2 pounds whole squid will serve about 4–6 persons as a sautéed appetizer.
❖3 pounds whole squid will serve about 4 persons as a sautéed main course.
❖Allow 1–2 whole bodies for stuffed-squid recipes.

Salade Niçoise

I may be dating myself, but there was a period when every restaurant had this dish on the luncheon menu. Fashions may change and dishes fall out of favor, but this salad is as good as ever, especially when the tuna fish is fresh and grilled. What a nice party dish this is; I have served it, among other occasions, to three dozen happy women at a baby shower. Many of the ingredients can

be prepared ahead. Prepare the potato salad and vinaigrette in the morning or the day before; marinate the tuna, blanch the beans, and prepare the salad greens in the morning. All that really needs to be done just before serving is to cook the tuna and assemble the salad. This is a dish that rewards attention to presentation, so allow yourself enough time to assemble it carefully.

Alternative fish: swordfish, shark, or firm-fleshed fish such as salmon that grills well, or the traditional canned tuna

Salade Niçoise (continued)

2 lb tuna steaks, ¾–1 inch thick
2 Tb red wine vinegar
1 Tb fresh thyme
¼ cup olive oil
1 large head loose-leaf or Boston lettuce
1½ lb green snap beans
1 cup *Vinaigrette* (page 365)
4 cups *Potato Salad Vinaigrette* (page 90)
4 large ripe tomatoes
6 hard-boiled eggs
½ cup pitted small black Niçoise olives
One 2-oz tin flat anchovies packed in oil
2 Tb chopped shallots
2–3 Tb chopped parsley
Lemon wedges

In a nonaluminum-lined pan or dish large enough to hold the tuna in one layer, place the tuna steaks. In a small bowl, combine the vinegar, thyme, and oil, and pour the mixture over the fish. Turn the tuna in the marinade until coated on all sides, cover, and refrigerate for at least 1 hour. Wash and spin-dry the lettuce, place it in a large plastic bag with paper towels to absorb extra moisture, prick a few air holes in the bag, and refrigerate.

Remove the stem ends of the beans, cut large beans on the diagonal into 2-inch-long pieces, and leave small beans whole. Bring a large pot of water to a boil and set a bowl of ice water to one side. Drop the beans into the boiling water, bring the water back to a boil over high heat, and cook the beans 3–5 minutes, or until they are just tender. Drain them and immediately drop them into the ice water to stop the cooking action; refresh the cooling water with more ice water as necessary to chill the beans quickly. Drain the cool beans, pat them dry with a cloth towel, put them in a large plastic bag with paper towels to absorb extra moisture, prick a few air holes in the bag, and refrigerate.

Shortly before serving, place the tuna on a preheated grill, cook for 5 minutes, turn, and grill the other side for 5 minutes, or until the tuna is just barely pink in the center. Watch the grill enough to avoid overcooking, which dries out and toughens the flesh. Remove the tuna to a rack or plate to cool slightly.

To assemble the salad, toss the lettuce with a few tablespoons of the vinaigrette and arrange the lettuce around the edges of and in the center of a large serving

platter. Add a bit of the vinaigrette to the potato salad, if it needs it, and arrange the potato salad along one side of the platter. Toss the beans with ¼ cup of the vinaigrette and arrange them on the other side of the platter from the potato salad. Break the tuna into chunks or slice it, and place it on the lettuce in the center of the platter. Core and quarter the tomatoes, and peel and halve the eggs. Arrange the tomatoes, eggs, and olives decoratively about the platter. Drizzle a little vinaigrette over the tuna, tomatoes, and eggs. Garnish the tuna and the eggs with the anchovies, sprinkle the shallots over the beans, sprinkle the potato salad with the parsley, and garnish the platter with lemon wedges. Spoon the remaining vinaigrette over the beans and tuna, if desired. SERVES 6

❖Substitute endive spears, watercress, radicchio, or other greens for the lettuce.
❖Substitute *Grilled Potato Salad* (page 89) for the *Potato Salad Vinaigrette.*
❖Substitute *Green Bean and Seared Red Onion Salad* (page 79) for the beans.

Green Bean, Red Pepper, and Tuna Salad

We always have loads of green beans in our garden. Add a little leftover tuna for protein and plenty of beans, and you have a salad worthy to be a main course at lunch or supper.

Alternative fish: cooked swordfish, shark, mahi mahi, or other firm-fleshed fish

1 lb green beans
1 red pepper
2 tsp Dijon-style mustard
1 Tb red wine vinegar or fresh lemon juice
½ cup olive oil
Salt and freshly ground pepper
½–1 lb cooked flaked fresh tuna (1–2 cups)
½ cup thinly sliced red onions
1–2 Tb capers

Trim the stem ends off the beans. If the beans are large, cut them diagonally into 1½–2-inch pieces. Set aside. Cut the pepper in half lengthwise, remove the stem, seeds, and white membrane, and slice into thin strips. Set aside.

Drop the beans into a large pot of boiling water and cook until just tender, about 5–8 minutes. Drain the beans immediately in a colander and run them under cold water, or drop them into a bowl of ice water to stop the cooking action. Drain again, pat dry, and set aside in a large bowl.

In a small bowl, combine the mustard and vinegar or lemon juice, stir, and gradually whisk in the oil. Season with salt and freshly ground pepper.

Add the red pepper strips, tuna, onions, and capers to the beans, pour the vinaigrette over the vegetables and fish, toss well, and serve.   SERVES 4

❖The smoky flavor of blackened red peppers changes the taste of this salad. Take 2 red peppers instead of 1 as above. Place them under a preheated broiler and turn to blacken on all sides. Remove and drop into a brown paper bag for about 10 minutes. Remove, and when cool enough to handle, pull off the charred skin. Cut the peppers in half, remove the stems, seeds, and white membrane, and slice into ¼-inch strips. Proceed with recipe as above.

❖Lacking cooked fresh fish, substitute a large can of tuna, drained.

Fresh Tuna and Cauliflower Salad

Here is a great way to use up the grilled or broiled fish left over from last night's dinner. In *The Victory Garden Cookbook* I have a similar salad in which the cauliflower is blanched. I like the crunchiness of the raw cauliflower in this version, but the very fact that it is raw makes it essential that the cauliflower be very fresh from your garden or market.

Alternative fish: cooked swordfish or shark

½–¾ lb cooked fresh tuna
½ lemon
7 Tb olive oil
1–1¼ lb cauliflower
½ cup sliced or chopped pimento-stuffed olives
½ cup pitted small black olives (Niçoise-style, if possible)
2 Tb drained capers
2 tsp Dijon-style mustard
2 Tb red wine vinegar
Salt and freshly ground pepper

Flake the fish into a small bowl. (You should have 1–2 cups.) Squeeze the juice of half a lemon over the fish, add 2 tablespoons of the olive oil, toss, and set aside.

Trim, core, wash, and pat the cauliflower dry. Remove the stem and peel off the thick outer skin. Break the top of the cauliflower into flowerets and thinly slice the flowerets and the peeled stems. (You should have 4–5 cups.) Place the cauliflower, olives, capers, and fish in a large bowl.

To make a vinaigrette, whisk the mustard and vinegar together in a small bowl, and then gradually whisk in the remaining 5 tablespoons of oil. Pour the vinaigrette over the cauliflower and tuna, toss well, season with salt and freshly ground pepper, cover, and marinate in the refrigerator for 1 hour before serving.

SERVES 4–6

❖Use a 7½-ounce can of tuna fish. Use only the 5 tablespoons of oil for the vinaigrette and omit the tossing of the canned tuna with 2 tablespoons oil and lemon juice at the beginning of the preparation.

❖Add chopped anchovies.

Main Courses

Mixed Fish Grill with Arctic Char and a Warm Herb-and-Caper Vinaigrette

Whether a mixed fish grill is an elaborate affair for a crowd or a simple supper for four, the principles of preparation are the same. Choose two or more of the freshest firm-fleshed fish available in your market when you shop. I am specifying four that are regularly available to me and that I relish: rosy-pink Arctic char, bright orangy-pink salmon, glistening white halibut, and translucent deep-red tuna.

Next, head to the garden for herbs for the vinaigrette and to select a vegetable accompaniment. If you have grill space, grill an assortment of vegetables.

For a quick and simple supper, try foolproof *Roast Sliced Potatoes* (page 336) and, to provide color and crunch, *Whole Green Beans with Lemon Butter and Shallots* (page 320). The fish can be marinated and refrigerated until you are ready to grill. The vinaigrette can be prepared ahead and heated just before serving. Green beans take only a few minutes to cook; or they can be boiled, refreshed under cold water, and set aside to reheat before serving. The potatoes are peeled, sliced, and roasted 45 minutes before mealtime.

Opposite: Marian grilling bass—with a platter of grilled vegetables alongside.

A note on grilling different fish at the same time: If a fish is particularly thick or dense, I start cooking it slightly before the rest, but basically I start cooking all the fish at once and carefully monitor their progression; as they finish cooking, I move them to a warm platter. I leave the skin on fish fillets because it helps to hold the fish together and prevents the flesh from sticking to the grill. You can remove it after grilling or leave it for its crispy charred taste.

Fish and Marinade

1 lb Arctic char fillet, with skin on
¾ lb salmon fillet, with skin on
1 lb halibut steak, ¾ inch thick
½–¾ lb tuna steak, ¾ inch thick
3 Tb fresh lemon or lime juice, or
    a combination of both
⅓ cup vegetable oil

Herb-and-Caper Vinaigrette

2 tsp Dijon-style mustard
3 Tb fresh lemon or lime juice, or
    a combination of both
¼ cup vegetable oil
¼ cup light olive oil
2 Tb chopped shallots
2 Tb chopped parsley
1 Tb chopped tarragon

ARCTIC CHAR

ARCTIC CHAR IS A firm-fleshed cold-water fish, with rosy-pink flesh that cooks to pale pink; it has a robust yet delicate flavor—somewhere between the taste of salmon and of trout. Like wild salmon, Arctic sea-run char live in salt water but swim up freshwater rivers to spawn; all such anadromous fish are subject to parasites and should be eaten only fully cooked or after commercial freezing to kill any parasites. There are landlocked char in deep, cold European lakes. British food writer Jane Grigson noted that potted freshwater char from Windermere Lake was a popular delicacy in eighteenth- and nineteenth-century England; the shallow fish-decorated white pottery dishes in which the potted char was packed are now collector's items. Eskimos have long made these circumpolar fish, which run up to 30 pounds in the wild, a staple in their diet, and Arctic char is also very popular in Canada.

I first heard about it two years ago, when Russ came home from a business dinner at Jasper White's Jasper's Restaurant, in Boston, raving about his serving of "Arctic char." In the interim the fish has grown in popularity in New England because of the availability of "farmed" char. At Legal Seafood, our outstanding Boston-based chain of fish markets and restaurants, Roger Berkowitz found that wild Arctic char varied considerably in quality, depending on the season, habitat, diet, and age of the fish. Then he tried char from a fish farm in Iceland and found the quality consistent. As a result, the level of sales has skyrocketed.

Arctic char is widely available now as a whole fish of about 2–4 pounds or as fillets, from 8 ounces to over a pound. Although I feature it in only one recipe, I treat it as I would any firm-fleshed fish and particularly as a substitute in any of the salmon recipes. Fish lovers who find salmon a bit strong-tasting have gravitated to the more delicate flavor of char.

Yields: A 3-pound whole Arctic char yields 2 skin-on fillets of approximately 15 ounces each, which in turn yield 2 skinned fillets of 12 ounces each, making 4 6-ounce servings.

Mixed Fish Grill with Arctic Char (continued)

1 Tb drained capers
1–2 tsp chopped lovage or chervil (optional)
Salt and freshly ground pepper

Sprigs parsley, for garnish

To prepare the fish: Pressing down lightly, run your fingers over the top of the Arctic char to feel for bones. With tweezers or needle-nose pliers, remove the line of small bones that start at the thick end and taper off toward the tail end. Check the salmon the same way and remove any bones. Leave the skin on both fish. Cut the char fillet in half crosswise; you will have a thick section and a thinner tail section. Place all the fish in a large glass or nonaluminum-lined pan that will hold the fish in one layer.

To make the marinade: Combine 3 tablespoons lemon or lime juice and ⅓ cup vegetable oil, and pour the mixture over the fish. Turn the fish in the pan to coat on all sides with the marinade. Cover and refrigerate for at least 20 minutes.

To grill the fish: Heat the grill and oil the grill rack. If the grill does not have a lid, fashion a cover of aluminum foil that will enclose the fish but not press against it. Place the tuna and halibut steaks on the grill; add the Arctic char and salmon, skin sides down. Cover the grill and cook the fish for 4 minutes. Uncover the grill and turn the tuna and halibut over with a large spatula. If the salmon is very thick, turn it also. Cover the grill and cook for 2 minutes. At this point, begin checking the fish, which is done the instant the flesh is opaque all the way through. When the Arctic char and salmon fillets are almost done, turn them over, if you wish, with a large spatula to quickly brown the flesh side. The thinner tail section of the char will be done first, followed in order by the thicker section of char, the salmon, the halibut, and the tuna. You may want to remove the tuna when its center is still pink. Remove each cooked fish to a warm plate; they will all be done within a few minutes of one another.

To make the vinaigrette: While the fish is cooking, combine the mustard and lemon or lime juice in a small saucepan and gradually whisk in the vegetable oil and the olive oil. Just before serving the fish, heat the mixture and stir in the shallots, parsley, tarragon, capers, and lovage or chervil, if desired. Season with salt and freshly ground pepper.

To serve: Divide each fish into 4 pieces and place a portion on each of 4 serving plates. Spoon the warm vinaigrette over the fish and garnish with parsley sprigs.   SERVES 4

❖ Use this vinaigrette as a lovely topping for poached or baked fish.

❖ Broil the fish under a preheated broiler instead of grilling it.

❖ For a large crowd, use several grills at once. Coat the fish with oil or with a simple marinade, as above. Place fish of the same thickness or density on the same grill. For example, one grill might have tuna, shark, and swordfish steaks; another might have salmon, bluefish, and amberjack fillets; another, Arctic char or bass and halibut or snapper; another, skewers of shrimp, scallops, and chunks of monkfish. Use one grill just to open clams, oysters, and mussels, and consult directions for cooking mussels on the grill in *Clambake for Fifty* (page 204). Use one or two grills for vegetables, such as thickly sliced onions, zucchini and pattypan squash, eggplant, and peppers.

Steamed Black Sea Bass with Scallions and Ginger

It baffles me that black sea bass has not become a very popular fish in American markets. Its flesh is simply delicious, delicate but firm, with a lovely pure taste. To get as much as I wanted for the restaurant on Nantucket, I sometimes resorted to begging lobstermen to bring me any of this rockfish that may have wandered into their traps. When you see a nice fresh black sea bass, treat yourself and buy it. For this dish, which has obviously combined elements of both Oriental and Occidental cookery in a happy marriage, you need a steamer. A bamboo or metal steamer with racks that enables you to steam more than one fish at a time is ideal. However, you can improvise as I have on occasion. I've used high-sided baking pans with cake racks fitted inside; I've also used a Pyrex pie plate sitting on a trivet over an inch of boiling water in a covered pot. You will also need a heatproof plate large enough to hold the fish and small enough to fit comfortably into the steamer.

Alternative fish: small firm-fleshed rockfish, small hybrid farmed striped bass, red snapper

One 2–3-lb black sea bass
2 Tb rice wine
2 Tb light soy sauce
2 oz peeled fresh ginger
6 scallions
3 paper-thin slices Kentucky ham or prosciutto
Chili oil (optional)

DIPPING SAUCE

⅓ cup rice wine
⅓ cup light soy sauce
2 Tb white vinegar

2 Tb sesame oil

Have the whole fish scaled and gutted, leaving the head on but making sure the gills are removed. Wash the fish and pat dry with paper towels. With a sharp knife, make short cuts down to the center bone about 1 inch apart across one side of the fish, holding the knife at a 45-degree angle so that the cuts are diagonal rather than straight across the side of the fish. Place the scored fish in a dish, cut side up.

Combine the rice wine and 1 tablespoon of the soy sauce in a cup and rub the mixture onto the fish, allowing it to go into the scored cuts. Then refrigerate the fish to marinate for 30 minutes.

Cut the ginger into a very fine julienne and set aside. Remove the dark tops of the scallions and peel off any dry or damaged outer skin. Set aside 3 of the 4–5-inch-long cleaned scallions; cut the remaining 3 scallions into 1½-inch-long pieces, slice each piece lengthwise into a fine julienne, and set aside.

Steamed Black Sea Bass with Scallions and Ginger (continued)

When you are ready to cook the fish, cut the slices of ham into enough pieces to insert into the scored cuts of the fish. Place the 3 whole scallions evenly across a heatproof plate and set the fish, scored side up, on top of the scallions. Sprinkle the julienne of ginger and half of the julienned scallions evenly across the top of the fish, pour the remaining tablespoon of soy sauce over the fish, and sprinkle the fish with a few drops of chili oil, if desired. Place the plate of fish on a steamer rack over boiling water, cover, and steam for 15–20 minutes over high heat, making sure that all of the boiling water does not evaporate, or until the fish is opaque at the center and beginning to flake. (To test, prick with a sharp knife or fork.)

To make the sauce, while the fish is steaming, combine all the dipping sauce ingredients in a small bowl and set aside.

Serve the fish on its cooking plate or carefully lift the fish to a warm platter. Spoon any juices from the steaming over the fish. In a small pan, heat the sesame oil to very hot. Scatter the remaining julienned scallions over the fish, pour the hot oil over all, and serve immediately with the dipping sauce.   SERVES 2

❖Crush a piece of peeled ginger into the rice wine that the fish marinates in.

❖For a different flavor, add crushed cloves garlic to the steaming water.

❖Sprinkle the finished dish with chopped fresh parsley or cilantro.

Poached Striped Bass with White Butter Sauce and Boiled New Potatoes

When the Straight Wharf Restaurant opened in Nantucket, there were only four main courses on the menu, so terrified were my cooking partner, Susan Mayer, and I of what we had gotten ourselves into. The lead entrée was this classic dish. It became our signature dish and would probably never have lost its top billing except that this glorious fish became endangered from pollution and overfishing. We immediately replaced striped bass with other fish, but none could really match it. Today striped bass is gradually coming back to the market, but only in fish much larger than the beautiful 8–10 pounders we once poached whole; when it is available at your market, try this wonderful fish. The white butter sauce can be made ahead but must be kept warm over water that is the same temperature as the sauce; if it is kept over very hot water, it may separate. Use a heavy-bottomed pan to ensure the even heat control you will need to make the sauce. The butter sauce I made at the restaurant contained no cream but was trickier to make and to hold; for a safer experience, use the optional cream. Boiled new potatoes sop up the butter sauce, and I wouldn't dream of serving the bass without them.

Alternative fish: whole fillets of black sea bass, hybrid farmed striped bass, salmon, halibut, cod

1½–2-lb skinned striped bass fillet

WHITE BUTTER SAUCE

½ cup red wine vinegar
3 Tb chopped shallots
¼ cup heavy cream (optional)
¾ cup *chilled* unsalted butter, cut
    into ¼-inch pieces
Salt and freshly ground pepper

To make the White Butter Sauce: Put the vinegar and shallots in a heavy-bottomed nonaluminum-lined saucepan and bring the vinegar to a boil. Cook until the reduced liquid (about 2 tablespoons) just films the bottom of the pan. If you are using the cream, add it now and cook until the mixture is reduced by half. Turn the heat down very low. Whisking constantly, slowly add the butter piece by piece. As you add the butter, the sauce will gradually thicken and become creamy and turn a light golden color. Season with salt and freshly ground pepper. Keep warm over water that is the same temperature as the sauce.

MAKES ABOUT 1½ CUPS

12 baby new potatoes, 1½–2 inches round
Salt

Remove any bones from the fish and cut off the dark flesh on the skinned side of the fillet, if you wish. Cut the fillet into 4 equal portions and refrigerate until ready to cook.

Prepare the white butter sauce and keep warm.

To boil the potatoes: Wash the potatoes, put them in a saucepan, cover with water, add a teaspoon of salt, and bring the water to a boil. Reduce the heat and cook gently for about 15 minutes, or until they are just tender. Immediately drain the potatoes, return them to the pan, and roll them around to evaporate any excess moisture; partially cover the pan to keep the potatoes warm.

To poach the fish: While the potatoes are cooking, fill a wide, high-sided pan two-thirds full of water and bring to a boil. Drop the bass pieces into the water and adjust the heat so that the water returns only to a simmer and shivers just under a boil. Poach the bass for 8 minutes (or up to 10 minutes if the pieces are thick) or until the flesh is just opaque at the center. Remove the fish to double-folded paper towels and pat dry.

To serve: Place the fish on 4 warmed serving plates, spoon over the white butter sauce, and distribute the potatoes 3 to a plate.   SERVES 4

❖Thinner fish like black sea bass and farmed striped bass fillets may be cooked through in 6 minutes.

Kep Sweeney's Sunflower Seed–Crusted Striped Bass with Spaghetti Squash and Herb Beurre Blanc

Good cooks seem to move around like good recipes. When a chef-friend left Nantucket's 21 Federal restaurant, Kep moved in, kept up the standards of his predecessor, and began creating lovely dishes of his own, including this striped bass dish. Then Kep moved on to open the Atlantic Pearl in Boulder, Colorado, where he still highlights fresh seafood. I love the flavors and texture of this dish. The herb beurre blanc is a luscious addition, but if you are watching calories, have no fear; this dish can stand alone with-

out the sauce. If you do make the sauce, you will need a food processor or blender. Keep the sauce warm until served in a double boiler over water that is the same temperature as the sauce (if the water is too hot, the sauce may separate). The spaghetti squash can be cooked ahead of time and kept warm or quickly reheated before serving.

Alternative fish: salmon, Arctic char, thick halibut fillets, sturgeon

SPAGHETTI SQUASH

1 spaghetti squash
1–2 Tb butter
1 finely chopped clove garlic
Salt and freshly ground pepper

HERB BEURRE BLANC

1 cup fresh spinach leaves
10 leaves fresh basil
10 sprigs parsley, heavy stems removed
1 minced shallot
½ cup dry vermouth or white wine
⅛ cup white wine vinegar
⅛ cup heavy cream
½ lb *chilled* unsalted butter, cut in small pieces
Salt and freshly ground white pepper

STRIPED BASS

Four 8-oz pieces skinned striped bass fillet
¼ cup roughly chopped sunflower seeds
⅛ cup fresh bread crumbs
1 tsp salt
Pinch of black pepper
½ cup buttermilk
1–2 Tb olive oil

To prepare the squash: Cut the squash in half lengthwise and clean out the seeds and stringy membranes. Place the halves, cut side down, in a baking pan with 1 cup water in the pan. Cook in a preheated 350-degree oven for 40 minutes, or until the squash is tender. Remove from the oven and as soon as the squash is cool enough to handle, pull out the flesh in long spaghetti-like strands with a fork. (You can set the squash aside at this point and reheat as follows just before serving.) In a wide sauté pan, heat the butter,

continued on page 118

SPECIAL INFORMATION ABOUT

BASS

STRIPED BASS, HYBRID FARMED STRIPED BASS, AND BLACK SEA BASS

FORTUNATELY, THIS is a cookbook and not a reference work on marine life. The marine biological families that include bass contain hundreds of freshwater and saltwater fish relatives, and it would take an entire book to do justice to their variety. I will limit my attention to two of them, one very large and one very small, both equally delicious, and to a new hybrid market substitute for one of them.

The large fish—my most favorite fish of all—is the striped bass, familiarly known as "striper" and also sometimes called rockfish. Stripers are magnificent fish with large heads and handsome striped bodies, and their fighting qualities have made them renowned as an adversary in sport fishing. If you have a chance, do read *Striper* by John N. Cole, a fine book about this fabulous fish.

The kitchen is where I truly celebrate the striped bass. Its flesh is firm and moist and takes beautifully to virtually every method of fish cookery, although I most like to poach it. The way a striper's flesh flakes is quite distinctive; it holds together in big chunks and doesn't become mushy or stringy. We so appreciated this fish that we made it the logo of the Straight Wharf Restaurant and featured *Poached Striped Bass with White Butter Sauce and Boiled New Potatoes* (page 114) as the first, or featured, main course on the menu, where it remained until 1983, when the striped bass fell on hard times.

Russ's striped bass catch circa 1970, well before the 36-inch limitation. This was our first poached bass with white butter sauce.

Unfortunately, once you remove the large head, guts, frame, and skin of a striper, you have removed almost two-thirds of its weight. It took a lot of stripers to satisfy demand, and suddenly the striped bass was almost an endangered species because of overfishing and high levels of PCB contamination. We immediately stopped serving it, and many concerned markets and restaurants also stopped providing it. The management of commercial fishing has recently brought stripers back but in limited quantities of fish that have to be at least 3 feet long. There is an active lobby to eliminate commercial harvest altogether and make striped bass a sport fish only. Through the rest of the 1980s we looked for substitutes. I found that red snapper has many of the properties of striped bass and that thick fillets of halibut also work well. One of the purveyors of fish to the restaurant promoted substitutes such as channel bass—also known as red drum—or tilefish, which has flesh somewhere between cod and striped bass.

In the end, my favorite substitute was a small rockfish, black sea bass. Tiny in size compared to stripers and with a much more delicate texture, this fish nevertheless has sweet, clean white flesh and a flavor reminiscent of striped bass. Black sea bass hang around rocks and reefs and rough ocean floors, and are not the easiest fish to catch commercially, but they are a treat and take to every cooking method including steaming, where they excel. You will find black sea bass in many Chinese whole-fish preparations, and consequently, it is usually available in Chinese markets.

To fill the market void caused by the diminished supply of stripers, commercial fish farmers have crossed striped bass with

BASS

STRIPED BASS, HYBRID FARMED STRIPED BASS, AND BLACK SEA BASS

freshwater white bass and are marketing these hybrid fish from coast to coast. The hybrid farmed striped bass are small and have a delicate white flesh that is quite good but reminds me more of perch than of striped bass. My advice is to keep looking for striped bass—the fish without equal; try black sea bass for the stellar qualities of its own, and accept hybrid farmed striped bass as a new and fine-tasting fish on the market.

Buying: Depending on the condition of the striped bass population, a limit for commercial fishing is set each year, and once the figure is reached, the commercial fishing of stripers ends until the following year. So striped bass has become a seasonal pleasure from late spring until August or September, when the quota is reached. All the more reason to grab it when you see it in the market. You won't find it whole since, as I said, the minimum length is about 3 feet and may rise; it would take a bathtub to poach a fish that large. But beautiful thick fillets can be found. The skin should still be on, showing the 7–9 distinctive stripes running down the fillet. Expect to pay a high price for this premium fish.

The hybrid farmed striped bass are much smaller. They are available year-round as whole gutted fish, averaging 2 pounds, or in fillets.

Black sea bass are plump, shiny blue-black fish that can grow as large as 8 pounds but more typically weigh from 1½–3 pounds. They are marketed whole or in fillets that run from 4–8 ounces. They are available year-round but may be expensive if the supply is limited.

The flesh of bass fillets should be white, firm, and sparkling, translucent rather than dull or opaque, and there should be no gaps in the flesh. The fillets should smell fresh without any fishy odor. Whole fish should be firm, and if you push your finger into the flesh, the flesh should be resilient. The skin should glisten, and the eyes should be clear and flush with the surface of the head. Cloudy or depressed eyes mean that the fish has been around for a while. If the fish still has its gills, they should be bright red.

Storage: Like all fish, bass should be rushed home and refrigerated as quickly as possible. Check whole fish to make sure they have been gutted and gilled and are thoroughly clean inside. Wash and pat the fish dry, as necessary, before refrigerating. I store fillets and whole fish in nonaluminum-lined pans covered with waxed paper or butcher's paper and topped with ice packs. Use as soon as possible.

Preparation: When skinning striped bass fillets, you might want to remove the brownish dark meat on the skinned side of

the fish. Check for, and remove, any pin bones in fillets of any bass. Whole fish should be washed and patted dry. Remove the gills if that has not been done at the market.

Cooking: Like salmon, wild striped bass are anadromous, living in salt water but spawning in freshwater rivers; all such fish are subject to parasites, and the flesh should either be fully cooked or, if it is eaten raw or undercooked, should first be commercially frozen (see *Parasites,* page 367). I have never heard of this infestation in striped bass, but better to be cautious than sorry.

Yields: Skinned striped bass fillets yield 100 percent meat; allow 6 ounces per serving. If you are lucky enough to catch a striped bass above the present minimum length, figure that you will have about one-third of its total weight as edible flesh.

❖ A 2-pound whole hybrid striped bass (about 14 inches long) yields 1 pound 5 ounces when headed and gutted, and unskinned fillets weighing 13 ounces. After skinning, the 2 fillets total 10 ounces, enough to serve 2 people. Skinned fillets are 100 percent yield.

❖ You will need at least a 2-pound whole black sea bass for 2 people, for once again the skinned fillet yield is about one-third of the original weight. Skinned fillets are 100 percent yield.

Kep Sweeney's Sunflower Seed–Crusted Striped Bass (continued)

stir in the garlic, and add the spaghetti squash, turning the strands to coat with the butter and heating as necessary for 1–2 minutes. Season with salt and freshly ground pepper.

To prepare the herb beurre blanc: While the squash is cooking, bring a small pot of water to a rolling boil and prepare a bowl of ice water to one side. Drop the spinach, basil, and parsley into the boiling water and blanch just until they are limp. Immediately drain them and drop them into the ice water to stop the cooking action and set their color. Drain them again, squeeze them dry gently, place them in a food processor or blender with 2 tablespoons ice water, process to a purée, and set aside. In a heavy-bottomed, nonaluminum-lined saucepan, combine the minced shallot, vermouth, and vinegar; bring the mixture to a boil and reduce by boiling until only 2 tablespoons of liquid remain. Add the cream and cook over medium heat for 2 minutes to reduce the liquid again. Piece by piece, gradually add the butter, whisking constantly and adjusting the heat so that the mixture does not get too hot. As the butter is added, the sauce will thicken to a creamy emulsion. Whisk in the herb purée and season with salt and freshly ground white pepper. Keep the sauce warm in the top of a double boiler.

To prepare the fish: Remove any bones from the striped bass. In a pie pan, combine the sunflower seeds, bread crumbs, salt, and pepper. Pour the buttermilk into another pie pan. In a wide sauté pan, heat the oil. Dip the top rounded side of each piece of bass into the buttermilk, and then into the seed-and-bread-crumb mixture. Place the fish, coated side down, in the sauté pan and cook for 1–2 minutes, or until the coated side is golden brown. Transfer the fish pieces, coated side up, to a baking pan and finish cooking in a preheated 350-degree oven for about 4 minutes, or until the fish is just cooked through and not translucent. (Cooking time will depend on the thickness of the fish.)

To assemble: Place a pile of hot spaghetti squash in the center of each of 4 warmed serving plates. Place a piece of fish, crusted side up, in the center of the squash. Surround the squash with a pool of the herb beurre blanc.   SERVES 4

❖To serve as an appetizer, which is the first way I encountered the dish and a delightful way to serve it,

slice the striped bass into ⅜–½-inch-wide slices. Coat and sauté as above, then either turn and sauté the other side of the fish slices for 2–3 minutes to complete the cooking, or place the fish slices in the oven for 2–3 minutes. Serve smaller portions of spaghetti squash, top with 1 or 2 slices of fish, and surround with the sauce, if desired.

SERVES 8–10 AS AN APPETIZER

❖Use other sauces, such as a *Sweet Pepper Sauce* (page 195) or *Sorrel Sauce* (page 229).

Broiled Striped Bass

Naturally oily fish—bluefish or mackerel, for example—need only a brushing of vegetable oil before submitting them to the intense heat of a broiler and broiler pan, but many fish, striped bass certainly among them, will dry out quickly under the searing heat. Moistening the less oily fish with a butter mixture before broiling helps them remain tender. The coating of butter does add some calories to the dish, but in the cooking, much of the butter runs off, leaving behind a delicious added flavor. The second key to moist, tender fish is to watch it carefully and remove it from the broiler at the right moment—when the flesh is opaque but still tender—not a smidgen overdone. Be sure to ask your fish market for a piece cut from the thick part of a fillet rather than from the tapered tail end of a striped bass fillet.

Alternative fish: firm-fleshed thick white fish fillets or steaks, such as halibut, cod, cusk, or snapper; salmon fillets or steaks; or thick steaks of swordfish or shark

2½-lb striped bass fillet, the thick end
6 Tb softened butter
2 Tb fresh lemon juice
1 Tb Dijon-style mustard
Lemon wedges

Remove the skin and any bones from the fish. Cut the fillet crosswise into 1-inch-wide pieces and refrigerate until ready to cook. In a small bowl, beat together the butter, lemon juice, and mustard.

When ready to cook, place the pieces of fish on the rack of a broiler pan, with one of the freshly cut surfaces down. Spread half the butter mixture evenly on top of the fish and place the rack 3–4 inches under a preheated broiler. Cook for 6 minutes. Turn the fish, spread the remaining butter mixture on top, and broil 3–4 minutes. Serve with lemon wedges.   SERVES 6

❖For a fancier version, cut the fillet crosswise into 2-inch-wide pieces. Then cut most, but not all, of the way down through the middle of each piece, spread it open in a "butterfly," and broil first the opened butterfly side, as above, and then the opposite side.

❖Add fresh herbs to the softened butter mixture.

Grilled Whole Small Bass with Fennel

The anise, or licorice, flavor of fennel is a perfect foil for fish. In this recipe the stuffing is more to flavor the fish than for consumption, so don't worry if some falls out as you handle and grill the fish. Use even more fennel bulbs than are prescribed here if you like the taste of fennel as much as I do. This is a good recipe for small, farm-grown striped bass or for the black sea bass that I find very tasty. You can prepare and refrigerate the marinated fish and cook the fennel bulbs well ahead of serving; the final preparation and grilling go quickly.

Alternative fish: salmon trout or other small whole fish, such as porgy or snapper

    Four 1½–2½-lb scaled, gutted, and gilled
       whole bass
    Salt and freshly ground pepper
    2 fennel bulbs, with stalks and leaves
    ⅓ cup olive oil
    2 Tb Pernod or 2 tsp anise flavoring
    Lemon wedges

Make sure that the fish gills have been removed, and remove the fish heads and tails, if you wish. Wash the fish thoroughly and pat dry. Season the fish cavities with salt and freshly ground pepper.

Cut the fennel stalks and leaves off the bulbs. (Reserve the bulbs for later.) Chop enough of the leaves and stalks to loosely stuff the fish cavities. From other leaves, mince 2–3 tablespoons. Wet down and reserve the remaining stalks and leaves.

In a small bowl, combine the olive oil, Pernod or anise flavoring, and minced fennel leaves; season the mixture with salt and pepper. Lay the fish in a flat, nonaluminum-lined pan and pour the marinade over the fish, turning the fish and spooning the marinade until the fish are completely coated. Cover and refrigerate until ready to use.

Bring a pot of water to a boil, drop in the fennel bulbs, and boil for 10 minutes, or until they are just tender; cooking time will depend on the size of the bulbs. Drain the bulbs and run them under cold water to stop the cooking action. Cut each bulb in half lengthwise.

Preheat an oiled grill with movable rack until the coals are covered with gray ash and you can hold a hand above the rack for 5 seconds. Place the fish on the rack and cook for about 8 minutes. (Cooking time will vary with the heat of the fire and the distance from the fire to the rack.) Remove the fish, lift the grill rack, and throw the reserved dampened fennel leaves and stalks on the coals for smoke. Turn the fish and return them to the grill. Brush the fennel bulbs with some of the marinade and grill them, turning them once, while the fish cooks on the second side for about 8 minutes, or until the flesh just turns opaque. Remove the fish and fennel to a warm serving platter and serve with lemon wedges.   SERVES 4

❖Garnish with lemon mustard, herb-flavored sour cream, drawn butter, or fresh *Salsa* (page 7).

Fried Striped Bass on a Bed of Tomato Fondue

The thick, chunky flesh of striped bass is one of its principal charms for cooks and diners alike. The thinner tail sections, therefore, sometimes go begging in the fish market, but here is a perfect recipe for them or for whole fillets of the smaller hybrid farmed striped bass now available in markets. The length of time the piece of fish needs to sizzle in the frying pan will vary with its thickness. I top the cooked fish with a browned lemon butter, but you can, if you wish, simply garnish the fish and fondue with lemon wedges. You can make the tomato fondue ahead and reheat it just before serving.

Alternative fish: black sea bass, porgy, thick pieces of flounder, thin fillets of halibut, haddock, cod

Fried Striped Bass on a Bed of Tomato Fondue (continued)

TOMATO FONDUE

1 Tb butter
¼ cup minced onions or shallots
1 minced clove garlic (optional)
2 cups peeled, seeded, and chopped tomatoes
1 Tb fresh or 1 tsp dried basil, oregano, or thyme
Salt and freshly ground pepper

1½–2-lb farmed striped bass fillet, or tail sections or slices wild striped bass
Salt and freshly ground pepper
2 Tb butter
3 Tb vegetable oil
½ cup flour
2 eggs beaten with 2 Tb water

LEMON BUTTER (optional)

6 Tb butter
3 Tb fresh lemon juice
1 Tb chopped parsley

To make the tomato fondue: In a sauté pan, melt the butter, add the onions or shallots, and cook until they are softened. Add the garlic, if you are using it. Add the tomatoes and herb, and cook over medium heat for 4–5 minutes to evaporate some of the juices and slightly thicken the mixture; if it gets too dry, add a tiny bit of tomato juice. Season with salt and freshly ground pepper, and set aside.

Remove any skin and bones from the fish, and cut it into 4 serving portions. Season with salt and freshly ground pepper, and set aside.

In a nonstick sauté pan large enough to hold the fish in one layer (or in two pans, dividing the butter and oil between them), heat the butter and oil. Dip the fish pieces into the flour, shake off any excess, then dip them into the beaten eggs. Place the fish pieces in the sauté pan, cook for 4–5 minutes or until lightly colored, then turn them and sauté the other side until just cooked through, 3–4 minutes, depending on the thickness of the fish.

While the fish is frying, reheat the tomato fondue. Just before serving, spoon a portion of the fondue on each warmed serving plate, and place a serving of fish on top of the fondue.

To make the lemon butter: Immediately after removing the fish, wipe out the sauté pan, add the 6 tablespoons of butter and heat until it turns light brown. Swirl in the lemon juice and parsley, and spoon the mixture over each serving of fish.   SERVES 4

❖Prepare 1 whole fillet of farmed striped bass per person; cooking time will be about 2–3 minutes on each side. For black sea bass or thick flounder, cooking time could be 3–4 minutes on each side.

❖If you are using thick pieces of striped bass, cut them into ½-inch-thick slices and cook as above.

❖Substitute 1–2 tablespoons drained capers for the parsley in the lemon butter.

Broiled Bluefish with a Soy Marinade

This is really a simple marinade, but it imparts a very suitable and subtle Oriental flavor to the bluefish. In warm weather, *Chinese Cabbage and Spinach Salad with Ginger* (page 81) is a lovely light accompaniment to this dish, and for winter suppers I would recommend *Chinese Cabbage Stir-Fry* (page 324).

Alternative fish: amberjack, salmon, mackerel (adjust cooking times to the thickness of the pieces of fish)

1½–2 lb skinned bluefish fillets

SOY MARINADE

2 Tb vegetable oil
1 tsp sesame oil
1 Tb soy sauce
1 Tb sake (rice wine) or Scotch whisky
3 peeled slices fresh ginger

Pickled ginger (available in jars) (optional)
Soy sauce and sake for dipping sauce (optional)
Lemon wedges

Remove any bones and dark meat from the bluefish. Cut the fillets into 4 equal serving portions.

To make the soy marinade, whisk together the two oils, soy sauce, and sake or Scotch whisky in a small bowl. Pinch the slices of ginger between your fingers

to crush them slightly, and add them to the marinade.

Put the pieces of bluefish in one layer in a shallow dish or pan, pour the marinade over, and turn the fish until it is well coated. Set aside to marinate for at least 20 minutes.

Place the fish on an oiled broiler pan rack about 7 inches below a preheated broiler. Depending on their thickness, the fillets will cook in 8–12 minutes. To brown the top of the fillets, lift the pan closer to the broiler for the last few minutes of cooking. Remove the fish to a serving platter as soon as the flesh has turned opaque. Serve with thinly sliced pickled ginger, if you like, or with a dipping sauce made of equal portions of soy sauce and sake, also optional, but definitely serve lemon wedges on the side. SERVES 4

❖Add a thin julienne of scallions to the marinade.

❖Just before serving, drizzle a little warm sesame oil over the fish.

❖*To grill:* Leave on the skin of the bluefish and marinate as above. When ready to cook, place the fish on an oiled grill rack, skin down. Cook for 6–7 minutes, or until the skin is crisp and the flesh has begun to turn pale gray. Turn the fish and cook for 2–4 minutes, or until the flesh is just opaque throughout. Adjust cooking time to the thickness of the fish.

Broiled Baby Bluefish Fillets

The fillets from a 2½–3-pound bluefish make perfect individual servings. A brushing of olive oil or melted butter is sufficient to ready the fish for the heat of the broiler. Serve only with lemon wedges, or try the *Lemon and Caper Butter* variation for a lovely finishing touch.

> Four 8-oz skinned bluefish fillets
> Olive oil or melted butter
> Lemon wedges

Remove any bones from the fish and the dark meat, if you wish. Brush the fillets on both sides with oil or melted butter, place the fish on an oiled broiler pan rack just below the heat of a preheated broiler for 5–6 minutes, or until the flesh is just opaque throughout. Serve with lemon wedges.   SERVES 4

❖ *With Lemon and Caper Butter:* In a small sauté pan, heat 4 tablespoons of butter to golden brown, then swirl in 1–2 tablespoons fresh lemon juice and 2 tablespoons drained capers. As soon as the mixture is warmed through, pour it over the broiled fish and serve immediately.

❖ Top the broiled fish with your choice of one of the compound butters on pages 352–353.

Bluefish Broiled with a Mustard Mayonnaise

The origin of this method is unclear, but however it began, the practice of slathering mayonnaise on bluefish before broiling is a popular custom in New England. Certainly the bluefish doesn't need any more oil, but the mayonnaise does give an appealing golden-brown coating. My version of this method is to flavor the mayonnaise with mustard, anchovies, and lemon for a piquant taste.

> ½ cup mayonnaise
> 1 Tb Dijon-style mustard (grainy version, if
>   available)

> 2–3 tsp fresh lemon juice
> 1–2 tsp anchovy paste or puréed anchovies
> Salt and freshly ground pepper
> 1½–2 lb skinned bluefish fillets
> 2–3 Tb vegetable oil
> Lemon wedges

Put the mayonnaise in a bowl, beat in the mustard, stir in the lemon juice, and season the mixture to taste with anchovy paste or purée and freshly ground pepper.

Remove any bones and dark meat from the blue-fish. Cut the fillets into 4 serving portions, if you wish. Season the fish with salt and freshly ground pepper, and brush the skinned side with oil. Place the fish on an oiled broiler pan, skinned side down. Spread the mustard mayonnaise evenly over the fish and cook in a preheated broiler about 7–8 inches below the heat until just cooked through and beautifully glazed, about 8–10 minutes—a little longer if the fish is very thick. Serve with lemon wedges.   SERVES 4

❖ Bake the fish in one layer in a broiler-proof dish or pan in a preheated 400-degree oven until just cooked through, then spread the mustard mayonnaise over the baked fish and run the dish under a pre-heated broiler just long enough to glaze the top.

Grilled Bluefish Fillets with Dun Gifford's Bluefish Basting Sauce

The best way to assure that fish fillets on the grill will stay in one piece when they are turned is to put them in a flat, hinged, double-sided chrome basket. If you prefer to cook directly on the grill, oil both the grill and the fish very well to prevent sticking. Ways of protecting the delicate flesh of the fish include wrap-ping the fish in a protective covering, as in the recipe for *Grilled Bluefish Fillets with Bacon,* which follows this one, or leaving the skin on, grilling the oiled or marinated skin side first, and turning the flesh side down only for the final 2–3 minutes of cooking. Before grilling, cut the fish into pieces that can be turned easily with a wide spatula. The bluefish can be basted with a simple mixture of melted butter and fresh lemon juice, but a more flavored basting sauce can add another dimension to the dish. Our friends the Giffords are veteran bluefish fishermen, and I like Dun's sauce. I grill fish over hardwood charcoals prepared well in advance so that they are a smoldering hot gray. With grilled fish I like accompaniments that can be made ahead, leaving just the grilling for mealtime work. *Chunky Tomato and Cucumber Salad* (page 92) or *Potato Salad Vinaigrette* (page 90) complement grilled bluefish very well. Of course, corn on the cob and a plate of vine-ripened sliced tomatoes drizzled with balsamic vinegar are *always* appropriate with bluefish.

Alternative fish: salmon, amberjack

DUN GIFFORD'S BLUEFISH
BASTING SAUCE

½ cup melted butter
¼ cup olive oil
2 Tb Worcestershire sauce
Juice of ½ lemon or lime
1 Tb crushed fresh rosemary, thyme,
    marjoram, or oregano
Salt and freshly ground pepper

To make the basting sauce: In a bowl, combine the butter, oil, Worcestershire sauce, lemon or lime juice, and crushed herb, and season the mixture with salt and freshly ground pepper.

MAKES ABOUT I CUP

Two 1-lb bluefish fillets
Lemon wedges

Prepare the basting sauce and set aside.

If you are using a grill basket, remove the skin, any bones, and the dark meat from the bluefish. If you are grilling the bluefish directly on the grill rack, leave the skin on and remove it and any dark flesh after the bluefish is cooked.

Brush the basting sauce on both sides of the fillets until they are thoroughly coated. Place the fish in an oiled hinged grill basket or skin side down on a well-oiled grill rack. The cooking time depends on the thickness of the fish. Cook on one side for 4–8 min-

utes, then turn and cook on the other side for 4–8 minutes, basting throughout the cooking. If the fish is very thick, continue to turn and cook while basting until the fish is golden on the outside and just slightly springy to the touch. Thick fillets of bluefish can take 15–20 minutes to cook. Remove to a serving platter and serve with lemon wedges.   SERVES 4

❖Use a plain basting sauce of melted butter mixed with fresh lemon juice.

❖Use an Oriental basting sauce. Combine 2 tablespoons each rice wine, sesame oil, peanut oil, and soy sauce; baste as above. To broil the bluefish, see *Broiled Bluefish with a Soy Marinade* (page 120).

❖Rub the fish only with oil before grilling; then serve topped with a flavored butter, such as *Cilantro Butter Roll* (page 353) or *Anchovy Butter* (page 352). Or serve with a side sauce, such as *Cucumber-Dill Sauce* (page 354) or *Salsa* (page 7).

❖To broil, place the fish 5–6 inches under a preheated broiler and cook, turning once until the fish is just cooked through.

Grilled Bluefish Fillets with Bacon

The bacon makes two different contributions to this dish. It protects the flesh of the bluefish a little from the searing heat of the grill—thus the fish is moister—and the crisp texture and salty taste of the bacon balance the smooth richness of the bluefish. *Broiled Baby Bluefish Fillets* (page 122) shows how to broil without a bacon wrap, but do give this method a try.

Alternative fish: salmon, amberjack

1½–2 lb bluefish fillets
3 Tb olive oil
Salt and freshly ground pepper
4 strips bacon
Lemon wedges

Skin the bluefish and remove any bones and the dark meat. Cut the fillets into 4 serving portions, rub each piece on both sides with oil, and sprinkle with salt and freshly ground pepper. Wrap each piece of fish with 1 strip of bacon, overlapping the ends to encircle

Grilled Bluefish Fillets with Bacon (continued)

the fish. The oil rubbed on the fish should keep the bacon clinging to the fish, but secure the bacon wrap with toothpicks, if you wish. Another way to help the bacon and fish to bond is to wrap each piece of fish and bacon in plastic and refrigerate it for a while before cooking.

Grill the fish over hot coals on an oiled grill rack for about 3–4 minutes on each side, or until nicely browned on the outside and just cooked through. Remove the toothpicks, if you used them, and serve with lemon wedges.   SERVES 4

❖ Serve with a fresh peppery salsa on the side.

❖ *To broil:* Place the bacon-wrapped fish about 5–6 inches below a preheated broiler on an oiled broiler pan rack, and cook, turning once, just until cooked through.

Baked Bluefish with a Tapenade and Crumb Topping

Bluefish tastes so good with salty accompaniments that I like to bake it with a topping of tapenade—a strong, salty olive spread from the South of France composed of olives, anchovies, and capers. The tapenade can be made well in advance and any excess keeps well; it is a smooth tapenade, and you will need a food processor to prepare it. The fish bakes in about 10 minutes. Serve this dish with *Braised Broccoli de Rabe* (page 323) and *Boiled New Potatoes* (page 334). For extra deliciousness, dip the potatoes into any extra tapenade.

Alternative fish: amberjack, salmon, sable, bass, thick pieces of cod or of other fish from the cod family

TAPENADE SPREAD

½ cup pitted black olives, cured in oil
5 anchovies
1 peeled and split clove garlic
3 Tb drained capers
1 tsp Dijon-style mustard
1 tsp fresh lemon juice
3 Tb olive oil
1 Tb chopped fresh parsley

1½–2 lb bluefish fillets
2 Tb vegetable or olive oil
3 Tb butter
2 cups fresh bread crumbs
Lemon wedges

To prepare the tapenade spread: Put the olives, anchovies, and garlic into a food processor, and process until the mixture is smooth. Add the capers, mustard, and lemon juice, and process again until smooth. With the motor running, add the oil in a slow stream. Remove the mixture to a bowl and stir in the parsley. Cover and refrigerate until ready to use. (Makes about ⅔ cup)

Remove the skin and dark meat from the bluefish, and cut the fillets into 4 equal serving portions. Brush both sides of the fish with oil and place the fish in an oiled broiler-proof baking dish large enough to hold the fish in one layer.

In a sauté pan, heat the butter, add the bread crumbs, and cook, turning the crumbs frequently, until they are golden brown.

Bake the fish in a preheated 400-degree oven for about 8 minutes, or until almost cooked through. Remove the baked fish from the oven, spread a thin layer of tapenade over each piece, sprinkle the bread crumbs over the tapenade, and return the dish to the oven for another 2–3 minutes, or until the fish is just opaque. Run the dish under a preheated broiler for 30 seconds to brown lightly, if desired. Serve with lemon wedges and with more tapenade on the side.   SERVES 4

Baked Bluefish with Fennel

I love the combined flavors of bluefish and anise-like fennel.

Alternative fish: sliced tuna, whole small rockfish

2 lb fennel bulbs, with 1-inch stalks
4 Tb light olive oil
2 Tb butter
1½–2 lb skinned bluefish fillets
8 flat anchovies
Salt and freshly ground pepper
Lemon wedges

continued on page 126

SPECIAL INFORMATION ABOUT

BLUEFISH

MY INTRODUCTION TO bluefish couldn't have been more dramatic. Russ and I were talking with friends on the beach near our August rental on Martha's Vineyard, and the children, then young, were playing in some nearby mud banks. Suddenly people started screaming for everyone to get out of the water. I thought sharks must have been spotted, but all I could see was birds circling above a patch of churning water. Everyone grabbed children out of the surf, but our friend Peter grabbed a fishing rod and began to cast as the patch of wild water moved closer. Within a couple of minutes he had cast three times and pulled out of the surf three big bluefish, which we cooked later over an open fire. As quickly as the voracious school of bluefish appeared, they moved on out of sight and normal vacationing resumed.

The bluefish, celebrated in a fine book, *Blues,* by John Hersey, is a family of one. They inhabit warm waters in several parts of the globe, including the East Coast of the United States but not the West Coast. Named for their color, they have moderately stocky bodies that are dazzling sea-green-blue on the back, turning to silver on their bellies. Their jaws are lined with awesome conical, canine teeth with which they bite anything that moves when they are in a feeding frenzy. Not a fish to be around when they're hungry. Sport fishermen delight in the fighting qualities of this fish, which often escapes simply by

biting through even metal lines. Blues travel in packs and migrate north to New England waters in late spring, spend the summer at the shore just as we do, and head south again in October and November. They are so prevalent and catchable by everyone on Nantucket that we could scarcely sell any bluefish dishes at the Straight Wharf Restaurant. Bluefish come to the market anywhere from young 6–8-inch-long fish up to 10–15 pounders. Since the flesh of bluefish is very oily—perhaps because of a diet rich in oily menhaden—one has to be especially cautious about chemical pollution, which accumulates most readily in fatty tissue. The larger the fish, the greater the risk, and so one is advised to eat bluefish in the 4-pound (about 22-inch) range and smaller.

The meat of bluefish is dark, ranging from a light putty color to dark gray. There is a section along the midline that contains more oil and is dark red; it is edible but has a stronger flavor that many people do not enjoy. Bluefish has a smooth, dense texture and a rich full-bodied flavor that is more intense than the flavor of other oily fish, such as mackerel. I think of eggplant as the "meat" of the vegetable world, and I think of bluefish as the "meat" of seafood. A 6–8-ounce portion of a lean white fish might be a proper average serving, but 4–6 ounces of bluefish will be equally filling.

Buying: As is true of all oily fish, the sooner eaten after being

caught, the better. Handling is important; oily fish needs to be gutted and bled immediately after it is caught. The skin color fades after it is caught, and so the best tests of freshness are texture and luster. Bluefish flesh is soft to begin with and softens further as it ages. Small bluefish fillets should look and feel firm and should have a moist, clear sheen. Fillets from larger bluefish will be softer and may show slight separations in the flesh, but they should still have a fresh look, like the gleam of gunmetal. Any fillets that look dull, have pronounced separations, and look mushy-soft should be avoided. Though this fish can be steaked, it is most often sold as fillets.

Smoked bluefish has become more prominent in the market in recent years because of its slightly longer shelf life than fresh bluefish. It should be refrigerated just as carefully as fresh bluefish. All the PCB and other chemical-pollution considerations remain the same because smoking is not cooking, and cooking, especially high-temperature grilling or broiling, carries much of the pollutant away with the fish's natural fats and oils. I remove all of the dark flesh of smoked bluefish before using smoked bluefish in an uncooked preparation, because any pollutants would concentrate in the dark flesh. Ask for a taste of smoked bluefish before buying. The inner flesh should be slightly moist and firm. If it is soft and mushy inside, it wasn't smoked long enough or was too old before it was smoked.

SPECIAL INFORMATION ABOUT

BLUEFISH

Bluefish (continued)

Preparation: If you catch your own bluefish, gut and bleed it immediately. Keep it on ice, but when you fillet it, keep the ice from touching the flesh; water will quickly soften and discolor the meat.

❖To remove the dark red-brown fatty flesh that lies just below the skin, skin the fillet, then insert the point of a knife into the fatty section. With the knife parallel to the surface of the fish, and with a sawing motion, cut a thin layer of dark meat off the fish. That will leave a dark "V"-shaped section along the midline. Make a shallow cut along each side of the "V" and lift out the dark meat.

❖To remove the pin bones that extend a few inches down the midline, cut down on both sides

of the small ridge of bones in a narrow "V" shape and lift the bones out.

❖To portion a fillet, I cut serving pieces on a slight diagonal to give a more even distribution of thick and thin meat to each piece.

Cooking:

❖Sautéing is my favorite way to cook bluefish because it is easy and the finished texture is so good.

❖Broiling and grilling, which can be harsh methods for many lean white fish, are also good ways to cook bluefish. The inherent oil keeps the flesh from drying out too much. It actually helps that some of the oil cooks off, leaving the finished dish lusciously smooth. I recommend oiling the grill rack and the fish to prevent the fish from sticking and then breaking as you try to turn or remove it.

❖Bluefish bakes well with vegetable accompaniments.

❖Poaching or steaming bluefish further softens a fish that is soft to begin with; I use this method only when preparing a mashed spread or dip.

❖Deep-frying doesn't enhance a naturally oily fish at all.

❖If I need cold bluefish for a salad, I find that broiled, grilled, or even baked bluefish all have good texture and flavor when served cold.

Yields: About 40 percent of the weight of a gutted, head-on bluefish is edible flesh after head, skin, dark meat, and bones have been removed. A whole 4-pound fish, therefore, yields 1½ pounds skinned bluefish fillet, which in turn makes four 6-ounce servings.

Baked Bluefish with Fennel (continued)

Wash and trim the fennel bulbs, and cut them lengthwise into slices about ½ inch thick so that you have at least 8 slices.

In a wide frying pan, heat 2 tablespoons of the olive oil and the butter; add the fennel slices and lightly brown them on both sides. Cover the pan, reduce the heat to low, and cook about 10 minutes, or until the fennel is slightly softened. (Add a bit of water to the pan if the fennel seems to be sticking to the pan or browning too much.) Place the cooked fennel in an even layer in a buttered, broiler-proof baking dish.

Remove any bones and dark meat from the bluefish and cut into 4 equal serving portions. Rub the fish pieces on both sides with the remaining 2 tablespoons of oil. Arrange the fish on top of the sliced

fennel and top each serving of fish with 2 anchovies. Season with salt and freshly ground pepper. Bake in a preheated 400-degree oven for 10–15 minutes, depending on the thickness of the fish, or until just cooked through. Run the dish under a preheated broiler just long enough to brown the top. Serve with lemon wedges.   SERVES 4

❖Omit the anchovies and top the bluefish with thin slices of Bermuda onions before baking, or with strips of smoky ham, or with buttered bread crumbs.

❖Chop the feathery fennel tops as a garnish for the finished dish.

❖Cook the fennel in chicken broth or water rather than butter.

❖Cut the fennel into julienned strips, combine with other julienned vegetables such as carrots, and make a bed for the bluefish to bake on.

❖Broil this dish entirely until just cooked through instead of baking and broiling.

Bluefish Baked with Peppers and Onions (Pipérade)

Bluefish was not the most popular item on the menu of a Nantucket restaurant, because many residents catch it themselves regularly and eat it at home, so they look for something else when dining out. We tried diligently to create bluefish recipes that would coax this tasty fish out of the kitchen onto patrons' plates; this recipe worked well. The dark color of the fish is enhanced by the color of the vegetables, and the vegetables also add a crunchiness that complements the soft texture of the fish. Peppers come in many colors. I use green and red, but feel free to use yellow, purple, and even brown peppers to give a rainbow look to the dish.

Alternative fish: amberjack, striped bass, halibut, haddock, or other firm, thick white fish

1½–2 lb skinned bluefish fillets
3 Tb light olive oil
Flour
Salt and freshly ground pepper

PEPPER-ONION GARNISH

3 Tb light olive oil
1½ cups thinly sliced green peppers
1½ cups thinly sliced red peppers
3 cups thinly sliced onions
2 tsp minced garlic
1 Tb chopped fresh basil
1 tsp chopped fresh oregano
Salt and freshly ground pepper

½ cup dry vermouth or white wine
4 flat anchovies (optional)
½ recipe *Aïoli* (page 349) (optional)

Remove any bones and dark meat from the bluefish and cut it into 4 equal portions. In a sauté pan, heat the 3 tablespoons olive oil. Dredge the pieces of fish lightly in a plate of flour, shaking off any excess, and season the pieces with salt and freshly ground pepper. Sauté the fish quickly in hot oil on both sides, cooking it just long enough to seal the surface of the flesh but not long enough to brown the fish. Remove the fish to a plate, set aside, and wipe out the pan.

To make the pepper-onion garnish: In the same pan, heat another 3 tablespoons of olive oil, add the red and green peppers and onions, and cook, stirring, until the vegetables have just turned tender and the onions have turned golden, 8–10 minutes. Add the garlic, basil, and oregano, cook for 30 seconds, remove from the heat, and season the mixture with salt and freshly ground pepper.

To assemble the dish: Butter an 8 × 8-inch baking dish or other baking dish large enough to hold the fish, or butter 4 individual au gratin dishes. Place the fish in the baking dish and spoon the pepper-onion mixture over it. Add the vermouth or white wine and top with the anchovies, if desired. Cover the dish with aluminum foil and bake in a preheated 425-degree oven for 15–20 minutes, depending on the thickness of the fish. Uncover the pan and lift the fish with the pepper-onion topping out of the pan and onto 4 warm serving plates. Either boil down the cooking juices and pour them over the fish, or beat a little of the cooking juices into aïoli and serve on top or to the side. SERVES 4

❖Cook on top of the stove. Allow slightly more liquid by increasing the amount of vermouth or white wine or by adding fish stock. Cook, covered, over gentle heat until the fish is cooked through, about 8–15 minutes. Reduce the cooking juices, as above, and serve.

Bluefish Baked with Potatoes and Onions

When you are looking for a hearty dish that needs only a green vegetable or salad to complete the meal, consider this way of serving bluefish. The potatoes and onions can be prepared ahead of time; final assembly and cooking takes only a short time.

Alternative fish: amberjack, mackerel, salmon, or any firm, dense white fish

Bluefish Baked with Potatoes and Onions (continued)

1½ lb potatoes
6 Tb light olive oil
1 Tb fresh lemon juice
½ tsp crushed fennel seed
2–3 Tb shredded fresh herbs, such as basil or
    lemon thyme
Salt and freshly ground pepper
3 cups sliced onions
1½–2 lb skinned bluefish fillets
4 thinly sliced pieces smoked ham

Bring a pot of water to a boil, drop in the potatoes, and cook until they are just tender; drain the potatoes, and as soon as they are cool enough to handle, peel them and cut them into thin slices.

In a small bowl, combine 3 tablespoons of the oil, the lemon juice, fennel seed, and herbs, and pour the mixture over the potatoes. Toss the potatoes and dressing, and season the mixture with salt and freshly ground pepper. It should taste like a delicious potato salad.

In a saucepan, heat 2 tablespoons of the oil, add the onions, and cook until they are wilted and golden, about 10–15 minutes.

Remove any bones and dark meat from the bluefish. Cut the fillets into 4 portions, season them with salt and pepper, and wrap a slice of ham around each portion.

In an oiled 8 × 8-inch baking dish, spread the potatoes in an even layer. Spread three-quarters of the onions evenly on top of the potatoes, then place the fish wrapped in ham on top of the onions. Top each piece of bluefish with some of the remaining onions. Drizzle the remaining tablespoon of oil over all. Bake in a preheated 425-degree oven for 15–20 minutes, depending on the thickness of the fish, or until the fish is just cooked through.   SERVES 4

❖Substitute thin slices of prosciutto for the ham.

Sautéed Bluefish Fillets with Piquant Spanish Sauce

Bluefish has a distinctive character of its own; because it's an oily fish, it accepts sharp, acidic flavors beautifully without losing its mellow flavor, which is not at all harsh. I always make plenty of this piquant tomato-based Spanish sauce, because it tastes so good with bluefish and keeps so well. I serve this dish with fluffy mashed potatoes or rice and peas.

Alternative fish: amberjack, mackerel, whiting, cod, halibut

SPANISH SAUCE

2-oz thick slice prosciutto (optional)
3 Tb light olive oil
2 cups thinly sliced onions
1 cup thinly sliced red peppers
1 cup thinly sliced green peppers
¾ cup thinly sliced carrots
1–2 tsp minced garlic
4 cups peeled, seeded, and finely
    chopped tomatoes or crushed
    tomatoes
¼ cup red wine vinegar
Hot pepper sauce (optional)
Salt and freshly ground pepper

To make the Spanish Sauce: Cut the prosciutto, if you are using it, crosswise into paper-thin strips or matchsticks, and set aside.

In a 3–4-quart saucepan, heat 3 tablespoons olive oil. Add the onions, red and green peppers, and carrots, and cook, stirring occasionally, for 8–10 minutes, or until the vegetables are wilted and lightly colored. Stir in the garlic and cook the mixture for 30 seconds; then add the tomatoes, vinegar, and the prosciutto and hot pepper sauce, if you are using them. Bring the mixture to a boil, reduce the heat, cover, cook for 5 minutes, uncover, and simmer until the sauce thickens, about 10–12 minutes. Season with salt and freshly ground pepper.
                MAKES ABOUT 5 CUPS

1½–2 lb skinned bluefish fillets
3 Tb light olive oil
Salt and freshly ground pepper
Flour
2–3 Tb chopped parsley

Prepare the Spanish sauce and keep warm.

To cook the bluefish: Remove any bones and any dark meat, and cut into 4 equal portions. In a sauté pan wide enough to hold the bluefish in one layer, heat 3 tablespoons olive oil. Season the fish with salt and freshly ground pepper, dip the fish into a plate of flour, shaking off any excess, and sauté over medium heat, about 4–5 minutes, until lightly browned. Turn the fish and cook on the other side until the fish is just cooked through and lightly browned, about 4–5 minutes. Place a spoonful of sauce on each of 4 serving plates, place a piece of fish on the sauce, and top the fish with another dollop of sauce. Sprinkle with parsley and serve. SERVES 4

❖ *To bake:* Prepare the sauce as above. Heat the oil in a sauté pan and sauté the dredged fish quickly on both sides to lightly sear the fish and seal in its juices, but do not finish cooking. Remove the fish to a baking dish, spoon the sauce over it, and bake in a preheated 400-degree oven for 10–12 minutes, or until the fish is just cooked through.

❖ Dust the fish with cornmeal instead of flour.

Sautéed Bluefish with Lemon and Capers

This is my favorite bluefish recipe, based on one from the Four Seasons restaurant in New York. The lemons and capers provide the right acidic foil for the rich flavor of bluefish. Use them, just warmed lightly in butter, with other bluefish recipes, such as *Grilled Bluefish Fillets with Bacon* (page 123). I prefer instant flour as a coating because of its granular texture; whatever you use, dust the fish just before cooking it. Serve with boiled new potatoes.

Alternative fish: amberjack, salmon, yellowtail, or any firm-fleshed white fish

1½–2 lb skinned bluefish fillets
3 lemons
3 Tb *Clarified Butter* (page 351), or
    2 Tb butter and 1 Tb vegetable oil
Instant-blending flour (such as Wondra
    Quick-Mixing Flour)
3 Tb unsalted butter
⅓ cup drained capers

Sautéed Bluefish with Lemon and Capers (continued)

Remove any bones from the fish and the dark red meat, if desired (see Bluefish Box, page 126); cut the fish into 4 serving portions and set aside.

Remove the skin and white pith from the lemons. Section the lemons by cutting out the flesh between the white membranes all around each lemon. Do this over a bowl, saving all the juice. Combine the lemon sections with the juice and set aside.

In a nonstick sauté pan large enough to hold the bluefish in one layer without crowding, heat the clarified butter or combination of butter and vegetable oil. Dip the fish into a plate of the flour and shake off any excess. Place the fish in the sizzling clarified butter or butter-oil combination, and cook over medium heat until lightly browned, about 4–5 minutes. Turn and cook on the other side until browned and just cooked through, about 3–5 minutes, depending on the thickness of the fillets.

Remove the cooked fish to warm serving plates and wipe out the pan. Melt the unsalted butter over low heat, add the lemon sections, lemon juice, and capers. Warm gently so that the lemon sections don't disintegrate. Spoon the lemon-and-caper sauce over the fish and serve.   SERVES 4

❖Omit the lemon-and-caper sauce, and serve the sautéed bluefish with a favorite tomato sauce, such as *Tomato Muffuletta Sauce* (page 212) or *Portugaise Sauce* (page 298).

Fried Clams

Long before I lived in Massachusetts, I went on regular family summer excursions to Cape Cod, one feature of which always was to stop at roadside stands for a box of heavily battered fried clams. My standards may be higher these days, but I still love fried clams—especially clams fried at home. Read the warnings in the Clam Box (page 131) about digging your own and on buying clams. I use soft-shell clams for frying, and I steam them open before I fry them. I tried using raw shucked clams, but it was harder to remove the black skin of the siphon when it was raw, and the finished preparation was tougher. The clams can be steamed open, cooled, and refrigerated in their broth until ready to fry. The batter

should be made at least 30 minutes before cooking; here I use the same light batter I use in *Fish and Chips* (page 143). Always use impeccably clean fresh oil for frying. Six pounds of soft-shell clams that have been steamed open give you about 3 cups shucked meat.

6 lb soft-shell clams

BATTER

1 cup flour
¼ tsp salt
2 eggs, separated
1 Tb vegetable oil
1½ cups beer, at room temperature

Peanut oil
Lemon wedges
Tartar Sauce (page 363) (optional)

Gently scrub the clams. If you have dug your own or if you have bought clams that you are not entirely sure have been purged of their sand, put them in a pot and cover them with a salt-water mixture composed of 3 tablespoons salt and 1 tablespoon vinegar for each 2 quarts water; refrigerate for 2 hours. Drain the clams, rinse them off under cold water, and discard any open clams that do not close when handled.

Put ½–1 inch of water in a pot large enough to hold the clams, add the clams, cover, and bring to a boil. Steam the clams just until they open, about 8 minutes. Immediately remove the open clams to a large baking pan and spread them around so they will cool quickly. Leave unopened clams in the pot to steam a little longer, but discard any that have not opened after 10–12 minutes of steaming. Carefully pour the cooking broth into a bowl, discarding the last bit containing any sand, and set the broth aside to cool. Remove the clam meats from the shells; pull off the black siphon from each clam and discard it with the shell. Rinse the meats, if needed, in a little of the broth. Put the clam meats in a bowl, and if you are going to fry the clams sometime later, cover them with broth and refrigerate.

To prepare the batter: Put the flour and salt in a large bowl, add the egg yolks, vegetable oil, and beer, and whisk all together until smooth. Let the batter rest at room temperature for at least 30 minutes. Just before frying the clams, beat the egg whites until they form peaks, then fold them into the batter.

continued on page 133

CLAMS

CLAMS, I HAVE TO SAY, have been both a favorite sport and a favorite food of mine since childhood; that's how long I have been digging them on various New England shores and eating them. Like oysters, mussels, and scallops, they are bivalve mollusks that live in double-hinged shells. They live near the surface of the ocean floor, and each clam is a small circulating system taking in gallons of water each day, and therefore susceptible to ingesting pollutants that can be toxic to humans. For this reason, should you be gathering your own clams, always go to an approved, safe shellfish area, and never buy from anyone who is vague about where the shellfish came from. There are hundreds of species of clams scattered around the world. From the West Coast I have enjoyed sweet, tender Manila clams, introduced there by the Japanese; Pismo clams, littleneck clams that are different from our East Coast littlenecks; and little butter clams. I have even enjoyed the sweet taste and smooth texture of geoduck clam meat that has been pounded flat and then fried. Geoduck clams, with their long, fat siphon necks, are immense by East Coast standards; a quite average-size geoduck at 3 pounds will yield 1½ pounds of meat! Here on the East Coast I use two kinds of clams on a regular basis: hardshell quahog clams and soft-shell "steamer" clams.

Hard-Shell Clams (quahogs, pronounced có-hogs):
Quahogs, our most versatile clams, are graded and named by size, with the smallest being the most expensive and the largest ones used mainly for chowders. The gradings vary a little, but this is common:

❖ *Littlenecks,* 2–2½ inches across, are perfect for a raw bar or when lightly cooked or grilled.
❖ *Topnecks,* 2¼–2½ inches across, are my favorite size for raw bar or for *Chili Clams* (page 32). Many areas do not grade this size.
❖ *Cherrystones,* 2½–3 inches across, are a very popular size. They are versatile enough to be used in raw bars, but also a nice size for baking, grilling, and roasting.
❖ *Chowder quahogs,* 3 inches or more across, are hard-shell clams that are larger than cherrystones. They are perfect for baked stuffed clams, chowders, and recipes using clam meats.

Buying: Buy only from the most reputable of dealers and markets, and check that the market buys only from "approved" sources that are licensed by federal and state agencies and regularly inspected. Don't hesitate to ask to see the tag of origin that comes with the shipment from an approved source; if the market will not produce the tag, try another market. I myself avoid buying clams from markets that package the clams in wrapping so that I cannot handle them. An open clam should close when handled. You can buy shucked clams in containers, but I prefer to buy live clams and shuck them myself. If you are unsure of your shucking ability, ask the fish market to do it for you. If you are preparing a raw bar, ask the fish market to shuck the clams and pack them in their shells, covered with their top shells.

My favorite clam man, Oscar Bunting, gave me these tips. Good quahogs should be half meat and half juice, and should feel full and heavy. The color of the meat will vary with the clam's habitat—lighter meat if the clam lived in sand, darker if it lived in a muddy area. Clams will stay alive for 5–10 days under perfect refrigeration but will lose their juices gradually as they open and close, so the fresher they are, the better they are. Should you have the opportunity to gather your own, get a license and go to a designated safe shellfish area at low tide. Use a six-pronged "potato rake" to gently drag the surface of the ocean floor and dislodge the clams. If the bed is a thick one, you will be able to feel the clams just under the surface with your feet.

Storage: Keep clams refrigerated in a burlap bag, or in a paper bag with air holes to let the clams breathe, or loose in the vegetable drawer of your refrigerator. If possible, cover them with seaweed to give them moisture. *Never put them in fresh water.* They will die.

Preparation: Before serving clams raw or cooking them, scrub the shells with a stiff vegetable brush or a round plastic scrubber sold for nonstick pans and rinse them.

SPECIAL INFORMATION ABOUT

CLAMS

Clams (continued)

To shuck a clam: Clams sometimes open more easily if they have been buried in ice for a few minutes just before shucking. If you are right-handed, hold the clam in the palm of your left hand, with the hinged side against the heel of your palm. Insert the point of a clam knife, or a strong, thin knife, between the two shells next to the hinge. Push the knife into the clam with an upward motion to make the blade slide along the inside shell top, and at the same time twist the blade slightly. Run the blade along the upper shell from one side to the other, severing the muscle and separating the top of the clam from the shell. Twist off and discard the top shell. Use the knife to loosen the bottom of the clam, running the knife under the muscle to sever its connection to the bottom shell. The clam meat now sits unattached in its shell. With enough practice you might be able to match our restaurant clam opener who could open six clams in a minute or less! Place the clams in their half shells on a flat tray lined with a layer of rock salt to stabilize the shells and hold in the juices. Shuck clams as close as possible to serving time, but if you have to set them aside, put the top shells loosely back in place, cover the tray with a damp towel, and refrigerate. To serve, place the clams on dishes lined with a bed of ice.

To open clams with heat: Steam the clams for 5–10 minutes until open, or roast them in a pre-heated 450-degree oven for 2–3 minutes, or put them on a grill rack over hot coals until they open (discard any that don't).

Yields:
❖*Littlenecks:*
   about 10 clams per pound
   6 shucked meats with juice yield about ½ cup
   10 shucked meats without juice yield about ½ cup
❖*Topnecks:*
   about 6 clams per pound
❖*Cherrystones:*
   about 4 clams per pound
   4 shucked meats with juice yield about ½ cup
   6 shucked meats without juice yield about ½ cup
❖*Chowder quahogs:*
   2–3 clams per pound
   24–30 mixed-size clams yield about 4 cups meat and 4 cups juice
❖Allow 6 littleneck, topneck, or cherrystone clams per person for a raw bar.
❖1 quart shucked clams should serve 6, depending on the recipe.

Soft-Shell Clams (steamers, Ipswich clams, long-neck clams):
These old favorites are distinguished by their long, oval shape, thin gray-white shells, and long siphons, or necks, that do not retract completely into their shells. Follow the suggestions above for buying hard-shell clams. Use only reputable dealers and ask to see the tag of origin, which shows whether the clams came from an approved source monitored by government agencies. The best test for aliveness of a soft-shell clam is to touch the siphon, or neck; when you do, it should move and constrict, and if it doesn't, the clam should be rejected.

If you have the opportunity to gather your own soft-shell clams, get a license and go to a designated safe shellfish area at low tide to look for them in tidal flats. When you see their squirt holes in the sand, dig down and around the hole, scooping the clam up and out, taking care not to break the fragile shell. Using a rake may damage the shell, so your hands are the best tool. This elongated clam is standing on end with its siphon toward the ocean floor. You can get nasty scratches if you come directly down on it, so the technique is to dig around and under, and excavate it from the sand.

Storage: Refrigerate the clams in a burlap bag or in another container with plenty of air holes so that the clams can breathe. Their shelf life is not as long as that of hard-shell clams. I plan to use soft-shell clams almost immediately, certainly within 2 days. *Never store them or soak them in fresh water.*

Preparation: Scrub the shells with a stiff vegetable brush or a round plastic scrubber sold for nonstick pans before cooking the clams. Since the shells of soft-shell clams never close completely, they are likely to have sand or muck inside the shells. To purge the clams, refrigerate them for at least 2 hours submerged in a salt-

SPECIAL INFORMATION ABOUT

CLAMS

water mixture composed of 3 tablespoons salt and 1 tablespoon vinegar for each 2 quarts water (or, by another method, use 2 tablespoons cornmeal for each 2 quarts water). Change the water and additives once or twice during the purging so that the clams do not exhaust the oxygen in the water and suffocate.

To shuck raw soft-shell clams:

Insert a clam knife into the shell by the siphon, rotate it around the inner surface of the top shell, open the shell, then rotate the knife around the inside of the bottom shell to remove the meat. Slit the black skin of the siphon and pull the black skin off. (*Note:* I find that it is easy to open the clam but difficult to remove the black siphon skin

when it is raw; steaming the clam in the shell makes it easier to remove the black skin and in my experience makes the clam more tender when fried subsequently.)

Yields:
❖Our home-dug steamers average 8 to a pound.
❖Allow at least 12 per person, or 6 pounds for 4 persons.

Fried Clams (continued)

In a deep-fat fryer or very deep-sided saucepan, heat 4–5 inches of peanut oil to 375 degrees and maintain the temperature at a constant level with the help of a deep-fat-frying thermometer. Preheat an oven to 250 degrees and line a baking sheet with brown paper or a brown paper bag.

To fry the clams: If the clam meats have been refrigerated, drain them and pat them dry with paper towels. Drop a few clams at a time into the batter, remove, let any excess batter drip off, then carefully drop the clams into the hot oil. Cook for 2–3 minutes or until lightly browned, and remove with a wide, open-holed wire spoon, letting excess oil drip back into the fryer. Place the fried clams on the paper-lined tray and keep them warm in the oven as you fry more batches. Serve as soon as possible after frying with lemon wedges and with tartar sauce, if desired.

SERVES 4–6

❖Substitute half milk and half cold water for the beer in the batter.
❖If you buy shucked raw clams, remove any bits of shell and pat dry. If any clams still have the black skin on the siphon, slit it with a knife and pull it off, or, if you prefer, use just the clam bellies and cut off and discard the whole siphon, which can be chewy.
❖Toast hot dog rolls and serve the clams in them.
❖If this is a main course, you *must* serve *Coleslaw* (page 82).

Clams Cataplana-Style

The Portuguese make a wonderful dish of clams or mussels combined with sausage or ham or pork. It is cooked in a *cataplana,* a round domed pot with a tight hinged cover that goes right from stovetop to table; when the cover is opened, the fragrance of the shellfish and meat cooked with tomatoes, onions, and garlic is stunning. In place of a *cataplana,* use a wide, heavy-bottomed, 8–10-quart pot with a tight-fitting lid. The heavy bottom is important to prevent the tomatoes from scorching as the clams cook. You could also use a 14-inch-wide covered paella pan for this dish. The juices released from the clams thin the tomato-based sauce and turn it into an aromatic soup, so I serve the dish in deep soup bowls with crusty bread to soak up the delicious juices. I like to serve a *Caesar Salad* (page 84) before this dish and accompany the clams with corn on the cob when it is in season, or I will serve this dish first and follow it with *Green Salad with Saga Blue Cheese* (page 86).

My favorite instrument for scrubbing clams is the round plastic scrubber sold for nonstick pans; it doesn't snag on the ridges of the clams as some other scrubbers do. You can scrub the clams ahead of time and keep them refrigerated, and you can prepare the recipe, as indicated below, up to the point of adding the clams, set it aside, and reheat and cook the clams quickly just before serving.

Clams Cataplana-Style (continued)

Alternative shellfish: other small clams such as Manilas, or mussels

36 littleneck clams
¾–1 lb linguiça, chorizo, or kielbasa sausage
3 large onions or 2 large sweet onions
2 Tb olive or vegetable oil
½ tsp paprika
2 tsp finely chopped garlic
7–8 cups peeled, seeded, and chopped ripe
    tomatoes
½ cup dry vermouth or white wine
1 bay leaf
Hot pepper sauce
½ cup chopped fresh parsley

Scrub the clams very thoroughly because they will be cooking in their shells in the base sauce; discard any open clams that do not close tightly when you press them. Refrigerate the clams in a bowl until ready to cook.

Remove and discard the skin of the sausage, cut it into ½-inch-wide slices, and refrigerate.

Peel the onions and chop them into ½-inch chunks, and set aside. (Makes about 4 cups) Everything up to this point can be prepared well ahead.

In a heavy-bottomed, 8–10-quart pot, heat the olive or vegetable oil, add the sliced sausage, and cook over medium-high heat to lightly brown the sausage and render some of its fat. Remove the sausage when browned with a slotted spoon and set aside. Remove and discard all but 2 tablespoons of the oil and fat in the pan, add the onions, and cook, stirring occasionally, until the onions have wilted and are tender and golden, about 8 minutes. Stir in the paprika to coat the onions, then stir in the garlic and add the tomatoes, vermouth or white wine, and bay leaf. Bring the mixture to a boil, cover the pan, reduce the heat slightly, and cook for 4–5 minutes to release the juices from the tomatoes. Uncover the pan and cook until the juices are reduced and the mixture has thickened. (The mixture should be fairly thick because it will be thinned by the clam juices when the clams are cooked.) You can set the sauce aside at this point, if you wish, and reheat it later, shortly before you are ready to serve.

Stir in the sliced sausage and ¼ teaspoon hot pepper sauce or more, to taste, and bring the mixture to a boil. Add the clams to the sauce with their closed edges down so that as they open they will release their juice into the sauce. Cover the pot, adjust the heat so that the sauce boils gently, and cook until the clams open, about 10–14 minutes, depending on the size of the clams and the degree of heat. After the clams have cooked 4–5 minutes, uncover the pot long enough to stir the clams and sauce together, cover again, and resume cooking. Remove the cooked clams to a warm platter or bowl, discarding any clams that do not open. Ladle some of the tomato-sausage sauce into 4 soup bowls, divide the clams evenly on top of each bowl, spoon the remaining sauce over all, sprinkle with parsley, and serve with crusty bread.

SERVES 4

❖ To make a heartier meal, ladle the sauce and clams over cooked warm sliced potatoes or over toasted thick-sliced country bread.

❖ If you make the dish with small mussels, count on at least 12 mussels per serving. Just before cooking the mussels, remove the beards. The mussels will cook more quickly than the clams and release less juice, so you will not need to thicken the sauce quite as much when using mussels.

❖ If vine-ripened tomatoes are not available, use 4 cups drained canned tomatoes for color and flavor and 4 cups peeled, seeded, and diced tomatoes for texture, or use all canned tomatoes. Or use 6 cups drained, chopped canned plum tomatoes instead of 8 cups fresh tomato pulp, and omit the cooking step that reduces the tomato juices.

❖ *Vegetable Soup Variation:* When I make this dish for two I have leftovers, so the next day I supplement the leftover sauce with *cooked* vegetables (sliced potatoes, green beans, quartered pattypan squash, whatever I have on hand), add a little water, simmer enough to blend everything together, and I have a really good vegetable-clam-and-sausage soup. Or you could add cooked vegetables before you served the dish the first time.

Spaghetti Squash with White Clam Sauce

When I wrote *The Victory Garden Cookbook* in the early 1980s, spaghetti squash was a novelty; now you can find it in most supermarkets. It is classified as a winter squash and named for the way its flesh forms strands when cooked. The texture of spaghetti squash is delightful, but the vegetable has very little flavor, so it becomes a crunchy vehicle for sauces or seasonings.

Clam sauce turns spaghetti squash into a main course, and the taste and fragrance of the shellfish and garlic give the dish the punch it needs. A green salad is all you need to complete a delicious, low-calorie meal. You can prepare both the squash and the sauce ahead. I usually prepare the clam sauce up to the point of returning the clams to the broth, and reheat it just before tossing with the squash.

Alternative shellfish: mussels

1 large spaghetti squash

CLAM SAUCE

24–36 littleneck clams
½ cup dry vermouth or white wine
¼ cup olive oil
3–4 finely minced cloves garlic
Freshly ground pepper
¼ cup chopped parsley
Salt (optional)

To prepare the squash: Bring a pot of water large enough to cover the spaghetti squash completely with water to a boil, drop in the squash, and cook for 20–30 minutes, depending on the size of the squash, or until a fork goes easily into the flesh. Remove the squash from the water, let cool, and when it can be handled, split it lengthwise and remove the seeds and thin, stringy membranes. With a fork, "comb" the squash into long spaghetti-like strands. (Makes 6–8 cups) Keep the squash warm in a bowl until ready to combine with the sauce, or refrigerate for later use. Reheat by sautéing the squash in a little butter or oil, or by dropping it into boiling water and then quickly removing it, or by steaming it briefly.

To make the clam sauce: Scrub the clams well, discarding any that do not close when pressed, and put them in a pot. Add the vermouth or white wine, cover, bring the vermouth or wine to a boil, and steam just until the clams have opened. Lift the clams out of the pot, discarding any that did not open, remove the clam meats, and discard the shells. Pour the cooking broth carefully into a bowl, leaving behind and discarding the last bit containing any sand from the clams. Wipe out the pot, add and heat the oil, add the garlic and cook, stirring, for 30 seconds; then add the clam broth and generous grindings of pepper (about ½ teaspoon). Bring the mixture to a boil, lower the heat, and simmer for 5 minutes. Add the clams to the sauce, allow

Spaghetti Squash with White Clam Sauce (continued)

them to heat through for 1 minute, and pour the clam sauce over the hot or reheated spaghetti squash. Toss with the parsley, season with additional pepper and salt, if desired, and serve.   SERVES 4

❖Substitute pasta for the spaghetti squash.
❖Chop the clams into smaller pieces.

Pan-Fried Scrod Cod or Haddock in an Egg Coating

My husband says this is his favorite fish recipe, and if he ever has to request a last meal, this is it. The usual way of coating fish to be fried in a batter is to dip the fish in beaten eggs, then dredge it in flour. This recipe reverses the order; the egg wash on the outside of the floured fish produces a soft "skin," which makes the fish seem all the more tender. Serve this with home-made *Tartar Sauce* (page 363) and a crisp coleslaw or Russ's favorite *Sautéed Rutabaga Dice* (page 337).

Alternative fish: almost any firm-fleshed fish fillets

1½–2 lb skinned scrod cod or haddock fillets
½ cup flour
Salt and freshly ground pepper
3–4 Tb light olive oil
2 eggs beaten with 1 tsp water
Lemon wedges

Remove any bones from the fish and cut the fillets into 4 equal portions. Place the flour in a flat dish or pie pan and season it with salt and freshly ground pepper.

In a sauté pan large enough to hold the fish in one layer, or in two pans, heat the oil. Dredge the fish in the flour, shaking off any excess, then dip it in the beaten egg, letting any excess coating drip off. Place the fish in the pan and cook slowly over medium heat for 3–4 minutes, or until the bottom coating is golden. Turn the fish and cook about 3–4 minutes longer, depending on the thickness of the fish; thinner tail ends will be done first. Remove to a warm serving platter and serve immediately with lemon wedges.   SERVES 4

Scrod Cod or Haddock Sautéed in Fresh Bread Crumbs

Scrod refers to young cod or haddock weighing less than two pounds each. Some New Englanders limit the term to young cod, but I use it to designate both of these cousin fish. This dish takes just minutes to cook. With it serve made-ahead *Roasted Ratatouille* (page 326) or *Leeks Braised with Tomatoes, Garlic, and Olives* (page 329). If time is a consideration, quickly boil small potatoes and make the sautéed zucchini in *Sautéed Zucchini and Zucchini Tian* (page 343).

Alternative fish: any small fish fillets, including black sea bass, snapper, ocean perch (red perch), flounder

2 lb skinned scrod cod or haddock fillets
½ cup flour
Salt and freshly ground pepper
2 eggs beaten with 1 tsp water
1½ cups fresh bread crumbs
3 Tb butter
1 Tb vegetable oil
Lemon wedges

Remove any bones from the fish and cut the fillets into 4 equal portions.

Season the flour with salt and freshly ground pepper, and spread it in a flat dish or pie pan. Dredge the fish pieces lightly in the flour, shaking off any excess, then dip them in the beaten egg and turn them in the bread crumbs until they are well coated on both sides. Refrigerate the fish for 30 minutes to help the coating adhere to the flesh.

In a sauté pan large enough to hold the fish without crowding in one layer, or in two pans, heat the butter and oil. When the bubbles subside in the cooking liquid, add the fish and sauté slowly over medium heat for 3–4 minutes on each side, or until golden on the outside and just cooked through. Serve with lemon wedges. If you like, serve *Tartar Sauce* (page 363) or *Salsa* (page 7) on the side.   SERVES 4

❖Add chopped fresh herbs to the bread crumbs.
❖*Southern-Style Pan-Fried in Cornmeal:* Substitute 1 cup cornmeal for the flour, eggs, and bread crumbs above. In a wide, heavy sauté pan large enough to

continued on page 140

SPECIAL INFORMATION ABOUT

COD AND HADDOCK

(AND POLLOCK, HAKE, AND CUSK)

ALTHOUGH I WAS introduced to a variety of seafood as a child (my father's favorite spring meal was shad roe; my mother put up herring with pickles and onions; a neighbor sometimes brought us fresh-caught crabs; my best friend's dad took me clamming; and my mother dutifully cooked sunfish I caught in a Connecticut lake), the fact remains that most of our fish dinners at home were dishes of cod and haddock. The favorite fish for generations of New Englanders has been the noble Atlantic cod. Take my Yankee husband, Russ, anywhere and serve him the finest fish gilded with satiny sauces and elegant accompaniments, and he will say, "Well, it's nice, but not as good as a piece of fresh cod." From early Colonial days until the late-nineteenth century, the principal method of preserving this fish— so prolific as to give Cape Cod its name—was to salt it, and salt cod became a staple in the various exchanges that made up the slave and rum trades. In the late 1800s increased use of ice refrigeration made fresh fish more available and popular, and salting cod gradually declined in significance. About the same time, another member of the cod family—haddock—became a commercially important fish, both fresh and smoked as "finnan haddie." The codfish family includes a number of fish, the best known being Atlantic cod, Pacific cod, and haddock, with pollock, hake, and cusk being the lesser-known cousins. Nomenclature is a problem with this family, and you are best advised to deal with a reliable fish retailer where fish are accurately labeled. One major confusion concerns the word "scrod," which is frequently used as though it defined a fish when in truth it refers to the size of certain fish of the cod family. A scrod fish is a small, young fish (perfect for sautéing), and can be a scrod cod or a scrod haddock or a scrod pollock, etc., and should be so labeled. Here is a brief rundown of the cod family:

1. *Atlantic cod,* the foundation of the cod industry, is a heavy-bodied fish with a big head that takes up about one-quarter of the fish's length. A long pale line runs the length of its body—distinguishing it from haddock—the upper body is spotted, and the belly is white. Cooked cod meat is white and firm, with a sweet, mild taste. It flakes nicely, and because the flakes hold together well, cod is an excellent fish for fish chowder.

2. *Pacific cod* is also called true cod, gray cod, and sometimes sea bass. The designation "true cod" is to distinguish it from several other West Coast fish that are not really cod but are often referred to by names that include cod; for example, black cod is really sablefish. Most Pacific cod in the markets are in the 6-pound range. The white flesh flakes well, but I think is a little softer than the flesh of Atlantic cod.

3. *Haddock* has a dark lateral line and distinctive dark blotches on each side just over the pectoral fin. It is the most expensive of the cod family because the flesh has a delicate sweet taste and a tender, firm texture with finer grain than cod, and the supply is limited. It holds together better for pan-frying than any other member of the cod family.

4. *American pollock* has a deep-fat body and a distinctive olive-green skin color. The creamy flesh, darker just under the skin, is the darkest of any member of the cod family. Pollock has a coarser grain and meatier texture than cod, and spoils faster, so be alert to the freshness of pollock you buy. Be careful not to over-

SPECIAL INFORMATION ABOUT

COD AND HADDOCK

(AND POLLOCK, HAKE, AND CUSK)

Cod and Haddock (continued)

cook pollock because the flesh toughens quickly.

5. *Alaskan pollock:* If you come across a fish called Alaska scrod, you can be pretty sure it is Alaskan pollock, also known as walleye pollock, big-eye cod, and Alaska snow cod. The flesh is similar to that of its East Coast cousin, rather coarse and best when coated in batter and fried as in *Fish and Chips* (page 143). These fish are often caught, dressed, filleted, and quick-frozen at sea. Many are used for the new prefabricated seafood "surimi." The Japanese invented surimi as a way of using the millions of tons of pollock they were catching. The flesh of the fish is broken down into blocks of tasteless, odorless, colorless denatured fish product, which, with additives, can be reconfigured into fake crab legs, fake lobster chunks, etc. American and Russian companies now also make surimi.

6. *Hake.* Hake are biologically close to the cod family, but quite different in appearance and texture from their cod relatives. They are small, slender, soft-bodied fish. White hake and red hake are most frequently found in fish markets; both have off-white flesh that turns white when cooked. Silver hake is marketed as whiting. Whiting average under 2 pounds. The flesh is sweet but softens quickly after it is caught.

7. *Cusk.* Because it has tough,

leathery skin, cusk is usually sold as skinless fillets. The pin bones are more prominent in cusk than in other members of the cod family. A handy way to get rid of the pin bones is to cut the fillets lengthwise into strips, which are good for chowders and soups, or fish and chips. The meat is lean, white, quite firm, and a little coarse when cooked. Cusk is also marketed as whitefish or ocean whitefish.

8. *Tomcod.* This is not a true cod or a commercial fish. It is an inshore fish caught all along the Atlantic Coast from the Gulf of St. Lawrence to Virginia. At first glance it looks like a cod, but its body is more slender and it has smaller eyes. The largest run to about 15 inches. It's not a pretty fish, but it has delicious flesh; if you're lucky enough to find one, cook it and eat it.

Buying Fresh Cod: The cod family are incredibly versatile and can be purchased and cooked as whole fish, fillets, or steaks. Some members of the family are better than others for certain treatments, but among them you can find splendid fish to poach, steam, fry, sauté, bake, grill, and broil to your heart's content. Cod and haddock (as fillets, steaks, or whole) poach beautifully—better than cusk, pollock, and hake. Scrod cod or small haddock fillets sauté nicely, and hake can be sautéed quickly. Generally speaking, the cod family does not grill as well as fish with more oil and

denser flesh, but with proper protection, such as a wrapping, they adapt to this method. For fish kabobs you might prefer cusk over cod because of its ability to hold together. All members of the family excel in chowders, soups, and stews, and their frames make excellent stock.

Look for fish markets that buy from the most reputable fishermen, like Jerry Knecht of Portland, Maine. He became renowned for his "boxed" cod and haddock. Instead of dumping masses of fish into a hold, Knecht separated the fish immediately by shelves, or "boxes," to prevent damage during handling. I used his fish at the restaurant, and they were handled and dressed so expertly that they were worth any price. The flesh was clear, bright, firm, and delicious.

Special Forms of Cod and Haddock:

1. *Finnan haddie.* The Scottish nickname for haddock that was originally split and smoked by the Ross firm in Findon, Scotland. The fillets of haddock, with head removed but skin, backbone, and tail intact, are butterflied (or spread open), lightly salted to draw moisture out of the flesh, and then smoked. It is not necessary to soak finnan haddie as you would more heavily salted salt cod, but it does benefit from a gentle poaching, which firms up the flesh and makes it easy to remove the skin and bones. Finnan haddie has a golden color and should feel slightly moist; it has a gentle,

COD AND HADDOCK
(AND POLLOCK, HAKE, AND CUSK)

almost velvety, smoke flavor that is delicious and subtle.

To prepare: The fillets are often too long to fit into a pan, so snap the backbone in two or three places and then cut through the fish at those places. Place the sections in a pan, cover with water (or with milk if you are using the liquid for a chowder or baked dish), and bring to a simmer. Cover the pan, remove from the heat, and allow to steep for 10 minutes. Drain, and when the fish is cool enough to handle, remove the skin and bones. Now the flesh is ready to use in many different kinds of dishes.

2. *Smoked cod.* More and more stores are handling a skinless, boneless smoked cod fillet *and often calling it finnan haddie.* Perhaps it appeals to customers because it doesn't have to be skinned and boned. However, it still requires work because it does need the gentle poach described above for finnan haddie. Smoked cod is very good and perfectly usable for many recipes, but it has a stronger, harsher flavor than real finnan haddie, and the flesh has a larger grain.

3. *Salt cod.* Salt cod is simply cod that has been heavily salted to preserve it from spoilage. There are three different commercial methods of salting fish. Each produces varying results, depending on the size and age of the fish; the least salted is called Gaspé-cured. In some markets you can find whole sides of salt cod with skin and bones; elsewhere you may find it already boned and filleted,

packed in one-pound wooden boxes. I have found wide differences in quality from packer to packer. Salt cod has a fairly sharp, salty odor, but it should not have an unpleasant "fishy" smell. If it still smells strong and unpleasant after soaking, it was probably old before it was salted; look for another packer. Before cooking salt cod, it is important to "refresh" and poach it as described below.

To Prepare Salt Cod:

To refresh and remove salt: If you wish, cut the fish into serving pieces or into 2-inch sections. Rinse the fish under cold water for 5 minutes. Place the fish, whole or in pieces, in a glass or stainless dish or pan, cover with cold water, and refrigerate for 24 hours, changing the water 3–4 times.

To soften by poaching: Place 1 sliced small onion, 1 bay leaf, and 1 cup water in a 10-inch skillet. Bring to a boil and cook gently for 5 minutes to flavor the water. Add 2 cups cold water, place the fish in the pan, and add another 2 cups water, or enough to cover the fish by ½ inch. Bring to a simmer. As soon as the water simmers, cover the pan and remove from the heat. Let stand for 10 minutes. (Continuing to cook the fish over heat will toughen it.) The fish is now ready to use in a dish, or you can let it cool and then refrigerate it for 24 hours. Drain well again before using.

(*Note:* In some markets you may find a split side of wizened

dried fish that looks and feels like shoe leather. It is "stockfish," which is prepared by air drying, not salting; long soaking is required to bring it back to usable consistency.)

Yields of Fresh and Smoked Cod and Haddock:

❖When you buy fresh fillets in the market they might be prepared as whole fillets or "J"-cut fillets. You will have to remove the pin bones from the whole fillets. The J-cut fillets have pin bones removed, and you get totally boneless fish, which may be a little more expensive. When you check fillet prices, note how the fillets have been cut.

Cod family, fresh:

❖Cod and cusk yield about one-third the weight of the live fish in boneless filleted fish.

❖Haddock, hake, and pollock yield about 40 percent of the weight of the live fish in boneless filleted fish.

❖A 4-pound whole cod yields 2 boneless fillets of about 10–12 ounces each.

❖Allow 1 pound of whole fish per person.

❖Allow 6–8 ounces filleted fish per person.

❖1 pound raw filleted cod yields about 3 cups cooked fish.

Finnan haddie:

❖4 pounds whole split finnan haddie yield about 2 pounds skinned, boned flesh.

❖1 pound skinned, boned flesh yields about 3 cups cooked fish.

Scrod Cod or Haddock Sautéed in Fresh Bread Crumbs (continued)

hold the fish in one layer, or in two pans, heat ½ cup solid shortening or vegetable oil. When the shortening or oil is hot, dip the fish fillets into the cornmeal to coat both sides, shaking off any excess. Add the fish carefully to the sauté pan, being careful about spattering, and cook over medium heat for 3–4 minutes. Turn the fillets and cook another 2–4 minutes, depending on the thickness of the fish, or until the fish is golden brown. Remove thinner pieces after 2 minutes. Place the fried fish on brown paper to absorb any excess fat, then place on warm serving plates and serve as above. You can, if desired, dip the fish fillets into milk before dipping them into the cornmeal.

Sauté of Cod with an Eggplant and Tomato Sauce

Eggplant, tomatoes, and garlic give a rich Mediterranean flavor and fragrance to the thick sauce of this dish, which happily accepts fish fillets of all kinds. The instant flour for the coating doesn't lump the way ordinary flour may during dusting or dredging; it gives a nice light coating.

Alternative fish: bass or monkfish or almost any white fish; oily fish, such as bluefish or mackerel; thin slices of tuna, swordfish, or shark

  1½-lb eggplant
  Salt and freshly ground pepper
  3 lb ripe tomatoes
  Olive oil
  2 tsp minced garlic
  1½–2 lb cod fillets, not too thick
  2 Tb butter
  Instant-blending flour (such as Wondra Quick-
    Mixing Flour) or fine cornmeal

Remove the skin of the eggplant. Cut the flesh into ¾-inch-thick slices, then into ¾-inch-wide strips, then into ¾-inch cubes. Place the eggplant cubes in a colander, sprinkle them with 1 teaspoon salt, and let them drain for 30 minutes.

Core the tomatoes, place them in a roasting pan, and roast them in a preheated 450-degree oven for 10 minutes to loosen their skins and partially cook them. As soon as they are cool enough to handle, peel and seed them, roughly chop the tomato pulp, and place the pulp in a sieve to drain.

In a sauté pan, heat 2 tablespoons of the olive oil. Pat the eggplant dry with paper towels and sauté it in batches, so as not to crowd the pan, for 7–8 minutes, turning the cubes continually so that they brown on all sides; add more oil as needed. When all the eggplant is browned, return it to the sauté pan, add the garlic, toss together for 30 seconds, then stir in the tomatoes. Cover the pan, reduce the heat, and cook gently for 6 minutes, stirring occasionally. Remove the cover and cook for 1–2 minutes more. Season with salt and freshly ground pepper, and keep warm.

Cut the fillets into 4 serving pieces. In a sauté pan, heat the butter and 1 tablespoon olive oil over medium-high heat. Dust the fish with instant-blending flour or cornmeal, shaking off any excess, place the fish in the pan, and sauté for 4 minutes or until golden brown. Turn the fish and sauté the other side for about 4 minutes. (Timing depends on the thickness of the fillets; if they are scrod size, reduce the cooking time slightly; if the fillets are very thick, increase the cooking time slightly.)

To serve, divide three-quarters of the eggplant-tomato sauce on 4 warm serving plates, set a piece of fish on top of the sauce, then pour the remaining sauce over the fish.   SERVES 4

❖Add 2 tablespoons chopped parsley or basil or other herb to the sauce.

❖If fresh ripe tomatoes are not available, use a good canned variety. Drain the canned tomatoes, remove as many seeds as possible, and chop enough for a generous 2 cups.

Blackened Haddock

Paul Prudhomme, the chef and owner of K-Paul's Restaurant in New Orleans, took the restaurant world by storm with his Blackened Redfish. Redfish, which had been a relatively obscure and inexpensive fish, suddenly became expensive and hard to get at any price as chefs across the country tried to duplicate the original fiery dish. Back on Nantucket, I turned to the fish on hand. We were receiving "boxed" young scrod haddock that had been handled so well its flesh was extremely fresh and firm: just the right fish to stand up to the searing heat of Paul's method. It is important to use only the freshest and firmest fish fillets for this recipe; otherwise the flesh will fall apart. An iron frying pan large enough to hold the fish is essential. Do not attempt this recipe unless you have an exhaust fan above your stovetop.

When the fish is hot, it's nice to serve something very cool and refreshing with it. Try a cucumber salad, or serve the fish with *Cucumber-Dill Sauce* (page 354) on the side.

Alternative fish: redfish, snapper, bass, salmon, blue-fish, halibut, firm-fleshed fish that is not too thin

Heat a cast-iron frying pan to white-hot. Turn on the exhaust fan over the cooktop. Place the fillets in the pan and pour about 1 tablespoon butter over each piece of fish. (The pan will smoke immediately and excessively.) Cook for about 3 minutes, or until the fish is very brown but not burned. Turn the fillets over and pour about 2 teaspoons of butter over each piece again. Cook for another 3–4 minutes, depending on the thickness of the fish; the tail pieces will take less time. Remove to a warm plate and serve immediately with lemon wedges.   SERVES 4

❖Serve with a side dish of melted butter with fresh lemon juice squeezed into it.

Cod Messina-Style

In Sicily this dish is traditionally made with dried or salted codfish, but it is a delicious and simple way to cook fresh cod as well. Of course, you can use salt cod if you wish; just soak and refresh it in water for 24 hours as instructed in *To Prepare Salt Cod* (page 139). Serve this richly flavorful dish with rice, cannellini beans, or wide noodles and broccoli.

Alternative fish: prepared salt cod; or pollock, haddock, grouper, halibut, or other white firm-fleshed fish

BLACKENED SEASONING MIXTURE

7 Tb paprika
3 Tb cayenne pepper
2 Tb black pepper
2 Tb dried thyme
2 Tb dried basil
2 Tb dried oregano

To make the Blackened Seasoning Mixture: In a small bowl, combine all the seasonings and mix thoroughly. Store until needed in an airtight jar or container. Keeps indefinitely with proper storage.

MAKES I CUP

¼ cup golden raisins
1½ lb cod fillets
4 Tb light olive oil
Flour
Salt and freshly ground pepper
1 thinly sliced onion
1 cup thinly sliced celery
½ tsp minced garlic (optional)
2½ cups peeled, seeded, and finely chopped tomatoes
½ cup halved pitted Mediterranean-style black olives
2 Tb drained capers
2 Tb pine nuts

2 lb skinned scrod haddock fillets
⅔ cup melted *Clarified Butter* (page 351)
Lemon wedges

Prepare the Blackened Seasoning Mixture.

Cut the fish into 4 equal portions. Brush one side of each piece of fish with the melted butter and sprinkle a generous coating of the seasoning mixture over the buttered fish. Turn the fish and repeat the buttering and seasoning on the other side. Cover the coated fish with waxed paper and refrigerate it for at least 30 minutes before cooking to help the coating adhere nicely.

Soak the raisins in a cup or bowl of warm water for 15 minutes.

Remove any skin and bones from the fish, and cut the fillets into 4 equal serving portions. In a wide

Cod Messina-Style (continued)

sauté pan, heat 2 tablespoons of the olive oil. Dust the fish pieces lightly with flour, shaking off any excess, season with salt and pepper, and place the fish in the sauté pan. Cook on one side for about 1 minute to brown lightly, turn, and sauté the other side until lightly browned. The fish will not be cooked through. Remove the fish to a plate, set it aside, and wipe out the pan. Heat the remaining 2 tablespoons of oil in the sauté pan, add the onion and celery, and cook about 8 minutes until the vegetables are wilted. Stir in the garlic, if you are using it, and cook for 1 minute. Drain the raisins and add them to the sauté pan along with the tomatoes, olives, capers, and pine nuts. Stir the mixture and cook gently for 10 minutes. Return the fish to the pan, spooning the sauce over the fish pieces. Cook gently for about 8 minutes, or until the fish barely turns opaque at the center. Remove to a warm serving platter.   SERVES 4

❖Omit the pine nuts and substitute thinly sliced almonds.

❖Use Italian black or green olives.

Sautéed Cod Tongues and Cheeks

I have seen recipes in English cookbooks for stuffed head of cod. Even though cod connoisseurs consider the meat from the head to be the sweetest of all, the idea of it doesn't appeal to me. What little head meat there is consists of "tongues" (really the meaty throat muscle at the base of the tongue) and "cheeks" (round chunks of flesh cut from the jowls). Since most of us prefer to use a cod head for fish stock rather than as a main-course centerpiece, fish markets here sell the tongue and cheek meat separately. The morsels are very sweet, good for soups, and especially delicious done this way. Try serving the dish with *Sautéed Brussels Sprouts and Sweet and Sour Cabbage* (page 322).

2 lb cod tongues and cheeks
Salt and freshly ground pepper
Clarified Butter (page 351) or a mixture of
    half butter and half vegetable oil
Instant-blending flour (such as Wondra
    Quick-Mixing Flour) or fine cornmeal,
    for dredging
Lemon wedges

Pat the cod pieces dry, cut them into bite-size pieces, and season them with salt and freshly ground pepper. In a sauté pan, heat 2 tablespoons of clarified butter. Working in batches, toss a few pieces of cod at a time with flour or cornmeal, drop them into the pan, and sauté until the fish is golden on all sides but still springy to the touch. Keep the cooked fish warm in a 200-degree oven while you cook the remaining pieces, adding more butter to the pan as needed. Transfer the sautéed fish to a warm serving platter and serve with lemon wedges.   SERVES 4–6

❖Deep-fry the fish as in *Fish and Chips* (this page).

Codfish Hash

When you see "hash" in the title and already cooked, flaked fish specified in the list of ingredients, you may jump to the wrong conclusion that this is a dish the family eats in private to clean leftovers out of the refrigerator after the guests have left. It is a fine dish for leftover fish, but it's also a dish worth poaching up some fish for and a main dish for a brunch that weekend guests will demand the recipe for. A 10-inch, nonstick frying pan is ideal for this recipe. All you need is a green salad as an accompaniment.

Alternative fish: Use all kinds of leftover fish or use soaked salt cod.

    1 lb cooked cod
    3 thick strips bacon (optional)
    5 Tb butter
    3 Tb olive oil or vegetable oil
    1 chopped large onion
    1 chopped red pepper
    3 cups diced cooked potatoes
    ¼ cup heavy cream
    2–3 Tb chopped fresh parsley
    Salt and freshly ground pepper
    Fresh lemon juice

Flake the fish into a bowl. (You should have about 2–2½ cups.)

In a 10-inch, nonstick frying pan, sauté the bacon (if you are using it) until it is crisp, drain it well on brown paper, crumble it into small pieces, and set it aside.

Wipe out the pan, heat 1 tablespoon of the butter and 1 tablespoon of the oil, add the onion, and cook for 2 minutes. Add the red pepper and cook for 4–5 minutes, or until the vegetables are wilted.

In a bowl, combine the potatoes, the cooked onion and pepper, the bacon (if you are using it), and the cream and parsley. Fold the fish into the mixture and season with salt and freshly ground pepper and a squeeze of lemon juice.

Wipe out the frying pan again and heat 2 tablespoons of the butter and the remaining 2 tablespoons of oil. Add the fish mixture, press it down into the pan to form a "cake," and cook over medium heat until the bottom forms a crust, about 10–15 minutes, regulating the heat as necessary so that the bottom browns but does not burn. Shake the pan occasionally so that the hash moves in one piece. Stir the mixture up to incorporate the crusty bottom into the hash, add 1 tablespoon of the butter, and press the mixture down again. Cook another 10 minutes, shaking the pan occasionally; then stir the crust into the hash again, add the remaining tablespoon of butter, and press the hash down into a cake again. Cook for another 10 minutes. Remove the hash from the pan by placing a warm plate over the pan and inverting the pan so that the hash turns onto the plate crust side up. Serve immediately.   SERVES 4–6

❖Serve topped with a poached egg. Offer homemade tomato sauce or ketchup.
❖Serve with a fresh, cold spicy salsa.
❖Add other cooked vegetables, such as chopped beets, fennel bulb, or carrots, and reduce slightly the amount of fish and potatoes.
❖Add fresh herbs.
❖Use soaked (see *To Prepare Salt Cod,* page 139) and poached salt cod.

Fish and Chips

I remember our first trip to England in 1958, when one could—and we did!—do Europe on five dollars a day. How grateful we were for all the economical fish-and-chips shops, where the fried fish of the day was listed as cod or hake or haddock or flounder. We would walk out of the shop with our choice, crisply fried, wrapped in the customary newspaper and bundled with "chips"—the quaint English term for the strips of deep-

Fish and Chips (continued)

fried potatoes we call French fries—both fish and chips sprinkled with salt and vinegar. Now we all avoid deep-fat-fried foods as a steady diet, but every once in a while it's fun to indulge; what better way than with crunchy yet tender fish. When possible, I serve this with *Coleslaw* (page 82).

Ideally, potatoes should be fried twice to ensure maximum crispness. In this case, the double frying is perhaps an advantage because the first step can be done way ahead, and then the final cooking just before serving takes only a minute or two. Use potatoes with as low a moisture content as possible; a starchy baking potato is perfect for French fries. And use absolutely fresh cooking oil.

I like to use a very light batter to get nicely crisp fish. The batter should be made at least 30 minutes before frying the fish. All the cod family and the flounder family and many other white fish can be deep-fried, but this is a good place to use less expensive fish, such as cusk (see *Fried Fish Dogs,* page 145). The same oil can be used for both the fish and the chips.

French Fried Potatoes, or "Chips"

Peanut or vegetable oil
2 lb peeled baking potatoes
Salt

Fried Fish

1 cup flour
2 eggs, separated
Salt and freshly ground pepper
Peanut or vegetable oil
1½ cups beer, at room temperature, or a
    combination of half milk,
    half cold water
2 lb skinned cusk, haddock, pollock, cod or
    combination fillets
Lemon wedges
Tartar Sauce (page 363)

To fry the potatoes: Heat 4–5 inches of oil in a deep-fat fryer or deep saucepan to 325 degrees, using a deep-fat-frying thermometer. If you are using a frying basket, warm it in the oil (a cold basket will cool down the oil when you begin cooking). Cut the potatoes length-wise into ⅜-inch-thick slices, then cut the slices into ⅜-inch-wide strips. Rinse them off and pat them dry with paper towels to prevent their sticking together as they cook. Drop the potato strips in small batches into the hot oil, using a basket or a large wire spatula. Stir them, if necessary, to keep them from sticking together. Beware of overflowing bubbles created by the moisture released from the potatoes and rising through the fat. Cook the potatoes for 2–3 minutes until cooked through but not browned. Bubbles will still be rising. Lift the potatoes from the fryer and drain them in another wire basket or on a brown paper bag. Continue in batches until all the potatoes have had this first-stage cooking. Cool them until just before serving. Before giving the potatoes their second fry, make the fish batter and allow it to sit for 30 minutes.

Reheat the same oil to 375 degrees. Plunge the potatoes in batches back into the oil for 3–5 minutes, or until they are nicely browned and the fat has almost stopped bubbling, indicating that the potatoes have given up most of their moisture. The potatoes should be crisp. Transfer them to a brown-paper-lined baking sheet and keep them in a warming oven at 250 degrees until all the batches are cooked. Sprinkle with salt and serve.

If you are in a hurry, the potatoes can be prepared in one cooking. Drop them into 375-degree oil and cook until the bubbles have just about disappeared in the oil. Drain and serve immediately with salt.   SERVES 4

To fry the fish: Put the flour in a large bowl and whisk in the egg yolks, ¼ teaspoon salt, 1 tablespoon peanut or vegetable oil, and the beer or combination of milk and water. Let the batter rest at room temperature for at least 30 minutes. Just before using the batter, beat the egg whites until they form peaks and fold the beaten whites into the batter.

Remove any bones from the fish and cut the fillets into portions about 2 inches × 3 inches; pat the fish dry.

Heat 4–5 inches of oil in a deep-fat fryer or deep saucepan to a temperature of 375 degrees, using a deep-fat-frying thermometer, and adjust the heat as needed to keep this temperature constant. Preheat an oven to 250 degrees and line a baking sheet with brown paper.

Drop a few pieces of fish at a time into the batter, remove them, letting excess batter drip back into the bowl, and drop the coated pieces into the hot oil. Cook for 4–5 minutes or until golden brown, turning the fish occasionally to prevent the pieces from sticking together. Remove the fish, let it drain for a moment, and keep it warm in the oven as the brown paper absorbs any excess oil. As soon as all the fish is cooked, serve immediately—with chips—and provide lemon wedges, salt and pepper, and tartar sauce or, in the English manner, sprinkle malt vinegar and salt over all. SERVES 4

❖If you are using a flat fish such as flounder, cut the pieces into 3 × 5-inch size.

❖*Fried Fish Dogs:* This is fun to do. Cusk fillets, because of their long lengthwise lines of pin bones, have to be divided in long strips as the bones are removed. This gave one clever entrepreneur the idea of cutting cusk into hot dog–length strips, deep-frying the strips, and serving them in toasted hot dog rolls. You can do it yourself. Cut cusk fillets lengthwise into strips 1 inch wide and about 5 inches long. Dip the strips in batter, fry as above, and serve in a toasted hot dog roll with a mustard-flavored tartar sauce!

❖*No-Batter Shallow-Fry:* This method is both delicious and simple. Use a sauté pan instead of a deep-fat fryer. Cut cusk into 1–2-inch-long pieces. Heat a thin layer of vegetable oil in a sauté pan, preferably a nonstick pan. Dip the pieces of cusk into milk, then into dried bread crumbs, tossing to coat on all sides. Place the coated pieces in the hot oil and fry, turning, about 5 minutes, or until golden brown and tender.

Fried Whiting

When you see small whole whiting or any small whole white fish at your fish market, think about this fast fish fry. Fried fish dishes always make me think of *Coleslaw* (page 82) and French-fried potatoes, but a made-ahead dish of *Easy Eggplant Parmesan* (page 328) is quite delicious with fried fish.

4 scaled, cleaned whole small whiting (½–¾ lb each) or other small whole white fish
4 cups peanut oil or vegetable oil
1 cup milk
Coarse (kosher) salt
Instant-blending flour (such as Wondra Quick-Mixing Flour), semolina flour, or cornmeal, for dredging
Lemon wedges

Wash and pat the fish dry.

Pour the oil into a wide, high-sided skillet; the oil should be at least 1 inch deep in the pan. Heat the oil to 360 degrees, using a deep-fat-frying thermometer.

Put the milk in a shallow bowl, dip the fish in it, sprinkle the fish with salt and dredge it in the flour or cornmeal, shaking off any excess. Carefully lower the fish, two at a time, into the hot oil, and deep-fry for about 5 minutes, turning the fish as necessary until they are golden brown on all sides. Remove the fish to a baking dish lined with brown paper and place in a preheated 200-degree oven to keep warm. Continue frying until all the fish are cooked. Serve with lemon wedges. SERVES 4

❖Use larger whiting. Take two 1½–2-pound whiting, remove and discard the heads and tails, and cut 1-inch-wide sections across the fish and through the soft backbone. Coat and deep-fry as above.

"Dry"-Poached Haddock with Warm Vinaigrette

A simple treatment is the finest complement to fresh fish; here haddock is cooked in the juices it releases in the pan, then lightly flavored with the clean taste of good vinegar, oil, and fresh herbs. Keep this meal simple and light with *Green Beans with Shallots and Garlic* (page 320) and *Roast Potato Chunks* (page 336).

Alternative fish: thick flounder, thin cod, halibut fillets, snapper, other light lean fish

VINAIGRETTE

1 tsp Dijon-style mustard
1 Tb balsamic vinegar
2 Tb red wine vinegar
½ cup virgin olive oil
Salt and freshly ground pepper

2 lb skinned haddock fillets
Salt and freshly ground pepper
2 Tb softened butter
2 Tb minced shallots
2 Tb chopped fresh parsley
1 Tb chopped fresh thyme

"Dry"-Poached Haddock with Warm Vinaigrette (continued)

To make the vinaigrette: In a small bowl, combine the mustard and the two vinegars, and whisk all together. Gradually whisk in the oil in a thin stream. Season the vinaigrette with salt and freshly ground pepper, pour it into a small saucepan, and set aside.

Remove any bones from the fish, cut the fillets into 4 equal serving portions, and sprinkle them with salt and freshly ground pepper. Coat the flat surface of a wide, nonstick sauté pan with 1 tablespoon of the butter. Cut a piece of waxed paper or aluminum foil to the size of the sauté pan, and coat one side of the paper or foil with the remaining tablespoon of butter. Place the fish in the pan in one layer and place the paper or foil over it, buttered side down. Cover the pan and set it over medium heat. Cook for 8 minutes. If the fish is very thick, remove the pan from the heat and allow it to "repose," still covered, for another 6 minutes.

Remove the fish to a warm serving platter. Heat the vinaigrette, mix in the shallots, parsley, and thyme, and pour the sauce over the fish.   SERVES 4

❖Balsamic vinegar gives the vinaigrette a distinctive, sweet oaky taste. You can make the vinaigrette without it or substitute a bit of sweet sherry wine.

❖Make the vinaigrette with lemon juice instead of vinegar and add chopped mint along with the parsley and thyme.

❖Experiment with other fresh herbs.

❖For a sharper taste, reduce the amount of oil in the vinaigrette to 6 tablespoons.

❖ *"Dry"-Poached Fish with Warm Mignonette Sauce:* For a piquant variation that does not use oil, pour warm *Mignonette Sauce* (page 14) over the dry-poached haddock or other lean white fish. Try using balsamic vinegar in the Mignonette Sauce.

Poached Cod with a
Warm Aïoli (Garlic) Sauce

Poached white fish is always delicious dressed only with a squeeze of fresh lemon, but it also accepts an infinite variety of sauces. If you like garlic as I do, and plenty of it, try this dish. The sauce, by the way, is great on many kinds of fish. If you are concerned about making this traditional sauce from scratch using raw eggs, use pasteurized eggs in liquid form, such as Simply Eggs, or substitute *Aïoli* (page 349), made with store-bought mayonnaise, and heat it gently. I like to serve plain braised, boiled, or steamed vegetables with this dish so that the vegetables can be dunked in the delicious aïoli. Try braised leeks, as in *Leeks Vinaigrette with a Mediterranean Topping* (page 34), along with colorful boiled carrots.

Alternative fish: striped bass, haddock, halibut, salmon, snapper, turbot

WARM AÏOLI SAUCE

2 Tb minced garlic
Salt and freshly ground pepper
⅔ cup light olive oil
⅔ cup vegetable oil
2 egg yolks
1 tsp Dijon-style mustard
1–2 Tb fresh lemon juice or red
    wine vinegar
Hot pepper sauce (optional)

To make the Warm Aïoli Sauce: Mash the garlic and ¼ teaspoon salt together with the back of a knife to make a purée. In a separate bowl, combine the two oils and set aside.

In a mixing bowl that will fit into a 4-quart saucepan, beat the egg yolks until they are pale-colored and whisk in the puréed garlic, mustard, and 1 tablespoon of the lemon juice or vinegar.

Bring 2 inches of water to a boil in a 4-quart saucepan. Remove the saucepan from the heat and place the mixing bowl with the egg mixture in the hot water. Whisk in the oil, beginning very slowly with a few drops and gradually increasing in a small but steady stream until the mixture has thickened to a thick mayonnaiselike consistency. Season with salt and freshly ground pepper and with hot pepper sauce, if you like, and with more lemon juice or vinegar, if needed. Keep warm in a double boiler or in a pan over water that is the same temperature as the sauce. Water that is too hot may cause the sauce to separate.   MAKES 1⅓ CUPS

1½–2 lb thick cod fillets
½ lemon

Prepare aïoli sauce and keep warm.

To cook the fish: Cut the fillets into 4 serving portions, removing any bones in the fish. Put 3 inches of water into a wide, high-sided saucepan, bring the water to a boil, squeeze the juice of the lemon half into the water, reduce the heat, add the fish, and cook, uncovered, with the water just "shivering" below a simmer for 6–8 minutes, depending on the thickness of the fish. Remove the fish to folded paper towels, pat off any moisture, place the fish pieces on 4 warm serving plates, spoon aïoli over each serving, and serve.   SERVES 4

❖ To your taste, add or subtract the amount of garlic.
❖ For a lighter version of the aïoli sauce, beat 2 egg whites and fold them into the warm sauce.
❖ For a slightly thicker aïoli sauce, add ¼ cup fresh bread crumbs with the egg yolks and mash the crumbs into the mixture.
❖ In place of *Warm Aïoli Sauce,* make chilled *Aïoli* (page 349), and serve as a side dish instead of spooning it over the warm fish. Cold aïoli can be made well ahead.

❖ Poach and serve fish steaks instead of fillets. For a nice touch, poach the fish steaks, gently pull off the outer skin, lift out the center bone, and arrange the steak on the plate with warm aïoli between the fillet sides.
❖ Serve with other warm sauces, such as *Egg Sauce* (page 354) or *Fresh Tomato Sauce* (page 364).
❖ *Cold Poached Cod:* Poach the fish as above or in *Court Bouillon* (page 219) and serve cold. Cook the fish fillets for 6 minutes, then remove the pan from the heat and let the fish cool in the cooking liquid for 20–30 minutes. Fish poached in a court bouillon will pick up flavors from the liquid. Drain the fish, pat dry, cover, and refrigerate. Serve with *Aïoli* (page 349) or *Cucumber-Dill Sauce* (page 354).
❖ *Whole Poached Cod:* We were on Martha's Vineyard one time, at Poole's Market in Menemsha, when a cod boat pulled in. Our host, Peter McGhee, snagged an 8-pound cod and headed for the kitchen. That night we dined on some of the most succulent poached fish I've ever had, served with boiled new potatoes and *White Butter Sauce* (page 114). Poach a whole cod according to the instructions for *Whole Poached Salmon* (page 219); decorate the dish with cherry tomatoes warmed in a bit of butter.

Grilled Fillet of
Haddock with Herbs

The many different fish making up the cod family are often ignored in grilled fish menus because their delicate flesh tends to fall apart over the intense heat. This "sandwich" of haddock, however, cooks like a charm directly on the grill rack. The secrets of success here are to use very fresh—and therefore very firm—fish and to use a well-oiled grill rack to prevent sticking. If you are nervous about the sticking, use a hinged grill basket. It is best to cover the fish partially with a grill cover or a tent of aluminum foil for part of the cooking. I serve this with fresh tomato slices and potato salad, and with *Cucumber-Dill Sauce* (page 354) or *Tomato-Citrus Fondue* (page 364) on the side.

Alternative fish: scrod cod (young cod)

1½–2-lb haddock fillet, with skin on
⅓ cup olive oil
Juice of 2 lemons
1 bay leaf, broken into pieces
1 crushed clove garlic
2 Tb chopped parsley
1 Tb chopped fresh thyme
1 tsp chopped fresh sage
1 tsp chopped fresh rosemary
Salt and freshly ground pepper
Lemon wedges

Remove any bones from the fish, including the small pin bones that run along the side of the fillet. Cut the fillet in half crosswise into a thinner tail section and a thicker front section.

In a small bowl, combine the oil, lemon juice, bay leaf, and garlic. Combine the parsley, thyme, sage, and rosemary to make an herbal seasoning; add half the seasoning to the flavored oil and reserve the other half. Season the oil mixture with salt and freshly ground pepper.

Place the fish in a glass or stainless bowl or pan, pour the flavored oil mixture over it as a marinade, and let the fish sit for 15–20 minutes, turning it occasionally in the marinade.

Remove the thinner tail half of the fillet to a flat plate or work surface, skin side down. Sprinkle the remaining herb seasoning mixture over it, and drizzle a little of the marinade over the top. Remove the thicker half of the fillet from the dish, reserving the marinade, and place it, skin side up, on top of the thinner piece to make a sandwich; try to position the two pieces of fish so that you have a sandwich of uniform thickness. If the fish is fresh and firm, it will stay together during the grilling, but you may insert some toothpicks by way of precaution.

Place the fish on a well-oiled rack over preheated coals. Pour a bit of the reserved marinade over it. Cook for 1 minute to get grill marks on the fish. With two large spatulas, carefully turn the fish 45 degrees on the grill to make a crosshatch pattern on the skin of the fish. After the fish has been on the grill for 4 minutes, partially cover it and cook for 4 minutes more. Turn the fillets over carefully and baste again with a little of the marinade. Repeat the crosshatching procedure, if you like. Cook, partially covered, for 6–8 minutes, depending on the heat of the coals. Lift the fillets apart slightly to check the interior flesh; it should be just barely opaque when you remove the fish from the grill. Remove the fish to a serving platter, garnish with lemon wedges, and serve with a sauce on the side, if desired.   SERVES 4

Creamy Cod and Leeks

Even the tougher members of the cod family prosper in this recipe because the fish gently braises with the leeks and benefits from the moisture of the vegetable.

Alternative fish: cusk, pollock, haddock, other firm-fleshed white fish

2 Tb butter
5–6 cups chopped leeks (white and light green
    portions)
1 cup thinly sliced celery
Salt and freshly ground pepper
½ cup heavy cream
2-lb skinned cod fillets

In a wide saucepan, melt the butter, add the leeks and celery, and stir until well coated with the butter. Add ½ cup water, cover, and cook gently over medium-low heat for 8 minutes, or until the vegetables are wilted, stirring occasionally. Uncover, season the mixture with salt and freshly ground pepper, stir in the cream, and cook for 3–4 minutes to reduce the cream slightly.

Remove any bones from the fish and cut it into 4 equal portions. Season the fish with salt and freshly ground pepper, arrange it on top of the braised leeks, cover the pan, and cook over low heat until the fish is springy to the touch, about 8 minutes.   SERVES 4

❖To avoid animal fats, braise the leeks in virgin olive oil and substitute 1 cup of your favorite fresh tomato sauce for the cream.

❖Braise ½ cup thinly sliced carrots with the leeks and celery.

❖Braise 1 cup thinly sliced red peppers with the leeks and celery.

❖ *Creamy Cod and Leek Stew:* This version uses extra broth. Boil 2 cups dry white wine or fish stock until it reduces to 1 cup. Add 1 cup heavy cream and simmer the liquid mixture for 2 minutes. Stir this sauce into the braised leeks before adding the fish. Cut the fish into chunks and carefully stir the fish into the leek mixture. Cover and cook until the fish is springy to the touch, about 6–8 minutes. Add other kinds of fish or shellfish, if desired.

❖ *Baked Creamy Cod, Leeks, and Potatoes:* Peel and slice 1½ pounds of potatoes and boil them until just tender. Drain and place the potatoes in a buttered baking dish. Spoon the braised leeks over the potatoes. Place the fish pieces on top of the leeks, brush the fish with melted butter or with vegetable oil, and season with salt and freshly ground pepper. Sprinkle buttered browned bread crumbs over all, if desired. Bake, uncovered, in a preheated 400-degree oven for 12–15 minutes, or until the fish just turns opaque.

❖All versions of this dish can be baked in a 400-degree oven rather than cooked on the stovetop.

Broiled Whiting Fillets

This recipe may be the winner in the "How to Cook the World's Fastest Dinner" Sweepstakes. Small (4-ounce) fillets cook in a minute or less under a hot broiler, and they are as delicious as they are quick. I top the fillets with a hot lemon butter, but you could omit the butter and lemon juice in this recipe, and brush the fish with oil or just a tiny bit of melted butter. *Braised Peas and Scallions* (page 332) and *Roast*

Sliced Potatoes (page 336) make a complete meal.

Alternative fish: any small, thin fish fillets, such as porgy, black sea bass, hybrid farmed striped bass, salmon trout

    2 lb skinned small (4-oz) whiting fillets
    ½ cup melted butter
    2 Tb fresh lemon juice
    3 Tb finely chopped fresh parsley
    Lemon wedges
    Salt and freshly ground pepper

Remove any bones from the fish. Preheat the broiler to very hot. In a small saucepan, combine the butter and the lemon juice. Place the fillets on a buttered baking sheet and brush the tops of the fish with some of the lemon butter. Slide the baking sheet directly under the broiler and cook for 45 seconds to 1 minute, or until the fish is just opaque throughout. Lift the fillets off the sheet gently with a wide spatula and arrange them on warm serving plates. Heat the remaining lemon butter to sizzling, sprinkle the fish with the parsley, and pour over the hot butter. Serve with lemon wedges and salt and pepper.   SERVES 4

❖Add drained capers to the sizzling butter.

❖Omit the lemon-butter garnish; substitute a sauce, such as *Sorrel Sauce* (page 229) or *Moroccan Spice Tomato Sauce* (page 208), putting a small pool of sauce on each serving plate and placing the cooked fish on top of the sauce.

Baked Cod Fillets

I find that greens and fish are very good together and very simple to prepare. While the cod bakes, I quickly sauté *Wilted Spinach with Garlic and Lemon* (page 339), which I will use as a bed on which to serve the fish.

Alternative fish: haddock, pollock, grouper, cusk, ocean perch, almost any thick, firm-fleshed fish fillets

    1½–2 lb cod fillets
    ⅓ cup melted butter
    2 Tb fresh lemon juice
    Salt and freshly ground pepper
    Lemon wedges

Baked Cod Fillets (continued)

Remove any skin and bones from the fish, and cut the fillets into 4 equal portions. Combine the butter and 1 tablespoon of the lemon juice, brush the mixture on both sides of the fish pieces, and season the fish with salt and freshly ground pepper. Pour the remaining butter into a baking dish large enough to hold the fish in one layer, place the fish in the baking dish, and bake in a preheated 400-degree oven for 8–12 minutes, depending on the thickness of the fish, or until the fish is just opaque throughout. Serve with a garnish of lemon wedges.   SERVES 4

❖To omit butter from the recipe, brush the fish with light olive oil and film the bottom of the baking dish with dry white wine or water.

❖Add chopped fresh herbs to the butter.

❖Turn the butter-brushed fish in 1½ cups fresh bread crumbs or sprinkle with *Blackened Seasoning Mixture* (page 141) and bake as above, turning the fish over midway through the baking.

Gladys Porter's
Whale Rock Point Baked Cod

At the family compound on Narragansett Bay in Rhode Island, Pebble Gifford says that her mother has cooked cod—and every other fish, even swordfish—this way for forty years. The original recipe calls for steeping the fish in milk to make it tender, but you can omit this step; the milk bath that the fish cooks in keeps it nicely moist. "Sometimes the milk curdles," Pebble adds. "That's how I remember the dish; it's perfectly all right that way." Gladys Porter always serves this dish with fresh corn and rice to sop up the juices.

Alternative fish: all members of the cod family or salmon, snapper, halibut, thick flounder, or almost any white fish

2 lb skinless cod or haddock fillets
4 cups (approximately) milk, at room
   temperature
Salt and freshly ground pepper
1 cup grated Cheddar cheese
2 Tb butter

Remove any bones from the fish. Arrange the fillets in one layer in a baking dish and add enough milk to come at least three-quarters of the way up the sides of the fish. Allow the fish to steep in the milk for 30 minutes, if you like. Sprinkle the fish with salt and freshly ground pepper and the grated cheese. Dot with butter and bake in a preheated 375-degree oven for 15 minutes, or until the fish is opaque at the center. Run the dish under a preheated broiler just long enough to brown the cheese topping lightly, and serve.   SERVES 4

Olga Hamwey's Tartoor—Baked
Haddock and Sesame Sauce

This recipe came from a local Oriental rug dealer, who said my book would not be complete without this recipe from his wife. The flavor of the sesame sauce enrobing the fish is a delightful change of pace. Mrs. Hamwey served it at room temperature, which makes it perfect for a buffet spread. The recipe is for two persons but is easy to increase. I like to add other Middle Eastern dishes as accompaniments, such as *Tabbouleh* (page 28) or a big *Greek Salad* (page 85).

Alternative fish: cod, snapper, striped bass, salmon, bluefish

¾–1-lb haddock fillet
2 Tb light olive oil or vegetable oil
½ Tb butter
2 Tb pine nuts
½ cup sesame paste (tahini)★
Juice of 1 lemon, more as desired
1 small clove garlic puréed with ¼ tsp salt
2 Tb water
Paprika
Chopped parsley

★Tahini is available in jars in most supermarkets and in Middle Eastern food markets.

Remove any skin and bones from the haddock and pat dry. Rub the fish with oil, place it in a baking dish that can come to the table, and drizzle any remaining oil over the fish.

Place the fish in a preheated 350-degree oven and bake for 20 minutes, or until the fish is just cooked through; cooking time will vary with the thickness of the fillet. Remove the fish from the oven and let it cool.

In a small frying pan, heat the butter and sauté the pine nuts until lightly browned, and set aside.

In a bowl, combine the sesame paste, lemon juice, and garlic purée. The mixture will turn white and should have a tangy taste. Adjust the amount of lemon to your taste. Add the water until the consistency is a thin sauce. Once the fish has cooled, pour the sesame sauce over the fish and sprinkle the fish with paprika, parsley, and the sautéed pine nuts. Serve at room temperature with Syrian bread. SERVES 2

Lettuce-Wrapped Fillets of Haddock

In the comparatively innocent 1970s and early 1980s our patrons at the Straight Wharf Restaurant would often book reservations deliberately on the nights when we were serving either Striped Bass in Brioche or *Coulibiac* (page 243), a rich assembly of salmon, crêpes, rice, and egg sauce. Both dishes were enrobed in buttery brioche dough to keep the fish succulent in the dry oven, and both dishes were served with plenty of delicious white butter sauce. Those plates were certainly clean when they came back to the kitchen. Of course, now we realize that, for health reasons, a little butter can go a long way, and for the most part, we should avoid the most butter-rich dishes. There are delicious alternatives; this lettuce-wrapped fish will keep taste buds happy and consciences clear. Serve this with the juices from the pan, or thicken the juices with just a tiny bit of cream and butter, or serve the haddock with one of the several tomato sauces in this book.

Alternative fish: any firm-fleshed white fish fillets weighing about a pound

Two 1-lb haddock fillets
10 large outer leaves iceberg lettuce
½ lb escarole
2 Tb olive oil
1 tsp minced garlic

½ cup fresh bread crumbs
Juice of ½ lemon
Salt and freshly ground pepper
2 Tb chopped shallots
½–¾ cup dry vermouth or white wine
1 Tb butter plus 3 optional Tb
Lemon wedges
¾ cup heavy cream (optional)

Remove any bones from the fish; remove the skin, if desired. Cover and refrigerate.

Bring a pot of water to a boil, drop the iceberg lettuce leaves in, blanch for 1 minute, drain, and run under cold water to stop the cooking action; drain, lay out on a towel, and pat dry. Wash, spin-dry, and finely chop the escarole. In a wide sauté pan, heat the olive oil, stir in the garlic, add the escarole, and turn it to coat with the oil; cook gently until the escarole is wilted and tender, about 6–7 minutes. Turn up the heat for a moment to evaporate any extra moisture in the pan. Stir in the bread crumbs, add the lemon juice, and season with salt and freshly ground pepper. Remove from the heat and let cool.

Sprinkle the shallots in the bottom of a buttered long, ovenproof dish. Spread the lettuce leaves over the shallots in two rows, side by side, down the length of the dish and slightly overlapping where the rows meet. Place one of the fish fillets lengthwise down the center of the dish, skinned side down. Season it with salt and pepper. Spread the escarole mixture on top of the fish fillet, then top with the second fillet, skinned side up, matching a thinner end of one fillet to the thicker end of the other so that the resulting sandwich is of uniform thickness. Season the second fillet with salt and pepper. Fold the lettuce leaves up and over the fish to encase it, and tuck in the ends. The fish should be entirely covered with lettuce. Pour in enough vermouth to cover the bottom of the dish, and dot the lettuce-wrapped fish with 1 tablespoon of the butter. Cover the fish with parchment or waxed paper, then cover the dish with a lid or with aluminum foil and bake for 20–25 minutes in a preheated 400-degree oven, or until the fish smells good and the flesh is opaque. Cooking time will depend on the thickness of the fillets; test for doneness by inserting a sharp paring knife into the thickest part of the fish.

Remove the fish from the oven to a warm serving platter, pour the cooking juices into a small saucepan, and boil to reduce by half; then spoon the juices over the fish and serve with lemon wedges. If desired, add

Lettuce-Wrapped Fillets of Haddock (continued)

heavy cream to the cooking juices and boil until reduced to a syrup consistency. Then remove the pan from the heat, beat in the 3 optional tablespoons butter, and spoon this sauce over the fish.   SERVES 6

❖Use any lettuce with a broad outer leaf, or use savoy cabbage; trim any thick stems and blanch as above.

❖Vary the stuffing: use sautéed spinach, *Braised Cabbage and Collard Greens* (page 323), braised leeks, or mushroom duxelles.

Fish Timbales with Curried Cabbage and Tomato Sauce

Depending on the size and number of baking dishes you use, this recipe will make a delicious dinner for six or a lovely first course for eight. The tomato sauce and curried cabbage add color and texture to the soft delicacy of the cod mousse. A food processor is an essential here. You can prepare the tomato sauce well ahead. You can prepare the fish mousse, fill the molds, and refrigerate for up to six hours before baking. This dish relies on plenty of heavy cream for its light quality, so it is not a dish for dieters.

Alternative fish: gray sole, petrale sole, hake, halibut

TOMATO SAUCE

2 Tb light olive oil
1 cup finely chopped onions
4 cups peeled, seeded, and chopped ripe
    tomatoes★
1 Tb tomato paste
½ tsp thyme
½ tsp curry powder
Salt and freshly ground pepper

COD MOUSSE

1½ lb cod fillets
1 egg plus 1 egg white
2 Tb fresh lemon juice
Salt and freshly ground pepper

Pinch of cayenne pepper
Pinch of grated nutmeg
½ tsp curry powder (optional)
1½–2 cups *chilled* heavy cream

CURRIED CABBAGE

3 Tb butter
1–2 tsp curry powder
8 cups thinly sliced cabbage
Salt and freshly ground pepper

To prepare the Curried Cabbage: Melt the butter in a wide sauté pan. Stir in the curry powder to your desired taste. Add the sliced cabbage and mix thoroughly. Cover and cook gently for 5 minutes, or until just tender, stirring occasionally. Season with salt and pepper.

MAKES 4–5 CUPS

★If you do not have fully ripe tomatoes, use half fresh tomatoes and half canned tomatoes.

To make the tomato sauce: In a 4-quart saucepan, heat the oil. Add the onions and cook until wilted, about 4–5 minutes. Add the tomatoes, tomato paste, thyme, curry powder, and ¼ teaspoon salt, and bring the mixture to a boil. If you are using fresh tomatoes, cover the pan and cook gently for 5 minutes to release the juices of the tomatoes, then uncover the pan and boil gently, stirring occasionally, about 15 minutes, or until the sauce has reduced and thickened. Season with salt and freshly ground pepper, and set aside to reheat later. (Makes 2½–3 cups)

To prepare the cod mousse: Remove any skin and bones from the fish and cut it into small chunks. Put the fish into the bowl of a food processor and blend (in two batches if you have a small machine) until the fish is puréed. Add the egg and egg white, lemon juice, ½ teaspoon salt, a few grindings of pepper, the cayenne pepper, nutmeg, and curry powder, if desired, and process to blend. With the motor running, gradually add 1½ cups cream and process until the mixture is smooth. Add the remaining cream if the mixture seems dense. (Makes 4–5 cups mousse)

For a main course, butter six 10-ounce Pyrex molds; for an appetizer course, butter eight 6-ounce molds. Divide the mixture into the molds, smooth the tops with a rubber spatula, and cover each mold with a round of buttered waxed paper or aluminum foil.

Place the filled molds in a large baking pan with 2-inch-high sides and pour in boiling water to come halfway up the sides of the molds. Cook in a pre-heated 375-degree oven for 25–30 minutes for the large molds, 20–25 minutes for the small. The tim-bales are done when the mousse shrinks slightly from the sides and a knife inserted in the center comes out clean and the mousse feels springy to the touch, or when the temperature reaches 140 degrees on an instant thermometer.

While the mousse is cooking, prepare the curried cabbage and keep it warm.

When you are ready to serve, reheat the tomato sauce and remove the fish molds from the oven. Before unmolding the mousse to serving plates, it is necessary to drain off any excess liquid in the molds. Remove the waxed paper or aluminum foil from the top of the molds. Holding a small plate over most of the mold to keep the mousse in place, tip the mold over a bowl to catch the excess liquid that drains from the open crack between the plate and the mold. Tip the mold upright again and remove the plate.

Arrange a portion of curried cabbage on each serving plate. Turn the individual molds out onto each bed of curried cabbage. Spoon a dollop of tomato sauce over the mousse and serve.

SERVES 6 FOR A MAIN COURSE, 8 FOR AN APPETIZER COURSE

❖Omit the cabbage. A sauté of spinach, Swiss chard, or sharp green broccoli de rabe makes a color-ful and tasty bed for these timbales.

❖Spoon the fish mousse into a buttered 6-cup ring mold, or 6-cup loaf pan, and bake as above. Increase the cooking time to 50–60 minutes, or until a knife inserted into the center of the mold comes out clean. Line the molds with thin slices of smoked fish, if you wish. Serve hot, or serve cold, sliced, as part of a salad plate.

❖Combine the cod with some flounder, scallops, or shrimp. Or put a surprise shrimp in the center of the mousse.

❖Use fresh herbs instead of a curry butter for the cabbage. Cook the cabbage in plain butter or broth. Add chopped fresh dill or a combination of herbs to the mousse and to the tomato sauce.

Salt Cod Fish Balls or Cakes

From childhood summers in Nova Scotia, my mother-in-law came to have a high regard for codfish balls and has never stopped recommending them. Ordinarily I have no trouble passing up salt cod in favor of fresh cod, but I have to admit these are pretty darn good. Their versatility is also to be recom-mended. You could serve this dish for a simple sup-per, a hearty breakfast, a buffet dish, a cocktail appetizer, or even as the first course for a dinner party. When I serve them for supper, I add big bowls of *Stir-Fried Broccoli with Garlic* (page 322).

1 lb salt cod
1 lb potatoes
2 eggs, beaten
1 Tb grated onions
Salt and freshly ground pepper
Vegetable or peanut oil

Soak and poach the salt cod as in *To Prepare Salt Cod* (page 139).

Boil the potatoes just until tender, drain them and peel them, put them through a ricer if you have one, or mash-whip them. (You should have about 2 cups fluffy mashed potatoes.)

Drain the cod, pat it dry, and flake the flesh into a bowl. Stir the potatoes into the cod with a fork. Add the eggs and onion, season the mixture with salt and freshly ground pepper, and mix well. Cover and chill the mixture for at least 30 minutes.

In a high-sided saucepan, heat 2 inches of oil to 375 degrees, using a deep-fat-frying thermometer. Form the codfish mixture into 1½-inch-round balls. Drop a few at a time into the hot oil, fry for 2–3 min-utes, turning them in the oil so that they brown on all sides, lift them with a slotted spoon, and place them on brown paper to drain off any excess oil. Keep each batch warm in a preheated 200–250-degree oven while you fry the remainder. Serve with *Tartar Sauce* (page 363) or *Tomato-Citrus Fondue* (page 364) or a traditional *Egg Sauce* (page 354).

SERVES 8–10; MAKES ABOUT 24–30
CODFISH BALLS—ALLOW 3 PER SERVING

Salt Cod Fish Balls or Cakes (continued)

❖These are tasty cocktail snacks. Shape into ¾-inch balls, fry for 2 minutes, and serve with *Tartar Sauce,* as above, or *Cucumber-Dill Sauce* (page 354).

❖Add horseradish sauce, to taste, to the codfish mixture.

❖Add 2–3 tablespoons grated cheese to the codfish mixture.

❖*Codfish Cakes:* Form the fish mixture into flat cakes 3 inches × ¾ inch. Heat 3 tablespoons butter and 3 tablespoons oil in a frying pan, and cook the cakes on each side until they are lightly browned, adding more butter and oil as needed.

❖Fold in 1 cup finely chopped cooked vegetables such as carrots or beets, or cooked greens such as kale or spinach.

❖*Codfish Pancake Appetizers:* Replace the grated onions with ¼ cup finely chopped scallions in the codfish mixture. Form very small, pancake-like codfish cakes. Sauté them in butter and oil until golden on both sides, drain on brown paper, and keep them warm in a 200-degree oven until cooking is completed. Serve as a first course with *Tomato-Citrus Fondue* (page 364) or top with sour cream and caviar.

❖Use poached fresh cod in place of the salted cod.

Smoked Haddock or Smoked Cod Fritters with Peppers and Herbs

Jamaicans serve an irresistibly named dish called "Stamp and Go." It consists of salt cod fritters fried in deep fat, and it is part of the Caribbean cuisine influenced by the salt cod trade of years ago. Stamp and Go inspired me to do this dish using smoked haddock or smoked cod and peppers, which I serve with a fresh salsa to remind me of the region where the fritters originated. I sauté the fritters in a film of oil rather than deep-frying them, and I think they are wonderful for brunch or supper. They go well with *Sautéed Corn* (page 325) or *Succotash* (page 341) or for more of a Caribbean flavor, *Grilled Parsnips and Bananas* (page 330). You can prepare the fritter mixture ahead up to the point where the egg whites are folded in.

Alternative fish: smoked pollock or other smoked fish, soaked and poached salt cod

½ lb smoked haddock or cod
¾ cup flour
2 tsp baking powder
Salt and freshly ground pepper
2 eggs, separated
½ cup finely chopped red peppers
½ cup finely chopped onions or scallions
2 tsp finely chopped hot peppers
1 Tb chopped parsley
1 Tb chopped cilantro
Hot pepper sauce (optional)
Peanut oil
Lemon wedges
Salsa (page 7)

Place the smoked haddock or cod in a saucepan, cover with water, bring the water to a simmer, cover the pan and remove it from the heat, and let the fish steep for 10 minutes. Taste the liquid in the pan after 5 minutes. If it still tastes very smoky or salty, drain off the liquid, cover the fish with fresh water, and repeat the simmer-and-steep procedure once more. Drain the fish after the steeping, let it cool to the touch, and flake it into small pieces.

In a bowl, combine the flour, baking powder, and ¼ teaspoon salt. Whisk in ½ cup water, then whisk in the 2 egg yolks until the mixture is fairly smooth. Add the fish, red peppers, onions or scallions, hot peppers, parsley, and cilantro to the bowl, and fold all the ingredients together. Season with salt and freshly ground pepper, and with a few drops of hot pepper sauce, if desired. Beat the egg whites until they are just firm. Stir one-quarter of the beaten egg whites into the fish mixture to lighten it slightly, then fold in the remaining whites.

Film the bottom of a sauté pan with peanut oil, heat the pan, and when the oil is hot, begin gently dropping heaping tablespoons of the fish mixture into the pan, cooking the fritters in batches. Heaping tablespoons should form about 3-inch pancake-like fritters. Cook each fritter until the bottom is golden and bubbles are appearing on top of the batter, then turn and sauté the second side to golden brown, about 2–3 minutes on each side. Regulate the heat and add more oil as necessary so that the fritters cook through without burning and do not stick to the pan.

Place the cooked fritters on a brown-paper-lined baking sheet to absorb excess oil, and keep them warm in a 200-degree oven while the remainder of the fritters are cooked. Serve immediately with lemon wedges and the fresh salsa.

MAKES 20–24 FRITTERS

❖For a Sunday breakfast, top the fritters with poached eggs.

❖Though the fritters are best served immediately, you can reheat them in a 350-degree oven.

❖Make the fritters smaller and serve as cocktail appetizers.

❖Add some finely chopped smoked ham or sausage.

❖Use clarified butter instead of oil.

❖Deep-fry the fritters in 2–3 inches of 350-degree peanut oil, carefully dropping the fritter mixture by heaping tablespoons into the oil, frying them for about 5 minutes or until golden brown, removing and draining as above. Fritters cooked this way will be round.

Naomi's Finnan Haddie

My mother-in-law considers finnan haddie the ultimate food treat. She always serves it with mashed potatoes and cooked carrots. Sometimes she makes the dish with smoked cod; since it has a stronger flavor than finnan haddie, she tastes the water after the first steeping and repeats the process with fresh water if the steeping water tastes too strong or salty.

1½-lb side of finnan haddie or 1 lb smoked cod
2 cups light cream
2 Tb butter
Freshly ground pepper
Toast or mashed potatoes (optional)
Paprika (optional)
Chopped parsley (optional)

Place the finnan haddie in a frying pan, add enough water to cover it, and bring the water to a simmer. Cover the pan, remove it from the heat, and let it stand for 10 minutes to steep in the hot water. If you use smoked cod, taste the water after 5 minutes of steeping; if it tastes strong or too salty, drain off the water, cover the fish again with fresh water, bring to a simmer, and let it stand to steep a second time.

While the fish steeps, heat the cream gently in a saucepan. Drain the fish, remove the flesh from skin and bones, flake it into chunks, and add it to the warm cream. Dot the top with butter and grind pepper generously over the top. Heat gently and serve on toast or mashed potatoes, if desired. Top each serving with a sprinkling of paprika and chopped parsley, if you like.

SERVES 4

❖You can bake this dish in the oven, if you prefer. After you have steeped and drained the fish, removed the skin and bones, and flaked the flesh, place the chunks of fish in a baking dish, pour the warm cream over it, dot with butter, and season with freshly ground pepper; then cover and bake in a preheated 375-degree oven for 20 minutes.

❖Cook 1 cup sliced onions in 1 tablespoon butter until the onions are wilted and lightly colored. Add to the warm cream and proceed as above.

❖If you like a little thicker sauce, reduce the cream slightly by boiling. Add a crushed garlic clove to the cream for flavor while it reduces.

Baked Finnan Haddie

Naomi's Finnan Haddie, which precedes this recipe, is essentially fish served in cream; here is a more robust version, with the finnan haddie baked in an egg-laced cream sauce. This dish can be prepared way ahead, refrigerated, and baked just before serving. Serve it with mashed potatoes and a green salad or *Seared Red Pepper Salad* (page 88) for a Sunday night supper, or spoon this comforting dish over toasted English muffins for a buffet breakfast.

    1½-lb side of finnan haddie
    6 Tb butter
    1 cup fresh bread crumbs
    4 Tb flour
    2 cups warmed milk
    Salt and freshly ground pepper
    Fresh lemon juice
    3 quartered hard-boiled eggs
    ½ cup grated Swiss cheese (optional)

Lay the finnan haddie in sections in a sauté pan large enough to hold the fish in one layer. Cover the fish with water, bring to a simmer, cover, and remove from the heat. Let it steep for 10 minutes. Drain the fish, remove any skin and bones, break the flesh into large pieces, and set aside.

Wipe out the sauté pan, melt 2 tablespoons of the butter in it, add the bread crumbs, and sauté, stirring, until the crumbs have separated and are golden. Set aside.

In a 2-quart saucepan, melt the remaining 4 tablespoons of butter, whisk in the flour, and cook, stirring, for 2 minutes. Remove from the heat, pour in the milk, and whisk until the mixture is smooth. Return the pan to the heat, bring to a boil, and boil gently, stirring, for 4–5 minutes. Season with salt, freshly ground pepper, and lemon juice. Fold in the hard-boiled eggs and the finnan haddie.

Butter a shallow, 2-quart baking dish and spoon the finnan haddie mixture into it. Sprinkle the bread crumbs over the top and the grated cheese, if you are using it. (Refrigerate the dish at this point, if you wish, and bake at a later time, allowing a little more baking time if the dish is cold.) Bake in a preheated 400-degree oven until the fish mixture is bubbly and the top is lightly browned, about 20 minutes.   SERVES 4–6

❖Sauté ½ pound sliced or quartered fresh mushrooms in butter and fold them into the fish mixture before adding the topping and baking.

❖Add sautéed onion slices or sautéed fennel or leeks to the fish mixture.

Finnan Haddie with Chilies and Cheese

You might think of this casserole as a crustless quiche. Served hot, it makes a fine supper or brunch dish; cold, it makes small appetizer squares for home or to take on a picnic.

    ¾ lb boned and skinned finnan haddie
    8 skinned whole mild chili peppers (three 4-oz
        cans)
    2 cups grated Muenster cheese
    2 cups grated Cheddar cheese
    4 eggs
    1 cup buttermilk or milk
    ⅓ cup flour
    Hot pepper sauce

Break the finnan haddie into small flakes and set aside. Split the chili peppers in half, remove any seeds, and drain. In a bowl, combine the two cheeses. In another bowl, beat the eggs, then beat the buttermilk or milk and flour into the eggs until the mixture is smooth; season the mixture with a few drops of hot pepper sauce.

Butter an 8 × 8-inch baking dish or a high-sided round baking dish. Place 4 chili peppers opened flat in the bottom of the dish. Spread half the finnan haddie over the peppers. Spread half the grated cheese over the fish. Repeat the same layering with the remaining ingredients in the same order, finishing with the cheese. Pour the egg mixture over all and bake in a preheated 350-degree oven for 40 minutes, or until a knife inserted in the center comes out clean.

                                            SERVES 6–8

❖Use fresh peppers, if you like. Char the peppers on all sides under the broiler. Drop them into a brown paper bag, close the bag, and allow them to steam for 15 minutes. Remove them, allow to cool slightly, then split them lengthwise; remove the stems, cores, seeds, and white membranes, and peel off the charred skins. Proceed as above.

Salt Cod, Onions, and Potatoes Gratin

There are similar versions of this dish on both sides of the Atlantic, from Canada to Scandinavia to France to Portugal and back again. It is a very widely practiced way to prepare salt cod. The recipe can be completed way ahead up to the point of final baking, refrigerated, and baked just before serving, which makes it a very handy dish for a buffet meal. The gratin uses a traditional cream sauce as the binder, but you can, if you wish, substitute your own favorite tomato sauce. This is a great dish for using up leftover fish. I serve it with a green vegetable, such as *Braised Broccoli de Rabe* (page 323), and colorful carrots.

Alternative fish: poached fresh cod, haddock, pollock, cusk, salmon, or any other poached fish of your choice

1 lb salt cod
1½ lb potatoes
2 Tb vegetable oil
4 cups sliced onions
2 Tb butter
½ cup fresh bread crumbs

CREAM SAUCE

3½ Tb butter
4½ Tb flour
1½ cups milk
1½ cups light cream
Salt and freshly ground pepper
Pinch of nutmeg
Fresh lemon juice

½ cup roughly grated Swiss cheese
½ cup freshly grated Parmesan cheese

Soak and poach the salt cod as in *To Prepare Salt Cod* (page 139).

Boil the potatoes just until tender, drain and peel them, cut them into ⅜-inch-thick slices, and set aside.

In a sauté pan, heat the oil, add the onions, cook them until wilted and lightly colored, 8–10 minutes. Remove the onions to a sieve over a bowl to drain off excess oil and juices.

Wipe out the sauté pan, heat 2 tablespoons butter, add the bread crumbs, and cook, stirring, until they are lightly colored. Remove and set aside.

To make the cream sauce: In a 2-quart sauté pan, melt the 3½ tablespoons butter and whisk in the flour until it blends in with the butter. Cook, stirring, over low heat for 2 minutes. Remove the pan from the heat, pour in the milk and cream, and whisk until the mixture is smooth. Return the pan to the heat and cook over medium heat, stirring, until the mixture thickens. Reduce the heat and cook gently, stirring, for 5 minutes. Season to taste with salt, freshly ground pepper, nutmeg, and lemon juice.

Butter a shallow, 2-quart baking dish. Spoon a thin layer of the sauce on the bottom of the dish. Spread the potatoes in an even layer on the sauce. Add a layer of onions over the potatoes. Flake the cod over the onions, and pour and spread the remainder of the sauce evenly over all. Combine the cheeses and sprinkle them over the sauce, and top with the bread crumbs. (You can refrigerate the dish at this point, if you wish, and bake it later just before serving.) Bake in a preheated 400-degree oven for 20 minutes, or until the dish is bubbly and lightly browned.

SERVES 8

❖Use the white part of leeks in place of onions, or a combination of sautéed onions and celery, or sautéed onions and fennel.
❖Substitute all milk for the combination of cream and milk in the cream sauce.

Sautéed Soft-Shell Crabs

One of my sons-in-law would cancel any other plans if offered a dinner of these delicacies. The soft-shell crabs we get in the market are usually blue crabs. As the crab ages, it periodically sheds its too small hard shell and in its place has a new soft shell that will harden in a few hours unless it is lifted from the salt water to interrupt the hardening. Soft-shell crabs are quickly packaged live, nestled in straw, or frozen, then shipped to market and graded by size (see pages

Sautéed Soft-Shell Crabs (continued)

161–162). I allow 3 mediums or hotels, or 2 primes per person. The crabs should be alive when you buy them. While the fish market can prepare them for you, it is better to clean them just before cooking them because they lose juices after they have been cleaned. See *To "dress" (clean) a soft-shell crab,* page 163. Since you want the crabs to brown and crisp and not get mushy from simmering, do not crowd them in the pan. Ideally you should cook one serving of two or three crabs in a pan at a time, using two pans to enable you to cook two servings at a time. Cook in batches as necessary, but serve the sautéed crabs as quickly as possible after cooking them. I like to use my oblong iron frying pans, but you can use heavy-bottomed, nonstick sauté pans. Fine vegetable accompaniments would be *Dilled Peas and Cucumbers* (page 332) or *Okra and Tomato Stew* (page 330), and *Boiled New Potatoes* (page 334).

6 "medium" soft-shell crabs
6–8 Tb butter
Instant-blending flour (such as Wondra Quick-
    Mixing Flour)
1 Tb fresh lemon juice
Lemon wedges

Prepare the crabs as in *To "dress" (clean) a soft-shell crab,* page 163. To cook 2 servings at a time, heat 2–3 tablespoons of the butter in each of two sauté pans until the butter is lightly browned. Quickly dredge the 6 crabs in a plate or shallow bowl of flour, shaking off any excess, and place 3 crabs in each pan, back side down. Sauté for 3 minutes over medium-high heat to brown and crisp the crabs, turn them, and sauté for 2 minutes longer. Lift the crabs to warm serving plates. Quickly scrape the residue of butter and brown bits out of one pan, and add 2 more tablespoons of the butter to the cleaned pan. Cook the butter until it is brown and sizzling, remove the pan from the heat, swirl in the lemon juice, and pour the browned lemon butter evenly over the sautéed crabs. Garnish with lemon wedges and serve immediately.

SERVES 2

❖*With Garlic:* After the crabs are cooked, wipe out one pan, add 3 tablespoons butter and cook until brown and sizzling. Remove the pan from the heat, add 1 tablespoon lemon juice and 1 tablespoon minced garlic, swirl all together, spoon the garlic butter over the crabs, and serve.

❖*With Capers:* After the crabs are cooked, wipe out one pan, add 3 tablespoons butter, and cook until sizzling. Remove the pan from the heat, swirl in 1 tablespoon lemon juice and 3 tablespoons drained capers. Spoon the caper butter over the crabs and serve.

Judy Miller's Giant Maryland Crab Cakes

There are three secrets to these exceptional crab cakes, which were featured at the Millers' famously exuberant parties. Judy did not believe in heavy binders and lots of seasonings and spices; she believed in crab cakes made of impeccably fresh crabmeat—lots of it—and very little else in the cakes. Second, she put the mixture briefly in the freezer to firm it before shaping and frying the cakes. Third, she prefried the cakes on both sides, set them aside, and finished cooking them in the oven just before serving. The chilling in the freezer is brief and the mixture should not be frozen; the same effect can be obtained by refrigerating the mixture for several hours. I've altered her recipe a bit, cutting down somewhat on the size of the cakes but keeping them fat, replacing her capers with a little red pepper, and adding some cracker crumbs. I promise that your guests will like these cakes, which I serve with *Curried Cabbage* (page 152) or *Braised Cabbage and Collard Greens* (page 323).

2 lb fresh lump crabmeat
2 Tb butter
1 cup finely minced celery
½ cup finely minced red peppers
1 cup saltine cracker crumbs (about 30 crackers)
1 egg, beaten★

⅓–½ cup mayonnaise
3 Tb chopped fresh parsley, dill, or a
    combination of both
Hot pepper sauce
Salt and freshly ground pepper
⅓ cup vegetable oil
Lemon wedges
Tartar Sauce (page 363) or *Salsa* (page 7)
    (optional)

★Judy preferred to use only mayonnaise as a binder. She acknowledged that the egg was helpful but thought its yellow color disguised somewhat the beautiful white color of the crabmeat. Try the recipe both ways and see which you prefer.

Pick over the crabmeat, removing any bits of shell or cartilage, and place it in a large bowl that will fit in your freezer. In a sauté pan, heat the butter, add the celery and peppers, and cook for 4–5 minutes, or until the vegetables are wilted and tender; remove from the heat and let cool slightly. To the crabmeat in the bowl, add the cooled vegetables, ½ cup of the cracker crumbs, the egg, mayonnaise, and parsley or dill, and season the mixture with a few drops of hot pepper sauce and with salt and freshly ground pepper. Fold the ingredients together gently to keep from breaking up the lumps of crabmeat, cover the bowl, and place in the freezer for 20–30 minutes (or refrigerate for an hour or more). (Makes about 6 cups)

Spread the remaining cracker crumbs in a pie pan. Divide the crabmeat mixture with your hands into 6 portions, make 6 round balls, then flatten the balls into fat cakes, about 4 inches wide and 1 inch thick. Handle the mixture as little as possible to keep it light-textured. Turn each cake carefully in the cracker crumbs to coat, place the cakes on a plate or tray, and return them to the freezer for 15–30 minutes (or refrigerate for a few hours) until the cakes are very cold.

In a large, nonstick frying pan, heat the oil, add the cakes, and sauté on each side for 2–3 minutes or until lightly browned, using a wide spatula to turn them carefully and gently. Place the browned cakes on a baking sheet and bake in a preheated 375-degree oven for 8 minutes. Turn the cakes carefully and bake for another 6 minutes, or until they are completely hot. Serve with lemon wedges and, if you wish, pass tartar sauce or salsa.

SERVES 6

continued on page 164

CRAB

A PSYCHIATRIST FRIEND, Bob Mayer, first showed us how to catch blue crabs in the salty ponds of Tisbury on Martha's Vineyard. His foolproof method was to tie a big old fish head on the end of a heavy test line, cast the bait as far as possible into the pond, and slowly pull it back. As the bait came back in sight, we would see from two to ten crabs hanging on, snatching at the bait. Bob would scoop the gullible crabs up with a big net and either dump them into a bucket to take home to a steaming pot, or we would build a fire on a nearby ocean beach and eat freshly caught and cooked crabmeat as the rays of the late-afternoon sun glistened across the waves. One never forgets those tastes and sights.

There are no fewer than eight kinds of crabs available in our markets, and they vary even in the part of the crab we covet for eating: in some, the claw meat is the best; in others, it's the leg meat, and in still others, the body meat.

1. Blue crab. Found along the Atlantic Coast from Cape Cod down into the Gulf of Mexico, blue crabs are the most frequently caught and consumed crabs in the United States. These are the famous crabs of the Chesapeake Bay, honored in William Warner's Pulitzer prizewinning *Beautiful Swimmers*. The live crab has a dark green-brown shell, sometimes with traces of blue, and the shell turns red when cooked. While there is some market for hard-shell blue crabs in the shell (whole or as claws), most

hard-shell blue crab is marketed as crabmeat already removed from the shell. Blue crabs are especially appreciated because they are the crabs we eat whole in their soft-shell stage. Many times, as they grow and mature, blue crabs shed their too small hard shell, and for a few hours the molting crabs have very soft shells; if one of these crabs is removed from salt water when the shell is soft, it will not harden, and it can be shipped to market to be eaten whole with only the "face" (eyes and mouth), the gills, and the apron removed. Soft-shell crabs were incredibly popular at our restaurant and are very simple to prepare.

2. Jonah crab. Most abundant off the shores of New England and the Middle Atlantic States, Jonah crabs have red-purple upper shells and yellow underbellies. They average about a pound in weight, and the main meat is in the claws because they are walking crabs rather than swimmers. Their meat

is very sweet, and the claws are perfect for "cocktail claws," where the shell is scored and easily lifted off to expose the cooked meat. Jonah crabmeat is also processed and sold as packaged crabmeat.

3. Rock crab. A smooth-shell, speckled, smaller relative of the Jonah crab, the rock crab measures 4–5 inches across and weighs 8–10 ounces. It is often referred to as the Maine crab—where it is available year-round—because it likes cold water. This crab frequents shallow waters where the water is cold, and it is sold whole or for its picked meat, which is very sweet and has a reddish color.

4. Red crab or deep-sea red crab. Named for their bright red uncooked shells, red crabs inhabit deep water and are found along the entire eastern seaboard and at least as far south as Cuba. They are sometimes referred to as Cape Cod crabs because of the exten-

CRAB

sive marketing from that area. Weighing from 1½–3 pounds, they are sold whole, cooked, as crab legs or claws or cocktail claws, and as cocktail meat in both fresh and frozen form. Incidentally, another deepwater crab of unusual color is the golden Gulf crab from the Gulf of Mexico with a shell that remains golden when cooked.

5. Stone crab. Found from the Carolinas through the Gulf of Mexico, this crab is often referred to as Florida's crab; even people who haven't been to Florida have heard of Joe's Stone Crab restaurant in Miami Beach, home of the "stone crab with mustard sauce" feast. Only the claw meat of this extremely hard-shell crab is eaten. The claws, cooked and then sold fresh or frozen, have a distinctive coloring of black tips on a cream-colored claw and knuckle tinted with red. They are often served cracked, with the top of the shell removed to expose the delicious meat.

6. Dungeness crab. People from the West Coast hail this crab—named for a Washington fishing village—as the finest-tasting of all, and I have to say that the ones I've had have been sublime. Harvested from Alaska to southern California, Dungeness crabs average about 2½ pounds. They are marketed as cooked whole, in sections, in single legs, as cocktail claws, and as picked crabmeat, both fresh and frozen. This crab's very sweet, tender, moist flesh makes it a premium crab, and its

price is high, reflecting its quality and limited availability.

7. King crab. As is the case with Dungeness crabs, only the males of king crabs are harvested. Of the several known king crabs, the most notable harvested in Alaskan and north Pacific waters are red king crab and blue king crab. They average from 5–10 pounds, and their legs contain the most meat. The largest section of leg meat, located just below the shoulder, is the merus; the most expensive way to buy king crab is to buy just the white merus meat with its covering of red membrane. The most common form of king crab in the market is the single leg or claw—sometimes split for convenience—but one can also buy sections, or "clusters," composed of three legs and a claw with the shoulder attached. The ratio of meat to shell in king crab legs is about 50:50. Although king crab legs are often frozen in the market, they have already been cooked and need only enough further cooking to warm the meat.

8. Snow crab. This rather frightening-looking creature, which can weigh from 1–5 pounds and measure as much as 3 feet from tip to tip, has delicious meat. Snow crab in our markets has usually been harvested and processed in Alaska, and it comes to us most frequently as a section, or cluster, of three legs, a claw, and a shoulder. Individual claws and legs are also marketed. Some of the legs are sold as "snap 'n eat," which

means they have been cut at intervals and the shells will snap open easily at the cuts.

Buying:
Hard-shell crabs: If you are buying fresh uncooked crabs, make sure they are moving; never buy a dead fresh crab. Hard-shell crabs are usually sold already cooked. If they are whole, the consumer must clean them by removing the gills and the guts located under the hard top shell; then the meat can be picked. Choose whole crabs that feel heavy and packed with meat, that have no odor other than a fresh sea smell, and do not sound of water inside when shaken. Commercial packaging of parts (legs or claws or sections including legs and a shoulder) of hard-shell crabs can vary tremendously, depending on the species. Your selection from what is available will depend very much on how you intend to serve the crab. Sometimes you will find whole cooked crabs or parts of crabs where the meat adheres to the shell and is almost impossible to get out; these are called "stickers," and the problem usually results from the crab not having been processed quickly enough or from being refrozen after thawing.
Soft-shell crabs: These crabs are shipped live to markets nestled in wet straw or seaweed. Do not buy them unless you can see from movement that they are alive. They are graded according to the width of the upper shell into five groups: whales—over 5½ inches; jumbos—5–5½ inches; primes—

CRAB

Crab (continued)

4½–5 inches; hotels—4–4½ inches; mediums—3½–4 inches. The larger the size, the fewer needed per serving. I usually serve 3 hotels or mediums per person, or 2 primes. They are usually sold by the piece and are usually available from late spring to early fall.

Crabmeat: Picked crabmeat is sold fresh, frozen, and canned. Impeccably fresh crabmeat is preferable because it loses some of its tenderness and sweetness when frozen. Some crabmeat is pasteurized (sealed and heated just to a temperature to kill growing microorganisms) to extend its shelf life. Crabmeat should always smell and taste sweet and fresh. Reject any with a musty or ammonia odor. The color of the meat is usually a combination of white and red or pink. Some leg meat might have a slight brownish color, but if the meat looks definitely brown, it may have had inadequate refrigeration. The meat is graded in four major categories:

1. *Lump or backfin:* large pieces of white meat removed from the backfin appendage chamber; it is the most desirable crabmeat and the most expensive.
2. *Flake:* much smaller pieces of white meat removed from other body chambers.
3. *Claw:* meat extracted from the claws; it tends to be darker than body meat.
4. *Mixed:* a combination of all the forms of crabmeat.

Storage: Live hard-shell crabs should be kept cool and moist in a place with good air circulation; a good choice is a dampened burlap bag or a container with seaweed in it. Cook within 24 hours.

Cooked whole crab or parts of crab will keep for 24 hours under refrigeration; freeze, if necessary, to keep longer before preparing and serving.

Cooked crabmeat out of the shell is best kept in a container on ice in the refrigerator. Fresh cooked crab has a shelf life of 1–2 days. Fresh pasteurized crab should be stored the same way; although some say it will store for months, I always use it within 2 weeks.

Live soft-shell crabs will keep for a day or two in a single layer in the wet straw they were shipped in; their durability will depend on how long they had been in the fish market. Once they have been cleaned, place them in a single layer on a waxed-paper-lined tray, cover, and refrigerate; cook as soon as possible.

Defrost frozen crab, such as legs and claws or sections, by placing them on a plate or tray, covering them with waxed paper or plastic wrap, and letting them thaw in the refrigerator for 8–10 hours or overnight.

Basic Preparation and Cooking:

To cook live hard-shell crabs: Bring a large pot with enough water to cover the crabs you are cooking to a boil, adding 2 table-spoons of salt for each quart of water. Drop the crabs into the water one by one so that the

water will come back rapidly to a boil; add more boiling water to cover, if necessary. If you are cooking a number of crabs, allow 15–25 minutes of cooking time after the water has returned to a boil; timing will depend on the number of crabs. The crabs will turn completely red when they are cooked. For large crabs, estimate about 6 minutes per pound. Cooking blue crabs in a flavored water using packaged "Crab Boil" seasoning or pickling spices is very popular in the South. Add one 3-ounce package of Crab Boil for every 12 crabs that you will cook. You can add coarsely chopped onions or celery or sliced lemon for additional flavor. Boil the water and seasoning together for 20–30 minutes to make a rich-flavored broth before adding the crabs. Drain the crabs and serve hot, or cool them to room temperature, refrigerate, and serve cold.

Or steam the crabs by bringing an inch of water to a boil in a large pot. Place a steamer rack in the bottom of the pot and place the crabs in the basket. Steam, covered, for 15–20 minutes, or until the crabs are bright red, allowing extra time if you have a large number of crabs in the pot. Remove the crabs, rinse them with cold water, cool to room temperature, and chill in the refrigerator; or, if you wish to serve them hot, rinse them under cold water just until they are cooled enough to handle, prepare as in *To pick a cooked crab* (page 163) and serve with melted lemon butter. If your guests are

CRAB

picking their own crabs, prepare them for a happy but messy time with oversized napkins and bowls of lemon water to wash their hands.

To pick a cooked crab: Carefully twist off the legs and claws where they meet the body, and set them aside. With a small knife or fork, clean any meat out of the sockets where the legs were attached. Use a knife to pry off the top shell, discarding it or washing it well and setting it aside if you wish to use it as a dish. Remove and discard the spongy gills, stomach sac, outer veins, and white membrane from the exposed body. Scoop out any tan innards in the center (if you wish to use it) as you would lobster tomalley. Break the body in two or cut it lengthwise with a heavy knife and pick out the chunks of meat from each side. Lay each claw, in turn, on a flat surface and sharply rap it near the juncture with the back of a knife or with a hammer if the shell is very hard, taking care to crack it, not shatter it, thereby avoiding shell splinters in the meat. Pull the two sections of shell apart. Since the meat will adhere to the pinchers, break the stationary pincher off and cut the meat away from the remaining pincher with a knife or skewer. Extract the meat from each section of the arm of the claw in similar manner. After cracking the center of each section, run a thin knife between the shell and meat to extract the meat.

To prepare and reheat cooked parts of shell-on crab: Cooked legs, claws, and shoulders of crab need only quick reheating, which can be done by steaming, sautéing, broiling, grilling, baking, or adding to soups and stews for the final 5 minutes of cooking. Sections, or "clusters," can be separated by cutting or breaking the legs apart at each joint. Use a large, heavy knife to cut or score the back side of the leg shells. Break the shoulder into two or three pieces. Crack the claw shells if they are heavy. To steam, put 1 inch of water in a pot large enough to hold the crabs in their steamer basket, bring the water to a boil, add the basket of crabs, reduce the heat, cover, and steam for 5 minutes, or until the crabs are thoroughly heated. Or sauté pieces of legs or claws for 5 minutes; or grill or broil for about 5 minutes, 5 inches from the heat; or bake in a preheated 400-degree oven for a few minutes just until heated through.

To sauté large pieces of cooked crabmeat, turn them in melted butter or in a little broth for 3–5 minutes, or until thoroughly heated through.

To "dress" (clean) a soft-shell crab: Turn the crab on its back, and using a sharp knife or kitchen shears, cut a slice across the front of the crab just behind the eyes, separating the "face" from the body, and discard the face. Remove the grayish bile sac exposed by the cut. Lift up and out, and pull or cut off the apron, or flap, that folds under the rear of the body. (The apron is triangular in female crabs and T-shaped in male crabs.) Lift up the loose flaps on either side of the crab and remove the spongy gills. The crab is ready to cook (see *Sautéed Soft-Shell Crabs,* page 157).

Yields:

❖*Hard-shell blue crabs:* 1 pound of whole crab yields only about 1½ ounces meat; it takes about 6 crabs to get 1 cup crabmeat.

❖*Soft-shell crabs:* Everything but the face, bile (or stomach) sac, apron flap, and gills is edible.

❖*Jonah and Rock crabs:* 1 pound whole crab yields about 2 ounces picked meat.

❖*Red crab:* About 25 percent of the weight of the whole crab is meat.

❖*Stone crab claws:* medium grade, less than 3 ounces meat, so 6–8 claws to get 1 pound meat; large grade, 3–5 ounces meat per claw, so 4–6 claws to get 1 pound meat; jumbo grade, over 5 ounces meat, so 1–3 claws to get 1 pound meat

❖*Dungeness crab:* 1 crab body with top shell and membranes removed, weighing from 1–1¼ pounds, yields ½ pound meat.

Servings:
Cooked meat: 3–4 ounces per person
Cooked legs or claws: 6–8 ounces per person
Cooked claws: 6–8 per person for a main course, 3–4 per person for an appetizer
Soft-shell crabs: 2–3 per person, depending on grade (see pages 161–162)

Judy Miller's Giant Maryland Crab Cakes (continued)

❖Make the cakes smaller or larger. Divide the mixture into 12 portions and make cakes 3–3½ inches wide and ¾ inch high, then bake for 5 minutes on each side; or make Judy's giant cakes by dividing the mixture into 4 portions and make cakes 4 inches wide and 1½ inches high, baking them 10 minutes on each side. Add a little more beaten egg and bread crumbs as binder if you make smaller cakes; the smaller cakes can be fried on both sides to completion, omitting the baking step.

❖Substitute tartar sauce for mayonnaise in the recipe; or add Dijon-style mustard to the mayonnaise.

❖Add 2 tablespoons of drained capers, or substitute capers for the peppers.

Dungeness Crab Cakes
with Two Tomato Sauces

Whenever I can get to the Pike Place Market in beautiful, friendly Seattle, with its colorful stalls of fresh seafood and produce, I bring home wonderful Dungeness crabmeat. Of course, any sweet crabmeat will be fine for these delicate cakes bound by a light white sauce and accompanied by two sauces: a cold tomato mayonnaise made well ahead and a warm tomato fondue made just before serving. The crab mixture should be made well ahead and thoroughly chilled before the cakes are formed. Try serving mustard greens or sautéed collard greens with these cakes.

TOMATO MAYONNAISE

¾ cup mayonnaise
½ cup peeled, seeded, and diced tomatoes
1 Tb fresh lemon juice
1–2 tsp grated horseradish
¼ tsp cayenne pepper
1 Tb drained capers (optional)

CRAB CAKES

1 lb cooked crabmeat
5 Tb butter
2 Tb flour

¾ cup milk
2 tsp Dijon-style mustard
1 Tb fresh lemon juice
Salt and freshly ground pepper
½ cup finely chopped onions
½ cup finely chopped celery
¼ tsp hot pepper sauce
1 tsp cracked black pepper
2 Tb vegetable oil

TOMATO-CAPER FONDUE

1 Tb butter
1–2 Tb minced onions or shallots (optional)
2 cups peeled, seeded, and diced tomatoes
2–3 Tb drained capers
Freshly ground pepper

To make the tomato mayonnaise: Combine all the ingredients, including the capers, if desired, in a bowl; mix well, cover, and chill for 2 hours or longer.

To make the crab cakes: Pick through the crabmeat, removing any bits of shell and cartilage, and set aside in a bowl.

In a saucepan, melt 2 tablespoons of the butter, blend in the flour, and whisk together for a minute to cook the flour. Remove the pan from the heat and whisk in the milk. Return the pan to medium-high heat and cook, whisking constantly, until the white sauce comes to a boil, then lower the heat and cook for 2–3 minutes. Whisk in the mustard and lemon juice, season with salt and freshly ground pepper, and set aside.

In a sauté pan, heat 1 tablespoon of the butter, add the onions and celery, and cook gently for about 5 minutes, or until the vegetables are wilted and golden. Combine the vegetables and the white sauce with the crabmeat and mix well. Stir in the hot pepper sauce and cracked pepper, and add more salt and pepper if needed. Cover and refrigerate the crab mixture until chilled.

When the crab mixture is thoroughly chilled, shape it with your hands into 8 even-sized cakes. In a large sauté pan, heat the oil and remaining 2 tablespoons of butter; add the crab cakes and sauté over medium-high heat for 5–6 minutes, turning once, or cook until they are golden brown on both sides, adding more butter and oil if needed. Serve 2 cakes per person as a main course or 1 cake as an appetizer, accompanied by the two sauces.   MAKES 8 CAKES

To make the tomato-caper fondue: In a saucepan, melt the butter, add the onions or shallots, if desired, and cook for 1 minute; then add the tomatoes and capers, and cook over medium-high heat for 4–5 minutes to evaporate some of the juices and thicken the sauce. Season with freshly ground pepper.

❖Add 1–2 tablespoons drained capers to the crab mixture.

❖Add fresh chopped dill, parsley, tarragon, or other fresh herbs to the crab mixture.

❖Add minced pimento to the crab mixture.

❖To stiffen the mixture, add 2 beaten eggs and ½ cup fresh bread crumbs.

❖Coat the crab cakes with bread crumbs before cooking. Sprinkle the cakes with flour, dip them into a mixture of egg beaten with ¼ cup water, turn them until coated on all sides in 2 cups fine fresh bread crumbs, and sauté as above.

Crab and Broccoli Quiche

In the 1960s everyone was serving quiche and a salad for lunch; some restaurants offered as many as eight to ten variations. Gradually quiche declined in popularity, perhaps because diners began to shy away from eggs and cream, perhaps because the dish was overused, became tiresome, and gave way to the next rage. Nevertheless, quiche can make a convenient and economical lunch or supper dish. I use fresh broccoli and crabmeat here, but don't hesitate to substitute leftover cooked salmon or bluefish or lobster, or other combinations of fish and shellfish, and leftover spinach, cabbage, leeks, corn, or other vegetables. The amounts are not engraved in stone; if you have a cup of cod and a cup of kale, put them into a quiche. Use your favorite crust for a 9-inch shell or use the recipe below; if you are pressed for time, put the filling and egg mixture in a crustless pie dish and bake. A food processor mixes the piecrust in seconds, but start the crust well ahead to allow time to chill the dough and partially prebake the shell.

PIE SHELL

1¼ cups flour
¾ tsp salt
¼ cup *chilled* shortening
3 Tb *chilled* butter, cut into small pieces
3–4 Tb ice water

FILLING

1½ lb broccoli
1 cup crabmeat
1–2 Tb butter
1–2 Tb chopped shallots
3 large eggs
1 cup light cream or milk
Salt and freshly ground pepper
Hot pepper sauce
½ cup grated Jarlsberg cheese (optional)

To make the pie shell: Put the flour, salt, chilled shortening, and chilled butter into the bowl of a food processor, and pulse the processor for 2–3 seconds to break up the shortening and butter into pea-size pieces. Turn the processor on and add just enough ice water so that the dough begins to mass on the blade (about 10 seconds of processing). Remove the dough to a lightly floured surface and knead with the heel of your hand a few times to work the dough and smooth it. Shape the dough into a 5-inch-wide round, wrap in waxed paper, and refrigerate for at least 1 hour. (Makes dough for one 9-inch pie shell)

When the dough has chilled, roll it out on a lightly floured surface into a circle 2 inches larger than the pie pan. Fit the dough into the pan, pressing excess dough down slightly inside the pan to make the sides thicker. Make a decorative edge on the pastry, and prick the bottom and sides with a fork. Refrigerate again for 30 minutes. Place a piece of aluminum foil slightly larger than the pie pan, shiny side down, into the shell and fill the shell with dried beans or washed pebbles. Bake in a preheated 425-degree oven for 10 minutes. Remove the pan from the oven, remove the weighting and the foil, straighten the sides of the pastry if they have sagged, prick the bottom and sides again, return the pan to the oven, and bake for another 4–5 minutes to lightly brown and set the dough. Remove to a pie rack.

To make the filling: Remove and peel the stems of the broccoli and cut into ½-inch pieces; divide the top of the broccoli into flowerets. Bring a pot of water to a boil, drop in the broccoli, and cook for 3–5 minutes, or until it is just tender. Drain immediately and run under cold water to cool quickly. Drain again

Crab and Broccoli Quiche (continued)

and chop the broccoli into small pieces, place in a sieve, and set aside. (You will have about 1½ cups cooked broccoli.)

If the crabmeat is very moist, drain it and remove any bits of shell and cartilage. In a sauté pan, heat the butter, add the shallots, and cook until they are wilted. Add the crabmeat, turn it in the butter and shallots, and cook just long enough to evaporate any excess moisture, about 1–2 minutes; remove from the heat and set aside. In a small bowl, beat the eggs, stir in the cream or milk, season with salt and freshly ground pepper, and add a few drops of hot pepper sauce.

To assemble the quiche: If the broccoli is damp, pat it dry with paper towels; spread it over the bottom of the partially baked shell. Spread the crabmeat evenly over the broccoli and pour the egg mixture over all. Sprinkle the top with cheese, if desired. Bake in a preheated 375-degree oven for 35 minutes, or until the quiche has puffed up and is lightly browned.

SERVES 4–6

❖For a richer filling, use a combination of heavy cream and light cream.

❖Add a thin layer of grated Jarlsberg cheese in the bottom of the shell.

❖Sauté the broccoli or any other vegetable you are using in butter and add seasoning to taste.

❖Sprinkle crumbled, crisply cooked bacon in the bottom of the quiche shell.

Deviled Crabmeat
in Scallop Shells

This is one of the first party dishes I ever made. It was quite extravagant for our budget thirty years ago, but it was easy to make and always well received. Back then I made a quick white sauce to bind the crabmeat, but now I take an even simpler approach and bind it with mayonnaise. The recipe is easy to enlarge to accommodate more guests. For a buffet, I may serve the deviled crabmeat in mushroom caps (see variation); otherwise I bake and serve the dish in scallop shells that are available in most kitchen stores. Other presenta-tions could use ramekins or a one-quart baking dish. The dish can be assembled and refrigerated, and then baked just before serving, or it can be whipped up in minutes just before serving. I like to serve *Sugar Snap Peas and Carrot Logs* (page 333) or *Braised Broccoli de Rabe* (page 323) as the accompanying vegetable.

Alternative shellfish: cooked diced lobster meat, cooked diced shrimp

1 lb lump crabmeat
3 Tb butter
⅓ cup finely chopped onions
⅓ cup finely chopped green peppers
⅓ cup finely chopped red peppers
⅓ cup finely chopped celery
¼ cup chopped scallions
½ cup mayonnaise
4 tsp Dijon-style mustard
1 tsp Worcestershire sauce
Hot pepper sauce (optional)
1¼ cups fresh bread crumbs
1–2 Tb chopped parsley
Salt and freshly ground pepper
Small sprigs parsley
Lemon wedges

Pick over the crabmeat, removing any bits of shell and cartilage, and place it in a large bowl. (If the crab-meat is juicy, let it drain in a strainer while you pre-pare the other ingredients.)

In a sauté pan, heat 1½ tablespoons of the butter, add the onions, green and red peppers, celery, and scallions, and cook for 4–5 minutes, or until the veg-etables are wilted. Remove from the heat and allow to cool slightly. In a small bowl, mix together the mayonnaise, mustard, Worcestershire sauce, and a few drops of hot pepper sauce, if desired.

Into the large bowl with the crabmeat, add the cooked vegetables, ½ cup of the bread crumbs, and the parsley; gently fold in the mayonnaise mixture and season with salt and freshly ground pepper. Divide the crabmeat mixture evenly among 4 scallop shells (about 5 inches wide each), mounding the mix-ture up in the center. In a small saucepan, heat the remaining 1½ tablespoons of butter, add the remain-ing bread crumbs, and cook until lightly browned. Spoon the bread crumbs over the crabmeat mixture and place the shells on a baking sheet. (Refrigerate the shells at this point for later baking, if you wish.)

Place the shells in a preheated 375-degree oven

and bake for 20 minutes or until thoroughly heated through. Decorate with parsley sprigs and serve with lemon wedges. SERVES 4

❖*Deviled Crabmeat–Stuffed Mushrooms:* Remove the stems from 16 cleaned large mushrooms about 2½–3 inches in diameter. Reserve the stems for another use; brush the outside of the caps with vegetable oil. Spoon the crabmeat mixture evenly into the inside of the caps, mounding the mixture in the center. Sprinkle with bread crumbs and bake as above. Serve on a platter for a buffet dinner or serve 2 stuffed mushrooms as an appetizer course. Or stuff and bake smaller mushroom caps for a cocktail tray.

❖Place the deviled crabmeat in a casserole dish, top with bread crumbs, and bake for 25–30 minutes.

❖Divide the mixture among 6 scallop shells for an appetizer course for 6.

❖Add finely diced hot peppers to the crabmeat mixture.

❖Use pimentos in place of chopped red peppers.

❖Add the juice of 1 lemon to the mixture, or for a softer texture, add more flavored mayonnaise.

Flounder Meunière

The simple treatment of dusting fish with flour and sautéing it in butter is surely one of the most delicious ways ever invented to cook fish. Fillets of almost any young, small, firm-fleshed fish take well to "meunière"-style sautéing, but so do slices of large fish, such as swordfish and tuna. (See *Sautéed Swordfish,* page 286.) There are distinct differences in the firmness of flesh among the varieties of flounder available in our markets. Gray sole and young plaice are well suited for this sauté because of their firm flesh, and very fresh English Dover sole is ideal. I use oblong black frying pans that I bought in France many years ago; they are just right in heat retention for a meunière, but nonstick frying pans are a workable substitute. The fillets need to lie flat in the pan without crowding, so use two pans, if necessary. This is not a dish for someone reluctant to cook in butter. Clarified butter gives the best results, but a combination of butter and oil also works nicely. I always serve *Boiled New Potatoes* (page 334) with this dish.

Alternative fish: young small cod or haddock (scrod)

fillets, black bass, ocean perch, small bluefish, salmon trout, hybrid farmed striped bass, snapper, thin slices of swordfish or tuna

1½–2 lb skinned flounder fillets, 5–8 oz each
½ cup flour
Salt and freshly ground pepper
4 Tb butter★
1 Tb vegetable oil★
4 Tb unsalted butter
1 Tb fresh lemon juice
Chopped fresh parsley (optional)
Lemon wedges

★Or use 4 Tb *Clarified Butter* (page 351) to sauté the fish, and omit the oil.

If you do not have 4 fillets, cut the fillets lengthwise as necessary to make 4 equal portions. Remove any bones and pat the fillets dry. To prevent the fillets from curling as they cook, make very shallow diagonal cuts about 1 inch apart on the skinned (or darker-colored) side of each piece. Season the flour with salt and freshly ground pepper, and spread it on a flat dish or pie pan.

Heat 2 tablespoons of the butter and ½ tablespoon of the oil in each of two sauté pans or just in one pan if you are going to cook in batches. If the fish is crowded in the pan, it will simmer and not turn brown and crispy. When the butter is very hot but not brown and the bubbles in it begin to subside, dip both sides of each piece of fish lightly in the flour and shake off any excess to leave just a light dusting. Lay the fish gently into the butter in the pan, skinned side up, keeping space around each piece, and cook over medium heat for 2–3 minutes, or until the bottom side is golden. With a long spatula turn the fish very carefully and cook until golden on the second side, about 1–2 minutes; cooking time will vary with the thickness of the fillet. The goal is to get a thin, light brown crust on the outside while the inner flesh just turns opaque and remains very tender.

Carefully lift the fillets with a long spatula or two flat spatulas to warm serving plates, keeping the cooked fillets warm in a 200-degree oven if you are cooking in batches. Wipe out the pan and heat the 4 tablespoons unsalted butter until it is hazelnut-brown. Swirl in the lemon juice. Pour the lemon butter over the fish and sprinkle the fish with parsley, if desired. Garnish with lemon wedges and serve at once. SERVES 4

Flounder Meunière (continued)

❖ Add 1 tablespoon drained capers to the butter with the lemon juice or in place of the lemon juice.

❖ Omit the browned-butter-and-lemon sauce, and dress the fish with lemon wedges and capers, as in *Sautéed Bluefish with Lemon and Capers* (page 129).

❖ Cook small whole fish, 6–8 ounces each, cleaned, in the same manner; cook for about 5–6 minutes on each side.

Heat the oil and 1 tablespoon of the butter in a sauté pan large enough to hold the fish and banana in one layer. Add the fish and sauté on one side until lightly browned. Turn the fish and add the banana to the pan. Cook the banana on both sides while the second side of the fish cooks to a light brown. Remove the fish to a warm plate and place the banana slices across the fish. Wipe out the pan, add 1 tablespoon of the butter, and brown the butter. Pour the butter over the fish. Garnish, if you like, with 4 ounces each of cooked broccoli, carrots, and boiled potatoes.   SERVES I

Pan-Fried Fillet of Dover Sole (or Espada) with Banana

When "The Victory Garden" visited the island of Madeira, the chef of Reid's Hotel, Acacio Afonseca, took me through the fish market. Among the fish I'd never seen before was espada, a long black fish resembling a fat eel, with a vicious set of teeth. Underneath the ugly exterior was a delicious, white, firm-fleshed fish. Chef Acacio gave me his restaurant-based espada recipe for a single serving. Since many of us will never have access to espada, I turned to comparably firm-fleshed Dover sole imported from England as my most preferred alternative, but any of the alternative fish recommendations are worth trying, for combining fish and bananas is an inspired idea. I suggest cooking the fish and bananas in separate pans when you prepare this dish for more people; increase the oil and butter as necessary.

Alternative fish: gray sole, any firm-fleshed flounder, slices of salmon or striped bass, thin slices of swordfish

One 6-oz Dover sole fillet
Salt and freshly ground pepper
1 small banana
1 Tb vegetable or olive oil
2 Tb butter

Remove any bones from the fish and pat it dry. To prevent the fillet from curling as it cooks, make very shallow diagonal cuts about 1 inch apart on the skinned side of the fillet. Season the fish with salt and pepper. Peel the banana and slice it in half lengthwise.

Simple Sole Supper with Peas and Potatoes

I'm afraid dinnertime has fallen away from the old ideal of the family gathering for a gracious meal of good food punctuated with unhurried conversation. Too often the cook has just arrived home from a job, and everyone in the family is racing to catch a meeting, a date, or a ball game. Here is a one-dish meal that is quickly prepared, nutritious but with low calories, and so tasty that everyone in the house will find a way to stop long enough to enjoy it.

Alternative fish: any firm-fleshed flounder, ocean perch, orange roughy, Dover sole

Four 6–8-oz skinned gray sole fillets
4 large potatoes
8 small shallots or onions, or 2 large onions
Vegetable oil
Salt and freshly ground pepper
2–3 Tb sliced fresh sage (optional)
¾–1 lb sugar snap peas
2 Tb melted butter (optional)
1 Tb fresh lemon juice (optional)
Lemon wedges

Place the fish fillets on a flat work surface, skinned or darker side up, and make very shallow diagonal cuts about an inch apart across the fillets to prevent curling when they cook. Place in a glass or nonaluminum-lined dish, cover, and refrigerate them until ready to cook.

Peel the potatoes and cut them into 1–1½-inch chunks. Peel the shallots or onions, leaving shallots or
continued on page 171

SPECIAL INFORMATION ABOUT

FLATFISH

FLOUNDER, SOLE, AND HALIBUT

IN THE FINAL SCENE of Arthur Miller's play *The Crucible,* the hero, John Proctor, cries out in anguish, "How may I live without my name? I have given you my soul; leave me my name." Well might flatfish in general, if they had souls, adopt Proctor's line, for nothing in the world of fish is more confusing than the names given various kinds of flatfish in different parts of the country. Flounder may be called sole, fluke may be called flounder, dab may be called plaice—the confusion is on such a scale as to drive you to reliable and knowledgeable fish dealers who can tell you exactly what you are buying. In Europe, flatfish are often sold whole, so the shopper can identify the fish by size, shape, color, and markings. In the United States, most flatfish is sold as skinned fillets or steaks; even so, if you study what's available over a period of time, you will begin to identify different fish by the color and texture of the flesh and by the size of the fillets or steaks.

Flatfish get their name from their shape, which has evolved as a perfect adaptation to their habits as bottom feeders flattening themselves against the ocean floor and often covering themselves with sand except for their watchful eyes. Their dark top sides blend into the ocean floor, and if they rise toward the surface, their light lower sides help them avoid the attention of predators who

lose sight of them against the surface of the water. There are seven families of flatfish. The ones that concern us for cooking are commonly known as lefteye flounders, righteye flounders, and the true sole family, to which English Dover sole belongs. The eye designation is fascinating. Flatfish begin life looking pretty much like other fish, but rather quickly one eye floats over close to the other eye, so that both eyes are on one side of the body; in one family the eyes are on the left; in the other, on the right.

English Dover sole, truly a sole and not a disguised flounder, is a remarkably delicious fish, with glistening white flesh of a dense texture that keeps its shape and firmness when cooked but is also moist and tender. In England this flat, football-shape fish is often served whole and filleted at the table. Dover sole is imported whole and in fillets, and can be distinguished in part by its price as the most expensive sole or floun-

der. Do not confuse true imported Dover sole with the California flounder called Dover sole (quite mushy by comparison and different in taste and texture) or with another West Coast flounder called English sole.

My candidate for the native fish closest to imported Dover sole is witch flounder, commonly referred to as *gray sole.* It is found in New England and Canadian Atlantic waters, and yields a long, narrow fillet of white, firm flesh, with a lovely cooked texture and taste. It is excellent for preparations in which the fillet is folded or rolled. An extended visit to heavenly Santa Barbara, California—where the shrimp were exceptional—convinced me, however, that fish from cold eastern waters generally have finer-textured flesh than comparable fish from warmer Pacific waters. Of the Pacific flounders, I found myself preferring petrale sole, followed by rex sole—both of which are flounders, not true sole. Back East, I recommend *blackback flounder*—also called *winter flounder*—marketed in sizes ranging from very small ones called peewees to larger fish over 4 pounds that are called lemon sole. Blackback fillets have a pronounced color difference between the dark side and the light side of the fillet. I am fond of *plaice*—which is really a dab—also called sea dab, sand dab, American plaice, and Canadian

Flatfish (continued)

plaice; it has a thick, meaty fillet. Other popular eastern flounders include the thicker summer flounder, or fluke; and the *yellowtail flounder,* with slightly milky-colored flesh, soft texture, and a distinctive dark stripe under the skin of the dark side of the fish.

The category of flatfish includes two fish less thin than flounder: turbot and halibut. Genuine *turbot* is harvested only in northern European waters. Like Dover sole, it is an expensive imported fish here, available both in fillets and steaks. It is not to be confused with the Pacific arrowtooth flounder, which is marketed as turbot, or with Greenland turbot, which has oilier, softer, and less flavorful meat than European turbot.

Halibut is the biggest and fattest member of the flatfish families. There are two true halibuts available—Atlantic and Pacific—neither of which should be confused with California halibut, a flounder caught off the coast of California and Mexico with flesh that does not compare in quality to true halibut. Atlantic halibut, which is sold in long, thick fillets or in steaks or in pieces of the face cut into "cheeks," is one of my favorite fish. When striped bass became unavailable to the Straight Wharf Restaurant, I often turned to thick fillets of halibut for their delicious moist white flesh.

Buying: Most flatfish are harvested well out at sea by trawlers dragging nets across the ocean floor. The quality of the flatfish in the market will depend on the quality of the handling after the fish was netted and how quickly the trawler came back to port. In our markets you will mainly find flounder as fillets and halibut as fillets or steaks. The meat should be shiny and fresh-looking; pass up any pieces that are dull or limp or have separations in the flesh. They should have no more than a mild fresh sea smell. Flounder fillets can run from a few ounces to 10–12 ounces or more. They have usually been trimmed on the sides to remove the outside perimeter strip and may also have a small "V" cut along the center lateral line where pin bones were removed. Fillets have no waste, so buy poundage according to the amount you wish to serve. Halibut steaks will have a center bone and skin, so allow for some weight loss after trimming. I like to buy halibut fillets that can be portioned just as you would portion a salmon fillet; if, therefore, you want to serve each person 6 ounces of fish and you are serving 4 persons, buy 1½ pounds of halibut fillet.

Storage: Fish needs to be kept cold (32 degrees is ideal); bacteria grow quickly when fish is stored at a temperature above 40 degrees. Rush your fish home from the market and put it in the refrigerator. I store flatfish in a stainless, glass, or nonaluminum-lined dish covered with butcher's paper or waxed paper, topped with an ice pack, and set in the coldest part of the refrigerator. If I use plastic wrap to seal the storage dish, I leave an opening to allow air circulation around the fish. I try to purchase flatfish the day I am serving it—no earlier than the day before serving. Frozen fish should be gradually defrosted in the refrigerator.

Preparation: Flatfish can harbor roundworms, the tiny curled orange nematodes that are aesthetically unpleasant but are killed in the process of cooking the fish and are not a health threat. Most of them are removed when the fish is processed on its way to market, but occasionally you may find one or two. Their presence does not mean the fish is old or inedible; just remove them. Fillets should be checked for pin bones. Remove any center pin bones by cutting a narrow "V" along the lateral line of the fillet. If the fillet is too large for a single serving, you can divide it in half lengthwise down the center line of the fillet. Fillets will curl when cooked in the direction of the skinned side unless you lightly score the flesh. Place the fillet on a work surface, skinned side up. Using a sharp, thin knife, cut very shallow lines at a slight diagonal across the flesh about 1 inch apart. Halibut steaks can be cooked with backbone and skin intact, or you can remove the skin and separate the flesh from the bones. Very small halibut fillets are lovely for pan-frying. Larger fillets can be portioned into 6–8-ounce pieces,

SPECIAL INFORMATION ABOUT

FLATFISH

FLOUNDER, SOLE, AND HALIBUT

or butterflied as in *Sautéed Butterflied Salmon* (page 222), or cut in thin diagonal slices and prepared like salmon in *Sliced Salmon with Sorrel Sauce* (page 229).

Cooking: Flounder are delicate fish, with very little oil or fat in their flesh, and need only the simplest cooking treatments. They sauté beautifully and are excellent to poach or braise. Baking is best if the fillets have been combined with a sauce, liquid, or moist vegetables. Broiling should be done quickly and with some lubrication to keep the flesh moist. Flounder fillets are not suited for grilling.

Halibut can be cooked in just about every way. Halibut steaks will hold together on the grill or under the broiler but should be well basted because of their lean flesh. Grill racks should be clean, oiled, and very hot to prevent sticking. When broiling, you can add ⅛ inch of liquid to the broiler pan to help keep the fish moist.

Yields:
❖Flatfish fillets are 100 percent edible. Allow 6–8 ounces per serving.
❖Halibut steaks lose some weight when the skin and backbone are removed. A 1½-pound, 1-inch-thick, bone-in steak with skin can yield 14 ounces of meat after being skinned and boned.

Simple Sole Supper with Peas and Potatoes (continued)

small onions whole but cutting large onions into chunks. Pour 3–4 tablespoons of vegetable oil into a baking dish large enough to hold the vegetables in one layer, add the potatoes and onions, and turn them in the oil until they are well coated on all sides. Sprinkle the vegetables with salt and freshly ground pepper, and with the sage, if you are using it. Place the baking dish in a preheated 450-degree oven and bake for 30 minutes, or until the vegetables are tender, turning the vegetables once or twice as they cook.

While the vegetables are cooking, pull the stem of each sugar snap pea down one side of the pea and the strings of both sides come off. Discard the strings and set the peas aside.

About 5 minutes before the potatoes and onions are done, brush the fish fillets with oil on both sides, and place them, cut side down, on an oiled baking sheet. Place the sheet in the oven with the potatoes and onions. Cook the fish for 4–6 minutes, depending on its thickness, or until the fillets are just opaque. (If you are unsure about timing, finish cooking the potatoes and onions first, then cook the fish; the vegetables will hold well while the fish cooks.)

While the fish is cooking, put the sugar snap peas in a wide sauté pan, add ½ cup water, cover, and cook over medium heat for 3–4 minutes, or until the peas are just tender. Uncover, drain any liquid from the pan, add the melted butter and lemon juice (if you are using them), toss, and season with salt and freshly ground pepper.

Place the fish on 4 warm serving plates and arrange the potatoes and onions and the steamed sugar snap peas around the fish. Garnish the fish with lemon wedges.   SERVES 4

❖Combine the potatoes with chunks of celery or ripe tomatoes instead of onions.
❖Use *Sautéed Corn* (page 325) or *Sautéed Cucumbers* (page 326) instead of sugar snap peas.

Sole in Parchment

The presentation of this dish is irresistible, and once I started offering the dish at the restaurant, there was no turning back. A waiter would present the puffed-up parchment to the diner, dramatically slit open the pouch, and out would waft the sweet smell of fresh cooked fish, mousse, and wine. We made up dozens of servings every day and always sold out. At our restaurant we served the sole with a side cruet of *White Butter Sauce* (page 114) and found that about half the diners

Sole in Parchment (continued)

used the sauce and half were happy just to sauce the fish with the natural juices left in the parchment.

You will need a food processor to make the mousse in this recipe. It is worth the effort to get to a cookware store for the parchment because the visual effect is so winning, but you can use aluminum foil in a pinch. Every part of this dish can be prepared ahead: the parchment envelopes can be cut; the fish mousse can be prepared and refrigerated; you can even assemble the dish in the parchment the morning before you serve it—just as long as you refrigerate the fish on a tray until right before serving and you use impeccably fresh fish. *Sugar Snap Peas and Carrot Logs* (page 333) is a colorful and crunchy side dish. In case any guests have allergies, remember to tell them that the mousse in this dish contains shellfish.

Alternative fish: thin, firm-fleshed flounder fillets, Dover sole, orange roughy

Parchment paper
Four 6–7-oz gray sole fillets

MOUSSE

½ lb gray sole or other flounder
5 extra large (26–30 count) raw shrimp
¾–1 cup heavy cream
2 Tb lemon juice
Salt and freshly ground pepper

6 Tb melted butter
½ cup dry vermouth or white wine
2 Tb *chilled* butter
Salt and freshly ground pepper

Cut 4 parchment-paper rectangles, each about 20 inches long and the width of the paper, which is usually 12 inches. Fold each rectangle in half to make a doubled sheet 10 inches × 12 inches. Starting at one end of the 10-inch-long folded edge, cut a semicircle, curving up to the middle of the open side of the fold and then back down to the far end of the 10-inch folded edge. The semicircle you have cut will open into an oblong circle. Set the parchment semicircles aside.

Remove any bones from the fish. To help the fillets curl in the right direction, place them on a work surface with the skinned, or darker, side up and make shallow diagonal cuts across the fillets an inch apart.

Cover and refrigerate until ready to assemble the dish.

To make the mousse: Remove any bones from the gray sole or other flounder and peel and devein the shrimp. Cut the sole and shrimp into small pieces, place them in the bowl of a food processor fitted with a steel blade, and process in rapid on-and-off pulsing motions to break the seafood down into a rough purée. Gradually add the cream, with the processor on, until the mixture has a firm, smooth consistency that will softly hold its shape when lifted with a spoon. Add the lemon juice, 1 teaspoon salt, and a few grindings of pepper, and process the mixture enough to mix in the seasonings.

To assemble: Open up the parchment circles. Brush all but the outer 2 inches of each parchment circle with melted butter. Place 1 fish fillet, cut side up, in the middle of one of the semicircles established by the folding of the parchment. Place about one-quarter of the mousse in the center of the fillet and fold the edges of the fillet up around the mousse to make a packet. Care-

fully turn the fish packet over so that the seams of the fold are down against the parchment. Pour 2 tablespoons of the vermouth over each fish packet, place ½ tablespoon of the chilled butter on top of each packet, and season with salt and freshly ground pepper. Fold the bare semicircle of parchment over the semicircle holding the fish packet, match up the edges of the two semicircles, and make a 1-inch-wide fold (see photograph) all along the double edge of parchment to close the seam tightly. The wrapped fish will look like a filled turnover. Brush the top of the parchment with a little melted butter, and set the finished packet on a baking sheet. Complete this preparation for each serving. Do not crowd the parchment packets; use two baking sheets or put each packet in an aluminum pie pan. If you wish, refrigerate the packets and bake later.

When ready to serve, place the trays or pie pans in a preheated 400-degree oven and bake for 20 minutes. If you are using big baking sheets and have two ovens, bake one sheet in each oven.

Bring the sole in parchment to the table on a flat plate. Cut a large "X" in the top of the puffed and browned parchment, or unfold the folded edge, and lay back the top parchment to reveal the cooked fish and release the fine aroma. Using two large, wide spoons, lift the cooked sole and mousse to a warm serving plate, and spoon the juices from the parchment over the fish. Repeat the process for each serving. Serve with a side of *White Butter Sauce* (page 114), if desired, or another favorite sauce, or lemon wedges.   SERVES 4

❖ Any leftover mousse can be dropped by soupspoonfuls into simmering water and poached.

Gray Sole with Herbs and a Fresh Tomato Coulis

For a meal in which you want to practically eliminate fat, this dish is a winner, and delicious, too. Serve with steamed carrot and parsnip logs and fresh blanched sugar snap peas for an assembly of flavors and bright colors.

Alternative fish: thin, firm-fleshed flounders, flattened or butterflied salmon fillets

*Gray Sole with Herbs and a Fresh Tomato Coulis
(continued)*

> Four 5–6-oz skinned gray sole fillets
> 4 large ripe tomatoes
> 1 Tb minced shallots
> ½ tsp minced garlic
> ½ cup chopped fresh parsley, lightly packed
> ½ cup chopped fresh mint, lightly packed
> Grated rind of 2 large lemons (about 1½ Tb)
> 1 tsp fresh lemon juice
> Salt and freshly ground pepper

Remove any bones from the fish. Place the fillets on a work surface, skinned side up, and make a few shallow diagonal cuts across each fillet to prevent it from curling as it cooks. Refrigerate the fish until ready to cook.

Bring a pan of water to a boil and prepare a bowl of ice water to one side. Core the tomatoes, drop them into the boiling water for about 10 seconds or just until the skins begin to split, then immediately remove the tomatoes and plunge them into the ice water to stop the cooking action. As soon as the tomatoes are cool enough to handle, remove them from the water, slip off the skins, halve the tomatoes, squeeze out the seeds, and finely dice the tomato pulp. Set aside.

Combine the shallots, garlic, parsley, mint, lemon rind and juice, ⅛ teaspoon salt and a pinch of pepper in a food processor, and process until the mixture is finely minced. Place the fillets, scored side up, on a flat work surface. Spread the herb mixture evenly over the fillets; roll up each fillet, starting at the narrow or tail end, and set into a baking dish, seam side down. Bake in a preheated 375-degree oven for 15 minutes, or until the fish just turns opaque. While the fish is cooking, gently heat the diced tomato pulp in a nonmetallic saucepan and season, if you wish, with salt and freshly ground pepper.

To serve, remove the baked sole to 4 warm serving plates, and spoon the warm tomatoes evenly over and around the fish.   SERVES 4

❖Substitute basil or other fresh herbs for the mint.
❖Sauté the diced tomatoes with minced shallots in 2 tablespoons of butter and add fresh herbs, if desired.
❖Chill the baked sole. Slice the rolled fillets diagonally into rings and serve cold with sliced tomatoes and a lemon mayonnaise.

Fillet of Gray Sole
with a Crabmeat Topping

Underneath the festive look of this dish provided by its crabmeat topping is a simple, easy-to-prepare meal. I serve steamed snow peas and rice with the fish.

Alternative fish: any thin, firm-fleshed flounder fillets, Dover sole, ocean perch

> Four 6-oz skinned gray sole fillets
> 4–6 oz cooked crabmeat
> 2 Tb softened butter or margarine, for buttering the pan
> 2–4 Tb dry vermouth or white wine
> 3 Tb butter
> 1 Tb fresh lemon juice

To prevent the fillets from curling as they cook, make shallow diagonal cuts an inch apart on the darker, or skinned, side of each fillet. Remove any bones or cartilage from the crabmeat. Set the fish and crabmeat aside.

Butter a nonstick sauté pan large enough to hold the fish in one layer, or use two pans. Cut a round of waxed paper the same size as the pan and butter one side of it. Place the fillets in the pan, add 2 tablespoons vermouth or white wine per pan, and top with the buttered waxed paper, buttered side down. Cover the pan with a lid and set it over medium heat. Cook for 4–8 minutes, depending on the thickness of the fillets, or until the fish has just turned opaque at the center. Remove the fillets to warm serving plates. Immediately wipe out the sauté pan, add the 3 tablespoons butter, and heat the butter to sizzling. Stir in the crabmeat and cook for 1 minute, then swirl in the lemon juice. Spoon the crabmeat and lemon-butter juice evenly over the servings of fish and serve.

SERVES 4

❖Substitute sliced cooked lobster or small cooked shrimp for the crabmeat.
❖After garnishing the fish with the crabmeat, put 2–3 tablespoons drained capers in the sauté pan, add 1 tablespoon lemon juice, swirl together over high heat, and distribute over the crabmeat topping.
❖Prepare the gray sole as in *Flounder Meunière* (page 167) and top with crabmeat.

❖Use fish broth in place of vermouth, if you wish.

❖Heat the crabmeat in a microwave oven, in a steamer, in a saucepan with a little broth, or in a sauté pan sprayed with vegetable spray if you wish to eliminate all butter from this recipe.

Baked Fillet of Flounder with Bulb Fennel and Anchovy

The dinner menu at our house is sometimes shaped by what I can quickly put together at the end of the day from a fast trip to the market for protein and a swift raid on the garden to gather whatever is ripe and ready. Fresh flounder is always available, I've found. In this preparation I add the mellow anise, or licorice, flavor of fennel and the salty accent of anchovies, because they add dimension to the delicate flounder without overpowering it. But as you will see in the variations below, this method of baking flounder with vegetables will work well with many different vegetables. Gray sole—the Cadillac of flounders—is ideal for this dish, but other thin, flexible flounder fillets will work well. You can cook the fennel ahead, cool it, roll up the fish and fennel, and refrigerate it in its baking dish until ready to cook. If you wish, add a favorite sauce or my favorite fresh *Tomato Fondue* (page 363).

Alternative fish: thin fillets of firm-fleshed flounder, such as fluke, plaice, or lemon sole; thin fillets of ocean perch

1½–2 lb gray sole fillets
1½–2 lb bulb fennel
6 flat anchovies, more if desired
2 Tb butter or light oil
Salt and freshly ground pepper
¼ cup dry vermouth or white wine
Lemon wedges (optional)

To keep the fish fillets from curling in the wrong direction, place them on a work surface, skinned (or darker) surface up, and with a sharp knife make a few shallow diagonal cuts across each fillet. Divide the fillets into 4 equal serving portions; depending on the number and size of the fillets, it may work to cut some of the fillets in half lengthwise along the center line so that a portion includes both a whole fillet and a half fillet. Cover and refrigerate the fish until ready to assemble the dish.

Trim off the stalk ends of the fennel and any withered outer skin. Cut the bulb or bulbs in quarters without removing the core that holds the layers together. Holding each quarter on a cutting surface, slice around the core thinly just as you would slice cabbage for coleslaw. (You will have about 4 cups sliced fennel.)

Slice or chop the anchovies into small pieces. In a sauté pan, heat the butter and add the fennel. Turn the fennel in the butter to coat, then cover and cook over low heat, stirring occasionally, for 10 minutes. Uncover, stir in the anchovies, and continue cooking until the fennel is softened, stirring the fennel and anchovies together so that the anchovies soften and purée into the fennel. Add more anchovies to taste, if you wish. Season the mixture with freshly ground pepper. Remove the mixture from the heat and allow to cool slightly, or if you are cooking the final dish at a later time, cool the mixture completely, cover, and refrigerate.

To assemble the dish, place the fish fillets, scored side up, on a work surface. Evenly divide the fennel mixture among the fish pieces, placing it by spoonfuls in the center of each piece. Curl the ends of each piece up over the filling to make a packet. Turn each packet over and place it seam side down in a buttered baking dish or in individual buttered au gratin dishes. Season the tops of the fish packets with salt and freshly ground pepper. Pour in enough vermouth or white wine just to film the bottom of the dish or dishes, and cover with aluminum foil. Refrigerate the dish at this point, if desired, and bake just before serving it.

Place the fish in a preheated 400-degree oven and bake for 18–20 minutes—18 minutes for thin fillets, 20 for slightly thicker fillets. Lift the fish packets to warm serving plates and spoon the pan juices over the fish. For a more concentrated flavor, lightly cover the fish with aluminum foil to keep it warm, pour the pan juices into a small saucepan, quickly reduce the juices over high heat, then spoon them over the fish. Serve with lemon wedges, if desired, or a favorite sauce.

SERVES 4

❖Substitute thinly sliced celery for the fennel.

❖To keep the dish without fat, braise the fennel and anchovies in chicken or fish broth instead of butter and oil.

Baked Fillet of Flounder with Bulb Fennel and Anchovy (continued)

❖Omit the anchovies and use fresh herbs, such as sage, parsley, or lovage.

❖Braise any combination of vegetables that you like as a filling for these fish packets. Try a combination of thinly julienned carrots and parsnips, or the aromatic trio of carrots, celery, and leeks. Try thinly sliced red peppers and zucchini, or fill the fish with *Braised Cabbage and Collard Greens* (page 323) or *Curried Cabbage* (page 152) or *Braised Chopped Spinach* (page 338). Let your imagination take wing: how about caramelized onions?

❖Fill the fish with a purée of winter squash, parsnips, or potatoes and leeks cooked in butter.

❖This is an excellent place for leftover vegetables; check to make sure they are perfectly seasoned.

❖For a more dramatic presentation, bake the fish packets in parchment as in *Sole in Parchment* (page 171).

❖Add cooked mushrooms to the vegetable filling.

Gray Sole and Spinach Paupiettes

The slightly fancy name of this dish makes it sound complicated to prepare, but actually it's an easy dish to make and, because all the preparation before final cooking and serving can be done way ahead, a perfect party dish. You will need molds for individual servings; I use 10-ounce Pyrex dishes that are readily available in hardware or cookware stores, but any ovenproof 8–10-ounce mold will work. The recipe calls for gray sole because the fillets are thin and firm, and therefore curl in the molds nicely, but any thin, firm-fleshed flatfish can be substituted. While I once would have topped the paupiettes with a white butter sauce—a tasty combination—now I would recommend warm *Herb Vinaigrette* (page 365) or warm *Roasted Red Pepper Purée* (page 360) or a favorite tomato sauce, or I might serve them with no sauce or dressing at all. All you need to serve with this is a colorful vegetable, such as carrot logs or *Sautéed Rutabaga Dice* (page 337).

Alternative fish: any thin, firm-fleshed flatfish, thin ocean perch, orange roughy, tilapia

3 lb fresh spinach
1 Tb vegetable oil
2–3 Tb butter, plus more to taste
1 finely chopped medium onion
Salt and freshly ground pepper
Nutmeg
Juice of ½ lemon
1¼–1½ lb gray sole fillets
Lemon wedges

To blanch the spinach, bring a large pot of water to a rolling boil. Wash the spinach thoroughly and remove any heavy stems. Drop the spinach into the boiling water a little at a time so that the water keeps boiling, and cook for 2–4 minutes, or until the spinach just turns limp and tender. Cooking time will vary with the size of the spinach. Immediately place the pot in the sink and begin to run cold water into it so that the cold water exchanges with the hot; if the force of the water is not excessive, the spinach will not run over the side of the pot. When the water in the pot is completely cold, drain the spinach and gently squeeze it to remove all its water. (You will have about 3 cups.)

Finely chop the spinach. In a wide sauté pan, heat the vegetable oil and 1 tablespoon of the butter; add the onions and sauté until they are wilted and golden. Add the spinach and cook, stirring, until any excess moisture is evaporated, then stir in 1 tablespoon of the butter and season the mixture carefully with salt, freshly ground pepper, a dash of nutmeg, and the lemon juice. Set aside to cool slightly, or refrigerate until ready to use.

Butter the insides of four 10-ounce Pyrex glass molds or other molds of about the same size. Cut the fillets lengthwise down their center line, and place them, skinned (or darker) side up, on a flat work surface. Lightly score (cut) the fillets crosswise at 1-inch intervals to counter the natural curl of the fish. Divide the fish pieces into 4 portions and line the sides of each of the molds with one of the portions, placing the lighter, unscored side of the fillets against the sides of the molds and leaving the bottom of the mold uncovered with fish. Fill the inside of each mold with one-quarter of the spinach mixture. Dot the center of each filled mold with a small piece of butter, if you like. If you are not going to bake the molds at once, cover and refrigerate them.

When ready to bake, cover each of the molds with aluminum foil, or, if you prefer, cover all of the molds with one sheet of aluminum foil after they have been placed in the baking pan. Set the molds into a baking pan deep enough to allow boiling water to reach halfway up the sides of the molds. Set the pan on the slightly pulled-out rack of a preheated 400-degree oven, add boiling water to the pan up to the halfway mark of the molds, carefully slide the rack into the oven, and cook for 20 minutes. Remove the molds from the oven and drain by holding a small plate over each mold and tipping the mold until juices run out the crack between the mold and the plate. Save the juices for a sauce, if you wish. Unmold the sole and spinach onto warm serving plates, garnish with lemon wedges, or serve with a sauce.

SERVES 4

❖Make a cream sauce using the fish juices and extra fish stock or unsalted chicken broth. In a saucepan, melt 2½ tablespoons butter, add 3½ tablespoons flour, and cook, stirring to blend the butter and flour, for 2 minutes, or until the mixture is lightly colored. Remove the pan from the heat and whisk in 1 cup fish juices supplemented with fish stock or chicken broth, and 1 cup milk. Return to the heat and cook over medium heat, stirring with a wooden spoon so that no particles of flour stick to the bottom of the pan. Simmer for 3–4 minutes, thinning with more milk, if desired. Season with salt and freshly ground pepper and with a pinch of nutmeg and a little lemon juice, if desired.

❖Sauté the spinach in light olive oil.

❖Use other blanched greens or chopped sautéed broccoli or broccoli de rabe, or sliced sautéed cabbage.

Gray Sole Dugléré

In French culinary terminology, *dugléré* indicates that a dish has a tomato-enriched sauce. Poaching folded fillets of fish in the oven is a versatile technique, and we used it with many variations at the Straight Wharf Restaurant. The fish is always prepared the same way, and the sauce as well, but the shellfish or vegetable enrichments can vary dramatically, as you will see in the notes following the recipe. You can poach the fish ahead if necessary, cool it, then cover and refrigerate it. Shortly before serving, place the fish in indi-

vidual au gratin dishes, cover each with aluminum foil, and reheat for 10–15 minutes in a preheated 350-degree oven. You can also make the base sauce ahead, leaving out the tomatoes and the optional hollandaise sauce. Combine the base sauce and tomatoes when you reheat the sauce, then fold in the hollandaise and run the sauced fish under a preheated broiler; or omit the hollandaise and lighten the sauce by folding in ½ cup whipped cream before running under the broiler.

Alternative fish: any thin, firm-fleshed flounder, Dover sole, orange roughy

1½–2 lb gray sole fillets
Salt and freshly ground pepper
3 Tb minced shallots
⅔ cup dry vermouth or white wine
⅔ cup fish broth or unsalted chicken broth
1½ Tb butter
2 Tb flour
½–¾ cup heavy cream
2 cups peeled, seeded, and diced tomatoes, well drained
Fresh lemon juice
⅓ cup *Hollandaise Sauce* (page 356) (optional)

Divide the fish into 4 serving portions; if necessary, cut some fillets in half lengthwise to get the right apportionment. Lightly score (cut) the skinned, or darker, side of the fillets with a sharp knife crosswise at 1-inch intervals, and season the fish with salt and freshly ground pepper. Fold over the ends of each fillet so that they slightly overlap and make a flat roll with the scored side on the inside of the roll.

Butter a baking dish large enough to hold the fish in one layer, and sprinkle the shallots in the bottom of the dish. Place the fish in the dish with the overlapping ends down against the bottom of the dish, and pour in the vermouth or white wine and broth. Cover the fish with a sheet of buttered waxed paper or aluminum foil, place the dish in a preheated 400-degree oven, and poach for 6–10 minutes, depending on the thickness of the fish; it should be just cooked through and springy to the touch.

Remove the baking dish from the oven, pour off the cooking liquid into a small saucepan, leaving the waxed paper over the fish, and boil the juices rapidly until they reduce to 1 cup.

In a medium saucepan, heat the butter and whisk in the flour. Cook the mixture for 2–3 minutes, remove from the heat, and whisk in the reduced

Gray Sole Dugléré (continued)

cooking juices. Add any other juices exuded by the
cooked fish and bring the sauce to a boil. Whisk in ½
cup of the cream, bring the mixture to a boil, reduce
the heat, and cook gently for a few minutes longer, or
until the sauce has thickened enough to coat a spoon.
Add the remaining cream, if desired, and fold in the
tomatoes to warm in the sauce. Season the sauce with
lemon juice and with salt and pepper. Remove the
sauce from the heat and fold in the hollandaise sauce
(if you are using it).

Either leave the fish in its baking dish or arrange it
in 4 au gratin dishes. Spoon the sauce over the fish
and run it under a preheated broiler just long enough
to glaze the top.   SERVES 4

❖ If you have used the hollandaise sauce, you can
fold ½–¾ cup whipped cream into the sauce to turn
it into a lighter mousseline sauce before spooning the
sauce over the fish and running it under the broiler.

❖ Add 1 tablespoon minced fresh herbs, such as
parsley, tarragon, lovage, or chervil, to the sauce.

❖ *Gray Sole Florentine:* Prepare *Braised Chopped
Spinach* (page 338). Spoon ½–¾ cup spinach into
each of 4 buttered au gratin dishes; place the cooked
fish on top, cover with sauce, and broil briefly as
above. If you are preparing the dish ahead, reheat the
spinach, fish, and sauce separately and then combine
them for the final light broil. Substitute other cooked
vegetables for the spinach under the fish. Try
chopped *Braised Cabbage and Collard Greens* (page
323) or a purée of winter squash.

❖ *Gray Sole with Mushrooms:* Sauté 2–3 cups sliced
mushrooms in butter, season the cooked mushrooms
with lemon juice, salt, and freshly ground pepper, and
spoon the mushrooms over the fish before adding the
sauce.

❖ *Gray Sole with Lobster or Crab:* Prepare the fish
and sauce as above, omitting the tomatoes. Sauté
1½–2 cups cooked sliced lobster meat or cooked
crabmeat gently in butter. When the fish has been
cooked and drained of its cooking juices, place even
portions of the cooked shellfish in 4 buttered au
gratin dishes. Place the portions of cooked fish on top
of the shellfish and proceed with the saucing as in the
main recipe. Stir a bit of tomato paste—or lobster
bisque, if you have some—into the sauce.

Lettuce Packets of Sole and Smoked Salmon

Wrapping fish in brioche dough or puff pastry or filo
dough before baking it insulates the fish from the drying effect of the oven, and thus keeps the fish moist.
But wrapping the fish in green lettuce leaves accom-
plishes the same purpose with far fewer calories, and
the bright green package is very appetizing. *Sautéed
Cucumbers* (page 326) are an ideal delicate vegetable to
accompany this dish.

Alternative fish: thin fillets of any flatfish

8 large leaves iceberg, butterhead, or other crisp
   lettuce
Four 6-oz skinned gray sole fillets
Salt and freshly ground pepper
8 paper-thin slices smoked salmon
2–3 Tb chopped shallots or white of leeks
¾ cup dry vermouth or white wine
1½ Tb softened butter (optional)
½ cup heavy cream (optional)
2 Tb *chilled* butter, cut into small pieces
   (optional)
Fresh lemon juice (optional)

Bring a large pot of water to a boil and set a bowl of
ice water to one side. Drop the lettuce leaves into the
boiling water, push them down with a perforated
spatula, and cook for 1 minute or less, until the lettuce just wilts. Lift the lettuce immediately with the
spatula to the ice water to cool and set its color. Drain
the lettuce leaves, place on paper towels, and pat dry.

Place the fish fillets on a flat work surface, skinned
(or darker) side up, and score (cut) them lightly with a
sharp knife at 1-inch intervals crosswise on the fillets.
Season the fish with salt and freshly ground pepper.
Place 2 slices of smoked salmon on each fillet and fold
the ends of the fillet up and over the salmon to make an
envelope with the salmon enclosed. Lay out 2 lettuce
leaves, partly overlapped, for each packet of fish. Place 1
fish packet in the center of each lettuce wrapping. Fold
the lettuce wrapping up and over the fish, and tuck in
the ends of the leaves to make a complete wrapping.

Butter a sauté pan and sprinkle the shallots or leeks
across the bottom. Place the lettuce-wrapped packets of
fish in the pan, seam side down. Pour in the vermouth

or wine, and dot the top of each packet with a portion of the softened butter, if you wish. Cover the fish packets with a sheet of waxed paper or parchment paper and bring the vermouth to a boil. Cover the pan with a lid, reduce the heat, and simmer for 8–10 minutes, or until the fish is just opaque; you can make a small slit in one packet to check. Remove the fish packets to a warm platter. Serve plain, or with a favorite sauce, or use the pan juices to make a cream sauce. To make the cream sauce, strain the pan juices into a saucepan, add the cream, bring to a boil, and cook until the mixture reduces to a medium-thick consistency. Remove the pan from the heat and piece by piece beat in the 2 tablespoons chilled butter. Season the sauce with salt and freshly ground pepper and a little lemon juice. Serve with the wrapped fish.   SERVES 4

❖In place of cooking the fish on the stovetop, bake it in a preheated 400-degree oven for 10–12 minutes, or until the fish is just opaque.

❖Omit the smoked salmon and spread an herb or anchovy butter over the fish before wrapping it in lettuce, or sprinkle the fish with chopped fresh herbs and finely grated lemon zest.

❖Top the cooked packets of fish with a dollop of salmon caviar before serving.

Poached Halibut with Rosemary Cream Sauce

A fragrant herb can give life to a dish. Here, a fresh rosemary sauce transforms succulent but mild-flavored halibut. The sauce, which can be made ahead and reheated before serving, is awfully good; spoon any extra sauce over an accompaniment of boiled potatoes, rice, or pasta. Halibut is the largest member of the flat-fish family—single fish weighing more than 200 pounds have been caught—but regardless of its size, it has the same kind of delicate flesh typical of its smaller flounder cousins. Perfectly fresh halibut, which this recipe demands, is very firm and shiny; as halibut ages, it gets yellowish and the flesh begins to separate. I ask for fillets of halibut even though it is often marketed as steaks. Sometimes I can find small halibut the size of flounder, but more often it is a fillet from a larger fish. The poaching time, which is not long in any case, will

vary somewhat with the thickness of the fish.

Alternative fish: salmon, Arctic char, black bass, striped bass, haddock, cod, snapper, almost any firm-fleshed white fish

One 2-lb halibut fillet, about ¾–1 inch thick

ROSEMARY CREAM SAUCE

1 cup fish broth or unsalted chicken
   broth
½ cup dry vermouth or white wine
2–3 sprigs fresh rosemary
1–2 Tb chopped shallots (optional)
2 Tb butter
2 Tb flour
1 cup heavy cream
1 beaten egg yolk (optional)
Juice of ½ lemon
2–3 Tb finely minced fresh rosemary
Salt and freshly ground pepper

To make the Rosemary Cream Sauce: In a small saucepan, combine the broth, vermouth or wine, rosemary sprigs, and chopped shallots (if you are using them). Bring the mixture to a boil, reduce the heat, and simmer, covered, for 10–15 minutes. Remove the sprigs and set the flavored broth aside. In another saucepan, melt the butter, stir in the flour, and whisk together for 2 minutes, regulating the heat so that the mixture does not brown. Remove the pan from the heat and whisk in the rosemary-flavored broth. Return to the heat, stirring the mixture until it thickens, and simmer for 5 minutes. Add the heavy cream and simmer 2–3 minutes more. If you are using the beaten egg yolk, whisk a bit of the sauce into the egg to warm it. Remove the sauce from the heat, whisk in the warmed egg yolk (if desired), lemon juice, and minced rosemary, and season the mixture with salt and freshly ground pepper. If you are serving shortly, keep the sauce warm; if you are serving later, let the sauce cool, cover the surface with plastic wrap, and refrigerate until ready to reheat and serve.

MAKES 1½ CUPS

Poached Halibut with Rosemary Cream Sauce (continued)

Remove any skin and any pin bones from the halibut fillet; if you have difficulty removing the skin, you can poach the fish first and then easily pull the skin off. Cut the fish into 4 equal-sized portions, cover, and refrigerate until ready to poach.

Prepare the rosemary cream sauce.

To poach the fish: Fill a high-sided pan that is wide enough to hold the fish in one layer two-thirds full of water and bring to a boil. Reduce the heat so that the water simmers and place the fish in the water. Adjust the heat so that the water stays at a shiver just below the boil. Poach the fish for 8 minutes, then lift it with a wide, slotted spatula onto double-thick paper towels and blot the top of the fish with other paper towels. If the fish has been poached with its skin on, turn it skin side up and gently pull off the skin.

To serve: Reheat the sauce, if necessary. Place the halibut on 4 warm serving plates and spoon over the sauce.   SERVES 4

❖Substitute fresh tarragon for the rosemary.

❖Reduce the poaching time for small fillets or thin ends of halibut. Don't hesitate during poaching to lift a piece out, cut into it to test for doneness, and then return it to the pan if it needs further cooking.

Baked Halibut with Radishes and Scallions

This is a delicately delicious dish that just happens to be an ideal diet dish. Since the dish contains no fat, I think of it as a perfect dish for spring when you are thinking about getting into a bathing suit again, and the first tender radishes and scallions are ready in the garden. The radishes provide a significant part of the flavor of this dish; make sure, therefore, that they are young, crisp, and mild-tasting, not big and strong-tasting. Serve this with blanched snow peas or asparagus dressed with a bit of lemon juice, and a bowl of plain rice.

Alternative fish: cod, haddock, bass, salmon, snapper, redfish, wolffish, rolled fillets of flounder

1½–2 lb skinned halibut fillets
20–30 young radishes
12 scallions
1 Tb finely chopped fresh ginger
1 Tb soy sauce
2 Tb rice wine or dry vermouth
2 tsp sesame oil
1–2 Tb chopped chives (optional)

Remove any skin and bones from the halibut. Cut the fish into 4 equal portions, cover, and refrigerate.

Trim the stems, wash and dry the radishes. Cut any large radishes in halves or quarters. (You should have about 1½ cups radishes.)

Trim the scallions and cut the white and pale green sections into thin diagonal slices. (You should have about ½ cup sliced scallions.)

Place the fish in a glass, ceramic, or stainless baking dish large enough to hold the fish in one layer. Scatter the radishes and scallions around the fish and sprinkle each piece of fish with the ginger. In a small dish combine the soy sauce, rice wine or dry vermouth, and sesame oil, and spoon the mixture over the fish. Cover the dish tightly with a lid or with aluminum foil, and bake in a preheated 400-degree oven for 20 minutes. Remove the fish to 4 warm serving plates. Distribute the radishes and scallions around the fish, and spoon the juices in the baking dish over the fish. Sprinkle with fresh chives, if desired.   SERVES 4

❖If you like the distinctive grassy or earthy taste of cilantro, add ¼ cup roughly chopped cilantro leaves to the fish before baking it.

Broiled Halibut or Cod Steaks

Big fat halibut or cod are often cut across the girth of the fish and sold as "steaks" including the center bone rather than as fillets. These steaks take well to poaching, but another simple, effective method is to broil them. Adding some liquid to the pan in which they are broiled helps to keep these lean white fish from drying out under the intense heat of the broiler. When it is cold outside, I like to serve broiled fish

with vegetable purées; try *Mashed Rutabaga* (page 337) or *Squash and Apple Purée* (page 247).

Alternative fish: pollock or other thick, lean fish steaks or thick fillets

Four ¾–1-inch-thick halibut or cod steaks
Salt and freshly ground pepper
2 Tb softened butter
1 tsp Dijon-style mustard (optional)
½–1 cup dry white wine or a combination of
    milk and water
Lemon wedges

Pat the fish steaks dry and season them with salt and freshly ground pepper. Place the steaks in a buttered, broiler-proof baking dish. Mix the softened butter with the mustard, if desired. Spread the butter mixture evenly on top of the fish. Pour the wine or combination of milk and water into the baking dish to cover the bottom to a depth of ¼ inch.

Place the fish about 3 inches below a preheated broiler and cook for 5–8 minutes, or until the fish is just opaque throughout and slightly springy to the touch. Serve with lemon wedges.   SERVES 4

❖Substitute a slice of *Escargot Butter Roll* (page 353) or a spoonful of *Mustard-Paprika Basting Butter* (page 235) for the plain softened butter or the mustard butter.

❖Brush the fish only with vegetable oil before cooking.

Steamed Lobster and Boiled Corn on the Cob

On the New England coast there are only two honored ways to cook a lobster, steaming or boiling; every other way is merely gilding the lily. I prefer steaming because the water is ready faster and the lobsters don't get waterlogged. But there are critics who say boiling is more merciful to the lobster. I leave it up to you. If you wish to boil lobsters, see *Boiled lobster* (page 186). Please refer to the Lobster Box (page 183) before buying lobsters. The traditional accompaniment to lobster is corn on the cob. As much as I prefer to steam lobster, I prefer to boil corn, although it can be prepared either way;

Steamed Lobster and Boiled Corn on the Cob (continued)

chalk that up to ornery New England habits. If you want to add one more treat to this luxurious combination, prepare *Boiled "Salt" Potatoes* (page 334) and dip them in the melted lobster butter.

> Lobsters
> Melted unsalted butter
> Fresh lemon juice
> Freshly shucked ears corn

Put 2 inches of water into a large kettle or lobster pot. Place a steamer basket or an inverted pie or cake tin in the bottom, or use the steamer insert that comes with a lobster pot. Cover the kettle and bring the water to a rolling boil. Curl the tails of the lobsters under, and drop the lobsters headfirst into the kettle. Don't crowd the kettle. Cover and cook as follows:

> 1¼-pound lobsters, 12 minutes
> 1½-pound lobsters, 15 minutes
> 2-pound lobsters, 20 minutes
> 2½-pound lobsters, 25 minutes
> 3-pound lobsters, 30 minutes

If you cram 5–6 small lobsters or 3–4 big lobsters into the same pot, count on a slightly longer cooking time.

Using tongs, remove the lobsters, and serve immediately or, for the convenience of your guests, partially prepare the lobster for eating as follows: handling each lobster with hot pads, put it on its back on a cutting board with a drain to catch the juices. Slice down the length of the body and tail, but do not cut all the way through and do not open the cut. With a hammer—or with the back of a heavy knife, if you are careful—give each claw one good crack. Place the lobster, right side up again, on a plate and serve with melted butter seasoned with lemon juice.

To boil corn on the cob: Bring a pot of water to a boil, drop the ears of corn into the water, and boil for 4–7 minutes, depending on the size and age of the corn. Remove one ear after 4 minutes and sample it; it should be still slightly crisp when removed from the cooking water. Lift with tongs to a warm serving platter and serve immediately with butter, salt, and pepper.

❖ *To steam corn on the cob:* Put 1 inch of water in a steamer and bring it to a boil. Place the corn in a steamer rack and steam for 6–10 minutes, depending on the size and age of the corn. Test for doneness as in the instructions above for boiled corn.

Lobster and Scallion Stir-Fry

If you are in the mood for a Chinese banquet, add this dish to the menu; lobster is delicious with Chinese seasonings. You can cut up the lobster, refrigerate the pieces ahead of time, and even prepare the seasonings in advance. Shortly before serving, make some rice. The final cooking of the lobster takes only a few minutes.

> Two 1½-lb lobsters
> 2 slices fresh ginger
> 2 cloves garlic
> 10 scallions
> 3 Tb soy sauce
> 3 Tb rice wine
> 3 Tb tomato paste
> 2 tsp white vinegar
> 1 Tb sugar
> ⅛ tsp salt
> ¼ cup vegetable oil
> 1 cup chicken broth or water
> 1 Tb sesame oil

Prepare the lobsters as in *To cut an uncooked or partially cooked lobster for stir-frying* (page 186). If you prefer, you can kill the lobsters by the *Fast-Boil Method* (page 185) and then cut them into pieces for the stir-fry. Refrigerate the lobster pieces in a bowl until ready to cook.

Finely chop the ginger and the garlic. Trim the scallions and cut them on a diagonal into ½-inch-long pieces.

In a small bowl, mix together the soy sauce, rice wine, tomato paste, vinegar, sugar, and salt.

Heat the oil in a hot wok, swirling the oil around the sides of the wok. Over medium heat, add the ginger, garlic, and scallions, and stir-fry for 20 seconds. Turn the heat up, add the lobster pieces, turn them in the oil, and cook, stirring, for 3 minutes. Add the soy-sauce mixture and stir to coat the lobster with it. Add the broth or water, cover, and steam for another 3 minutes. Uncover, cook a little longer to reduce the liquid, and stir in the sesame oil. Serve with rice.

SERVES 2 AS A SINGLE DISH, 4 WHEN
SERVED WITH OTHER DISHES

❖ For a spicier version, substitute 1–2 teaspoons hot chili oil for the sesame oil.

LOBSTER

WHEN I WAS ELEVEN years old, I accompanied my physician cousin and his family on a trip along the coast of Maine. Every township was trying to woo him into settling there as the local doctor. One village outdid themselves; they put on a clambake that would put *Carousel* to shame. The whole beach was dotted with smoldering fires, and for the finale, hundreds of steaming, sea-sweet succulent red, red lobsters were unveiled. All of my life lobster has been a special food to me, and I am not alone; lobster is a favorite of most diners. It's hard to believe there was a time when lobsters were so abundant they were used for garden fertilizer. Lobstering as a business began in Massachusetts in the mid-1800s, but it prospered most in Maine. First there was a canned lobster industry, and then a fresh lobster industry developed as methods were devised to hold lobsters in large seawater enclosures and rapidly ship them to local markets. Now live lobsters can be purchased in fish markets and supermarkets throughout the country. Lobsters, like most seafood families, come in several forms:

1. *American lobster.* This is the only real lobster we have in the United States; it is found in coastal waters from Canada as far south as the Carolinas. The solid upper shell that covers the internal organs is called the carapace, or "lobster body." What most distinguishes the American lobster is its foremost of five sets of legs that have evolved into meaty claws, one of which—

the crusher claw—is larger than the other—the ripper claw. These claws make the lobster a formidable adversary in the water. The lobster body is attached to a segmented tail, which is the largest source of meat in the lobster.

2. *European lobster. Homard* in France, the European lobster inhabits waters from northern Europe as far south as the Mediterranean. It is a true relative of the American lobster but generally smaller, and it can be cooked with all the methods appropriate to American lobsters.

3. *Lobsterette.* These smallest members of the lobster family are found on continental shelves of all the oceans and are identified regionally by different names: Norway lobster, Dublin Bay prawn, langoustine, lobsterette, and *scampo*. This is the shellfish used in authentic Italian scampi recipes. Lobsterettes lack the exaggerated claws of the American and European lobsters.

4. *Spiny lobster, rock lobster, crayfish.* These shellfish in dozens of species inhabit warm waters throughout the world, including the southern

LOBSTER

Lobster (continued)

coastal waters of both our coasts. Distinguished by their lack of the great claws of the American lobster, and by the tiny spines that cover their shells, they are strictly speaking closer relatives of crabs and shrimp and crawfish. The word "crayfish" specifies the saltwater species and "crawfish" the freshwater cousin, but the terms are often confused, and to make matters worse, the freshwater crawfish is a miniature replica in appearance of the true lobster. In France this shellfish is *langouste;* in Spain, *langosta;* in Australia, eastern rock lobster; and in New Zealand, spiny rock lobster. Though I brag about the delicious qualities of the American lobster, I remember sitting one afternoon at a long picnic table in an olive grove on the isle of Corfu. A white monastery sat on a knoll to the right; otherwise we had only azure sky and the turquoise Aegean Sea to look at under our canopy of grape leaves. We were offered wine, tomatoes, olives, and the largest lobster tail I had ever seen. Carried to the table on a board, then sliced and served like a roast of beef, this lobster meat from a spiny lobster was as fine and as sweet as any shellfish I had ever had. Spiny lobsters are available live in southern and western markets in this country, and everywhere as frozen lobster, usually just tail meat, often imported.

Color: The natural pigment of lobster is a combination of red, blue, and yellow that yields a shell that is dark green with touches of red. There are lobsters of other colors, and some attempts have been made to breed different colors into the shells of some lobsters in order to track their migratory habits; but shell color has nothing to do with taste, and every cooked lobster shell turns that wonderful red.

Molting: Lobsters, like crabs, outgrow their shells several times as they mature, and have to divest themselves of the old shell and grow a new one. During this molting period and as they harden a new shell, lobsters are not at their best for eating; they are known as "shedders," they feel lighter, and the shell isn't rigid. The meat is less firm. A lobsterman I know puts it this way, "When you pick 'em up, there's no one home." Avoid soft-shelled lobsters and lobsters with new-looking shells lacking the scars and scratches from living among the rocks.

Buying: The lobster should be active and angry-looking and flexing its tail; reject limp and listless ones. The shell should be hard and the lobster should feel heavy, packed with meat. If you want roe, ask the fish merchant for a female (the first pair of swimmerets on the underside of a lobster are soft on a female, hard on a male). If you are buying a whole cooked lobster, make sure its tail is curled—a sign that it was alive when it was cooked. Unfortunately, some markets will hastily cook dead or dying lobsters and sell them cooked. It's always safer to buy a vigorously alive lobster and cook it yourself. Cooked lobster meat should be sparkling white and pink and smell sweet; don't accept cooked lobster that smells at all of ammonia or is otherwise "fishy"-smelling, or cooked lobster that is yellowing or is at all slimy or slippery to the touch.

In American lobster the liver is called tomalley; it is beige-green when raw and turns pale green when cooked. Its special flavor is considered a delicacy, as is the roe of the female lobster. Both the tomalley and the roe can be eaten as is or incorporated into sauces for lobster dishes. However, if there is any chance that the lobster came from polluted waters or suspect areas, it is wise to discard the tomalley, since contaminants will tend to concentrate in the liver.

Size: Lobsters are sold either as "chickens" (below 1¼ pounds) or by weight, with 1½–2-pound lobsters commanding the highest prices. Larger lobsters actually go down in price per pound. "Culls," lobsters with only one claw, often are the cheapest of all, but if you can buy a cull with the larger, crusher claw, you will be getting almost as much meat as with a two-claw lobster.

Storage: Live lobsters need cold, moist conditions to survive out of seawater. I store them on their stomachs in a large high-sided pan in the refrigerator so that they will have plenty of air circulation. Another storage area is

SPECIAL INFORMATION ABOUT

LOBSTER

the vegetable drawer, left slightly ajar to allow air circulation. I have kept lobsters alive in this manner for 2–3 days without visible signs of listlessness. A weakening lobster will slow its movement, stop flexing its tail, and may even foam at the mouth. Cook lobster while it is still alive; its flesh deteriorates very rapidly after it dies. Make sure lobster claws are banded or pegged so that they can't harm one another. *Never* store lobsters in fresh water; *never* store them in seawater either, unless you have a tank with a circulator to keep oxygen in the water.

Cooked lobsters should be thoroughly chilled before wrapping them for storage. Whole cooked lobster should not be held longer than 2 days. Very fresh shelled lobster meat will keep in the refrigerator for up to 4 days; if you have not cooked the lobster meat yourself, use within 2 days. Frankly, the sooner you use cooked lobster meat, the better.

Frozen cooked lobster meat should be thawed slowly in the refrigerator, allowing 12 hours for an 8-ounce package. If necessary, thaw the lobster faster in its package under cold running water. If you are going to cook the lobster meat further, do so as soon as it is thawed. *Frozen cooked meat in shells, or just the shells,* can be taken directly from the freezer and heated in a stock or stew. *Frozen, partially cooked lobster in the shell* should be cooked (steamed or boiled) directly from the freezer.

Freezing lobster meat in a home freezer is not recommended; shellfish should be frozen very quickly and is best done by commercial packers. If you must freeze at home, use only very fresh cooked lobster meat; do not freeze lobster that has already been refrigerated for a time. Lobster meat frozen at home should be used within a month, and even then the flesh may be stringy and watery.

To freeze cooked lobster meat, either leave the meat in the tail and claw shells and wrap each piece tightly, or wrap shelled meat in small packages. Always use heavy wrap designed specifically for freezers. Before freezing lobster bodies, remove the stomach sacs, intestinal tracts, and spongy gills; then freeze in freezer bags to use later in soups and stocks.

Preparation: The hardest task for many cooks is killing the lobster. There are two humane ways to do it. The lobster's brain lies between and just behind its eyes, and its heart is about 1 inch behind its brain. Both are shielded by the hard upper shell. The fastest way to kill a lobster is to thrust a sharp, heavy knife down through the top shell just behind the eyes and then to cut down the length of the body shell, severing both the brain and the heart and instantly killing the lobster; any further movement is due to muscle reflex action only.

Fast-Boil Method: The second method is to bring a big pot of water to a rolling boil, adding 1 tablespoon of salt for each quart of water. Plunge the lobsters headfirst (and one by one to try

to keep the heavy boil) into the water. Cook for 1–2 minutes after the water returns to a rolling boil. Remove the lobsters and cool immediately to stop the cooking action by running them under cold water or refrigerating them.

To partially cook lobsters: Continue the Fast-Boil Method slightly longer if you wish then to remove the meat from the shell and sauté it, use it in a quick stir-fry, or add it to a soup, stew, or paella.

Claws only: 3 minutes or less

Lobsters of 1 pound or less: 4 minutes

1–1½-pound lobsters: 5 minutes

1½–2-pound lobsters: 6 minutes

2–3-pound lobsters: 7–8 minutes

3–4-pound lobsters: 12 minutes

To cut an uncooked or partially cooked lobster in half: Grip the lobster firmly just behind the claws and set it, back side up, on a cutting board sitting in a pan or tray that will catch all the lobster juices to be used later for stock or stew. Insert a sharp, heavy knife through the upper shell just behind the eyes and cut down and completely through the center of the length of the body and tail. Turn the lobster end for end and cut through the head so that the lobster is separated into two equal halves. Discard the stomach sac at the front of the body cavity, just beneath the eyes; it is a translucent beige sac usually containing grit, and since you may have cut it in

LOBSTER

Lobster (continued)

two when you cut the lobster in half, look for the sac on both sides of the shell. Remove the long threadlike intestinal tract. Reserve the liver, or tomalley (if you wish to use it), which is a beige-green color but turns pale green when cooked. If the lobster is female, save the roe (if you wish to use it), which is a dark green-black but turns orange-red when cooked. You may want to remove the tip of the head where the eyes are located and the antennae are attached, along with the long antennae.

To cut an uncooked or partially cooked lobster in pieces: Proceed as above for cutting an uncooked or partially cooked lobster in half, but instead of cutting down through the entire length of the lobster from the head through the tail, stop when you come to the place where the body section ends and the tail begins. Turn the lobster end for end and finish cutting the head end in two. Turn the lobster on its back and cut crosswise where the tail and body meet to separate them. Cut the tail crosswise into equal sections. Remove the claws and elbows (or knuckles) from the body. As above, remove the stomach sac and intestinal tract and the eyes and antennae, and remove and reserve the tomalley and any roe, if desired.

To cut an uncooked or partially cooked lobster for stir-frying: Proceed as in *To cut an uncooked or partially cooked lobster in pieces,* above, and in addition, cut between the elbow

joints and chop each claw in two, separating the pincers, and then chop the larger pincer in two.

To butterfly an uncooked or partially cooked lobster: To kill a lobster that you wish to butterfly, thrust a sharp, heavy knife down through the top shell just behind the eyes and cut down through the body for several inches to sever both the brain and the heart. Do not cut completely down the length of the lobster shell.

Turn the uncooked lobster or a partially cooked lobster on its back, and split the underside of the lobster in half from end to end without going through the back shell. Spread the halves of the lobster apart in a butterfly shape. (Don't worry if some of the bottom shell cracks a bit.) Clean the body cavity as above.

Cooking:

1. *Steamed lobster.* This is my preferred method of cooking lobsters to eat as is, or for obtaining cooked lobster meat.

Put 2 inches of water into a large kettle or lobster pot. Place a steamer basket or an inverted pie or cake tin in the bottom, or use the steamer insert that comes with a lobster pot. Cover the kettle and bring the water to a rolling boil. Curl the tails of the lobsters under, and drop the lobsters headfirst into the kettle. Do not crowd the kettle. Cover and cook on the following schedule:

    1¼-pound lobsters,
       12 minutes
    1½-pound lobsters,
       15 minutes
    2-pound lobsters, 20 minutes

    3-pound lobsters, 30 minutes
If you cram 5–6 small lobsters or 3–4 big lobsters in the same pot, count on a slightly longer cooking time.

Using tongs, remove the lobsters and serve, or cool and remove the meat.

2. *Boiled lobster.* Fill a large kettle two-thirds full of water and bring to a rolling boil. Drop the lobsters in headfirst, making sure not to crowd the pot or spill the water over the side. Cover the pot and bring the water back to a rolling boil, reduce the heat until the water boils gently, and start timing the cooking on the schedule above for steamed lobster.

3. *Poached lobster.* This technique is often found on restaurant menus. The lobsters are cooked in a court bouillon, or flavored broth. Some cooks think that the gentle poach yields a more succulent lobster, and others suggest that the seasonings in the broth enhance the lobster's flavor. After a number of experiments, I find very little difference, but I happily instruct you how to do it so that you can experiment yourself. Prepare a *Court Bouillon* (page 219), multiplying the recipe as necessary to accommodate the number of lobsters you are cooking. Bring the finished broth to a full boil, drop in the lobsters headfirst and one by one so as not to cool the water too rapidly from the temperature of the lobsters, and allow to boil for 1 minute. Reduce the heat and poach gently (that is, cook just under a simmer), using the schedule for steamed lobster above.

LOBSTER

4. *Roast lobster.* This is a particularly good method for a very large lobster that won't fit handily into any of your kettles. Large lobsters are cheaper per pound, and they can be spectacular to serve to a group. One 8-pound lobster will yield 1½–2 pounds of meat, enough for 4 diners. Roasting seems to intensify the flavor of lobster; if your fish market can provide seaweed to put around the lobster while it roasts, the seaweed will help to keep the lobster moist and will give off a nice fragrance during the roasting.

Preheat the oven to 475 degrees. Put ⅜ inch of water into a large, covered roasting pan. Plunge a sharp, heavy knife into the upper shell of the lobster just between and behind the eyes, and cut down and back through the shell 2–3 inches to kill the lobster instantly. Place the lobster in the roasting pan, cover with seaweed if you have it (if you don't, check the water level in the pan occasionally as the lobster roasts and add more water, if necessary), and cover the pan. Cook as follows:

1–1½-pound lobster,
    15 minutes
1½–2-pound lobster,
    20 minutes
3-pound lobster, 30 minutes
4–6-pound lobster,
    45 minutes
8–10-pound lobster,
    60 minutes

Drain and present the cooked lobster, then remove the meat and serve with melted butter. Reserve any juices from opening the lobster to remove the meat for making a stock or sauce.

5. *Grilled Lobster* (see page 188)

6. *Baked lobster* (see *Baked Stuffed Lobster for Two,* page 202)

7. *Broiled Lobster* (see page 189).

8. *To cook lobsterettes:* Prepare a *Court Bouillon* (page 219), and when it is completed, bring it to a boil again, drop the lobsterettes into the boiling water, reduce the heat, and simmer for 12–15 minutes or until cooked through. Serve in the shell. Use uncooked tails for scampi recipes; cooked tail meat can be used much like lobster or shrimp. This method is equally appropriate for the freshwater crawfish that resembles the lobsterette in size.

9. *To cook spiny lobster tails:* If you live where lobster tails are only available frozen, thaw them in the refrigerator or, if you are in a hurry, under cold running water. Slit the undershell, if desired, before cooking to facilitate removal of the meat. Drop the tails into boiling water and cook about 1 minute per ounce. The lobster tails are done when they lose their translucent look and the meat turns opaque. Raw or cooked, the meat may be substituted for most lobster recipes. I do not recommend using frozen lobster meat for mousses because the thawed meat still retains moisture from the freezing that can affect the consistency of the mousse. If you must use frozen meat, make sure it is thoroughly defrosted, press as much moisture from it as you can, and pat it dry before further cooking. If you want to cook the meat partially

before using it in a recipe, drop the tails into boiling water, cook for 5 minutes after the water returns to a boil, drain, and cool immediately.

There are a few special cooking techniques for the spiny lobster tail:

"Piggyback" lobster tail. With the back or top side of the shell up, insert sharp scissors and cut lengthwise down the center of the shell, from the end where the body was attached down to just above the tail fans. Lift the raw flesh up through the slit so that it rests on top of the shell in a piggyback fashion. Brush the flesh with melted butter and broil about 6 inches from the heat.

"Butterflied" lobster tail. With the back or top side of the shell up, insert sharp scissors and cut lengthwise down the center of the shell, from the end where the body was attached down to just above the tail fans. Slice the meat inside the shell down to the undershell and spread the opening in the shell apart to form a butterfly shape. Brush the flesh with melted butter and broil about 6 inches from the heat.

"Fan-cut" lobster tail. With the back or top side of the shell down against the work surface, cut off the undershell with sharp scissors, leaving the tail fans in place. Bend open smaller tail shells or use skewers on larger tails to ensure that the tails will lie flat during cooking. Brush the flesh with melted butter and broil about 6 inches from the heat. This method is practical for charcoal grilling larger lobster

Special Information About

LOBSTER

Lobster (continued)

tails; the hard top of the shell protects the flesh. Baste with butter or a favorite marinade and grill until the flesh turns opaque. Small tails prepared with a fan cut are perfect for a batter deep-fry.

To cut a cooked lobster in half: Cut lengthwise through the top and bottom shells and flesh with a heavy knife. Spread the lobster open, remove the stomach sac at the front of the body cavity just below the eyes, and the intestinal tract that runs the length of the body and tail. Crack the claws, if desired.

To remove meat from a cooked lobster: With a twisting motion, separate the tail of the lobster from the body. Break off the fans at the end of the tail and push the tail meat out the wider end where the tail was attached to the body. Twist or break off the knuckles and claws. Crack the knuckles and push or fork the knuckle

meat out. Crack the claws gently so as not to tear or crush the meat inside, and break off the small pincers. Either cut away the top shell with strong shears to remove the meat in one piece, or carefully fork out the meat. Break off the legs and, if you are endowed with great patience, pick out the meat. Inside the body there are some particularly sweet nuggets of meat; the larger the lobster, the more your search for them will be rewarded. If you are going to cook the body shell, be sure to remove the stomach sac.

Yields: The ratio of the weight of a live lobster to its usable meat is approximately 4:1. If the lobster has recently molted, the ratio may be closer to 5:1. With this ratio in mind you can compare the relative costs of buying live lobsters or shelled, cooked lobster meat for recipes in which you do not need lobster in the shell. If the price per pound of cooked lobster meat is significantly more

than four times as much as the price per pound of live lobster, economy is on the side of buying live lobsters. If you carefully buy live lobsters, you also have the advantage of knowing the meat is very fresh, and you can use the juices and shell for stock.

❖ A 1-pound lobster yields 4–4½ ounces of meat
❖ A 1½-pound lobster yields 6 ounces of meat
❖ A 2-pound lobster yields 8 ounces of meat
❖ A 3-pound lobster yields 12 ounces of meat
❖ A 5-pound lobster yields 1 pound, 4 ounces of meat
❖ 1½ pounds of lobster tails, shell on (about six 4-ounce tails), yield 1¼ pounds of meat
❖ 5 shelled lobster tails yield 1 pound of meat
Since lobster meat shouldn't be packed down, count on 6 ounces of meat being close to a cup in bulk measure; 12 ounces will be about 1¾–2 cups.

Grilled Lobster

Grilling is a treatment that adds a lovely flavor to lobster and gets one out of the kitchen to prepare it. It looks and is simple, but there are some pitfalls to beware of. One way to grill lobster is to halve a live lobster and grill it raw; but if that is not the best way for you, then you can use the *Fast-Boil Method* (page 185) to kill the lobster before grilling it. This method also seems to help keep the lobster meat from sticking to the shell during the grilling. Do not cook the lobsters more than 1–2 minutes by the *Fast-Boil Method* before transferring

them to the grill. (I have tried to grill partially steamed lobsters, but the meat tasted mushy.) Grill the lobsters over medium heat; if the fire is too hot, the lobster meat will taste burned. A cover for the grill or a tent of aluminum foil over the lobsters is essential during grilling to enable them to cook evenly. Once you get the hang of it, you'll be grilling lobsters all the time. Serve with a Greek salad or potato salad, and enjoy presiding over the cooking from a deck chair.

Four 1½-lb lobsters
Vegetable oil
⅔ cup melted butter
Lemon wedges and fresh lemon juice (optional)

Prepare each lobster as in *To cut an uncooked or partially cooked lobster in half* (page 185), using the *Fast-Boil Method* (page 185) to kill the lobsters, if you wish. Clean out the body cavities as instructed on page 186, and if you plan to use the tomalley or any roe, place it back in the upper body cavity. Crack the top side of the claws and knuckles, trying not to tip them and lose any of their juices. Rub the shells with vegetable oil and spoon the melted butter evenly over the lobster meat and, if you can, into the cracks of the claws and knuckles. Place the lobster bodies, shell side down, on a grill rack over medium heat. Place the claws and knuckles, cracked side up, on the rack. Cover the lobsters with the grill lid or a tent of aluminum foil and cook for 8–15 minutes, depending on the heat of the fire, or until the meat is opaque (white) and firm. Serve with lemon wedges and, if desired, with more melted butter seasoned with fresh lemon juice.   SERVES 4

❖Grill larger or smaller lobsters and adjust the grilling time accordingly.

❖Add dried fennel branches, mesquite, or wood chips to the fire to create smoke that will further flavor the lobster.

❖Use melted *Escargot Butter Roll* (page 353) as the basting butter, or use one of the other flavored butters from page 352. Or baste the lobsters with virgin olive oil or a flavored oil in place of the melted butter.

❖*To grill-steam lobsters:* Kill the lobsters by cutting through the upper shell just behind the eyes as instructed in *Roast lobster* (page 187). Place each lobster on a large piece of aluminum foil and fold the foil around the lobster to make a loose package. Pour ½ cup water into each package and seal the foil tightly. Place each package, sealed side up, on a grill rack 6–7 inches above the coals. Cook for 20–25 minutes, rotating the packages occasionally or covering the packages with a grill lid or foil tent to ensure even cooking, or until the meat is white and firm. (To test, undo one package and cut into the tail meat; if the meat is not completely cooked, wrap the package up again and grill a little longer.)

❖*Broiled Lobster:* Prepare each small lobster as in *To butterfly an uncooked or partially cooked lobster* (page 186), or each large lobster as in *To cut an uncooked or partially cooked lobster in half* (page 185). Clean out the body cavity (page 186), leaving the tomalley (if you wish to use it) and any roe in the cavity. Remove the claws and knuckles from the lobster bodies and crack

them slightly on their top sides. Oil the shells with vegetable oil and liberally baste the lobster meat with melted butter, spooning some into the cracks of the claws and knuckles if you can. Place the claws and knuckles, cracked side up, on a broiler rack about 5–6 inches from the heat and cook for 3–4 minutes, then add the lobster bodies, flesh side up. Baste often so that the meat will not dry out. Cook for 8–15 minutes, depending on the heat of the broiler, or until the meat has just turned opaque. Top with buttered bread crumbs, if you like, and toast briefly again under the broiler. Serve with lemon wedges and melted butter or with a dipping sauce.

Lobster Fra Diavolo

The Italian equivalent to Lobster Américaine (see page 191) is this superb dish of lobster cooked in a sauce of ripe red tomatoes. I have had glorious versions of this dish in the Italian North End of Boston, some of them laced with clams, mussels, scallops, or squid and inspiring the variations in the notes at the end of the recipe. In summer months I use garden tomatoes, but out of season I use two parts canned Italian plum tomatoes for flavor to one part fresh tomato pulp for texture. You will need a wide, high-sided sauté pan to hold all the lobster pieces and their sauce.

> Three 1½-lb lobsters
> ½ cup olive oil
> ½ cup cognac
> ½ cup chopped onions
> 2–3 tsp finely chopped garlic
> 1–1½ cups dry vermouth or white wine
> 3 Tb tomato paste
> 4 cups peeled, seeded, and chopped tomatoes
> ¼ cup chopped parsley, plus more for garnish
> 2 Tb chopped fresh basil or 1 Tb dried
> 1 Tb chopped fresh oregano or 1 tsp dried
> ⅛ tsp red pepper flakes
> Salt and freshly ground pepper
> Hot pepper sauce (optional)

Prepare the lobster as in *To cut an uncooked or partially cooked lobster in half* (page 185), using the *Fast-Boil Method* (page 185) to kill the lobsters if you like. Clean out the body cavity (see page 186), reserving

Lobster Fra Diavolo (continued)

the tomalley and any roe, if you wish to use them. Cut the body and tail sections in half crosswise, twist off the claws, separate the claws and elbows, and slightly crack each claw.

In a wide, high-sided sauté pan large enough to hold half the lobster without crowding in one layer, heat ¼ cup of the olive oil, add half the lobster pieces, and sauté on all sides, turning them, for 3–4 minutes until the shells turn red. Pour ¼ cup of the cognac into the pan, flame it, and shake the pan until the flames die out. Remove the lobster to a warm platter and repeat the process with the second batch of lobster, starting with the heating of ¼ cup of oil in the pan.

After the second batch of lobster has been cooked and removed to the warm platter, drain all but 2 tablespoons of oil from the pan. Add the onions and cook over medium heat for 3–4 minutes, or until the onions are wilted; then add the garlic and stir all together. Pour in the vermouth or wine, bring the mixture to a boil, and cook until the liquid is reduced by half. Combine the tomato paste with the tomatoes and add the mixture to the pan along with the parsley, basil, oregano, red pepper flakes, and 1 teaspoon salt. Stir to combine all together. Bring the mixture to a boil, return the lobster to the pan, cover, and cook gently over lowered heat for 15–20 minutes, basting occasionally.

If you wish to use the tomalley and roe, remove the lobster pieces again to a warm platter and sieve the tomalley and roe into the sauce by pressing through a fine strainer. Stir well and simmer for 1–2 minutes until the roe turns red. Season, as needed, with salt and freshly ground pepper, and with drops of hot pepper sauce, if desired.

Serve with linguine or rice and top with additional chopped parsley; or serve in bowls with crusty Italian bread.   SERVES 6

❖Add hard-shell clams or mussels—3–4 littleneck clams or mussels per person. Scrub the shellfish under cold water, then add to the sauce for the last 10 minutes of cooking.

❖Cut cleaned squid into thin rings and add to the sauce for the last 2 minutes of cooking.

❖Add scallops for the last 4 minutes of cooking.

❖Use a favorite homemade tomato sauce. Prepare the lobsters as above, and add the sauce immediately after the lobster has been flamed in cognac. Finish cooking as above.

Lobster, Artichokes, and Chicken

Lobster meat is expensive, and since one point of cooking is not to break the bank, it is economical to combine it with complementary flavors and textures. Here is a trio of lobster, artichokes, and chicken, all enrobed in a light sauce and each retaining its own fine character without being overridden by the companion ingredients. The chicken and lobster can be prepared ahead, and the fresh artichokes can be cooked ahead as well. If fresh artichokes are not available, feel free to use frozen artichokes or canned, drained, and rinsed artichokes, artichoke hearts, or quartered artichoke bottoms.

FRESH ARTICHOKES

8 baby artichokes
1 lemon, cut in half
½ cup flour
2 Tb fresh lemon juice
1 tsp salt

SAUCE

2 Tb butter
¼ cup chopped shallots
2 Tb flour
1¼ cups dry vermouth or white wine
2 cups *Lobster Stock* (page 358) or
     chicken broth
1 Tb finely chopped fresh marjoram
Salt and freshly ground pepper
½ lemon

½ cup light olive oil or vegetable oil
4 crushed cloves garlic
¼ lb trimmed and quartered mushrooms
1½ lb boneless skinned chicken breasts, cut into
     1–1½-inch pieces
Salt and freshly ground pepper
1 Tb butter
¾–1 lb cooked lobster meat, cut into 1-inch
     pieces

To prepare the fresh baby artichokes: Wash the artichokes, break off the outer leaves down to the tender pale green leaves, trim the stems, and cut about ⅜ of an inch off the top of each artichoke. Rub all the cut areas with fresh lemon to prevent discoloration. In a saucepan, whisk together the flour and ½ cup water; then beat in 1 quart water, the lemon juice, and salt. Bring the mixture to a boil, reduce the heat, and simmer for 5 minutes to make a flour-water, or blanc, in which the artichokes can cook without discoloring. Add the artichokes to the pan, making sure they are covered by the liquid. Simmer them for about 15 minutes, or until just tender when pierced by a small knife. Remove the artichokes, drain them, and scoop out the fuzzy chokes from their centers. If the artichokes are bite-size, leave them whole; if they are larger, cut them in thirds or halves, and set aside.

To make the sauce: In a saucepan, melt 2 tablespoons butter, stir in the shallots, and cook them for 2 minutes. Sprinkle the flour into the butter-and-shallot mixture and cook, stirring, for another 2 minutes. Remove the pan from the heat and whisk in 1 cup of the vermouth or wine and the lobster stock or chicken broth. Continue whisking until the mixture is smooth, then return the pan to the heat and add the marjoram. Bring the sauce to a boil, whisking, and boil gently for about 15–20 minutes, or until the sauce has reduced to 1–1¼ cups. Season the sauce with salt and freshly ground pepper and a squeeze of lemon juice.

While the sauce is cooking, heat ¼ cup of the oil in a large sauté pan over medium heat. Add the garlic, and stir it with the oil for 1 minute to release its perfume to the oil, but do not let the garlic brown. Add the artichokes and mushrooms, toss to coat with the oil, and cook for 4–5 minutes or until lightly colored. Remove the artichokes and mushrooms to a warm plate, and remove and discard the garlic.

Sprinkle the chicken with salt and freshly ground pepper. Wipe out the sauté pan, heat 2–3 tablespoons oil, add chicken, and cook over medium-high heat, stirring, for 4–5 minutes, or until the chicken is cooked through. Transfer to a warm plate.

Wipe out the sauté pan again and heat 1 tablespoon butter and 1 tablespoon oil. Add the lobster meat and toss over medium-high heat for 1 minute. Add the remaining ¼ cup of vermouth or wine and boil rapidly until the liquid in the pan has almost evaporated. Return the artichokes and the chicken to the pan. Add the reduced sauce to the pan and fold it into the artichokes, chicken, and lobster. Heat thoroughly. Season with salt and pepper, and serve with rice.   SERVES 4

❖Add a little heavy cream to enrich the sauce.

Lobster Américaine

The origins of Homard à l'Américaine, also referred to as Lobster Américaine in a melding of two languages, are subject to dispute. Some authorities say the dish was created in Brittany and named for a province where lobsters were plentiful; other sources assert that the dish was created by a French chef who loved tomatoes for a favorite American patron. The traditional method involves cooking the lobster and the sauce together, but I prepare the sauce first to ensure that the lobster meat is not overcooked. I use whole lobsters, but the dish is suitable for lobster tails only. The dish is awfully good and very quickly prepared: sautéed lobster briefly simmered in a flavored fresh tomato sauce. There are two stopping points along the way for make-ahead preparation to take pressure off the cook at mealtime. I like to serve this with a mixture of white and wild rice, and with sautéed corn and a green salad.

Three 2-lb lobsters
½ cup light olive oil
4 Tb butter
1½ cups chopped leeks or onions
1 cup chopped carrots
1 tsp mashed garlic
4 cups peeled, seeded, and chopped tomatoes
3 Tb tomato paste
1 cup fish stock or chicken broth
1 cup dry vermouth or white wine
1 Tb fresh tarragon or 1 tsp dried
¼ cup chopped parsley
Salt and freshly ground pepper
⅓ cup cognac or Pernod
Fresh lemon juice
Hot pepper sauce
3 Tb softened butter (optional)

Prepare the lobsters as in *To cut an uncooked or partially cooked lobster in pieces* (page 186), using the *Fast-Boil Method* (page 185) to kill the lobsters if you wish, and then cut the lobsters into pieces. Reserve the tomalley and any roe (if you wish to use them). Refrigerate the lobster pieces and the optional tomalley and roe.

To prepare the sauce, heat 2 tablespoons of the oil and 1 tablespoon of the butter in a saucepan. Add the

Lobster Américaine (continued)

leeks or onions and carrots, and cook about 5 minutes, or until the vegetables are lightly colored and wilted. Add the garlic, tomatoes, tomato paste, fish stock or chicken broth, vermouth or white wine, tarragon, and 2 tablespoons of the parsley. Cover and cook gently for 5 minutes, then uncover and cook for 8–10 minutes more to reduce the juices. (You can refrigerate the sauce at this point and continue the recipe later.)

To sauté the lobster, cook in three batches to avoid overcrowding. In a sauté pan that is large enough to eventually hold all of the lobster, heat 2 tablespoons of the oil and 1 tablespoon of the butter until very hot; stir in one-third of the lobster, toss, season with salt and freshly ground pepper, and sauté until the shells turn red, about 3–4 minutes. Remove the lobster from the pan and continue with the other two batches, adding 2 tablespoons of the oil and 1 tablespoon of the butter to the pan for each batch.

Return all the lobster to the sauté pan, place over medium heat, pour in the cognac or Pernod, flame it, shaking the pan until the flames die out, and cook the lobster for 3 minutes more. (You can set both the lobster and the tomato sauce aside in the refrigerator at this point, to finish later. You can also remove the lobster meat from the shells, if you prefer.)

Flavor the tomato sauce with a few drops of lemon juice, a dash of hot pepper sauce, and salt and freshly ground pepper. Pour the sauce over the lobster, stir well, and cook gently for 5–6 minutes to finish. While the lobster is cooking in its sauce, blend the tomalley and roe (if you are using them) with the softened butter in a small bowl. Remove the lobster pieces to a warm platter. Beat a cupful of the warm sauce into the tomalley butter, then whisk the mixture back into the rest of the sauce. Heat gently, stirring, to thicken the sauce. Pour the sauce over the lobster, sprinkle with the remaining parsley, and serve.   SERVES 6

❖Traditional recipes use only butter to cook the sauce and sauté the lobster. You can do that, or you can eliminate the butter completely and use only olive or vegetable oil. Omit the tomalley butter completely in the latter case.

❖This dish is traditionally served with rice or risotto, but it is also very good served on top of pasta (try corkscrew or shell shapes).

Lobster in Puff Pastry

By merely changing the size of the puff-pastry rectangles and the amount of lobster meat, you can make this dish into either a luxurious appetizer or a sumptuous main course. Homemade puff pastry is delicious, but preparing it is time consuming. There is very good ready-made puff pastry available in boxed packages of pastry sheets in the frozen-food section of supermarkets; I use the Pepperidge Farm brand pastry sheets. Note that the thickness of the pastry sheets determines the cooking time and the height of the cooked puffs: see the instructions for using a thicker sheet of homemade puff pastry in the *Using homemade puff pastry* variation that follows this recipe. Always try to keep the pastry as cold as possible as you work with it. If you wish to avoid butter sauces, try the *Sweet Pepper Sauce* (page 195) or *Sauce Américaine* (page 357). Or omit a sauce completely and heat the lobster in a sauté pan with just a film of wine or broth or even water, and serve it on the puff pastry with a garnish of lemon wedges. Serve boiled baby red potatoes to dip into the sauce, and accompany the lobster with a side dish of steamed or roasted vegetables.

Alternative fish or shellfish: big lumps of crabmeat; a combination of poached fish such as monkfish and cooked shellfish

> 1 package puff pastry (2 pastry sheets, each
>   about 9 inches × 10 inches)
> Flour for rolling the pastry
> 2½ lb lobster meat (5 oz per person)
> *Lemon Butter Sauce* (page 357) or *White Butter
>   Sauce* (page 114)
> 1 egg beaten with 1 tsp water
> 2 Tb butter
> 1 Tb light oil
> 2 Tb chopped shallots
> Fresh sprigs of parsley for garnish

The packaged puff pastry sheets that I use come pre-rolled to a thickness between ⅛ inch and ¼ inch. There are 2 sheets of pastry to a package, each about 9 inches × 10 inches in size. One sheet will be enough for 8 light rectangular puffs that will be split in the middle for the lobster stuffing. If you like a high and impressive puff-pastry rectangle, see the variation that follows this recipe for making double-height puffs using 2 sheets of pastry.

Flour a smooth—and cold, if possible—work surface, and place one sheet of the pastry on the surface. Roll the sheet into a 10 × 10-inch square. Cut out 8 rectangles, each approximately 2½ inches × 5 inches. Spread the rectangles on a baking sheet, cover and refrigerate for at least 20–30 minutes.

Cut the lobster meat into bite-size pieces, place in a bowl, and refrigerate.

Just before you cook the puff pastry, make the lemon butter sauce or white butter sauce and keep the sauce warm in a double boiler.

Decorate the top of the pastry rectangles, if you wish, by making intersecting diagonal lines with a sharp knife. Brush the tops of the pastry with the egg beaten with water, but do not let the egg glaze run down the sides of the pastry. Let the glaze sit for 1 minute, then repeat with a second brushing. Bake the pastry rectangles in a preheated 450-degree oven for 10–12 minutes or until puffed and browned. (You can bake the rectangles slightly in advance of serving and hold them in a warm oven.)

While the pastry is baking, combine the butter and oil in a wide, nonstick sauté pan, heat them over low heat, stir in the shallots, and add the lobster meat. Turn the lobster pieces in the pan until well coated and gradually warm the lobster mixture until it is hot and sizzling.

Split the baked puff pastries in half horizontally. Place the bottom halves on 8 warm serving plates and evenly divide the lobster meat on top, lifting the lobster from the sauté pan with a slotted spoon to drain off any excess butter or oil. Spoon the lemon butter sauce or white butter sauce over the lobster and set the pastry tops on the sauced lobster at a slight angle from the pastry bottoms. Garnish, if you like, with a sprig of parsley.   SERVES 8 AS A MAIN COURSE

❖If you wish to have a higher puff-pastry rectangle, cut 16 rectangles using 2 sheets of the packaged pastry. Instead of splitting each puff rectangle in half, use 2 rectangles for each serving. Place one rectangle on each serving plate, top with the lobster and sauce as above, and top the sauced lobster with another puff-pastry rectangle.

❖*Using homemade puff pastry:* If you use homemade pastry, roll it to a ¼-inch-thick sheet. This will give you a higher cooked puff rectangle than the prerolled packaged sheets. Cut the pastry into rectangles as above, and push a skewer down through each rectangle in two or three places. This will stabilize the thicker pastry and the top will not tip over as it bakes. Bake at 450 degrees for 15–18 minutes, or until puffed and lightly browned. Split the baked puff pastries in half horizontally. Remove any inner layers of pastry that are slightly undercooked in these thicker puffs.

Sautéed Lobster with an Aromatic Vegetable Cream Sauce

This richly delicious dish can be served in its own juices or on top of fresh pasta or steamed rice. It is virtually a meal in itself for four lucky people.

> Two 1½-lb lobsters
> 4 Tb butter
> 1 cup finely chopped carrots
> 1 cup finely chopped leeks
> 1 cup finely chopped celery
> 3 Tb light olive oil
> ¼ cup cognac
> 1 cup heavy cream
> 2 cups peeled, seeded, and chopped tomatoes
> Salt and freshly ground pepper
> 1 Tb chopped parsley
> 1 Tb chopped fennel leaves

Prepare the lobsters as in *To cut an uncooked or partially cooked lobster in pieces* (page 186), using the *Fast-Boil Method* (page 185) to kill the lobsters if you like. Clean out the body cavity (see page 186). Remove the claws and separate them from the knuckle joints. With a hammer or the back of a heavy knife, make a crack in each of the claws and knuckles. Reserve all the lobster pieces in a bowl.

In a small sauté pan, melt 2 tablespoons of the butter, stir in the carrots, leeks, and celery, cover, and cook gently about 8 minutes, stirring occasionally, or until the vegetables are wilted and tender. Set aside.

In a sauté pan large enough to hold the lobster pieces in one layer without crowding, heat the olive oil, add the lobster pieces, and sauté for 3–4 minutes, stirring, until the shells begin to turn red. Add the remaining 2 tablespoons of butter and continue cooking for 3 minutes more. Pour in the cognac, flame it, and shake the pan until the flames die down. Add the cream, tomatoes, and reserved vegetables,

Sautéed Lobster with an Aromatic Vegetable Cream Sauce
(continued)

and season with salt and freshly ground pepper. Cook
for 4–5 minutes to reduce and thicken the sauce,
turning the lobster pieces occasionally.

Remove the lobster pieces to a warm serving platter. Mix together the parsley and fennel, and stir two-
thirds of the mixture into the sauce. Pour the sauce
over the lobster and sprinkle the remaining herbs
over all.   SERVES 4

Lobster in a Cabbage Leaf with a Sweet Pepper Sauce

Cabbage leaves are used in dishes from many different
countries as a wrapping for delicious stuffings. In this
instance, the stuffing is sweet cooked lobster meat.
The pale green packets are steamed and then served
with a sweet pepper sauce that looks wonderful
against the cabbage and complements the flavors of
both the cabbage and the lobster. This lobster dish is a
good candidate if you are looking for a comparatively

low-calorie way of serving lobster. All the steps, including the final assembly of the lobster-cabbage packets, can be prepared ahead.

Alternative shellfish or fish: Combine lobster with chunks of poached monkfish or with scallops.

SWEET PEPPER SAUCE

1½ lb sweet red peppers
2 Tb olive oil
1 cup chopped onions
¼ cup chopped celery, stalk and
    leaves
1 tsp minced garlic
1½ cups peeled, seeded, and
    chopped tomatoes
½ tsp thyme
Salt and freshly ground pepper

To make the Sweet Pepper Sauce: Peel the red peppers as instructed on page 360. Cut the peppers lengthwise into strips and set aside. In a sauté pan, heat the oil, add the onions and celery, and cook until wilted and golden, about 4–5 minutes. Add the garlic and cook for 30 seconds. Stir in the peppers, tomatoes, and thyme, and season the mixture with salt and freshly ground pepper. Cover the pan and cook for 5 minutes, then uncover and simmer for 15–30 minutes or until thickened; cooking time will depend on the juiciness of the tomatoes. Purée the mixture in a blender, food processor, or food mill until it is smooth. Add more salt and pepper, if necessary.

MAKES ABOUT 2½–3 CUPS

LOBSTER IN A CABBAGE LEAF

1 head savoy cabbage
2 Tb butter
Salt and freshly ground pepper
2 lb cooked lobster meat
Lemon wedges (optional)

Prepare the sweet pepper sauce and set aside.

To prepare the cabbage and lobster: Core the cabbage and carefully remove 8 of the largest, best-looking leaves. Bring a pot of water to a boil, drop in the 8 leaves, and blanch for 2–3 minutes until they are wilted. Drain the leaves and run them under cold water to stop the cooking action, drain again, and pat dry with paper towels. With a sharp paring knife shave off some of the thickest part of the midrib so that all parts of the cabbage leaf are of uniform thickness. This will make the cabbage leaf easier to roll. Finely slice the remaining raw cabbage until you have 3–4 cups sliced cabbage. In a sauté pan, heat the butter, add the sliced cabbage, and cook over low heat, stirring, until it is wilted and tender. Season the sautéed cabbage with salt and freshly ground pepper. Set aside to cool slightly. (You will have about 2 cups.)

Slice the lobster meat into bite-size pieces.

To assemble the packets: Spread out one of the large blanched cabbage leaves with the inner side of the leaf facing up. Place one-eighth of the lobster meat in a mound on the lower third of the leaf's surface closest to the rib end. Spread about ¼ cup of the cooked sliced cabbage over the lobster meat. Fold the rib end of the leaf over the filling, then fold the two sides of the leaf up over the filling, and roll the filled cabbage

Lobster in a Cabbage Leaf with a Sweet Pepper Sauce
(continued)

over to the top of the leaf to make a tight packet.
Secure the packet with a toothpick, if you wish.
Complete this step for each of the 8 leaves.

Place the packets on a perforated steamer rack or
on a plate that will fit into a steamer, and steam them
for 8 minutes or until heated through.

To serve: Reheat the pepper sauce, if necessary.
Place a puddle of sauce on each warm serving plate
and top with a single cabbage-lobster packet for an
appetizer course and with 2 packets for a main course.
Garnish with lemon wedges, if desired.

SERVES 8 AS A FIRST COURSE, 4 AS A MAIN COURSE

❖Peeled roasted red peppers in jars can be substituted for fresh red peppers. Drain before slicing.

Lobster and Chicken Stew

This dish has plenty of color from bright red peppers
and juicy ripe tomatoes. It has the distinctive fragrance
of fennel. And it has a winning blend of flavors: the
sweet taste of lobster, chicken, and peppers; the acidic
balance contributed by the tomatoes; and the pleasant
mild anise, or licorice, accent from the fennel. Rice or
cooked white beans would be a perfect accompaniment. Although the recipe looks to have a number of
steps, there are several stop points. Most of the recipe
can be done ahead, with just a few minutes of final
cooking. It is the ideal recipe to use "culls" (lobsters
with only one claw) for the lobster pieces.

Four 1–1¼-lb lobsters
2 lb fennel bulbs
3 large red peppers
½ cup light olive oil or vegetable oil, plus extra
4 Tb butter
1 chopped carrot
2½ cups chopped onions
1 cup dry vermouth or white wine
4 cups chicken stock
1 large tomato, cut in half
2 Tb tomato paste
Two 3-lb frying chickens
Salt and freshly ground pepper

Paprika
4 cups peeled, seeded, and chopped
    ripe tomatoes
1 Tb puréed garlic
Pinch of sugar
¼ cup chopped parsley

Prepare the lobsters as in *To cut an uncooked or partially
cooked lobster in pieces* (page 186), using the *Fast-Boil
Method* (page 185) to kill them and then cut them into
pieces, if you wish. Clean out the body cavities as
instructed on page 186, reserving the tomalley and
any roe, if you wish to use them. Cut the shells of the
body cavities into pieces and refrigerate them.
Refrigerate the lobster pieces with meat and the
tomalley and roe, if desired.

Wash and trim the fennel bulbs and quarter them
lengthwise without removing the cores. Holding
each quarter by the core, thinly slice the fennel
around the core much as you would slice cabbage for
coleslaw. (You will have about 6 cups sliced fennel.)

Peel the red peppers as instructed on page 360. Cut
the peeled pepper flesh into 1-inch pieces and set
aside.

To make the stock, heat 2 tablespoons of the oil
and 1 tablespoon of the butter in a large, deep-sided
sauté pan; add the carrot, ½ cup of the chopped
onions, and the reserved pieces of lobster body shell,
and sauté for 4–5 minutes. Add the vermouth or
wine, chicken stock, tomato halves, and 1 tablespoon
of the tomato paste, bring the mixture to a boil,
reduce the heat, and simmer for 30 minutes. Strain
the mixture through a fine mesh sieve and set the
strained lobster stock aside in a bowl. (You will have
about 3½ cups.)

While the stock is simmering, cut each chicken
into 8 trimmed pieces, removing the backbones and
wing nubbins. Rinse the chicken pieces, pat them
dry, and sprinkle with salt, freshly ground pepper, and
paprika. Wipe out the sauté pan, add and heat 2 tablespoons of the oil, add the chicken pieces and brown
them on all sides, cooking in two batches and adding
a little more oil for the second batch, if necessary.
Remove the chicken to a plate and set aside.

Wipe out the sauté pan, add and heat 2 tablespoons
of the oil and 1 tablespoon of the butter; add the
reserved lobster pieces with meat and sauté, turning
on all sides, until the shells have turned red. Remove
the lobster to a plate and set aside.

Wipe out the sauté pan again, add and heat 2 tablespoons of the oil and 2 tablespoons of the butter, stir in the remaining 2 cups chopped onions and the sliced fennel bulb, cover, and cook gently for 10 minutes, stirring occasionally. Uncover, stir in the tomalley and roe (if you are using them), and cook for 2 minutes. Add the chopped tomatoes, garlic, reserved lobster stock, the remaining tablespoon of tomato paste, and a pinch of sugar; bring the mixture to a boil, reduce the heat, and simmer for 20–25 minutes to thicken the mixture. (The recipe can be prepared ahead up to this point. Refrigerate the peppers, chicken, lobster, and sauce separately. Resume final cooking by reheating the tomato stew base in the large sauté pan.)

Shortly before serving, add the chicken pieces to the tomato base and cook gently for 10 minutes. Add the lobster pieces, red peppers, and 2 tablespoons of the parsley, and cook for an additional 8 minutes. Season with salt and freshly ground pepper as needed and garnish with the remaining parsley. Provide lobster crackers and plenty of napkins.   SERVES 8

❖In place of whole chickens, use 2 whole boned chicken breasts. Lightly brown the breasts, cut them into several pieces, and set aside. Add them to the stew with the lobster pieces for final cooking, and cook for 8 minutes.

❖For less mess, remove the lobster meat from the shells before serving.

❖For a Spanish-style variation, make a paste of the tomalley and 1 cup ground, peeled, and toasted almonds. Add 2 tablespoons chopped parsley and additional puréed garlic to taste. Stir the mixture into the sauce before adding the chicken.

Dinner-Party Lobster—Five Ways

Lobster is a very special treat to serve to guests at a dinner party, but serving a whole steamed lobster can be a formidable challenge to guests in dinner-party clothes. Here are five different ways to serve lobster in a no-mess, easy-to-eat presentation. In each case you will prepare and partially cook the lobsters earlier in the day, remove the lobster meat from the shells, cut it into bite-size pieces, and return it to the cleaned shells. You also prepare one of the vegetable, herbal, or spiced sauces to enhance the lobster. Hard work in

the morning, to be sure, but very simple and quick to reheat and serve at dinnertime when you want to give your guests your full attention. All the following recipes start with partially steamed and filled lobster shells.

Partially Steamed and Filled Lobster Shells:

   Two 3-lb lobsters

Adapt the recipe to the number of dinner guests; each person will be served half a lobster. Buy larger or smaller lobsters, if you prefer.

In a large pot fitted with a rack for steaming or with a pie pan or cake pan upside down in the bottom, bring 2 inches of water to a full boil, drop the lobsters in headfirst, cover, and steam them for 8 minutes. Remove the lobsters and set them aside until they are cool enough to handle. Separate the claws and knuckles from the lobster bodies. Remove and discard the long feelers, if you wish. Slice the lobsters in half lengthwise with a heavy knife, and remove and discard the stomach sacs and intestinal tracts. Remove the tomalley and any roe; since the lobsters are not fully cooked yet, the roe may still be a dark green-black. Use the tomalley and roe as suggested in the following recipes, if you wish, or discard them.

Remove the tail meat from the shells. Keeping the tail shell attached to the rest of the body shell, wipe out each half shell with paper towels. The half shell will be the serving dish for the portion of lobster. Cut the tail meat into bite-size pieces and return it to the tail shells in an even distribution among the shells. Crack the claws and knuckles, remove the meat, cut it into bite-size pieces, and distribute this meat evenly among the body-cavity part of the shells. Cover the filled shells with plastic wrap and refrigerate.

4 PARTIALLY PREPARED SERVINGS

Steamed Lobster with Chinese Seasonings

For this fragrant, fat-free fixing for lobster you do need to rig a special steamer for the final cooking of the dish. What you need is a firm, flat rack that will sit in a steamer pot. A double-tiered Chinese metal steamer is ideal. You can improvise by using two pots

Dinner-Party Lobster—Five Ways (continued)

with racks, or even a large roasting pan with a cake rack fitted into it as a platform for the lobster meat in the shells.

Aluminum foil
Two 3-lb *Partially Steamed and Filled Lobster Shells* (page 197)
1 cup chicken broth
⅓ cup rice wine
2 Tb soy sauce
3 Tb finely chopped ginger
3 Tb minced scallions
½ tsp sugar
4 scallion flowers (optional)
8 chives, with flowers if possible (optional)
Dipping sauce (optional)

Cut 4 pieces of aluminum foil, each large enough to make a "basket" to set one of the half lobster shells in; the aluminum foil basket, which is to hold the juices that will accumulate when the lobster is cooked, should come up the sides of the lobsters but not over the top at all. Place the lobsters in their aluminum foil baskets just before steaming.

In a saucepan, combine the broth, rice wine, soy sauce, ginger, scallions, and sugar. Bring the mixture to a boil, reduce the heat, and simmer for 2 minutes. Meanwhile, bring 2 inches of water to a boil in the steamer you have rigged. Spoon the sauce over the lobster halves, place the lobsters in their aluminum foil baskets on the rack of the steamer, cover, and steam for 8–10 minutes, or until the lobsters are completely heated through and the meat is opaque.

Using mitts or tongs, carefully lift the lobster halves from their foil baskets to serving plates. Pour any accumulated juices in the foil baskets evenly over the lobster meat. Garnish each serving, if you wish, with a scallion flower and place 2 chives in a crossing pattern over the top of each lobster shell. Serve with a dipping sauce, if desired.   SERVES 4

❖*Soy-Sake Dipping Sauce:* Combine equal parts soy sauce and sake.

❖*Yakitori Dipping Sauce:* Combine ¾ cup dark soy sauce, ½ cup sake, 3 tablespoons mirin (sweet rice wine), 2 tablespoons sugar, bring to a boil, and cook for 2 minutes.

No-Mess Steamed Lobster

Two 3-lb *Partially Steamed and Filled Lobster Shells* (page 197)
1 cup melted butter (optional)
¼ cup lemon juice (optional)
Lemon wedges

Place the filled lobster half shells in aluminum foil baskets, and rig a steamer, as described in the instructions for the preceding recipe, *Steamed Lobster with Chinese Seasonings*. Bring 2 inches of water in the steamer to a boil, carefully place the lobsters in their baskets in the steamer, cover, and steam for 8–10 minutes, or until the lobster meat is completely cooked through and opaque. Lift the lobster halves out of their foil baskets to serving plates, using mitts or tongs.

Combine the butter and lemon juice, if you wish, and serve in small bowls on the side. Garnish the lobster with lemon wedges.   SERVES 4

❖Spoon a favorite sauce or a flavored vinaigrette over the lobster just before serving.

Roast Lobster with Warm Salsa

Tomatoes and lobster are meant for each other; the rich-tasting lobster meat is tempered by the acidic bite of tomatoes. For final cooking, the lobsters are roasted in this treatment and then served with a warm tomato-herb salsa. The salsa can be prepared ahead and reheated while the lobsters are roasting.

WARM SALSA

2 Tb light olive oil
½ chopped large red onion
3 peeled, seeded, and chopped tomatoes
1 peeled, seeded, and chopped green tomato
1 seeded and minced chili pepper
2 tsp red wine vinegar
2 Tb chopped cilantro
2 Tb chopped parsley
Hot pepper sauce
Salt
Sambal oelek★ (optional)

ROAST LOBSTER

Two 3-lb *Partially Steamed and Filled Lobster
    Shells* (page 197)
⅔ cup melted butter
2 Tb lemon juice
Lemon wedges

*Sambal oelek is a fresh, ground chili paste avail-
able in many Chinese and Mexican markets and
in specialty-food stores.

To make the warm salsa: In a saucepan, heat the oil, add
the onion, and sauté it until it wilts and turns golden.
Add the red and green tomatoes, cover, and cook over
medium heat for 5 minutes. Uncover the pan, add the
chili pepper and vinegar, and cook gently to evaporate
some of the liquid and thicken the sauce for 5 minutes.
Add the cilantro, parsley, a dash of hot pepper sauce,
and season with salt. Add small amounts of sambal
oelek, if you like, or other hot chili paste or more hot
pepper sauce to taste. Remove from the heat and set
aside or refrigerate until shortly before serving.

To roast the lobsters: Put the lobster halves on a baking sheet. Combine the butter and lemon juice, and
spoon the mixture over the lobster meat in the shells.
Roast the lobsters in a preheated 500-degree oven
about 10 minutes, or until they are cooked through.

Just before serving, bring the salsa to a boil. Place
the roasted lobster halves on serving plates and spoon
the hot salsa partially over the lobster. Garnish the
plate with lemon wedges.   SERVES 4

❖Serve the salsa on the side rather than spooning it
over the lobster, and garnish the lobster with lemon
wedges.

*Roast Lobster with Tarragon
and Mousseline Sauce*

We called this dish Lobster Valdosta when we first
created it at the Straight Wharf Restaurant, but for
the life of me I can't now remember why. What I do
remember is that it was an instant hit. A frequent
patron of the restaurant once asked me to make 130
Lobster Valdosta servings for a wedding rehearsal din-

ner; do you think I did it? The dish is very rich and
therefore not something to have regularly, but once
in a while it is a very special treat.

Reserved tomalley and any roe from the
    prepared lobster shells (if you wish to use
    them)
¾ cup melted unsalted butter
1 tsp Dijon-style mustard
1 Tb fresh lemon juice
2 Tb chopped fresh tarragon
1 Tb chopped fresh parsley
Hot pepper sauce
Two 3-lb *Partially Steamed and Filled Lobster
    Shells* (page 197)
1½ cups *Hollandaise Sauce* (page 356)
½ cup heavy cream

Place the reserved tomalley and any roe (if you wish
to use them) in a saucepan, add ¼ cup of the melted
butter, and whisk together. Cook the mixture over
very low heat, stirring, until the roe turns red. Transfer the mixture to a blender or food processor and
purée it to a smooth consistency. Place the tomalley-
and-roe purée in a bowl, cover, and refrigerate; bring
it to room temperature before folding it into the hollandaise sauce.

To roast the lobsters: In a bowl, combine the remaining ½ cup of the melted butter, mustard, lemon juice,
tarragon, parsley, and a few drops of hot pepper sauce.
Place the lobster halves on a baking sheet, and spoon
the seasoned melted butter over the lobster meat in
the shells. Roast the lobster halves in a preheated 500-
degree oven for about 10 minutes, or until thoroughly
heated through, allowing a few extra minutes if the
lobster halves come directly from the refrigerator.

While the lobsters are roasting, fold the tomalley-
roe purée (if you are using it) into the hollandaise
sauce and keep the sauce warm in a double boiler.
Whip the cream and keep it cold. Remove the
roasted lobsters from the oven, fold the whipped
cream into the hollandaise, and spoon the lightened
sauce evenly over the lobster meat in the shells.
Immediately place the sauced lobsters under a preheated broiler just long enough to brown the tops
lightly. Serve immediately.   SERVES 4

❖*With Basil:* Substitute fresh basil for the tarragon.
❖*With Basil and Tomatoes:* When summer vine-

Dinner-Party Lobster—Five Ways (continued)

ripened tomatoes are at their ripest, prepare 1½ cups peeled, seeded, and finely chopped ripe tomato pulp. In a sauté pan, heat 2 tablespoons butter and 1 tablespoon oil, add 2 tablespoons finely minced shallots, and cook briefly until the shallots have softened. Add the tomatoes, cover, and cook over medium heat for 5 minutes. Remove the cover and cook gently to evaporate some of the juices and thicken the sauce. Season with salt and freshly ground pepper, and add chopped fresh basil to taste. Spoon some of the tomato mixture into the cleaned lobster shells before filling them with the cut-up lobster meat. Proceed as above, using fresh basil in place of tarragon.

À la Lobster Savannah

There are a few classic American lobster dishes, and Lobster Savannah is one of them. It was created at Locke-Ober's in Boston, where they poached the lobster strapped to a straight implement to keep its tail from curling, removed and sauced the claw and knuckle meat, and served the meat in a cavity formed by cutting open the back shell of the lobster. Somehow I prefer my easier method of preparation!

     Two 3-lb *Partially Steamed and Filled Lobster Shells* (page 197), but steamed for 20 minutes
5 Tb butter
3 Tb flour
1½ cups warmed light cream
1½ tsp paprika
Salt and freshly ground pepper
½ cup thinly sliced mushroom caps
¼ cup minced green peppers
¼ cup minced red peppers or pimentos
½ cup good dry sherry
½ cup fresh bread crumbs
¼ cup freshly grated Parmesan cheese

Prepare the lobsters as in *Partially Steamed and Filled Lobster Shells*, but steam them for a full 20 minutes. Remove all the lobster meat and cut it into bite-size pieces; clean the shells, but do not return the meat to the shells. Reserve the tomalley and any roe, if you wish to use them. If you are doing this part of the preparation ahead, cover and refrigerate separately

the tomalley and the roe, the lobster meat, and the lobster shells until ready for final cooking.

     In a small saucepan, melt 3 tablespoons of the butter and stir in the flour. Remove the pan from the heat and whisk in the warmed cream. Return the pan to the heat and bring the mixture to a boil while whisking, then reduce the heat and cook until slightly thickened. Whisk in the reserved tomalley and roe, if desired. Stir in the paprika and season with salt and freshly ground pepper. Set aside.

     In a deep-sided sauté pan, melt the remaining 2 tablespoons of butter, add the mushrooms and green and red peppers, and cook, stirring, for 7–8 minutes; let any pan juices evaporate, but do not let the vegetables brown. Add the lobster meat and the sherry, stir together, and cook down to reduce the sherry by half. Stir in the reserved cream sauce, turning the lobster in the sauce until it is well coated. Season with more salt and pepper as needed.

     Spoon the lobster mixture into the shells, and arrange the shells on a baking sheet. Mix the bread crumbs and the cheese together, and sprinkle over the lobster filling. Bake in a preheated 400-degree oven for about 15 minutes, or until the sauce is bubbling. Run under a preheated broiler, if you wish, just long enough to brown the top lightly. Serve immediately.   SERVES 4

Lobster Crêpes

For cooks and guests who want to enjoy a lobster dish without dealing with the shells, this dish is an excellent choice and, in the world of lobster dishes, comparatively inexpensive because it requires only 4 ounces of lobster meat per serving. In the innocent old days, we made the sauce with 3 cups of heavy cream and a cup of Swiss cheese, with a bit of arrowroot to thicken the mixture. The version here uses a much lighter basic white sauce. The dilled crêpes can be made days ahead and refrigerated or frozen, the sauce can be made a day ahead and reheated, and the entire dish can be prepared ahead and refrigerated. A 6-inch, nonstick sauté pan is by far the best pan for making the crêpes. A green salad is all that is needed to complete this lobster dinner.

     Alternative shellfish: cooked shrimp, crabmeat, scallops, or a combination

     Alternative fish: almost any poached white fish

DILLED CRÊPES

1 cup instant-blending flour (such as
     Wondra Quick-Mixing Flour)★
¼ cup all-purpose flour★
½ tsp salt
3 large eggs
¾ cup milk
¾ cup water
3 Tb vegetable oil
3 Tb chopped fresh dill
Peanut oil or vegetable oil, to coat pan

★Using instant-blending flour for the crêpes makes the batter ready to cook immediately, though I do add some regular flour to enhance the texture. The notes following the recipe indicate how to make the crêpes using only all-purpose flour.

To make the Dilled Crêpes: In a bowl, combine the instant-blending flour, all-purpose flour, and salt. In a mixing bowl, beat the eggs with a whisk, and add the milk and water. Gradually pour the flour mixture into the liquid, beating constantly until the mixture is smooth. Add the oil and dill, and stir until well blended. (Makes about 2¾ cups batter)

Preheat a 6-inch frying pan with sloping sides (nonstick, if available) over medium heat and wipe it lightly with oil. When the oil coating begins to smoke, remove the pan from the heat, pour a scant ¼ cup batter into the pan, quickly tilt the pan back and forth so that a uniform thin film of batter covers the bottom of the pan, set the pan over the heat, and cook the crêpe for about 1 minute, or until the batter is bubbly and the edges have begun to brown. Shake the pan (the crêpe should move easily), turn the crêpe over with a spatula or flip it over with a flick of the wrist, and cook the second side for 15 seconds. Slide the cooked crêpe onto a cooling rack or waxed-paper-lined baking sheet. Wipe the pan again lightly with oil and repeat the procedure until the batter is used up.

MAKES 12–15 CRÊPES

❖If making the crêpes ahead, stack them between sheets of waxed paper, wrap the stack with plastic wrap, and refrigerate for up to a week or freeze.

❖To make the crêpes entirely of all-purpose flour, substitute 1¼ cups all-purpose flour for the two flours in the recipe and then let the batter "rest" in the refrigerator for 2 hours so that the flour particles will swell enough to ensure a light crêpe.

❖Substitute other herbs for the dill, or make the crêpes plain without herbs.

LOBSTER AND SAUCE

1½ lb cooked lobster meat
3 Tb butter
4 Tb flour
3 cups milk
½ cup ricotta cheese
¼ cup light cream
1–2 Tb chopped fresh dill
Salt and freshly ground pepper
½ lemon
1 cup grated Swiss cheese

Prepare the crêpes and set aside.

To prepare the lobster and sauce: Cut the lobster meat into bite-size pieces, cover, and refrigerate. In a saucepan, melt the butter, remove the pan from the heat, whisk in the flour, return the pan to the heat, and cook for 2 minutes to slightly cook the flour. Add the milk and whisk the mixture over low heat until smooth and thick. Combine the ricotta cheese and cream, and add them to the basic white sauce. Add the dill and season the sauce with salt, freshly ground pepper, and lemon juice to taste.

Spoon about ½ cup of the sauce into a buttered 9 × 13-inch ovenproof dish that can go under a broiler and spread the sauce in a thin layer. Sprinkle ⅓ cup of the grated Swiss cheese over the layer of sauce. Pour 1 cup of the sauce over the lobster meat and turn the lobster and sauce together until the lobster is well coated. Place one-twelfth of the lobster mixture (about 2 ounces or 2 heaping tablespoons) along the

Lobster Crêpes (continued)

center of each of 12 crêpes. Roll up the crêpes and set them in the baking dish, seam side down. Cover the crêpes with the remaining 1½ cups of sauce and sprinkle the remainder of the grated cheese over the top. (The dish can be assembled, covered, and refrigerated until ready to bake—a day ahead, if you wish.)

Bake in a preheated 400-degree oven for 20 minutes or until bubbly. Run the dish under a preheated broiler just long enough to brown the top lightly, if you like.   SERVES 6, 2 CRÊPES PER SERVING

❖For a more generous amount of lobster, increase the total amount of lobster meat to 2 pounds.

❖To help your budget, combine the cooked lobster meat with chunks of poached fish, such as monkfish, wolffish, or other firm-fleshed white fish.

❖For individual servings, place 2 filled crêpes in each of 6 buttered au gratin dishes and cover with sauce before baking.

❖To turn the crêpes into a vegetarian meal, omit the lobster and substitute 4 cups of a chopped, sautéed vegetable, such as broccoli or spinach.

Baked Stuffed Lobster for Two

What a dish! A history of restaurant menus would show this as a featured dish in one restaurant after another, often with fanciful stuffings to turn it into the chef's signature creation. Then nouvelle cuisine arrived and dishes like this withered away. But many lobster lovers longingly remember the crunchy topping over the smooth sweet lobster meat in the shell underneath. The herbal stuffing protects the tender lobster meat from the dry heat of the oven and adds some nice flavor. It really is a nice dish for the diner— and for the cook, too, since the whole preparation can be done ahead and refrigerated until time to pop it into the oven shortly before serving. The recipe multiplies easily. I like to serve baked lobster with a few colorful vegetables on a side plate: *Sugar Snap Peas and Carrot Logs* (page 333), *Stir-Fried Broccoli with Garlic* (page 322), and *Seared Red Pepper Salad* (page 88).

Two 1½-lb lobsters

STUFFING

4 Tb butter
3 Tb chopped shallots
1 tsp minced garlic
2 cups fresh bread crumbs, lightly packed
2 Tb chopped pimentos
2 Tb chopped fresh tarragon
2 Tb chopped parsley
2 tsp fresh lemon juice
¼ tsp Dijon-style mustard
Salt and freshly ground pepper

Lemon wedges
Sprigs parsley

Bring a pot of water to a boil, adding 1 tablespoon of salt for each quart. Drop the lobsters into the boiling water headfirst, one at a time so as not to reduce the boil, and cook for 3 minutes. Remove the lobsters from the pot and run under cold water to cool them enough to handle. Break the claws and knuckles off, crack them open, remove the meat, cut it into small chunks, and set aside. Turn the lobsters over on their backs and split down the middle lengthwise, taking care not to cut through the back shell. Spread the lobster halves apart in a butterfly shape. Remove and discard the translucent beige stomach sacs under the eyes, the spongy gills, and the intestinal tract running down the body and tail. Remove and discard the tomalley and any roe. Carefully lift the tail meat out in one piece, cut into bite-size pieces, and return to its original position in the tail shell. Wipe out the inside of the body cavities and place the chunks of

claw meat in the cavities. Place the lobsters on a baking sheet, cover with plastic wrap, and refrigerate while you make the stuffing.

To make the stuffing: In a sauté pan, melt the butter, add the shallots, and cook for 2 minutes or until tender. Stir in the garlic and then the bread crumbs, and cook over medium heat, stirring, until the crumbs have absorbed the butter, separated, and dried slightly; do not let them brown. Remove mixture to a bowl, add the pimentos, tarragon, parsley, lemon juice, and mustard, and stir together; season with salt and freshly ground pepper. Take half the stuffing and spread it over both the chunks of claw meat in the body cavity and the tail meat of one of the lobsters. Spread the remaining stuffing over the second lobster. (Cover and refrigerate the stuffed lobsters at this point, if you wish, until ready to bake.)

Bake in a preheated 475-degree oven for 15 min-

utes. The tails will curl up from the heat, so when you remove the lobsters from the oven, make a small incision down the middle of the tail ends to force them to lie flat. Place each lobster on a warm serving plate and garnish with lemon and parsley.   SERVES 2

❖Vary the stuffing by adding chopped celery, hot red pepper, or a bit of sautéed vegetable, such as chopped leeks or spinach. Add grated cheese, flakes of cooked crabmeat, or small shrimp.

❖Substitute other fresh herbs, such as basil or oregano, for the tarragon.

❖Use a light olive oil instead of butter, and with it use Italian seasonings, such as oregano and sage.

❖Drizzle on more oil or melted butter, if you wish, just before baking the stuffed lobsters.

❖Use 2-pound lobsters and bake 18 minutes.

CLAMBAKE FOR FIFTY

YES, YOU READ IT correctly—a clambake for 50 people. A clambake is a glorious feast with several foods but lobster above all, and it is the happiest kind of event when many people share the very considerable amount of work involved. A few Nantucket experiments—one of which was televised on "The Victory Garden"—persuaded us that the ideal bake occurs when three host couples invite about 20 guests each, with acceptances running to about 50 people. Since lobster can be expensive, each guest receives an invitation with a recommended "freewill offering" for the lobster and a promise that when the check is in hand, the host will forward a map to the beach location where the clambake will happen. Parents of hosts, newlyweds, and children are always invited without a freewill offering. It is very likely that Indians did their own clambakes on New England shores hundreds of years ago when lobsters were so prevalent that one could hardly give them away. Dun Gifford, who is our bakemaster and an authority on food lore and local history, says that 10–15-foot mounds of shells have been found in Nantucket coves as evidence of Indians' cooking seafood in a pit over hot rocks. The essence of a modern clambake is to line a beach pit with rocks, build a bonfire on the rocks to make them very hot, line the heated pit with seaweed, place lobsters, corn, and clams on the seaweed, cover the food with more seaweed and a tarp, and let it all steam to glorious perfection. We add chicken and potatoes to the wonderful assemblage of foods under the seaweed and tarp. By the way, I think this lobster tour de force is called a "clambake" because the steaming clam juices permeate the air with a dazzling fragrance one will not forget.

FOOD EQUIPMENT

Sturdy plastic plates, bowls, cups, and glasses; cutlery, chef's knives, clam knives, lobster crackers, grill forks and tongs; big paper napkins, paper towels, newspapers, garbage bags; can openers, corkscrews; cutting boards; pots for melting butter; kettle for quahogs; 60 small brown paper lunch bags; thermoses for coffee; cheese-cloth; string; scissors; coolers with ice; radio or portable cassette player for dance music

FOOD LIST

Fifty to fifty-five
    1¾-2-lb lobsters
1 bushel steamer clams
1 bushel mussels
½ bushel littleneck clams
20 lb quahogs
15 quartered chickens
15 large Spanish onions
60 ears of corn
60 large red potatoes
10 lb chorizo sausage
Bowls of red and yellow
    cherry tomatoes
Bowls of washed and
    stringed sugar snap peas
Watermelon
Brownies
Homemade breads
Plenty of butter and lemons
Cocktail sauce
Horseradish
Beer, wine, soft drinks,
    coffee

Mix all ingredients together with sun, sea, blue sky, and loved ones.

Early preparation—a few weeks before: Plan location, get beach-fire permit, complete guest list, mail invitations, prepare maps to site, plan the menu, make shop-

CLAMBAKE FOR FIFTY

ping lists, make work assignments (very important), and notify everyone of the assignments.

Week before to a few days before: Order the seafood; send a detail of strong young men with a pickup truck to gather enough rocks (about the size of a football) to line a sand pit 8 inches deep and about 10 feet in diameter and deliver them to the clambake site; commission others to collect fire material (wood—preferably hardwood— kindling, newspapers, and matches); commission others to gather a great quantity of "rockweed"— seaweed with small polyps that release moisture when heated; round up wire bushel baskets and wooden crates and any other large containers good for holding food in the sea while the fire is being prepared; find or sew together some canvas, sailcloth, or plenty of burlap to make the tarp to cover the baking pit; shop for all nonperishable supplies; sew colorful flags and banners to decorate the site; locate volunteers to bring two charcoal grills and hardwood coals for preparation of hot appetizers, canvas chairs for the older set, beach umbrellas for same, at least four pairs of protective mitts for the cooks, buckets for water, a 16-foot sailboat, a powerboat and water skis, kites, dogs to pet and chase, and bunches of wildflowers in throwaway can-vases; send husband, Russ, with a small detail

to gather driftwood and old boards to build the necessary "'furniture'": one or two buffet tables to hold food, a square clam-shucking table, and a variety of benches to sit on and low tables to sit around, and a bar for serving drinks.

Day before: Shop for perishables other than seafood; gather branches to tie into brooms to sweep the fire ashes; locate shovels and strong iron rakes; lug fire equipment and furniture to the site; bake breads and brownies; pray for good weather.

The day: In the morning the bake-master takes a group of draftees to the beach, where they dig the pit (about 10 feet in diameter and about 8 inches deep) and line it completely with rocks, then lay a large bonfire on top. They also

soak the tarp in the ocean. The seafood is picked up from the supplier, and all the supplies and equipment are brought to the site. The furniture is arranged and the site decorated. About 11:00 the fire is lighted, and it is frequently replenished with more wood so that it burns intensely for 2–3 hours, making the rocks underneath hot to their very core. A large kettle filled with quahogs and 5–6 inches of water is placed by the fire to heat: the intense heat actually brings the water to boiling, and the quahogs open and release their juices. They are sacrificed for their broth alone, which will be used to dip the cooked steamers in. Beer, wine, soft drinks, and shellfish are stored in the ocean water to cool.

Guests begin arriving about noon and join the work in progress. The corn is prepared by pulling down the husks, removing the silk, tying the husks back up around the ears, and then soaking the corn in the ocean for a while so that the husks will keep the corn from drying out in the bake. Thick slices of onion, a quarter of a chicken, and a pat of butter are placed in each of 60 individual brown paper lunch bags, and the bags are tied up with string and kept in coolers until ready to bake. Steamers (about a dozen per serving) are tied up in cheesecloth bags. Brooms are assembled and

CLAMBAKE FOR FIFTY

*Clambake for Fifty
(continued)*

tied from the branches and sticks gathered earlier. The two grills are fired up for the mussels and sausage, which everyone begins consuming as soon as the coals are hot and the cooking can begin. When the coals are white-hot, mussels that have been rinsed off in the ocean but not debearded are spread across the grill, and a saucepan of melted butter and lemon juice is kept on the outer edge of the grill; as soon as the mussels pop open, they are ready to dip into the

butter and enjoy. The second grill is used to cook large pieces of sausage, a spicy contrast to the sweet mussel meats, which are grilled until brown on all sides, removed to a cutting board, cut into bite-size rounds, and served with toothpicks. (If you wish to reduce spattering as the sausage cooks, prick the sausage with a fork and blanch it in boiling water for 5 minutes to release some of the fat before bringing it to the beach.) Bowls of cherry tomatoes and sugar snap peas from the garden replace potato chips at our clambakes. Volunteers take turns opening littleneck clams, and crisp Sanford Winery Sauvignon Blanc

along with guest donations of favorite wines and beers are opened at the bar to toast the day.

At 1:30 the bakemaster and his assistants rake the charred wood off the pit with iron rakes and brush the rocks clean of coals with the homemade brooms. The ensuing period of work is done with real concentration. A 4–6-inch layer of seaweed is spread across the heated rocks with the iron rakes. The potatoes are spread on the seaweed, topped by the chicken in brown bags, and the chicken is topped in turn by the corn. The lobsters go on top of all, and the steamers in cheesecloth bags are placed around the edge (don't

worry—the bags will not burn). Another layer of seaweed is spread on top of the food, and then the wet tarp is carried from the water, laid over the pit, and secured at the edges by heavy stones. It is a wonderful sight. Soon the tarp will billow from the pressure of the steam generated from the hot rocks against the seaweed. The food is cooked in the pit for 1 hour. At 3:00 sharp, Dun gives the signal, "Break the bake!" and the guests who have been flying kites or sailing or sunning for an hour gather for the exciting moment when the tarp is rolled back, releasing a great whoosh of steam and thrilling everyone with the intense fragrance of lobster, clams, chicken, and the sea. Four men wearing mitts pull the food from the pit, and others carry it to the serving tables, where the lobsters are split open for easy eating and all the delicious hot food is laid out. The broth from the kettle of quahogs is poured into bowls to dip the steamers into. We eat until the driftwood furniture threatens to collapse under us. Then as the tide creeps in, we turn on the radio and dance on the beach to the sound of music and gentle surf until well after the orange setting sun has silhouetted the bouquets of wildflowers on the tables.

Lobster and Leeks au Gratin

Gratin is the French term for the thin crust formed on top of dishes when they are run under the broiler or put into a very hot oven; the crust is achieved with butter, bread crumbs, or cheese. Thus a recipe baked and browned in a shallow fireproof dish has become known as a gratin. More often than not, the dish contains a basic cream sauce, béchamel, or a flavored version of it. This dish uses braised leeks as a bed for lobster meat; it can be prepared in advance and baked just before serving, but if you are baking a dish that has been refrigerated, allow a little more baking time.

Alternative shellfish: poached scallops or shrimp, cooked crabmeat

Alternative fish: poached cod, monkfish, or other cooked white fish

1 cup chicken broth or water
5–6 cups chopped leeks
Salt and freshly ground pepper
3 Tb butter
2 Tb light olive oil or vegetable oil
1 cup fresh bread crumbs
1½ lb cooked lobster meat (page 186)
2 cups *Béchamel Sauce* (page 350)
¼ cup Madeira wine
1 Tb Dijon-style mustard

In a large sauté pan, heat the chicken broth; add the leeks, stirring them into the liquid, cover, and cook over low heat for 8–10 minutes, stirring frequently to make sure the leeks don't brown. When the leeks are tender, remove the cover and cook uncovered to reduce any liquid in the pan. Season the leeks with salt and freshly ground pepper. (You will have about 3 cups braised leeks.) Spread the cooked leeks in the bottom of a buttered au gratin dish or shallow oven-proof baking dish.

Wipe out the sauté pan, heat 1 tablespoon of the butter and 1 tablespoon of the oil, and add the bread crumbs. Stir the crumbs until well coated with the butter and oil, and sauté until the crumbs are lightly browned. Remove the crumbs to a bowl and set aside.

Cut the lobster into bite-size pieces. Wipe out the sauté pan again, heat the remaining 2 tablespoons of butter and 1 tablespoon of oil, add the lobster meat, and sauté over gentle heat for 5–6 minutes. In a saucepan, heat the béchamel sauce, stir in the Madeira and mustard, and season with salt and pepper as needed. Spread the lobster meat on top of the leeks in the au gratin dish, spoon the sauce over the lobster meat, and sprinkle the bread crumbs over all. Bake in a preheated 375-degree oven for 15 minutes or until bubbly, run the dish under the broiler just long enough to brown the top lightly, and serve. SERVES 6

❖Divide the prepared ingredients among 6 individual au gratin dishes.
❖Omit the bread crumbs and top the dish with a combination of grated Swiss and Parmesan cheeses or with crumbled feta cheese.
❖Substitute other vegetables, such as braised cabbage, fennel, or spinach, for the leeks.
❖If you want to substitute poached fish for the lobster meat, flake the fish into bite-size chunks and gently fold the fish chunks into the sauce before baking as above.

Pan-Roasted Mackerel with a Moroccan Spice Tomato Sauce

If a fisherman wished to cook a mackerel immediately after catching it, he might very well build an open fire, heat an iron frying pan over it, and put the cleaned fish in the hot pan to fry. The simple method that follows for pan-roasting a fish is very much like the fisherman's way. I use a nonstick sauté pan, and in addition to scaling, gutting, and removing the head, tail, and fins of the mackerel, I butterfly and trim the fish and remove the backbone and line of center bones (see Mackerel Box, page 210); it requires a bit of time, but it isn't difficult, it can be done ahead, and it makes eating the fish less messy for guests. You will need a food processor or blender to purée the sauce, and one or two nonstick sauté pans large enough to hold the fish in one layer. Just as the fish can be prepared ahead and refrigerated until it is cooked shortly before serving, so, too, can the sauce be made ahead and reheated later. The sauce has a subtle flavor from the seasonings that adds character to the dish but doesn't overpower the fish; it is a sauce worth trying with other fish or using as a dipping sauce for grilled

*Pan-Roasted Mackerel with a Moroccan Spice Tomato
Sauce (continued)*

shrimp and other shellfish dishes. I like to serve this
dish with *Mashed Rutabaga* (page 337) and *Sautéed
Corn* (page 325) or *Sautéed Eggplant* (page 328). Cous-
cous is also a nice accompaniment and can be dressed
with extra sauce from the fish.

Alternative fish: small bluefish, amberjack, salmon
trout, Arctic char, hybrid farmed striped bass or
salmon

Four 1¼–1½-lb whole gutted mackerel

MOROCCAN SPICE TOMATO SAUCE

2 Tb olive oil
½ cup chopped shallots
2 tsp chopped garlic
2 cups peeled, seeded, and chopped
    tomatoes
1 Tb ground coriander
1 Tb cumin
¼ tsp turmeric
Grated rind and juice of 1 lemon
¾ cup fish stock or chicken broth
¼ cup orange juice
Hot pepper sauce
Salt and freshly ground pepper

To make the Moroccan Spice Tomato Sauce:
In a saucepan, heat the oil, add the shallots, and cook them for 2 minutes. Stir in
the garlic, add the tomatoes, and cook for
5 minutes, stirring occasionally. Stir in the
coriander, cumin, turmeric, lemon rind
and juice, and fish stock or chicken broth,
bring to a boil, reduce the heat, and cook
gently for 15 minutes. Pour the sauce into
a food processor or blender and purée
until smooth. Return the sauce to the
saucepan, add the orange juice, and
reheat. Season with a few drops of hot
pepper sauce and with salt and freshly
ground pepper. If you are making it
ahead, cover and refrigerate until reheating just before serving   MAKES 2–2¼ CUPS

Have your fish market dress the mackerel—remove
the heads, tails, and fins of the fish; butterfly them;
remove the backbones, side bones, and center line of
bones; and trim the belly flap. Or do it yourself following the directions on page 210. If the market prepared the fish, check them again to remove any
bones. Pat the fish dry, close the 2 fillets of each fish
so that they resume the shape of a whole fish, cover,
and refrigerate until ready to cook.

Prepare the Moroccan spice tomato sauce and
keep warm.

To cook the fish: Heat a nonstick sauté pan wide
enough to hold the fish in one layer, or use two pans.
(Do not use butter or oil in this preparation.) Place
each fish (2 fillets together) skin side down in the hot
pan and place a lid or heat-proof plate smaller in diameter than the pan directly on top of the fish; the cover is
more of a weight to keep the fish from popping open
than a cooking cover, and there should be air space
between the cover and the sides of the pan. Cook over
medium-high heat for 6 minutes, lift the cover, turn
each fish over with a long spatula while holding the top
fillet in place with your fingers as you turn it, replace
the cover, and cook for another 6 minutes. Remove
the fish to a flat work surface, and with a knife gently
scrape the skin off all of the fillets and, if you wish,
remove the thin layer of dark meat as well.

To serve: Place a puddle of warm sauce on each of 4
warmed serving plates. Place 1 whole fish (2 fillets) on
each plate, opening the fillets into a butterfly shape
with the skinned side down. Spoon another stripe of
sauce across the fish and serve.   SERVES 4

❖Cook the dressed mackerel in the pan as above,
but remove the bones and trim the belly flap when
you remove the skin from the cooked fish.

*Broiled Mackerel Served
with Warm Applesauce*

Fish and applesauce may sound like unlikely partners,
but I can tell you that my grandchildren love the
combination. Mackerel is at its prime in the fall, just
when a new crop of cooking apples is coming to market. The cooked apples bring out the sweetness of the
(continued on page 211)

MACKEREL

WHETHER YOU LIKE or dislike mackerel has probably been determined or at least heavily influenced by the freshness of the mackerel you've eaten. If it is very fresh, mackerel has a pleasantly assertive, almost sweet taste that fishermen frying fresh catches rave about and that many lovers of sushi relish. But mackerel is an oily fish that can go "off" very rapidly to a mushy texture and a tinny taste if it has not been properly gutted, bled, and iced when caught, well refrigerated in transit, and available in your market within 5–7 days from the time it was caught. I read that well-handled mackerel should have a shelf life of 18–20 days, but I think a week from boat to table would be my outside limit.

Mackerel, of the same family as tuna and bonito, is a migratory species that appears and disappears in schools of fast-moving fish. *Atlantic mackerel*—known in my area as Boston mackerel—range from Labrador down to Cape Hatteras and are harvested from spring until late fall when they head for deeper waters. Adult Atlantic mackerel run from 1¼–2½ pounds and are at their fattest in the fall. In early spring one can get small mackerel called "tinker mackerel," which weigh up to a pound and have a slightly milder flavor than adult mackerel.

Spanish mackerel, weighing 2–3 pounds, are caught from the Chesapeake Bay south into the Gulf of Mexico. A close cousin— *cero*—is also found in warm southern waters; it runs slightly larger than Spanish mackerel. *King mackerel* (sometimes referred to as kingfish, but not to be confused with northern whiting, which is also sometimes called kingfish) may weigh as much as 100 pounds, but the ones caught in Florida are more often in the 20-pound range.

The West Coast *Pacific mackerel* is also found on the East Coast, where it is called chub mackerel to distinguish it from Atlantic mackerel. It is smaller than Atlantic mackerel. *Jack mackerel,* which schools and tastes like mackerel, is really a member of the jack family along with amberjack and Florida pompano; it is a West Coast fish.

When cooked, mackerel shows a band of darker, fattier flesh that is a place where any contaminants in the fish's diet would concentrate; this darker flesh can be trimmed off, if you prefer, down to the lighter flesh underneath. Because of its high oil content, mackerel takes well to broiling and grilling, which dissipates some of the fat. It can be substituted in many bluefish recipes. The distinctive taste of mackerel accepts acidic sauces, such as the several tomato sauces in this book, or brush it with marinades, such as *Dun Gifford's Bluefish Basting Sauce* (page 123). Applesauce brings out a subtle sweet flavor in this fish. Skinned mackerel fillets need only be sautéed for a few minutes in butter, oil, or bacon fat, or dipped in flour and sautéed as in *Flounder Meunière* (page 167).

The Japanese use mackerel in sushi and sashimi, the Latin Americans use it in ceviche, and the Scandinavians cure it with the same technique used for salmon in *Gravlaks* (page 14). Because of its high fat content, mackerel smokes well, and commercially smoked mackerel can be very good. Use it as a substitute for *Smoked Bluefish Pâté* (page 4).

SPECIAL INFORMATION ABOUT

MACKEREL

Mackerel (continued)

Buying: To avoid an old or rancid taste, buy only impeccably fresh mackerel. They are usually marketed whole, either fresh or frozen, and the skin should be clear with a blue-green upper body and a glistening silver-white belly. A freshly caught mackerel has a beautiful iridescent shine that fades after death, but the skin should still have a shiny, wet look in the market, not a cloudy look or a slimy feel. Make sure the mackerel has been gutted and that the belly looks clean and without belly burn (see page xiii). Most mackerel is marketed with the head and tail on, and it can be grilled with only the gills and side fins removed; if you are going to remove them anyhow, have the market remove the head, tail, gills, and side fins just to minimize the odor in your garbage can. I always split my own mackerel, as in the directions below, but you can ask the market to do it. Smoked mackerel should be just as firm as you would expect fresh fish to be, so pass up any that is mushy; the smoked fish is often packaged as a whole fish cut into sections.

Storage: Excellent refrigeration is essential for fresh mackerel. Wrap the fish in butcher's paper after making sure the belly is completely cleaned out, and store on a bed of ice in the coldest part of the refrigerator with ice packs on top of the wrapped fish. Fillets can be wrapped and laid on ice or placed in a nonalu-minum-lined dish with ice packs on top. Do not let the flesh get wet from melting ice.

Preparation: I like to split the mackerel down the center in a butterfly cut, remove the center bone, and trim the side bones and belly flap. I leave the skin on for cooking because it helps to hold the soft flesh of the mackerel together and is easily removed after cooking; however, if you want to pan-fry the fillets, you can remove the skin before cooking.

To remove the head and tail of a gutted fish: Place a sharp knife underneath the back of the side fin close to the head, and slide the knife under the fin and then down through the body to sever the head. Turn the fish over and cut off the fin on the other side. Cut off the tail, and wash the inside and outside of the fish thoroughly.

To butterfly a mackerel: Holding the fish belly up, run a sharp knife lengthwise down through the fish, cutting down to and around and under one side of the center backbone, but not cutting through the skin on the back of the fish. The mackerel will fall open and lie flat on its back. Slide the tip of the knife under the backbone at one end and run it along just under the backbone so that the bone can be lifted out. If you wish to split the mackerel, slice through the skin lengthwise in the middle of the butterflied fish.

To trim the butterflied fish: After removing the backbone, slip the knife under the bones that come over the flesh on each half of the fish; slide the knife under the bones down to the belly flap and cut off the flap, freeing the bones with the flap. Repeat on the other half of the fish. Trim any ragged edges on either side of the fish. A line of small bones remains down the center strip of each fillet. You can leave those in and remove them after cooking when they lift out easily, or you can remove them next.

To remove the center line of pin bones: With a sharp knife, cut through the flesh on each side of the center strip of bones in each fillet without cutting through the skin. Holding one end of the strip of bones firmly, gently pull the strip out. Now you have a boneless butterflied mackerel, skin side down.

Yields: A 1½-pound whole gutted fish weighs about 1 pound after removal of the head, tail, and backbone; after removal of the belly flap and side bones, each of the 2 fillets will weigh about 6 ounces. Removing the skin reduces each fillet to about 5 ounces. After the fillet is cooked and the line of center bones and the dark meat have been removed, 4 ounces of cooked meat remains in each fillet.

❖Allow 1 whole gutted 1–1½-pound mackerel per person, or 2 small ¾-pound tinker mackerel per person.

❖Smoked mackerel: ¾ pound of sections of whole mackerel yields 10 ounces after removal of skin and bones, or about 2 cups of flaked meat.

Broiled Mackerel Served with Warm Applesauce
(continued)

fish. Homemade applesauce is easy to prepare and so much better-tasting than store bought. Make it just before serving, or make it ahead and reheat to serve; and don't hesitate to double or triple the applesauce recipe so you can have plenty of leftovers. Broiling is one of the best preparations for mackerel, which has enough oil to stand up well to the heat of the broiler. The fish can be prepared for cooking, refrigerated, and then broiled quickly just before serving. Try *Sautéed Swiss Chard* (page 285) and *Sautéed Rutabaga Dice* (page 337) with the broiled fish.

Alternative fish: small bluefish, amberjack, shad, Arctic char, hybrid farmed striped bass or salmon

APPLESAUCE

4 lb Cortland apples, or your
favorite cooking apples
½ cup water

To make the Applesauce: Peel, core, and quarter the apples. Place the apples in a heavy-bottomed saucepan and add the water. Cover and cook over medium-high heat for 10–15 minutes, until the apples have softened. Regulate the heat as necessary so that the apples do not stick to the pan and brown. Remove the pan from the heat and let sit, covered, for 10 minutes, while the apples soften completely. Mash the apples to a coarse texture with a potato masher or purée until smooth in a food processor or blender. Keep warm if serving shortly, or allow to cool, cover, and refrigerate.

MAKES 4 CUPS

Two 1¼–1½-lb whole gutted mackerel★
3–4 Tb melted butter
Lemon wedges for garnish
Salt and freshly ground pepper

★If your market sells mackerel fillets, buy four 6-ounce skin-on fillets instead of whole fish.

Prepare the applesauce and keep warm, or refrigerate and gently reheat before serving.

To prepare and cook the fish: Ask your fish market to fillet the fish, leaving the skin on, and to remove the side bones and trim the belly flap; or do it yourself following the directions on page 210. You should have 4 fillets of about 5–6 ounces each. With a pair of tweezers or small pliers, carefully remove the center line of bones running down the length of each fillet. Pat dry and refrigerate until ready to cook.

Cover the rack of a broiler pan with aluminum foil, brush both sides of the mackerel fillets with melted butter, and place the fish flesh side down on the foil. Place the fish about 4 inches under a preheated broiler and cook for 2–3 minutes, or until the skin is brown and bubbling up. Turn the fish over with a wide spatula so that the flesh side is up, brush with more melted butter if you wish, and broil for 3–5 minutes, depending on thickness, or until the flesh is just opaque throughout. Serve immediately with lemon wedges, salt and freshly ground pepper, and warm applesauce on the side.   SERVES 4

❖Add fresh herbs or spices to the basting butter.

❖Omit the basting butter and baste the fish with oil or a sauce such as *Soy Marinade,* page 120.

❖Omit the applesauce and pour lemon butter with capers over the fish (see *Sautéed Bluefish with Lemon and Capers,* page 129).

❖*Grilled Mackerel:* Baste fillets with butter, oil, or a favorite basting sauce, and place skin side down on an oiled grill rack. Turn the fish after 2 minutes and cook for another 3–5 minutes, depending on the heat of the fire and the thickness of the fillets. Serve immediately.

❖Wrap partially cooked bacon around split fish fillets and broil or grill as above.

Broiled Monkfish with a Tomato Muffuletta Sauce

Broiling or grilling is an excellent way of cooking the firm flesh of monkfish. Because the mild, almost sweet taste of the fish cries out for an assertive partner, such as a highly flavored sauce, here I marinate the raw fish in a piquant dressing of lemon and lime before broiling it, and then serve it with a salty muf-

Broiled Monkfish with a Tomato Muffuletta Sauce (continued)

fuletta sauce. I call this sauce "muffuletta" because I have combined tomatoes with what is basically an olive salad, and olive salad is an essential part of an Italian muffuletta sauce. The sauce can be made well ahead and reheated at serving time. The fish can be cut and the marinade prepared in advance, but don't marinate the fish longer than 30 minutes before cooking it or it will begin to "cure" from the citric acid in the marinade. This very dish is good with mashed potatoes and peas.

Alternative fish: chunks of firm-fleshed fish, such as shark, tuna, or swordfish

TOMATO MUFFULETTA SAUCE

1 Tb olive oil
1 Tb minced garlic
4 cups peeled, seeded, and chopped
    tomatoes
¼ cup pitted and chopped green
    olives
¼ cup pitted and chopped black
    olives
¼ cup chopped pimentos
2 Tb drained capers
1 Tb fresh oregano or ½ tsp dried
Salt and freshly ground pepper

To make the Tomato Muffuletta Sauce: In a saucepan, heat the oil, add the garlic, and cook it for 30 seconds, but do not let it brown. Add the tomatoes, bring the mixture to a boil, cover, and cook over medium heat for 4–5 minutes. Uncover the pan, add the green and black olives, pimentos, capers, and oregano, and simmer for 4–5 minutes to reduce the juices slightly. Season with salt and freshly ground pepper. Keep warm if serving shortly, or cover and refrigerate for reheating later before serving.

MAKES ABOUT 4 CUPS

MARINADE

1 lemon
2 limes
1 tsp soy sauce
½ tsp freshly ground pepper
2 Tb olive oil

2–2½-lb skinned monkfish fillet, with
    membrane removed

Make the tomato muffuletta sauce and keep it warm.

To make the marinade: Grate the rind of the lemon and limes into a small bowl. Squeeze the juice of the lemon and limes, add the juice to the bowl of grated rind, stir in the soy sauce, pepper, and olive oil, and set aside.

Remove any thin gray-pink membrane and any thin layer of pink or yellow meat just beneath it so that the monkfish fillet is all white meat. Starting at one end, cut the fillet crosswise into ¾–1-inch slices. (You should have 12–15 slices.) Thirty minutes before cooking time, place the fish slices in a nonaluminum-lined dish, pour the marinade over the fish, and turn the slices in the marinade until they are completely coated. Cover and refrigerate for 30 minutes.

Just before serving, place the fish on the rack of a broiler pan and broil for 3–4 minutes in a preheated broiler; then turn the fish and broil the other side for 3–4 minutes, or until the fish is opaque throughout. Divide the fish into 4 equal portions on warm serving plates and serve with warm muffuletta sauce.   SERVES 4

❖Grill the fish, adjusting the cooking time to the heat of the fire.

❖Cut the monkfish fillet into 1-inch chunks and thread the chunks on skewers. Marinate as above, and grill or broil before serving with dipping sauces as a cocktail appetizer; try *Peanut Sauce* (page 360) or a pesto sauce, or mayonnaise with plenty of chopped cilantro and lime juice folded into it.

❖Monkfish takes well to other marinades. I sometimes slice monkfish, as above, marinate it with a teriyaki marinade, barbecue sauce, or in *Satay Marinade* (page 272) or *Curry Paste* (page 274), then broil it and serve it with *Sweet-and-Hot Grape Sauce* (page 43) and a side dish of *Cauliflower Relish* (page 351) or *Pickled Cucumber Salad* (page 272).

continued on page 214

SPECIAL INFORMATION ABOUT

MONKFISH (GOOSEFISH)

WHEN JULIA CHILD WAS formulating the dishes and menus for her "Julia Child and More Company" television series back in the 1970s, she decided to show her audience the deep-sea scaleless fish of notable ugliness well regarded in European cooking but scarcely known here: monkfish. She badgered her supplier, who somehow managed to acquire a whole monkfish— a 25-pound glistening monster with a gigantic head fitted with bulging eyes and a cavernous mouth filled with impressive teeth and a fleshy tongue. It gave you the shivers to touch the loose black skin. But Julia was in her glory as she held this aesthetic travesty up by its tail before the camera, prodded its belly for signs of a recent meal (the monkfish is known for its willingness to eat anything), and peered into its gaping mouth. I don't know how viewers reacted, but such was her influence that monkfish soon began to appear in American markets. This fish, technically named goosefish but commonly called monkfish, is known also by the names of lotte, bellyfish, or anglerfish, and is harvested from the Grand Banks to the Carolinas; much of the catch is exported to Europe, but domestic demand has grown.

From the extraordinary body of this fish, we eat only two round elongated fillets on either side of the tailbone. Between the loose, dark, thick skin of the fish and the milky white meat, there is a gray-pink membrane that should be removed before cooking. Monkfish tail fillets can range from 1–10 pounds, with those in the 1–4-pound range being most common in the market. The noted English food writer Jane Grigson thought that fillets in the 2–3-pound range had more flavor than smaller ones. Large tail fillets are often sliced crosswise into steaks. The boneless meat of this distinctive fish is firm and white, with a dense consistency more like the texture of lobster or scallops than of many fish. This texture is useful to the cook because it stands up to many preparations without falling apart, including stir-fries, skewering in chunks for brochettes, or incorporating into a fish soup or stew to give sub-

stance. I am not highly enthusiastic about the bland flavor of monkfish, but that very blandness makes it possible to combine monkfish for its texture with other, more assertive flavors which it absorbs. You can sauté slices of monkfish and then braise them in a highly flavored sauce such as in *Sautéed Bluefish Fillets with Piquant Spanish Sauce* (page 128) or in *Bluefish Baked with Peppers and Onions* (page 127). Jacques Pépin's cookbooks are worth consulting for many reasons, and especially for his monkfish recipes. Make a mental note to think of monkfish as a handy filler for shellfish salads. For a lobster salad on a tight budget, poach some monkfish (a 1-pound trimmed monkfish fillet cut into two sections takes about 18 minutes to poach in simmering water) and add it to cooked lobster meat.

Buying: The tail meat is sometimes sold skin on, but more commonly as elongated thick fillets with the skin and tailbone removed. Depending on the market, the membrane covering the meat may or may not have been removed. Some dealers, I have read, soak the tail meat in a phosphate dip to reduce natural drip loss, whiten flesh, and increase shelf life. If the outer ring of a cross section of the tail meat is whiter than normal, there is a chance the tail has been soaked. While properly used dips

MONKFISH (GOOSEFISH)

Monkfish (continued)

can improve color and shelf life, I prefer to reject such meat.

Storage: As is true of all fish, monkfish needs to be carefully stored in the coldest part of the refrigerator, wrapped in butcher's paper or waxed paper, sitting on ice, if possible, but without letting the flesh get wet from melting ice, and covered with ice packs.

Preparation:

To remove the outer skin: Remove any dark mottled outer skin by slicing through it with a sharp knife and then pulling it down

from the cut side of the fish, slicing skin away from flesh as you go. It is a loose skin and should come off without any trouble.

To remove the fillets from the tailbone: The two fillets lie on either side of the central tailbone. Cut down between the bone and the meat on each side, hugging the bone with your knife. Each boneless fillet will be wider at one end, narrower at the other.

To remove the membrane: Trim this gray-pink membrane off just as you would trim a layer of fat off a chunk of meat, removing both the membrane and any pink or yellowish fat beneath it and exposing the white meat of the

fillet. You may have to cut away small bits of the white meat in order to remove all of the membrane, but it's important to get it all because the membrane tightens up as it cooks and distorts the shape of the meat underneath.

Yields: A 6-pound whole tail with outer skin on yields about 4 pounds after the outer skin, central tailbone, and membrane have been removed; it is in the form of 2 boneless fillets of about 2 pounds each. Therefore the yield is about 67 percent. Allow 8 ounces of raw tail meat per person, as monkfish tends to shrink in cooking.

Broiled Monkfish with a Tomato Muffuletta Sauce (continued)

❖Omit the muffuletta sauce and serve the marinated, broiled slices of monkfish with a crisp relish, such as *Raw Bar Relish Al Forno* (page 14), or serve it plain with lemon wedges.

❖For a sharper flavor in the marinade, add chopped cilantro.

Monkfish and Eggplant Stew

Monkfish is a welcome addition to soups and stews because of its perfect firm texture. You could add chunks of monkfish to *Split Pea Soup with Celeriac* (page 60) or to any of the combination fish-and-vegetable soups in this book. In this recipe, monkfish borrows flavor from two of my favorite vegetables—eggplant and tomatoes. The vegetables can be pre-

pared ahead; in fact, the entire stew except for the fish can be made ahead, and the monkfish can be added just before the final baking.

Alternative fish: striped bass, haddock, cusk, or other firm-fleshed white fish

1½-lb skinned monkfish fillet, with
    membrane removed
1-lb eggplant
Salt and freshly ground pepper
6 Tb olive oil
1½ cups sliced onions
1 tsp minced garlic
Saffron threads (optional)
Cayenne pepper
1 bay leaf
4 cups peeled, seeded, and chopped tomatoes or
    drained, chopped canned plum tomatoes
2 Tb tomato paste
¼ cup chopped parsley
3 Tb butter
1 cup fresh bread crumbs

Remove any yellow or pink meat from the monkfish fillet (see Monkfish Box) so that you have just white meat. Cut the fillet crosswise into ½-inch-thick slices and then cut the larger slices into 1½-inch-square pieces. Cover and refrigerate until ready to cook.

Peel the eggplant and cut the flesh into 1-inch cubes. Place the eggplant in a colander, sprinkle 1 teaspoon of salt over the cubes, toss until all the cubes are coated with salt, and let drain for 30 minutes. With paper towels, rub any excess salt and moisture off the cubes, and pat them dry.

In a wide, high-sided sauté pan, heat 2 tablespoons of the oil, add the onions, and cook until wilted and lightly colored. Add 2 more tablespoons of the oil and stir in the eggplant, adding the remaining 2 tablespoons of oil if the eggplant absorbs most of the oil already in the pan; sauté the eggplant, stirring occasionally, for 5 minutes. Stir in the garlic, a pinch of saffron threads (if you like), a pinch of cayenne pepper, the bay leaf, tomatoes, and tomato paste, and cook, covered, for 5 minutes; uncover and cook 5 minutes more. Season with salt and freshly ground pepper.

Fold the pieces of monkfish and the parsley into the vegetable mixture, and spoon the entire mixture into a baking dish. In a small sauté pan, heat the butter, stir in the bread crumbs, and cook until the crumbs are lightly browned. Spoon the buttered crumbs over the top of the fish-vegetable mixture, place the dish in a preheated 425-degree oven, and bake for 15 minutes, or until the fish is tender and the stew is bubbly.   SERVES 4

❖ Turn this stew into a chowder by adding fish stock to the desired consistency and simmering the mixture on top of the stove just until the fish turns opaque.

Coriander-Crusted Mahi Mahi with Drunken Vegetables and Banana

Michael McSweeny, who has been a chef on the beautiful Hawaiian island of Kauai, generously gave me his favorite recipe for this fish, which became popular in Hawaii before being appreciated on the mainland. Michael has been a professional cook in many places, but he swears there is nothing to match Hawaiian waters for the variety of cooking fish. He recommends ono (wahoo) fish as a perfect substitute for mahi mahi; both are white, flaky, and delicately delicious. A large iron frying pan is ideal for this preparation; whatever pan you use, make sure it is capable of going from the cooktop to the oven. Michael recommends a cold beer as the perfect accompaniment to this dish.

CRUST

2 Tb coriander seeds
1 Tb black peppercorns
1 Tb cumin seeds
1–2 tsp kosher salt

VEGETABLES AND BANANA

1 lb onions
1 lb mixed sweet peppers
2 lb bananas
Juice of 2 limes

Four 7–8-oz mahi mahi fillets
3–4 Tb peanut oil
¼ cup dark rum
¼ cup softened butter

To make the crust: In a coffee grinder or blender, combine and pulverize the coriander seeds, peppercorns, cumin seeds, and kosher salt. Set the mixture aside in a pie pan. (If he has any left over, Michael tosses it with fried potatoes.)

To prepare the vegetables and banana: Peel and halve the onions, then either cut into thin slices or julienne strips; place in a bowl. Cut the peppers in half, remove stems, seeds, and white membrane, slice into thin julienne sticks, and add to the onions. Peel and slice the bananas, place in a small bowl, toss them with the lime juice, and set aside.

Pat the fish fillets dry and brush them lightly with a little of the peanut oil. Turn the fish into the crusting mixture, coating both sides. In a high-sided sauté pan large enough to hold the fish in one layer, heat the remainder of the oil. Place the fish in the hot oil, sear until browned on one side, then turn and sear until browned on the other side. Remove the fish to a warm plate and add the onions, peppers, and bananas to the sauté pan, mixing them gently. Simmer briefly,

SPECIAL INFORMATION ABOUT

MAHI MAHI

MAHI MAHI IS THE Hawaiian name for the dolphin *fish,* and the fish is most commonly marketed under the Hawaiian name so as not to confuse the fish with the very different *mammal* dolphin, or porpoise, which we all know, love, and protect. In Latin America this fish is often known as dorado, not to be confused with the Latin American freshwater dorado. Mahi mahi, or dolphin fish, can be found in warm waters in both the Atlantic and Pacific oceans. It is a delicious firm-fleshed fish, light pink when raw, white when cooked—the kind of fish that people who "don't like fish" will eat because it has delicate flavor and firm, juicy flesh. Once a fish known mainly to sport fishermen on vacation in Florida, mahi mahi is now widely available, fresh or frozen, in American markets. The best-tasting mahi mahi is bled at sea just after being caught and then quickly refrigerated at a very cold temperature.

One problem sometimes associated with mahi mahi is scombrotoxin poisoning (see *Scombroid Poisoning,* page 367). Fish that are not properly refrigerated can develop a histamine toxicity associated with decomposition at elevated temperatures. Because the toxic reaction can be severe, the FDA spot-checks mahi mahi for the presence of histamines. Make sure your supplier knows his fish has come from a reliable source.

Buying: Mahi mahi is usually available in fillets, steaks, or big chunks, but not as a whole fish. Some come to market fresh, some frozen. The skin may be on, but it is tough and not good to eat.

Storage: I buy fresh mahi mahi to order and use it the same day or the very next day. Keep this fish well chilled in the coldest part of the refrigerator, wrapped in butcher's paper, and sitting on ice, if possible, and topped with ice packs.

Preparation: Unless you have caught your own, you are most likely dealing with mahi mahi fillets or steaks from the market that need only be checked for bones and skinned before cooking, if desired. To remove the skin of a fillet, place the fillet skin side down on a flat work surface. Slip a long, sharp knife between the skin and flesh of the tail or narrower end and make about an inch-long cut. Grasp the separated skin firmly with the hand not holding the knife and pull the skin up toward you as you continue the knife along, cutting between the skin and the flesh. Eventually you will have the skin separated entirely from the fillet in one piece, and the skinned fillet will also be in one piece. It is fine to cook mahi mahi steaks with the skin on; when the cooking is completed, make a slit in the skin and pull it off.

Mahi mahi adapts to just about every cooking method, and the cooked flesh has nice large flakes. It can also be used raw in ceviche preparations, again after making sure that the fish has been inspected against the presence of histamines in the flesh.

Yield: The skin is the only part of the fillets, steaks, or chunks that you buy that is not edible, so you have almost 100 percent yield. A whole fish will yield about 45 percent edible flesh.

Coriander-Crusted Mahi Mahi with Drunken Vegetables and Banana (continued)

add the rum, and cook for a few minutes to allow the alcohol to burn off. Return the fish to the pan and place the pan in a preheated 400-degree oven for 5 minutes, or until the fish is just opaque. Remove the fish to 4 warm serving plates. Swirl the butter into the vegetables and fruit, smother the fish with the mixture, and serve.   SERVES 4

Salmon Steamed on a Bed of Winter Vegetables

From a recipe for a boiled fish-and-vegetable dinner in Jasper White's marvelous cookbook, *Jasper White's Cooking from New England,* I have devised this variation for a quickly prepared meal-in-one-dish full of good flavors, colorful, and blessedly low on calories.

When you're in Boston, his restaurant, called Jasper's, is not to be missed for refined food of eclectic inspiration. Use a pan for this recipe that is wide enough to lay out the salmon in one layer on top of the bed of vegetables. I use a pan about 10 inches square and 4 inches high for enough to serve 4 people. For more people, multiply the ingredients and the number of pans. The salmon and the vegetables can all be prepared well in advance and the vegetables cooked and the salmon added for final cooking just before serving. Serve with a green salad and crusty rolls.

Alternative fish: thick fillets of bass, cod, haddock, halibut, Arctic char, sturgeon

1½-lb skinned salmon fillet
1 lb celeriac
1–2 Tb fresh lemon juice
4 carrots (about ¾–1 lb)
Three to four 1-inch-thick leeks
8 small red potatoes
4–5 cups kale leaves (about ½ lb stem-on kale)
2 Tb butter
2 Tb Dijon-style mustard
Lemon wedges
Salt and freshly ground pepper

Remove any bones from the salmon, divide it into 4 servings of about 6 ounces each, cover, and refrigerate until ready to cook.

Remove the skin from the celeriac, cut the flesh into 1-inch chunks, place the chunks in a bowl, cover with water, and add the lemon juice to the water to keep the celeriac from darkening. Set aside.

Peel the carrots and cut them on the diagonal into 1-inch-long pieces. Set aside.

Remove the root end and dark green leaves of the leeks. Wash the leeks well and cut into 2-inch-long pieces.

Wash the potatoes and cut them in half.

Wash the kale and remove any stems. Keep small leaves whole and tear large leaves into 4-inch pieces.

Place the celeriac, carrots, leeks, and potatoes side by side in a large pan, cover with water, bring the water to a boil, reduce the heat, partially cover, and cook until the vegetables are almost tender, approximately 15 minutes. Add the kale leaves and continue to cook until the kale is tender, about 5 minutes.

Pour off most of the cooking liquid, leaving about ½ inch of liquid in the pan. Add the butter to the cooking liquid and place the pieces of salmon on top of the veg-

etables. Cover the pan and cook gently for 10 minutes, or until the salmon is opaque all the way through.

Remove the salmon to a warm platter or 4 serving plates. Lift the vegetables out and arrange them around the salmon. Immediately stir the mustard into the remaining cooking liquid and boil rapidly to reduce to a light syrup consistency. (You should have ½–¾ cup reduced juices.) Spoon the reduced juices over all. Serve with lemon wedges, salt and freshly ground pepper, and with more mustard, if desired.   SERVES 4

Poached Salmon with Lentils and Sun-Dried Tomato Sauce

Poaching salmon is the surefire method for treating it right; it always comes out tender and moist. At the drop of a hat, I poach salmon for my grandchildren, because it is cooked in 8 minutes, provides their protein, and they happily eat it without seasonings or sauces because they like its color and flavor without embellishment. This dish is actually a simple and healthy variation of the classic poached salmon with hollandaise sauce. The earthy lentils are a lovely contrast to the pink salmon and red sauce. If I am putting lentils in a soup or stew, I usually ignore any directions on the package to soak them before cooking them; but when I use them as a vegetable, I do soak them because they seem to hold their shape better. You could choose to omit the soaking and cook them a little longer. The lentils can be soaked in advance and then cooked just before serving, or they can be completely cooked ahead and gently reheated. The sauce can be cooked in advance and reheated at serving time. The salmon can be prepared for cooking, refrigerated, and then poached in just 8 minutes before serving. Ripe fresh tomatoes are essential for this sauce, as is a food processor or blender. I serve this dish with *Sautéed Cucumbers* (page 326), or with crunchy blanched green beans tossed with lemon juice and savory, or with a crisp cucumber salad.

Alternative fish: firm-fleshed fish fillets, such as striped bass, black bass, halibut, swordfish, snapper

LENTILS

1⅓ cups dried lentils
Salt and freshly ground pepper
2 Tb olive oil

Poached Salmon with Lentils and Sun-Dried Tomato Sauce (continued)

Sun-Dried Tomato Sauce

16 sun-dried tomato halves★
3 cups peeled, seeded, and chopped
    fresh, ripe tomatoes
1 lemon

★*To soften sun-dried tomatoes:* If the sun-dried tomatoes are packed in oil, there is no need to soften them by soaking, but they should be drained. To soften dry-packed sun-dried tomato halves, place them in a small bowl, pour 1 cup of boiling water over them, cover, and let soak for 30 minutes; drain before using.

To make the Sun-Dried Tomato Sauce: Place the chopped fresh tomatoes in a saucepan, bring to a boil over medium heat, cover, lower the heat to a gentle boil, and cook for 5 minutes to release some of the juice from the tomatoes. Add the sun-dried tomatoes, cover the pan, and cook for 15–20 minutes, stirring occasionally to release more of the tomato juices. Uncover and cook for 5–10 minutes more to reduce the juices and thicken the mixture. Transfer the tomatoes to a food processor or blender and purée. Return the sauce to the pan and stir in the juice of half the lemon, or more to taste.

MAKES ABOUT 1½ CUPS THICK SAUCE

❖The tomato sauce may thicken if stored. Thin it with a bit of tomato juice as you reheat before serving.

Salmon

Six 6–8-oz pieces salmon fillet
Lemon wedges

To prepare the lentils: Rinse the lentils well, put them in a 4-quart saucepan, cover them with 2 inches of water, and let them soak for 1 hour. Drain the lentils and rinse them again, wipe out the saucepan, and return the lentils to the pan; cover with 1 inch of water, add 1½ teaspoons of salt, bring to a boil, reduce the heat, and cook very gently for 12–15 minutes to keep the lentils from breaking up, or until they are tender. Drain the lentils in a sieve and return them to the saucepan. Stir in the olive oil and season with salt and freshly ground pepper. (Makes about 4 cups of cooked lentils)

Prepare the sun-dried tomato sauce and set aside.

To prepare the salmon: Run your fingers over the salmon, pressing gently, to feel for any bones; some bones are just below the surface, and you will feel them with your fingertips. Remove any bones with tweezers. Remove the skin or leave it on, as you prefer. Cover and refrigerate until ready to cook.

Fill a wide, 4-inch-deep saucepan about two-thirds full of water, bring the water to a boil, and lay the salmon pieces in the pan, skin or skinned side down. The cool salmon will drop the water temperature below the boil. Adjust the heat so that the water returns only to a simmer just under a boil and poach the salmon for 8 minutes or, if the fish pieces are thicker than ¾ inch, for 10 minutes. (To test for doneness, remove one piece and gently cut into its center with a small paring knife; it should be opaque all the way through.) Remove the pan from the heat, but leave the salmon in the poaching water while you assemble the rest of the dish; then remove the salmon from the water, pat it dry and serve.

To assemble the dish: Reheat the lentils and sauce, if necessary. Lift each salmon piece onto a double layer of paper towel, skin side up if it hasn't been skinned. Lift an edge of the skin with a paring knife and pull the skin off. Pat the fish with paper towels to remove any excess moisture. Spoon some lentils on each of 6 warm serving plates to make a bed for the salmon. Place a piece of salmon half on the lentils and half on the plate. Spoon some of the tomato sauce onto the salmon so that it runs a bit onto the lentils. Garnish with lemon wedges.   SERVES 6

❖Cook the lentils in a combination of chicken broth and water, and add a bouquet garni.
❖Flavor the olive oil with garlic before stirring it into the cooked lentils.
❖Add chopped herbs to the lentils or crunchy

vegetables, such as a little chopped scallions, red onions, celery, or hot or sweet peppers.

❖Add fresh lemon juice to the lentils.

❖Revert to the classic presentation: Poach the salmon as above and serve it with *Hollandaise Sauce* (page 356) and *Boiled New Potatoes* (page 334).

Whole Poached Salmon

Nothing I can think of is as certain to cause a sensation when you present it at your dinner table as a whole poached salmon of about 6 pounds. The color and form of the whole fish are spectacular. A slow poach will make the salmon flesh so succulent that it needs no enhancement; however, you might want to add the accoutrements of a traditional Fourth of July dinner: *Hollandaise Sauce* (page 356), *Braised Peas and Scallions* (page 332) fresh from the garden, and *Boiled New Potatoes* (page 334). A fish poacher—an elongated pot with a removable tray—is extremely useful. Mine is 27 inches long, just right for a 6-pound salmon, which will be about 26 inches long from snout to tip of tail; if I had only a 24-inch poacher, I would remove the salmon's head, and if I had only a 20-inch poacher, I would snip off its tail. Life is accommodation. Occasionally I have had to improvise and poach a whole salmon wrapped in cheesecloth for easy lifting and curled in an upright swimming position around the inside of a deep roasting pan. I like to poach the fish in a flavored water, or court bouillon. It is convenient to prepare the cooking liquid right in the poaching pan, but one has to know how much liquid it will take to cover the fish. I happen to know that it takes 8 quarts of water to cover a 6-pound fish in my 27-inch poacher, but if I didn't know, I would put the fish on its rack into the pan, measure cold water into the pan until the fish was covered, then remove the fish and rack and either use the water in the actual cooking or, if the water had particles of flesh and blood in it from the fish, empty out the pan and remeasure the same amount of clean water back into the poacher. A special advantage of cooking a whole fish is that there is likely to be some left over, and with salmon, that is a real treat.

Alternative fish: whole cod, haddock, snapper, or Arctic char

COURT BOUILLON

Water to cover fish in poaching pan
2 peeled and sliced large carrots
    (about 1½ cups)
3 sliced stalks celery, with leaves on
    (about 1½ cups)
2 quartered onions (about 1½ cups)
3 bay leaves
3–4 sprigs fresh thyme or 1 tsp dried
2 tsp salt
½ cup red wine vinegar

To make the Court Bouillon: Place the fish poacher or other poaching pan over two cooktop burners. Add enough water to cover the fish later, along with the carrots, celery, onions, bay leaves, thyme, and salt; bring the mixture to a boil, reduce the heat, and simmer, covered, for 30 minutes. Remove the cover and let the flavored water cool for 45 minutes to an hour, longer if convenient, then add the vinegar. This can be done well in advance.

1 scaled, gutted, gilled, and washed 6-lb salmon
Zucchini Slice "Scales" (optional, see directions
    below)
Thin slices lemon (optional)
Sprigs parsley (optional)
Lemon wedges (optional)

Prepare the court bouillon and allow to cool.

To prepare the salmon: Place the salmon in a poacher. If the bouillon doesn't cover the fish, add more water until the fish is submerged. Turn the burners to high heat, and when the bouillon comes just to a simmer, turn down the heat and cover the poacher. Maintain the bouillon at a bare shiver, keeping the temperature between 180–190 degrees if you have a liquid thermometer. Cook the salmon for 20 minutes, uncover, and turn off the heat. Let the salmon rest in the poacher for another 20 minutes.

To serve: Lift the fish on the rack out of the bouillon

Whole Poached Salmon (continued)

and tip the rack slightly to let excess liquid drain back into the poaching pan for about 30 seconds. Place the rack parallel to a serving platter, tip the rack, and gently slide the salmon sideways onto the platter. Remove and discard the skin on the top side of the salmon from the base of the head back to the tail. Remove the back fins with a knife and discard. Lightly scrape the dark fatty flesh off the top of the salmon and discard.

If desired, overlap zucchini slices to make a pattern like scales. Add a necklace of lemon slices and garnish the platter with parsley sprigs and lemon wedges.

To serve: Divide the top fillet in half lengthwise by running a knife along the center, cutting down to the center bone. Cut across the fillet halves every 3–4 inches to make serving pieces, lifting the pieces up with a flat server and checking for bones on the underside. When the top fillet has been served, remove the center bone and any visible small bones, and cut and serve the bottom fillet, turning each portion over to remove the skin and any dark flesh.   SERVES 8–10

❖ *Zucchini Slice "Scales":* Wash and dry 2–3 long, narrow zucchini and slice them into paper-thin rounds. Drop the zucchini into a pot of boiling water, blanch them for 30 seconds, drain, pat dry, and cut each round in half. Or make the zucchini rounds well ahead, blanch them in boiling water, drain them, and drop them into ice water to stop the cooking action. Drain on paper towels, pat dry, and set aside or refrigerate, covered, until ready to use. Just before the salmon is ready to serve, drop the reserved zucchini rounds into boiling water for 5 seconds and proceed as above (or reheat in a microwave oven).

❖ Poached salmon can be served plain, with lemon wedges, or with a sauce. In addition to a hollandaise sauce, try *Lemon Butter Sauce* (page 357), *Sorrel Sauce* (page 229), or warm *Fresh Tomato Sauce* (page 364).

❖ *Cold Whole Poached Salmon:* Cook the salmon as above, but let the salmon cool to room temperature in the poaching liquid. Remove the salmon to a work surface, carefully remove the skin and back fins, and scrape off the dark fatty flesh under the skin. Cover the fish with waxed paper or plastic wrap and chill for several hours or overnight. Make scales of thinly sliced cucumbers instead of zucchini, omitting the blanching step. Serve with crème fraîche and lemon wedges or a mixture of dill mayonnaise and sour cream, or a horse-radish-mustard cream.

Poached Salmon and Scallops with Ginger-Lime Butter Sauce

Ten years ago my husband came home from a business trip to Paris raving about a sauce that tasted like sweet lime. I devised one of honey and lime, but later replaced the honey with syrup from jars of stem ginger available in Asian markets. At the Straight Wharf Restaurant this dish became so popular that we went through cases of stem ginger every summer. The sauce uses a lot of butter, but even a small portion transforms the fish. Butter sauces will separate if mishandled; use a heavy-bottomed pan, keep the heat low, count on the cream to stabilize the sauce, and hold the sauce over warm rather than very hot water until ready to serve, and you will have a memorable sauce.

Alternative fish: bass, snapper, halibut, other white fish. Salmon is ideal, however, because its color as well as taste works so well with the other elements in this dish.

GINGER-LIME BUTTER SAUCE

½ cup fresh lime juice (about 4 fresh
   limes)
6 Tb ginger syrup
½ cup heavy cream
2 sticks plus 4 Tb *chilled* butter,
   cut into small pieces
½ cup finely chopped stem ginger

To make the Ginger-Lime Butter Sauce: Whisk together the lime juice and ginger syrup in a heavy-bottomed pan, adding more of either to suit your own taste. Bring the mixture to a boil and reduce by half. Stir in the cream and cook to reduce by half again. Turn the heat to low and gradually whisk in the butter. The sauce will get creamy and thicken. Stir in the chopped ginger and keep the sauce warm over barely simmering water.

MAKES 2 CUPS

FISH AND GARNISH

2-lb skinned salmon fillet
⅔ lb small sea scallops
1 lime
Grated lime rind (optional)

Prepare the ginger–lime butter sauce and keep it warm.

To prepare the fish and garnish: Remove any bones from the salmon and cut it into 6 even portions. Remove the tough piece of cartilage from the side of the scallops, wipe off any bits of shell, and pat them dry. Cut the lime into thin slices and make a small cut halfway across each slice.

Fill a wide pan two-thirds full of water and bring it to a boil. Lay the salmon in the water, regulating the heat so that the water just shivers below the boil. Simmer for 8 minutes. Two minutes before the salmon is ready, drop the scallops into the water.

Remove the salmon and scallops from the cooking liquid at the same time, using a slotted spoon for the scallops; place them both on paper towels and quickly pat dry.

Place a piece of salmon on each warmed serving plate. Place an equal portion of scallops on top and to the side of each piece of salmon. Spoon the sauce all over and decorate each plate with a twisted slice of lime. Sprinkle grated lime on the salmon, if desired.

SERVES 6

❖ Serve the salmon and scallops with a fresh tomato sauce or sorrel sauce, or just with lemon.

Sautéed Butterflied Salmon

I learned the technique of butterflying salmon from the Norwegian television cooking star Ingrid Espelid Howig. The technique works so nicely for so many kinds of fish that I think you will use it again and again. It's easy to do and, as Ingrid says, makes a small piece of fish look like quite a generous serving (see illustration on facing page). In the notes following the recipe, there are instructions for making two excellent quick sauces to serve with the salmon, but you could also serve this versatile presentation just with lemon wedges or chutney, or with a butter, tomato, or sorrel sauce.

Alternative fish: any firm-fleshed thick fish, such as bass, snapper, sturgeon, halibut, bluefish, shark

1¾–2-lb center-section salmon fillet
    (8 inches long)
3 Tb butter
2 Tb light olive oil or vegetable oil
Salt and freshly ground pepper
Lemon wedges

Remove the skin and any bones from the salmon fillet, and trim off any dark flesh on the skin side of the fillet. Slice the fillet crosswise at 1-inch intervals to make 8 individual pieces. The width of the original fillet now becomes the length of each of the 1-inch-wide pieces. With a thin, sharp knife, slice lengthwise down through the center of each piece, but do not cut quite all the way through. Open the cut with your hands, turning each side down flat. You now have 8 pieces of ½-inch-thick butterflied salmon that look rather like salmon steaks but have no bones.

Divide the butter and oil between two preferably nonstick sauté pans, heat the butter and oil until it bubbles, place 4 pieces of salmon in each pan, and sauté over medium heat for 2 minutes. Season with salt and freshly ground pepper, then turn and cook for 2–3 minutes on the other side or until just cooked through. Serve with lemon wedges and, if you like, with a sauce.   SERVES 4, WITH 2 PIECES PER PERSON

SERVES 8 AS AN APPETIZER

❖*With Shallot, Crème Fraîche, and Dill Sauce:*
2 Tb butter
2 Tb chopped shallots

⅓ cup dry vermouth or white wine
½ cup *Crème Fraîche* (page 353), sour cream,
    heavy cream, or a combination
2–3 Tb chopped fresh dill

Remove the sautéed salmon to a warm serving platter. Wipe out one of the pans the salmon cooked in, melt the butter in the pan, stir in the shallots, cook for 30 seconds, then add the vermouth or wine and boil until reduced by half. Stir in the crème fraîche or cream and dill, and heat thoroughly. Arrange 2 slices of salmon on each of 4 serving plates and spoon the sauce next to the salmon.

❖With *Shallot, Olive, and Red Pepper Topping:*
2 Tb light olive oil
2 Tb chopped shallots
⅓ cup dry vermouth or white wine
½ cup finely diced, roasted and peeled red peppers (pimentos)
3 Tb finely diced black olives
Lemon wedges

Remove the sautéed salmon to a warm platter. Wipe out one of the pans the salmon cooked in and heat the oil in it. Add the shallots and cook for 30 seconds; then add the vermouth or wine and cook until reduced by half. Add the red peppers and heat, stirring, for 1 minute. Add the olives, stir all together, and cook just until heated through. Arrange 2 slices of the salmon on each of 4 serving plates and drizzle one-quarter of the sauce across each serving. Serve with lemon wedges.

SPECIAL INFORMATION ABOUT
SALMON

WHEN IN DOUBT, SERVE salmon. It is surely Americans' first choice for a fish dinner, just as shrimp is the most popular choice among shellfish. Many consider salmon to be the world's finest eating fish. Just the color of the raw flesh—ranging from delicate pink to orange to deep red—is enough to draw one to this fish. The high oil content in salmon makes the meat silky and luscious, but unlike other oily fish such as mackerel or bluefish, salmon has a mild flavor that appeals even to those who "don't like fish." Because of its firm, close-grained texture, salmon lends itself to steaks, fillets, butterfly cuts, chunks, and thinly sliced escalopes without falling apart. Cooks praise its versatility, for it can be poached, steamed, sautéed, braised, baked, or roasted; and because of the oils that retain moisture even under intense heat, it can be very successfully broiled and grilled as well. The wild salmon we find in our markets is anadromous salmon—salmon that is born in a freshwater river and migrates to the ocean, where it spends much of its life, and then returns to the river of origin to spawn and die. I shall never forget standing at the base of a high waterfall in Scotland watching salmon fighting their way up and over the formidable and treacherous obstacle between them and their spawning grounds. It was all I could do not to get into the water, take them in my hands, and carry them up to the next

plateau above the falls. A "Victory Garden" crew of five was with me, and after an hour of watching the remarkable determination of these beautiful creatures, we were all almost in tears.

Wild Atlantic salmon have been commercially overfished and affected by polluted waters to the point of becoming an endangered species; unless you have the good fortune to catch one (they are magnificent fighters in sport fishing), at the fish market you will usually find farmed Atlantic salmon that has been raised in commercial saltwater farms and fed a diet of fish products, wheat, and other nutrients. Farm-raised salmon is superbly rich and fatty, sometimes almost marbled in texture, and, provided that handling and storage have been expert, very uniform in quality. It is available year-round; veteran suppliers say that anyone anywhere in the country can get an Atlantic salmon that has been out of the water for less than 24 hours.

SALMON

Salmon (continued)

What farmed salmon lacks is a certain pronounced taste that wild salmon gets from its different diets and environments, and from its migratory life. The wild salmon available to us is Pacific salmon—most of it from Alaskan waters—harvested from early spring until midfall. The combination of fresh wild Pacific salmon during its season and the always available fresh farmed salmon from the Atlantic overwhelms the market at midyear; consequently, a good deal of the Pacific catch and some of the farmed Atlantic salmon come to the market frozen. If the salmon has been swiftly and carefully frozen at sea and kept under proper conditions, frozen salmon can be very close to the quality of perfectly handled fresh salmon and superior to fresh salmon that has not been handled properly. There are six species of salmon available in American markets, one from the East Coast and five from the West Coast:

ATLANTIC SALMON

Atlantic salmon is often identified by its country of origin—Norway, Canada, etc.—but it is all the same species, and now most of the market supply is farmed Atlantic salmon. Suppliers may confuse the issue by calling their salmon "Norwegian" and charging a premium price when, in fact, because of recent regulations and tariffs, the amount of Atlantic salmon imported from Norway has sharply declined. The flesh of Atlantic salmon is pink, and because of its high oil content, it smokes well and grills well. Most of the farmed salmon is harvested and marketed in the 6–9-pound range.

PACIFIC SALMON

Each of the five wild Pacific salmon species differs in size, color, and fat content. Salmon store up fat in preparation for the long and arduous journey upriver to spawn; during the journey they do not eat, but live off their stored fat. The longer the journey, the fatter the fish needs to be at the start. A spawning journey up the Yukon River may be 2000 miles long, and lovers of salmon flesh prize—and will go out of their way to get—a salmon that has just prepared itself for such a trip. We have had the good fortune to dine on Columbia River and Copper River salmon, relishing every mouthful.

1. *Chinook salmon.* The largest of all the salmon—and for that reason often called "king" salmon—chinook have a flesh color that, depending on diet, ranges all the way from red to such a pale pink as to be called "white." Their high fat (or oil) content makes them ideal for smoking, broiling, or grilling. Chinook salmon account for only about 1 percent of the Alaskan catch—another reason why they are expensive and sold largely either to the restaurant trade or to commercial smoking establishments. Blackmouth salmon is a smaller, immature chinook without the incomparable taste of fully mature wild chinook.

2. *Coho salmon* (also known as silver, medium reds, redsides, silversides) are one of the last salmon to spawn, so they are harvested wild in late summer and fall, but they are also farmed in Chile and elsewhere. Their orange-red flesh holds its color well when cooked. Since the flesh has less oil than some other salmon species, the cook has to watch that the flesh does not dry out during cooking. Their size, 4–12 pounds, makes them ideal for steaks, and they are perfect for poaching, braising, and covered baking, as in a paupiette. Some farmed coho of 10-ounce to 2-pound size are marketed as "baby" or "yearling" salmon and are available whole and boned, with head and tail removed, or as fillets; they have a delicate taste and texture, and can be prepared like trout.

3. *Sockeye salmon* (also known as red or blueback). Once the foundation of the canned salmon industry, these darkest of all salmon, with deep, rich red flesh and oil (or fat) content second only to chinooks, have been rediscovered as a fresh or frozen table fish. They have firm texture, fine flavor, and good color retention after cooking, and average 3–5 pounds dressed. They are harvested from late spring through midsummer. A good part of the catch is frozen and exported to Japan, where it is in great demand. An excellent salmon for steaks, sockeyes are

SALMON

also alder-smoked by some pack-agers and sold in a pouch that requires no refrigeration.

4. Chum salmon (the brightest known as silverbrite and not to be confused with coho salmon when it is called silver salmon). Harvested from September through November, chum has the least oil content of all the salmons, making it less desirable for direct-heat cooking such as grilling. Its skin is bright silver when the fish is fattest and dark-ens during river runs, so it is best to buy chum skin-on and to be sure the skin is silvery. The deep orange flesh can be delicious, and chum is available, frozen, year-round. Its price often makes it an attractive buy, and its aver-age weight is about 7 pounds whole.

5. Pink salmon. Pinks, at an aver-age 3 pounds, are the smallest and most abundant of the salmons, and now the heart of the salmon canning industry. They do appear in markets fresh or frozen, but the flesh, which is a light rose color, is delicate and requires careful handling, so buy with care.

Note: A *steelhead* (also called a salmon trout or steelhead salmon) is really a seagoing trout that can be treated for cooking in much the same way as salmon.

SMOKED SALMON

Nothing is better as a first course than a plate of thinly sliced smoked salmon served with warm toasts and a choice of lemon wedges, capers, sliced onions, and a sweet butter or piquant mustard-dill sauce. Salmon can be home-smoked, but since the commercial prod-uct is so good and readily avail-able, it is simply much easier to serve. Before being smoked, the salmon is salted in brine or with a coating of dry salt to release liq-uids from the flesh and act as a preservative. Then it is rinsed and air-dried, leaving a glossy film (the pellicle) that preserves the color and texture of the fish as it smokes. *Hot* smoking cooks the fish at temperatures up to 180 degrees and produces a flaky flesh that tastes more like canned than fresh salmon; it is difficult to slice hot smoked salmon thin. *Cold* smoking dries the salmon at temperatures up to 90 degrees, and the flesh retains the translu-cency and texture of raw fish more than that of cooked fish. It is easily sliced or comes presliced for convenience and uniformity. Commercial smokehouses vary in methods and recipes, so shop for one you like. I always refrig-erate both hot and cold smoked salmon, even if the hot smoked variety has been vacuum-sealed and essentially canned.

LOX

Lox is not smoked salmon. It is unsmoked raw salmon preserved by heavy salting. This was the original method of preserving salmon before refrigeration or canning. The salmon is quite heavily salted in a brine, then soaked to remove much of the saltiness, but it characteristically has a saltier taste than smoked salmon.

Be aware: Cold smoking and salting do not kill the parasites that can be present in the flesh of fish. Blast-freezing to −40 degrees for 15 hours, or commercial freezing to −10 degrees for 7 days, is rec-ommended by the FDA to kill parasites in fish to be eaten raw or undercooked. The parasite anasakis simplex—a potential health hazard to humans—could be present in cold-smoked or salted fish, and tapeworms could be present in anadromous fish such as wild salmon that has not been commercially frozen at some point before being served. See *Parasites* (page 367).

Salmon "caviar": A tasty addi-tional benefit of salmon is the female roe, often referred to as salmon "caviar." The reference is a little presumptuous. Real caviar is the processed roe of sturgeon. The most famous, delicious, and expensive caviar comes from three species of sturgeon that live mainly in the Caspian Sea bor-dering Russia; in descending order of cost, these are beluga, osetra, and sevruga, each named for its sturgeon. Processing the roe consists of a careful washing, sorting, and salting to preserve the eggs and highlight their deli-cate flavor. The salting is critical, because too much salt harms the flavor of the eggs and too little will not preserve them. The finest-quality Russian caviar is called "malossol," which means "little salt." There are many species of sturgeon around the world, including sturgeon from

SALMON

Salmon (continued)

American waters, from which a very tasty roe is processed that can legitimately be called American caviar. The eggs of other fish can, of course, be processed the same way. Whitefish roe is sometimes referred to as golden caviar. Salmon roe is the largest-grained of all these processed roes, with each egg looking like a tiny orange pea. Each grain has an almost translucent quality and is juicy, with a pop-in-your-mouth texture. The flavor is relatively mild, and the saltiness varies from one producer to another. I find salmon "caviar" to be quite different from real caviar but very good in its own right, and I use it to garnish both salmon dishes and many other fish dishes. An added appeal is that the price is right.

Buying: Look for these signs in buying salmon: The skin should have an iridescent sheen and should be clear of marks indicating rough handling; if the fish has scales on, check that the scales are undisturbed—a poorly handled or old fish will lose scales. The color under the gills should be vivid, not gray. The flesh should be moist-looking rather than dry, firm rather than mushy; its color should be rich, and it should look almost translucent rather than opaque. Separations in the flesh suggest aging; dark red patches suggest bruising. While I have said that other fish should have little or no odor, salmon does have a characteristic odor peculiar to itself, but

it is not an unpleasant "fishy" odor. Your fish market should be able to identify the species of salmon you are buying (which will determine the best ways to cook it) and the source. Always ascertain if the salmon is entirely fresh or if it was frozen and then thawed by the retailer. Previously frozen and thawed fish may be softer-textured and not as suitable for some recipes that involve broiling or grilling. The price should reflect the species: the price of chum and of pink salmon, for example, should be less than that of chinook, coho, sockeye, or Atlantic salmon.

Salmon is marketed whole, as large cross sections of the whole fish (often of the tail section, which does not cut into uniform steaks), in steaks, or in fillets. Steaks are cut from the cross section of the salmon, including the center bone and skin, and are usually ¾–1-inch thick, although your market will undoubtedly cut them to a different thickness for you if you order ahead. Fillets are the flesh sides of the fish removed from the backbone that are sold as whole fillets or sliced into fillet portions.

While this book is directed principally to the cooking of fresh fish, I advise buying commercially frozen salmon for any preparations using salmon raw, marinated, or not completely cooked. The best frozen fish is flash-frozen immediately after being caught, gutted and bled, and then thawed slowly at home on ice in the refrigerator over a period of 24–48 hours. The cri-

teria for quality in frozen-thawed fish are the same as for fresh fish, but check also for yellowing along the belly flaps, which is a sign that the fish was improperly frozen or frozen too long, and as a result, the oil is separating in the flesh. Frozen-thawed flesh should be resilient like fresh fish; an indentation made by poking around the spine with your fingers should spring right back.

Storage: Store fresh salmon wrapped in butcher's paper in the coldest part of the refrigerator and topped with ice or ice packs. Do not let any water from melting ice come in contact with the flesh of the fish. I cook all fish as soon as I get it home, but you can keep salmon up to 48 hours, if necessary.

Preparation: Salmon is usually marketed skin-on. Many recipes are best cooked with the skin on to help hold the fish together, and the skin can easily be lifted off the flesh after cooking. However, some recipes call for special cuts, and in that case you should buy a whole salmon fillet. You can ask your fish market to remove the skin, or you can remove it yourself; I feel that a piece of fish stores better with its skin intact.

To remove the skin from a whole fillet: Place the fish skin side down on a flat work surface. Using a sharp, 8-inch-long knife, cut a small slit about an inch long between the skin and the flesh at the tail end of the fillet. Hold the end of the skin with a firm grip, and with your other hand, slide

SPECIAL INFORMATION ABOUT

SALMON

the knife away from you between the skin and flesh at a slight angle. Angle the blade so that its edge is slightly up toward the flesh, and use a gentle sawing motion as you work the knife down the length of the fillet, pulling the skin toward you slightly as you cut.

Salmon has a thin layer of dark meat under the skin that turns a dark gray when cooked; it is muscle hemoglobin, and while it is perfectly edible, it has a slightly bitter taste compared with the sweeter meat next to it. It also somewhat spoils the look of the otherwise handsome cooked salmon flesh. To remove it, run a sharp, thin-edged knife just under the dark meat, slicing it off in small sections. Once the dark meat has been removed, turn the salmon fillet skinned side down, and run your fingers over the top of the fillet to detect any of the pin bones that run down the cen-

ter of the fillet from the nape of the salmon's neck about halfway to its tail. When you feel bones, pull them out with tweezers or needle-nose pliers.

Yields: A whole 7½-pound salmon, 27 inches long, contains 5½ pounds of flesh in the form of 2 fillets, or sides, each weighing 2¾ pounds. If you cut a whole

gutted and headed fish into steaks, you will get about 60 percent yield of meat; if you fillet a whole gutted and headed fish, you will get a yield of 70–75 percent meat.

❖ I count on 6–8 ounces of meat per serving.
❖ An 8-ounce steak with bone and skin removed yields 5½–6 ounces of meat.
❖ An 8-ounce fillet with skin removed yields 7 ounces of meat.

If the price per pound between steaks and fillets remains equal, fillets are the better buy. Even with some price differential, fillets can be the better buy. At $9.00 per pound, 8 ounces of salmon steak costs $4.50 but yields only $2.75 worth of meat after removing bone and skin. At $10.00 per pound, 8 ounces of salmon fillet costs $5.00, but after removing the skin, I have $4.36 worth of meat.

Salmon Paillardes with Parsley, Sage, Rosemary, and Thyme

In kitchen parlance, paillardes are flattened slices of food, often of meat or poultry, that have been pounded very thin and cooked very quickly. Salmon can be prepared the same way. I use a plumber's rubber mallet for pounding, but the bottom of a round plastic food con-

tainer will do nicely. The salmon will spread out considerably from the pounding, so plan to serve this dish on wide, flat plates. Just for fun, I have coated these paillardes with the herbs in the title of Paul Simon's famous folk song. The pounded, seasoned paillardes should sit in the refrigerator at least an hour before cooking, and the *Spaetzle* (page 362) that I recommend to accompany the fish can be prepared in the morning or even the day before. Spaetzle is a classic accompaniment to veal paillardes; it is equally good with salmon. If you want to be very nice to your guests, begin this meal with a vegetable course of *Waltham Butternut*

Salmon Paillardes with Parsley, Sage, Rosemary, and Thyme (continued)

Squash "Pillows" with Fresh Sage (page 340), which can be prepared ahead, or use the squash as accompaniment to the paillardes in the main course.

Alternative fish: bluefish, bass, or monkfish medallions, or almost any firm-fleshed fish that can be sliced horizontally without breaking apart; or unsliced flounder or orange roughy

Alternative shellfish: abalone steaks

1½-lb salmon fillet, 1 inch thick
3 Tb finely chopped parsley
1½ tsp minced fresh sage
1½ tsp minced fresh rosemary
1 Tb minced fresh thyme
1 Tb finely grated lemon rind
Pinch of cayenne pepper
⅓ cup light olive oil
Salt and freshly ground pepper
Lemon wedges

Remove any skin and bones from the salmon. Cut the fillet in half crosswise to make 2 equal portions, each 1 inch thick. Holding your knife parallel to the work surface, cut the 2 pieces in half horizontally to make 4 pieces, each now ½ inch thick. Place each slice between sheets of waxed paper and pound to a thickness of about ¼ inch.

In a small bowl, combine the parsley, sage, rosemary, thyme, lemon rind, cayenne pepper, and olive oil. Rub this mixture over all sides of the paillardes, season with salt and freshly ground pepper, and place them in the refrigerator for at least 1 hour.

Just before serving, heat two large, nonstick sauté pans. Place the paillardes in the pans and cook for 1 minute on each side. Lift the fish with a wide spatula to warm serving plates and serve with lemon wedges.

SERVES 4

❖Substitute cilantro for parsley, or lemon thyme for plain thyme, or try other herbs.
❖Omit the herbs and sprinkle the salmon with *Blackened Seasoning Mixture* (page 141).
❖Omit the herbs, sauté the salmon paillardes, remove the fish to serving plates, swirl and heat 2–3 tablespoons drained capers and 2 tablespoons lemon juice in the sauté pan, pour the lemon-and-caper sauce over the paillardes, and serve.

Sautéed Salmon Fillets with Sweet Red Pepper Compote

There is something wonderful about the color combination of light pink salmon and bright red peppers, and about how the sweet taste of each—fish and vegetable—complements the other. With this dish I like to serve *Portuguese Peas* (page 240) to get the accent of green and the spicy flavor of sausage cooked with peas.

Alternative fish: bluefish, tuna, swordfish, or any thick, firm-fleshed white fish

1½–2-lb salmon fillet
3 red sweet peppers
1 sliced small onion
¾ cup water, tomato juice, or a combination of both
2 Tb fresh lemon juice
3 Tb light olive oil
¼ cup flour, preferably instant-blending flour (such as Wondra Quick-Mixing Flour), for dredging
1 crushed clove garlic
3–4 Tb sliced basil leaves
Salt and freshly ground pepper

Remove any skin and bones from the salmon, cut it into 4 equal portions, and set aside.

Halve the peppers, remove the stems, seeds, and white membranes, and cut into slices lengthwise. Place the peppers, onion, ¼ cup of the water or tomato juice, and lemon juice into a food processor, and chop the vegetables into small pieces. In a nonstick sauté pan wide enough to hold the salmon later on in one layer, heat 1 tablespoon of the oil, then add the pepper-onion mixture. Cook over medium heat, stirring, for 3–4 minutes until the vegetables are wilted and the liquid in the pan is almost evaporated. Remove the mixture to a bowl and set aside.

Wipe out the sauté pan, and add and heat the remaining 2 tablespoons of oil. Lightly flour the pieces of salmon, shaking off any excess, and place in the pan skinned side up. Cook over medium-high heat for 4 minutes or until golden brown, then turn and cook on the other side for 4 minutes. Remove the fish to a warm plate. Return the pepper-onion mixture to the pan and reheat, stirring in the remaining ½ cup of water or tomato juice, the garlic, and the basil. Season with salt and freshly ground pepper. Place the salmon pieces on top of the pepper-onion mixture, cover, and cook over medium heat for 5–6 minutes, or until the salmon is just cooked through; cooking time will depend on the thickness of the salmon. Lift the salmon to warm serving plates and garnish with the pepper mixture. SERVES 4

❖Add some Middle Eastern spices, such as cumin and/or cardamom, to the pepper mixture.

Sliced Salmon with Sorrel Sauce

I always forget how good sorrel sauce is until I make it again. Sorrel, also known as sour grass because of its tart lemony taste, is a leafy green that looks somewhat like a flat-leafed spinach. It makes a flavorful addition to vegetable soups, but my favorite use for it is in this sauce. There are many versions of sorrel sauce, some as simple as stirring shredded sorrel leaves into reduced heavy cream, but I prefer this version for its versatility; it can be made ahead and reheated, and taking time to "stew" the stems in the broth base increases the vividness of the flavor. The sauce is thickened with beurre manié, which is nothing more than a paste of softened butter and flour. The recipe calls for a cup of heavy cream and several tablespoons of butter, but the sauce is enough to serve 8–10 people or it can even be stretched to serve 12, so the fat and calories are widely distributed. Halve the recipe if you are serving only a few people. I count on 6 ounces of fish per serving. Serve a side dish of sweet carrot or parsnip logs and boiled potatoes, and there you have it: a perfect main course for a dinner party because the distinctive sauce can be made ahead and the fish cooks in only a couple of minutes just before serving—how nice for the cook!

Alternative fish: firm-fleshed fillets that will hold their shape when sliced—striped bass, halibut, snapper, sturgeon, sable

2½-lb skinned salmon fillet

BEURRE MANIÉ

1 Tb softened butter
2 Tb flour

SORREL SAUCE

½ lb sorrel stems and leaves
1 Tb butter
4 Tb roughly chopped shallots
1 cup dry vermouth or white wine
2 cups salmon broth or unsalted
    chicken broth
1 cup heavy cream
½ lemon
Salt and freshly ground pepper

To make the Sorrel Sauce: Wash the sorrel and remove the stems by holding the folded leaf in one hand and pulling the stem down the back of the leaf with the other hand. (You will have about 5–6 cups loosely packed leaves and about ¼ pound stems.) Spin-dry the leaves, stack them in piles, and cut them in very thin chiffonade strips. (You will have about 4 cups sliced leaves.)

In a nonaluminum-lined saucepan, heat the tablespoon of butter, add the shallots, and cook for 1 minute. Add the vermouth or wine, broth, and sorrel stems, bring the mixture to a boil, and cook for 8–10 minutes, or until the liquid is reduced to about 2 cups. Stir in the cream, bring the mixture back to a boil, and cook for 5 minutes more. Pour the mixture through a sieve into a bowl, pressing the sorrel stems and shallots in the sieve to extract their juices. Discard the solids, return the sauce to the pan, and gradually whisk bits of the beurre manié into the sauce, cooking for 4–5 minutes until the sauce has thickened. If the sauce seems lumpy, strain it through the sieve again and return the strained sauce to the pan. Stir in the sliced sorrel leaves and the juice of half a lemon, and season the sauce with salt and freshly ground pepper. Keep the sauce warm if you are serving shortly, or bring it to room temperature, cover, and refrigerate if you are making it ahead, and reheat over low heat before serving. MAKES 3 CUPS

Sliced Salmon with Sorrel Sauce (continued)

4 Tb melted butter or vegetable oil

Remove any bones and dark fatty meat from the salmon, and cut the fillet into ¼-inch-thick slices with a diagonally angled cut. Cover and refrigerate until ready to cook.

To make the beurre manié: In a small bowl, work the softened butter and flour together with your fingers until they make a paste. Set aside.

Prepare the sorrel sauce and keep warm.

Brush the salmon slices with melted butter or oil and spread them out on baking sheets. Place one sheet at a time under a preheated broiler and cook until the salmon just turns opaque, about 1–2 minutes. Repeat until all of the salmon is cooked.

To serve: Spoon some of the sorrel sauce onto the center of each warm serving plate. Using a long spatula and dividing the salmon slices evenly among the plates, place the salmon slices on the sauce in an overlapping fan pattern. Spoon a little sauce in a line across the top of each serving.   SERVES 4

❖Sauté the salmon in butter in a nonstick sauté pan.

Chunky Salmon Hash

This hash is loose enough that you can see all of the ingredients. It's an ideal way to use leftover cooked fresh salmon, and it's good enough to be worth cooking up some salmon if there are no leftovers in the refrigerator. Broccoli tossed in melted butter flavored with lemon juice is a nice accompaniment.

Alternative fish: any firm-fleshed cooked fish

4 cups cooked salmon, broken into large flakes
3 Tb butter
1 Tb vegetable oil
1 sliced onion
1½ lb cooked, peeled, and sliced potatoes
2 peeled red peppers, cut into strips
Salt and freshly ground pepper
½ cup roughly chopped Italian parsley
Lemon wedges
Tartar Sauce (page 363) (optional)

Carefully remove any bones from the salmon and set it aside.

In a large skillet, melt 2 tablespoons of the butter and the vegetable oil. Add the onion slices and potatoes, and cook over medium-high heat, turning occasionally, for 15 minutes, or until the vegetables are lightly browned and crisp. Add the peppers, folding them into the onions and potatoes, and cook for another 10 minutes, turning occasionally. Add the remaining 1 tablespoon of butter to the skillet and carefully fold in the salmon, trying not to further break the flesh apart. Season with salt and freshly ground pepper and continue cooking for another 5–8 minutes, or until the salmon is heated through. Fold in the parsley and check the seasoning once more. Serve with lemon wedges and with tartar sauce, if you like.   SERVES 4

❖I love to serve this with poached eggs and ketchup on top.

❖Use pimentos if you do not have red peppers.

Salmon with a Potato Crust

A creative French chef invented a fish dish with a potato crust, and versions of it swept through restaurants and cookbooks. My adaptation is based on a recipe developed by one of my culinary heroes, Jacques Pépin. Its strength is its very simplicity. The dish actually benefits from early preparation and refrigeration to encourage the potato slices to adhere to the fish.

Alternative fish: snapper, bass, halibut, bluefish, or amberjack (none of which looks as pretty between the potato layers as salmon does)

1½-lb salmon fillet
2 large potatoes
4 Tb melted butter
Salt and freshly ground pepper
1 Tb chopped fresh thyme
3 Tb vegetable oil

Remove the skin and any bones from the salmon and trim off any dark meat on the skin side. Divide the salmon into 4 equal portions of about 6 ounces each. Pat the fish pieces dry with paper towels. Peel the potatoes and cut them lengthwise into paper-thin slices.

For each serving, cut an 8-inch square of plastic wrap or waxed paper. Place 3 slices of potato, slightly overlapping, in a diagonal line in the center of the wrapping material. Brush both sides of a piece of salmon with melted butter and set the salmon on top of the potato slices. Season the salmon with salt and freshly ground pepper and a sprinkling of thyme. Top the fish with another 3 slices of potato and brush the potato with butter. Depending on the size of the salmon pieces, you may need fewer or more than 3 slices of potato to cover each side of the fish. Wrap each fish parcel tightly and refrigerate until final cooking.

For final preparation, heat the oil in a large, non-stick sauté pan. Carefully unwrap the fish parcels and transfer them to the pan. Sauté the fish and potatoes over medium heat for 4–5 minutes, turn carefully with a large spatula, and sauté for another 4–5 minutes, or until the potatoes are browned and the salmon is just cooked through. SERVES 4

❖Serve with *Roasted Ratatouille* (page 326).
❖*Oven-Roasted:* Unwrap the fish parcels and place them on an oiled baking sheet. Roast in a preheated 450-degree oven for 10–12 minutes. Run the baking sheet under the broiler to brown the potatoes, if desired.

Chopped Braised Leeks and Salmon

The leeks and salmon braise together in a one-pan, no-fuss meal. You can prepare the chopped leeks a day ahead, if you like, and the final cooking is just a few minutes. Braised baby carrots or carrot logs would be an ideal side dish. Carrots taste very good with leeks and add a complementary color; sprinkle them with some chopped chives, too.

Alternative fish: halibut, cod, bass, snapper, Arctic char

1½-lb skinned salmon fillet
4 lb whole leeks
3 Tb butter
½ cup chopped celery
½ cup chicken broth
Salt and freshly ground pepper
¼ cup chopped chives
2 Tb salmon caviar (optional)

Remove any bones in the salmon, cut the fillet into 4 equal portions, cover, and refrigerate.

Remove any withered outer leaves of the leeks, and cut off and discard the green upper leaves down to the point where the dark green begins to pale. Quarter the leeks lengthwise from the top down to within 1½ inches from the base, and gently fan out the leaves so that any soil or grit on the leaves is easy to remove. Fill the sink or a deep pot with lukewarm water and plunge the leeks up and down in the water until they are clean, then pat them dry. To chop, cut across the leeks in ¼-inch slices. (You will have about 8 cups chopped leeks.)

In a large frying pan, melt the butter, add the celery and the chopped leeks, and stir to coat the vegetables with butter. Pour in the chicken broth and cook for 3–4 minutes, or until the vegetables are just wilted. Season with salt and freshly ground pepper. (To serve as a vegetable without the fish, continue cooking for 2–3 minutes more, covered, stirring occasionally.)

Place the salmon fillets on top of the chopped, braised leeks, cover, reduce the heat, and braise gently for 10 minutes, regulating the heat so that the leeks don't brown. Remove the braised leeks to warm serving plates, top each bed of leeks with a piece of salmon, sprinkle chopped chives over the leeks and salmon, and garnish with salmon caviar, if you like. SERVES 4

❖Omit the butter and cook the leeks and salmon in the broth alone, adding a bit more if needed.
❖Substitute *Curried Cabbage* (page 152) for the leeks. Braise the cabbage for 4–5 minutes or until just tender, place the salmon on the cabbage, and proceed as above.

Fresh Fish Cakes with Tomato-Basil Butter Sauce

Take my word for it, this is an absolutely delicious dish, thanks to the inspiration of Leslie Mackie, a talented chef who worked with me at the restaurant. It can be made with an array of poached fishes, but I think my favorite combination is salmon, cod, and halibut. The different fishes contribute their own flavors and textures, and the salmon adds a lovely pink color to the cakes. The first steps should be done well ahead of serving so that the

2 eggs, beaten
Juice of 2 large lemons
⅓–½ cup chopped parsley
1–2 Tb chopped fresh basil (optional)
Salt and freshly ground pepper
Hot pepper sauce (optional)
Egg wash (2 eggs beaten with a little water)
4 or more cups finely ground fresh bread
    crumbs

TOMATO-BASIL BUTTER SAUCE

¼ cup red wine vinegar
¼ cup fresh lemon juice
3 Tb heavy cream
¾–1 lb *chilled* unsalted butter, cut
    into small pieces
1 cup peeled, seeded, and chopped
    tomatoes
¼ cup or more shredded basil leaves
Salt and freshly ground pepper

To make the Tomato-Basil Butter Sauce: In a
stainless or enamel saucepan, combine the
vinegar and lemon juice, and boil to reduce
to about 3 tablespoons. Add the cream and
boil the mixture again until it reduces to
about 3 tablespoons. Remove the saucepan
from the heat and immediately beat in 2
pieces of the chilled butter. Add another
piece of butter and return the pan to very
low heat. Whisking constantly, continue to
add pieces of butter. The sauce will thicken
and become creamy; the more butter you
beat in, the more sauce you will have.
Remove the pan from the heat as soon as all
the butter has been added, and fold in the
tomatoes and basil. Season with salt and
freshly ground pepper. Keep the sauce
warm in a double boiler over warm water
until ready to serve.

MAKES ABOUT 2 CUPS

Fresh Fish Cakes with Tomato-Basil Butter Sauce
(continued)

fish-cake mixture can chill before cooking. Although the
tomato-basil butter sauce is a perfect accompaniment,
you could substitute a fresh tomato sauce, if you prefer,
or serve the cakes plain with lemon wedges. A crunchy
green vegetable, such as broccoli de rabe or green beans,
is a nice side dish.

Alternative fish: haddock, snapper, monkfish,
almost any lean white fish

2-lb combination salmon, cod, and
    halibut fillets
2 large potatoes
3 Tb butter
2 cups finely diced vegetables (½ cup each
    carrots, celery, onions, red peppers)

⅓ cup *Clarified Butter* (page 351), or a
    combination of butter and light olive oil
    or vegetable oil, more as needed

Remove any skin and bones from the fish fillets. Bring a wide, 4-inch-high skillet half full of water to a boil, place the fish fillets in the boiling water, reduce the heat so that the water "shivers" just below the simmer point, and poach the fish until it is just springy to the touch and just opaque at the center, about 6–8 minutes, depending on the thickness of the fillets. Remove the fillets to a plate and set aside to cool.

Peel the potatoes and cut each one into a few chunks for faster cooking. Bring a saucepan of water to a boil, drop in the potato chunks, and cook until they are tender. Drain the potatoes, rice or mash them into small lumps (don't purée), and set them aside to cool slightly. (You will have about 2–2½ cups.)

In a sauté pan, heat the 3 tablespoons of butter, add the diced vegetables, and cook them over low heat, stirring occasionally, until they are tender. Remove from the heat and let cool slightly.

In a large bowl, combine the riced or mashed potatoes, the sautéed diced vegetables, the 2 beaten eggs, lemon juice, parsley, and basil, if you are using it. Flake the poached fish into the potato mixture and gently fold the mixture together again. Season with salt and freshly ground pepper, and with a few drops of hot pepper sauce, if desired. Cover and chill the mixture. When the mixture is chilled, shape it into thick patties. This is a light mixture; handle it gently. The patties should be about 3–3½ inches wide and about 1 inch high. (Makes 12 patties, 2 per serving as a main course) Dip the patties into the egg wash, then turn them in the bread crumbs to coat with the crumbs. Rechill until ready to cook.

Shortly before serving, prepare the tomato-basil butter sauce and keep warm.

Just before serving, heat 2 tablespoons of the clarified butter or combination of unclarified butter and oil in a wide, preferably nonstick sauté pan. Cook the fish cakes in batches, adding more butter as needed, over medium heat for about 4 minutes on each side or until lightly browned and heated through. Place the cooked fish cakes on a baking sheet lined with brown paper in a preheated 200-degree oven until all of the cakes have been cooked.

To serve: Slightly overlap 2 fish cakes on each serving plate and spoon the warm sauce over them.

SERVES 6

❖An alternate sequence is to prepare the fish-cake mixture up to the point of making the patties, cover, and chill it; then prepare the sauce, and make and coat the patties just before cooking them.

❖Sauté the fish cakes on each side for 1–2 minutes just until lightly colored. Remove to a baking sheet, then place them in a preheated 500-degree oven for 5–6 minutes to complete the cooking.

❖Serve 1 fish cake with sauce for an elegant first course for 12 persons.

❖*Fresh Fish and Crabmeat Cakes:* Use 1½ pounds poached fish combined with ½ pound fresh crabmeat and proceed as above.

Salmon Fillets with a Toasty Tomato Fondue

Toasted bread crumbs add body and flavor to this sauce or fondue made with fresh tomatoes, parsley, and thyme. When new potatoes are available from my garden or the market, I serve this dish with *Grilled Potato Salad* (page 89).

Four 4–6-oz salmon fillets, with skin on
3 Tb light olive oil
1 cup fresh bread crumbs
3 cups peeled, seeded, and chopped tomatoes
1 tsp minced garlic (optional)
⅓ cup chopped parsley
2 tsp fresh thyme or other herbs
Chopped zest of 1 lemon
Salt and freshly ground pepper

Remove any bones from the salmon and brush all sides with 1 tablespoon of the olive oil. Set aside.

Spread the bread crumbs on a baking sheet and run them under a preheated broiler, turning with a spoon until they are lightly toasted on all sides. Set aside.

In a nonstick sauté pan, heat the remaining 2 tablespoons of oil. Add the tomatoes and cook over medium-high heat for 4–5 minutes to evaporate some of their juices and thicken the sauce. Add the garlic, if you like, and the parsley, thyme, lemon zest, and toasted bread crumbs. Stir the mixture and cook until lightly thickened. Season with salt and freshly ground pepper, and keep warm; or set aside and reheat when you are ready to serve.

Heat a large, nonstick sauté pan over medium-high heat. Place the oiled salmon fillets, skin side

Salmon Fillets with a Toasty Tomato Fondue (continued)

down, in the pan and cook for 2 minutes. Turn the fillets and cook on the other side for 2 minutes. Transfer the fillets to a baking pan and bake in a pre-heated 350-degree oven until the salmon is just opaque in the center, 4–6 minutes, depending on the thickness of the fillets.

To serve, put a spoonful of the sauce on each serving plate, place the salmon fillet on the sauce, and top each fillet with another spoonful of sauce.   SERVES 4

Broiled Salmon on a Bed of Warm Potatoes

In the summer of 1991 my husband, Russell, and I traveled through Norway with our longtime friend Julia Child, videotaping a television show on Norwegian cookery. Since the sun scarcely set before it rose again in subarctic days, the shooting schedule was long every day, but we took time for memorable meals. Chef Michael Reddington at the SAS hotel in Bergen served salmon on top of a rich potato stew. My version drastically reduces the pound of butter Chef Michael put in his sauce, but it is still a luscious dish that reminds me of a jolly crew and a great television cook.

The salmon can be prepared for broiling well ahead and refrigerated. The potato "stew" can be made slightly in advance and reheated while the salmon broils just before serving.

> 1½-lb salmon fillet
> Vegetable oil
> 1½ lb peeled and sliced potatoes
> 2½ cups salmon stock, fish stock, or unsalted
>   chicken broth
> ½ cup dry vermouth or white wine
> 6 Tb butter
> ½ lb sliced mushrooms
> ½ cup sliced scallions (thin sliced on the diago-
>   nal)
> Salt and freshly ground pepper
> 1 Tb chopped fresh dill

Skin the salmon and remove any bones. Slice the fillet diagonally into ½-inch strips. Brush the strips with oil

and lay them on a nonstick baking sheet. Cover and refrigerate until ready to cook. Put the potatoes, stock, vermouth or white wine, and 4 tablespoons of the butter into a 4-quart saucepan and bring to a boil. Reduce the heat, partially cover, and simmer until the potatoes are just tender. Lift the potatoes with a slotted spoon to a flat dish or pan; measure 1 generous cup of potato and return it to the saucepan, then spread the remainder out in the flat dish. Pour the liquid and potato from the saucepan into a food processor or blender and purée the mixture. Return the purée to the saucepan and cook gently to reduce to about 2 cups of liquid.

Melt the remaining 2 tablespoons of butter in a sauté pan, add the mushrooms and scallions, and cook over medium heat until the vegetables are wilted and lightly colored. Add this mixture and the reserved potatoes to the puréed liquid and heat slowly. Season with salt and freshly ground pepper.

Place the tray of salmon strips under a preheated broiler 4 inches from the heat. Broil for 3 minutes or until just cooked through.

Divide the potato stew among 4 warm shallow soup plates or dishes with enough depth to accommodate the sauce. Place the salmon strips on top of the stew, sprinkle with the dill, and serve.   SERVES 4

❖Add other vegetables, such as blanched snow peas or finely chopped and sautéed red peppers.

Broiled Salmon with a Mustard-Tarragon Butter Sauce

There is no avoiding butter in this recipe; it is used to baste the fish as it broils and as a base for the sauce I serve with it. So this is a dish for those once-in-a-while days when you allow yourself the pleasure of good butter taste. Under the intense heat of the broiler, the paprika-flavored butter melts into the flesh of the fish to keep the fish moist and tender, and the paprika gives a rosy glow to the exterior. Mustard in the butter adds zest to the taste of the dish. Tarragon is a lovely herb to use with salmon, and if you shy away from the butter sauce, you can add chopped tarragon to a fresh tomato sauce to serve with the salmon. I wish I could claim credit for the mustard-tarragon butter sauce, but it was the brilliant California chef Wolfgang Puck who created it for a shrimp appetizer and inspired me to use it with salmon.

Make the basting butter ahead—it keeps in the refrigerator for weeks—so that it is chilled and hard before you put it on the salmon. Serve a side dish of *Sautéed Sugar Snap Peas and Cucumbers* (page 333).

MUSTARD-PAPRIKA BASTING BUTTER

4 Tb softened butter
1 tsp Dijon-style mustard
½ tsp paprika

MUSTARD-TARRAGON BUTTER
SAUCE

1 Tb finely chopped shallots
1 heaping Tb finely chopped fresh
   tarragon
½ cup dry vermouth or white wine
⅓ cup heavy cream
½–¾ lb *chilled* unsalted butter,
   cut into ¼-inch pieces
2 Tb grainy Dijon-style mustard
Salt and freshly ground pepper

To make the Mustard-Tarragon Butter Sauce: In a heavy-bottomed stainless saucepan, combine the shallots, tarragon, vermouth, and cream; bring the sauce to a boil and cook to thicken and reduce until the mixture coats the back of a spoon and becomes almost a glaze. Turn the heat to low and gradually whisk in the butter a piece at a time. With each addition the sauce will become creamier and will gradually become thicker. Stir in the mustard and season with salt and freshly ground pepper. Do not let the sauce boil; keep it warm in a double boiler over water the same temperature as the sauce until served.   MAKES ABOUT 1½ CUPS SAUCE

2-lb skinned salmon fillet
Small sprigs fresh tarragon (optional)

To make the Mustard-Paprika Basting Butter: In a small bowl, beat together the 4 tablespoons of butter, 1 teaspoon mustard, and the paprika. Cover and refrigerate until the mixture is hard.

Shortly before serving, prepare the mustard-tarragon butter sauce and keep it warm.

Remove any bones from the salmon and divide it into 6 equal portions. Preheat the broiler and brush the broiler rack with oil. Place the pieces of salmon, skinned side down, on the rack and place one-sixth of the basting butter on top of each piece. Place the rack 4–5 inches below the heat and broil for 7–8 minutes, or until the fish is just cooked through; cooking time will vary with the thickness and density of the fish.

To serve: Spoon some of the mustard-tarragon butter sauce onto each of 6 warm serving plates, set a piece of salmon on the sauce, and garnish with a sprig of tarragon, if you like.   SERVES 6

❖Substitute *Fresh Tomato Sauce* (page 364) with tarragon for the mustard-tarragon sauce, or try Dijon-style mustard combined with horseradish or *Horseradish Cream* (page 356), or serve the salmon plain with a garnish of lemon wedges.

❖Grill the salmon, lifting each piece with a wide spatula after about 4 minutes of cooking and rotating them about 45 degrees on the grill rack to make a cross pattern of grill marks.

Roasted Fillet
of Salmon with Bess's
Cucumber-Dill Sauce

In the summer of 1991, when Julia Child returned to Norway, where she had once lived when her husband was a diplomatic attaché, the American consulate gave a large garden dinner party in her honor, and, of course, salmon was served. Whole salmon fillets were briefly broiled, then partially roasted in the consulate kitchen and carried to the garden for a dramatic final grilling. It was served with a fresh cucumber-dill sauce and beautifully sliced tomatoes. You can dazzle your guests with the same elegant dish, but prepare it a little more simply in your kitchen. Bess Hopkins was an early volunteer helping with Julia's first television cooking shows; it seems appropriate to

Roasted Fillet of Salmon with Bess's Cucumber-Dill Sauce (continued)

use her sauce with a dish I first saw prepared in honor of Julia Child. Bess's sauce should be partially prepared a day before serving; for a faster sauce, see *Cucumber-Dill Sauce* (page 354). *Corn Pudding* (page 325), by the way, is awfully good with this salmon.

BESS'S CUCUMBER-DILL SAUCE

3 large cucumbers
1 sweet onion
½ cup fresh lemon juice
⅓ cup finely chopped fresh dill
¾ cup sour cream
Salt and freshly ground pepper

To make Bess's Cucumber-Dill Sauce: Peel the cucumbers, halve them lengthwise, and scoop out the seeds. Peel the onion. Using the large holes of the grater, grate the cucumbers and onion. Place the grated vegetables in a bowl, add the lemon juice, toss all together, cover, and refrigerate overnight. Before serving, squeeze the juice out of the vegetables (a potato ricer does this handily) until they are as dry as possible. Add the dill and sour cream to the grated vegetables and mix very well. Season with salt and freshly ground pepper.

MAKES ABOUT 2 CUPS

ROASTED SALMON

1½–2-lb salmon fillet, in 1 piece
Vegetable oil
½ tsp salt
¼ tsp paprika
⅛ tsp cayenne pepper
Lemon wedges

Prepare Bess's cucumber-dill sauce in advance, cover, and refrigerate.

To prepare the roasted salmon: If you have two ovens, preheat the broiler of one and preheat the other to 400 degrees. Otherwise, broil the salmon first and set

it aside while you switch the oven from broil to bake and preheat to 400 degrees.

Remove any bones from the salmon. Brush the surface of a shallow baking sheet with vegetable oil. Brush both sides of the salmon with oil and place it, skin side up, on the baking sheet.

In a small bowl, combine the salt, paprika, and cayenne pepper. Sprinkle half the mixture over the salmon. Place the baking sheet 4–5 inches below a preheated broiler and broil for 5 minutes. With two long, wide spatulas, carefully turn the salmon, sprinkle the remaining seasoning mix over it, and broil for 5 minutes.

Transfer the salmon to a preheated 400-degree oven to roast until the flesh just turns opaque at the center, from 15–25 minutes, depending on the thickness of the fish; begin checking after 15 minutes.

Carefully slide the salmon onto a warm serving platter. Cut the fillet into individual pieces, lifting the flesh off the skin, and serve with lemon wedges and the cucumber-dill sauce.   SERVES 4–6

❖Substitute other cold sauces: *Horseradish Cream* (page 356), *Tartar Sauce* (page 363), or *Salsa* (page 7), or combine 1½ cups sour cream with 1 heaping tablespoon each horseradish and Dijon-style mustard.

❖Serve with warm sauces, such as *Sorrel Sauce* (page 229) or *Mustard-Tarragon Butter Sauce* (page 235), or a warm herb vinaigrette.

❖Substitute other seasonings. Use only salt and freshly ground pepper, or sprinkle with a blackened mixture, or try an Oriental 5-spice powder.

❖Leaving the skin on helps to hold the fish together when you turn it. You can, however, cook a skinned fillet, but be very careful turning it. To facilitate the turning, if you wish, place a long piece of oiled aluminum foil under the fish before broiling and use it to roll the fillet over carefully.

Roasted Salmon with Prosciutto

The way the smoky saltiness of prosciutto picks up the subtle flavor of salmon without overpowering it makes this a really good dish. Many vegetable accompaniments complement this dish—for instance, *Sautéed Corn* (page 325)—but for a delicious contrast try the slightly sharp taste of one of my favorite greens, *Braised*

Broccoli de Rabe (page 323). *Tuscan-Style White Beans* (page 321), warmed in a garlic-infused olive oil, are an awfully good addition to this preparation of salmon, and can be made ahead and reheated at serving time. The salmon should also be prepared ahead so that it has a little time in the refrigerator before cooking; the broccoli de rabe can be prepared ahead of time and quickly sautéed while the salmon is roasting.

Alternative fish: halibut steaks

Four 8-oz salmon steaks
¼ lb very thinly sliced prosciutto
3 Tb olive oil
Lemon wedges

Using a thin, sharp knife, cut down either side of the center bone of each salmon steak and remove it. Cut through the skin where the center bone was, dividing the steak into two pieces, and remove the skin and any pin bones. Position the thick end of one piece of the steak next to the thin end of the other piece in order to make an oval boneless and skinless steak, keeping the skinned surfaces to the outside. Cut a slice of prosciutto in half lengthwise and place this half strip of prosciutto between the two pieces where they meet. Wrap another half slice or two, if necessary, lengthwise around each oval package of fish, and then wrap the package crosswise with one or two full-size pieces of prosciutto so that each serving is

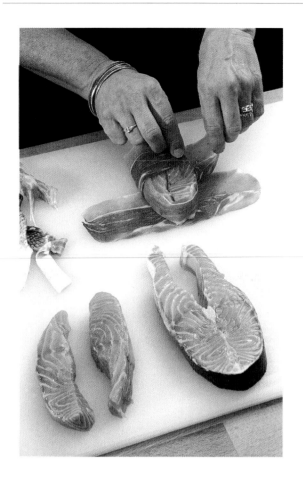

2 lb salmon fillet, with skin on
2 Tb butter
6 cups finely sliced green cabbage
Salt and freshly ground pepper
2 Tb vegetable oil
Lemon wedges

Remove any bones in the salmon but leave the skin on. Cut the salmon into 6 equal portions and set aside in the refrigerator.

In a large sauté pan, heat the butter, add the cabbage, and stir to coat with the butter. Cover, lower the heat, and cook gently for 5–6 minutes, or until the cabbage is tender, stirring occasionally. Set the cabbage aside, covered, to keep warm.

While the cabbage is cooking, season the salmon pieces with salt and freshly ground pepper. Heat the oil in an ovenproof skillet, using two skillets, if necessary, to cook the fish in one layer. Sear the salmon, unskinned side down, for 1 minute. Turn the fish over and transfer the skillet to a preheated 450-degree oven. Roast for 4–8 minutes, depending on the thickness of the salmon, or until the fish is just opaque throughout.

While the fish roasts, uncover the cabbage and cook it over high heat for a minute, stirring, to evaporate any excess moisture and to reheat it. Season with salt and freshly ground pepper.

To serve, divide the cabbage equally among warm serving plates and place a piece of salmon on each bed of cabbage. Serve with lemon wedges.   SERVES 6

❖Use *Curried Cabbage* (page 152) for the sautéed cabbage.

Roasted Salmon with Prosciutto (continued)

completely encased in prosciutto. Cover the packages with plastic wrap and refrigerate for a time so that the chilling will help the prosciutto adhere to the fish during cooking.

In a sauté pan, heat the oil to very hot, carefully place the wrapped fish packages in the pan, and cook for 1 minute on each side to lightly brown. Transfer the salmon to a lightly oiled baking pan and roast in a preheated 450-degree oven about 10 minutes or until just cooked through. Serve with lemon wedges.

SERVES 4

Roasted Salmon with Sautéed Cabbage

It sounds exotic to speak of "roasting" fish, but all the word refers to is cooking the fish uncovered in a hot oven—in this case, just for a few minutes. A bed of sautéed cabbage is all the "sauce" this salmon needs.

Alternative fish: bass, snapper, cod, haddock, halibut

Zucchini Salmon with a Seafood Mousse

This is a dramatic company dish, yet it is easily prepared well in advance. Don't be daunted by the length of the recipe; the steps are deceptively simple, and your guests will think you have just come home from cooking school. The one absolute necessity is a food processor to make a smooth, light mousse. You can slice the zucchini as much as a day ahead. Make the mousse and chill it while you butterfly the fish.

Arranging the zucchini slices to look like scales on the salmon takes a little time but is artistic fun. Once assembled, the dish can sit in the refrigerator for 3–4 hours before baking. Make the *Lemon Butter Sauce* (if you are using it) while the fish is baking. Serve with braised peas or steamed baby carrots or *Sautéed Zucchini* (page 344).

Alternative fish: bass, red snapper, sturgeon
Alternative shellfish for the mousse: scallops

Seafood Mousse

¼ lb raw shrimp
¼ lb sole or flounder
2 tsp fresh lemon juice
1 Tb fresh dill
Salt and freshly ground pepper
Pinch of nutmeg
2 large eggs, separated
⅔ cup heavy cream

Zucchini Salmon

½ lb small, narrow zucchini
2¼–2½-lb thick midsection of salmon fillet
Salt and freshly ground pepper
⅓–½ cup dry vermouth or white wine

Sauce and Garnish

Lemon Butter Sauce (page 357) (optional)
1 small jar salmon caviar
Sprigs fresh dill
Lemon wedges (optional)

To make the seafood mousse: Peel and devein the shrimp, cut the flesh into small pieces, and put the shrimp into a food processor. Cut the sole or flounder into small pieces and add it to the processor. Process the shrimp and sole briefly until they are minced. Add the lemon juice, dill, ½ teaspoon salt, a couple of grindings of pepper, a pinch of nutmeg, and 2 egg yolks. Turn on the processor and slowly add the cream. Process for 15–20 seconds, or until the purée softly holds its shape. Remove the mixture to a bowl and season with salt and freshly ground pepper to taste. Beat the egg whites until they are firm but not stiff. Stir one-third of the beaten whites into the mousse mixture to lighten it, then gently fold in the remaining whites. Cover the mixture and refrigerate.

To make the zucchini salmon: Wash and dry the zucchini and remove the ends. Cut the zucchini into fine cross-sectional slices with a sharp, thin knife or food slicer. Bring a pot of water to a boil and drop in the zucchini slices for 1 minute to blanch them. (If you have a fry basket that will fit the pot, put the zucchini in the basket and lower it into the boiling water for 1 minute.) As soon as the zucchini has barely wilted, remove it from the pot and run it under cold water or drop it into a bowl of ice water to stop the cooking action. Drain the zucchini slices and lay them out on double-thick paper towels. Pat them dry with more paper towels. (If you are preparing the zucchini ahead, place the slices on a cookie sheet lined with paper towels, cover with waxed paper, and refrigerate.) With a sharp knife, remove the skin of the salmon and the thin layer of dark flesh on the skin side, and pull out any bones with tweezers. Cut the fillet crosswise into 6 equal pieces of about 6 ounces each. Butterfly each piece by cutting it partway through in the middle, spreading it open, and turning each side down flat. Each piece will resemble a butterfly shape; see the photograph for *Sautéed Butterflied Salmon* (page 222).

Season the top of the salmon fillets with salt and pepper, and top each portion with spoonfuls of mousse, dividing and spreading the mousse evenly across each piece. Cut the zucchini slices in half, and starting at the narrow end of each piece of salmon, arrange the slices in overlapping rows to resemble the scales on a fish. Place each completed salmon portion in a buttered glass, ceramic, or stainless baking pan that is 2 inches high and large enough to hold all the portions without touching. (At this point you may refrigerate the dish, covered, for up to 4 hours before baking.)

Just before baking, pour the vermouth or wine down the side of the pan to make a thin layer of liquid in the bottom. Cover the pan tightly with a cover or aluminum foil, making sure that the cover does not touch the fish. Bake in a preheated 400-degree oven for 20–25 minutes, or until the mousse is firm and the salmon is cooked through. If the fish was refrigerated before cooking, it will take 25 minutes.

To serve: If you are using the lemon butter sauce, spoon some onto the center of each serving plate, set the salmon portion on top of the sauce, add a generous dollop of salmon caviar, and garnish with the dill sprigs.

If you do not use the lemon butter sauce, top the salmon portion with the caviar and garnish with dill and lemon wedges. SERVES 6

Zucchini Salmon with a Seafood Mousse (continued)

❖For an appetizer course, cut each of the 6 salmon pieces in half again, and assemble and bake as above.

SERVES 12

❖Use other herbs, such as tarragon or parsley, in the mousse, or substitute green peppercorns for herbs.

❖Add a bit of smoked salmon to the mousse.

❖Substitute a fresh tomato sauce, red pepper sauce, or sorrel sauce for the lemon butter sauce.

❖Garnish each plate with sautéed shrimp instead of salmon caviar.

❖I like the big orange caviar that pops in your mouth; if it is unavailable, use finely chopped, sautéed and peeled red peppers or pimentos for garnish.

Grilled Salmon with Portuguese Peas

Grill purists will be shocked to hear that I would consider grilling without a wood fire and fragrant smoke, but because gas grilling is so easy, we simply grill more often; once we acquired a gas grill at our summer house in Nantucket, which I think of as a wooden tent, even our traditional Fourth of July feast of whole poached salmon with fresh peas suddenly had competition. The days are more relaxed, less complicated, and I want cooking to reflect the change. Salmon with its natural oils stands up well to grilling. I use thick fillets and leave the skin on to help hold the fish together, but steaks can be grilled the same way. Oil the grill rack well, or use an oiled grill basket. New England seaports have populations descended from men who emigrated here from Portugal generations ago to fish, and this dish celebrates our affinity for their hearty cuisine by enriching a sauté-braise of peas with the linguiça sausage that flavors many Portuguese seafood dishes. Here is the order of battle: Prepare the salmon for the grill and refrigerate it. Shell the peas and prepare the remaining ingredients. Cook the onions, carrots, and linguiça before putting the salmon on the grill, and finish cooking them with the peas while the salmon grills. It isn't what my mother has in mind for the Fourth of July, but it's a wonderful dish, it *is* salmon and peas, and it liberates me from the stove; isn't that what the Fourth is all about?

Alternative fish: swordfish, shark, mahi mahi, bluefish, marlin, tuna, thick Arctic char

PORTUGUESE PEAS

3 lb unshelled garden peas
6 oz linguiça sausage
2 Tb olive oil
1 cup chopped onions
½ cup finely chopped carrots
⅓–½ cup roughly chopped cilantro
Salt and freshly ground pepper

To prepare and cook the Portuguese Peas: Shell the peas. (You will have 3½–4 cups shelled peas.) Chop the linguiça into ¼-inch dice. In a sauté pan, heat the oil, add the onions, carrots, and linguiça, stir all together, cover, and cook over medium heat, stirring occasionally, for 5–6 minutes, or until the onions and carrots are tender. Uncover and remove any excess oil released by the linguiça. Just before serving, add ¼ cup of water, stir in the peas, cover, and cook for 3–4 minutes, stirring occasionally, or until the peas are just tender. Stir in the cilantro and season with salt and freshly ground pepper.

SERVES 4–6

❖Use other cooked sausages, such as kielbasa, or use diced ham.

❖To remove excess fat from the linguiça before cooking it with the vegetables, prick it with a fork, put it in boiling water, and cook it gently for 5 minutes; then drain, cool, and chop into dice.

GRILLED SALMON

1½–2-lb salmon fillet, 1 inch thick, with skin on
Vegetable oil
4 Tb butter (optional)
Lemon wedges

Prepare the Portuguese peas and keep them warm.

To prepare and cook the fish: Remove any bones from the salmon cut into 4 equal portions and refrigerate until ready to cook. Just before cooking, preheat the grill and oil the grill rack. Brush the salmon on both sides with oil and place it, skin side down, on

the grill rack. To cook the fish more quickly, as I pre-fer, cover the grill with a lid or a tent of aluminum foil and grill for 5–6 minutes, turn, and grill the other side for 2–3 minutes, or until the fish is just opaque throughout. (Or cook uncovered and adjust the time, about 5–6 minutes on each side.) SERVES 4

❖ Grill the whole salmon fillet. Use long wide spatulas to turn the fish on the grill, or grill the fillet in an oiled fish basket.

❖ Broil the salmon.

❖ Top with warm *Tomato Fondue* (page 363).

❖ Lubricate the salmon with a flavored basting but-ter. Try *Mustard-Paprika Basting Butter* (page 235). The butter will melt into the salmon, the paprika will leave a rosy hue, and the mustard will add a piquant flavor. Place a heaping teaspoon of the butter on top of the salmon before grilling or broiling.

❖ Brush the salmon with a marinade of soy sauce and oil to give a salty taste and a golden glaze, or brush with a mixture of equal parts soy sauce, lime juice, and oil.

Fisherman's Eggs
Almost Benedict

Eggs Benedict is a well-established favorite for brunch, but as more people shy away from the salti-ness and fat of bacon and ham and in butter sauces, it makes sense to try a variation—perhaps eggs with salmon and a warm salsa. Served with a tossed salad, this dish makes a delicious light supper.

Alternative fish: thin pieces of gray sole, lemon sole, or plaice; thin slices of bluefish, tuna, haddock, bass, or other firm-fleshed white fish

Fisherman's Eggs Almost Benedict (continued)

¾-lb salmon fillet
2 Tb vegetable oil or melted butter
2 Tb butter (optional)
2 split English muffins
Salsa (page 7)
White vinegar
4 large eggs
Salt and freshly ground pepper

Remove the skin and any bones from the salmon. Slice the fillet at a slight diagonal angle to make 8 slices about ¼ inch thick. Brush the slices with the oil or melted butter and place them on an oiled baking sheet, oiled side of the salmon up. Set aside.

Butter the muffins, if you like, and place on a broiler pan. Lightly brown the muffins under a pre-heated broiler and warm the salsa in a saucepan. Remove the muffins and keep them warm.

Bring a saucepan of water to a boil, adding 2 table-spoons of white vinegar for every quart of water to help the eggs congeal. Reduce the heat until the water just simmers, crack the eggs gently into the water, and cook for 4–5 minutes, or until the eggs are set but the yolks are not hard. Remove the eggs with a slotted spoon to a warm plate and lightly pat dry with paper towels.

Place the salmon under a preheated broiler and cook for 1 minute. Season with salt and freshly ground pepper.

To assemble, place the toasted muffins on serving plates, top each muffin half with a slice of broiled salmon, then a poached egg, and spoon salsa over.

SERVES 4 FOR BREAKFAST OR BRUNCH, 2 FOR SUPPER

❖Use smoked fish, such as salmon, bluefish, cod, haddock, or sable, and just warm the fish briefly under the broiler.

❖For a crunchier texture, cut slightly thicker salmon slices, dip them in flour, and fry them in but-ter meunière-style; or prepare pieces of flounder in the same way.

❖Replace the salsa sauce with warmed lemon sections and capers as in *Sautéed Bluefish with Lemon and Capers* (page 129).

❖Top the muffins, salmon, and eggs with the tra-ditional *Hollandaise Sauce* (page 356) or *Sorrel Sauce* (page 229).

❖Add a heaping spoonful of chopped braised spinach on top of the muffin, then assemble as above.

Marilyn's Salmon with Artichoke Mousse and Tomato Hollandaise

Some of the best meals I've had have been prepared and served by Marilyn Benson and her partner, Deb-orah Goodman, caterers in Lexington, Massachusetts. Their salmon dish is perfect for parties because it can be prepared for the oven and then refrigerated until ready to bake just before serving. While the fish is cooking, there is just time to make the hollandaise. Marilyn serves this with a combination of wild and Italian rices flavored with fresh herbs.

Eight 4-oz pieces salmon fillet
1 can drained, rinsed, and quartered artichoke
    hearts
2 tsp chopped shallots
½ tsp thyme
2 egg whites, at room temperature
2 tsp Pernod
Salt and freshly ground pepper
Tomato Hollandaise (see below)

Remove the skin and any bones from the salmon. Place the fish pieces one by one on waxed paper, skinned side up, cover with another piece of waxed paper, and pound lightly to flatten. Set aside.

In a food processor or blender, combine the arti-choke hearts, shallots, thyme, egg whites, and Pernod, and purée until smooth. Season with salt and freshly ground pepper.

Place about 2 tablespoons of the artichoke purée in the center of each piece of salmon, spread the purée out slightly, and roll up the salmon. Place the rolled salmon pieces in a buttered baking dish, seam side down. (The dish can be prepared up to this point, covered, and refrigerated until shortly before serving.) Bake in a pre-heated 375-degree oven for 15 minutes. Serve immedi-ately with the tomato hollandaise sauce.   SERVES 8

❖*Tomato Hollandaise:*

2 egg yolks
3 Tb fresh lemon juice
1 Tb warm water
1 cup unsalted *Clarified Butter* (page 351)
2 Tb peeled, seeded, and diced tomatoes

In a double boiler over hot water, combine the egg yolks, lemon juice, and warm water, and whisk until thick, about 5–7 minutes. Remove from the heat and gradually whisk in the clarified butter. Fold in the tomatoes and serve.

Coulibiac

Of Russian origin, coulibiac (or kulebiaka) is a fish loaf baked in pastry with mushrooms, eggs, and rice. The version made with salmon is best known, but the dish can also be made with fillings of other fish, chicken, or even cabbage. When we first started offering it at the Straight Wharf Restaurant, adapting a recipe from the French cooking volume of the old Time-Life cookbook series and making pounds of our own brioche dough to create a giant coulibiac that was displayed on a specially hewn, long wooden platter, the dish was three days in the making, incredibly rich, and instantly popular; some patrons would plan their reservations around the availability of coulibiac, which we offered only on weekends. In the recipe below I have set out to simplify coulibiac by reducing the number of steps and amount of time necessary to complete the dish, by substituting store-bought puff-pastry sheets for homemade brioche, and by reducing the amount of fat used while still keeping the special character and flavor of this superb dish. It is an excellent choice for a special dinner party. Much of the preparation can be done ahead. You could begin on the morning of the day you are serving the coulibiac, but I find it easier to spread the preparation over two days. Take it step by step. You can prepare this version without the dilled crêpes, but I think they add an important texture and taste, so include them if you can. The salmon and its sauce must be baked ahead so that it can chill and firm in the refrigerator. The crêpes can be made ahead at your convenience, as can the rice mixture. If you prepare all the ingredients the day before you are serving, and then assemble the filling in the pastry the morning of your dinner party, all you have to do is pop the coulibiac into the oven when your guests arrive. If you are doing the entire preparation the day of the party, allow enough time after the final assembly for the dish to chill in the refrigerator for at least 30 minutes before baking. Essential equipment includes a glass or nonaluminum-lined baking pan measuring 9½ × 13½ inches, a 12 ×

17-inch baking sheet, 2 wide spatulas with a lifting surface of at least 3 × 6 inches, a pastry brush, and tweezers. Though the coulibiac contains only 2 pounds of salmon, it will serve 8–10 or even 12 people as a main course, with nothing more than a green salad or some colorful *Braised Carrot Logs* (page 333). For a buffet you can divide the coulibiac into 18–20 smaller servings. For a very rich treat, serve the coulibiac with salmon caviar and a *White Butter Sauce* (page 114) or with a favorite tomato or sweet red pepper sauce.

SALMON

2–2¼-lb skinned salmon fillet
¼ cup chopped fresh dill
Salt and freshly ground pepper
½ lb thinly sliced fresh mushrooms (the whitest available)
1 cup dry vermouth or white wine

SALMON SAUCE

½ cup or more unsalted chicken broth or *Salmon Stock* (page 361)
2 Tb butter
3 Tb flour
4 yolks, from large eggs
1–2 Tb fresh lemon juice
Salt and freshly ground pepper

RICE MIXTURE

2 cups cold water
2 tsp tapioca
1 Tb butter
¾ cup uncooked rice
Salt and freshly ground pepper
2 finely chopped hard-boiled eggs
⅓ cup chopped parsley

12 *Dilled Crêpes* (page 201)

DOUGH

2 packages puff pastry (2 sheets per package, each about 9 inches × 10 inches)
Egg glaze (2 eggs beaten with 2 Tb water)

3–4 Tb butter (optional)
Salmon caviar

Coulibiac (continued)

Step #1. One day in advance: Prepare the salmon, bake the salmon, and make its flavored sauce.

To prepare the salmon: Remove any dark fatty flesh on the skinned side of the salmon, if you wish. Carefully check for bones running down the center of the fillet and remove any with tweezers. Using a thin, sharp knife, slice the salmon with a diagonal cut into ¼-inch-thick slices. Butter a 9½ × 13½-inch glass or nonaluminum-lined baking dish and place the salmon slices across the bottom in two rows—the slices will overlap one another in the rows, and the rows will overlap where they meet so that the bottom of the dish is completely covered. Sprinkle the dill over the salmon and season with salt and freshly ground pepper. Spread the mushrooms evenly on top, pour the vermouth or wine over all, cover the dish with aluminum foil, and bake in a preheated 400-degree oven for 15–20 minutes, or until the salmon is just opaque and still resilient to the touch. (To test for doneness, lift one corner of the foil and cut into a slice of the salmon.) Leave the foil on the pan, but open one corner of the foil enough to pour the liquid from the pan into a 2-cup measure. Then remove the foil and set the salmon aside to cool. As it cools, the salmon will exude more juice; spoon any additional juice into the measuring cup. (You should have about 1 cup salmon cooking liquid.)

To make the salmon sauce: Add ½ cup of chicken broth or salmon stock, or more if needed, to the salmon cooking liquid in the measuring cup to make 1½ cups liquid. Melt the butter in a saucepan, remove the pan from the heat, and whisk in the flour. Return the pan to the heat and cook, whisking, for 2–3 minutes, or until the flour is lightly colored. Pour in the 1½ cups cooking liquid, whisking, bring the mixture to a boil, and boil gently for 5 minutes. Put the egg yolks into a large bowl and beat them lightly. Using a cup measure or ladle, gradually pour a little of the hot sauce into the egg yolks, whisking continuously, to warm the egg mixture gradually to prevent it from curdling. After whisking in about a cup of hot sauce, pour the egg-and-sauce mixture back into the saucepan with the rest of the hot sauce. Gently heat the sauce again just to a simmer and cook it for a few minutes, whisking continually, until the sauce has thickened slightly. Remove the pan from the heat and season the sauce to taste with lemon juice and salt and freshly ground pepper.

(1)

(2)

Drain or spoon off any liquid remaining in the pan of cooled salmon, and pour the hot sauce evenly over the salmon so that it is completely covered. Let the dish of sauced salmon cool slightly, then partially cover it (do not completely cover it if it is at all warm) and refrigerate for 2–3 hours until the sauce is firm, or, preferably, overnight. Once the dish is completely cool, cover it completely.

Step #2. One day in advance: Make the rice filling.

Put the 2 cups of cold water in a bowl, sprinkle the tapioca into it, and set it aside for 5 minutes for the tapioca to soften. In a saucepan, heat the butter, stir the rice into the butter, then stir in the tapioca with its water and ½ teaspoon salt. Bring the mixture to a boil, reduce the heat, cover, and simmer for 15–20 minutes, or until the rice is cooked and the liquid has been absorbed by the rice. The tapioca will slightly thicken the rice mixture and hold it together. Remove the

(3)

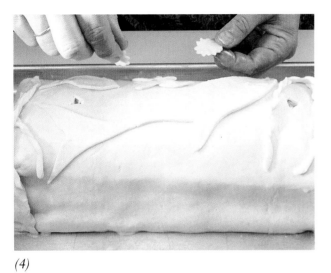

(4)

rice mixture to a large mixing bowl, fold in the hard-boiled eggs and parsley, and season with salt and freshly ground pepper. Let the mixture cool, then cover and refrigerate. (Makes about 3 cups)

Step #3. One day in advance or the morning of the meal: Make the crêpes.
Prepare *Dilled Crêpes* (page 201).

Step #4. The morning of the meal: Assemble the dish.

(Note: Keep puff-pastry dough as cold as possible while you are working with it, working on a cool work surface and refrigerating the dough whenever possible during the assembly to keep it chilled. Allow for at least 30 minutes of refrigeration to chill the assembled dish before baking it.)

Butter a sturdy 12 × 17-inch baking sheet and refrigerate it to chill. On a floured work surface, place

2 sheets of puff pastry end to end, overlapping the narrower 9-inch sides by ¾ inch and pressing the overlapping dough together with your fingers. With a floured rolling pin, roll the dough out to a rectangle measuring about 13 inches × 18 inches and transfer the pastry rectangle to the chilled baking sheet. Refrigerate the pastry on the sheet for 15 minutes while you assemble all the components of the dish: chilled salmon with sauce, rice mixture, and crêpes. With a sharp knife, cut down the center of the dish of salmon lengthwise to make two long strips of salmon and sauce. Divide the rice mixture into thirds. Remove the sheet of chilled dough from the refrigerator and assemble the coulibiac filling in the following sequence: crêpes, rice, salmon, crêpes, rice, salmon, rice, crêpes.

Overlap 4 crêpes down the middle of the length of the dough to make a 15-inch-long band, leaving about 1½ inches of pastry uncovered at each end. Spread one-third of the rice mixture evenly over the crêpes *(1)*. Slip the two long, wide spatulas under the ends of one of the long strips of salmon and sauce, and lift up the salmon strip carefully in one piece, center it over the band of crêpes, and turn it over so that the sauce side is down and the salmon side is up. Top the salmon with another band of 4 overlapping crêpes *(2)* and spread one-third of the rice mixture evenly over the second band of crêpes. Lift the second strip of salmon with the spatulas and set it down over the band of crêpes spread with rice, *but* this time with the sauce side *up*. Spread the remaining one-third of the rice mixture over the salmon sauce and complete the filling by covering the rice completely with a final band of 4 overlapping crêpes. You now have a layered loaf of salmon sitting in the center of a sheet of pastry. Trim the pastry so that it extends uniformly 1½ inches out from the loaf, saving the trimmings to use for decoration. Refrigerate the trimmings and the baking sheet of pastry and salmon loaf.

Place the remaining 2 sheets of chilled puff pastry end to end on a floured work surface, overlapping the narrower 9-inch sides by ¾ inch and pressing the overlap together with your fingers; with a floured rolling pin, roll the dough out to a rectangle about 12 inches × 18 inches. Remove the tray of pastry and salmon loaf from the refrigerator. Lift the 12 × 18-inch rectangle of pastry, center it over the salmon loaf, and lower it into place over the loaf. Working on one side of the assemblage at a time, fold one of the long sides of the top layer of puff pastry back over onto the top of the loaf to expose the underside of the dough, and brush at least 2

Coulibiac (continued)

inches of the edge of the underside with the egg glaze (*3*, page 245). Fold the 1½-inch exposed edge of the bottom layer of pastry on the same side up against the loaf and brush the exposed strip of pastry with egg glaze. Fold the top layer of pastry down so the glazed surfaces of pastry meet, and press them together to form a sealed pastry seam. Trim any excess dough, if necessary, and tuck the sealed pastry in along the side of the loaf to make it attractive. Repeat the same process on the other side of the coulibiac. Trim the corners of the dough on the ends of the assemblage, glaze both the top and bottom sheets of pastry where they will meet, and press the pastry together to seal the ends of the loaf in an attractive curved end. (You will have an oblong loaf completely encased in sealed dough measuring about 15 inches long, 6 inches wide, and 3½–4 inches high.) Using a small, sharp paring knife or two round pastry nozzles, cut two small ½-inch steam holes in the top of the pastry, placing one hole about 3 inches from each end. Refrigerate the coulibiac.

Using small cookie cutters or devising your own shapes with a paring knife, cut the reserved scraps of chilled pastry into shells or small fish shapes, cut narrow strips of pastry and twist them into seaweed shapes, or make other designs of your choosing.

Remove the chilled coulibiac from the refrigerator.

Brush the bottom side of each decoration with egg glaze and place on top of the coulibiac (*4*, page 245). In place of, or in addition to, cut-out pastry decorations, you can lightly score the top pastry with decorative markings. Brush all of the top and side pastry with egg glaze. Insert two pastry nozzles or two small handmade aluminum-foil funnels into the steam holes. Refrigerate the coulibiac for at least 30 minutes, longer if possible.

To bake: Place the coulibiac in a preheated 400-degree oven for 15 minutes. Reduce the heat to 375 degrees and continue baking for 40–45 minutes, or until the pastry is golden and puffed. Remove from the oven and let stand at room temperature for 15–20 minutes before cutting. If you wish, heat 3–4 tablespoons of butter and pour the melted butter into the steam holes on top of the coulibiac.

To serve: Using a bread knife or thin, flat-bladed knife, make a slightly diagonal cut across the coulibiac about 2–3 inches from one end of the loaf. Make the next cut parallel to and about ¾–1 inch toward the center of the loaf from the first cut. Run the knife under the bottom of the slice, and holding the top of the slice lightly with the fingers of your other hand, lift the slice up and place it on its side on a warm serving plate. Then move the 2–3-inch end of the loaf up against the open end of the coulibiac to stabilize the pastry and filling while you cut the next slice. Repeat the procedure until the two end sections become the final servings. Spoon a dollop of salmon caviar across each slice and serve with a favorite sauce, if desired.

SERVES 8, 10, OR 12, DEPENDING
ON THE THICKNESS OF THE SLICES

Sautéed Bay Scallops with Fall Purée of Squash and Apple

Family scalloping season in Massachusetts begins in October, a month before the commercial season does. We put on chest-high waders and carry nets to scoop up the delicate sweet shellfish. This simple sauté—no flour, no bread crumbs, no batter—is all the scallops need, and they are gone so quickly we are soon back in our waders looking for our nets again. The seasonal squash-and-apple purée accentuates the sweetness of the scallops; it can be made well ahead, allowing one to devote the day to scalloping.

SQUASH-AND-APPLE PURÉE

3 lb winter squash (Waltham butter-
    nut, buttercup, or other)
2 apples
Salt and freshly ground pepper
1–2 Tb finely grated orange peel
    (optional)
Pinch of ginger or cinnamon
    (optional)

To prepare the Squash-and-Apple Purée: Peel and halve the squash, remove the seeds, and cut the flesh into 1–2-inch cubes. Peel, core, and quarter the apples. Bring 1 inch of water in a steamer to a boil. Place the squash and apples in the steamer basket, cover, and steam until the squash is soft, about 15–20 minutes. Remove to a bowl and mash together to the consistency you prefer. Season with salt and freshly ground pepper, and add the grated orange peel and/or ginger or cinnamon, if desired. Keep warm if serving shortly, or cover and refrigerate and reheat just before cooking the scallops.   MAKES ABOUT 4 CUPS

❖Add 2 tablespoons butter to the purée, spread the purée into a buttered 1½-quart baking dish, dot the top with additional butter, if desired, and reheat in a preheated 350-degree oven for 30 minutes.

❖*Squash-and-Apple Purée in a Buttercup Squash Shell:* Cut a jack-o'-lantern-type lid on the top of a butternut squash, remove the lid, and scoop the seeds out through the opening. Place the squash in a shallow baking dish or roasting pan, replace the lid, and bake in a preheated 400-degree oven for 1 hour, or until the interior flesh is tender. (Set aside and keep warm if you are not ready to serve; if the squash cools, reheat it in the oven for 10 minutes.) To serve, spoon the squash-and-apple purée into the cavity of the squash, replace the lid, and serve, serving both the purée and sliced wedges of the baked squash.   SERVES 4–6

Sautéed Bay Scallops with Fall Purée of Squash and Apple (continued)

SAUTÉED BAY SCALLOPS

1½ lb bay scallops
4–6 Tb butter
Salt and freshly ground pepper
Lemon wedges

Prepare the squash-and-apple purée.

To prepare the scallops: Remove any tough cartilage on the sides of the scallops, wipe off any bits of shell, and pat dry. In a sauté pan large enough to hold the scallops in one layer without crowding (or use two sauté pans or cook in batches), heat 4 tablespoons of the butter. When the butter bubbles, add the scallops and cook for 2–2½ minutes, turning and tossing them after 1 minute of cooking. The scallops should just turn opaque. Remove the scallops to a warm serving platter, season with salt and freshly ground pepper, and serve with lemon wedges and the squash-and-apple purée.   SERVES 4

❖Use small sea scallops.

❖Sauté the scallops and serve with a *Tomato Muffuletta Sauce* (page 212) or a warm *Tomato Fondue* (page 363).

❖Use a fresh sweet virgin olive oil in place of butter to sauté the scallops.

❖Cook 2 tablespoons of finely chopped shallots in the butter until wilted before adding the scallops. Cook the scallops and shallots, remove the scallops to a warm platter, deglaze the pan with 2–3 tablespoons dry vermouth or white wine, and pour the deglazing sauce over the scallops.

❖Use the hot sautéed scallops to garnish the top of an arugula salad.

SPECIAL INFORMATION ABOUT

SCALLOPS

PICTURE THE OPEN sea on a calm autumn day. In the distance is a long spit of land, and in the middle of the frame a small group of people dressed in bulky rubber outfits appear to be walking on water. Two boats float close to them, and a white dog leaps about in the gentle waves. Something just under his paws keeps the white dog dancing and barking in excitement. The dog is our dog, Sam, and his frenzy is caused by scores of Nantucket bay scallops clapping their way across the edge of the sandbar he is prancing on, next to the eelgrass shoals where they thrive. An aerial view shows similar groups of scallopers dotted around the island, all hoping to bring home a haul of scallops for dinner. Euell Gibbons titled one of his books *Stalking the Blue-Eyed Scallop,* and indeed, scallops do have a line of sensory organs along the edge of their shells to guide them through their underwater world.

Catching the scallops using rakes, nets, and glass-bottomed viewfinders is actually the easier of two steps; then the scallops must be shucked from their shells with razor-sharp edges that can shred the hands of inexpert shuckers. The sweet meat of these beautiful creatures is worth a few Band-Aids.

A scallop is a bivalve with two lovely fluted shells, the familiar backdrop for Venus, the goddess of love, and the corporate logo of the Shell Oil Company. In addition to the blue "eyes" along the shell edge, the scallop has the capacity to detect certain enemies (but not Sam, I think) by scent. A large adductor muscle joins the two shells together and works the hinge that opens and closes them. The scallop propels itself in jerky or fluttery butterflylike movements by forcing water in and out around the hinge—a small-scale example of jet propulsion. Inside the shells, besides the adductor muscle, there are the digestive organs (stomach and liver), the crescent-shaped sex organ, or gonad, commonly referred to as the roe (mature male milt is opaque white, and mature female eggs are orange-red), and the "rim" or "skirt" or "frill" of sensory organs around the inner circumference of each shell. The adductor muscle, shaped much like a marshmallow, is what Americans know as a "scallop"; the rest of the scallop has usually been discarded before we see scallop meat in the market. In Europe, however, a scallop is usu-

ally served with the crescent-shaped gonad still attached to the adductor muscle. The orange female roe has a slightly stronger flavor than the white male milt, but both are delicate and complement the taste of the muscle meat. I'll always remember the first time I encountered a beautifully prepared dish of creamy scallops with their coral roe in a Parisian restaurant. The dish looked like a painting, and it was as delicious as it was handsome. Only recently have any scallops with roe attached appeared in American markets, and for several reasons, I think. It requires more work and more careful handling to dress a wild scallop with roe attached. The roe is more perishable than the muscle meat, and it also has to be inspected more carefully because the roe will absorb toxins from "red tide" pollution and other sources that the muscle meat does not take in. Farmed whole scallops are now being marketed that are delightful small-size scallops; you eat every bit, just like oysters or clams on the half shell.

There are over 360 species of scallops worldwide, but perhaps only a dozen or so make their way to the market. Three Atlantic species—sea scallops, bay scallops, and calico scallops—are most widely available across the United States, along with imported scallops from such countries as Canada, Japan, Peru, and Aus-

SCALLOPS

Scallops (continued)

tralia. One can find excellent regional varieties such as the Icelandic scallop, a subarctic species found off the East Coast; the purple-hinged rock scallop of Oregon (the only scallop that attaches itself to rocks); or the glowing pink scallop of the Northwest sold in its shell in Seattle markets.

1. *The Sea Scallop.* Sea scallops can have a life span of twenty years, and the size and characteristics of each one will vary with its maturity. The muscle meat of larger scallops can measure a generous 2 inches across. If you are able to buy scallop meat with roe attached, it will undoubtedly be from sea scallops. They are gathered from deep waters year-round and thus can be available fresh at any time. They are shucked at sea, and the shells and guts are thrown overboard. As soon as they are shucked, the scallops are stored in containers (often cloth bags) and iced down. They are not usually graded for size as shrimp are, though some markets will designate "baby seas" or "small seas" and charge more for them. Count on about 25 sea scallops per pound, with selected smaller ones running about 40–50 per pound. While sea scallops do not have the intense sweetness of bay scallops, they are very good indeed, and when impeccably fresh, they have a briny sweetness all their own.

2. *The Bay Scallop.* Bay scallops are smaller than sea scallops, live inshore, and have life spans of

only about two years. There are three subspecies along the East Coast, but the best known and most coveted is the eastern bay scallop harvested along the coast of Nantucket Sound and off Long Island, where harvesting is limited to scallops exhibiting the distinct second-year growth ring. Harvesting occurs from autumn until late spring; if you see "fresh" bay scallops in the market during the summer, you can assume they have been frozen and defrosted. Bay scallops are brought ashore in their shells (it is illegal to shuck them on board) and opened in "shucking" shacks by the flying fingers of experts. They vary in size, but a 50–60 count per pound would be typical. The smallest ones, at 80–100 count, are called "peanuts." Fresh bay scallops are incomparably sweet.

3. *The Calico Scallop.* Calico scallops are small scallops found in deep waters from the Carolinas all the way to Brazil. Florida, especially Cape Canaveral, is the heart of the calico industry, and

perhaps for that reason calicos are sometimes referred to as "Capes," a practice that enrages New Englanders who believe the less sweet calicos will be confused with eastern bay scallops. Since calicos are even smaller than bay scallops, they are brought ashore in the shell and steam-heated and opened mechanically—a process that partially cooks them. They are usually packed and marketed fresh and can run from 80–200 scallops per pound.

Farmed Scallops
In the growth of aquaculture, scallops have not been forgotten. Right here in Massachusetts, Rodman Taylor, a former Woods Hole Oceanographic Institute biologist, is growing from seed beautiful small Cape Cod Bay scallops. At Taylor Seafood, scallops are grown in carefully monitored waters inspected by state biologists for heavy metals and other pollution. Strict surveillance is especially important because these scallops are being marketed as whole scallops in their shells.

SCALLOPS

Taylor advocates eating the entire scallop, as Europeans have been doing for years. He has been given permission to harvest the scallops at a smaller size than regulations allow for wild bay scallops, and consequently they are a perfect bite-size, very easy to shuck, delicious raw, and can be eaten just as one would eat oysters or clams on the half shell. The scallops can also be steamed open in minutes and treated like mussels—see *Mussels Marinière* (page 35)—or clams—see *Steamed Soft-Shell Clams* (page 33) or *Clams Cataplana-Style* (page 133). They can also be used as a shellfish addition to soups and stews. Unlike wild scallops, these farmed scallops are now available year-round, and are even blast-frozen at −40 degrees Fahrenheit and marketed in frozen form. Aquaculture has brought, in these whole scallops, a new seafood to our table.

Buying
Look for shiny translucent meats with clear, bright color. Fresh sea scallops will be slightly creamy in color, bay scallops even more so. The partial cooking in the processing of calico scallops removes their sheen and gives them a white color. Aging scallops will be more opaque with a dull pallor or even grayish color. Scallops should be firm, not mushy or slimy, and they should not show any evidence of shredding. Scallops have a natural odor that builds up if they are kept in a closed container very long. You can come to identify this odor yourself. Exposure to the air or rinsing will dissipate

it; the smell is not sour or acrid or like iodine (avoid scallops with any such odors). Scallops have a high proportion of water in their meat, and once they are harvested, they begin to "drip" this water content and lose weight. To counteract this weight loss for commercial reasons and to make the scallops look plump, some wholesalers may dip them in a water-chemical solution to add weight and make them whiter in appearance. Having a trustworthy fish market is the best defense against excessive dipping of scallops, but you can also be a little wary of scallops that look too plump to be true or too pristine white.

Always ask if scallops have been previously frozen and then defrosted. Imported scallops that have been frozen and then defrosted and sold as "fresh" have become a significant part of the scallop market. Defrosted scallops have a tendency to exude more liquid than fresh scallops when they are cooked, and they are likely to shrink more during cooking. Avoid sautéing defrosted scallops or serving them in a fragile sauce such as a hollandaise or mousseline because their juices will seriously dilute the sauce.

Frozen scallops may come in bulk frozen packages or in packages in which each scallop has been individually frozen. With shrimp we find a comparative advantage in individually frozen shrimp, but with scallops the balance swings the other way. Individually frozen scallops may each have absorbed more water in the

freezing process and will exude more liquid and lose more weight in the cooking process. When they are available, I always prefer fresh scallops over frozen for taste, texture, and the way they cook up. This means that I would take a fresh sea scallop in June over a frozen bay scallop at that time of year.

Storage
Whole scallops. I store whole scallops in the shell in my refrigerator vegetable bin or in a large high-sided pan in the coldest part of the refrigerator. I cover them loosely with a damp cloth; do not cover them tightly, for they are alive and need air circulation. I shuck and cook them as soon as possible. Whole scallops in the shell will keep for two days in the refrigerator.

Shucked scallops. Scallops build up an odor if tightly sealed, so I always cover them loosely and provide vents for air circulation. I store scallops in a flat layer in a nonaluminum-lined pan in the coldest part of the refrigerator, covering them loosely with butcher's paper or waxed paper and topping them with ice packs or ice but making sure that the melting ice cannot directly touch the scallops. Since the scallops continue to lose moisture even under the best circumstances, the sooner they are cooked the better; typically, I take them home and cook them within a few hours. Refrigerating cooked scallops is not very satisfactory; once cooked and then chilled, they seem to get rubbery. If you must

SCALLOPS

Scallops (continued)

store cooked scallops, keep them moist in a fish broth, their cooking juices, lemon water, or a marinade or vinaigrette.

Freeze your catch of shucked scallops only when they are very fresh. Chill the scallops, then place them flat in freezer bags, pushing out the air so they will freeze evenly and quickly. The faster they freeze, the less the natural water of the scallops will expand and the less the fibers will break down or be damaged. I freeze scallops in 8-ounce packages, and they will keep that way for 3–4 months.

Never defrost scallops at room temperature. The fastest way is to place the watertight package of frozen scallops in cold water and keep more cold water running into the container, or keep them in still, cold water, replacing the water as it warms until the scallops are defrosted. Defrosting in the refrigerator will usually take 8–10 hours or more. Cook the scallops as soon as possible after they are defrosted.

Preparation
All scallops have a small connective cartilage strip attached to the shucked muscle meat—I call it gristle. It is edible but tougher than the other meat and detracts from the silky smoothness of the muscle meat. I always remove it on sea scallops by simply pulling it off with my fingers, and I remove it on bay scallops if they are not too small.

Fresh scallops might have bits

of shell or membrane attached to them. I prefer to pick and wipe these off rather than washing the scallop. Washing allows the scallop to absorb water, which affects the cooking quality, and it rinses out natural juices and taste. If scallops must be washed, it should be a fast rinse followed by an immediate drain and wiping or patting dry.

If scallops are quite uneven in size or very large, I cut them to similar size for cooking. Cutting across the grain is the better method; cutting down through the fibers may encourage the scallop to fall apart as it cooks.

If scallops have been frozen and defrosted before cooking and are going to be cooked in a sauce, it may help to poach them quickly for 1–2 minutes, and then drain them well to rid them of excess water from the freezing before doing the final cooking in the sauce.

Since nothing tops a scallop taken from the water and immediately shucked and cooked, I will tell you how to get the sweet muscle meat out of the shell.

To shuck a scallop:
1. Hold the scallop in the palm of one hand with the hinge facing your thumb and the curved or more convex shell down against your palm; clasp the top of the shell firmly with your thumb.
2. Insert a stiff-bladed paring knife between the shells near the wings and hinge where they gape. Twist the knife slightly up against the top shell and pry the knife enough to get the blade in to where the muscle attaches.

3. Cut the muscle away from the top shell with a scraping motion, then run the knife between the two shells and press the top shell back and open.
4. Hook the point of the knife into the rims and firmly pull the rims up to remove the rims and the viscera; the action is much like pulling a dress up over your head. Discard the viscera and the top shell.
5. Cut the muscle meat from the bottom shell, drop the meat into a container, and discard the shell. I have watched experienced shuckers do this in three motions so fast that if you blink, you miss it; they are paid by the weight of shucked meat, so speed is money.

Yields
Basically, what you buy is what you eat; scallops are a good buy. I remove the side cartilage, but that is only a small fraction of the scallop's weight. Yield will be affected by the amount of water the scallop has absorbed and will release when cooked. Fresh scallops shouldn't lose much weight during cooking, but frozen and defrosted scallops might. Because individual size varies, these are approximate numbers:

❖ Serving size of 6 ounces equals ⅔ cup
❖ ⅔ cup sea scallops equals 8–10 scallops
❖ ⅔ cup baby sea scallops equals 12–14 scallops
❖ ⅔ cup bay scallops equals 20–30 scallops
❖ ⅔ cup calico scallops equals 40–50 scallops

Scallops Sauté Meunière

"Meunière" is a delicious and practical way to cook shellfish and fish that cook quickly; the food is lightly floured and then quickly sautéed in a hot pan. The thin skin of flour seals in the juices that otherwise would be drawn out by the high heat, and also makes a tasty golden-brown coating. The pan and cooking liquid have to be very hot so that the food will brown and not simmer, and the food needs to be separated, not crowded, in the pan so it will sauté and not braise; therefore, cook in batches, if necessary, to keep the pan uncrowded. In the case of scallops, flouring should be done at the very last minute before cooking so that the flour doesn't soak up moisture from the scallop and become gluey and lumpy. Toss the scallops in flour, using instant-blending flour, if you have it, for the best results, and then shake them gently in a sieve to remove excess flour. I use a well-seasoned iron frying pan or a nonstick sauté pan. With these sweet morsels I serve *Roasted Ratatouille* (page 326), which I prepare well ahead of serving and reheat while the scallops are quickly sautéing.

Alternative shellfish: peeled and deveined shrimp

1½ lb scallops
6–8 Tb butter
¾ cup flour (preferably instant-blending flour, such as Wondra Quick-Mixing Flour)
Salt and freshly ground pepper
Lemon wedges

Remove any tough pieces of cartilage from the sides of the scallops, wipe off any bits of shell, and pat dry. Heat 3 tablespoons of the butter in a sauté pan large enough to hold the scallops comfortably in one layer without crowding, or cook them in two batches, using an additional 2 tablespoons of butter, if necessary. Place the flour in a pie pan or bowl, season it with salt and freshly ground pepper, and just before cooking, toss the scallops in it; remove the scallops to a sieve and shake to remove excess flour. Add the scallops to the hot butter, separating them in the pan with a spoon or spatula. Cook them for 30 seconds, then cook for another 1–2 minutes as you turn them in the pan to brown all sides equally. Remove the cooked scallops to a warm platter, wipe out the pan, add the remaining 3 tablespoons of butter, and cook

until the butter turns a rich brown color. Pour the brown butter over the scallops and serve sizzling hot with lemon wedges. SERVES 4

❖Although a classic meunière uses all butter, you can sauté the scallops in a combination of equal parts butter and oil, and you can omit the brown-butter topping.

❖ *With Capers:* Cook the scallops as above and remove to a warm platter. Heat 3 tablespoons butter, and when it begins to turn brown, add ⅓ cup drained capers. Swirl the capers into the butter and cook just until they release their juices and the butter browns. (Add 1 tablespoon red wine vinegar for additional acidity, if you wish.) Pour over the scallops and serve.

❖ *Almandine:* Cook the scallops as above and remove to a warm platter. Heat 3 tablespoons butter, and when it is light brown, add ⅓ cup sliced or slivered blanched almonds. Cook, swirling the pan, until both the butter and the almonds are brown. Pour over the scallops and serve.

❖ *With Garlic and Parsley:* Cook the scallops as above and remove to a warm platter. Heat 3–4 tablespoons butter, add 2 tablespoons minced shallots, and cook for 1–2 minutes or until wilted. Add 1 heaping teaspoon minced garlic and 2–3 tablespoons minced fresh parsley, and cook, swirling the pan for 30 seconds, until the butter is just golden brown. Pour over the scallops and serve.

Scallops Provençale

When I hear *à la Provençale,* I think of garlic, tomatoes, onions, and a fine French olive oil. This is a good dish to serve with pasta or rice.

1½ lb small sea scallops
3 Tb virgin olive oil
Instant-blending flour (such as Wondra Quick-Mixing Flour), for dredging
¼ cup finely chopped scallions
2 minced cloves garlic
2 cups peeled, seeded, and chopped tomatoes
½ cup dry vermouth or white wine
2 tsp chopped fresh basil
2 Tb chopped fresh parsley
Salt and freshly ground pepper

Scallops Provençale (continued)

Prepare the scallops by removing the tough cartilage on the side of the scallops, wiping off any bits of shell, and patting them dry.

Heat the oil in a large sauté pan. Toss the scallops in flour in batches, then immediately shake them in a sieve to remove the excess flour (flour the scallops just before they go into the pan). Sauté the scallops until lightly colored on all sides, about 1 minute. Add the scallions, garlic, tomatoes, and vermouth or white wine. Toss all together and cook briefly over high heat to thicken the sauce and finish cooking the scallops. Remove from the heat, stir in the basil and parsley, season to taste with salt and freshly ground pepper, and serve. SERVES 4

❖Before adding the tomatoes, add ¼ pound quartered small mushrooms that have been lightly sautéed in olive oil.

❖Divide the scallops into 4 individual buttered scallop shells. Top with grated cheese or buttered bread crumbs and run under the broiler to lightly brown.

Sautéed Scallops
with a Little Sauce

There is just enough vermouth and cream in this recipe to glaze the scallops lightly in a quick sauté. For some reason I love this dish with *Succotash* (page 341).

> 1½ lb bay or small sea scallops
> 3 Tb butter
> 1 Tb chopped shallots
> ⅓ cup dry vermouth or white wine
> ⅔ cup heavy cream
> 1 Tb chopped fresh dill (optional)
> Salt and freshly ground pepper
> Cayenne pepper

Remove any tough cartilage on the sides of the scallops, wipe off any bits of shell, and pat them dry. In a sauté pan, heat the butter. Add the scallops and let them cook for 1 minute, then begin tossing them occasionally as they cook for 2–3 minutes longer,

depending on the size of the scallops. Cook the scallops in batches, if necessary, to prevent crowding them in the pan. Lift the scallops out of the pan to a warm plate. Add the shallots to the pan, cook for 30 seconds, then add the vermouth and cook until it is reduced by half. Add the cream, stir, and cook until the sauce is reduced to about ½ cup. Return the scallops to the pan just long enough to reheat in the sauce, adding the dill, if you like. Season with salt, freshly ground pepper, and cayenne pepper. SERVES 4

❖*Normandy-Style:* After sautéing the scallops and removing them from the pan, add ½ pound of small peeled and deveined shrimp to the butter in the pan. Cook for 2–3 minutes, tossing occasionally, then remove to the same plate with the scallops and proceed, as above, to prepare the sauce. If desired, divide the creamed scallops and shrimp among individual buttered scallop shells and decorate each serving with a sautéed shrimp or a puff-pastry fleuron.

❖*With Pink Sauce:* Before returning the sautéed scallops to the pan to reheat in the sauce, stir ⅓ cup *Roasted Red Pepper Purée* (page 360) into the sauce.

❖Add chopped fresh herbs to the pan with the cream.

❖Add 2 tablespoons finely minced celery to the pan with the shallots.

❖Substitute orange or grapefruit juice for the vermouth. Omit the cayenne pepper and sprinkle the finished dish with finely grated orange zest.

Grilled Sea Scallops
with Green Tomato Salsa

While I would walk a mile to find small sweet bay scallops, I have found that big fat sea scallops are best for grilling. It is wise to take some steps to prevent their smooth, tender flesh from sticking to the hot grill rack. One could blanch them by dropping them into boiling water for 1 minute, then draining them immediately, and the quick blanching would firm them up for the grill. Or one could brush them with oil before placing them on the grill. In this case I have chosen to marinate them in a flavored oil before grilling. I try to pick out scallops of uniform size. Lace them on skewers to prevent them from dropping through any open spaces in the rack, or put the scallops in an oiled grill basket. By the way, if I am grilling a combination of seafood, I keep them separate during grilling because they are apt to have different cooking times. I make this salsa from some of the many green tomatoes in our fall garden. You could substitute tomatillos or use tougher unripened tomatoes from the supermarket, or a combination of both. The salsa preparation requires a food processor or blender; it can be made well ahead. Serve with *Succotash* (page 341), *Warm Radishes and Black Beans* (page 337), or grilled potatoes and a fresh vegetable.

Alternative shellfish or fish: shrimp, chunks of monkfish, eel

GREEN TOMATO SALSA

1 lb small to medium green
    tomatoes
2 large canned medium-hot
    jalapeño peppers
2 finely chopped, fresh hot peppers
½ cup finely chopped red or white
    onions
2–3 Tb chopped cilantro
Juice of 1 lime
Salt and freshly ground pepper

To make the Green Tomato Salsa: Core the tomatoes, cut them into quarters or large pieces, and put them in the bowl of a food processor fitted with a steel blade. Roughly chop the canned jalapeño peppers and add them to the bowl. Process the tomatoes and peppers to the consistency of a chunky sauce and remove the rough purée to a bowl for storage. Add the fresh hot peppers, onions, cilantro, and lime juice, season the mixture with salt and pepper, cover, and refrigerate until ready to use.

MAKES ABOUT 2 CUPS

1½–2 lb large sea scallops
¼ cup light olive oil
2 Tb fresh lime juice
1–2 Tb chopped cilantro
Salt and freshly ground pepper

Prepare the green tomato salsa and refrigerate.

To cook the scallops: Remove any tough pieces of cartilage on the sides of the scallops and any bits of shell, and put the scallops in a bowl. In a small bowl, combine the olive oil, lime juice, and cilantro, and pour the mixture over the scallops; toss until the scallops are well coated. Let the scallops marinate for 20 minutes, if you wish.

Preheat the grill and place the scallops on skewers, running the skewers through the side of the scallop, not from the top through the bottom. Sprinkle with salt and freshly ground pepper. Place the skewers on a well-oiled grill rack and leave over the heat for 2 minutes; then begin to turn the skewers to expose all sides of the scallops to the heat, using a large spoon or spatula to make sure the scallops are rotating on the skewers. Cook for a total of 3–6 minutes, depending on the size of the scallops, or until they are firm and opaque at the center. (To test, cut one open.) Remove the scallops from the skewers and serve with the salsa on the side.

SERVES 4

❖Broil the scallops.

❖In place of brushing the scallops with oil or marinating them, prepare them for the grill by blanching them for 1 minute in boiling water, then seasoning them with salt and freshly ground pepper, and placing them on the grill.

❖Serve the scallops with lemon wedges instead of salsa, or use another sauce such as the traditional and always delicious homemade *Tartar Sauce* (page 363).

❖Add a few skewers of chunks of cooked sausage—linguiça or kielbasa—to the grill; the smoky sausage contrasts nicely with the sweet scallops.

❖Add minced garlic to the salsa.

❖Substitute fresh parsley for the cilantro or omit it completely.

❖Adjust the amount of hot pepper in the sauce to your own taste.

Baked Scallops and Leeks

Cooked leeks have a mild, yet distinctive flavor and a nice firm, but not quite crunchy, texture. One could describe many shellfish and fish in exactly the same terms. Consequently, I serve leeks and seafood in combined dishes frequently because the leeks bring

Baked Scallops and Leeks (continued)

out, but do not overwhelm, the flavor of the fish. Two slightly different techniques for preparing the leeks are offered here. In the first, I gently boil, then slice the leeks; in the variation, I chop and braise them. I think you'll find both ways delicious.

 6 leeks, ½ inch in diameter
 1 lb bay or small sea scallops
 6 Tb unsalted butter
 2–3 Tb finely chopped shallots
 ⅔ cup *Buttered Bread Crumbs* (page 351)
   (optional)

Clean the leeks by trimming the root end, removing any withered or bruised outer leaves, and cutting off and discarding the dark leaves at the top where the leaves turn to pale green. Cut a 1-inch slit down through the top end of the trimmed leek, then give the leek a quarter turn and make another 1-inch-deep slit. The two crosscuts will enable you to spread open the top of the leek to clean it thoroughly. Plunge the leeks up and down in a pot or sinkful of water to remove any sand or soil that may be in the leaves. Bring a large pot of water to a boil. Tie the leeks together with string, if you like, to make it easier to remove them from the pot. Drop the leeks into the boiling water and cook for 5 minutes, or until they are just tender. Remove the leeks, run them under cold water to stop the cooking action, drain, pat thoroughly dry, and cut into ½-inch-thick rounds.

Remove any tough pieces of cartilage from the sides of the scallops, wipe off any bits of shell, and pat dry. Butter 4 scallop shells or individual au gratin dishes, and divide the scallops and leeks evenly among them. In a small sauté pan, melt the butter, add the shallots, and sauté them for 1–2 minutes to soften them slightly. Spoon the shallot butter evenly over the scallops and leeks, distribute the buttered bread crumbs evenly over all, bake in a preheated 400-degree oven for 12–15 minutes, then remove and run the dish under a preheated broiler briefly to brown the crumbs.   SERVES 4

❖ If you have large sea scallops, cut them into ½–¾-inch pieces for this recipe.
❖ *Baked Scallops and Braised Leeks:* Trim 3 pounds of leeks, make long slits almost all the way down the sides of the leeks, wash as above, and chop them. (You will have about 6 cups chopped leeks.)

In a wide saucepan, heat 2–3 tablespoons butter, add the leeks and cook gently, covered, for 8–10 minutes, stirring occasionally. Uncover, continue to cook until any excess moisture in the pan has evaporated, and season the leeks with salt and freshly ground pepper. Spoon the braised chopped leeks evenly into 4 buttered baking dishes or shells (use 6 shells if you are serving as a first course) and distribute the scallops evenly on top of the leeks. In a small sauté pan, melt 2 tablespoons butter, add the shallots, and cook until they are lightly colored; then spoon the shallot butter over the scallops and leeks. Top with bread crumbs, if desired, and cook as above.

SERVES 4 AS A MAIN COURSE, 6 AS A FIRST COURSE

❖Cook the leeks and shallots in equal amounts of butter and light olive oil.

Stir-Fry of Scallops, Shrimp, and Zucchini

Creamy scallops and pink shrimp, both with silky texture, and garden-fresh green zucchini quickly cooked to preserve crunchiness—a perfect marriage.

 1 lb bay or small sea scallops
 ¾ lb large (31–35 count) raw shrimp
 2–3 small zucchini
 2 Tb vegetable oil
 3 Tb butter
 ½ cup scallions, cut into ½-inch lengths
 ½ tsp minced garlic
 ½ cup dry vermouth or white wine
 2 Tb fresh lemon juice
 Dash of soy sauce
 Sesame oil (optional)
 Salt and freshly ground pepper

Remove any tough bits of cartilage on the sides of the scallops, wipe off any bits of shell, and pat the scallops dry. Peel and devein the shrimp.

Trim the ends off the zucchini, cut each zucchini into 4 strips lengthwise, then cut the strips crosswise into 1–1½-inch lengths.

In a large sauté pan or wok, heat the oil and 2 tablespoons of the butter, add the zucchini, and cook, tossing, for 2–3 minutes. Remove the zucchini to a warm plate. Turn the heat to high and add the shrimp to the pan. Cook, turning the shrimp, until they are lightly colored on all sides. Add the scallops and cook with the shrimp for 2–3 minutes, turning them after 1 minute, or until just cooked through. Remove the shrimp and scallops to a warm plate.

Add the remaining tablespoon of butter to the pan, then add the scallions, and cook for 1 minute. Stir in the garlic. Add the vermouth or wine and cook to reduce the mixture to a syrup, swirling the liquid to deglaze the pan. Return the zucchini, shrimp, and scallops to the pan. Add the lemon juice, soy sauce, and sesame oil, if desired, and toss all together. Season with salt and freshly ground pepper, and serve with pasta or rice.   SERVES 4

❖ Substitute roll-cut, peeled asparagus or sliced strips of red peppers or other raw vegetables for the zucchini; or use blanched vegetables, such as broccoli flowerets or carrot logs.

Fried Scallops

The secret to tasty fried scallops is fresh oil. Even the sweetest scallops taste like old grease if cooked in secondhand oil. Since oil is expensive, I shallow-fry the scallops in ¾ inch of oil in a heavy-bottomed saucepan rather than deep-fry them; however, a deep-fat-frying thermometer is still necessary to check the oil temperature. I don't think I could serve fried scallops or fried clams without a generous helping of *Coleslaw* (page 82).

1½ lb bay or small sea scallops
½ cup flour
Salt and freshly ground pepper
1 cup very fine, fresh bread crumbs
1 egg beaten with 1 Tb water
Peanut oil or vegetable oil
Lemon wedges
Tartar Sauce (page 363)

Remove any tough bits of cartilage on the sides of the scallops, wipe off any bits of shell, and pat them dry. Place the flour in a bowl; season it with salt and freshly ground pepper. In batches, toss the scallops in the flour until coated, then transfer them to a sieve

and shake them to remove any excess flour. Spread the bread crumbs on a plate. Roll the floured scallops in the beaten egg, drain slightly, then roll them in the bread crumbs. After coating the scallops well with bread crumbs, return them to the sieve and again shake off any excess coating. Refrigerate the coated scallops for 20 minutes to help the coating adhere.

Pour ¾ inch of oil into a wide, high-sided pan; heat the oil to 360 degrees. Add the scallops in one layer, cooking in batches, if necessary, to prevent crowding the scallops in the pan. Cook for 2–3 minutes, or until the coating is a rich golden brown. Remove the scallops with a slotted spoon and place them on double-thick paper towels or on brown paper for just a minute so any excess oil can be absorbed. Keep the scallops warm in a 200-degree oven if not serving immediately, or place them on a warm platter and serve with lemon wedges and tartar sauce.   SERVES 4

❖ Add seasonings such as cayenne pepper or paprika to the flour.
❖ Substitute stone-ground cornmeal for the bread crumbs.

Gladys' Scalloped Scallops

Dun Gifford, who goes scalloping with my husband in the fall, freezes much of his catch, and his wife, Gladys, uses this recipe often as she works her way through his stash. Mashed potatoes are delicious with this dish.

Alternative fish: chunks of firm-fleshed fish, such as monkfish, striped bass, sturgeon

1 lb bay or small sea scallops
3 Tb butter
3 Tb flour
1 cup light cream
½ cup milk
¼ cup dry vermouth or white wine
Salt and freshly ground pepper
¾ cup *Buttered Bread Crumbs* (page 351)

Remove any tough bits of cartilage on the sides of the scallops, wipe off any bits of shell, and pat the scallops dry. Cut large sea scallops into medium-sized pieces of about equal size; use bay scallops whole.

Gladys' Scalloped Scallops (continued)

In a sauté pan, melt the butter and cook until bubbly. Add the scallops and cook over medium heat, stirring constantly, until lightly colored and cooked through, about 2–4 minutes, depending on their size. Lift the scallops with a slotted spoon to a warm plate. Add the flour to the butter left in the pan and cook, stirring, for 1 minute. Remove the pan from the heat and whisk in the cream, milk, and vermouth or wine. Return the pan to the heat and cook, stirring, until the mixture thickens. Return the scallops and any juices to the sauce, and season with salt and freshly ground pepper.

Pour the scallops and sauce into a buttered baking dish and sprinkle the buttered bread crumbs over the top. Bake in a preheated 400-degree oven for 10 minutes, or until the bread crumbs are brown and the sauce is bubbly.   SERVES 4

❖ Add ½ cup sautéed sliced mushrooms to the sauce before baking.

Scallops Soffritto

The Italian *soffritto* is a mixture of aromatic vegetables; here these vegetables become a fragrant nest for baked scallops. Bring the bubbling scallops to the table in their baking dish and let your guests spoon them out onto a bed of rice, if you like. Accompany with green peas or beans. Or you can bake and serve these in 6–8 small shells as an appetizer.

Alternative fish: small chunks of monkfish, striped bass

1¼ lb bay or small sea scallops
4 Tb light olive oil
½ cup finely chopped onions
½ cup finely chopped celery
⅓ cup finely chopped carrots
⅓ cup finely chopped cured ham
1 tsp minced garlic
¼ cup dry vermouth or white wine
¾ cup fresh bread crumbs
2 Tb finely chopped parsley
Lemon wedges

5–6 cups cooked rice (optional)

Prepare the scallops by removing any tough bits of cartilage on the sides of the scallops, wipe off any bits of shell, and pat the scallops dry. If the scallops are very large, slice them across the grain into smaller pieces.

In a sauté pan, heat 2 tablespoons of the oil, add the onions, celery, and carrots, and cook until the vegetables are wilted and tender, about 10 minutes, taking care not to brown them. Add the ham and sauté for 2 minutes. Add the garlic and cook, stirring, for 30 seconds. Add the vermouth or wine and cook for a few minutes until the liquid is reduced and the vegetables are glazed.

Distribute the vegetable mixture among 4 oiled large-sized scallop shells or individual au gratin dishes and scatter the scallops evenly on top of the mixture.

Combine the bread crumbs and parsley with the remaining 2 tablespoons of oil and sprinkle the mixture over the scallops. Bake in a preheated 400-degree oven for 15 minutes, or until the scallops are just opaque. Serve with lemon wedges and, if you wish, with cooked rice as a bed for the baked scallops.

SERVES 4

❖ If you have large sea scallops, cut them into ¾–1-inch pieces for this recipe.

Coquilles Saint-Jacques au Gratin

If you order "Coquilles Saint-Jacques" from an American menu, you will usually get a dish of creamy baked scallops. In France, however, the phrase "Coquilles Saint-Jacques" refers to scallops in general, not to a particular recipe. On a French menu you might find Coquilles Saint-Jacques Provençale (scallops in a garlic-flavored tomato sauce) or Coquilles Saint-Jacques Mornay (scallops in a cheese-cream sauce), and so on. This recipe is for the familiar creamy version—scallops and mushrooms enrobed in a white wine sauce, baked, and gratinéed to a bubbly finish. The richness of the sauce stretches a pound of scallops to serve 4. It is a perfect dish to serve in scallop baking shells or individual au gratin dishes. You can prepare this dish in steps up to and including assembling the entire dish, then cover and refrigerate it until baking just before serving. I like to serve this with a side dish of *Braised Peas and Scallions* (page 332).

Alternative fish: Heretical as it seems to suggest another fish in place of scallops in this famous dish, you could enrobe poached chunks of a firm-fleshed fish such as monkfish, bass, or salmon in the same sauce and cook them the same way.

> 1 lb bay or small sea scallops
> ¼ lb mushrooms
> 1 cup dry white wine
> 2 Tb butter
> 2 Tb minced shallots
> 2 Tb flour
> 1 cup light cream
> ¼ cup milk (optional)
> 1 lemon
> Salt and freshly ground pepper
> 1 cup *Buttered Bread Crumbs* (page 351)

Remove any pieces of tough cartilage from the sides of the scallops, wipe off any bits of shell, and pat them dry. Wipe any particles of soil off the mushrooms and cut them into thin slices. In a stainless or enamel saucepan, combine the scallops and their juices, the mushrooms and the wine, cover, bring to a simmer, and poach for 3–4 minutes (2–3 minutes if you are using small bay or calico scallops). Lift the scallops and mushrooms from the pan to a bowl and set aside. Boil the poaching liquid until it is reduced to 1 cup, adding to it any liquid that drains from the reserved scallops.

In a saucepan, heat the butter, add the shallots, and cook until the shallots are wilted. Stir in the flour and cook the mixture for 2 minutes, then remove the pan from the heat and whisk in the poaching liquid. Return the pan to the heat and whisk until the mixture is smooth and has thickened slightly. Add the cream and cook, stirring, until the mixture thickens some more. Thin the sauce with milk, if desired, and season with the juice of a lemon, salt and freshly ground pepper. Add the reserved scallops and mushrooms, stir gently but well, and spoon the mixture into 4 scallop shells or individual au gratin dishes. Top with the buttered bread crumbs. Bake until bubbly in a preheated 400-degree oven, run the shells or dishes under a preheated broiler just long enough to brown the tops lightly, and serve. SERVES 4

❖If you have assembled, then covered and refrig-erated the whole dish, reheat at serving time in a pre-heated 400-degree oven for about 12–15 minutes or until bubbling, then run the dish under the broiler briefly to brown.

❖Substitute finely grated Swiss cheese for the bread crumbs, or add along with the bread crumbs.

❖Add 1 tablespoon of Dijon-style mustard with the cream.

❖Whisk in 1 teaspoon curry powder with the but-ter and shallots.

❖Replace a few of the scallops with small cooked shrimp.

❖Use ¾ cup cream if you want a very rich sauce.

❖Fold a bit of the sauce into 2 cups chopped braised greens, such as spinach, broccoli de rabe, col-lards, or kale. Spoon the greens evenly into individual au gratin dishes to form a bed for the scallops, mush-rooms, and sauce. Proceed as above.

❖If you have large sea scallops, cut them into ½–¾-inch pieces for this recipe.

Scallops Mousseline

The persistent popularity of Eggs Benedict is itself sufficient proof of the claim that just about everyone loves hollandaise sauce. Even in our fat- and calorie-conscious time, an occasional rich sauce is a welcome treat. Adding whipped heavy cream to the hol-landaise in this recipe transforms it into a light and airy mousseline sauce.

This recipe needs your attention at mealtime. You can assemble the individual scallop dishes in advance, and you can prepare the ingredients for the sauce ahead, but since letting an egg-based sauce sit out is not a good idea, you should make the hollandaise while the scallops cook and, if necessary, keep it warm for a short time over a double boiler of water the same temperature as the sauce. I prefer absolutely fresh scallops for this dish because previously frozen scallops lose a great deal of juice as they cook; and I like to serve it in individual au gratin dishes or in deep scallop-shaped shells. Because this is a rich dish, I serve it with something simple, such as green beans blanched and tossed with fresh lemon juice and savory or rice flavored with fresh herbs, and a green salad. By the way, the lobster variation makes an ele-gant beginning or main course for a dinner party.

Scallops Mousseline (continued)

1½ lb bay or small sea scallops
½ lb mushrooms
3 Tb butter
½ cup heavy cream
1 cup *Hollandaise Sauce* (page 356)

Remove any pieces of tough cartilage from the sides of the scallops, wipe off any bits of shell, and pat the scallops dry. Wipe any particles of soil off the mushrooms and cut them into thin slices.

In a sauté pan, heat the butter, add the mushrooms, and cook until they are wilted and lightly colored. Lift the cooked mushrooms from their pan juices to a shallow bowl, let them cool slightly, then spread them evenly across the bottom of 4 individual au gratin dishes. Distribute equal amounts of the scallops evenly over the mushrooms. Cover each serving with aluminum foil. (You can prepare the dish ahead to this point and refrigerate.)

Just before cooking the scallops, whip the cream to soft peaks and refrigerate it. Prepare the hollandaise sauce while the scallops are baking and keep it warm over a double boiler. Bake the scallops in a preheated 400-degree oven for 15 minutes. After 15 minutes, open one of the foil covers and check the scallops. They should be opaque throughout. Make a test cut in one, if you wish. If the scallops are too crowded, they may not cook uniformly on all sides. Use a fork to separate the scallops as much as possible. If necessary, cover and cook for another 5 minutes.

When the scallops are ready, remove the dishes from the oven. Open one end of the foil on each dish and drain off any excess juices that may have accumulated in the dish. (Save these juices, if you wish, for soups or sauces.) Quickly and gently fold the whipped cream into the hollandaise to make a mousseline sauce. Uncover each dish completely and spoon the mousseline sauce evenly over the baked scallops. Immediately run the dishes under a preheated broiler long enough to lightly brown the top of the sauce. Serve immediately.

SERVES 4 AS A MAIN COURSE, 6–8 AS A FIRST COURSE

❖Replace the mushrooms with a bed of vegetables. Spread chopped braised spinach or Swiss chard in the bottom of the shells or dishes, top with scallops, and bake as above.

❖Add some finely sliced sun-dried tomatoes to the mushrooms when you line the shells or individual au gratin dishes.

❖*Scallops and Lobster Mousseline:* Prepare as above, using 1 pound of scallops and ½ pound of cooked lobster meat. Distribute the scallops and lobster meat evenly—4 ounces of scallops and 2 ounces of lobster meat per serving; spread over the mushrooms. Or change the ratio to half scallops and half lobster meat.

❖If the scallops you have are large sea scallops, cut them into ½–¾-inch pieces for this recipe.

Baked Shad
and Boiled Asparagus

If you're looking for dependable signs to herald the arrival of spring, consider these: when shad begin their run from the sea to freshwater spawning grounds, and when the first fresh asparagus breaks the surface of the ground. These two harbingers combine to make a traditional spring dinner. Be sure to buy already boned shad, and even then check for bones again. Trim the asparagus well ahead and cook it while the shad bakes. I top the baked shad with broiled buttered bread crumbs to add a crisp textural contrast to its soft flesh. Sometimes I add boiled potatoes, but in truth this meal is just grand with nothing more than a dish of poached rhubarb for dessert.

BOILED ASPARAGUS

2–2½ lb asparagus
¼ cup *Lemon Vinaigrette* (page 365) or
    more to taste
Lemon wedges

BAKED SHAD

Two 1¼–1½-lb boned shad fillets with skin on
3–4 Tb melted butter or vegetable oil
Salt and freshly ground pepper
½–¾ cup *Buttered Bread Crumbs* (page 351)
Lemon wedges

To prepare the asparagus: Peel off the tough outer skin from the bottom of the spears. Cut a thin slice off the

(continued on page 262)

SHAD AND SHAD ROE

I CAN STILL SEE the delight on my father's face when he brought home the first shad roe of the spring season. Most of us, I suspect, have certain things that we look forward to seasonally—the first sun-ripened tomato, the first spring spear of asparagus, the first sweet parsnip dug after the first frost—and the anticipation makes the event all the more gratifying when it arrives. Fortunately for my father's passion for shad roe, we lived near the Connecticut River, which had a flourishing shad industry, and as soon as the shad began to run in the spring, we were guaranteed as much shad as we could eat for several weeks. Shad are physically among the largest members of the vast herring family of fish. They are native to the Atlantic Coast but were successfully transplanted to Pacific waters in the late 1800s and can be found there all the way from Alaska to Mexico. On the East Coast their range is from the Gulf of St. Lawrence to the Gulf of Mexico, but they are most abundant from Connecticut to North Carolina. Like salmon, for example, they are anadromous—spawned in freshwater rivers, migrating to the sea, returning to the river of origin again to spawn. In warmer waters shad may begin their spawning runs in December, but in Connecticut the run occurs in early spring, just about the same time their smaller cousins—the alewife herring—begin their run. Shad gravitate to the larger rivers to spawn, the alewives to smaller streams. Although shad can reach weights of about 12 pounds, most

are in the 3–8-pound range. The male is smaller and thinner than the female. When the female enters the freshwater river, she carries two large sacs of roe containing thousands of tiny eggs—the delicacy my father loved. The meat of the shad is very much worth eating as well, but between the fillets and the diner lie an incredible number of bones.

The shad has an unusual skeleton of floating parallel layers of bones that run through the fish from head to tail. If you or I attempted to bone and fillet a shad, the result would be a shredded mess. Even my excellent local fish market in Massachusetts won't attempt to bone a shad; the market relies on a "secret" source, a couple in Connecticut who have been preparing shad for twenty-five years. The meat of the shad is light and sweet, very much worth going to the trouble to bone, and there are river towns along the Connecticut and Hudson rivers that have shad festivals where hundreds of people feast on the spring run of shad. One of the traditional ways to serve shad is in a dish called planked shad, so called because each serving of fish is baked on a seasoned oval-shaped piece of wood about an inch thick, and the fish is surrounded on the plank by a ring of mashed potatoes.

Buying: Buy boned fillets of shad. Don't attempt to bone them yourself unless you are very experienced, or unless you want to spend a great deal of time and wind up with a miserable mess.

They are usually sold with the skin on. There may be cuts in the flesh from the boning, but the fillets should have been shaped back together. Fillets from the female shad tend to be larger, fattier, and thicker than those of the male shad. Flesh color ranges from white to pink to light beige, and the flesh should be glistening and bright to proclaim freshness. Please try, if you haven't, the delicious shad roe. Each female has a pair of flattened roe sacs that are encased in thin membranes. A pair of sacs will range in weight from 4 ounces to 1 pound; at my market they are typically 12 ounces to a pair or 6 ounces to a sac. The color of the roe will vary from light to dark rosy-red; the eggs should be firm and look like tiny berries. There should be no odor at all. Avoid buying roe with a torn outer membrane, or if the eggs look large and soft and mushy.

Storage: Shad fillets should be stored like any other fresh fish fillets. I put them in a glass or nonaluminum-lined dish, cover them with plastic wrap, and place ice packs on top of the wrap. Shad roe is very delicate, and you should treat it with kid gloves. You do not want the membrane to break, and you want to use it as soon as you buy it—old fish eggs are not desirable. Remove the roe from any paper it might have been wrapped in as soon as you get it home; otherwise it will exude juices and stick to the paper. I store the roe in a covered flat

SPECIAL INFORMATION ABOUT

SHAD AND SHAD ROE

Shad and Shad Roe (continued)

glass or stainless container and use it as soon as possible.

Preparation: Boned shad fillets are best cooked with the skin on to hold the delicate flesh in place.

Fillets can be broiled, baked, or sautéed, and larger fillets can be cut into portions and prepared like snapper or bass. Perhaps the simplest method, and one of the best, is *Baked Shad* (page 260). How to prepare shad roe for cooking is explained in *Sautéed*

Shad Roe with Bacon and Balsamic Onions (below).

Yields: Allow 6–8 ounces of boned shad fillet per person. Allow 4–6 ounces of shad roe per person.

Baked Shad and Boiled Asparagus (continued)

base of each spear of asparagus. Insert a small, sharp paring knife under the thicker skin at the base of each spear and work it up toward the tip, making the cut shallower as the skin becomes thinner; taper the cut off completely about 3–4 inches from the tip. Use a vegetable peeler to peel the asparagus, if you prefer. Set the peeled asparagus aside until the fish goes in the oven.

To cook the asparagus: Just before putting the shad in the oven, start the water for the asparagus. Fill three-fourths full of water a large rectangular or oval pot or high-sided sauté pan that is large enough to hold the asparagus lying down, cover, and bring to a boil. Drop the peeled asparagus into the boiling water, partially cover the pot until the water returns to a boil, uncover, reduce the heat to a medium boil, and cook for 4 minutes, or until the tip of a sharp knife easily pierces the spear. Timing depends on the size and age of the asparagus. Do not overcook; the asparagus should retain its texture and not be soggy or limp. Using 2 large spatulas, lift the asparagus to a clean dry towel for a minute to absorb any excess moisture, then place the spears on a warm serving platter and keep warm until ready to serve.

Remove any remaining bones from the shad. Brush the top of the fillets with the melted butter or oil, place the fillets on a buttered or oiled baking pan, and season with salt and freshly ground pepper. Bake for 12–15 minutes in a preheated 400-degree oven, or until the fish is just opaque throughout (test by inserting a sharp knife into the thickest part of the fillet).

Remove the pan of cooked shad from the oven,

turn off the oven, and turn on the broiler. Spread the buttered bread crumbs evenly over the top of the shad fillets, and place the pan on a rack about 5–6 inches below the preheated broiler. Broil for 2–3 minutes, or until the bread crumbs are lightly colored and crisp.

To serve the shad, cut across each fillet to divide into equal portions. Slide a wide spatula between the flesh and the skin, lift the shad off the skin, and place each portion on a warm serving plate. Garnish with lemon wedges and serve with the boiled asparagus, dressed with the lemon vinaigrette.

SERVES 4–6

❖Use virgin olive oil or melted butter in place of vinaigrette on the asparagus.

Sautéed Shad Roe with Bacon and Balsamic Onions

My father, who was a professional chef, sautéed shad roe very gently and carefully, and that is the method I prefer, using a nonstick sauté pan. A safer method is to poach the roe briefly to firm it up, then finish with a gentle sauté (see variation). Roe has an inclination to explode when heated, and the poaching seals the surface. Because the roe should be cooked slowly, clarified butter, which is less likely to brown, is the preferred cooking fat. You can use unsalted butter, but watch that it does not brown too much, or you can add a little vegetable oil to the butter to stabilize it. The rich, sweet flavor of shad roe reminds me of another favorite meal: sautéed calves liver. I like to serve both with the same garnish: sweet onions and bacon. With this dish I serve tender green asparagus fresh from the spring garden.

Alternative roe: alewife herring roe; cod roe is sometimes available

1½ lb red onions, or Spanish, Walla Walla, or
    Maui onions
4–8 strips bacon (optional)
2 pairs shad roe, about ¾ lb per pair
Clarified Butter (page 351)★
2 Tb fruity olive oil
2 Tb balsamic vinegar
Salt and freshly ground pepper
Lemon wedges

★If you do not have clarified butter, use unsalted butter and watch it carefully so that it doesn't brown; or use 2 parts unsalted butter to 1 part vegetable oil so that the oil will stabilize the butter.

Peel and halve the onions, and slice them into ¼–½-inch-thick circles or semicircles. Set aside.

Using a sauté pan that is just large enough to hold the 2 pairs of roe without crowding, fry the bacon (if you are using it) until it is crisp and drain it on brown paper. Keep the bacon warm and wipe out the sauté pan.

Handling the roe gently to keep the outer membrane intact, cut the membrane between the two sacs to separate them and remove any excess membrane. Rinse the sacs of roe, if necessary, to remove any blood veins and pat dry.

In the sauté pan, heat 4–5 tablespoons of clarified butter over medium heat. Add the roe, reduce the heat to low, and sauté *very gently,* covered, for 5–6 minutes. Uncover, carefully turn the roe with one long spatula, holding the top of the roe with your fingers, or two wide spatulas, and sauté very gently, uncovered, for 6–8 minutes more. If you are cooking the roe too fast, you will see the roe start to pop through the membrane. If so, reduce the heat even more. Depending on the size of the roe, it will take from 10–15 minutes to cook through until they are

just opaque and firm to the touch.

While the roe is cooking, heat the olive oil and vinegar in a sauté pan. Add the onions and cook for 5–6 minutes over medium heat, stirring, to brown and soften them. Season with salt and freshly ground pepper. Set aside and keep warm.

Remove the cooked roe to a warm plate and serve with strips of bacon, if desired, and a side garnish of the balsamic onions and lemon wedges.   SERVES 4

❖For a crisper surface to the roe, dust them with flour just before sautéing.

❖*With Lemon-Caper Butter:* After cooking the roe and removing it to a warm plate, wipe out the pan, add 3–4 tablespoons unsalted butter, cook the butter to a toasty-brown color; then swirl in the juice of 1 lemon and 1 tablespoon drained capers. Pour the flavored butter over the shad roe and serve.

❖*Poach-Sauté Method:* To a pan that is wide enough to hold the roe, add enough water to cover the roe completely. Before adding the roe to the pan, bring the water to a boil, squeeze in the juice of 1 lemon, turn the heat down to a simmer, gently lower the roe into the simmering water, and cook for 2 minutes. Remove the pan from the heat, allow it to cool slightly, then put the pan under the tap and gradually replace the hot water with cold water. Carefully lift the roe out of the water and pat it dry. Sauté as above.

Broiled Shrimp Scampi

A *scampi* is actually a miniature European lobster, but in this country the word has come to refer to shrimp cooked in a particular way with seasonings dominated by garlic—my favorite seasoning. Plain rice served with broccoli tossed with lemon is delicious with this dish.

2 lb extra jumbo (16–20 count) raw shrimp
⅓ cup butter
⅓ cup light olive oil
2 Tb fresh lemon juice
1 Tb minced garlic
Salt and freshly ground pepper
¼ cup finely chopped parsley
Lemon wedges

Broiled Shrimp Scampi (continued)

Peel and devein the shrimp, leaving on the last tail-shell segment. Pat the shrimp dry with paper towels and place them in a large bowl.

In a small bowl, combine the butter, oil, lemon juice, garlic, ½ tsp salt, and several grindings of black pepper to make a basting sauce. Pour the sauce over the shrimp and toss until the shrimp are well coated. Spread the shrimp in one layer on a baking sheet or, for ease of turning, thread the shrimp on skewers (presoaked in water if they are wooden) and place the skewers on a baking sheet. Reserve any basting sauce left in the bowl.

Preheat the broiler to very hot, place the shrimp 3–4 inches from the heat, and broil for 2–3 minutes. Turn the shrimp, baste them with the reserved sauce, and broil until they are pink on the outside and opaque at the center. Remove the shrimp to a warm serving platter and pour over any juices from the broiler pan. Sprinkle the shrimp with parsley and serve with lemon wedges.   SERVES 6

❖ *Sautéed Shrimp Scampi:* In a large sauté pan, heat the butter and oil. Sauté the shrimp in batches to give them plenty of room in the pan, tossing frequently, until they are pink on the outside and opaque at the center. Remove the shrimp to a warm serving platter. Add the lemon juice and garlic to the cooking liquid in the pan and swirl together for 30 seconds. Add salt and freshly ground pepper and parsley, swirl once more, pour the sauce over the shrimp, and serve with lemon wedges.

Broiled Shrimp with Fresh Tomato-Orange Sauce

The tomato-and-orange sauce looks so inviting and tastes so tangy with grilled or broiled shrimp that one scarcely notices how simple it is to prepare; the sauce is delicious with almost any fish or shellfish. The shrimp can be marinated well ahead of cooking time and left in the refrigerator until the grill is ready.

Alternative shellfish: scallops
Alternative fish: chunks of swordfish, tuna, shark, monkfish, or other firm-fleshed fish

2 Tb fresh lemon juice
1 tsp minced garlic
3 Tb olive oil
Dash of hot pepper sauce
Salt and freshly ground pepper
1½ lb peeled and deveined colossal
  (16–20 count) raw shrimp

TOMATO-ORANGE SAUCE

½ cup orange juice
1 cup peeled, seeded, and finely
  chopped tomatoes
2 Tb butter or olive oil
2 Tb chopped fresh mint or parsley
1 Tb finely grated orange rind
½ lemon
Salt and freshly ground pepper

To make the Tomato-Orange Sauce: In a small saucepan, bring the orange juice to a boil and cook over high heat until reduced by half. Add the tomatoes and butter or oil, and cook for 3–4 minutes to boil down the mixture slightly. Stir in the mint or parsley and orange rind. Season to taste with a squeeze of lemon juice and salt and freshly ground pepper.

MAKES I CUP SAUCE

In a bowl large enough to hold the shrimp, combine the lemon juice and garlic, and whisk in the oil. Add a dash of hot pepper sauce and season with salt and freshly ground pepper. Add the shrimp and toss to coat well. Cover and refrigerate until just before grilling.

Prepare the tomato-orange sauce and keep warm.

Before grilling the shrimp, thread them on metal or presoaked wooden skewers, thrusting the skewer through the tail and head of each shrimp so that it is held on the skewer in a "C" shape. Grill or broil about 4 minutes, turning once, or until shrimp are pink on the outside and opaque at the center. Spoon a pool of sauce on each of 4 serving plates and place equal portions of shrimp on top of the sauce.   SERVES 4

❖ Substitute a cold *Cucumber-Dill Sauce* (page 354).

SHRIMP

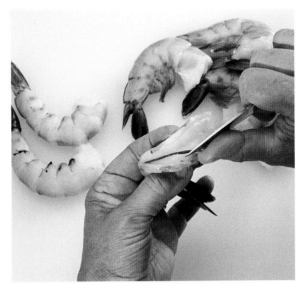

WHEN I WAS A CHILD, shrimp were a special-occasion luxury; their appearance was a reliable indicator of the importance of the occasion. The usual presentation consisted of 5 or 6 boiled shrimp hooked over the side of a glass dish or goblet filled with shredded lettuce in which nested a jigger of cocktail sauce. "Shrimp cocktail" evokes memories of fancy restaurants, wedding receptions, anniversaries, and graduations, maybe even a landmark birthday. How things change in a lifetime. Now I see shrimp everywhere I go—in the supermarket deli case, at fast-food restaurants, and, of course, still on those special occasions at fancy restaurants. Every restaurant chef will tell you that a shrimp dish on the menu is one of the surest items to sell out. From a luxury item for the few at the turn of this century, shrimp have become the most valuable seafood commodity in the world, a development related largely to fishermen moving from coastal waters out to deeper waters, where they found larger shrimp in teeming abundance. Literally hundreds of species of shrimp are harvested around the world. Shrimp fishers work in both salt and fresh waters (but mainly salt), from the Tropics to the cold sub-arctic region, and to the wild catch is added the substantial produce of commercial shrimp farms in Thailand, China, Indonesia, Ecuador, India, and elsewhere. Americans consume virtually all of the domestic catch and production, and, their appetites still unfulfilled, they import countless tons of shrimp from scores of countries.

What is the appeal of this curious crustacean with five sets of walking legs and five sets of swimmerets on its belly? Its flesh is firm and smooth, very pleasant to the palate; its flavor is mild and sweet in a way that is both delicious in itself and complements many other foods and flavors; and its color is attractive, ranging from light pink to red. Every cook likes the fact that shrimp cook very quickly and take readily to virtually every cooking method: grilling, broiling, deep-frying, sautéing, boiling, steaming, and baking.

Fresh shrimp are a treat available only to lucky folks who live near or are traveling in an area where shrimp are brought to port or are farmed. I've eaten fresh Gulf shrimp in Florida, small ridge-back and larger spotted shrimp in Santa Barbara, California, and tiny northern shrimp along the coast of Maine. In those rare marketplaces where fresh shrimp are available whole, one can see what many of us have never seen—that we consume only the tail meat of the shrimp. The head and body, which account for two-thirds of the body mass, have been removed from almost all shrimp before wholesalers ship it to our markets. Usually I—like you—buy, cook, and eat shrimp harvested far away, quick-frozen, transported, and sold still frozen or already thawed. The customer, therefore, is at the mercy of many unknowns: the quality of the shrimp's original environment, the care in handling and quickness of freezing, and even the local market's care in handling, storing, and thawing shrimp. The best course is to buy shrimp (and all seafood) from your most trusted source, even if that entails a higher price.

Warm-water shrimp dominate the market, and about 70 percent of them are imported frozen from other countries. They are classified in three groups that are distinguished by the color of the shell. White shrimp are usually considered the premier shrimp because they

SPECIAL INFORMATION ABOUT

SHRIMP

Shrimp (continued)

have the least frequent traces of iodine smell and taste; the level of iodine in shrimp depends on the feeding area and what the shrimp consumed. Pink shrimp have a pink or pinkish-brown shell when raw and a slightly deeper pink color when cooked than white shrimp. Brown shrimp have the darkest shell of the three groups. In general, the level of iodine increases from white to pink to brown shrimp, thus establishing an order of preference for me and most cooks. One of the shrimp I like most to cook and eat is individually frozen white shrimp that come from the Gulf of Mexico labeled "Campeche."

Basically, the colder the water, the smaller the shrimp. Cold-water shrimp, also called northern or pink shrimp, are much smaller than the warm-water species. Most of them are sold as peeled and cooked shrimp because they are too time-consuming to peel at home. They are not subject to iodine smell and taste. Except for these tiny northern shrimp, I rarely purchase cooked shrimp and then only from a trusted source. It's so simple to cook your own, and it seems to me they taste much fresher. Most of the shrimp recipes in this book will be for raw shrimp that you cook yourself, but when I refer to "poached" shrimp in a recipe, you can, if you like, use purchased cooked shrimp.

Shrimp are subject to a certain amount of confusion of terminology. Restaurants often use the word "prawn" to describe large shrimp, and the Food and Agricultural Organization of the United Nations uses the same word "prawn" to distinguish freshwater shrimp from saltwater shrimp. Many restaurants use the word "scampi" to refer to shrimp sautéed with garlic, but the word also applies more accurately to the tail meat of a lobsterlike crustacean found off the coasts of northern Europe, Africa, and South America, and in the Mediterranean. "Langostino" is another term sometimes used for shrimp, but it refers more properly to a small European lobster (also known as Dublin Bay prawn or scampi) and to an entirely different crustacean from South America. Perhaps we would all be better off just calling a shrimp a shrimp.

Buying
Fresh shrimp: Fresh shrimp spoil quickly unless cooked or frozen, so if you are fortunate enough to be where you can buy them, check them carefully for freshness. Sometimes they are available with their heads on, and you can remove and clean the heads to make stock. The shells should be firm and glistening, and should have a "dry" feel rather than any trace of slick or slime that would indicate aging. The flesh should have a fresh, clean smell without any hint of ammonia or pronounced odor or flavor

of iodine from feeding areas (not dangerous, but unpleasant).

Thawed, previously frozen shrimp: These are the shrimp we often find on display at fish markets, on ice or under refrigeration, sometimes inaccurately labeled "fresh." Check for a fresh, clean smell. Reject shrimp with any hint of ammonia odor (sign of aging) or with a strong odor or flavor of iodine. The flesh and shell should be firm, not mushy. White patches can be a sign of dehydration from inferior freezing or storage. Black spots on the shell or flesh can also indicate aging; they are from inferior freezing or storage. Top-quality shrimp are usually quite uniform in size.

Frozen shrimp: Fish markets commonly offer frozen shrimp to their customers in two ways—either in blocks of many shrimp frozen together and not separable unless the whole block is thawed (often in 5-pound packages) or in packages of individually quick-frozen shrimp that are separable from the rest while still frozen (often in 3-pound packages). Block-frozen shrimp are good for a large party when you will use the entire package, but I prefer individually quick-frozen shrimp for taste and texture, and because I can use part of a package, reseal the container, and return the shrimp to the freezer for later use. Check for any signs (staining of the package or sticking together of individually frozen shrimp, for example) that might indicate that the shrimp

Shrimp

were frozen, then accidentally or negligently defrosted, and then refrozen; reject all refrozen shrimp. Frozen shrimp are available both raw and precooked.

Grading or Sizing: There are two systems for referring to the size or weight of shrimp, and fortunately, the two systems are correlated. First, shrimp are designated by terms that imply a difference in size: "colossal," "jumbo," "medium," etc. Most of us are familiar with these terms from menus and fish markets even if we are not always clear precisely what they mean. Second, shrimp are commonly referred to in the industry by numbers indicating the number of shrimp of that approximate size per pound. More and more this number system is being used also in fish markets and supermarkets for the benefit of the customer. The number system is preceded by the letter "U" for unit, meaning units or number of shrimp per pound; another designation uses the word "count" after the number. Usually the numerical system consists of a quotation of two numbers, indicating no fewer than the smaller number of shrimp to a pound, and no more than the larger number. The smaller the number, the larger the shrimp. A "U-5" or "5 count" shrimp indicates 5 shrimp to a pound, each weighing almost a quarter of a pound, ideal for grilling. A "U-220" or "220 count" shrimp would be a very tiny cold-water shrimp, ideal for use in a stuffed avocado, for

example. Here is how the numerical system is correlated with the verbal designations. The rule of thumb in grading is that shrimp lose a grading size when they go from shell-on to peeled, and another grading size when they go from peeled to cooked. When I specify a certain size shrimp, the recipes in this book will indicate the recommended grade of shrimp in both verbal and numerical terms. Cold-water northern, pink, or salad shrimp can have counts from over 70 per pound to 250–500 per pound.

If I indicate in a recipe *peeled* shrimp—for example, a 21–25 count—and you prefer to buy shell-on shrimp and peel them yourself, consult the chart below. You should buy shell-on 16–20 count shrimp to get 21–25 count peeled shrimp. However, don't feel bound to use exactly the recommended count of shrimp as indicated for each recipe. Use your own judgment and take availability into account.

Storage

Fresh shrimp and thawed but previously frozen raw shrimp should be refrigerated immediately in the coldest part of the refrigerator, surrounded top and bottom with ice packs, and wrapped loosely enough in butcher's paper, waxed paper, or unsealed plastic bags so that air can circulate around them. Store them so that melting water does not directly touch the shrimp. I typically cook raw shrimp the same day I hasten home with it, but with adequate storage methods, you could keep it refrigerated for 24–48 hours before using. Do not refreeze shrimp that have already been frozen and then thawed.

If possible, defrost frozen shrimp gradually in the refrigerator for 8–10 hours, or longer as needed. If you need to thaw shrimp quickly, place the shrimp in a watertight bag in a container of ice water; renew the cold water occasionally as it warms

Descriptive Grade Name	Raw Headless Shell-On	Peeled	Cooked
Extra Colossal	Under 10	Under 15	16–20
Colossal	Under 15	16–20	21–25
Extra Jumbo	16–20	21–25	26–30
Jumbo	21–25	26–30	31–35
Extra Large	26–30	31–35	36–40
Large	31–35	36–40	41–45
Medium Large	36–40	41–45	46–50
Medium	41–50	46–55	51–60
Small	51–60	56–65	61–70
Extra Small	61–70	66–75	71–80
Tiny	Over 70	Over 75	Over 80

SPECIAL INFORMATION ABOUT

SHRIMP

Shrimp (continued)

from exposure to room temperature.

Store cooked shrimp on top of a bag of ice in the coldest part of the refrigerator. Loosely cover the shrimp with parchment paper, waxed paper, or plastic wrap, and then put another bag of ice on top of everything.

Preparation

Peeling: I peel and devein raw shrimp before cooking them, but you can cook first, if you prefer. To peel, place the tips of your fingers or a small knife between the swimmerets (legs) at the thicker end of the shrimp and work back along the tail, peeling off each shell segment and pulling it away from the flesh, leaving the last tail segment with its tail feathers on for decoration, if you like. For ridgeback or rock shrimp, it is necessary to cut along the harder shells with scissors and then pry off the shells as best you can—the sweet meat is worth the effort.

Deveining: Make a shallow cut (about ⅛ inch) with a sharp knife along the center line of the back or outer curve of the shrimp, and pull out the dark or orange-colored intestinal vein, which is unsightly and sometimes gritty. The larger the shrimp, the more reason to remove it. If the vein is colorless, you can either remove it or leave it in place. (See illustration on page 265.)

Poaching: The cooking method for so-called "boiled

shrimp" is actually a poach. Peel and devein the shrimp. Bring a large pot of water to a rolling boil, using enough water to cover the shrimp by 1 inch. Add 1 tablespoon of salt for each 2 quarts of water. Prepare a large bowl of ice water to one side. Drop the shrimp into the rapidly boiling water. The cold shrimp will cool the water slightly, eliminating the boil, and the shrimp will poach in the hot water. If the water returns to a boil, reduce the heat immediately until the water is barely simmering. Large shrimp should poach in 1–2 minutes, small shrimp more quickly. (Note: Red shrimp and rock shrimp need only seconds to cook, and overcooking makes the meat tough.) Poach the shrimp until the tails curl, the outside turns pink, and the center turns from translucent gray to opaque white. If you want to check for doneness, make an incision in one of the shrimp; if the shrimp is not cooked through, you will be able to see a difference in color and texture between the outer part that is cooked and the inner part not yet cooked, and you can continue cooking as necessary. Lift the shrimp from the pot and immediately plunge them into the ice water to stop the cooking action. Drain them, pat them dry, and store until needed in the refrigerator between bags of ice. I store them in a glass or nonaluminum-lined bowl or dish, covered with plastic wrap and topped with an ice

pack. Individually frozen shrimp do not need to be thawed before poaching, but the cooking time will be a little longer; use the interior test of opaque whiteness at the center to indicate doneness. Block-frozen shrimp should be thawed enough to separate them before poaching. Flavor the poaching water, if you like, with sliced onion, sliced lemon, and a bay leaf, or with a commercial Shrimp Boil Mix.

Yields

Raw shrimp will shrink to about two-thirds their original size when peeled and cooked. One pound of shell-on raw shrimp yields 13–14 ounces peeled and deveined shrimp, which yields 10–11 ounces cooked shrimp.

Allow ⅓ pound or more cooked shrimp per serving (½ pound or more unpeeled raw shrimp).

One pound of peeled, cooked 16–20 count shrimp yields about 4 cups sliced, loosely packed shrimp.

Be Aware: Many people are allergic to shellfish and to shrimp in particular. It is not clear whether allergic reactions are triggered by the shrimp themselves or by chemicals used to prevent moisture loss after they are caught. Always notify guests if shrimp or other shellfish is included in a dish, especially if it is disguised in a stock or puréed mousse or is hidden among other ingredients.

Shrimp, Broccoli, and Snow Pea Stir-Fry

The contrasting colors and textures of crunchy forest-green broccoli and smooth pastel-pink shrimp appeal to me so much that I have included two stir-fry recipes using them together but with different seasonings—a spicy Oriental dish and another fragrant with garlic—that make these quick meals strikingly different in taste. As with all stir-fry dishes, the secret is to prepare all of the ingredients ahead of time, anticipating that once the quick cooking begins, there is no stopping. This dish is equally good served with rice, fresh Chinese noodles, or pasta.

1½ lb peeled and deveined extra jumbo (21–25 count) raw shrimp

SHRIMP MARINADE

1 Tb peanut or vegetable oil
1 tsp sesame oil
1 Tb rice wine or fresh lemon juice
1 tsp tomato paste
½ tsp soy sauce

2 cups broccoli flowerets
2 cups trimmed snow peas

Shrimp, Broccoli, and Snow Pea Stir-Fry
(continued)

SHRIMP SAUCE

¼ cup chicken broth
2 Tb rice wine
2 tsp cornstarch
1 tsp sesame oil
½ tsp sugar
½ tsp soy sauce
½ tsp freshly ground pepper

3 Tb peanut or vegetable oil
1–2 tsp finely sliced fresh ginger
1 tsp minced garlic (optional)
½ cup toasted raw peanuts or cashews

Pat the shrimp dry and place them in a large bowl. In a small bowl, whisk together all of the ingredients of the shrimp marinade. Pour the marinade over the shrimp, toss to coat the shrimp thoroughly, cover, and refrigerate for at least 30 minutes.

Bring a large pot of water to a boil and prepare a bowl of ice water to one side. Drop the broccoli into the boiling water and cook for 3–4 minutes, or until the flowerets are just tender but have not lost their crunchiness. Lift them out with a slotted spoon and drop them into the ice water to stop the cooking action. Drop the snow peas into the boiling water, blanch them for 30 seconds, and immediately remove them to the ice water to cool. Drain the vegetables when cool, pat them dry, and set aside.

When you are ready to cook, combine all of the ingredients of the shrimp sauce in a small bowl and set aside. Heat a wok or a wide, high-sided sauté pan (preferably sloped), add the oil, and heat until very hot. Add the shrimp and cook, tossing continuously, until the shrimp are pink on all sides, the tails curl, and the centers of the shrimp are opaque. Remove the shrimp to a warm bowl. Reheat the oil in the wok and add the ginger and the garlic, if you are using it. Stir-fry for 5 seconds, then add the broccoli and stir-fry for 30 seconds. Add the shrimp sauce and cook, tossing, until the mixture begins to thicken. Add the shrimp, snow peas, and toasted peanuts or cashews, and cook, tossing, just until heated through.

SERVES 4

Shrimp with Broccoli and Garlic Stir-Fry

When you add the bright red of a pepper to pink shrimp and green broccoli, you have a visual delight; and when you flavor all of them with the tang of garlic, you have a very tasty stir-fry. Serve this with pasta or rice or, if you like garlic as much as I do, with *Garlic Mashed Potatoes with Brown Onions* (page 335). You can prepare and blanch the broccoli, and peel and slice the pepper and garlic in advance; the final cooking takes just a few minutes.

Alternative shellfish and fish: scallops, medallions of monkfish

1½ lb broccoli
1 large red pepper
4 cloves garlic
¼ cup light vegetable or peanut oil
1½ lb peeled and deveined extra jumbo
    (21–25 count) raw shrimp
Fresh lemon juice
Salt and freshly ground pepper
Hot pepper sauce or flakes (optional)

Wash the broccoli and separate the stems from the flowerets. Peel off the tough outer skin of the stems with a paring knife or vegetable peeler. Cut the stems diagonally into ¼-inch-thick slices. Cut the flowerets into 1-inch pieces. Bring a large pot of water to a boil, drop in the broccoli, and cook for 2–4 minutes, or until the broccoli is just barely cooked through. Drain the flowerets and immediately run them under cold water to stop the cooking action, then pat them dry. Cover and refrigerate until ready to do the final cooking.

Cut the pepper in half lengthwise and remove the stem, seeds, and white membrane; cut the flesh lengthwise into narrow strips, and then cut the strips crosswise into pieces about 1½ inches long. Set aside.

Peel the garlic, cut it into thin slices, and set aside.

In a large, deep-sided sauté pan or wok, heat the oil, stir in the garlic, and cook it, tossing continuously, just until the garlic is lightly colored; avoid overcooking or browning it, as garlic turns bitter when overcooked. Remove the garlic to a brown paper bag to drain. Add the red pepper pieces to the sauté pan or wok, sear them quickly, and remove the peppers to a warm serving dish. Add the shrimp to the pan, toss it so that it will brown lightly on all sides, and cook about 2–3 minutes, or just until the flesh is opaque at the center. (To test for doneness, cut into one of the shrimp.) Remove the shrimp to the serving dish.

Lower the cooking heat slightly, add the broccoli to the pan, and cook just until it is heated through. Return the peppers and shrimp to the pan with the broccoli, tossing all together until hot. Squeeze in fresh lemon juice to taste. Season with salt and freshly ground pepper, and with hot pepper sauce or flakes, if desired. Add the garlic to the pan, toss once more, and return all to the warm serving dish.   SERVES 4

Sautéed Shrimp with Shallots and Vermouth

The gentle onion flavor of the shallots will not overpower the natural sweet taste of shrimp. A shallot-and-vermouth sauce gives a lovely finish to shrimp. Three variations pair shallots with other ingredients in equally delicious ways. To carry shallots into the accompaniment, serve this dish with *Roasted Shallots* (page 338).

    1½ lb extra jumbo (16–20 count) raw shrimp
    1 Tb butter
    2 Tb vegetable oil
    2 Tb finely chopped shallots
    Salt and freshly ground pepper
    ½ cup dry vermouth or white wine
    Lemon wedges (optional)

Peel and devein the shrimp, leaving the last tail-shell segment on for decoration, if you like. Pat the shrimp dry with paper towels.

Heat the butter and oil in a large sauté pan, or divide it between two smaller sauté pans; do not crowd the shrimp in the pan. When the combined butter and oil is hot, add the shrimp and the shallots, toss them in the pan, and cook for 2 minutes. Toss the mixture again, season with salt and freshly ground pepper, and cook for 1–2 minutes more, or until the shrimp are pink on the outside and opaque at the

center. Remove the shrimp to a warm serving platter. Pour the vermouth or wine into the pan and stir with any bits clinging to the bottom of the pan. Bring to a boil and cook until the vermouth or wine is reduced to a light syrup consistency. Pour over the shrimp and serve with lemon wedges, if you like.   SERVES 4

❖ *With Shallots, Pernod, and Cream:* When the shrimp and shallots have been cooked and removed to a warm plate, as above, add 3 tablespoons Pernod to the sauté pan and stir with the bits clinging to the bottom of the pan. Immediately stir in ¾ cup heavy cream. Bring to a boil, reheat the shrimp and shallots in the sauce, and serve.

❖ *With Shallots, Garlic, and Vermouth:* Add the shrimp and shallots to the pan, as above, and cook for 1 minute. Add 1 tablespoon minced garlic and toss with the mixture for 10 seconds. Add ½ cup dry vermouth and cook until the shrimp are pink on the outside and opaque at the center. Remove the shrimp to a warm serving platter and boil the pan juices until they are a light syrup consistency. Whisk 2 tablespoons fresh lemon juice into the pan juices and pour the sauce over the shrimp.

❖ *With Shallots and Chinese Seasoning:* Add the shrimp and the shallots to the pan, as above, and cook for 2 minutes. Add 1 teaspoon minced garlic, ¼ teaspoon sesame oil, and ½ teaspoon soy sauce, toss all together, and cook for another 1–2 minutes, or until the shrimp are pink on the outside and opaque at the center. Remove the shrimp to a warm serving platter. Add ½ cup dry vermouth to the pan juices and boil until the sauce is a light syrup consistency. Pour the sauce over the shrimp, squeeze some fresh lemon juice over all, and serve.

Shrimp Satay with a Pickled Cucumber Salad

In kitchen parlance, "satay" means the grilling or broiling of skewers of meat or poultry coated with Indonesian seasonings. Shrimp are delicious satayed. The spicy coating for the shrimp can be made well in advance, and the shrimp need to sit in the marinade for at least 30 minutes before cooking. (Try this marinade with other fish, such as slices of monkfish.) If

Shrimp Satay with a Pickled Cucumber Salad (continued)

you can't grill or broil this dish, quickly roast it in a hot oven or sauté the shrimp on top of the stove. The pickled cucumber salad is a cool and refreshing contrast to the spices of the marinade, but you can also "heat up" the salad, if you wish, by adding hot pepper flakes; it can be made ahead. I like to serve one or two dipping sauces, such as *Sweet-and-Hot Grape Sauce* (page 43) or *Peanut Sauce* (page 360). To complete a main course of Shrimp Satay, serve steamed rice or *Sesame Chinese Noodles* (page 276).

Alternative fish: chunks of very firm-fleshed fish, such as monkfish, swordfish, shark, tuna, or striped bass

PICKLED CUCUMBER SALAD

4 large cucumbers (about 3 lb)
Salt
3 Tb white wine vinegar
1 tsp sugar
¼ cup finely sliced scallions
    (optional)
Freshly ground pepper
½ tsp hot pepper flakes (optional)

To make the Pickled Cucumber Salad: Trim the ends of the cucumbers, peel them, and score the flesh lengthwise with the tines of a fork. Halve the cucumbers lengthwise, scoop out the seeds, and thinly slice the halves crosswise. (You will have about 6 cups.) Put the cucumber slices in a colander, toss them with ¼ teaspoon salt, and let them drain for 30 minutes. Gently press out the moisture from the slices and pat them dry with clean towels or paper towels. Remove the cucumbers to a large bowl. In a small bowl, combine the vinegar and sugar (the sugar will dissolve), and pour the mixture over the cucumbers. Add the scallions, if desired, season the salad with salt and freshly ground pepper, and add the hot pepper flakes, if you like. Cover and refrigerate until ready to serve. Add a bit more vinegar before serving, if you wish.

MAKES ABOUT 4 CUPS

SATAY MARINADE

1 large lemon
⅓ cup chopped onions
1 Tb chopped garlic
1 Tb chopped fresh ginger
2 tsp ground coriander
1 tsp cumin
1 tsp turmeric
1 tsp sugar
½ tsp salt
1 Tb vegetable oil (optional)

1–1¼ lb extra jumbo (16–20 count) raw shrimp
Lemon wedges (optional)
Sweet-and-Hot Grape Sauce (page 43)
    (optional)
Peanut Sauce (page 360) (optional)

Prepare the pickled cucumber salad and refrigerate.

To make the satay marinade: Grate the lemon rind. Squeeze the juice of the lemon and set aside. (You should have 2–3 tablespoons.) In a food processor, combine the lemon rind, onions, garlic, and ginger. Process, scraping down the sides once or twice, to a very fine mince. Remove the mixture to a small bowl, add the coriander, cumin, turmeric, sugar, salt, the oil (if you are using it), and the lemon juice; mix well. (Makes ½ cup)

Peel and devein the shrimp, leaving the last tail-shell segment on, if desired. Place the shrimp in a large bowl, add the marinade, and toss until the shrimp are well coated. Cover and refrigerate for at least 30 minutes.

Thread each shrimp through its tail and head in a "C" shape on a metal skewer or on a wooden skewer presoaked in water so it will not burn. Place the skewers on a grill rack over hot coals or under a preheated broiler for 2–3 minutes, turning once, until the shrimp are pink on the outside and just opaque at the center. Serve with the pickled cucumber salad and, if desired, with lemon wedges and side dishes of sweet-and-hot grape sauce or peanut sauce to dip the satayed shrimp in.

SERVES 4

❖For a larger group, or with cocktails or in a buffet, use bite-size shrimp and decrease the cooking time accordingly. Thread the shrimp on long skewers to cook, then unthread them onto a serving platter and add toothpicks and a dipping sauce.

❖Dissolve 1 generous tablespoon dried tamarind in ¼ cup warm water; strain and use in place of lemon juice in the satay marinade.

❖Add 1 tablespoon chopped fresh cilantro, mint, or dill to the cucumber salad.

Extra Colossal Grilled Shrimp on a Bed of Cabbage and Collard Greens

Here's an unlikely match: eye-catching big shrimp with two humble vegetables—collards and cabbage. But what a triumph: the light and dark green of the braised vegetables are a perfect backdrop for the toasty pink shrimp. The collards and cabbage you've usually encountered boiled to death are here cooked gently to tenderness in less than ten minutes.

Slicing the vegetables can be done way in advance or just before cooking. Marinate the shrimp at least an hour before cooking, or earlier, if you like. Allow 2–3 shrimp per person and make sure that you have eight metal skewers or wooden skewers that have been soaked in water. When you are ready to cook, begin by sautéing the vegetables. You can grill the shrimp while the greens braise, but if your timing is off, the greens will wait nicely while the shrimp cooks.

Alternative shellfish: raw lobster tails

¾ lb collard greens, with stems
¾ lb green cabbage
1½–2 lb extra colossal (5–7 count) raw shrimp
3 Tb fresh lemon juice plus 1 tsp
2 tsp minced garlic
2 tsp minced fresh thyme
5 Tb fruity virgin olive oil
Salt and freshly ground pepper
Lemon wedges

To prepare the greens: Wash the collard greens, and with a sharp paring knife, cut the heavy stems off the large leaves, including the part of the stem that runs down the back of the leaf. If the collards are very small, just cut off the stems at the base of the leaf. Spin-dry the leaves and slice them into thin diagonal slices. (You should have about 6 cups.) Cut the cabbage into large wedges, and holding the cabbage by

the core, slice the leaves into thin strips. (You should have about 6 cups.) Combine the sliced collards and cabbage in a bowl and refrigerate until ready to use.

To prepare the shrimp: Leave the shells on. Holding the rounded back side of the shrimp against a work surface, split the shrimp with a sharp knife, cutting from the underside of the shrimp down through the shrimp almost to the shell. Open the shrimp like a butterfly. Remove the dark intestinal tract. Put the shrimp in a bowl.

In a small bowl, whisk together 3 tablespoons of lemon juice, 1 teaspoon of the garlic, the thyme, 3 tablespoons of the olive oil, and season with salt and freshly ground pepper. Pour the mixture over the shrimp, turn the shrimp to coat with the marinade, cover, and refrigerate for at least 1 hour.

When you are ready to cook, lift the shrimp out of the marinade and drain them so that you can handle them easily. Reserve the marinade. Lay the shrimp on a flat surface, aligning the tail end of one shrimp next to the thick end of another shrimp. Thread two or three together using two skewers, running the skewers through the shrimp at either side to keep them flat. Repeat with the remaining shrimp.

Begin by cooking the vegetables. While they are braising, grill the shrimp.

To cook the cabbage and greens: Heat the remaining 2 tablespoons of oil in a large, high-sided sauté pan. Stir in the remaining teaspoon of garlic and add the combined greens to the oil in the pan a little at a time, stirring, until they are coated with the oil and have wilted. Add ½ cup water to the pan, cover, and braise the greens gently until they are just tender, about 8 minutes, stirring occasionally to make sure they are not cooking too quickly and sticking to the pan. Uncover the pan and cook for a minute, or until any excess moisture evaporates. Stir in the remaining teaspoon of lemon juice, season with salt and freshly ground pepper, and add a bit more olive oil, if you like. (You will have about 4 cups cooked greens.)

To cook the shrimp: Place the shrimp on an oiled grill rack, flesh side toward the heat, and cook for 2 minutes. Baste with any extra marinade. Turn the shrimp and cook for 2 minutes more, or until the flesh has just turned opaque.

To serve: Arrange the cooked greens on warm serving plates, slide the shrimp off the skewers, and place 2 or 3 shrimp on each plate, flesh side up, slightly overlapping the greens. Serve with lemon wedges and a bowl to put the shells in.   SERVES 4

Extra Colossal Grilled Shrimp on a Bed of Cabbage and Collard Greens (continued)

❖Broil the shrimp under a preheated hot broiler.

❖You can skewer the shrimp before you marinate them. Set the skewered shrimp on baking sheets and brush liberally with the marinade, cover, and refrigerate.

❖Add a bit of soy sauce or sesame oil to the shrimp marinade. Add hot pepper sauce, if you like.

❖Change the herbs in the shrimp marinade; try fresh tarragon or sage.

❖Add more garlic or lemon juice to the greens to taste.

❖Try other greens as a bed for the shrimp; see *Braised Broccoli de Rabe* (page 323).

❖Serve the shrimp with *Portuguese Peas* (page 240).

Shrimp and Shallot Curry

When "The Victory Garden" went to Singapore once to videotape special garden features, I interviewed a young cook named Hong at the famous Raffles Hotel. As she demonstrated her method for making their popular Tiffin Curry, what caught my eye was the curry paste she used. She had ground up various herbs and spices, and bound them in a paste with some oil. With this fragrant base at hand, the rest of the dish was a breeze. The curry powder we know has little to do with Asian cooking; there, native cooks grind their own spices, often daily. Hong liked to use star anise in her curry paste. While many authentic Asian spices are now available in specialty shops, I have devised a curry paste from ingredients commonly available in the home kitchen. Traditionally done with a mortar and pestle, the grinding gets done for me with less time and effort in a food processor. Cover any unused curry paste with oil, refrigerate it, and it will be available to use again over a period of time. I offer several condiments to garnish this curry: a chutney such as *Mango and Cilantro Chutney* (page 359), peanuts or toasted slivered almonds, sliced bananas, raisins, and grated coconut. Serve this curry on either plain boiled rice or saffron rice.

Alternative shellfish: scallops

Alternative fish: slices of monkfish or chunks of striped bass or other firm-fleshed fish

CURRY PASTE

3 hot red peppers
½ cup chopped shallots or onions
1 Tb grated lemon rind
2 Tb chopped fresh ginger
2 Tb chopped garlic
2 Tb ground coriander seed
1 Tb ground cumin
1 tsp ground turmeric
½ tsp nutmeg
¼ tsp cinnamon
¼ tsp cardamom or mace
Pinch of salt
3 Tb vegetable oil

To make the Curry Paste: Halve the red peppers lengthwise, remove the stems, seeds, and veins, and finely chop the flesh. (Makes about 2 tablespoons) Place the peppers in a food processor along with the shallots or onions, lemon rind, ginger, and garlic. Process until everything is very finely chopped. Add all of the spices and 2 tablespoons of the oil, and process to make a paste; the paste will not be totally smooth. Remove the paste to a small bowl, film with the remaining tablespoon of oil, cover, and refrigerate until ready to use.

MAKES ABOUT ⅔ CUP

❖This recipe makes enough to double the shrimp and shallot curry recipe. Make a larger amount of curry paste, if you like, film the top with oil, cover, and refrigerate for later use.

❖Substitute 2 chopped 3-inch pieces fragrant lemongrass for the lemon rind.

❖Add ½ teaspoon ground mustard seeds; experiment with different amounts and kinds of herbs and spices.

❖Add 1 teaspoon shrimp paste (trassi) or anchovy paste.

SHRIMP AND SHALLOT CURRY

1½ lb peeled and deveined extra jumbo
    (21–25 count) raw shrimp
4 Tb vegetable oil
1 cup sliced shallots
1 lemon
4 heaping Tb curry paste (above)
One 14-oz can coconut milk
Chopped fresh cilantro (optional)

Prepare the curry paste.

To make the shrimp and shallot curry: Pat the shrimp dry with paper towels. In a large sauté pan, heat 3 table-spoons of the oil. Add and cook the shrimp in two batches, tossing them frequently, until they just turn pink on all sides; they will not be cooked through. Remove them, batch by batch, to a warm plate. Add the remaining tablespoon of oil to the sauté pan, stir in the shallots, and cook over medium-high heat, stirring, until the shallots are a rich brown. Cut the lemon in half and squeeze the juice into the pan. Stir in the curry paste and cook for 2 minutes. Stir in the coconut milk, bring the mixture to a boil, and cook for 3–4 minutes, stirring, or until the mixture thickens. Return the shrimp to the pan and cook for 1 minute longer, or until the center of a shrimp sliced open to test for done-ness has turned opaque. Remove the curry to a warm serving dish. Sprinkle with cilantro, if you like. SERVES 4

❖Omit the lemon juice and add 2–3 inches of chopped fresh lemongrass when you add the shallots to the cooking pan.

❖Combine scallops or chunks of firm-fleshed white fish with shrimp.

Maltese Scampi

The idea behind this dish was to scale classic paella down a little to a simpler dish. Thinking Mediter-ranean, thinking smaller, I thought of Malta! You will find this a very colorful, tasty dish. Shrimp both pick up flavor and tenderize under the influence of a good marinade. Here the shrimp should be marinated at least two hours before cooking, but for the conve-nience of advance preparation, it is fine to place the

shrimp in the marinade either the morning of the day you are serving or even the night before. All the other scampi ingredients can be assembled and pre-pared ahead as well so that at mealtime you need only 20 minutes to cook the rice and a few minutes to complete the final scampi sauté. Serve the dish on rice or rice pilaf, and garnish each serving with sautéed cherry tomatoes, sprigs of parsley, and lemon wedges.

GARLIC-FLAVORED SHRIMP
MARINADE

⅓ cup olive oil
⅓ cup vegetable oil
⅓ cup fresh lemon juice
2 Tb tomato paste
¼ cup chopped parsley
1 Tb chopped fresh oregano or
    2 tsp dried
½ tsp salt
2 Tb minced garlic
½ tsp hot pepper sauce

To make the Garlic-Flavored Shrimp Marinade: In a small bowl, whisk all the ingredients together. Set aside until ready to use.

MAKES 1½ CUPS

MALTESE SCAMPI

2 lb peeled and deveined colossal (16–20 count)
    raw shrimp
¼–½ lb smoked sausage, such as kielbasa or
    chorizo
1–1½ lb garden peas
½ lb small sea scallops
1 lb mussels
5 Tb butter
3 Tb vegetable oil
18 cherry tomatoes
8 cups cooked rice or *Easy Rice Pilaf* (page 354)
Sprigs parsley
Lemon wedges

Maltese Scampi (continued)

Prepare the garlic-flavored shrimp marinade.

To make the scampi: Place the shrimp in a large bowl, add about 1 cup of the marinade, toss to coat well, cover, and refrigerate at least 2 hours or overnight.

Bring a pan of water to a boil, prick the sausage in several places with a fork, drop the sausage into the boiling water, and blanch for 5 minutes to release some of the fat. Remove the sausage, let it cool, slice it diagonally into ¼-inch-thick pieces, and set aside.

Shell the peas. Clean and refill the pan with water, bring to a boil, drop in the peas to blanch for 30 seconds, drain, run the peas under cold water to stop the cooking action, drain again, and set aside.

Remove any pieces of tough cartilage from the sides of the scallops, wipe off any bits of shell, and pat them dry.

Scrub the mussels and pull off their beards. (See Mussels Box, page 37, if you wish.)

(*Note:* The sausage, peas, and shellfish can be prepared ahead and refrigerated until later final cooking. It is better in this case to wait to debeard the mussels until just before cooking them. If you refrigerate debearded mussels, be sure to check them before cooking to make sure they are alive. Press any with opened shells; if they do not close when touched, discard them.)

When ready for final cooking, divide 4 tablespoons of the butter and 2 tablespoons of the oil between two wide sauté pans. (Do not crowd everything into one pan—the shellfish should be sautéed, not simmered.) Heat the butter and oil. Remove the shrimp from the marinade and divide the shrimp, scallops, and mussels evenly between the pans. Sauté over high heat about 3 minutes, shaking the pans occasionally, until the shrimp are pink on one side. Turn the shellfish, add the sausage, and sauté for 2–3 minutes, still shaking the pans, or until the shrimp, scallops, and sausage are lightly browned and the mussels have opened. Add the peas during the last minute of cooking.

While the shellfish is cooking, heat the remaining tablespoon of butter and the remaining tablespoon of oil in a sauté pan, and gently warm the cherry tomatoes.

To serve: Put a portion of rice or rice pilaf on each of 6 serving plates and divide the scampi preparation among the plates. Garnish each plate with 3 cherry tomatoes, a sprig of parsley, and a lemon wedge.

SERVES 6

❖Extra marinade keeps well in the refrigerator.

Broiled Thai Shrimp with Roasted Sugar Snap Peas and Sesame Chinese Noodles

This is what I call a "bar meal." It is special enough for company, yet casual and easy to prepare. The components can be prepared early in the day or the day before, and the cook need only spend a few minutes at the stove before serving. The sesame noodles can be refrigerated a day ahead and brought to room temperature before serving. The shrimp should sit in their marinade at least an hour, and up to twelve hours. I recommend *Sweet-and-Hot Grape Sauce,* which can be prepared days in advance, as an accompaniment to the shrimp. From a shellfish, a vegetable, and a pasta, one gets an appealing range of tastes, textures, and colors in this combination.

Sweet-and-Hot Grape Sauce (page 43) (optional)

SESAME CHINESE NOODLES

Sesame seeds
½ lb fresh Chinese noodles★
Sesame oil
Light soy sauce (optional)

To make Sesame Chinese Noodles: Amounts here are not important; prepare as much of the noodles as you like. Heat a nonstick sauté pan and pour in a thin layer of sesame seeds. Cook over medium heat, shaking and stirring the seeds until they are lightly browned or toasted. Set aside. Bring a large pot of water to a boil, drop in the noodles, and cook until they are just tender. Drain well and place in a large bowl. Add sesame oil and sesame seeds to taste and toss well. Season with light soy sauce, if desired. Unless you are serving shortly, cover and refrigerate.

★Available in Asian markets; otherwise use packaged dried Chinese noodles, which are widely available.

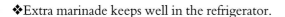

*Hot chili oil is available in many supermarkets and Asian markets. I like Chef Chow's Hot Spicy Oil, which is flavored with peppercorns, chili, sesame oil, and anise seeds.

Prepare the sweet-and-hot grape sauce, if desired, as a dipping sauce.

Prepare the sesame Chinese noodles.

To prepare the shrimp: Peel and devein the shrimp, leaving on the last tail-shell segment. Make a shallow cut along the center line of the underside of each shrimp to partially butterfly it. In a large bowl, whisk together the garlic, coriander, chili oil, lemon juice, ¼ cup of the oil, salt, and hot pepper flakes. Add the shrimp, toss them in the marinade to coat well, cover, and refrigerate 1–2 hours.

To prepare the peas: String the peas by snapping off the stem and pulling the strings attached to it down the sides of the pea. Refrigerate until ready to cook.

When you are ready to cook, thread the shrimp on long skewers for ease of handling, if you like. Insert the skewer through the thicker head end of the shrimp ½ inch from the end, and then through the underside of the tail end just in front of the remaining tail shell, forming a "C" shape. Put as many shrimp on each skewer as you can with the butterflied sides all facing in the same direction.

Toss the peas with 1 tablespoon of oil or less to coat them lightly. Spread them in a single layer on a baking sheet and sprinkle them with salt, if desired.

If you have a separate oven and broiler, preheat the oven to 450 degrees and preheat the broiler. If you have one oven with a broiler, broil the shrimp first, then immediately turn the oven to 450 degrees, and when it is ready, roast the peas.

Place the shrimp butterflied side down on the broiler rack for 3–4 minutes; turn and cook for 1–2 minutes more, or until the center of the shrimp have turned opaque.

Roast the peas for 3–4 minutes.

Remove the shrimp from the skewers and serve with the peas, noodles, and the sweet-and-hot grape sauce to dip the shrimp into, if you like. Serve 2 shrimp for an appetizer first course or 4–5 shrimp for a main course. SERVES 4–5 AS A MAIN COURSE, 8–10 AS AN APPETIZER

❖Grill the shrimp instead of broiling them while you are roasting the peas.

SHRIMP

2 lb extra colossal (7–10 count) raw shrimp
1½ tsp minced garlic
1½ tsp ground coriander
2 Tb hot chili oil*
2 Tb fresh lemon juice
¼ cup peanut or vegetable oil plus 1 Tb
Dash of salt
Dash of hot pepper flakes

SUGAR SNAP PEAS

¾ lb sugar snap peas
Salt (optional)

Broiled Thai Shrimp with Roasted Sugar Snap Peas and Sesame Chinese Noodles (continued)

❖The roasted sugar snap peas are wonderful as a snack by themselves.

❖Make an easy dipping sauce with equal parts soy sauce and sake.

Shrimp and Vegetable Tempura

The Japanese technique of deep-frying shrimp and vegetables that have been dipped in a light batter yields a superb dish. Unfortunately, it is not a dish that the cook can prepare ahead and then relax and join his or her guests. Tempura is best cooked in small batches so that the oil will stay very hot and keep the tempura crisp instead of soggy, and it is best served almost immediately after coming out of the wok or deep fryer. A high-sided wok with a draining rack or a deep fryer with a separate rack to drain the cooked ingredients is essential. Amounts in this dish can be adjusted easily to the number of diners. I would count on 1½ pounds of peeled, deveined, butterflied (and the larger the better) shrimp for 4 persons, plus the collection of vegetables you select to accompany the shrimp. The batter is very light and gives a crisp, lacy coating; you can make the coating lighter or heavier by adjusting the amount of ice water in the batter. Do not make the batter ahead of time; make it just before cooking, and as you run low, quickly make more. I drain the cooked shrimp and vegetables on brown paper, and then serve the tempura in baskets or on plates lined with absorbent paper to take up any additional excess oil. I like to use parchment paper for the baskets, because it looks nice, but you can use brown paper or even double-thick paper towels.

COOKING EQUIPMENT

Peanut oil
A deep-sided wok or a deep fryer
Draining racks
Absorbent paper
Tongs
Deep-fat-frying thermometer

ACCOMPANIMENTS

Dashi Dipping Sauce:
1 cup liquid dashi★
¼ cup sweet rice wine
⅓ cup soy sauce
½ cup grated daikon radishes★ or white turnips
1–2 tsp grated fresh ginger

Soy and Sake Sauce (equal parts soy sauce and rice wine)
Wasabi★
A prepared sweet-and-sour sauce (optional)
A prepared mustard sauce (optional)
Parchment paper, brown paper, or paper towels for serving baskets

★Powdered dashi in cans that can be dissolved to make liquid dashi, daikon radishes, and wasabi in cans can be purchased in Oriental markets, specialty-food stores, and some supermarkets.

SHRIMP AND VEGETABLES

Peeled, deveined shrimp with last tail-shell segment left on
Thinly sliced vegetables, such as winter and summer squash, sweet potatoes, onion and turnip rounds, wide flat carrot strips, peeled and diagonally sliced broccoli stalks, diagonal slices of celery or fennel, cross sections of eggplant
Stemmed vegetables, such as whole green beans, large spinach leaves, scallions, squash blossoms
All-purpose flour or (preferably) instant-blending flour (such as Wondra Quick-Mixing Flour), for dredging

BATTER

1 egg
1 cup ice water or more
1 cup sifted flour
Salt

To make the dipping sauce: Mix powdered dashi and water in proportions as directed on the can of powder to make 1 cup dashi liquid. In a small pan, heat together the dashi liquid, rice wine, and soy sauce, then stir in the grated radishes or turnips and the ginger.

To prepare the shrimp: Place the shrimp on a work surface and cut about halfway through the shrimp along the center line of the inside curve, or underside, to ensure even coating of the batter and even cooking. Pat the shrimp very dry and refrigerate until ready to cook.

To make the batter: Just before cooking, beat together the egg and ice water in a bowl with a fork or chopsticks. Add the flour and salt, and mix with a fork or chopsticks until just combined but not smooth. The batter should be barely mixed together, still lumpy.

To deep-fry the shrimp and vegetables: Heat at least 2 inches of oil to 360 degrees in the wok or deep fryer, using a thermometer and adjusting the heat to keep the temperature at 360 degrees during the cooking.

Pat the shrimp dry again, if necessary, to ensure that they are very dry before cooking. Cook a few at a time. Dip the shrimp into the plate of flour or instant-blending flour, shake off the excess, then dip them into the batter and let the excess drip back into the bowl. Slide the shrimp into the hot oil. Large bubbles will form around the shrimp, and the bubbles will gradually get smaller. When the shrimp turn golden and their flesh is just opaque (test by cutting into one) and the bubbles diminish, the shrimp should be done. Cooking time will vary with the size of the shrimp; large shrimp should cook in 2–3 minutes. Remove the shrimp with tongs to a draining rack and then to brown paper, which will absorb some of the oil. Transfer to a paper-lined warm platter or a paper-lined basket and serve immediately with the dipping sauce and other accompaniments.

To cook the vegetables: Pat the vegetables very dry with paper towels. Just before cooking, dip them into the flour and shake off any excess. (The flour helps the batter adhere to the vegetable. The flour coating should be very thin, and instant-blending flour works best for me in this regard.) Dip the vegetables into the batter, letting excess batter drip back into the bowl. Slide the vegetables into the hot oil, cooking just a few at a time. Cook for 3–4 minutes, or until the vegetables have a delicate, barely cooked crust. Remove them with a slotted spoon to a draining rack, then transfer them to brown paper so the extra oil can be absorbed. Place the drained cooked vegetables on a warm paper-lined platter or in a paper-lined basket, and serve immediately with the dipping sauce and other accompaniments.

❖Combine the shrimp with small pieces of thin, firm-fleshed flounder such as gray sole, or with thin slices of monkfish, or substitute pieces of fish for the shrimp.

Baked Shrimp with a Vegetable-Bread Topping

Shrimp have a natural juicy tenderness that the drying heat of an oven can transform into toughness if one does not take steps to protect the shrimp. In *Baked Shrimp with Tomato Concasse* (page 280), for example, we protect the shrimp with a moist sauce; another method, employed here, is to protect the shrimp with a delicious but simple stuffing mixture heaped on top of the butterflied shrimp. In the summer I'll add *Coleslaw* (page 82), *Fresh Pea Salad* (page 88), or a *Vine-Ripened Tomato Salad* (page 92); in the cold months I like *Shell Bean Succotash* (page 320) and *Spaetzle* (page 362), with these shrimp.

 1½ lb peeled and deveined extra jumbo
  (21–25 count) raw shrimp
 ⅓ cup light olive oil
 1 cup finely chopped onions
 ½ cup finely chopped celery
 ½ cup finely chopped red or green peppers
 1½ cups fresh bread crumbs
 1 Tb chopped fresh thyme or other herbs
 Salt and freshly ground pepper
 Lemon wedges

Butterfly the shrimp by placing them on their back on a work surface and slicing down through the center line of the inside curve, or curl, of the shrimp but not cutting quite all the way through. Cover and refrigerate until ready to cook.

To make the stuffing, heat 3 tablespoons of the oil in a sauté pan; add the onions, celery, and peppers, and cook for 2–3 minutes, or until the vegetables are wilted. Add the bread crumbs and thyme, stir all together, cook for another minute, and season with salt and freshly ground pepper.

Place the shrimp, split side up, on an oiled baking sheet. Spread a spoonful of stuffing over each shrimp, drizzle the remaining oil over all, and bake in a pre-

Baked Shrimp with a Vegetable-Bread Topping
(continued)

heated 450-degree oven for 6–8 minutes, or until the shrimp are opaque and the stuffing is hot and toasty. Serve with lemon wedges.   SERVES 4

Baked Shrimp with Tomato Concasse

Just a small amount of sauce—in this case a fresh tomato sauce—is all that is needed to keep succulent shrimp from drying out in the heat of the oven. If you have some on hand, the optional sun-dried tomatoes heighten the flavor of this dish. I would complete the meal by adding plain rice and a crisp green vegetable or a green salad.

3 Tb olive oil, butter, or a combination of both
1 tsp minced garlic
3 cups peeled, seeded, and chopped tomatoes
2 Tb fresh lemon juice
1–2 Tb chopped fresh basil
2 Tb minced softened sun-dried tomatoes
  (see page 218) (optional)
Salt and freshly ground pepper

1½ lb peeled and deveined extra jumbo
  (21–25 count) raw shrimp

In a wide, nonaluminum sauté pan, heat the oil or butter or combination. Stir in the garlic, then add the tomatoes, lemon juice, and basil. Bring the sauce to a boil and cook for 2–3 minutes to evaporate most of the liquid. Add the sun-dried tomatoes (if you are using them) and season the mixture with salt and freshly ground pepper.

Pat the shrimp dry and place them in a baking dish or in 4 individual au gratin dishes. Spoon the sauce evenly over the shrimp and bake in a preheated 450-degree oven for 8–9 minutes, or until the shrimp are just opaque throughout.   SERVES 4

❖*With Wine:* Substitute ¼ cup dry white wine or vermouth for the lemon juice.

❖*With Feta Cheese:* Stir crumbled feta cheese into the sauce just before spooning it over the shrimp.

Shrimp Chili

To purists, chili means small pieces of beef or pork cooked with chilies (or chili powder) and a few spices such as cumin. Adventurous cooks have stretched the definition of chili to include tomatoes and beans, and about everything else imaginable. All that unites these dishes is that they are reddish, chunky, and fragrant with chili and spices. Occasionally I like to make chili with shrimp. Firm shrimp is a nice contrast to soft beans.

3 Tb vegetable oil
2 cups chopped onions
1 cup diced red peppers
1 cup diced green peppers
½ cup chopped celery
1 tsp minced hot peppers (optional)
2 tsp minced garlic

SPICE AND HERB MIX

3 Tb chili powder
2 tsp oregano
2 tsp cumin
1 tsp thyme
1 tsp black pepper
1 tsp cayenne pepper
1 tsp paprika
½ tsp salt

4 cups peeled, seeded, and chopped very ripe
  tomatoes
2 Tb tomato paste
2 cups clam juice, strong *Fish Stock* (page 355),
  or chicken stock
½ cup dry vermouth
4 cups cooked kidney or pinto beans, drained
1½–2 lb peeled and deveined extra large
  (31–35 count) raw shrimp
3–4 Tb chopped cilantro (optional)
Sour cream or *Salsa* (page 7) (optional)

In a heavy, 6–8-quart pot, heat the oil. Add the onions and cook until they are wilted and golden, about 8–10 minutes. Stir in the red and green peppers, the celery, and the hot peppers, if you like, and cook 3–4 minutes. Add the garlic and stir in the ingredients of the spice and herb mixture. Add the tomatoes, tomato paste, clam juice or fish stock or chicken stock, and vermouth, stir well, and bring to a boil. Reduce the heat and boil gently for 45 minutes, or until the tomatoes have released their juices and the mixture has thickened. Add the beans, stir, and cook for 5 minutes. Add the shrimp and cook for 4–5 minutes until they are cooked through. Taste for seasonings, and serve in warm bowls. Sprinkle with cilantro if desired. Garnish with sour cream or salsa, if desired, and pass some corn bread.   SERVES 8–10

❖If the available fresh tomatoes are not very ripe, use half fresh tomatoes and half peeled and seeded canned tomatoes.

❖Use 1½ pounds shrimp and ½ pound other seafood, such as squid, scallops, monkfish, or lobster.

❖Use less black and cayenne pepper if you prefer a milder chili.

❖Use cooked shrimp; stir them in for just a minute or two to warm through.

BIG Shrimp
with a Lobster Stuffing

This is definitely a party dish, combining two almost universally popular shellfish—shrimp and lobster. I like to make it with extra colossal (7 count) shrimp. Since it is a rich dish, I accompany it with simply steamed vegetables tossed with lemon juice and herbs. Try green beans or chunks of zucchini and yellow squash.

32 extra colossal (7 count) raw shrimp

LOBSTER STUFFING

1 lb cooked lobster meat
1 cup peeled, seeded, and chopped tomatoes
½ cup grated Swiss cheese
2 cups fresh bread crumbs
⅓ cup melted butter
1 Tb fresh lemon juice, or more as desired
2 Tb chopped parsley
2 Tb chopped basil
Salt and freshly ground pepper
Hot pepper sauce

¼ cup grated Swiss cheese
3–4 Tb butter (optional)
Dry vermouth or water
Sprigs parsley
Lemon wedges

Peel the shrimp, leaving on the last segment of the tail shells for decoration. Make a shallow cut along the center of the back side of each shrimp and remove the dark intestinal vein. Turn the shrimp back side down and cut into, but not all the way through, the center line of the underside from the head end back to the tail shell to "butterfly" the shrimp. Cover and refrigerate until ready to assemble and cook.

To make the lobster stuffing: Cut the lobster meat into ½-inch pieces. In a bowl, combine the tomatoes, ½ cup grated Swiss cheese, bread crumbs, melted butter, 1 tablespoon of the lemon juice, parsley, and basil. Add the lobster and fold together until well mixed. Season to taste with salt and freshly ground pepper, a few drops of hot pepper sauce, and more lemon juice, if you like.

To assemble and cook: When ready, place 4 shrimp, tails upright, in each of 8 individual au gratin dishes, alternating head and tail ends, or put all the shrimp, tails upright and alternating head and tail ends in each row, into a large baking dish that can go under a broiler.

BIG Shrimp with a Lobster Stuffing (continued)

Mold about 2 heaping tablespoons of the lobster stuff-ing onto the top of each shrimp and press down slightly to fill the butterfly cut. Sprinkle ¼ cup grated Swiss cheese over the lobster stuffing, dot each shrimp with butter, if you like, and film the baking dish or dishes with vermouth or water. Cover loosely with aluminum foil, being careful not to flatten the stuffing, and bake in a preheated 500-degree oven for 15–20 minutes. Remove cover to check the shrimp—some ovens are hotter than others and you don't want to dry these out; they should be just opaque. Remove the foil and run the dish or dishes under a hot broiler for 30 seconds to crisp the shrimp lightly. Garnish with parsley sprigs and serve with lemon wedges.   SERVES 8

❖Substitute shrimp or crabmeat for the lobster in the stuffing.

❖Substitute light olive oil for the melted butter in the stuffing and eliminate the dotting with butter just before baking.

❖Substitute chopped tomatoes or other vegetables for the shellfish in the stuffing.

❖Reduce the serving portions of this rich dish from 4 to 3 shrimp each.

Shrimp Gumbo

Although our word "gumbo" comes from an African word for okra, *ochinggombo,* the word has come to denote a southern dish rather than the vegetable itself. Still, while cooking times and stock bases and ingredient lists for gumbos vary remarkably from cook to cook, every true gumbo does contain okra. I have retained the traditional roux as a thickening and flavoring agent. It can be made in advance, refrigerated, and reheated at will. Some southern cooks tell me that file powder is not put in gumbo if okra is already in it, but other cooks tell me it's quite acceptable; I've made it optional.

½ lb ham
1 ham hock
1 lb meaty veal bones
¾ cup flour
½ cup vegetable oil
1 lb okra
3–4 Tb bacon fat or vegetable oil
1 Tb butter
1 tsp minced garlic
1½ cups chopped onions
1½ cups chopped green peppers
½ cup chopped celery
1½ cups peeled, seeded, and chopped tomatoes
1 tsp hot pepper sauce
½ tsp cayenne pepper
1 tsp Worcestershire sauce
1 bay leaf
½ tsp thyme
Salt and freshly ground pepper
1 lb crabmeat
1½–2 lb peeled and deveined medium large
    (41–45 count) raw shrimp
2 Tb file powder (optional)
8–10 cups cooked rice

In a large pot cover the ham, ham hock, and veal bones with 3 quarts of water. Bring the water to a boil. Cover, reduce the heat, and simmer for 2 hours. Strain the stock and cook it again to reduce the liquid to 2½ quarts. Set aside.

To make the roux, stir together the flour and ½ cup vegetable oil in a heavy, 4–6-quart saucepan. Cook over medium-high heat for 15–20 minutes, whisking constantly, until the mixture turns a rich mahogany color. (Cooking it over a very low flame gives a fine mellow flavor but takes a great deal longer.) Set aside or refrigerate until ready to use.

Wash and trim the okra and cut it into 1-inch pieces. Heat the bacon fat or vegetable oil in a deep sauté pan or saucepan, add the okra, and sauté it for 5–10 minutes, or until it is lightly browned and has stopped "roping," or giving off strings of almost colorless material. Drain the okra and reserve. In the same pan, melt the butter, add the garlic, onions, peppers, and celery, and cook until the vegetables are wilted. Stir in the tomatoes and reserved ham stock, bring to a boil, reduce the heat, and simmer for 10 minutes.

Stir the roux; if it has cooled, reheat it over low heat, stirring constantly. Whisk the warm ham stock and vegetables into the warm roux to combine well. Add the okra, hot pepper sauce, cayenne pepper, Worcestershire sauce, bay leaf, thyme, 1 teaspoon salt, and a pinch of freshly ground pepper. Stir in ½ pound of the crabmeat and simmer, partially covered, for 1 hour. Add the shrimp and the remaining crabmeat. Simmer 5 minutes, remove from the heat, cover, and let steep for 5 minutes. Add the file powder, if you like, just before serving. Serve surrounding a mound of rice in individual bowls.   SERVES 8

❖You may substitute 2½ quarts shrimp or fish stock for the ham stock. In that case, add 1–1½ pounds chopped smoked sausage when you add the okra to the stock.
  ❖Add lobster meat or cleaned soft-shell crabs.
  ❖Add or substitute chicken for the ham.
  ❖Reduce the amount of roux to give a thinner texture.

Shrimp Creole

Prepare the spicy, hot Creole sauce in advance, if you like, then reheat it and add the shrimp for the final few minutes of cooking; this is a great dish for make-ahead cookery. When fresh ripe tomatoes are not available, I use 3 parts chopped canned tomato pulp to 1 part fresh chopped tomato pulp. During final cooking or reheating of the Creole sauce, prepare plain boiled rice as a base for the servings.

Shrimp Creole (continued)

2–2½ lb peeled and deveined jumbo
　　(26–30 count) raw shrimp
7–10 cups cooked rice

CREOLE SAUCE

2 Tb vegetable oil or chicken fat
2 cups chopped onions
2 Tb butter
1 cup chopped celery
1 cup chopped green peppers
2 tsp minced garlic
4 cups peeled, seeded, and chopped
　　tomatoes
¼ cup tomato paste
1 Tb fresh lemon juice or red wine
　　vinegar
1 bay leaf
2–3 Tb fresh basil or 1 Tb dried
1½ Tb fresh thyme or 2 tsp dried
1 tsp salt
1 tsp black pepper
½ tsp cayenne pepper
½ tsp paprika
¼ tsp hot pepper sauce
1 tsp sugar
2 cups *Shrimp Broth* (page 361) or
　　Fish Stock (page 355) or chicken
　　broth

To make the Creole Sauce: In a large pan heat the oil or chicken fat. Add 1 cup of the onions and cook, stirring, over medium heat for 8–10 minutes to brown the onions; this browning will give a nice flavor to the sauce. Add the butter, the remaining cup of onions, celery, and green peppers, and cook for about 5 minutes, or until these vegetables are wilted but not brown. Stir in the garlic and cook for 30 seconds. Stir in all the remaining ingredients of the sauce. Bring the mixture to a boil, reduce the heat, and cook gently for about 20–25 minutes, or until the sauce has thickened. After 15 minutes, taste the sauce for seasoning and adjust to make it hotter or spicier, if desired.

MAKES 8 CUPS

If you are making the sauce in advance, remove it from the heat at this point, let it cool, and refrigerate until ready to reheat and serve.

Just before serving, add the shrimp for the final 2–4 minutes of cooking; the time will depend on the size of the shrimp. Serve in warmed bowls over plain boiled rice.
SERVES 6–8

❖Double or triple the recipe for a crowd.

❖Add cubes of smoked ham for flavor.

❖Substitute smoked sausage for some of the shrimp. Prick the sausage in several places with a fork, drop it into a pan of boiling water, and cook for 5 minutes to release the fat. Remove and slice it into ¼-inch-thick rounds. Add the sausage with the shrimp.

❖Add cooked chicken or pieces of uncooked chicken breast, or substitute chicken for some of the shrimp.

Shrimp Baked with Escargot Butter

Most people watch their butter intake these days, but if you can indulge yourself occasionally, you will find this dish flavored with butter, garlic, shallots, and parsley a delicious treat. *Roast Sweet Potato Slices* (page 342) is an unusual and pleasant companion to this dish.

Alternative shellfish: scallops

Alternative fish: small chunks of monkfish, swordfish, or shark

1½ lb peeled and deveined extra jumbo
　　(21–25 count) raw shrimp
¼ cup dry vermouth
1 cup fresh bread crumbs, lightly toasted
½ cup fresh parsley
3 Tb minced shallots
1 Tb minced garlic
Salt and freshly ground pepper
½ cup melted butter

Butter 4 baking scallop shells or au gratin dishes and divide the shrimp equally among them. Pour an equal amount of vermouth into each dish. In a small bowl, mix together the bread crumbs, parsley, shallots, and garlic, and season the mixture with salt and freshly ground pepper. Sprinkle the mixture over the shrimp and drizzle the melted butter over all. Bake in a preheated 400-degree oven for 10–12 minutes, or until the center of one of the shrimp tested with a knife has turned opaque.   SERVES 4

Braised Yellowtail Snapper with West Indian Garlic and Thyme Sauce

Chef Claude Williams prepared this dish in front of a television camera at the Caneel Bay Resort in the Virgin Islands, and we broadcast the event for viewers of "The Victory Garden." He cooked at a grill set on a magnificent beach with the sparkling Caribbean as a backdrop, and I can remember wanting to watch the details of the preparation but being drawn to the beauty of the whole scene. Fortunately, the camera caught all of the preparation, which didn't take very long.

Alternative fish: red snapper or other small snappers; small whole rockfish, such as black sea bass; porgy, small farmed striped bass, or small fillets or steaks (see variation below)

Four 2–2½-lb cleaned whole yellowtail
    snappers
Salt and freshly ground pepper
4 finely chopped cloves garlic
¼ cup olive oil
½ cup chopped scallions
½ cup chopped red peppers, in ½-inch pieces
½ cup chopped green peppers, in ½-inch pieces
3–4 sprigs fresh thyme
Pinch of ground cloves
½ cup diagonally sliced celery
1 cup peeled, seeded, and chopped tomatoes, in
    ½-inch dice
2–3 cups crushed fresh or canned tomato pulp

Remove and discard the heads of the fish, wash the fish well, and pat them dry. Cut several shallow diag-

onal gashes across the skin of the fish. Rub the fish with salt, freshly ground pepper, and 2 teaspoons of the chopped garlic.

In a sauté pan large enough to hold the fish in one layer, or using two pans, heat the oil, add the fish, and sear on both sides until the fish is a deep golden brown. Remove the fish to a warm plate. Add the scallions, red and green peppers, the remaining garlic, thyme, and cloves, and sauté, stirring, for 1 minute. Add the celery, tomatoes, and crushed tomato pulp, stir all together, bring the mixture to a boil, and cook for 3–4 minutes, stirring occasionally. Season the sauce with salt and pepper. Return the fish to the pan, nesting the fish in the sauce and spooning the sauce over the fish. Cook at a gentle simmer for 5–10 minutes, depending on the thickness of the fish, or until the fish is just opaque at the center.   SERVES 4

❖Cook fillets or steaks in the same manner but slightly reduce the cooking time to take into account the thinner portions.
❖Use less garlic.
❖Add a few drops of hot pepper sauce when you add the tomatoes.

Roasted Red Snapper with Sautéed Swiss Chard

Greens are good with roast fish, and Swiss chard is one of my favorite greens. I specify red Swiss chard for this recipe because its color works nicely with the lovely color of red snapper, but you can certainly use the standard variety of chard. In *The Victory Garden Cookbook,* I have a recipe for a 4–5-pound snapper stuffed with Swiss chard, but I find that my fish market frequently carries smaller red snapper in a 1½–2-pound range for which a different treatment is best used. For a simple but wonderful dinner, serve this fish and its sauté of greens with noodles. The fish doesn't really need a sauce, but if you wish, you could accompany the snapper with *Fresh Tomato Sauce* (page 364), *Lemon Butter Sauce* (page 357), or another sauce from this book. The Swiss chard can be boiled ahead, refreshed in cold water, drained, and set aside until time for its final sauté.

Alternative fish: other small snappers, Arctic char, salmon trout, hybrid striped bass, bluefish, black sea bass

Roasted Red Snapper with Sautéed Swiss Chard
(continued)

SWISS CHARD

1½ lb red Swiss chard
2–3 Tb fruity olive oil
1–2 Tb balsamic vinegar
Salt and freshly ground pepper

ROASTED RED SNAPPER

Two 1½–2-lb cleaned whole snappers
Salt and freshly ground pepper
2 sliced lemons
Vegetable oil or combination oil and
    melted butter
Lemon wedges

To prepare the Swiss chard: Wash the Swiss chard and separate the stems from the leaves. Cut the stems diagonally into ½-inch-long pieces and tear the leaves into large pieces. Bring a large pot of water to a boil. If the stems are thick, drop them into the boiling water first, and after the water returns to a boil, cook the stems for 2–3 minutes, then add the leaves. If the stems are young and small, place the stems and leaves in the water at the same time. Boil the leaves for 4–5 minutes until they have wilted and the stems are tender. Drain the Swiss chard in a colander and run cold water over it until the chard is completely cooled. Set aside to drain. (Makes about 6 cups)

To roast the snapper: Remove the gills of the fish if they have been left on; trim the tail, if you wish, and rinse and pat the fish dry. Season the cavity of each fish with salt and freshly ground pepper, and slip slices of lemon into the cavity of each fish. Brush the fish on both sides with oil or a combination of oil and butter, and place the fish in a large baking pan. Roast in a preheated 450-degree oven for 10 minutes, then spoon a bit more of the oil over each fish. Roast the fish another 10–15 minutes, testing for doneness by pulling a small section of the fin; it should come out of the flesh easily. The fish will have popped open from the heat of the oven. The interior of the belly cavity should be opaque. (To test that the fish is just opaque throughout, cut into one fish.)

Just before the fish is fully cooked, finish preparing the Swiss chard. Heat 2–3 tablespoons of olive oil in a

wide, nonaluminum-lined sauté pan and stir in the reserved Swiss chard. Cook, stirring, just long enough to evaporate any excess moisture in the pan and to heat it completely. Season the chard with balsamic vinegar and salt and freshly ground pepper.

To serve: (This is the trickiest part of the recipe.) Run a sharp knife down the skin of the back of one of the fish from the neck to the tail, keeping the knife just above the back center bone. Slip the knife (a wide-blade fish knife is ideal for this) into the flesh at the neck end just above the backbone and slide the knife across the width of the fish and then down the length of the fish, keeping the knife close to the backbone as you slice. What you are doing is freeing the whole top fillet in one piece from the bone structure of the fish. Lift this fillet to a warm serving plate. Now slide the knife just under the backbone and work it along to separate the whole bone structure from the bottom fillet. Gently lift up and discard the bone frame and remove any pin bones that did not remain attached to the bone frame. Lift the bottom fillet to a second serving plate. Repeat the procedure with the second fish to cut fillets for the third and fourth serving plates. Each fillet will be about a 7-ounce serving. Serve with the sautéed Swiss chard and lemon wedges or a sauce of your choice.   SERVES 4

❖Roast any whole fish in the same manner and adjust the timing to the size of the fish. A 1-pound fish should take about 15–20 minutes; a 1–3-pound fish, 20–25 minutes; a 3–6-pound fish, 25–35 minutes; a 6–8-pound fish, 35–45 minutes; an 8–10-pound fish, 45–60 minutes.

❖Reduce the oven temperature to 400 degrees and increase the roasting time a little.

❖Substitute fresh lemon juice for balsamic vinegar.

Sautéed Swordfish

People usually broil or grill swordfish, but its firm flesh is perfect for a sauté; the fish is quickly cooked, thereby avoiding the danger of drying out under the intense heat of a broiler or grill. The fish will simmer rather than sauté to a crisp brown finish if it is crowded in the pan, so use two pans or cook in batches to ensure against overcrowding. I prefer my trusty old black iron

(continued on page 288)

RED SNAPPER AND COUSINS

I REMEMBER BEING at Jim Burke's Tuscan Grill not long ago and ordering red snapper. Jim rubbed the snapper with good olive oil, lemon juice, and spices, then grilled and served it with two grilled oysters on the half shell as garnish. It was a simple but perfect way to treat the succulent flesh of American red snapper.

There are many cousins, but there is only one American red snapper, and its dense but delicate flesh makes it a premium fish. The geographical range of this species is from the coastal waters of North Carolina south into the Gulf of Mexico, with Florida being the center of the red snapper trade for this country. At the fish market you will recognize red snapper immediately by its bright pink-red skin, more vivid on its back and fading toward the belly, and by the trademark bright red eyes. Red snapper can run as large as 30–35 pounds, but the ones that we usually see in our markets range from 1½–6 pounds.

There are over 180 species of snapper around the world, and the few that can sometimes be found in our markets are almost as fine as American red snapper—among them, lane snapper (also known as spot snapper), mutton snapper, mangrove snapper, and yellowtail snapper. At the Hawaiian fish auction in Honolulu, I've also seen onaga and lehi, both snappers but with characteristics very different from American red snapper. Possible confusion with genuine red snapper is compounded by the existence of fish with similar names such as northern ocean perch—often called redfish—and the redfish of the Gulf of Mexico made famous by Paul Prudhomme's recipe for "blackened redfish"; these latter fish are a species of drumfish and not a snapper at all. On the West Coast some members of the rockfish family can legally be called "red snapper" or "Pacific red snapper," but no fish other than the American red snapper can be shipped interstate and sold as red snapper. The point to be emphasized here is not that American red snapper is the only snapper worth eating—many snappers provide delicious eating—but rather that cousins and pretenders should not be sold at the premium price commanded by American red snapper.

Buying: Florida law requires that real red snapper be marketed with its easily identifiable and handsome skin on. There is a very good chance that skinned fillets you may find at a market called "red snapper" are something other than American red snapper. Red snapper is most frequently sold whole, gutted, but with the head on. You may also find skin-on fillets, and in some areas the cheeks (round head sections) and throats (meat from the front of the belly area) are sold along with strips of snapper meat called "fingers." The whole fish should be shiny, translucent, and firm, without any odor. Fillets are medium thick, and the flesh is white with a slightly rosy glow; the flesh should be firm, glistening, and clear.

Some snapper in our markets is imported, such as a southern red snapper found in the Caribbean and in Central America south of where American or northern red snapper is harvested, and frozen snapper imported from Thailand and Taiwan is also available. Be aware that snappers, like groupers, are reef fish and can be affected by ciguatera poisoning (see page 367), depending on where they come from. While the threat is more likely to affect the sport fisherman, the consumer should always buy snapper from a reliable dealer who knows the origin of all his fish.

Storage and Preparation: Store fresh red snapper in the coldest part of your refrigerator and handle it as you would any other lean, firm-fleshed fish. First remove the gills of the whole fish if the dealer hasn't done so, wash the fish well, pat it dry, and place it in a non-aluminum-lined pan; cover the pan with butcher's paper or plastic wrap loosely enough to allow air to circulate around the fish and

SPECIAL INFORMATION ABOUT

RED SNAPPER AND COUSINS

*Red Snapper and Cousins
(continued)*

place ice packs on top of the fish, making sure that water from the melting ice packs does not come in contact with the flesh of the fish. Store fillets the same way. Fillets are often sold without the pin bones having been removed; remove them in a "V" cut before cooking the snapper. My practice is typically to cook the fish the

same day I bring it home, but with proper storage you can keep snapper for 24–48 hours before cooking.

You can remove the skin before cooking snapper, if you like. I usually leave the skin on fillets because it is thin and quite edible. The skin of American red snapper does not curl as it cooks, but the skin of other snappers may curl—another way of telling if you are cooking real American

red snapper or a cousin. The flesh of this fish is firm, moist, and mild but distinctively flavored; snapper can be substituted in many recipes for striped bass or salmon.

Yields: A whole red snapper, gutted, but with the head on, yields about 50 percent edible flesh. A 2-pound whole gutted fish serves 2. Allow 6–8 ounces of skin-on fillet per person.

Sautéed Swordfish (continued)

frying pans for this sauté, but any heavy-bottomed pans will suffice. Serve the sautéed swordfish plain with lemon wedges, or season it with garlic in the variation offered by my friend Chef Joe Hyde—I don't know anyone who has had it and been less than enthusiastic—or accompany it with a favorite sauce. Tomato-based sauces always go well with swordfish; see *Swordfish with Portugaise Sauce* (page 298). Fresh crunchy green beans and small boiled or steamed red-skinned potatoes complement this dish nicely. By the way, small pieces of sautéed swordfish served with toothpicks make a good hot appetizer.

> 1½ lb swordfish, sliced into four ½–¾-inch-
>   thick pieces
> 4 Tb butter
> 2 Tb olive oil or vegetable oil
> Flour (preferably instant-blending flour, such as
>   Wondra Quick-Mixing Flour), for dredg-
>   ing
> Lemon wedges

Remove the dark skin and any white inner membrane from the swordfish, and pat the fish dry. Heat 2 tablespoons of the butter and 1 tablespoon of the oil until bubbly and light brown in each of two frying

pans, reducing the amount of butter and oil slightly if cooking in one pan that is large enough to hold all of the fish. Dredge the pieces of fish in a pie pan or plate of flour, shake off any excess flour, and place the fish in the pans. Cook for 3–4 minutes, or until the fish is medium brown, then turn and cook the other side for 3–4 minutes, or until the fish is opaque throughout. (To test for doneness, lift one of the pieces with a spatula on the seam of one of the rings so that you can see a cross section of the next inner ring—the flesh should be opaque—then drop the lifted rings back into place. There should be no trace of your having disturbed the fish.) As soon as it is cooked, immediately remove the swordfish to warm serving plates and garnish with lemon wedges.   SERVES 4

❖ Omit the butter as cooking liquid and use all oil.

❖ *With Browned Butter:* After the fish is cooked and removed to serving plates, wipe out one pan and return it to the heat. When the pan is hot, add 3–4 tablespoons butter and cook, swirling the pan, until the butter turns a deep brown. Remove from the heat, swirl in a little fresh lemon juice, if desired, and pour the butter over the fish and serve.

❖ *With Browned Butter and Capers:* Brown 4 tablespoons butter as in the preceding variation, remove the pan from the heat, swirl in 2–3 tablespoons drained capers, spoon the sauce over the fish, and serve.

❖*With Garlic:* For this treatment by Chef Joe Hyde use as much garlic as your taste will tolerate. After the swordfish is cooked and removed to serving plates, wipe out one pan and return it to the heat. Add 4 tablespoons butter to the pan when the pan is hot, and cook until the butter turns a deep brown. Remove the pan from the heat, swirl in 2 tablespoons (more or less to taste) finely chopped garlic, spoon the sauce over the fish, and serve.

Broiled Swordfish with a Fresh Pepper Relish

A perfectly cooked piece of harpooned swordfish, with a browned surface and a moist interior, is hard to beat, especially if served with a refreshing relish of crisp vegetables. If you broil swordfish as regularly as our restaurant patrons seemed to order it, alternate the relish with a flavored butter and a dipping sauce (see the variation below with citron butter and cucumber-dill sauce). Chop the vegetables for the relish ahead of time, but don't combine them until just before serving so the relish will be crisp when served. *Boiled New Potatoes* (page 334) always taste good with broiled fish; if you try the cucumber-dill sauce, dip the potatoes into it as well.

Alternative fish: steaks of tuna, mahi mahi, shark, halibut, salmon

1½–2 lb swordfish steaks, ¾ inch thick
Vegetable oil
½–¾ cup dry vermouth or white wine
2 Tb softened butter (optional)
Paprika (optional)

PEPPER RELISH

1 cup finely chopped red sweet peppers
3 Tb finely chopped red or green hot peppers
    (or more or less to taste)
½ cup finely chopped celery
½ cup chopped cilantro or Italian parsley
1 Tb minced garlic
¼ cup fresh lime juice
Salt and freshly ground pepper

Lime wedges and twists of sliced lime
Sprigs cilantro or parsley

Remove the dark skin and any white inner membrane and, if desired, the dark brown flesh of the swordfish steaks. Rub or brush both sides of the fish with oil and place the fish in a broiler pan. Pour enough of the vermouth or wine into the pan to cover the bottom by ⅛ inch to help prevent the fish from drying out under the intense heat of the broiler. Place the broiler pan 2–3 inches from the heat of a preheated broiler. After 2–3 minutes, baste the fish, if you wish, with the butter mixed with a little paprika, if desired, to add color to the surface of the fish. Broil the fish a total of about 8–10 minutes, or until the flesh is opaque throughout but still slightly springy to the touch; cooking time will vary with the heat of the broiler and the density of the fish. (To test for doneness, lift a swordfish steak with spatulas on two sides so that it opens along one of the seams of the rings of flesh, enabling you to see a cross section of the interior—the flesh should be opaque—and then lower the flesh back into the pan.)

Just before the swordfish is done, combine all of the ingredients of the pepper relish in a bowl and season the mixture with salt and freshly ground pepper.

Remove the cooked fish to a platter, cut it into 4 equal serving portions, and serve the relish on top of, or to one side of, the fish. Decorate with lime wedges, twists of lime, and sprigs of cilantro or parsley.   SERVES 4

❖If the swordfish steaks are very thick, brown them under the broiler and then transfer them to a 400-degree oven to finish cooking so that the outer flesh doesn't dry out under the broiler before the inner flesh is cooked. The thicker the steaks, the more helpful it is to baste the fish occasionally as it broils or bakes.

❖*Broiled Swordfish with Citron Butter and Cucumber-Dill Sauce:* Prepare the swordfish as above. Immediately after you remove the swordfish from the heat, place a slice of *Citron Butter Roll* (page 352) or other flavored butter, such as *Escargot Butter Roll* (page 353), on top of each serving. Serve with a side ramekin of *Cucumber-Dill Sauce* (page 354) in place of the fresh pepper relish.

❖Use the same toppings for grilled swordfish.

Grilled Swordfish
with Briny Sautéed Eggplant

The acknowledged popularity of swordfish may be due to its pleasantly firm, "meaty" texture, and perhaps also to its relatively bland taste. I confess that I find the taste of plain swordfish a bit dull, and for that reason I like to serve it with something aggressive, such as this sauté of eggplant colored with sweet red pepper and spiced with salty anchovies and capers. Since the intense heat of the grill tends to dry fish out, I cover the fish as it cooks to speed up the process and minimize the drying. To add moisture and interest, you can lubricate the fish as it grills with pats of plain or flavored butter, or top the swordfish with a slice of flavored butter as it comes off the grill; another way to add moisture is to serve the grilled fish with a dipping sauce, such as the easy *Cucumber-Dill Sauce* (page 354). You lessen the amount of cooking oil that eggplant absorbs by salting and draining the eggplant before cooking it. You can prepare the eggplant and peppers well ahead of time and then cook the eggplant mixture just before you put the fish on the grill. Serve with *Corn on the Cob* (page 181) or *Boiled New Potatoes* (page 334).

Alternative fish: steaks of tuna, shark, mahi mahi, salmon, marlin

1½–2 lb swordfish steaks, ¾–1 inch thick

SAUTÉED EGGPLANT

1½ lb eggplant
Salt
1 large red pepper or 2 small red peppers
Olive oil
1 Tb finely chopped garlic
2 Tb drained capers
6 chopped flat anchovies
1–2 Tb sliced sage (optional)
2–3 Tb chopped parsley
Freshly ground pepper

Vegetable oil
Anchovy Butter (page 352) (optional)
Lemon wedges
Sprigs parsley

Remove any inner white membrane from the swordfish, but leave the skin on to help hold the fish together on the grill. Divide the steaks into 4 equal serving portions and refrigerate until ready to grill.

Peel the eggplant and cut it crosswise into ½–¾-inch slices; then cut the slices into ½–¾-inch-wide strips, and cut the strips into ½–¾-inch cubes. (Makes about 5–6 cups cubed eggplant) Put the cubes in a colander, toss with 2 teaspoons salt, and allow to drain for 30 minutes; pat the eggplant dry to remove excess salt and moisture, and set aside.

Cut the pepper or peppers in half lengthwise and remove the stem, seeds, and white membrane. Cut the pepper halves lengthwise into ½-inch-wide strips and cut the strips into ½-inch pieces. (You will have about 1 cup.) Set aside.

To cook the eggplant: Just before grilling the fish or just as the fish goes on the grill, heat 3–4 tablespoons olive oil in a large, nonstick sauté pan. Add the eggplant and peppers and cook over high heat, stirring, until the vegetables are browned on all sides. Add more olive oil, as necessary, if the eggplant absorbs all the oil in the pan. When the vegetables have browned, reduce the heat slightly and continue to cook until the eggplant is tender, about 8 minutes. Stir in the garlic, capers, anchovies, and sage (if you are using it). Cook all together for 1 minute, add the parsley, and season with freshly ground pepper. Keep the eggplant mixture warm until the swordfish is grilled.

To grill the swordfish: Preheat the grill and oil the grill rack. Brush both sides of the swordfish pieces with vegetable oil, place the fish on the grill, and cover with the grill lid or a tent of aluminum foil. Cook for 5–6 minutes, turn the fish over, cover again, and cook for another 3–4 minutes, or until the center is just opaque. Cooking time will vary with the thickness of the fish and the temperature of the grill. (To test for doneness, carefully lift up two sides of a steak with spatulas; the steak will open along the seam of one of its natural rings, allowing you to see a cross section of the interior of the steak. After checking to see that the flesh is opaque, lower the fish back to its original position in the pan.) Remove the cooked fish to a warm platter and top each piece, if you like, with a slice of Anchovy Butter. Serve the swordfish and eggplant garnished with lemon wedges and parsley sprigs.   SERVES 4

(variations on page 295)

THE BIG FISH:

SWORDFISH, TUNA, AND SHARK

THESE THREE FISH are of very different biological species, but in the kitchen they can be interchanged in many recipes, provided the cook adjusts cooking times as needed to take into account the density of each fish. Swordfish is the best known of the three big fish, but tuna and shark are working their way steadily up the popularity charts. I like swordfish and shark cooked until the flesh is just opaque throughout, but tuna tastes better to me when slightly pink at the center.

SWORDFISH

At the Straight Wharf Restaurant we changed most of the menu daily, but a few fish were always on the menu in some treatment because patrons were always looking for them. Nothing was more popular than swordfish, with its mild flavor, flesh so firm as to be meat-like, and its blessed absence of bones. In the course of tracking down the best the market had to offer, I came to prefer swordfish from local waters caught the traditional way—by harpoon. Harpooned fish are boated, bled, gutted, and iced quickly, which makes the flesh of excellent quality. Cost efficiency has brought two other fishing methods—

From top: swordfish, tuna, and shark

longline and gillnet fishing—to the forefront of the swordfish industry, but with these methods the fish *may* spend so much time dangling on line or trapped in nets that they die before they are harvested, and they are not promptly bled, gutted, and iced; this delay can seriously affect the quality of the flesh. I admit that I have had longline-caught swordfish that was well handled and that it tasted as good to me as harpooned swordfish. Your best assurance is to deal with a fish market that is relentless in its pursuit of the highest-quality fish.

Swordfish are caught in many places around the world, but unlike the situation with other fish such as flounder or salmon, it is all the same species of fish. The color of the flesh will vary from area to area—pinkish in New England, whiter in California, redder in the Gulf of Mexico—but that is due to variations in diet. Swordfish like temperate waters and migrate to find them, coming north to New England in late May or early June and heading south again in October. So I get fresh local swordfish in the summer, fresh Florida or Gulf swordfish flown in during the winter, and frozen swordfish year-round both from local sources, which freeze some of the summer catch, and from Japan or Taiwan or other countries that export swordfish.

As a restaurant chef, I first started working with whole swordfish carcasses. In commercial fishing, as distinguished from sport fishing, swordfish heads (with the distinctive swordlike projection of the upper jaws) and tails are removed and discarded at sea; then they are wholesale-marketed as gutted carcasses or in large cross-section chunks called "wheels." Handling a

SPECIAL INFORMATION ABOUT

THE BIG FISH:

SWORDFISH, TUNA, AND SHARK

The Big Fish (continued)

50–100-pound carcass, or wheel, of swordfish was exciting. It taught me, however, that swordfish are subject to parasites that one doesn't see in local market steaks—most dramatically to cestodes, or large tapeworms—which are ugly but harmless and, fortunately, easy to cut out. You might find swordfish steaks in your market with small white parasites noticeable toward the belly flesh; pass them up and look for cleaner steaks. More serious than the parasites is the potential for these big fish to eat other fish with high concentrations of mercury. The concentration can build up through a long food chain, each fish in the chain passing on a higher concentration to the next larger predator. For a while in the 1970s, the FDA banned swordfish from interstate trade because of high mercury levels, but then the permissible level of mercury was raised and the ban was lifted. Nevertheless, high-risk consumers such as pregnant women are still advised not to eat swordfish.

Buying: The flesh of swordfish, regardless of its origin, should be shining and translucent, and the red muscle meat that flares out slightly to both sides from the lower center of a steaked piece should be bright red or pink-red. The longer the dark flesh is exposed to air, the darker it gets,

until it is brown-red or even dark brown; as the fish ages, the dark meat will actually bulge out. Swordfish flesh should feel squeaky clean and "dry," not at all slimy; and like all fresh fish, it should smell clean and of the sea, without odor. When the center bone is cut out of a swordfish carcass, there are two long, boneless sides, or "slabs," that can then be crosscut into steaks. The side of the steak that was on the bottom of the fish tapers to a narrow section, which is the belly flap. Some markets cut these flaps off into smaller pieces and sell them at a lower price. Some markets keep all or some of their swordfish in large chunks that can be sliced to the customer's request, usually ¾–1½ inches thick; other markets display only already-cut steaks. The center portion of the slab of swordfish is preferable because the texture of the meat toward the tail is slightly grainier. Professional cooks vary in their preferences as to what size swordfish makes the best eating. I prefer steaks cut from 50–100-pound medium swordfish, but other cooks prefer steaks from 200–300-pound fish, feeling that the larger fish have a higher fat content. Other cooks swear it makes no difference at all. Sometimes the flesh of a swordfish will unaccountably be jellylike; if you happen to buy such a piece, take it back to the dealer because it is useless to try to cook it. All swordfish should have the skin on when you buy it. Occasionally,

unscrupulous dealers will take the rough skin off shark and sell it as swordfish for the higher price swordfish commands. Swordfish has smooth skin, and it also has characteristic rings in its flesh (like tree rings) and shark does not. Be wary of fish described as swordfish but with its skin already removed. Much of the frozen swordfish imported from abroad is of good quality, especially the premium fish known as "clippers" that were flash-frozen at sea; many of these are defrosted and sold as "previously frozen," and the price should be less than that of fresh swordfish. Imported frozen swordfish has been spot-checked for mercury by U.S. inspectors. Check the center of defrosted swordfish for softness or mushiness that might indicate poor freezing methods.

Storage and Preparation: I place several steaks together to form a chunk, skin side up, and set them on a nonaluminum-lined tray in the coldest part of the refrigerator, covering the fish with butcher's paper topped with ice or putting watertight ice packs directly on the fish–in either case, making sure that the fish is protected from water or ice melting into the flesh. I typically cook swordfish the day I bring it home, but with proper storage you can keep impeccably fresh swordfish up to 24 hours before cooking. Defrost frozen swordfish for 8–10 hours or longer, as needed, in the refrigerator.

SPECIAL INFORMATION ABOUT

THE BIG FISH:

SWORDFISH, TUNA, AND SHARK

While old-time New Englanders either bake or broil swordfish, this versatile fish adapts well to grilling, braising, sautéing, or even poaching. Most recipes in this book will call for the removal of the skin before cooking swordfish, and all recipes in this book will call for the removal of any white inner membrane still attached to the steak. (Some markets remove it before selling swordfish, some don't.) Some cooks remove the dark meat before cooking swordfish, but it is perfectly edible. Watch swordfish especially carefully during broiling or grilling because its flesh easily dries out under intense heat.

Yields: Once the skin is removed, swordfish is 100 percent edible. Allow 6–8 ounces per person. One-half pound of cooked swordfish yields about 1 cup flaked fish.

TUNA

Americans consume more canned tuna than any other kind of fish. Fresh tuna has only recently made significant inroads on our fish marketplace—distinguishing us from, for example, Spain and Portugal, where fresh tuna has long been a familiar part of cookery, or Japan, where the finest grades of raw tuna are used in sashimi and sushi. Wherever one finds a long-established market for tuna, one finds a complex and discriminating set of buyers and standards. I have watched fish brokers in Hawaii select among tuna that had

notches or holes cut in the flesh so that the broker could press the flesh to judge its oil content, and I have seen prices there vary from $3 to $30 per pound, depending on the quality and the cut of the fish. Tuna are members of the same family of fish that includes mackerel, bonito, and wahoo. They are found in temperate and tropical waters around the globe and are caught on both coasts of the United States. The several species of tuna include the following, which are most prominent in cooking:

1. *Bluefin tuna.* Bluefin is the largest of the tuna (average weight is about 150–200 pounds, but it can run as high as 1,000 pounds) and the first choice of the Japanese for raw fish preparations. It has the darkest and fattiest flesh. It looks like a piece of red meat when cut, with a darker strip of muscle running through the midsection of the fish next to the bone. All tuna has this darker streak of meat, which is an accumulation of myoglobin stored by the fish for energy. The Japanese call this darker meat *chiai* and may retain it in sushi or sashimi, but you may want to remove it for its stronger taste—it is somewhat bitter and strong even when cooked.

2. *Bigeye tuna.* Once I made an early morning visit to the fish market at Funchal, on the island of Madeira, and found the market dominated by fresh tuna carcasses, and wheels and sides being cut to order for demanding and critical customers. The bigeye tuna that

were being sold were large, running sometimes to 500 pounds, but they were not quite as dark-fleshed and fatty as bluefin tuna.

3. Three smaller tuna, running between 4 and 25 pounds, are *skipjack tuna*—found in the Pacific and very popular in Hawaii, where it is called *aku*—and *little tuna* and *blackfin tuna,* both from Atlantic waters. I have never cooked these smaller tuna, but I am told that the meat is lighter in color than bluefin and bigeye and that the flavor is somewhat stronger than the flavor of yellowfin or albacore tuna.

4. *Yellowfin tuna*—not to be confused with yellowtail fish, which is a member of the jack family—is a popular tuna for its delicious flavor and much used in Hawaii, where it is called *ahi.* Yellowfin flesh lightens considerably as it cooks. This is the tuna we often find in our markets because much of the bluefin tuna catch has been exported to Japan for the high price it commands there.

5. *Albacore tuna,* also a Pacific fish, provides the well-known "white meat" of canned tuna fame. The most valuable tuna for the canning industry, it is the only tuna that can be labeled "white meat" in the United States.

Buying: Tuna, like swordfish and shark, is usually sold in fish markets as steaks, often with the skin removed and sometimes with the strip of very dark red muscle meat trimmed off so that it does not bleed into the surrounding lighter

SPECIAL INFORMATION ABOUT

THE BIG FISH:

SWORDFISH, TUNA, AND SHARK

The Big Fish (continued)

flesh. Tuna flesh should be sparkling, not dull or grayish. Many retailers identify only two grades—sashimi grade and fry grade—but more knowledgeable dealers break the tuna down into many different cuts and grades. Most of the tuna we buy is caught at sea and quickly bled, gutted, and flash-frozen. While purists might be horrified, flash-frozen tuna that is properly handled and defrosted makes superb sushi and sashimi. Tuna can spoil very rapidly if not refrigerated quickly after being caught, as I learned to my dismay in one restaurant cooking experience. An excellent local fish market called the island restaurants to offer tuna just caught in a fishing tournament. I bought some of it, and the second patron to whom I served it complained of the taste being off; we immediately pulled it from the menu. It looked fine and smelled good, but the taste had a sharp bite to it. Unknown to the restaurants that accepted the tuna, the fish had been kept outside in hot sunlight for hours during a photography session before being iced. Some tuna have high levels of histidine, which high temperatures and certain bacteria convert into histamine, which in turn can cause scombroid poisoning (see page 367). The toxin is ordinarily not life-threatening, but it can make a person miserably sick for a day, and it did so to all the patrons who ate it that night in island

restaurants. The moral is, Always check that sport fishermen who offer you their catch have handled it properly.

Storage and Preparation: The preceding anecdote shows how important the proper handling of fish is at every step between harvesting and cooking. Thus you will perhaps understand why I take a cooler with ice along with me when I go to buy fish if I know that I might be delayed at all getting the fish home to the refrigerator. I put tuna in a non-aluminum-lined pan after wrapping it in butcher's paper, and I completely cover it with ice or ice packs, making sure that no melting water from the ice can come in contact with the flesh of the fish. If you have a piece of tuna with the dark red hemoglobin muscle meat attached, you may want to remove it before storing the fish; this meat is perfectly edible, and you may or may not like its richer, stronger flavor, which can be somewhat bitter when cooked. I typically cook fish the same day I bring it home, but with proper storage you can, if necessary, keep fresh tuna up to 24 hours before cooking.

Some recipes recommend soaking dark-fleshed strong tuna for 1 hour in the refrigerator in a saltwater solution of ¼ cup of noniodized salt per quart of water in order to remove excess blood and lighten the flesh. I have never thought it necessary to do this brining step. The real secret of

cooking tuna, to my mind, is to undercook it. Impeccably fresh raw tuna has a smooth, soft, luscious taste, and cooking tends to firm the flesh, lighten the color, and intensify the flavor. Overcooking makes tuna tough and tasteless, like sawdust. I like tuna cooked to "medium rare," with the surface of the cooked fish light-colored and firm and the inner flesh light pink and tender. Tuna can be cooked in the same way as swordfish and shark (try it as kabobs in *Grilled Seafood with Sweet-and-Hot Grape Sauce,* page 43), but remember to keep it slightly underdone.

Yields: Since most tuna is sold as skinless steaks and has no bones, a clear piece of tuna will have 100 percent yield. Unless you happen to like it, do not buy pieces of tuna with large sections of the very dark red muscle meat because it becomes waste as you remove it. Tuna is a rich fish; allow about 6 ounces per person.

SHARK

Of the known 250–300 species of shark scattered in salt waters around the world, about a dozen are commercially marketed. A good piece of shark can be very delicious and will cook up as firm white meat; for cooking purposes, treat it much as you would swordfish. Chunks of shark are adaptable for grilling and for adding to soups and stews. Some species are preferred to others as table fare. On the East Coast, *mako shark*

SPECIAL INFORMATION ABOUT

THE BIG FISH:

SWORDFISH, TUNA, AND SHARK

heads the list, followed by *porbeagle shark;* Florida is the center of the shark fishing industry. *Thresher* may be the most popular West Coast shark, but be aware that thresher sharks of Atlantic and Gulf waters are not the same species as the Pacific thresher, nor are they edible. Other edible shark are the *blacktip shark,* the *sandbar* or *brown shark* (often marketed as blacktip), *silky shark* (its flesh breaks apart much like the flesh of cod), *dogfish shark, angel shark, soupfin shark,* and *bonito shark.* California, the center of the West Coast shark industry, made a big push in the 1970s to increase sales of shark meat, and the amount of harvested thresher shark did rise dramatically into the 1980s, but then it began to decrease as overfishing depleted the supply. Sharks are slow reproducers, so overfishing can easily reduce the supply and make suppliers turn to less desirable species.

There are two complications involved in buying and cooking shark. Since the skin is tough and inedible, it has often been removed before the consumer sees it at the fish market, and with

the skin removed, it is very hard to distinguish the species of shark from looking at the flesh. Thus one is very dependent on the reliability of the fish market. The second complication is tied to the anatomy of the shark. Like rays and skates, sharks are cartilaginous fish lacking a urinary tract. Urea is carried in a shark's blood and body tissue, and is expelled through the skin by osmosis. When a shark is killed, there is urea in the system, and if the shark is not properly and immediately bled, too much urea remains in the flesh and turns to ammonia within 24 hours. Even with the best handling, there can be a faint ammonia odor to shark flesh.

Buying: Shark is marketed in steaks, much like swordfish. Buy shark only from a very reputable dealer and check for an ammonia odor in the flesh before buying. Ask your market what species of shark you are buying. Each species seems to cook up differently, and by trial you can discover your own preferences and seek them for subsequent cooking. Often the skin has been removed from the

shark offered at your market; if not, you might want to ask the dealer to remove the skin because it can be very tough.

Storage and Preparation: Although the shelf life of fresh shark is often described in the industry as anywhere from 3–10 days, I cook shark as soon as I get it—that is, the same day. While waiting to cook it, I keep the fish in the coldest part of the refrigerator, covered with butcher's paper, and then with ice or ice packs, making sure that water from the melting ice does not come in contact with the flesh of the shark. If there is a trace of ammonia odor to the fish, you can soak it in a mixture of ice water and vinegar or fresh lemon juice, using enough ice water to cover the fish and 1 tablespoon of vinegar or lemon juice for each pound of fish; keep the soaking fish in the refrigerator for 4–5 hours.

Yields: Since there are no bones and shark is often marketed without its skin, the yield is 100 percent. Allow 6–8 ounces per person.

Grilled Swordfish with Briny Sautéed Eggplant (variations)

❖Use other flavored butters or a dipping sauce.

❖Speed up the cooking of the vegetables by covering the pan after they have browned.

❖Substitute *Portuguese Peas* (page 240) for the sautéed eggplant.

❖*Grilled Swordfish Marinated in Soy Sake:* In a small

saucepan, combine ½ cup soy sauce and ½ cup sake; stir in 1 teaspoon sugar, 1 tablespoon grated fresh ginger, and 1 tablespoon of chopped garlic, bring the mixture to a boil, and cook to reduce it slightly, then strain. Let the sauce cool, then pour it over the swordfish steaks and marinate them for 2 hours before grilling. Serve the grilled swordfish with sautéed cabbage or bok choy and Chinese noodles in place of the eggplant.

Roast Swordfish and Clams with Cherry Tomatoes and Olives

As I put the finishing touches on this cookbook in 1993, Tuscan cooking is being freshly celebrated in other cookbooks. This dish has Tuscan roots. In 1989 I visited the home of wine makers Patrizia and Walter Filiputti in the hills of Tuscany, Italy. Patrizia had driven out of her way that day to bring home a whole sea bass for dinner. Her aromatic treatment of that whole braised fish cooked with mussels and black olives inspired me to do a similar dish using swordfish and clams. Serve with crusty bread and a side dish of *Sautéed Corn* (page 325) or corn on the cob.

Alternative shellfish: other small clams, such as Manila clams, mussels

Alternative fish: steaks of tuna, shark, mahi mahi; thick fillets of firm-fleshed white fish, such as striped bass or snapper; or cleaned whole fish, such as sea bass or black bass

 1½ lb swordfish steak, 1½ inches thick
 ¼ cup virgin olive oil
 3 lb (about 18) topneck clams★
 16 pitted Mediterranean-style black olives
 8 or more large green olives with pimentos
 24 cherry tomatoes
 1 cup sliced sweet onions
 ¼ cup drained capers
 Small sprigs fresh thyme
 ¾ cup dry vermouth or white wine

 ★If topneck clams are not available, use 2 lb littleneck clams (about 20–24).

Remove the dark skin and any inner white membrane from the swordfish and cut the fish into 4 equal servings. Pour the oil into a large, nonaluminum-lined baking pan large enough to hold the fish and clams in one layer. (I use a 10 × 14-inch Pyrex or stainless pan.) Place the swordfish pieces in the pan and turn them in the oil until well coated. Scrub the clams to remove any sand or mud, discarding any that are open and do not close when handled. Place the clams around the pieces of swordfish. Add the black

and green olives and cherry tomatoes to the pan, spreading them around the fish and clams. Spread the onion slices over and between the other ingredients in the pan. Sprinkle the capers over all and tuck in the sprigs of fresh thyme. Add the vermouth or wine, place the pan in a preheated 475-degree oven, and cook for 20 minutes, or until the fish is opaque throughout and the clams have opened. Discard any clams that do not open. As soon as the pan is removed from the oven, pour off the cooking juices into a saucepan, bring the liquid to a boil, and cook for 4–5 minutes to reduce the amount and concentrate the flavor. Keep the pan of baked fish in a warm place while reducing the pan juices.

To serve, arrange on each of 4 serving plates or shallow, wide soup bowls a piece of swordfish, 4–5 clams, 2 green olives, 4 black olives, 6 cherry tomatoes, and some onion slices and capers. Spoon the reduced juices over all; if you are serving in soup bowls, you can increase the amount of juices with each serving.   SERVES 4

❖Substitute 12 plum tomatoes cut in half for the cherry tomatoes.

❖If you increase the recipe to serve more people and use a larger pan, use enough vermouth or wine to film the bottom of the pan; use red wine, if you like.

❖Add more olives and tomatoes.

❖Add sliced peppers or chopped hot peppers.

❖Use whole small shallots instead of sliced onions.

Swordfish with Mushrooms and Cream

When I was just beginning restaurant cooking on Nantucket, a master chef and caterer named Joe Hyde came for the first summer to tutor our staff in the fine art of surviving in this very demanding work. He showed us how to manage eighteen-hour workdays and seven-day workweeks, and while our own confidence and inventiveness developed, he shared his recipes so that we would have a reasonably complete menu. His swordfish cooked with mushrooms and butter and loads of cream quickly became a staple. I have dramatically reduced the butter and cream but have still retained the fabulous flavor of the original dish. The swordfish gently and quickly braises in

the sauce, becomes incredibly tender, and absorbs the compatible flavor of the mushrooms. I serve it with rice, wide noodles, *Spaetzle* (page 362), or tiny boiled potatoes and a crisp green salad.

Alternative fish: tuna, shark, marlin

1½ lb swordfish steaks
¾ lb mushrooms
2 Tb light olive oil or vegetable oil
2 Tb butter
Flour
3 Tb chopped shallots
½ cup dry vermouth or white wine
½ cup heavy cream
Juice of ½ lemon
Salt and freshly ground pepper
Paprika (optional)

Ask your fish market to cut the swordfish steaks ½ inch thick, or buy 1-inch-thick steaks and slice them in half. Cut the ½-inch steaks into 4 equal portions and refrigerate until ready to cook.

Wipe the mushrooms to remove any dirt particles. Leaving the stems on, lay the mushrooms on their sides and cut into slices that include both cap and stem. Set aside. (You will have about 4 cups sliced mushrooms.)

Swordfish with Mushrooms and Cream (continued)

When you are ready to cook, pat the swordfish dry and remove any dark skin and any white inner membrane. In a sauté pan (ideally a nonstick pan) large enough to hold the fish in one layer without crowding, heat 1 tablespoon of the oil and 1 tablespoon of the butter. Quickly dip both sides of the fish pieces in a plate of flour and shake off excess flour so that the fish will be only lightly coated. Place the swordfish in the pan and cook both sides just long enough to brown the fish lightly; it will not be cooked through. Remove the swordfish to a warm serving platter.

Heat the remaining tablespoon of oil and the remaining tablespoon of butter in the pan, stir in the shallots, and cook for 1 minute. Add the mushrooms and cook over medium heat until they lightly color while you stir up the brown bits in the bottom of the pan. Reduce the heat to low and cook the mushrooms for 4 minutes, or until they are wilted and begin to exude their juices.

Push the mushrooms to the sides of the pan, return the fish to the pan in one layer, and spoon the mushrooms over and around the fish. Add the vermouth or wine and boil the sauce for 1 minute. Add the cream and boil rapidly for 3–4 minutes, shaking the pan occasionally, to reduce and thicken the sauce. The mushroom juices and browned bits from the pan will give the sauce a lovely brown color. Season with lemon juice, salt and freshly ground pepper, and a sprinkling of paprika, if desired. Shake the pan to distribute the seasonings, remove the fish and sauce to the serving platter again, and serve.   SERVES 4

Swordfish with Portugaise Sauce

A comparatively dense-fleshed and oily fish such as swordfish benefits from a tomato-based sauce because the acidity of the tomatoes tempers the rich taste of the fish. The sauce can be made ahead and reheated just before serving. To carry out the theme, serve *Portuguese Peas* (page 240) as a side dish.

Alternative fish: tuna, shark, mahi mahi, bluefish, mackerel, amberjack, monkfish, or fillets of other firm-fleshed white fish

1½ lb swordfish steaks

PORTUGAISE SAUCE

3 Tb olive oil
1 cup scallions, cut into ½-inch
    lengths
1 tsp chopped hot peppers or dash
    of hot pepper sauce
2 tsp minced garlic
4 cups peeled, seeded, and chopped
    ripe tomatoes
2 Tb drained capers
1 Tb red wine vinegar
Saffron
1 bay leaf
2 whole cloves
½ tsp Worcestershire sauce
Salt and freshly ground pepper

To make the Portugaise Sauce: In a large sauté pan, heat the oil, add the scallions, and sauté them until they are lightly browned. Add the hot peppers or dash of hot pepper sauce and garlic, cook the mixture for 30 seconds, then add the tomatoes, capers, vinegar, a pinch of saffron, the bay leaf, cloves, Worcestershire sauce, and salt and freshly ground pepper to taste. Bring the sauce to a boil, lower the heat, cover, and cook for 5 minutes; then uncover the sauce and cook at a gentle roll for 30 minutes until it is thickened. Remove the cloves and bay leaf. Keep the sauce warm until ready to serve, or cool and reheat later.

MAKES ABOUT 2 CUPS

4 Tb butter
Flour
Lemon wedges

Ask your fish market to cut the swordfish steaks ½ inch thick, or buy 1-inch-thick steaks and slice them in half. Cut the ½-inch-thick steaks into 4 equal portions and refrigerate until ready to cook.

Make the Portugaise sauce and keep warm.

Trim any dark skin and any white inner membrane off the swordfish. In a sauté pan large enough to hold the fish in one layer without crowding (or cooking in two pans or in batches in one pan), heat the butter. When the butter is hot, quickly dust the swordfish pieces with flour, shaking off any excess, place them in the pan and sauté for 3–4 minutes; then turn and sauté the pieces for another 3–4 minutes, or until the fish is just cooked through and browned.

To serve: Place a few spoonfuls of sauce on each serving plate and top with a piece of sautéed fish. Top the fish with another spoonful of sauce, garnish with lemon wedges, and serve.   SERVES 4

❖Substitute vegetable oil or a combination of butter and oil for the cooking butter.

❖*Appetizer Swordfish Portugaise:* Slice the swordfish ¾ inch thick and then cut it into 1–1½-inch pieces. Flour the pieces and sauté as above until cooked through. Serve the pieces as a hot appetizer, with the sauce as a dipping sauce, or put the sautéed pieces in a baking dish, pour the sauce over the fish, let cool, and serve as a cold appetizer.   SERVES 8

❖For thicker fillets, sauté until browned on each side, add the sauce, cover the pan, and braise the fish in the sauce until the fish is just cooked through.

Michael McSweeny's Grilled Ahi (Tuna) Steaks with Macadamia Pesto

Michael McSweeny brought the background of Italian culinary training to the position of executive chef at the Poipu Bay Resort in Kauai, where he treasured the fresh fish available from Hawaiian waters. The tuna of this stuffed-tuna dish is cooked rare, and the pink-red of the rare tuna contrasts handsomely with the green pesto stuffing. Michael serves this dish with large triangles of roasted red, yellow, and green peppers seasoned with the best olive oil, cracked pepper, and fresh lime juice. In Hawaii it is customary to serve fish with sticky rice, but Michael often serves it with soft polenta and Asiago cheese, or a firm polenta that he brushes with olive oil and grills. A food processor and a pastry bag make the preparation of this dish much easier.

Four 5–7-oz thick yellowfin tuna steaks

MACADAMIA PESTO

2 cloves garlic
⅓ cup pickled ginger★
½ cup cilantro leaves
¾ cup toasted macadamia nuts (see *To Toast Pine Nuts,* page 301)
1 Tb sesame oil
½ cup olive oil
2 oz Asiago cheese

Olive oil
Lime wedges

★Pickled ginger is available by the jar in Asian food stores and in many supermarkets. You can substitute fresh peeled ginger, but you must dice it very fine so that it does not turn into a mass of strings in the food processor.

Make a stuffing pocket in each tuna steak by inserting a boning knife through the side of the steak into the center, and while keeping the incision cut narrow on the outside, move the knife back and forth inside the steak to create a pocket; be careful not to make additional holes in the exterior of the fish as you maneuver the knife to make the pockets. Refrigerate the steaks while you make the pesto stuffing.

To make the macadamia pesto stuffing: Peel the garlic and put it in the bowl of a food processor fitted with a steel blade. Rough-chop the garlic, then add the ginger, cilantro, and macadamia nuts, and process until the ingredients are well blended. With the motor running, gradually drizzle in the sesame oil and olive oil, then add the cheese.

Put the pesto mixture into a pastry bag and squeeze one-quarter of the pesto into the cavity of each steak; each steak should hold about 2 ounces of pesto. Brush the tuna steaks on both sides with olive oil and place them on the oiled grill rack over a preheated grill. Grill on one side until the outer part of the tuna steaks are opaque but the center around the pocket of pesto is still pink or red, to your preference. Turn the steaks and grill the other side until it too is opaque on the outside but pink or red toward the center. Remove the steaks to warm serving plates, cut each serving into slices, and fan the slices out on the plate. Serve with lime wedges.   SERVES 4

Grilled Tuna with Wild Rice and Scallion Salad

Sun-dried tomatoes add a rich earthy flavor to this fish-and-salad combination. The salad can be prepared in advance, even a day earlier, refrigerated, and served cold. All that is left to do at serving time is to whisk together a vinaigrette to dress the tuna and to grill the fish. It also works well to cook the two rices shortly before serving, let them cool slightly, combine them with the other salad ingredients, and serve the salad at room temperature. Arrange the salad on serving plates just before grilling the fish.

Alternative fish: swordfish, marlin, shark

GRILLED TUNA

2 Tb chopped softened sun-dried tomatoes
  (see *To soften sun-dried tomatoes*,
  page 218)
¼ cup olive oil
2 Tb fresh lemon juice
Salt and freshly ground pepper
Four 6-oz tuna steaks, ¾–1 inch thick
¼ cup vegetable oil

Washed lettuce leaves
½ lb feta cheese (optional)
Lemon wedges

WILD RICE AND SCALLION SALAD

½ cup toasted pine nuts★
5 cups cooked long-grain white rice
    or brown rice
3 cups cooked wild rice
½ cup chopped softened sun-dried
    tomatoes (see *To soften sun-dried
    tomatoes*, page 218)
2–2½ cups chopped scallions
¾ cup chopped parsley
⅓ cup chopped mint
1–2 tsp chopped fresh thyme
4 Tb fresh lemon juice
Salt and freshly ground pepper
6 Tb virgin olive oil

★*To Toast Pine Nuts:* Toast the pine
nuts by spreading them in one layer in
a nonstick sauté pan. Heat the pan and
let the nuts brown over medium heat,
shaking the pan frequently so that the
nuts brown lightly on all sides.
Remove the nuts from the pan and set
aside.

To make the Wild Rice and Scallion Salad: In a
large bowl, combine the white or brown
rice, wild rice, sun-dried tomatoes, scallions,
parsley, mint, thyme, and pine nuts. In a
small bowl, combine the lemon juice and 1
teaspoon salt, and whisk in the olive oil.
Pour this dressing over the salad, mix well,
and season with salt and freshly ground pepper. If you are not serving shortly, cover and
refrigerate until ready to serve.

MAKES 8 CUPS,

EASILY ENOUGH TO SERVE 8–10 PEOPLE

Prepare the wild rice and scallion salad.

To grill the tuna: In a small bowl, purée the softened sun-dried tomatoes with the olive oil and whisk
in the lemon juice. Season the mixture with salt and
freshly ground pepper, and set this vinaigrette dressing aside. Brush the tuna on both sides with the vegetable oil and season the fish with salt and freshly
ground pepper. Place the tuna on an oiled grill rack
over a hot fire and cook for 3–4 minutes, then turn
and grill the other side for 3–4 minutes. The center
should be slightly pink, so watch carefully and do
not overcook. (To test, bend one of the steaks
enough to make the meat separate; the center
should be barely cooked, slightly translucent rather
than opaque.)

To serve: Place lettuce leaves on one side of each
serving plate, spoon the wild rice and scallion salad on
top, and, if desired, place a slice of feta cheese next to
the salad or sprinkle crumbled feta cheese over the
salad. Place a piece of grilled tuna on each plate, drizzle the reserved vinaigrette dressing over the fish, garnish with lemon wedges, and serve. SERVES 4

❖*To broil the tuna:* Brush the fish with vegetable
oil, season it with salt and pepper, and place under a
preheated broiler for 4–5 minutes on each side.

Main Course
Pasta and Rice
Dishes

Smoked Bluefish with Pasta

When I want to keep meals simple—for example, when I am more or less on vacation on Nantucket—I frequently think of using pasta as a main course. Bluefish, fresh or smoked, is readily available; tomatoes, basil, and parsley are a step away in the garden ready for picking; together they dress pasta into a lovely main dish. This recipe can also be used with leftover fish, especially what may be left from a meal of grilled fish.

Alternative fish: smoked haddock, cod, leftover cooked fish

¾ lb smoked bluefish
5 Tb olive oil
3 cups peeled, seeded, and chopped tomatoes
2 tsp minced garlic
1 lb pasta
⅓ cup shredded fresh basil
2 Tb chopped fresh parsley
Salt and freshly ground pepper
6 strips cooked, drained, and crumbled bacon
    (optional)
Freshly grated Parmesan cheese (optional)

Remove the skin, any bones, and any dark meat from the bluefish, flake the fish with a fork, and set the flaked fish aside.

Opposite: Marian prepares Paella *(page 315).*

In a sauté pan, heat 2 tablespoons of the oil, add the tomatoes and garlic, and cook over medium-high heat for 4–5 minutes.

Meanwhile, bring a large pot of water to a boil, drop in the pasta, and cook until just tender, or al dente.

In a second sauté pan, heat the remaining 3 tablespoons of oil, add the flaked bluefish, and cook, tossing and turning the fish frequently, until the fish is lightly colored on all sides. Keep the fish warm, as necessary, until the rest of the dish is ready to be assembled.

Drain the pasta in a colander, then return it to the pot it cooked in. Stir the basil and parsley into the tomatoes. If the tomatoes have released a great deal of liquid as they cooked, drain off most of it. Pour the tomato mixture over the pasta, then pour the sautéed bluefish over all. Season with salt and freshly ground pepper, and toss all together. Taste again for seasoning. Sprinkle the top of the pasta, if desired, with bacon bits and/or Parmesan cheese. SERVES 4

❖*Fresh Bluefish with Pasta:* Substitute cooked fresh bluefish, preferably broiled or grilled fish, for smoked bluefish, increasing the amount of fish to 1–1¼ pounds; or use a comparable amount of any other leftover unsmoked fish.

❖Add chopped onions or shallots; sauté them in olive oil for 2–3 minutes before adding the tomatoes to the pan to sauté.

❖Omit the bacon; substitute cubes of smoked ham or slices of smoked sausage.

Clams, Garlic, Parsley, and Angel Hair Pasta

Light, delicate angel hair pasta makes a perfect partner for small sweet clams. Garlic adds a pungent fragrance to the dish, and the parsley makes two contributions: a fresh herbal taste and a bit of bright color to offset the pale colors of the pasta and clams. I serve this with a mixed green salad of some of the stronger greens, such as arugula and chicory dressed with a mustard-garlic-flavored vinaigrette—a crisp, assertive contrast to the pasta dish. You can steam open the clams and reserve their meat and broth well in advance; and if you try the spaghetti squash variation in the notes after the main recipe, you can prepare the squash ahead as well.

Alternative shellfish: If littleneck clams or other small clams such as Manilas are not available, use larger clams such as cherrystones and cut the clam meats into small pieces.

3–4 lb (30–40) littleneck clams
1½ cups dry white wine
1 lb angel hair pasta
¼ cup olive oil
3–4 minced cloves garlic
¼ tsp hot pepper flakes
Juice of 1 lemon
½–¾ cup roughly chopped Italian parsley
Salt and freshly ground pepper

Scrub the clams to remove any mud or muck, discarding any clams that are open and do not close when handled. Place the clams in an 8-quart nonaluminum-lined pot, add the wine, cover, and bring to a boil. Steam the clams until they open. Smaller clams will take 2–4 minutes, larger clams 5–7 minutes; if the clams are of mixed sizes, remove the smaller clams as they open and give the larger ones a few more minutes. Discard any clams that do not open. Lift the clams with tongs to a colander set over a shallow bowl to catch any juices. Carefully pour the clam cooking broth into a bowl, leaving behind the last bit of broth containing any sand or debris, set the bowl of broth aside, and clean out the pot. Remove the meats from the clams, discarding the shells, and place the meats in a bowl. Cover them with a little cooking

broth and set aside. You can do this preparation ahead, cover the bowls with plastic wrap, and refrigerate. (You will have about 1½ cups clam meats and about 1¼ cups broth.)

Shortly before serving, bring a large pot of salted water to a boil, drop in the angel hair pasta, and cook 8–10 minutes, or until it is just tender, or al dente. While the pasta is cooking, heat the oil in a large saucepan or pot, stir in the garlic, and cook about 1 minute until the garlic is golden but not brown. Add the hot pepper flakes and the clam broth, and bring the mixture to a boil. Add the lemon juice, parsley, and clam meats with their juices and cook just until the mixture is heated through. (Be careful not to boil the clams, or they will become tough.) Drain the pasta in a colander and shake it well to remove all the excess moisture. Pour the drained pasta into the pan with the clam mixture, fold all together, and season with salt and plenty of freshly ground pepper.

SERVES 4

❖Adjust the amount of garlic to your taste.

❖Substitute linguine or spaghetti for the angel hair pasta.

❖Add 1–2 cups peeled, seeded, and chopped tomatoes; stir them into the oil after the garlic has cooked.

❖Shuck the clams rather than steam them open. Reserve their juices in a separate bowl and add enough wine to the juices to make 1½ cups liquid. Heat the olive oil and gently cook the clam meats (whole, if small; chopped, if large) for 1–2 minutes, remove them to a bowl, add the garlic and hot pepper flakes, and proceed as above.

❖Add sliced rings of squid to the sauce. Heat the oil, cook the squid rings quickly in the oil, add the garlic, and proceed as above.

❖Substitute mussels for the clams.

❖*With Spaghetti Squash:* Make the same dish using spaghetti squash in place of pasta. Prick a large spaghetti squash in several places with a long-tined fork to prevent the squash skin from bursting in the hot oven. Bake the squash in a preheated 350-degree oven for 40 minutes to 1½ hours until the flesh is tender; or boil the squash in a large pot with enough water to cover for 20–30 minutes. Remove the squash from the oven or pot and let it cool enough to handle. Split the squash lengthwise and remove the seeds and stringy portion. With a fork, "comb" the squash flesh, and the "spaghetti" will pull out in long strands. This preparation can be done well ahead. Just before serving, reheat the long strands of squash in olive oil, butter, or in a bit of water; or reheat it by steaming it briefly, then fold the squash into the clam mixture.

September Pasta with Finnan Haddie

The smoky taste of creamy finnan haddie appeals to me at the very end of summer. Evenings are cool. There is a hint of fall in the air. But days are still warm, and there are still fresh tomatoes and basil in the garden for this recipe.

> 1½-lb side of finnan haddie
> 2 cups light cream
> 1 large crushed clove garlic
> 1 lb linguine
> 2 Tb butter
> 3–4 cups peeled, seeded, and chopped tomatoes, drained
> ¾ cup sliced basil leaves
> ¾ cup freshly grated Parmesan cheese
> Salt and freshly ground pepper

Cut the finnan haddie into 2-inch sections and rinse under cold running water for 5 minutes. Place the fish in a glass or stainless pan, cover with cold water, and refrigerate for 24 hours, changing the water three or four times.

Before cooking the fish, remove the skin and any bones, flake it into bite-size pieces, and set aside.

In a saucepan, combine the cream and garlic, and simmer until the cream is reduced almost by half. Remove the garlic, add the finnan haddie, and keep warm.

Bring 4 quarts of water to a boil in a large pot, drop in the linguine, and cook until it is done al dente. Drain it well and return it to the same pot.

While the linguine is cooking, heat the butter in a saucepan, stir in the tomatoes just to warm them through, and then stir in the basil.

Toss the drained pasta with ¼ cup of the cheese, fold in the cream-and-fish mixture, season with salt and freshly ground pepper, and toss again.

To serve, turn out the pasta-and-fish mixture onto a warm serving platter, top it with the tomato mixture, sprinkle some of the remaining cheese over the dish, and pass the rest of the cheese.   SERVES 6

❖If fresh tomatoes are not available, use well-drained and seeded canned plum tomatoes or substitute sliced and sautéed red and green peppers.

Crabmeat and Cabbage Pasta Crêpes with a Fresh Marinara Sauce

Marie Caratelli showed me how to make pasta crêpes as her Italian mother taught her. They are easy to make without a pasta maker, are thin and light, can be made ahead, and are fun to prepare. Crabmeat and cabbage are a happy partnership, and in this dish they make a very light and delicious casserole. The dish is economical because 1 pound of crabmeat wrapped in the crêpes stretches to feed 8–10 persons, and it is perfect for a buffet. The sauce is made with fresh garden tomatoes, but in the winter I use half fresh market tomatoes for texture and half drained, peeled, and canned Italian plum tomatoes for color and flavor. The crêpe batter must be made two hours before cooking so that the batter can rest, and other components of the dish can be prepared in advance as well. The finished dish can be assembled just before baking, or it can be assembled ahead and refrigerated until you are ready to cook. A food processor is useful in this preparation.

Alternative fish and shellfish: cooked salmon or Arctic char, or other cooked, firm-fleshed white fish; cooked lobster or shrimp or a combination of cooked fish and shellfish

PASTA CRÊPES

> 1 cup flour
> 4 eggs
> 1 cup milk
> ⅓ cup water
> 1 tsp salt
> Vegetable oil to coat frying pan

*Crabmeat and Cabbage Pasta Crêpes with a
Fresh Marinara Sauce (continued)*

MARINARA SAUCE

2 Tb olive oil
1 cup chopped onions
⅓ cup chopped carrots
1–2 tsp minced garlic (optional)
5 cups peeled, seeded, and chopped
    tomatoes
1½ cups tomato juice
Salt and freshly ground pepper
1 Tb chopped fresh oregano or 1 tsp
    dried
1 Tb chopped fresh basil or 1 tsp
    dried
¼ cup chopped fresh parsley

To make the Marinara Sauce: In a nonaluminum-lined, 4-quart saucepan heat the oil, add the onions and carrots, and cook for 4–5 minutes, or until the vegetables are wilted. Add the garlic (if you are using it) and the tomatoes, bring the mixture to a boil, reduce the heat, and cook gently, covered, for 5 minutes. Partially uncover the pan, stir, and cook for 10 minutes more. Remove the mixture to the bowl of a food processor and process with a pulse motion just enough to make a slightly chunky purée, or put the mixture through a food mill to get the same consistency. Return the mixture to the pot, add the tomato juice, 1 teaspoon salt, freshly ground pepper to taste, and the oregano and basil. Simmer, partially covered, for 20 minutes. Stir in the parsley, season again as needed with salt and pepper, and set aside.

MAKES A GENEROUS 4 CUPS

CRAB-AND-CABBAGE MIXTURE

1 lb cooked crabmeat
3 Tb butter or vegetable oil
8 cups thinly sliced cabbage
½ cup sour cream
Salt and freshly ground pepper

To make the pasta crêpes: Put the flour, eggs, milk, water, and salt into the bowl of a food processor fitted with a steel blade and process to a very smooth emulsion. Remove the mixture to a bowl, cover, and refrigerate for 2 hours. While the crêpe batter is resting, prepare the other ingredients.

To cook the crêpes: Rub a small, 6-inch (preferably nonstick) frying pan with vegetable oil and heat the pan until it just begins to smoke. Using a ¼-cup measure, pour slightly less than ¼ cup of batter into the pan, tilt the pan in all directions to distribute the batter evenly, cook until the batter is just set, then flip the crêpe over or turn it over with a flexible spatula; cook each side less than a minute, and do not let the crêpe brown. Slide the crêpe out of the pan onto a waxed-paper-lined baking sheet and continue cooking more crêpes, re-oiling the pan as necessary. You should be able to fit 3 cooked crêpes across a standard baking sheet. Top each layer of cooked crêpes on the baking sheet with another layer of waxed paper, and continue the layering until you are done. Allow the crêpes to cool, cover the baking sheet with plastic wrap, and refrigerate until ready to use. (If you want to make the crêpes ahead, you can remove them from the baking sheet and store them in one single pile. Once the crêpes are cooled, stack with waxed paper between them, place the pile in a plastic bag, and store in the refrigerator.) (Makes 18–20 crêpes)

Prepare the marinara sauce and set aside.

To make the crab-and-cabbage mixture: If it is moist, drain the crabmeat and remove any bits of shell or cartilage; refrigerate until ready to cook. In a wide, high-sided sauté pan, heat 2 tablespoons of the butter or oil, add the cabbage, and stir to coat the cabbage with the butter. Cover the pan and cook over low heat, stirring occasionally, about 10 minutes, or until the cabbage is tender. Uncover and cook for 1–2 minutes to evaporate any excess moisture in the pan, then remove the cooked cabbage to a large bowl. (Makes about 3 cups cooked cabbage) Add the remaining tablespoon of butter or oil to the pan, then add the crabmeat and cook for 1–2 minutes to evaporate any excess moisture. Spoon the crab over the cooked cabbage, mix gently, fold in the sour cream, and season with salt and freshly ground pepper. (Makes about 5 cups)

To assemble: Spoon a thin layer of the marinara sauce across the bottom of a 10 × 15-inch baking dish or two smaller dishes. Spoon about ¼ cup of the crab-and-cabbage filling across the center of each crêpe, roll the crêpe up, and place it seam side down in the baking dish. If you are using one large dish, arrange the crêpes in three rows across the dish and cover with the remaining marinara sauce. Cover the dish with aluminum foil and bake in a preheated 350-degree oven until hot and bubbly, about 20–30 minutes.   SERVES 8–10 WITH 2 CRÊPES PER PERSON

❖Make the filling of cabbage and sliced leeks or other cooked greens to combine with the crabmeat.

❖Add 1½ cups of a combination of grated mozzarella cheese and freshly grated Parmesan cheese to the top of the dish before baking.

❖*Crab and Cabbage Strudel:* Prepare the crab-and-cabbage mixture as above. Replace the pasta crêpes with 10 sheets of store-bought filo dough. Melt 8 tablespoons butter and have ⅓ cup fine dried bread crumbs or cracker crumbs prepared and set aside. Place a sheet of filo dough on a damp towel. Brush the top of the sheet with melted butter and sprinkle it lightly with crumbs. Place another sheet of filo dough on top and repeat the butter-and-crumb application. Continue the procedure until the filo dough is five layers thick. Then spread half of the crab-cabbage mixture across the narrow end of the top layer of filo, about 4 inches in from the end and leaving a 1½-inch border on each side. Form the filling into a rough rectangle about 1 inch high and 4 inches wide. As if wrapping a package, fold the side borders over the filling, and then fold the 4-inch border at the end over the filling. Using the towel, roll the filo-covered filling down the length of the filo sheet. Set the rolled strudel on a buttered baking sheet, seam side down. Repeat the procedure for the second strudel, using the remaining 5 sheets of filo and the other half of the filling. Brush both strudels with melted butter and either cover and refrigerate until ready to bake, or bake in a preheated 375-degree oven for 25–30 minutes, or until the strudels are crisp and golden brown. Serve with the marinara sauce, if desired, or with sour cream.   SERVES 8

Lobster Tetrazzini

This dish is a takeoff on Chicken Tetrazzini, which was named for a famous coloratura soprano who loved pasta. Preparing it offers the perfect opportunity to pull out of the freezer the lobster stock you made from past lobster shells and cleverly stored away. If you forgot to do that, you can use a fish broth, shrimp broth, or even chicken broth.

Alternative shellfish: Use a combination of cooked shellfish, such as scallops, lump crabmeat, squid, abalone.

1½ lb cooked lobster meat
3 Tb butter
1 Tb light olive or vegetable oil
½ lb sliced mushroom caps
3 Tb flour
2 cups lobster stock or fish, shrimp, or chicken broth
1 cup heavy cream
¼ cup sherry
Nutmeg
Salt and freshly ground pepper
¾ lb spaghetti
⅓ cup freshly grated Parmesan cheese (optional)
Sliced black olives (optional)

Cut the lobster into bite-size pieces and set aside.

In a saucepan, heat 1 tablespoon of the butter and the olive or vegetable oil, add the mushrooms, and cook for 4–5 minutes, or until the mushrooms are wilted and lightly colored. Remove the mushrooms to a bowl and keep them warm.

Heat the remaining 2 tablespoons of butter in the saucepan, stir in the flour, and cook for 2 minutes. Remove the pan from the heat and beat the lobster stock or broth into the slightly cooked flour mixture; return the pan to the heat and continue whisking over low heat until the mixture is smooth and thickened. Add the cream and sherry, and cook for 5 minutes, stirring, then season with a pinch of nutmeg, salt, and freshly ground pepper.

Lobster Tetrazzini (continued)

While the lobster sauce is cooking, bring a pot of water to a boil, drop in the spaghetti, and cook until the pasta is just tender, or al dente. Drain the spaghetti well, return it to the pot, add the grated cheese (if you are using it), and toss well. Add the mushrooms and the lobster meat to the lobster sauce and cook just until heated through.

Arrange the spaghetti on a warm serving platter, spoon the lobster-and-mushroom mixture on top, garnish with the olives, if desired, and serve.   SERVES 4

Pasta Timbales of Lobster, Leeks, and Prosciutto

While working with me one summer, Leslie Mackie, a talented chef, created a dish composed of fresh pasta squares shaped into timbales using 10-ounce ovenproof glass molds. We experimented with several kinds of fillings, but the following combination of lobster and leeks was the most popular. As fancy as this dish seems, it becomes very manageable with advance preparation. If you cook your own lobsters, do it the day before. The leeks can be cooked the day before also. The whole dish can be assembled the morning of the day it is served. You do need eight 10-ounce baking dishes; I use the Pyrex ones available in most hardware stores.

Alternative shellfish: cooked crabmeat, cooked shrimp
Alternative fish: cooked salmon, cooked sable, or experiment with a fish of your choice

    4 Tb butter
    6 cups chopped leeks
    Salt and freshly ground pepper
    Eight 8 × 8-inch squares fresh pasta★
    1 egg
    1 cup ricotta cheese
    2 cups cooked lobster meat, cut into
        bite-size pieces
    ½ cup thinly sliced prosciutto, cut into
        small strips
    1 Tb fresh lemon juice
    2 Tb melted butter
    Lemon wedges

★Many pasta shops will sell fresh pasta in sheets or cut to order; you will need 1 pound of pasta sheets. Ask the pasta shop to roll the pasta to the thickness of thin lasagna. See the variation below to substitute store-bought dry lasagna for the fresh pasta.

With 1 tablespoon of the butter, butter the insides of eight 10-ounce ovenproof baking dishes. Set aside.

In a high-sided sauté pan, heat the remaining 3 tablespoons of butter, add the leeks, and cook, covered, over low heat, stirring occasionally, until the leeks are wilted and tender, about 8–10 minutes. Season with salt and freshly ground pepper, and set aside to cool. (Makes about 3½–4 cups)

Bring a pot of water to a boil, drop in the squares of pasta, and cook for 3–4 minutes, or until just al dente. Drain the pasta, run it under cold water to stop the cooking action, drain again, lay it on clean towels, and pat dry. Place a pasta square in each of the baking dishes, pressing it gently to fit against the sides of the dish. The pasta square will be large enough to hang over the rim of the dish.

In a large bowl, beat the egg and stir in the ricotta cheese. Add the leeks, lobster, prosciutto, and lemon juice, and mix all together. Season the mixture with salt and freshly ground pepper. Divide the mixture evenly among the 8 pasta-lined dishes. Carefully fold the excess pasta over the filling mixture, trimming off any unneeded pasta with sharp scissors, and brush the top of the pasta with the melted butter. Cover and refrigerate until shortly before serving.

Place the timbales in a preheated 500-degree oven and bake for 15 minutes, or until the tops are crisp and browning. The very high heat will result in a crisp top

and a luscious creamy filling. Remove from the oven and turn the timbales upside down on a serving plate. Serve plain with lemon wedges or with a flavored sour cream or with *Tomato-Basil Butter Sauce* (page 232) or with *Fresh Tomato Sauce* (page 364).   SERVES 8

❖If you lack your own homemade pasta or fresh store-bought pasta, you can use packaged lasagna. You will need twenty-four 8-inch-long pieces. Cook the lasagna according to the package instructions, drain, run under cold water, drain again, lay on clean towels, and pat dry. Cut the curly edge off the lasagna. Use 3 pieces of lasagna for each baking dish. Put the first piece into the dish, molding it against the bottom and sides with one end hanging over the rim. Turn the dish a little and repeat with the second strip of lasagna, and again with the third strip. With a bit of trial and error you will see how much to overlap the 3 strips so that they completely cover the bottom and sides of the dish. Fill the

timbales as above, fold over the extra lasagna to cover the filling, trimming off any excess, brush the top with melted butter, and bake and serve as above.

❖Substitute chopped cooked cabbage or spinach or caramelized onions or other greens and vegetables for the leeks.

❖Substitute vegetable or olive oil, or a combination of both, for the melted butter.

Peppers, Pasta, and Lobster

While anyone would be happy to have this dish served as a main course, accompanied perhaps by a side dish of steamed broccoli flowerets, anyone would be equally pleased to find this dish before them as the first course of a fine dinner party.

Peppers, Pasta, and Lobster (continued)

2 Tb olive oil
1 red pepper, cut into thin lengthwise strips
1 green pepper, cut into thin lengthwise strips
1 tsp chopped fresh hot peppers
1 Tb minced softened sun-dried tomatoes
    (see *To soften sun-dried tomatoes,*
    page 218), plus 2 tsp finely sliced
    softened sun-dried tomatoes (optional)
1 cup heavy cream
1 slightly crushed clove garlic
3 Tb butter
1 Tb chopped shallots
½ lb cooked lobster meat
½ lb rotelle (corkscrew pasta)
¼ cup freshly grated Parmesan cheese
    (optional)
¼ cup shredded basil leaves, plus 4 whole
    basil leaves
Freshly ground pepper

In a sauté pan, heat the olive oil, add the red and green pepper strips, and cook for 2–3 minutes, or just until they have softened. Add the hot peppers and the minced sun-dried tomatoes, if desired; set aside, but keep warm.

Place the cream and garlic in a small saucepan, bring the cream to a simmer, and cook at a simmer until the liquid is reduced to ¾ cup. Remove and discard the garlic clove and keep the cream warm.

In a sauté pan, heat the butter, stir in the shallots, and cook for 1 minute; then add the lobster meat and cook for 5–6 minutes, or until the lobster meat is heated through.

While the lobster is cooking, bring a pot of salted water to a boil, drop in the rotelle, and cook just until it is tender, or al dente. Drain it well in a colander and return the drained pasta to the pot it was cooked in. Add the Parmesan cheese (if you are using it) to the pasta and toss them together; pour the warm garlic-cream over the pasta and toss again. Add the red and green pepper strips, hot peppers, lobster meat, shredded basil, and sliced sun-dried tomatoes, if desired. Toss once more. Season the pasta and lobster with freshly ground pepper. Divide equally among 4 warm serving plates and garnish with the basil leaves. Serve with additional grated Parmesan cheese, if you like.

SERVES 4

Red Pepper Pesto Pasta

When the basil is lush and peppers have turned red on the vine in our garden at summer's end, this dish is a favorite at our house. Serve it either hot or at room temperature, as a course by itself, or as a side dish for grilled, broiled, or sautéed fish or shellfish. You will need a food processor or blender for this recipe. The peppers and pesto can be prepared well in advance and combined with the pasta just before serving, or you can prepare the complete dish, refrigerate it, and bring it back to room temperature before serving. When you have used up all the red peppers in your garden, substitute pimentos in this dish.

3 large red peppers

PESTO

2 tsp minced garlic
Salt and freshly ground pepper
2 cups packed basil leaves
1–2 Tb parsley leaves
½ cup peeled and chopped red peppers (from
    the prepared 3 peppers above)
½ cup olive oil

1 lb spaghetti
½ cup freshly grated Parmesan cheese
Salt and freshly ground pepper

To prepare the peppers: Follow instructions under *To peel peppers* (page 360). Cut the peeled pepper flesh lengthwise into strips and cut the strips into small pieces. (Makes about 1½ cups chopped peppers) Reserve ½ cup of the peppers for the pesto and set the remainder aside for final assembly of the dish.

To make the pesto: Mash the garlic and ½ teaspoon salt together to make a purée. Place the garlic-salt purée in the bowl of a food processor fitted with the steel blade, and add the basil, parsley, and the reserved ½ cup peeled and chopped peppers. Process until the mixture has a paste-like consistency, scraping down the sides of the bowl with a spatula, if necessary. With the motor running, add the oil in a slow stream, thickening the mixture. Remove the pesto to a small bowl. (Makes about 1 cup)

To assemble the dish: Shortly before serving, bring a

large pot of water to a boil, drop in the spaghetti, and cook until just tender, or al dente. Drain the spaghetti well in a colander, return it to the pot, and add the pesto and the remaining cup of chopped peppers. Stir all together, season with salt and freshly ground pepper, and stir in the cheese or pass it separately.   SERVES 4–6

Peas and Pasta
with Pancetta, Prosciutto, Parsley,
and Parmesan

For awesome alliteration and a superb main course, how about serving this pasta with, or as a prelude to, a piece of perfect *pesce?*

3 cups sugar snap peas
3 oz pancetta, sliced ¼ inch thick★
6 oz thinly sliced prosciutto (or ham)★
8 oz pappardelle (wide Italian egg noodles) or
    pasta bows
4 Tb olive oil
1 minced onion
⅓ cup chopped parsley
Salt and freshly ground pepper
Freshly grated Parmesan cheese

★Pancetta is an Italian cured bacon available in most supermarket delicatessen sections or in Italian markets. Prosciutto is the Italian word for ham. The generic term "prosciutto" used in this country refers to raw air-dried ham, or prosciutto crudo in Italian. Prosciutto cotto is cooked Italian ham. Use air-dried or cooked Italian ham, a combination of both, Westphalian ham, or a good smoked ham in this recipe.

Snap the stems of the peas and pull the attached strings down the sides of each pea. Cut the peas diagonally into 2 or 3 pieces each. (Makes a generous 2 cups) Cut the pancetta into ½-inch pieces. Cut the prosciutto into pieces about ½ inch × 1½ inches.

Bring a large pot of water to a boil, add a pinch of salt, and drop in the pasta. Cook about 7 minutes, or until it is just al dente. While the pasta is cooking, heat 2 tablespoons of the oil in a sauté pan. Add the pancetta and cook for about 1 minute. Add the prosciutto and

cook for 1 minute more. Add the onion and parsley, and cook for 2 minutes. Add the peas, reduce the heat, and cook for 4 minutes, stirring frequently.

Drain the pasta, add the remaining 2 tablespoons of oil, and toss. Add the meat-and-pea mixture to the pasta, toss together, season with salt and freshly ground pepper, sprinkle with the cheese, and serve.   SERVES 4

❖Add shelled fresh garden peas with the sugar snap peas.

Grilled Salmon and
Asparagus with Pasta

Nutritionists will cheer the combination of protein, vegetables, and carbohydrates here in one dish, but you will cheer the flavor and bright color of it, and the ease of preparation. Since the salmon is thinly sliced, this is a good dish for the tail end of a fillet. You can slice the salmon, blanch and roll-cut the asparagus well ahead, and refrigerate until ready for final cooking and serving.

Alternative fish: bass, haddock, sturgeon, and other firm-fleshed fish

1-lb salmon fillet
1½ lb asparagus
6 Tb butter
2–3 Tb fresh lemon juice
1 lb linguine
Olive oil
Salt and freshly ground pepper
Lemon wedges

Remove the skin and any bones from the salmon and cut the fillet on the diagonal into ¼-inch-wide slices. Set the slices aside.

Peel the asparagus. Insert a sharp paring knife under the skin at the base and work it up toward the tip, making the cut shallower as the skin becomes thinner. Taper the cut off completely about 2–3 inches below the tip. You can also use a vegetable peeler. Take a large pan that is wide enough to hold the asparagus lying down, fill it three-quarters full of water, and bring to a boil. Drop the asparagus into the water and cook at a rapid boil for 2–3 minutes, or until they are just barely tender. Drain immediately

Grilled Salmon and Asparagus with Pasta (continued)

and run the asparagus under cold water to stop the cooking action. Drain again and pat dry.

Roll-cut the asparagus following the instructions in the recipe for *Asparagus Chinois* (page 319).

Refrigerate both the sliced salmon and the roll-cut asparagus for later cooking, if you like.

Before you are ready to serve, melt the butter in a small saucepan and stir in the lemon juice.

Bring a large pot of water to a boil, drop in the linguine, and cook until just tender, or al dente. Drain and toss with just enough olive oil to give it a light coating; season with salt and freshly ground pepper.

Meanwhile, as the pasta is cooking, brush two baking sheets with the lemon butter. Lay out the salmon slices on one sheet and brush the top side of the slices with lemon butter. Toss the asparagus pieces with the remaining lemon butter and spread on the second sheet. Place the asparagus under a preheated broiler and broil for 4–5 minutes, turning the asparagus once or twice. Then place the salmon under the broiler and broil for 2 minutes.

To serve, divide the pasta evenly among 4 serving plates. Arrange equal portions of the asparagus and salmon on top of the pasta. Serve with lemon wedges.

SERVES 4

❖If you have two broilers, broil the salmon under one and the asparagus under the other.

❖Substitute olive oil for the butter to make the lemon sauce, if you like.

Sauté of Scallops and Artichokes Fettuccine

Not only do the artichokes taste good, they stretch a mere pound of scallops to serve four persons amply. If fresh baby artichokes are not available, use artichoke bottoms or artichoke hearts (see page 350 for preparation), or use frozen or canned baby artichokes, rinsing the canned artichokes and patting either kind dry before sautéing them. This dish is also good served with a combination of plain and wild rice; in fact, it is good served all by itself.

Alternative shellfish: peeled and deveined shrimp, or a combination of shrimp and scallops, or add sliced squid

10 baby artichokes
1 lemon, cut in half, plus 2 Tb fresh lemon juice
1 lb bay or small sea scallops
¾ lb fettuccine
2 Tb butter
3–4 Tb light olive oil
1 tsp minced garlic
Salt and freshly ground pepper
½ cup dry vermouth

Break off the outer leaves of the artichokes down to the tender pale green leaves. Trim the stems and cut about ½ inch off the top of each one. Rub the cut surfaces repeatedly with the lemon halves to prevent discoloration of the artichokes.

In a large saucepan, bring 1 quart salted water and the 2 tablespoons of lemon juice to a boil. Add the artichokes and simmer them about 15 minutes, or until they are just tender when tested by piercing one with a fork. Drain the artichokes, cut them in half lengthwise, remove and discard the chokes, and set the artichoke halves aside.

Remove any tough pieces of cartilage on the sides of the scallops, wipe off any bits of shell, pat them dry, and set aside.

Bring a large pot of water to a boil and drop in the fettuccine. When the fettuccine is almost cooked, heat the butter in a sauté pan, add the scallops to the hot butter, and cook for 1–2 minutes until the scallops are golden brown, tossing them in the pan after the first 30 seconds so that they brown on all sides. Remove the cooked scallops to a warm bowl.

Add 2 tablespoons of the oil to the sauté pan, heat the oil, and add the artichoke halves; cook the artichokes for 2–3 minutes to heat through and lightly brown, then add the garlic and return the scallops to the pan and cook, tossing, for 30 seconds. Season with salt and freshly ground pepper. When the pasta is just tender, or al dente, drain it well in a colander and return it to the pot in which it cooked. Add 1–2 tablespoons of oil, toss, and season with salt and freshly ground pepper. Combine the artichokes, scallops, and pasta, and toss all together; place in a warm serving bowl or platter. Pour the vermouth into the sauté pan, bring it to a boil, scraping up the cooking bits to deglaze the pan, and cook to reduce the liquid by half; then pour the reduced liquid over the scallops, artichokes, and pasta, and serve.   SERVES 4

❖If you are using large sea scallops, cut them into smaller pieces.

❖ If you wish to omit the pasta, remove the cooked artichokes and scallops to a warm platter, reduce the vermouth in the sauté pan, pour it over the artichokes and scallops, and serve.

Pasta with Shrimp and Cucumbers

Shrimp is a quickly cooked and delicious addition to pasta dishes, and so are warm cucumbers—often overlooked as a hot vegetable—excellent with pasta. It is necessary to cut, salt, and drain the cucumbers for at least 20 minutes before cooking them, or well in advance, if you prefer. The notes after the recipe offer several variations for the creamy vegetable topping.

> 2 lb cucumbers
> Salt
> 1 cup heavy cream
> 2–3 crushed cloves garlic
> ¾ lb fettuccine or other pasta
> Olive oil
> ¾ lb peeled and deveined large (36–40 count)
>   raw shrimp
> Freshly ground pepper
> 2 Tb butter (optional)

Peel and halve the cucumbers lengthwise and scoop out the seeds with a spoon. Slice the cucumber halves crosswise into ¼-inch-wide pieces. (Makes about 4 cups) Place the sliced cucumbers in a colander, toss with ½ teaspoon salt, let drain for 20 minutes, then pat dry with paper towels to remove any excess salt and moisture.

Place the cream and garlic in a small saucepan, bring the cream to a simmer, and cook at a simmer to flavor the cream until the liquid has reduced to ¾ cup. Remove and discard the garlic and set the cream aside, but keep it warm.

Bring a large pot of water to a boil. Drop in the pasta and cook for about 10–12 minutes, or until the pasta is al dente. When the pasta is almost done, heat

3 tablespoons of the oil in a large sauté pan. Pat the shrimp dry with paper towels, add them to the pan, and sauté, turning them frequently, for about 1 minute, or until they are just pink on all sides. Add the cucumbers and cook for 1 minute. Add the reserved warm cream, cook for 1 minute, season the mixture with salt and freshly ground pepper.

Drain the fettuccine in a colander and shake it gently to get rid of all the liquid. Return the pasta to the pot in which it cooked, toss it with a little butter or oil, if desired, and pour the shrimp-and-cucumber mixture over it. Mix gently but well and season again with salt and pepper, as needed.   SERVES 3–4

❖Add 2–3 tablespoons finely sliced small strips of Tasso ham or prosciutto or other smoked ham when you add the shrimp.

❖Add a little finely minced garlic to the pan just before cooking the shrimp.

❖Fold in fresh herbs.

❖Add a pinch of hot pepper flakes.

❖*With Peas:* Substitute 2–3 cups fresh shelled peas for the cucumbers, or combine cucumbers and peas.

❖*With Summer Squash:* Peel, seed, and dice or julienne zucchini or other summer squash. Salt, drain, and dry it as you would the cucumbers, and use in place of the cucumbers.

❖*With Broccoli:* Blanch the flowerets and peeled stems of broccoli in boiling water until just tender, cool immediately in ice water, drain and cut into ½-inch pieces, and use in place of the cucumbers.

❖*With Peppers:* Halve red and green sweet peppers lengthwise, remove the stems, seeds, and white membranes, and cut them into small strips or triangular pieces. Cook in the oil for 2–3 minutes, or just until they soften, and remove them to a warm plate. Add the shrimp to the sauté pan, cook for 2 minutes, and return the peppers to the pan to reheat with the shrimp. Toss the cooked, drained pasta with the shrimp, peppers, and cream. Season with salt and pepper and, if desired, with hot pepper flakes.

❖*With Tomatoes:* Omit the crushed garlic cloves. Heat the butter and oil, add 2 teaspoons minced garlic, and cook for 30 seconds; then add 2 cups peeled, seeded, and diced tomatoes, and bring the mixture to a boil. Add the shrimp and fresh herbs, such as strips of fresh basil, and cook for 2 minutes. Add the warm cream and cook another minute. Season with salt and pepper. Or omit the cream and use more tomatoes.

Eugenie Voorhees' Red Scallop Pasta

Every October for twenty years or so Eugenie has been a fellow scalloper searching with me and other devotees for the secret beds of incomparable Nantucket bay scallops. She cooks simply and elegantly, as, for example, in this recipe.

2 cups bay or small sea scallops
5 Tb unsalted butter
1 cup fresh bread crumbs
Salt and freshly ground pepper
1 lb spaghetti
4 Tb olive oil
2 peeled and minced cloves garlic
2 cups peeled, seeded, and chopped plum
     tomatoes or regular tomatoes
1 Tb red pepper flakes, or less to taste
¼ cup chopped flat Italian parsley

Remove any tough pieces of cartilage from the sides of the scallops, wipe off any bits of shell, pat them dry, and refrigerate until ready to cook.

In a large sauté pan, heat 2 tablespoons of the butter over medium heat, add the bread crumbs, and sauté them to a toasty golden color; remove the cooked bread crumbs to a small bowl and wipe out the pan.

Bring a large pot of water to a boil, add 1 teaspoon salt, drop in the spaghetti, and cook until the pasta is just tender, or al dente, about 15 minutes.

While the spaghetti is cooking, heat the remaining 3 tablespoons of butter and the oil in the sauté pan, add the garlic, and cook for 2–3 minutes until the garlic is lightly colored, but do not let the garlic cook to a darker brown or it may take on a bitter taste. Add the tomatoes and bring the mixture to a simmer, mashing the tomatoes in the pan with the back of a wooden spoon. When the tomato mixture is heated through, add the scallops and cook for 3 minutes. Season with salt and freshly ground pepper, fold in the pepper flakes and parsley, and cook 1 minute more.

Drain the pasta in a colander. Coat the bottom of the pot in which the pasta cooked with a few spoonfuls of the tomato sauce and return the pot to the stove over high heat. Return the pasta to the pot, add another spoonful of sauce, and toss to coat the spaghetti with the sauce. Immediately divide the pasta among 4 warm serving bowls. Divide the remaining sauce and scallops evenly over the pasta and sprinkle generously with the toasted bread crumbs. Serve immediately.   MAKES 4 LARGE OR 5 SMALL SERVINGS

Fall Risotto with Shrimp, Tomatoes, and Butternut Squash

Judith Barrett and Norma Wasserman's book *Risotto* inspired me to combine all sorts of vegetables and fish with short-grain Arborio rice. Their method of cooking risotto works well for me. Since risotto should be stirred all the while it is cooking, I try to have a friend on hand to spell me so that I can attend to other things, and I take care to have all the ingredients assembled in advance to enable me to prepare the dish without pausing and to serve it immediately. This is a delicious one-dish meal.

½ lb peeled and deveined extra jumbo
     (21–25 count) raw shrimp
5 cups hot chicken or *Shrimp Broth* (page 361)
3 Tb butter
1 cup peeled, seeded, and chopped tomatoes
1 cup diced butternut squash
Salt and freshly ground pepper
1 Tb vegetable or olive oil
½ cup chopped red or Spanish onions
1 Tb minced garlic
1½ cups raw Arborio rice
½ cup dry vermouth or white wine
2 Tb freshly grated Parmesan cheese

Cut the shrimp in half crosswise. Pour the broth into a large saucepan and bring it to a simmer.

In a small saucepan, heat 1 tablespoon of the butter, add the tomatoes and squash, bring the mixture to a boil, cover, reduce the heat, and cook for 5 minutes, shaking the pan occasionally. Uncover and cook for 1 minute. Season with salt and freshly ground pepper, and set aside.

In a large, heavy-bottomed saucepan (I use an 8-inch-wide pan), heat the remaining 2 tablespoons of butter and the oil. Add the onions and garlic, and cook, stirring, over medium heat for about 1 minute,

or until they are wilted and lightly colored. Add the rice and stir until it is totally blended with the onions and butter. Add the vermouth or wine and cook, stirring, until the liquid is absorbed by the rice.

Next comes the critical step in making risotto. Set aside ¼ cup of the hot broth. Stir the remaining broth into the rice about ½ cup at a time over medium heat, *stirring continuously,* so that the rice absorbs each addition of the broth gradually in about 2 minutes. When the rice has absorbed each addition of the broth, add another ½ cup. After about 12 minutes of this step, add the shrimp, then continue with the gradual addition of the broth. It should take about 18–20 minutes to complete this step, and you *must* stir the entire time. When all the broth has been added and absorbed, stir in the reserved ¼ cup broth, along with the tomato-and-squash mixture and the Parmesan cheese. Stir to mix all together and serve immediately.   SERVES 4

❖Small shrimp are fine in this dish and need not be cut in half.

❖Stir in 1 tablespoon chopped parsley or dill or fennel or other fresh herbs.

Paella

Paella is a Spanish dish. There are dozens of paellas, some made just with vegetables, others with beans, chicken, rabbit, pork, and, yes, fish and shellfish. The dish is traditionally cooked over an open wood fire. I usually cook paella on top of my stove, but if I am making large amounts, I start it on the stovetop and finish it in the oven. A 14-inch paella pan with sloping 3-inch-high sides is a good investment if you make paella frequently. Its design ensures that the rice cooks evenly over direct heat; it can also go into the oven, and the paella can be served directly from the pan. Making paella takes time and effort, but it is a great dish for parties; for easier eating for a buffet, I cut the chicken off the bone. Once I tripled this recipe for an evening bridal shower, and it easily fed 45 people with leftovers. Short-grain rice is classic for paella and a lovely texture for the dish, but I find that our long-grain converted rice doesn't stick together and guarantees perfect results. Much of the recipe can

Paella (continued)

be prepared in advance; there are two stopping points. So don't be daunted. It is fun to make and delicious to eat. Some Spanish restaurants serve paella at room temperature. I prefer to serve it steaming and fragrant, but it should rest at least 10–15 minutes between cooking and serving. I like to serve this with crusty bread and sangria.

2 lb extra jumbo (16–20 count) raw shrimp
    (about 36 shrimp)
½ cup olive oil, plus 1–2 Tb
2 Tb fresh lemon juice
1 tsp tomato paste
1 tsp finely minced garlic
18–24 small mussels
¾–1 lb small sea scallops
1½ cups shelled fresh peas
1 lb chorizo or smoked sausage
12 chicken thighs
¾ lb smoked ham, cut into cubes
1½–2 cups chopped onions
1½ cups green peppers, cut in 1½ × ¼-inch strips
2½ cups raw long-grain converted rice
¾ cup pimento strips or peeled red pepper strips
2 peeled cloves garlic
1½ cups peeled, seeded, and chopped tomatoes
One 19-oz can garbanzo or kidney beans
½ tsp paprika
1 bay leaf
½ tsp thyme
1 tsp salt
1 cup dry vermouth
4 cups chicken broth
Pinch of saffron threads
½ cup black olives
Lemon wedges

Peel and devein the shrimp, leaving the last tail-shell segment on for decoration. In a small bowl, whisk together 2 tablespoons of the oil and the lemon juice, tomato paste, and minced garlic. Pour the marinade over the shrimp and toss to coat the shrimp well; cover and refrigerate the shrimp.

Wash the mussels. Debeard them if you are going to proceed with cooking; if you are going to refrigerate them for later cooking, delay the debearding until just before cooking.

Remove any small pieces of tough cartilage from the sides of the scallops, wipe off any bits of shell, pat them dry, and refrigerate.

Prepare a bowl of ice water and set it aside. Bring a pot of water to a boil, drop in the peas, blanch them for 30 seconds, drain them, and immediately drop them into the ice water to stop the cooking action. Drain again and set aside. Refill the pot with water, bring to a boil again, prick the chorizo or sausage in several places with a sharp fork, drop it into the pot, and simmer it for 5 minutes to release some of its fat. Drain and slice the chorizo into ¼-inch-thick rounds.

In the paella pan or a large sauté pan, heat 1 table-spoon of the oil, add the chorizo, and cook until lightly browned. Remove the chorizo to a plate and set aside. Pat the chicken dry with paper towels. Heat 2 table-spoons of the oil in the paella pan, add the chicken, and brown on all sides, about 10 minutes in all, adding 1–2 more tablespoons of oil, if necessary. The chicken should be about halfway cooked. Remove the chicken to a plate or bowl (cut the meat from the bones and discard the bones, if you like), and set aside. (Everything to this point can be done in advance, covered, and refrigerated until ready for final cooking.)

Clean the paella pan after browning the chicken. Heat 2 tablespoons of the oil in the pan, add the ham cubes, and lightly brown them on all sides. Add the onions and sauté until wilted. Add the green peppers and sauté until slightly wilted and tender. Stir in the rice and cook the mixture until the rice is very lightly colored; do not brown the rice. Add the chicken and the chorizo. (You can set the paella aside at this point, refrigerated, and resume cooking about 45 minutes before serving.)

Add the pimento strips or peeled red peppers, garlic cloves, tomatoes, beans, paprika, bay leaf, thyme, and salt. Pour in the vermouth and broth, and bring the mixture to a simmer. Add the saffron. Mix all the ingredients once, and do not stir them again during final cooking. Regulate the heat to maintain a simmer for 20 minutes. The rice will begin to rise to the top in about 10 minutes as it absorbs the liquid; if it appears to be cooking too slowly, cover the pan for just a few minutes, then uncover for the remainder of the final cooking.

While the mixture simmers, place the mussels (debearding them first if you have not done so earlier) in a large saucepan, add a little vermouth or water, cover, and steam until the mussels open. Remove them from the heat and keep them warm; discard any mussels that have not opened.

When the liquid in the paella pan is almost absorbed and the rice is just turning tender, heat 1–2 tablespoons of the oil in a large sauté pan (or two small pans, as desired), add the shrimp and scallops, and sauté until the shrimp are pink on the outside and just opaque at the center, about 2 minutes, and the scallops are lightly browned on all sides, about 1–2 minutes.

Add the shrimp, scallops, and mussels to the paella pan, pressing them slightly into the rice, and scatter the peas and olives over the top. Cover loosely with a towel and let rest for 10–15 minutes. Serve with lemon wedges, crusty bread, and sangria.

SERVES 12 GENEROUSLY; TO SERVE 15,

ADD A FEW MORE CHICKEN THIGHS

❖If you like, cook the shellfish along with the rice. Do not marinate the shrimp. When you add the vermouth and broth, add the mussels hinged side down, and the shrimp if they are large. After the rice has simmered for 10 minutes in the broth, add the shrimp if they are small, and the scallops. Discard any mussels that do not open in this treatment by the end of final cooking. I think the presentation is more beautiful in the main recipe, but this way is perfectly delicious, too.

❖If the rice has not absorbed all of the liquid after 25 minutes of simmering, try putting the paella into a 400-degree oven for 5 minutes.

❖Cook the paella in the oven. After adding the broth and bringing the mixture to a simmer on the stovetop, transfer the pan to a 400-degree oven and cook for 30–40 minutes, or until the liquid has been absorbed by the rice.

❖Substitute small clams for mussels or boneless pork for ham. Add rings of squid or chunks of lobster. Cut raw lobster tails with their shells into chunks, sauté them lightly, then cook them with the rice.

Kedgeree

A knowledgeable Indian friend told me that in India *khicharie* refers to a one-pot "hodgepodge" dish of beans, rice, and spices—often without meat but sometimes containing meat or fowl, though rarely fish. Under returning British colonialists, the dish evolved into "kedgeree"—a familiar dish on English breakfast sideboards. In the process the beans vanished, and smoked fish became a basic ingredient. It's a nice dish

for a brunch or a supper. The finnan haddie can be prepared well ahead of time. Serve with fresh garden peas or *Portuguese Peas* (page 240).

1-lb side of finnan haddie
½ cup raisins (optional)
¼ cup rum (optional)
1½ cups long-grain rice
Salt and freshly ground pepper
4 hard-boiled eggs
4 Tb butter
1 cup chopped onions
1 Tb curry powder
¼ tsp cayenne pepper
3 Tb chopped fresh parsley

Cut the finnan haddie into 2 or 3 sections and place the pieces in a wide pan. Cover the fish with water and bring the water to a simmer. Cover the pan, remove it from the heat, and let it stand so the fish can steep in the hot water for 10 minutes. Drain the fish, and as soon as it is cool enough to handle, remove the skin and any bones. Break the flesh into large flakes. (Makes about 3 cups) Cover and set aside.

If you are going to use the raisins, place them in a small bowl and cover them with the rum (or water, if you prefer) for 10 minutes to plump them up.

In a saucepan, bring 3½ cups water to a boil and stir the rice in slowly so as not to disrupt the boil. Add 1 teaspoon salt, cover, reduce the heat, and simmer for 20 minutes, or until the liquid is absorbed. Remove from the heat and let sit, still covered, so that the rice can absorb any last bits of liquid.

Cut the eggs into small pieces by putting them through an egg slicer twice, or chop them by hand.

In a 4-quart saucepan, heat the butter. Stir in the onions and cook for 5 minutes, or until they are wilted and lightly colored. Stir in the curry powder and cayenne pepper, and cook for 1–2 minutes.

Add the rice to the onion mixture and cook for 2–3 minutes to heat all together. Add the flaked fish and the drained raisins (if you are using them). Gently stir all together, cooking enough to heat the mixture through. Stir in half the eggs. Season to taste with salt and freshly ground pepper. Combine the remaining eggs with the parsley and sprinkle the mixture over the top of the fish-and-rice mixture.   SERVES 6–8

❖For a creamier version, stir in warm heavy cream to the desired consistency.

Vegetable Dishes

Asparagus Chinois

The delicate flavor of asparagus should not be overpowered with aggressive sauces. This light Oriental-style dressing allows the asparagus to shine through. It is a nice side dish with grilled or sautéed shrimp. The asparagus can be peeled and cut well ahead, and the dressing prepared at the same time. Cooking takes only a few minutes before serving.

> 2 lb asparagus
> ⅛ tsp minced garlic
> 1 tsp minced ginger
> ½ tsp sugar
> 2 Tb light soy sauce
> 2 Tb rice vinegar
> 2 tsp sesame oil
> Freshly ground pepper

Cut the very end off each stalk of asparagus. Peel the asparagus by inserting a small, sharp knife under the skin at the base and working it up toward the tip, making the cut shallower as the skin becomes thinner. About 2–3 inches from the tip, taper off the peel completely. If you prefer, use a vegetable peeler.

Roll-cut the asparagus stalks into bite-size pieces. Make a diagonal crosscut about 1 inch from the base

Opposite: Marian picks a Chinese cabbage from the garden.

of the stalk with the stalk lying flat. Roll the asparagus a quarter turn and make a cut on the same diagonal, about an inch up the stalk from the first cut; continue rolling and cutting until you are just below the beginning of the asparagus tip.

In a small bowl, combine the garlic, ginger, sugar, soy sauce, rice vinegar, and sesame oil, whisk to blend well, and set aside.

Bring a large pot of water to a boil, drop in the asparagus pieces, and cook for 2–3 minutes until the asparagus is just tender. Drain the asparagus pieces in a colander, then spread them out on a towel-lined work surface and quickly pat them dry. Place the asparagus in a shallow serving bowl and season with freshly ground pepper. Whisk the dressing once more, pour the dressing over the asparagus, gently fold all together, and serve warm.   SERVES 6

Sautéed Fava Beans

Fava beans have big fuzzy pods that are hard to open, and once they've been shelled and blanched, the outer layer of skin has to be removed. It's almost enough to drive a cook to frozen peas, but fava beans are worth the effort. I cook these tender, very sweet beans only for a small group because no one would want to take the time to prepare enough for a crowd.

Sautéed Fava Beans (continued)

Their flavor is so delicate it doesn't need competition or enhancement, so I avoid adding herbs or strong seasonings.

2–2½ lb fava beans
2 Tb butter or olive oil
Salt and freshly ground pepper

Shell the beans. (Makes about 2 cups) Bring a pot of water to a boil, drop in the beans, and cook until they are just tender, about 4–8 minutes, depending on the size of the beans. Immediately run the beans under cold water to stop the cooking action, and drain. Carefully remove the pale skins around the beans so as not to crush the beans, and discard the skins. In a sauté pan, heat the butter or oil, add the beans, turn them carefully in the butter, and cook gently just until heated through. Season with salt and freshly ground pepper, and serve.   SERVES 4

Shell Bean Succotash

Something about this side dish reminds me of the Southwest, and I often serve it with grilled or broiled shellfish that is garnished with salsa, and with a crisp green salad.

2 cups fresh shell beans, such as lima or horticul-
    tural beans
1 strip bacon (optional)
Salt and freshly ground pepper
¼ cup chopped onions
1 cup peeled, seeded, and chopped tomatoes
2 cups corn kernels
1–2 Tb butter or virgin olive oil
1 Tb chopped fresh savory (optional)

Place the beans, the bacon (if you are using it), 1 tea-spoon salt, and onions in a saucepan and add 1 cup water. Bring the mixture to a boil, cover, reduce the heat, and simmer for 20 minutes. Stir in the tomatoes and corn, and simmer 10 minutes more. Remove the bacon, stir in the butter or oil and the savory, if desired, and season with salt and freshly ground pepper.   SERVES 4–6

Whole Green Beans with Lemon Butter and Shallots

When I've done this vegetable dish recently, I've used a new variety grown in the Victory Garden called "Label"; it is a baby French or green filet-type of stringless green bean that should be harvested when it is 4–6 inches long and less than ¼ inch thick. What a wonderful bean! I think it's best when cooked whole.

1 lb thin whole stringless green beans
2 Tb butter
2 Tb chopped shallots
1–2 Tb fresh lemon juice
Salt and freshly ground pepper

Trim the stem end off the beans. Bring a large pot of water to a boil, drop in the beans, and cook for 2–3 minutes, or until just tender. Drain the beans in a colander. Add the butter to the pot, melt it, and stir in the shallots. Return the beans to the pot and toss them in the butter and shallots. Add the lemon juice, toss again, season with salt and freshly ground pepper, and serve immediately.   SERVES 4–6

❖Use light olive oil instead of butter.
❖Omit the butter and shallots, and toss the beans with lemon juice or red wine vinegar or balsamic vinegar.
❖Blanch the beans in boiling water, drain them, and plunge them into ice water to stop the cooking action. Drain again, let cool, and reheat later.

Green Beans with Shallots and Garlic

I guess you know that I use garlic whenever I can.

1½ lb green beans
3–4 peeled, thinly sliced shallots
2–3 peeled, thinly sliced cloves garlic
Olive oil
Salt and freshly ground pepper

Wash and stem the beans and cut them diagonally into pieces. Bring a large pot of water to a boil, drop in the beans, and blanch them for 2–3 minutes until the beans have lost their raw hardness but are not yet tender. Holding a lid partially over the pot, carefully pour all but ¼ inch of liquid out of the pot. Add the shallots, garlic, and 1 tablespoon oil to the beans in the pot, and toss all together. Cover the pot and cook for 4–5 minutes, or until the garlic is just tender. Drain in a colander and then remove the vegetables to a warm serving bowl, season with salt and freshly ground pepper and with a little more olive oil, if you like, and serve.   SERVES 4

❖Instead of serving warm, let the dish cool to room temperature, add a dash of red wine vinegar and a bit more olive oil, and serve as a salad.

Tuscan-Style White Beans

Cooked dried beans are economical, healthful, and often the perfect accompaniment to a piece of fish. You will find that a delicious fruity olive oil gives a luscious flavor to the beans. The beans I was served in Tuscany were flavored with a favorite northern Italian herb, fresh sage. Often overlooked in American cooking, fresh sage is an ideal fragrance with beans; if you don't have fresh sage, substitute other fresh herbs, such as savory, basil, or marjoram. This dish makes a nice change from potatoes and pasta.

  1 cup dried cannellini beans or other dried
     white beans, such as Great Northern
  Salt and freshly ground pepper
  8 fresh sage leaves, or more to taste
  ¼ cup fruity virgin olive oil, plus extra for fla-
     voring
  Fresh lemon juice

Rinse and pick over the beans. Put them in a pot, cover them with 2 inches of water, bring to a boil, and cook for 2 minutes; then remove the beans from the heat and let them sit for 1 hour or more, even overnight. Drain the beans, rinse them under cold water, and return them to the pot. Cover with 2 inches of water, add 1 teaspoon salt, bring to a boil, reduce the heat, and cook according to package instructions, or

until the beans are tender. Cooking time will depend on the variety and size of beans you use. Drain well. (If you are going to serve the beans at a later time, rinse them under cold water to stop the cooking action, drain again, and set aside to be reheated.)

If the sage leaves are very large, shred them. In a large sauté pan, heat the oil, stir in the sage and beans, and cook, stirring to coat the beans with the oil, until they are heated through. Remove from the heat and season with lemon juice and salt and freshly ground pepper. Stir in more oil, if desired.   MAKES ABOUT 3 CUPS

❖Add 1–2 teaspoons minced garlic to the oil, stir for 30 seconds, then add the beans.
❖Add chopped red peppers and tomatoes; see *White Beans with Shrimp and Basil* (page 48).
❖Use other types of dried beans.

Purée of Brussels Sprouts and Potatoes

If my guess is accurate, this recipe will win over many who turn up their noses at Brussels sprouts. The potatoes mellow the cabbage flavor of the sprouts, and the combination is delicate both in flavor and in its soft lime-green color. I like to serve it as partner to orange winter squash. It can be made ahead and gently reheated over boiling water with a bit of liquid or butter. A food processor is almost a necessity to get the right consistency for this dish.

  2 lb Brussels sprouts
  1 lb potatoes
  1 Tb butter
  1–2 Tb light cream or milk (optional)
  Salt and freshly ground pepper
  Juice of ½ lemon or more

Trim the Brussels sprouts of outer leaves and knobby ends, and cut each sprout in half lengthwise. (Makes about 1½ pounds after trimming) Peel the potatoes, cut them into thick slices, and place them in a small saucepan. Cover the potatoes with water, bring to a boil, reduce the heat, and simmer until the potatoes are tender, about 15–20 minutes.

While the potatoes are cooking, place the Brussels

Purée of Brussels Sprouts and Potatoes (continued)

sprouts in a wide saucepan, add 1 cup water, bring to a boil, cover, reduce the heat, and cook gently about 8–10 minutes, or until the sprouts are tender, watching to make sure that the water does not boil away.

Drain the potatoes and Brussels sprouts in a colander. Place the drained vegetables in the bowl of a food processor fitted with a steel blade, add the butter and the cream or milk, if desired, and process to a thick purée. (Be careful not to process so much that the purée becomes as smooth as baby food.) Season with salt and freshly ground pepper and lemon juice to taste, and briefly process once more to incorporate the seasonings. Remove to a bowl and serve.   MAKES 4 CUPS

❖Omit the butter and cream or add more to your taste.

❖If confirmed Brussels sproutsphobes remain skeptical, add a little more potato the next time.

Sautéed Brussels Sprouts and Sweet and Sour Cabbage

On a cold winter night, a supper of creamy cod is enhanced by these two members of the cabbage family. The big cabbage in this partnership is red, smooth, and sweet-sour; the little cabbage (Brussels sprouts) is bright green and crunchy, its distinctive but cabbage-like flavor intensified by adding a little lemon juice. Of course they can be served separately as well. The Brussels sprouts can be blanched, cooled, and sliced well ahead of their final sauté, and the red cabbage can be completely cooked ahead, then reheated before serving.

SAUTÉED BRUSSELS SPROUTS

1 lb Brussels sprouts
3 Tb butter
Juice of ½ lemon
Salt and freshly ground pepper

Trim and wash the sprouts, removing any damaged or withered outer leaves. Cut a small "X" into the core at the base to allow for even cooking. Drop the prepared sprouts into a bowl of tepid water, swirl

them around, and drain. Bring a pot of water to a boil, drop in the sprouts, and cook until they are just tender, about 4–8 minutes, depending on their size. Immediately run the blanched sprouts under cold water to stop the cooking action and to cool them down. Pat them dry and cut each sprout in half through the base. These steps can be done ahead and the sprouts refrigerated until ready for final cooking.

In a large sauté pan, heat the butter, add the sprouts, and cook until just heated through. Add the lemon juice, season with salt and freshly ground pepper, toss gently, and serve.   SERVES 4–6

SWEET AND SOUR CABBAGE

2 lb red cabbage (about ½ large cabbage)
2 firm apples
2 Tb butter
3 Tb light brown sugar
¼ cup white vinegar
Salt and freshly ground pepper

Remove any damaged or withered outer cabbage leaves, and rinse and pat the cabbage dry. Cut the cabbage in half down through the base, and then cut one of the halves in half down through the base. Holding each of the quarters in turn by its base and core, slice all but the core into fine shreds. Continue until you have 8 cups shredded cabbage, using some of the second half of the cabbage, if necessary. Peel and core the apples, and grate them through the large holes of a grater.

In a high-sided sauté pan, melt the butter, stir in the cabbage and apples, and cook gently, stirring, for 3–4 minutes. Sprinkle on the sugar, add the vinegar, stir all together, cover, and cook slowly for 30 minutes. Uncover and cook, if needed, for 5 minutes more to evaporate any excess liquid in the pan. Season with salt and freshly ground pepper.   SERVES 4–6

Stir-Fried Broccoli with Garlic

This dish is so simple and flavorful that I make it over and over again, especially to set the crunchiness and bright green color of broccoli against the smoother texture and paler color of some fresh fish.

1 lb broccoli
3 Tb virgin olive oil or vegetable oil
2 tsp minced garlic
½ tsp salt
¼ tsp sugar
⅓ cup water
Juice of ½ lemon
Freshly ground pepper

Trim any leaves off the broccoli and separate the stems from the flowerets. Cut the flowerets into smaller flowerets, about ½ inch across. Peel the stems, cut very thick stems in half lengthwise, and cut all the stems diagonally into ¼-inch-thick slices.

In a large frying pan or wok, heat the olive or vegetable oil. Add the garlic and broccoli, and cook for 1 minute, tossing frequently, or until the broccoli turns bright green. Sprinkle on the salt and sugar, stir well, then add the water. Cover and cook for 2–3 minutes, or until the broccoli is just bite-tender. Uncover and cook over high heat, stirring, until the water has evaporated. Squeeze on the lemon juice, season with freshly ground pepper, and serve.   SERVES 4

Braised Broccoli de Rabe

Also known as rape, broccoli de rabe is a relative of the better-known broccoli. It is a leafy green with a distinctive sharp taste, and the whole plant is edible except the root. As with asparagus and regular broccoli, I peel off any tough skin on the stem, but if the plant has been harvested while young and tender, this should not be necessary. Braised broccoli de rabe is good by itself, even better as a topping for pasta, and best of all as a bed for fish.

1 lb broccoli de rabe
3–4 Tb olive oil
3 tsp chopped garlic
½ cup liquid (dry vermouth, chicken broth, or
    water)
Salt and freshly ground pepper

Rinse the broccoli de rabe; cut off the bottom of any large, tough stems and peel away any tough outer skin. Spin-dry and cut into 2–3-inch lengths.

In a large, nonaluminum-lined sauté pan, heat the

oil and stir in the garlic. Add the broccoli de rabe and stir until the vegetable is well coated with the oil. Pour in the liquid, reduce the heat to low, cover, and steam-cook for 6–8 minutes, stirring occasionally. Uncover, increase the heat, cook until most of the moisture in the pan has evaporated, and season with salt and freshly ground pepper.   SERVES 4

Braised Cabbage and Collard Greens

These two humble vegetables make a colorful, flavorful combination that would grace the fanciest meal. Slicing these storage vegetables and then cooking them with a sauté-braise technique cuts cooking time and makes both their texture and taste tender. Serve as a vegetable side dish or as an excellent bed for grilled fish or shellfish.

1 lb collard greens
1 lb green cabbage
2–3 Tb fruity olive oil
1–2 tsp minced garlic
1–2 tsp fresh lemon juice
Salt and freshly ground pepper

Wash the collard greens. If the collard greens are very small, simply cut off the stems at the base of the leaf; if they are large, cut off the stems with a sharp paring knife, including the part of the stem that runs down the back of the leaf. Spin-dry the leaves and slice them into thin diagonal slices. (You should have about 8 cups.)

Cut the cabbage into large wedges, and holding each wedge by the core, slice the leaves into thin strips. (You will have about 8 cups.) Combine the collard and cabbage in a bowl and refrigerate until ready to cook.

In a large, high-sided sauté pan, heat 2 tablespoons of the oil. Stir in the amount of garlic you like, and add the combined greens to the oil in the pan a handful at a time, stirring, until they are coated with the oil and have wilted. Add ½ cup water to the pan, cover, and braise gently until the greens are tender, about 8 minutes, stirring occasionally to make sure the greens are not cooking too quickly and sticking to the pan.

Braised Cabbage and Collard Greens (continued)

Uncover the pan and cook for another minute or two to evaporate any excess moisture. Stir in the lemon juice to taste and season with salt and freshly ground pepper. Add a drizzle more olive oil, if you like.

MAKES 5–6 CUPS; SERVES 4–6

Chinese Cabbage Stir-Fry

Chinese cabbage is so light and crunchy as to be almost best eaten raw; this quick stir-fry is the next best way.

2 lb Chinese cabbage
3 Tb peanut oil or vegetable oil
2 quarter-size pieces fresh ginger
2 Tb thin julienne of fresh red hot chili peppers
    or chopped dried hot red peppers (optional)
½ tsp sugar
1 tsp salt
2 Tb water or chicken broth

Wash and pat the cabbage dry, and cut it into crosswise slices about 1–1½ inches thick. In a wok or large frying pan, heat the oil, stir in the ginger, and toss for 1 minute. Add the cabbage and peppers, if desired, and cook, stirring constantly, for 2 minutes, lowering the heat if the cabbage begins to brown. Stir in the sugar and salt, add the water or broth, cover, and cook for 2–3 minutes, or until the cabbage is tender but still crunchy.   SERVES 4

❖Season with a few drops of sesame oil.
❖Add toasted pine nuts.

Carrots and Kohlrabi Julienne

Once you have made the carrot salad in this book using a Mouli julienne machine or a grater to produce long, delicate, intensely flavorful strands of orange carrots, you will want to use carrots the same way in other dishes. This wonderfully light vegetable dish pairs the well-known carrot with a delicious but underutilized vegetable, kohlrabi. You might like to consult the chapter on kohlrabi in *The Victory Garden Cookbook* for more ideas. Kohlrabi is just as good raw as it is cooked.

¾ lb carrots
1 lb kohlrabi
2 Tb butter
1 Tb vegetable oil
1–2 Tb chopped fresh chives or other herbs
    (optional)

Fresh lemon juice
Salt and freshly ground pepper

Peel and trim the carrots, and grate them into long, thin strands using a hand grater, a Mouli julienne machine, or a food processor fitted with a shredding blade. Slice off each end of the bulbous kohlrabi stems and peel off the outer thin layer of skin to reveal the inner flesh. Grate the kohlrabi by the same means used for the carrots. Place the grated carrots and kohlrabi in a bowl and toss together.

In a large sauté pan, heat the butter and oil, and stir in the grated vegetables until they are completely coated with the butter and oil. Add ½ cup water, cover, and cook for 3–4 minutes, stirring occasionally. Uncover and cook until the vegetables are wilted and tender, reducing any liquid in the pan. Stir in the herbs (if you are using them) and season with a few drops of lemon juice and salt and freshly ground pepper. SERVES 6

Braised Carrots and Celery

The flavor of apples, you will see, has a way of intensifying the flavor of both carrots and celery.

1 lb carrots
½ lb stalks celery
2 Tb butter
¾ cup apple cider or unsweetened apple juice
Chopped parsley (optional)

Trim and peel the carrots, and cut them diagonally into ¼-inch-thick slices. Trim and slice the celery the same way.

In a sauté pan, heat the butter, add the carrots, and cook, stirring occasionally, for 2–3 minutes. Add the celery and cook for 1 minute. Add the apple cider or unsweetened apple juice, bring the mixture to a boil, cover, reduce the heat, and cook gently until the vegetables are just tender, about 4 minutes. Remove the vegetables to a warm serving dish and rapidly boil down the cooking juices slightly. Pour the juices over the vegetables, sprinkle with parsley, if you like, and serve. SERVES 4

Sautéed Corn

The toasty flavor that this technique of sautéing gives the corn proves to be a fine complement to fish. For convenience you can husk and cut the corn way ahead and reserve the kernels in the refrigerator, covered, until ready to cook quickly and serve.

6 large ears corn
2 Tb butter
2 Tb vegetable oil
Salt and freshly ground pepper

Remove the corn husks and silk, and cut the kernels off the cobs. (Makes about 4–5 cups cut corn)

In a large sauté pan, heat the butter and oil. Add the corn and cook, covered, for 4 minutes over medium heat, stirring occasionally. Uncover and cook, stirring, until any excess moisture in the pan has evaporated and the corn is lightly colored, about 4 minutes more. Season with salt and freshly ground pepper, and serve. SERVES 4–6

❖*Mexican Corn:* Add 1½ cups chopped red and green peppers and 2 tablespoons minced hot pepper to the corn. After heating the butter and oil, sauté ½ cup chopped onion for 1 minute, add the corn-and-pepper mixture, and proceed as above. SERVES 6–8

Corn Pudding

In order of preference, my favorite way to prepare corn is boiled corn on the cob; my next favorite is sautéed fresh corn kernels; and this bake-ahead dish—corn pudding—is a close third. The cooking method concentrates the corn's natural sugars to make a creamy, candy-sweet casserole that is delicious with grilled or broiled fish. Sometimes I add some hot peppers from the garden for a little contrast in flavor. Now that "sweet gene" varieties of corn are available in many markets year-round, you can prepare this dish whenever you like; in these new varieties the sugar doesn't convert to starch as rapidly, taking the sweetness of the corn with it. You will find it invaluable to acquire a corn scraper if you scrape corn very often.

Corn Pudding (continued)

6–8 ears fresh corn
1 Tb flour (if corn is very milky)
1 tsp sugar (omit if corn is very sweet-tasting)
⅔ cup heavy cream
¼ cup finely chopped hot peppers (optional)
Salt and freshly ground pepper

Husk and scrape the corn. If you do not have a store-bought corn scraper, slice and scrape with a knife. Run a sharp knife down the center of each row of each ear of corn. Hold each ear over a shallow pan with one end of the ear touching the bottom of the pan. Push the back of a heavy knife down the rows of kernels all around each ear to force the flesh and milk of the corn down into the pan. Scrape enough ears to get 2 cups scraped corn.

In a bowl, combine the scraped corn, the flour (if needed), the sugar (if needed), the cream, and the peppers (if you are using them). Season the mixture with salt and freshly ground pepper. Pour the mixture into a buttered 4–6-cup baking dish and bake in a preheated 325-degree oven for 50–60 minutes, or until the pudding has firmed up. SERVES 4–6

Sautéed Cucumbers

Cucumbers are usually served as a raw vegetable, but well-cooked cucumbers—tender but still crunchy—have a refreshing and unique flavor that enhances the flavor of fish.

1½ lb cucumbers (about 3 large cucumbers)
2 Tb butter, more as desired
Salt and freshly ground pepper
2–3 Tb chopped fresh dill

Peel the cucumbers. Run the tines of a fork along the sides of the cucumbers lengthwise to make a decorative edge. Cut the cucumbers in half lengthwise and remove the seeds with a spoon. Cut each half in half lengthwise again. Now you have 4 long pieces from each cucumber. Make a series of zigzag diagonal cuts along each piece of cucumber so that it becomes a number of triangular-shaped, bite-size pieces. Cover and refrigerate if not serving immediately.

Shortly before serving, heat the butter in a wide, nonstick sauté pan, add the cucumbers, and cook over medium heat, tossing constantly, for 3–4 minutes, or until the cucumbers are tender but still retain some crunchiness. Reduce the heat during the cooking if the cucumbers start to brown. Season with salt and freshly ground pepper and add more butter, if you like. Add the chopped dill, toss once more, and serve immediately. SERVES 6

Roasted Ratatouille

Conventionally ratatouille is prepared by browning cubed eggplant, summer squash, onions, and peppers in plenty of olive oil, then combining them with ripe tomatoes, garlic, and herbs, and stewing the mixture; it is a divinely good dish, but the individual sautéing of the vegetables is both messy and time-consuming. This easier method of roasting the vegetables rather than sautéing them yields, in my view, as good a dish as the old-fashioned ratatouille recipe I have in *The Victory Garden Cookbook*. The perfect time to make ratatouille is when the summer garden is lush. Vine-ripened tomatoes make a great difference in this dish. I use peeled and seeded tomato pulp, but if you are in a hurry and don't mind tomato skins in the dish, use ripe unpeeled plum tomatoes; cut them in half, squeeze out the seeds, and cut them into chunks.

While I like to go into the garden an hour before dinner, gather the vegetables and herbs, and quickly assemble this dish, it can also be made a day or two ahead. What versatility! Ratatouille is good served hot, at room temperature, or cold, and the recipe can be either halved or doubled to fit the number of diners. All that one needs to add for a complete meal is a nice piece of fish.

2–2½ lb eggplant
½ cup olive oil plus 1 Tb
1½ lb zucchini or yellow summer squash
2 large red or green peppers (about ¾ lb)
1 large Spanish onion or 2 large regular onions
   (about ¾ lb)
1 Tb chopped garlic
6 cups peeled, seeded, and roughly chopped
   tomatoes
1 Tb fresh thyme
½ cup sliced fresh basil leaves
Salt and freshly ground pepper

Peel the eggplant, cut it crosswise into 1-inch-thick slices, then cut the slices into 1-inch cubes. (Makes about 8 cups) Place the eggplant in a large bowl, add 3 tablespoons of the oil, and toss all together. Spread the eggplant cubes on a baking sheet.

Wash and dry the zucchini or summer squash, remove the stems, and cut into 1-inch cubes. (Makes 7–8 cups) Place in the bowl used for the eggplant, toss with 2 tablespoons oil, and spread on another baking sheet.

Cut the peppers in half lengthwise and remove the stems, seeds, and white membranes. Cut the pepper halves lengthwise into 1-inch-wide strips and then cut the strips into 1-inch triangles. Place the peppers in the bowl used for the zucchini and set aside.

Peel the onion or onions and cut into 1-inch chunks. Place the onion chunks in the bowl with the peppers, toss with 2 tablespoons of the oil, and spread the onion chunks and pepper triangles on a third baking sheet.

Preheat the oven to 500 degrees. Put two of the

Roasted Ratatouille (continued)

baking sheets in the oven and roast the vegetables, stirring once, for 10 minutes. Remove from the oven and put the third baking sheet into the oven for 10 minutes and stir once. (If you have two ovens, you can roast all three sheets at one time.)

While the vegetables are roasting, heat 2 tablespoons of the oil in a large, high-sided, nonaluminum-lined pot. Stir in the garlic, add the tomatoes, bring the mixture to a boil, reduce the heat to a gentle boil, cover, and cook for 5 minutes; then uncover and cook for another 5–10 minutes, depending on the amount of juices in the pan, to reduce the tomato liquid. (You want to have the tomato pulp and about 1–1½ cups liquid.)

Add the roasted vegetables and the thyme to the pot, and cook all together, stirring occasionally, for 10 minutes, or until the mixture is hot and the vegetables are quite tender. Stir in the basil and season with salt and freshly ground pepper.

MAKES ABOUT 10 CUPS; SERVES 8–12

Sautéed Eggplant

Eggplant, which is often used in combination with other vegetables in such familiar and wonderful dishes as ratatouille, or served with a sauce, as in eggplant Parmesan, is a vegetable well worth cooking by itself quite undisguised. Salting and draining eggplant make the preparation longer in duration, but the consequence of doing these steps is that the eggplant absorbs less oil as it cooks. Once the salting and draining are done, the actual cooking of the eggplant goes very quickly.

   1½ lb eggplant
   Salt and freshly ground pepper
   ¼ cup light olive oil, plus extra olive oil
   1–2 tsp minced garlic (optional)
   2 Tb chopped parsley

Peel the eggplant and cut it crosswise into ½–¾-inch-thick slices. Then cut the slices into ½–¾-inch-wide strips and the strips into ½–¾-inch cubes. (Makes about 5–6 cups)

Place the eggplant cubes in a colander, toss with 2 teaspoons salt, and allow to drain for 30 minutes; pat the cubes with paper towels to remove excess salt and moisture, remove the eggplant to a bowl, and set aside.

In a large, nonstick sauté pan, heat 3–4 tablespoons of the oil, add the eggplant, and cook over high heat, stirring and separating the cubes until they are browned on all sides. Add more olive oil as necessary if the eggplant absorbs all the oil in the pan. When the eggplant has browned, reduce the heat slightly and cook about 8 minutes, or until the eggplant is tender, shaking the pan or stirring occasionally. If you wish, cover the pan for a few minutes to help the eggplant cook faster. Stir in the garlic, if desired, add the parsley, and season with salt and freshly ground pepper.

SERVES 4

Easy Eggplant Parmesan

In my first cookbook I have a recipe for a delicious eggplant Parmesan that I fed our family for thirty years. Now I often prepare this version, which eliminates salting the eggplant, breading the eggplant, and frying the eggplant in oil. Tedious steps are gone— and some calories, too—and still this version tastes awfully good. Homemade tomato sauce is best, but a good commercial tomato sauce is also fine. This dish takes well to being made ahead, refrigerated, and baked just before serving.

   2 lb eggplant
   ½ cup light olive oil or vegetable oil
   1 cup freshly grated Parmesan cheese
   2 tsp chopped fresh oregano
   ¾ lb sliced mozzarella cheese
   3 cups tomato sauce

Peel the eggplants and cut them crosswise into ⅜-inch-thick slices. Brush both sides of the slices with the oil and lay them in one layer on baking sheets. Run the sheets under a preheated broiler until the slices are lightly browned, then turn them and broil the other side until lightly browned.

Place half of the eggplant slices in a 9 × 13-inch baking dish. Sprinkle one-third of the Parmesan cheese and 1 teaspoon of the oregano over the egg-plant, then spread one-third of the mozzarella slices on top. Cover all with half the tomato sauce. Place the remainder of the eggplant in a layer on top of the tomato sauce, add one-third of the Parmesan cheese and the remainder of the oregano, then one-third of the mozzarella slices and the remainder of the tomato sauce. Complete the layering with the remainder of the mozzarella slices and then sprinkle the remainder of the Parmesan on the very top. Bake in a preheated 350-degree oven for 30 minutes or until hot and bubbly. Serve with a green salad and crusty bread.

SERVES 6–8

Grilled Leeks

Leeks have a way of hiding sand and soil inside their stems, so they require more elaborate washing than do some other vegetables; but the effort is more than worthwhile. The pleasant texture and mild but distinctive flavor of grilled leeks will greatly complement any grilled or broiled fish dish in this book.

8 leeks, each about ¾ inch thick
½ cup vegetable oil
Fresh lemon juice
Salt and freshly ground pepper
½ cup freshly grated Parmesan cheese (optional)
Lemon wedges

Trim the roots of the leeks and cut off the dark green leaves down to where they turn pale green, leaving about 1 inch of pale green leaves on each leek. Slit down one side of each leek from the top to within 1½ inches of the base. Wash the leeks in a large bowl of lukewarm water, plunging them up and down to remove any soil or sand inside the leek; run the leeks under water to make sure they are perfectly clean and pat them dry.

Put the oil in a shallow bowl and dip the leeks in the oil, turning them until coated on all sides. Place the leeks on a preheated grill, slit side up, about 2–4 inches from the heat, and cook, turning them as they brown, for 7–8 minutes, or until they are well charred on the outside and tender inside when tested with a skewer. Cooking time will vary with the heat

of the fire. (You can grill oiled fish steaks at the same time, turning them once.)

Remove the leeks from the grill and discard the outer charred layers. Season the leeks with lemon juice, salt and freshly ground pepper, and sprinkle with the cheese, if desired. Serve with lemon wedges.

SERVES 4

Leeks Braised with Tomatoes, Garlic, and Olives

This dish has such a medley of flavors and colors that it serves equally well as an appetizer, a luncheon main dish, or the only accompaniment to a piece of fish for supper. I always make more than I need because I like it cold the next day spread on toasted French bread. You can prepare the dish ahead, refrigerate it, and gently reheat it just before serving.

4 large or 6 medium leeks
2 Tb virgin olive oil
2 minced cloves garlic
1½ cups peeled, seeded, and chopped tomatoes
12 halved pitted black olives
Zest of 1 lemon
Juice of ½ lemon
Salt and freshly ground pepper
2 Tb chopped parsley (optional)
1 tsp chopped fresh thyme (optional)

Trim the leeks, remove the dark green tops, and peel off the tough outer layers. Wash the leeks carefully, as described in the preceding recipe. Pat them dry and cut them into 1–1½-inch lengths.

In a 2-inch-deep sauté pan, heat the oil, add the leeks, and cook, stirring occasionally, until they are lightly colored on all sides. Add the garlic, tomatoes, olives, lemon zest, and lemon juice, and stir well. Bring the mixture to a very gentle boil, cover, and cook for 10–15 minutes, stirring once or twice, or until the leeks are just tender. Uncover and cook another 5–10 minutes to reduce the tomato liquid, or until the sauce has thickened. Season with salt and freshly ground pepper and with a sprinkling of parsley and thyme, if you like.

SERVES 4–6

Okra and Tomato Stew

When you are having a crisp dish of southern fried fish, think about having some okra stew on the side.

1 lb okra
2 Tb butter
1 Tb vegetable oil
1 cup chopped onions
½ cup chopped celery
1 tsp minced garlic
2 cups peeled, seeded, and chopped tomatoes,
    in ½-inch pieces
1 minced small hot red pepper
Salt and freshly ground pepper

Wipe the okra with a damp towel, trim off the stem cap, and cut into ½-inch pieces. In a sauté pan, heat the butter and oil. Add the onions, celery, and okra, and cook until the vegetables are lightly colored, about 8–10 minutes. Add the garlic, tomatoes, and hot pepper, and stir all together. Bring the mixture to a boil, reduce the heat, cover, and simmer for 6–8 minutes, or until the okra is just tender. Uncover and cook long enough to reduce the liquid slightly. Season with salt and freshly ground pepper.   SERVES 4–6

Big Baked Onions

Although one instinctively thinks of this recipe in terms of big sweet onions, such as Spanish, Vidalia, Maui, or Walla Walla, actually any onion is delicious prepared this way. These onions are perfect with grilled, broiled, or roasted fish dishes and are a pleasant contrast to creamy combinations such as *Naomi's Finnan Haddie* (page 155).

4 onions, each 3–4 inches wide
Vegetable oil
Butter or sour cream (optional)
Freshly grated Parmesan cheese (optional)

Trim the onions, cutting a thin slice off the root end so that the onions will sit in the baking dish and not roll about. Prick each onion in several places with a fork to

release moisture as needed to prevent the onion from bursting while baking. Rub the onions with oil, set them in a baking dish, and film the bottom of the dish with water so that the onions will not stick to the dish. Bake in a preheated 400-degree oven for 1–1½ hours, or until the onions feel soft when pinched and a knife slides easily into the center. Serve the onions plain or topped with a pat of butter or dollop of sour cream; or cut them in half vertically, sprinkle with grated Parmesan cheese (or a combination of Parmesan and Swiss), and run the onions under a preheated broiler just until the cheese is lightly browned.   SERVES 4

Grilled Parsnips and Bananas

Sweet parsnips make a perfect marriage with grilled bananas. There is no better accompaniment to mahi mahi than this dish, and as you will see below, I even use this dish as a topping for dessert.

1 lb parsnips
3 Tb orange juice
2 Tb butter
1 Tb sugar or honey
2 large bananas
Candied orange zest (optional)

Wash, trim, and peel the parsnips, and cut them crosswise into 1-inch pieces. Put the parsnips in a pot, cover with water, bring to a boil, reduce the heat, and cook about 6–8 minutes, or until the parsnips are tender. Drain immediately and spread the parsnip pieces in a shallow baking dish that can go under the broiler.

In a small saucepan, combine the orange juice and butter, bring the mixture to a boil, add the sugar or honey, and cook for 1 minute.

Peel the bananas and cut them into 1-inch chunks. Spoon them over and around the parsnips. Pour the orange-butter sauce over all and turn the parsnips and bananas until they are well coated. Place under a preheated broiler and cook, turning the pieces occasionally, until the parsnips and bananas are lightly browned on all sides. Serve garnished with candied orange zest, if you like.   SERVES 4

❖Omit the orange juice and baste the parsnips and bananas with melted butter and sugar before broiling.

❖Cut the parsnips and bananas into smaller pieces and serve the dish as a topping over ice cream.

Macadamia Nut Parsnips

This combination of crunchy nuts and smooth parsnips, all of it sweet, is a perfect accompaniment to grilled fish.

    1 lb parsnips
    5 Tb butter
    ½ cup finely chopped macadamia nuts
    2 tsp honey

Wash, trim, and peel the parsnips, and cut them into "logs" all of about the same size. Put the parsnip logs in an ovenproof dish and set aside.

In a sauté pan, melt the butter, stir in the nuts, and cook until the nuts are lightly colored. Stir in the honey. Pour the mixture over the parsnips and stir to coat the parsnips well. Cover and bake in a preheated 350-degree oven for 30 minutes, then uncover and bake for 5 minutes more.   SERVES 4–6

❖Omit the honey and toss the cooked parsnips with 1–2 tablespoons chopped fresh parsley.

❖Cut the parsnips crosswise into thin slices instead of logs. Cook as above and serve warm over ice cream.

Roasted Parsnip "French Fries"

When my grandchildren stop by for lunch, I like to serve them something from the garden. They love French-fried potatoes, but making those takes time and loads of oil. Instead I roast lengths of parsnip—they are quickly cooked and require only one tablespoon of oil. They are so sweet my girls think that Grammy is giving them candy.

1 lb parsnips
1 Tb vegetable oil

Peel the parsnips and cut them into 2–3-inch-long pieces. Cut each piece into ¼-inch-thick slices, then cut the slices into ¼-inch strips or logs. You will have about 4 cups of parsnip strips or "French fries."

Put the parsnips into a bowl and toss with the oil to lightly coat all the pieces. Spread the parsnips out on a flat baking sheet and place in a preheated 400-degree oven for 30 minutes. After 15 minutes, turn the parsnips once or twice on the baking sheet to lightly brown on all sides. Serve immediately.

MAKES ABOUT 2½ CUPS OF PARSNIP "FRENCH FRIES"; SERVES 4

❖Add other vegetables cut into lengths. Try carrots, celeriac, or rutabaga.

Braised Peas and Scallions

12–15 scallions
2 Tb butter
4 cups shelled fresh peas
1 tsp sugar
½ cup water
1 Tb chopped fresh mint
Salt and freshly ground pepper

Trim the scallions, discarding the dark green tops, and cut them into ¾–1-inch lengths. In a saucepan, heat the butter, add the scallions, and cook them for 2–3 minutes. Add the peas, sugar, and water, stir all together, cover, and bring the mixture to a boil. Cook rapidly for 3–4 minutes, shaking the pan frequently, uncover, and cook for about 5 minutes to

reduce the cooking liquid. Stir in the chopped mint, season with salt and freshly ground pepper, and remove to a warm serving dish.   SERVES 4–6

Dilled Peas and Cucumbers

Both vegetables are delicious with fish dishes. You can prepare the peas and cucumbers in advance, and the final sauté takes only a few minutes. See the variations that follow for using sugar snap peas in place of garden peas in the pod.

2 lb peas in pod
1 lb cucumbers
2 Tb butter or light olive oil
1 Tb chopped fresh dill
Salt and freshly ground pepper

Shell the peas. (Makes about 2 cups) Bring a large pot of water to a boil, drop in the peas, bring the water back to a boil, and blanch the peas for 30 seconds if they are very small, otherwise for 1 minute. Immediately drain them in a colander, run them under cold water to stop the cooking action, drain again, and set the peas aside.

Peel the cucumbers. Run a fork down the sides to make a decorative edge. Cut the cucumbers in half lengthwise and remove the seeds with a spoon. Cut each half lengthwise into long strips about ½ inch wide, then cut the strips diagonally into 1-inch-long pieces.

In a large, nonstick sauté pan, heat the butter or oil, add the cucumbers, and cook over medium-high heat, tossing occasionally; reduce the heat if the cucumbers start to brown. In 3–4 minutes the cucumbers should be tender yet retain some crunchiness. Gently stir in the blanched peas and chopped dill, and cook just long enough to heat through. Season with salt and freshly ground pepper, and serve.

SERVES 4

❖ *To blanch sugar snap peas:* Substitute ½ pound sugar snap peas for the shelled garden peas. String the sugar snap peas by gripping the stem and pulling it down along the pod to pull off the strings on both sides of the pod at the same time. Bring a large pot of water to a boil and drop in the peas. Cook for 30 seconds, drain immediately, and run them under cold water to stop the cooking action. Drain again and set aside. Add them to the sauté pan with the cooked cucumbers just long enough to heat through before serving.

❖ *Sautéed Sugar Snap Peas and Cucumbers:* Substitute ½ pound young small sugar snap peas for the shelled garden peas. String the sugar snap peas by gripping the stem and pulling it down along the pod to pull off the strings on both sides of the pod at the same time. Prepare and cook the cucumbers as above, adding the sugar snap peas to the sauté pan with the cucumbers. Cook until the vegetables are just tender yet retain some crunchiness. Add the dill and season with salt and freshly ground pepper.

Sugar Snap Peas and Carrot Logs

Sugar snap peas hadn't been invented when my grandmother set her table and served only peas that had to be shelled from their tough pods. But vegetable combinations familiar to my grandmother—peas and carrots, for example—still have great appeal. With a sugar snap pea, you get to eat the whole pea, pod and all, and sugar snaps are delicious just by themselves. But I like to serve them with carrots so that their crunchiness contrasts with the smoothness of the carrots, and as my grandmother knew very well, the colors are brilliant together. Penny-diced carrots were standard in the old days, but I prefer to cut the carrots into log shapes that echo the shape of the sugar snaps and cook very evenly. String the peas ahead of time, but cook them just before serving. The carrots can be prepared and cooked ahead, then reheated in butter or in a little broth or water just before serving; or you can skip the boiling steps in both cases and sauté the peas and braise the carrots (see variations after the main recipe).

1 lb sugar snap peas
1–1½ lb carrots
Salt and freshly ground pepper
2 tsp sugar (optional)
4–5 Tb hot melted butter
1 lemon

String the peas by snapping off the stem tip toward the flat side of the pod and gently pulling downward; the strings will pull right off. Set aside.

To prepare the carrot logs, peel the carrots and cut them into approximately 3-inch lengths. Depending on the thickness of the section of the carrot, cut the 3-inch pieces lengthwise into halves, thirds, or quarters in order to make the logs all about ½ inch thick.

Bring a pot of water to a rolling boil and add 1 teaspoon salt; if the carrots are older storage carrots that have lost their sweetness, add the sugar (carrots fresh from the summer garden or dug out of the ground of the winter garden will not need the sugar). Drop the carrot logs into the water and cook at a medium boil for 4–8 minutes, or until the carrots are barely tender, still firm, and not limp. Drain and keep the carrots warm while you cook the peas. (If preparing ahead of time, run cold water into the pan to stop the cooking action and cool the carrots, then drain them well and refrigerate until ready to reheat either in butter or in a small amount of broth or water.)

Just before you are ready to serve, bring a pot of water to a boil, drop in the peas, and cook for 2–3 minutes, or until the peas are tender but still crunchy. Drain immediately. Season the melted butter with fresh lemon juice and salt and freshly ground pepper. Pour 3 tablespoons of the seasoned butter over the carrots and toss to coat the carrots well. Stack the carrot logs down the center of a warm serving platter. Toss the sugar snaps with the remaining seasoned melted butter and place them on either side of the carrots.   SERVES 4–6

❖ Omit the butter and season the vegetables with lemon juice, salt, and pepper.

❖ Grandmother's shelled garden peas can be prepared the same way. Drop the shelled peas into boiling water and cook for 30 seconds–3 minutes, depending on the age and size of the peas.

❖ *Sautéed Sugar Snap Peas:* Sauté the peas instead of boiling them. In a large sauté pan, heat 2 tablespoons butter, stir in the peas, cover the pan, and cook over medium heat for 2–3 minutes, shaking the pan occasionally.

❖ *Braised Carrot Logs:* Peel 1 pound of carrots and cut them into logs as described above. Place the logs in a saucepan, add 1 cup beef or chicken broth and a pinch of salt, cover, bring to a boil, and cook for 5 minutes. Uncover and cook a little longer so that the liquid is reduced and forms a glaze over the carrots. Season with salt and freshly ground pepper.

Boiled New Potatoes

A favorite meal when I was growing up consisted of boiled new potatoes garnished with cottage cheese and chopped fresh scallions or chives—everything seasoned with plenty of freshly ground black pepper. Few foods are as delicious as freshly dug new potatoes boiled with skins on just until tender. The term "new potato" doesn't refer to a variety of potato, but rather to any potato freshly dug and not put into storage. It can be any size—from the size of a marble to big potatoes that I cut into chunks for roasting or mashing. You might like to consult the chapter on potatoes in *The Victory Garden Cookbook* for its information on types of potatoes and their cooking properties. When I am serving plain boiled potatoes, I remember the rule that low-starch or waxy potatoes are best for boiling. I usually select small 1½–2-inch potatoes for a plain boil, and I try to keep them pretty uniform in size so that they will cook in the same period of time. New potatoes have thin skins and do not need to be peeled unless you prefer to do so.

Twelve 1½–2-inch new potatoes
Salt

Wash the potatoes, place them in a saucepan, cover with water, and add a teaspoon of salt. Bring the water to a boil, reduce the heat, partially cover the pan, and cook gently for about 15 minutes, or until the potatoes are just tender when pierced with a fork. (Adjust the cooking time to the size of the potatoes.) Immediately drain the potatoes; then return them to the pan and roll them around to evaporate any excess moisture. Partially cover the pan to keep the potatoes warm until served, or if you need to hold them for a longer period of time, put them in the top of a double boiler over hot water.   SERVES 4–6

Steamed Baby
New Potatoes

The skins of new potatoes, especially the baby ones, are as tender as their flesh. Since steaming takes less time when the potatoes just cover the bottom of the steamer basket, I mainly use this method when I am cooking just a few small potatoes.

1 lb small new potatoes (about 10–12 potatoes)
3 Tb butter (optional)
Coarse salt
Freshly ground pepper

Wash the potatoes well. In a steamer pot, bring 1–2 inches of water to a boil and place the potatoes in the steamer basket above the water. Cover the pot, reduce the heat so that the water boils gently, and steam the potatoes until they are tender; potatoes 1½ inches in diameter should be tender in about 15 minutes. Remove the potatoes to a warm bowl, add the butter, if you are using it, and roll the potatoes in the butter after it melts. Season with coarse salt and freshly ground pepper, and serve.   SERVES 4

❖Sprinkle chopped fresh parsley, dill, or sage over the cooked potatoes and toss gently.

Boiled
"Salt" Potatoes

If you dip these cooked potatoes into the melted butter for a steamed lobster dinner, you can gratify all your self-indulgences in one meal. The salt that disqualifies this dish for anyone on a low-sodium diet gives the potato skins a white glaze and the taste of the sea.

12 small new potatoes
Kosher salt
Melted unsalted butter (optional)

Wash the potatoes and place them in a saucepan. Cover the potatoes with water by at least 2 inches and pour kosher salt into the pan until the potatoes begin to float; one pound of potatoes will take about 1 cup of salt. Bring the water to a boil and cook at a gentle boil for about 15 minutes, or until the potatoes are tender when pierced with a fork. Drain and keep warm until served. The potatoes will have a faint white salt film. Serve with melted butter for dipping, if desired.   SERVES 4

Easy Creamed Potatoes

A small serving of this wonderful but rich dish is all one needs—but don't be surprised if guests beg for more—and for that reason I think of it as perfect for holiday meals when there are lots of dishes to sample. The initial cooking softens the potatoes, and the final baking firms the dish. It is very important to dry the sliced potatoes so that the reduced cream will effectively coat the potatoes. You can prepare and assemble the dish for final baking early in the day or the day before, and bake just before serving. The recipe is easy to adjust to a larger or smaller group.

> 2 lb potatoes
> 1 cup heavy cream
> 1 cup half-and-half
> 2 crushed cloves garlic
> Salt and freshly ground pepper
> Pinch of nutmeg
> ¾ cup grated Jarlsberg cheese
> 2 Tb butter (optional)

Peel the potatoes, thinly slice them, and pat them as dry as possible with clean kitchen towels. Put the potato slices in a heavy-bottomed, 4-quart saucepan and cover them with the cream and half-and-half. Push the garlic cloves down into the cream and season the liquid with salt, freshly ground pepper, and a pinch of nutmeg. Bring the mixture to a boil, reduce the heat, and cook at a low boil until the potatoes are tender and the cream has reduced, about 30 minutes. Remove the garlic and transfer the creamed potatoes to a buttered 9-inch casserole that can go under the broiler, and sprinkle the cheese over the top. If not baking immediately, let the potatoes cool, cover, and refrigerate.

If you are proceeding to bake immediately, dot the top of the cheese with butter, if you wish, and bake in a preheated 400-degree oven for 10 minutes, or until the potatoes are bubbly; then run the dish under the broiler long enough to brown the cheese lightly.

If you have refrigerated the assembled casserole, dot the top with butter, if you wish, cover with aluminum foil, and bake in a preheated 400-degree oven for 20 minutes, or until the potatoes have heated through; then remove the foil and bake for another

10 minutes, or until the potatoes are bubbly. Reheating time will vary, depending on how cold the refrigerated casserole was. Run the dish under the broiler to brown the cheese, and serve.   SERVES 8

❖For a large crowd, this makes a great pan dish. Take any amount of peeled, sliced, towel-dried potatoes, put them in a heavy-bottomed pan, add enough equal parts of heavy cream and half-and-half to cover them, season with salt, freshly ground pepper, and crushed garlic cloves, and cook at a gentle boil until the potatoes are just tender—not pulpy-soft—and the cream has reduced. The larger the amount of potatoes, the longer the cooking time. Layer the creamed potatoes in buttered baking trays, cover with cheese, let cool, cover, and refrigerate. They will keep well for 1–2 days before baking. Reheat as above. The thicker the layers of potatoes, the longer the reheating time. Count on 30–45 minutes for large trays of potatoes. Cover the trays with aluminum foil and reheat until the potatoes are hot all the way through, then uncover and continue to bake until the top begins to brown and the cream is bubbling around the sides of the pan. Run under the broiler, if desired, to get a crusty top.

Garlic Mashed Potatoes with Brown Onions

My mother used to make mashed potatoes drizzled with onions that had been browned in butter, and I still have a vivid memory of that aromatic dish. You can omit the buttered onions from this recipe, if you like, but I believe that if you try them once, you'll find it hard not to serve them every time.

> 1 head garlic
> 5 Tb softened butter
> 2 lb peeled potatoes, cut into chunks
> Salt and freshly ground pepper
> ½ cup warm milk
> ½ cup chopped onions

Remove the outer white skin of the head of garlic and break it into cloves. Bring a pan of water to a boil, drop in the garlic cloves, and cook them for

Garlic Mashed Potatoes with Brown Onions (continued)

10–15 minutes, or until they are very soft. Drain the cloves, rinse them under cold water, peel them, and mash the flesh into a purée in a small bowl. (Or break the head of garlic into cloves and give each clove a whack with the flat side of a heavy knife; the skin will "pop" off. Mince the garlic, sprinkle it with a pinch of salt, and mash it into a purée using the back edge of a knife.) Mash 3 tablespoons of the softened butter into the garlic.

Cover the potatoes with water in a saucepan, add 1 teaspoon salt, bring to a boil, and boil for 20 minutes or until tender. Drain the potatoes, then mash them or put them through a ricer, adding small amounts of warm milk alternately with spoonfuls of garlic butter. Season with salt and freshly ground pepper.

While the potatoes are cooking, heat the remaining 2 tablespoons of butter in a small sauté pan, add the onions, and cook until the onions are lightly browned. Put the potatoes in a warm serving dish, pour the browned onions over the top, and serve.

SERVES 4–6

Hash Brown New Potatoes with Garlic, Parsley, and Lemon

Everyone loves hash browns. I make these hash browns from new potatoes that have been cooked just until tender, or I use leftover new potatoes that I may have served with fish the night before.

1½ lb new potatoes, boiled just until tender
1 tsp finely chopped garlic
3 Tb chopped parsley
Minced zest of 1 lemon (about 1 Tb)
Salt and freshly ground pepper
2 Tb vegetable oil
2 Tb butter

It's not necessary to peel new potatoes; the skins give color and texture, which I like, but peel them if you want to; then cut them into ¼-inch-thick slices. In a small bowl, combine the garlic, parsley, lemon zest, ¼ teaspoon salt and a few grindings of pepper. In a large

sauté pan, heat the oil and butter, add the sliced potatoes, and cook over medium-high heat, tossing occasionally, for 8–10 minutes, or until the potatoes are browned on all sides. Add the garlic-herb mixture and toss with the potatoes. Add more salt and freshly ground pepper, if desired.   SERVES 4

❖Omit the garlic, lemon zest, and lemon juice.

Roast Sliced Potatoes

What could be simpler than roast sliced or chunked potatoes? They are a standby at our house, and we never tire of them.

4 large baking or all-purpose potatoes
Vegetable or olive oil

Peel the potatoes and slice them into ¾-inch-thick slices. Rub the potato slices with oil until they are completely coated, place them in a baking dish, and roast them in a preheated 450-degree oven, turning them once or twice, until they are tender and brown, about 30–40 minutes. Serve immediately.   SERVES 4

❖Sprinkle the roast potatoes with kosher salt and freshly ground pepper.
❖Cook garlic cloves along with the potato slices.
❖Toss the cooked potatoes with fresh herbs.

Roast Potato Chunks

My mother always served these potatoes with a Sunday roast. Although you could omit the preboiling or blanching, I think you will find that the extra step gives a nicer texture to the finished potatoes.

4 large baking or all-purpose potatoes
Vegetable or light olive oil
Salt and freshly ground pepper

Peel the potatoes and cut them into large, 1½–2-inch chunks. Place the potatoes in a large saucepan, cover them with water, bring the water to a boil, and cook for 5–6 minutes. Drain the potatoes, and as soon as they are cool enough to handle, rub the chunks with oil until well coated; they can be prepared in advance to this point, and the potatoes will not darken if they have been thoroughly coated. Place the oiled potatoes in a baking dish and roast in a preheated 400-degree oven, turning occasionally, for 45–60 minutes, depending on the size of the chunks, or until the centers are soft and the outsides are brown and crispy. Season with salt and freshly ground pepper, and serve immediately.   SERVES 4

❖Cook garlic cloves along with the potatoes.

❖Toss the roast potato chunks with fresh herbs and grated or finely chopped lemon zest.

❖Lightly oil the potato chunks and place them alongside a poultry or meat roast. Turn occasionally in the fat released from the roast. If the temperature for the roast is 350 degrees, allow the potatoes to cook for 50–60 minutes.

Sautéed Rutabaga Dice

Rutabaga has a lingering dismal reputation from the days, not so long ago, when strong-tasting varieties were boiled to death to make them edible. The variety of rutabaga we grow in our garden now is so sweet and crisp that I enjoy eating it raw. It's a wonderful, old-fashioned root vegetable of such versatility that I even used it in a pie in *The Victory Garden Cookbook*. Providing just what the in-a-rush cook needs, the rutabaga in this recipe cooks in under 15 minutes and offers both delicious flavor and heartwarming nutrition. Our garden produces rutabaga up to 4 pounds in weight, but this recipe calls for a more conventional size.

1¼-lb trimmed rutabaga
2 Tb butter
1 Tb vegetable oil
Salt and freshly ground pepper

With a sharp knife, cut off all the tough skin of the rutabaga. (You should have about 1 pound flesh.) Cut the rutabaga into ⅜-inch-thick slices, cut the slices into ⅜-inch-wide strips, and cut the strips into ⅜-inch cubes. (You should have 4–5 cups cubes.)

In a wide sauté pan, heat the butter and oil, add the rutabaga cubes, and sauté over medium-high heat, tossing, for 3–5 minutes to brown on all sides. Reduce the heat to low, cover the pan, and cook, stirring occasionally, for another 8 minutes, or until the rutabaga is tender. Season with salt and freshly ground pepper, and serve.   SERVES 4–6

❖ *Mashed Rutabaga:* Cut the same amount of peeled rutabaga into small chunks and place them in a saucepan. Add 1 inch of water, bring it to a boil, cover, and boil gently for 15–20 minutes, or until the rutabaga is soft, watching that the water does not boil away. Drain and mash with a potato masher. I like to keep rutabaga a little lumpy. Add 2 tablespoons butter, if desired, and season with salt and freshly ground pepper. Combine with mashed potatoes, if you like.

MAKES ABOUT 2½–3 CUPS, SERVING 4–6

Warm Radishes and Black Beans

For color and texture, this hearty legume side dish—which goes well with big fish, such as swordfish, shark, and tuna—gives you red-and-white radishes and green scallions, both crunchy, to contrast with soft black beans.

1 cup sliced radishes
½ cup finely sliced scallions
2–3 Tb chopped cilantro
3 Tb olive oil
1 Tb red wine vinegar
2 cups cooked black beans
Salt and freshly ground pepper

In a small bowl, combine the radishes, scallions, and cilantro. In a sauté pan, heat the oil, stir in the vinegar, add the beans, and stir gently until the beans are heated through. Season with salt and freshly ground pepper. Add the radish mixture to the pan, stir it into the beans, and cook for 1–2 minutes until the mixture is warmed through.   SERVES 4

❖Add cooked corn kernels or other colorful vegetables to the pan with the cooked beans.

Roasted Shallots

Shallots are the "refined" member of the onion family. Their mild flavor has made them the minced onion of choice for many elegant sauces and salads. But they deserve more than a supporting role; they merit a dish of their own. Use them as an alternative whenever you are thinking of serving cooked onions as a side dish; they would be perfect as a companion to simple broiled or sautéed fish, perhaps with another vegetable or salad to add color.

½–¾ lb large shallots
2 Tb light olive oil
Salt and freshly ground pepper (optional)
Butter or sour cream (optional)

Peel the shallots and cut a tiny "X" in the root end of the larger ones. Rub them with olive oil. Place the shallots on a baking sheet in a single layer, sprinkle them with salt and freshly ground pepper, if desired, and roast in a preheated 450-degree oven for 15 minutes, or until the tip of a sharp paring knife easily pierces the flesh. Serve with butter or sour cream, if you like.   SERVES 4

❖Leave the skin on the shallots until after they are roasted; rub off the skins as soon as the shallots are cool enough to handle.

Braised Chopped Spinach

When spinach is in season, my husband, Russell, would be pleased to see it on the table every night. Sometimes, toward the end of a busy day, I find his appetite for spinach quite irritating. If the spinach is young and can be quickly rinsed and cooked in just the water that clings to the leaves, I am not bothered. But older spinach is another story; it can be a real pain to prepare, and I don't have to tell you how many spinach leaves it takes to make a serving. I have decided that the best way to look on the time it takes to wash and stem older spinach is as a time for meditation or mental list-making. The washing, stemming, blanching, and chopping of raw spinach can all

be done way ahead—I even recommend it—and the spinach refrigerated in a nonaluminum-lined bowl covered with plastic wrap, or in a plastic bag, until ready to use. This recipe for braised spinach is delicious, particularly for big, tough, or packaged spinach. The creamed version is always requested for special-occasion dinners at my house.

4 lb spinach (or six 10-ounce packages)
3–4 Tb butter
2 Tb finely chopped shallots or onions
    (optional)
½ cup chicken broth or beef broth
Salt and freshly ground pepper

To wash and stem the spinach: Fill the sink with slightly warm water. Place the spinach in the water and stir it around to loosen any soil clinging to the leaves. Remove a leaf at a time from the water and fold the leaf over lengthwise, with the underside of the leaf facing out. Hold the folded leaf in one hand and with the other hand pull the stem down the length of the leaf until it pulls off. Discard the stem, put the trimmed leaf on the drainboard, and continue with the rest of the spinach. Once the spinach is stemmed, rinse it again in a sinkful of fresh water and place the spinach in colanders to drain.

To blanch and chop the spinach: Bring a large pot of water to a boil; the pot should be large enough to hold the spinach without the leaves overflowing the pot or being crushed. Add 1 teaspoon or more of salt to the boiling water and drop in the spinach by big handfuls, pushing it down into the water with a long spoon. Cook for 2–3 minutes, or just until the spinach is wilted. Immediately remove the pot to the sink and run cold water into it—the spinach won't run over the sides. As soon as the cold water has completely replaced the hot water, drain the spinach in a colander. Gently squeeze a handful of the spinach at a time to remove as much water from it as you can and set it aside. Chop the spinach and braise it right away. Or place it in a nonaluminum-lined bowl, cover, and refrigerate until ready to proceed to the next step.

To braise the spinach: In a wide, high-sided, nonstick or nonaluminum-lined sauté pan, heat 3 tablespoons of the butter, add the shallots (if you are using them), and stir them into the butter. Add the chopped spinach and cook over medium-high heat for 3–5 minutes to evaporate the moisture in the spinach; the spinach will begin to stick to the bottom of the pan when all the moisture has evaporated. Stir the chicken or beef broth into the spinach and cook gently, partially covered for 4–5 minutes, stirring the spinach until it has absorbed the broth. Season with salt and freshly ground pepper, and add additional butter to taste, if desired.   SERVES 4–6

❖ *Creamed Spinach:* Replace the broth with heavy cream. If you want the dish to be very creamy, stir 1–2 tablespoons flour into the spinach after you have sautéed it in the butter. Cook the spinach and flour for 2 minutes, add 1 cup heavy cream, and let the spinach and cream braise together, partially covered, stirring frequently, until the spinach has absorbed most of the cream. Season as above

Wilted Spinach with Garlic and Lemon

Forget big pots of water to blanch spinach that you will serve immediately; this recipe lets you simply wilt spinach in flavored olive oil. Wash and spin-dry the spinach ahead of time, if you like, and refrigerate it until ready to cook in paper-towel-lined plastic bags with a few air holes for circulation.

> 1½–2 lb spinach
> ¼ cup olive oil
> 1–2 tsp finely chopped garlic
> Zest and juice of 1 lemon
> Salt and freshly ground pepper

Remove the stems from any large spinach leaves, and wash and spin-dry all of the spinach. In a wide, high-sided sauté pan, heat the oil, stir in the garlic, and add the lemon zest. Add the spinach a handful at a time, turning it in the oil as it wilts and cooks. When it has all wilted to tender, pour the lemon juice over it and season with salt and freshly ground pepper. Lift the spinach out of the pan with a slotted spoon or spatula to a warm serving dish, leaving the cooking liquids behind, and serve.   SERVES 4

❖ Omit the lemon zest and juice, and the garlic.

Roasted Summer Squash

This recipe might very well tempt you to plant more summer squash in your garden.

> 2 zucchini squash
> 2 yellow squash
> 1 red pepper
> 2 Tb pine nuts
> 6–8 cloves blanched garlic★ (optional)
> 2 Tb light olive oil
> Salt and freshly ground pepper
> 12 thinly sliced large basil leaves
> 1 Tb balsamic vinegar or fresh lemon juice

★ *To blanch the garlic:* Peel the garlic cloves, drop them into a pan of boiling water, cook at a rapid boil for 5 minutes, and drain.

Wash the two kinds of squash and the pepper, and pat them dry. Remove the squash stems and cut the squash into 1–1½-inch chunks. Cut the pepper in half lengthwise, remove the stem, seeds, and white membrane, and cut the flesh into 1–1½-inch pieces.

Place the pine nuts in a small, nonstick sauté pan and cook over medium heat, stirring, until they are lightly browned. Set aside.

Place the squash, pepper, and garlic, if you are using it, on a baking sheet. Drizzle the oil over the vegetables, sprinkle them with salt and freshly ground pepper, turn them in the oil until they are lightly coated, and spread them out across the sheet. Roast in a preheated 500-degree oven for 10 minutes. Remove the vegetables and let them cool slightly. Place the vegetables in a bowl, add the basil, and toss with the vinegar or lemon juice. Sprinkle the top with the pine nuts and serve.   MAKES ABOUT 4 CUPS

Sautéed Squash Chunks

This recipe happily accepts any kind of summer squash—yellow summer squash, zucchini, pattypan squash—and is a perfect way to prepare large squash. I

Sautéed Squash Chunks (continued)

blanch the whole squash ahead of final cooking to keep it from releasing so much juice when sautéed that it simmers instead; for convenience, blanch the whole squash in the morning, cut it, store in the refrigerator, and then spend a very few minutes cooking it just before serving. We used to blanch 20–30 pounds of squash in the morning at the restaurant, then sauté it to order that night. Use clarified butter to keep the butter from browning, or a combination of butter and oil, or all olive oil.

> 2–2½ lb summer squash
> 3 Tb *Clarified Butter* (page 351) or half butter
>   and half olive oil
> Salt and freshly ground pepper
> Chopped fresh herbs (optional)
> Fresh lemon juice (optional)

To blanch the squash, bring a large pot of water to a boil, drop the whole squash into the water, and cook until a long-tined fork pierces the flesh easily. Watch this step carefully; you want the squash to be just tender enough for the fork to go in, but the flesh should still be firm, not limp. Immediately place the pot in the sink and run cold water into the pot to replace the hot water, stopping the cooking action and chilling the squash down. Drain the squash and pat it dry.

Cut the squash lengthwise into strips and then crosswise into pieces about 1½ inches long; I think it looks best if the cuts are slightly on the diagonal. I cut pattypan squash into triangular chunks, but there is no reason for you not to experiment with other cuts. If you are reserving the squash for later cooking, pat the pieces dry as best you can, spread them out in a nonaluminum-lined pan, cover, and refrigerate until ready to use.

In a large sauté pan, heat the clarified butter, add the squash, and cook for 3–5 minutes, or until the pieces of squash are just tender and hot. If you have cut the squash into larger pieces, they may need to cook a minute or two more while covered. Season with salt and freshly ground pepper, and sprinkle with fresh herbs and lemon juice, if desired.   SERVES 4–6

❖ Cook the squash in olive oil. Heat the oil, stir in 1–2 teaspoons finely minced garlic, and sauté the squash as above.

❖ Young squash fresh from the garden can be thinly sliced and sautéed without the blanching step.

Waltham Butternut Squash "Pillows" with Fresh Sage

These pillow-shape bundles of squash are my version of squash gnocchi that I tasted at the guest house of Livio Felluga's vineyard in Friuli, the glorious northeast region of Italy. The chef knew no English and I knew very little Italian, but with gestures she showed me how to make them. What in Italy is called gnocchi could here be called dumplings, but the particular way these bundles are shaped reminds me of pillows. This dish makes a lovely and unusual appetizer, but it could also be a main course accompanied by a side dish to provide protein. The shaping of the pillows sounds harder than it actually is; it goes quickly and is fun to do. It is better if the squash is cooked and puréed the day before so that it will be well drained before it is shaped into pillows—leftover squash would be ideal to use. You can shape and poach the pillows in the morning or even the day before, refrigerate them, and bake them just before serving. To keep the bundles from getting leaden, I use a combination of cake flour and all-purpose flour and as little of it as possible, just enough to bind the puréed squash together lightly. The amount of flour to use is determined by the looseness of the squash; use less rather than more. I love the unique flavor of fresh sage, but you can heat the pillows in a favorite tomato sauce, if you prefer.

> 2 cups puréed cooked squash
> 2 large eggs, beaten
> ¾ cup cake flour★
> ½ cup all-purpose flour
> 1 tsp salt
> Freshly ground pepper
> 1 Tb finely grated fresh Parmesan cheese
>   (optional)
> 4–8 Tb butter
> 12–18 fresh sage leaves
> ½ cup shaved fresh Parmesan cheese (optional)

★ Add more flour as needed if the squash has a soft or loose texture.

Place the puréed squash in a sieve to drain any excess moisture (it is important that the squash be firm, not wet and loose). Place the drained squash in a bowl and stir in the eggs. Combine the cake and all-purpose flours and gradually beat the mixed flour into the squash, along with 1 teaspoon salt and the grated Parmesan cheese, if you are using it. Season with more salt, if desired, and with freshly ground pepper.

Bring a large pot of salted water to a rolling boil, then reduce the heat enough to keep the water at a gentle boil.

Use two equal-sized oval soupspoons or tablespoons to shape the squash pillows. Lift out a walnut-size scoop of the squash mixture with the first spoon. Holding both spoons in front of you at a slight angle to each other, slide the edge of the second spoon under the squash and at the same time rotate the first spoon enough so that the squash mixture rolls from the first spoon into the bowl of the second spoon; the rolling action will shape the squash into a "pillow." Then, holding the spoons over and as close to the water as you safely can, slide the first spoon under the squash and rotate the second spoon, but this time, instead of rolling the squash from one spoon to the other, use the first spoon to guide the squash pillow off the second spoon into the water in a rolling motion. The squash will sink to the bottom, but in less than a minute it will float to the surface. Continue making the pillows, either dipping the spoons into the cooking pot to remove any buildup of squash or rinsing the spoons in a jar of warm water kept next to the pot. After the pillows float back to the surface, let them cook another 5–6 minutes to lightly firm them and cook the insides. Cook about 8–12 pillows at a time, removing them with a slotted spoon when they are done, allowing them to drain, and placing them in a baking dish. (At this point you can cool the squash "pillows," and cover and refrigerate them until ready to bake later.)

In a small saucepan, melt as much of the butter as you want to use and stir in the fresh sage. Pour the mixture over the squash pillows and bake in a preheated 425-degree oven for 10–15 minutes, or until the butter is bubbly and the squash is completely heated through. Serve topped with shaved Parmesan cheese, if you like, and pass a pepper grinder.

MAKES ABOUT 24 SQUASH PILLOWS;
SERVES 6 AS AN APPETIZER, 4 AS A MAIN COURSE

❖The fresh sage gets toasty in the oven, a texture that I like. If you prefer, you can add the sage to the butter a few minutes before the squash finishes baking, and the leaves will be tender.

❖If you are serving the squash pillows immediately, keep them warm after they are removed from the water. Bake them as above or sauté them. Heat the butter and sage in a large, nonstick sauté pan, place the squash in the pan, and cook until the pillows are hot, turning them in the butter. You may want to add more butter or some heavy cream.

❖If you want to be very fancy, trim the pillows with scissors after the squash is poached so that all the sides are smoothly shaped.

❖Control the size of the pillows by the amount of squash you shape for each one. Use teaspoons instead of soupspoons or tablespoons to make smaller pillows.

❖Shape the squash as above, but omit the butter and sage; reheat the pillows in a favorite tomato sauce, salsa, or cream sauce.

Succotash

Succotash is a great partner for fish. For many years I made it the usual way with lima beans and corn, but when we began to grow a favorite English bean—fava—in our garden, I switched to fava beans in my succotash. There is an extra step because you have to slip off the outer skin of the fava beans after cooking them unless they are very young beans, but I think the result is worth the effort. If you don't have fava beans, by all means use the tried-and-true limas.

    2 cups shelled fava beans or lima beans
    1 strip bacon (optional)
    3 Tb butter
    ½ cup diced onions
    2 cups fresh corn kernels
    ¼ cup heavy cream
    Salt and freshly ground pepper
    Chopped fresh chives, for garnish

Bring a pot of water to a boil and drop in the fava beans and the bacon, if you are using it. Cook until the beans are tender, usually 6–10 minutes, but longer if the beans are large. Drain, discarding the bacon, and run the beans under cold water to stop the cooking action. Slip the skins off the beans (not necessary if you are using lima beans), discarding the skins. (Makes about 1 cup skinned beans)

In a sauté pan, heat the butter, add the onions, and sauté for 1–2 minutes. Stir in the corn and cook gen-

Succotash (continued)

tly for 2 minutes. Add the cream and beans, and cook until just heated through, about 2–3 minutes. Season with salt and freshly ground pepper. Serve garnished with fresh chives.   SERVES 3–4

❖Slightly reduce the amount of butter, if you like, or omit the heavy cream.

Roast Sweet Potato Slices

Forget the candied sweet potatoes! This is better.

    1 lb sweet potatoes
    Vegetable oil
    Salt and freshly ground pepper

Peel the sweet potatoes and slice them into ¼-inch-thick pieces. Toss the potato slices in a bowl with a few tablespoons of oil until the slices are lightly coated on all sides. Spread the slices in a single layer on a nonstick baking sheet and roast them in a preheated 500-degree oven for 10 minutes. Season with salt and freshly ground pepper.   SERVES 4

Broiled Tomatoes with an Herb-Crumb Topping

A tasty serving of fish needs nothing else if there is a toasty broiled tomato by its side.

    4 large ripe tomatoes
    4 Tb olive oil
    1 heaping cup fresh bread crumbs
    1 tsp minced garlic
    ⅓ cup chopped fresh parsley
    1–2 tsp chopped fresh thyme or other herbs
    Salt and freshly ground pepper

Wash, dry, and stem the tomatoes. Cut them in half horizontally and place them, cut side up, in a baking dish that can go under the broiler. Cut a thin slice as

necessary off the bottom of any of the tomato halves to make them sit stably in the dish. Brush the top side with oil.

In a small bowl, combine the bread crumbs, garlic, parsley, thyme, ½ teaspoon salt, and a few grindings of pepper. Add the remaining oil and mix all together.

Place the tomatoes about 4–5 inches below a preheated broiler and cook for 3–5 minutes to soften slightly and brown lightly; cooking time depends on how ripe the tomatoes are, but you don't want them to become mushy. Remove the tomatoes and spoon the crumb mixture evenly over the tops. Return the tomatoes to the broiler, this time about 8 inches below the heat, and broil for 3 minutes, or until the crumb topping is golden brown and crusty on top.
SERVES 4–8

Helen Cohen's Marinated Zucchini Strips

One of my sons-in-law is a master at the grill, and his mother, from whom I extracted this recipe, is an excellent cook. How lucky can you get? Use this as a vegetable side dish or as a first-course starter. Add olive oil as needed to fry the zucchini, and use a very good vinegar to taste.

    6–8 zucchini
    5–6 cloves garlic
    Vegetable oil, olive oil, or a combination of
        both
    Dried oregano to taste
    Salt and freshly ground pepper
    Red wine vinegar

Wash, dry, and trim the ends of the zucchini. Halve crosswise any zucchini longer than 5–6 inches. Then cut the zucchini lengthwise into strips ¼ inch thick and 3–5 inches long.

Peel the garlic and slice it into thin slivers.

Heat about ¼ inch of oil in a large skillet or, if you are making a large amount, in two skillets. Fry batches of zucchini strips in a single layer, turning them until they are lightly browned on both sides. Add a few slivers of garlic with each batch to flavor

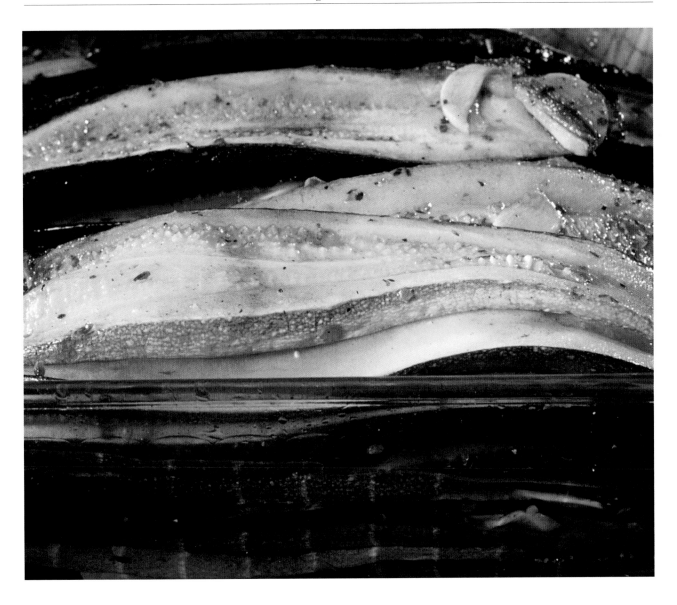

Sautéed Zucchini and Zucchini Tian

the oil, removing the garlic when it is light brown and avoiding blackened garlic, which gives an acrid taste. Lift the browned zucchini from the skillet to a large, flat serving dish with sides high enough to contain any juices, and spread the strips in an even layer. Sprinkle the layer with oregano, salt, freshly ground pepper, and a splash of vinegar. Add cooked garlic slivers to the layers in the serving dish as you go. Continue cooking, layering and seasoning until all the zucchini has been fried. Pour a little hot oil from the last batch of zucchini into the serving dish to give a good balance of oil, vinegar, and seasonings.

Serve the zucchini warm, at room temperature, or chilled; serve with Italian or French bread to sop up the delicious juices. SERVES 6–8

This "two-dishes-for-the-price-of-one" recipe offers the options of sautéing zucchini and serving it in that form, or of adding a slightly more elaborate step and baking the sautéed zucchini with rice, cheese, and bread crumbs. I have called the second step a tian, which is an earthenware container often used to bake this kind of dish, but I could also have called the dish a gratin because of the buttered crumb topping that browns as it bakes. The second stage of the recipe uses partially cooked rice, which then absorbs the natural juices of the zucchini as it finishes cooking in the baking dish. The zucchini needs at least 30 min-

Sautéed Zucchini and Zucchini Tian (continued)

utes of salting and draining to release some of its juice before it is sautéed; this preparation can be done in the morning or even the day before, and the prepared zucchini can then be refrigerated until final cooking. We used great quantities of zucchini at the Straight Wharf Restaurant, and the problem was how to squeeze so much of it. Once we even tried putting it in a fresh, clean pillowcase and placing it in a washing machine on the spin cycle; what emerged was something like shredded tissue paper. Eventually we settled on having two people twist a towel full of grated zucchini in opposite directions to wring out the juice—hard labor, but it worked.

SAUTÉED ZUCCHINI

2½ lb zucchini
1 tsp or more salt
2 Tb butter
1 Tb oil
½–1 cup chopped onions
1 minced clove garlic (optional)
Freshly ground pepper

To prepare and sauté the zucchini: Wash and dry the zucchini and trim off the stem ends. Grate the zucchini through the large holes of a grater. (Makes about 8 cups) Place the grated zucchini in a colander, sprinkle it with 1 teaspoon salt, and toss well. Allow to stand for 30 minutes so that the salt can draw liquid out of the zucchini. Then take handfuls of zucchini and squeeze out as much of the remaining liquid as you can. (You should now have about 6 cups zucchini.)

In a nonstick sauté pan, heat the butter and oil, add the onions, and sauté until the onions are slightly wilted. Stir in the garlic, if you are using it, add the grated zucchini, and cook for 3–4 minutes, stirring occasionally. Season with freshly ground pepper and, if needed, with more salt.

SERVES 3–4 AS A SIDE DISH

TIAN

½ cup raw rice, cooked 5 minutes in 1 cup
    water and drained
1 recipe *Sautéed Zucchini*
¾ cup grated Swiss cheese
Salt and freshly ground pepper
1 cup *Buttered Bread Crumbs* (page 351)

To make the tian: Combine the partially precooked rice, the sautéed zucchini, and ½ cup of the Swiss cheese in a bowl, and season the mixture with salt and freshly ground pepper. Place the mixture in a buttered, low-sided, 1½-quart baking dish, top with the remaining cheese and the buttered bread crumbs, and bake in a preheated 400-degree oven for 25 minutes.   SERVES 4–6

❖Rinse off the salt, if you wish, before squeezing and sautéing the zucchini.

❖In place of the zucchini, use 4 cups sautéed greens, such as broccoli de rabe, chicory, cabbage, or collard greens; or use other vegetables of your choice.

Mixed Vegetable Grill

I think of this dish as a variation on ratatouille, the Mediterranean eggplant and summer vegetable dish fragrant with garlic and basil (see *Roasted Ratatouille*, page 326). Traditionally each vegetable in ratatouille is cooked separately, and then they are combined and cooked further together. Here the vegetables are grilled, combined, and served without further cooking, so that each one retains its distinctive grilled flavor and texture.

If your grill does not have a cover, make a tent of aluminum foil with which to cover the vegetables while cooking. All the vegetables can be prepared for cooking ahead of time and set aside, or the completed dish can be made ahead and served later at room temperature, or refrigerated and served cold.

1 Tb minced garlic
Salt
½ cup olive oil
2 eggplants, about 1 lb each, or 2 lb small ones
3 zucchini, yellow squash, or a combination of
    both (2 lb total)

2 large Spanish onions
3 large red peppers
1 lb small plum tomatoes (8–10) or 1 lb cherry
    tomatoes
12 or more large fresh basil leaves
1–2 Tb balsamic vinegar or red wine vinegar
Freshly ground pepper

Mix the garlic with ½ teaspoon salt and purée the mixture with the back of a knife. Place the purée in a small bowl, add the oil, and stir.

Trim both ends of each eggplant. Peel the eggplants, leaving some lengthwise strips of skin showing, if you like, for decoration. Cut the eggplant lengthwise into 3 pieces, brush both sides of each piece with the garlic-oil mixture, and set the pieces on a tray or baking sheet. If the eggplants are very small, cut them in half lengthwise and leave the skins on if they are tender.

Trim the zucchini or squash, cut each in half lengthwise, brush the pieces with the garlic oil, and add them to the tray of eggplant.

Trim and peel the onions, slice each one crosswise into 3 pieces, brush the pieces on both sides with the garlic oil, and add them to the vegetable tray, using a second tray or baking sheet, if necessary.

Halve the red peppers lengthwise and remove the stems, seeds, and white membranes. Brush the pieces with the garlic oil and add them to the vegetable tray.

Thread the tomatoes on long skewers and coat them with the garlic oil; set aside.

Preheat the grill. Place the eggplant and zucchini on the grill, cover, and sear over high heat for 2–3 minutes; turn the vegetables, cover again, reduce the heat to medium, and cook the vegetables until they are just tender, about 4–8 minutes, depending on their thickness. Remove the eggplant and zucchini to a tray.

Bring the grill back to high, place the onions and peppers on the grill, cover, and sear for 2–3 minutes, or until the peppers have blackened. Turn the vegetables, cover again, reduce the heat to medium, and cook for 3 minutes; remove the peppers to the tray and cook the onions for another 3–4 minutes, or until they are slightly tender but not soft. Remove the onions to the tray and place the skewered tomatoes on the grill for just a minute or two; do not let them soften.

Scrape the charred skin off the grilled peppers as soon as they are cool enough to handle, cut them into ¾-inch chunks, and put them in a large bowl. Cut the eggplant, zucchini, and onions into ¾-inch chunks and add them to the peppers. Cut the tomatoes in half, or leave whole if they are very small, and add them to the vegetables. Roll up the basil leaves, cut them into fine julienne strips, and add them to the vegetables.

Mix the vinegar with 1–2 tablespoons of the remaining garlic oil, if you like, and drizzle over the vegetables. Fold all together and season with salt and freshly ground pepper. Serve at once, or marinate for 1–2 hours and serve at room temperature, or chill and serve cold.

SERVES 8

❖If you are using a charcoal grill, adjust the distance from heat to rack to sear or to cook at medium heat, or move the vegetables from the center to the edges of the grill.
❖Broil all the vegetables instead of grilling them.
❖Add other chopped fresh herbs.
❖Serve individual grilled vegetables as a vegetable course without combining.

Appendixes
and Index

Basic Recipes

Aïoli

Aïoli, a pungent garlic-flavored mayonnaise, is a fragrant addition when stirred into fish soups or served as an accompaniment to poached fish or grilled vegetables. The traditional recipe uses raw egg yolks and oil to create the thick mayonnaise emulsion, but since it is not wise to use raw eggs in any uncooked recipe, this version substitutes store-bought mayonnaise. (If you wish to make aïoli the classic way, see the recipe in *The Victory Garden Cookbook* and substitute liquid pasteurized eggs if you are concerned about using raw eggs in an uncooked recipe.) The amount of garlic is up to you, but I think the more the better. A food processor is handy for this sauce, which can be made well ahead and refrigerated.

    1–2 Tb minced garlic, or more to taste
    Salt
    ½ cup fresh bread crumbs, lightly packed
    2–3 tsp fresh lemon juice
    1⅓ cups mayonnaise
    1–2 tsp Dijon-style mustard (optional)
    Freshly ground pepper

Food Processor Method: Place the minced garlic on a work surface, sprinkle ¼ teaspoon salt on the garlic, and mash the garlic and salt together with the back of a heavy knife to purée the garlic. Adding more salt helps to purée the garlic, but you do not have to get the gar-

lic perfectly smooth. Put the puréed garlic in the bowl of a food processor fitted with a steel blade, add the bread crumbs and 2 teaspoons of the lemon juice, and process to combine the ingredients. Add the mayonnaise and the mustard (if you are using it), and process to blend until smooth, scraping down the sides of the bowl with a rubber spatula, if necessary. Season with more salt and lemon juice, if you like, and with freshly ground pepper.   MAKES ABOUT 1⅓ CUPS

❖*Hand Method:* Purée the garlic with the salt, as above, and place the puréed garlic in a bowl. Add the bread crumbs and the lemon juice, and pound the mixture into a paste with a pestle; then add the mayonnaise and the mustard, if desired, and blend to smooth. Season with more salt and lemon juice, if desired, and with freshly ground pepper.

❖See the pimento-flavored garlic mayonnaise *Rouille* (page 360).

Artichokes

    Whole artichokes
    1 lemon, cut in half
    Acidulated water (water with a little fresh
        lemon juice or vinegar added)

Artichokes (continued)

To prepare artichoke bottoms: (A whole artichoke bottom is the trimmed fleshy bottom of the artichoke with the tender pale leaves that cover the fuzzy inner choke removed; the choke itself is removed after cooking.) Cut off the stem from the base of each artichoke. Holding an artichoke in one hand by its top, start breaking off the leaves nearest the base with your other hand. Bend each leaf back until it snaps, leaving the fleshy base of the leaf still attached to the artichoke. Work around the artichoke in circles until you have trimmed the leaves up beyond the curve of the fleshy inner artichoke bottom. Rub the cut surfaces with half a lemon as you work so that the juice from the lemon will keep the artichoke from discoloring. Place the artichoke on its side on a work surface, and with a sharp, heavy knife, cut the artichoke in half crosswise, severing and discarding all the remaining untrimmed leaves above the curve. With a small, sharp paring knife, trim off any dark green portions of the leaves you snapped around the base of the artichoke. Drop the trimmed artichoke into the acidulated water to keep it from darkening until you are ready to cook it. (You will remove the inner fuzzy choke after cooking.)

To prepare artichoke hearts: (A whole artichoke heart is the trimmed fleshy bottom of the artichoke with the tender pale lower leaves that cover the fuzzy choke still attached; the choke itself is removed after cooking.) Trim the stem and snap off the leaves around the base as in the directions above for artichoke bottoms, but do *not* cut the artichoke in half crosswise and discard the top leaves; instead, continue snapping off the leaves until only the pale inner leaves that cover the bottom and the choke remain. Trim off any remnants of dark green leaf from the leaves around the base with a paring knife, as above, and rub all cut surfaces with half a lemon as you work. Drop the prepared artichoke into acidulated water until you are ready to cook. (You will remove the inner fuzzy choke after cooking.)

To cook whole artichoke bottoms or hearts: Artichokes need to be cooked in a solution called a blanc—flour and lemon juice mixed with water—to keep the flesh from darkening while they cook.

¼ cup flour
6 cups water
¼ cup fresh lemon juice
6 whole artichoke bottoms or hearts

Place the flour in a 4-quart saucepan and gradually beat in 3 cups water, whisking until the mixture is smooth. Heat the mixture to a boil, reduce the heat until the mixture just simmers, and add the remaining 3 cups of water and the lemon juice, whisking to keep the mixture smooth.

Drop the artichoke bottoms or hearts into the water, adding more water, if necessary, to make sure they are covered with liquid. Bring the liquid back to a boil, reduce the heat, and cook 15–30 minutes, depending on the size of the artichokes or until the artichoke flesh is tender when pierced with a knife. Remove from the heat and let the artichokes cool. They can be kept in their cooking liquid, refrigerated, for 2–3 days. Before you use them, rinse them off, pat them dry, and scoop out the inner fuzzy choke with a teaspoon.

Béchamel Sauce (Basic White Sauce)

2½ Tb butter
3 Tb flour
2 cups hot milk
Salt and freshly ground pepper

In a saucepan, melt the butter, add the flour, and whisk the mixture to remove any lumps. Cook the butter and flour over medium-low heat for 2 minutes, or until the flour is golden but not browned. Remove the pan from the heat, add the hot milk, and whisk the sauce vigorously until smooth. Return the pan to the heat, bring the mixture to a boil, add ½ teaspoon salt, and reduce the heat so that the mixture just simmers. Cook slowly for at least 5 minutes to eliminate any floury taste; simmering longer will improve the taste and thicken the sauce slightly. Thin the sauce with a little milk if it is too thick. Season with the salt and freshly ground pepper.   MAKES ABOUT 1½ CUPS

❖Change the consistency of the sauce by decreasing (to thin) or increasing (to thicken) the amount of flour.

❖*Velouté Sauce:* Use fish stock or chicken broth rather than milk, or half fish cooking liquid and half milk.

❖*Parsley Sauce:* This is very nice with a poached white fish, such as cod, bass, or halibut. Stir ¼ cup finely chopped parsley into the simmered sauce. Season with salt and freshly ground pepper, and with 2 teaspoons fresh lemon juice.

Buttered Bread Crumbs

2–3 Tb butter
1 cup fresh bread crumbs

In a sauté pan, heat the butter, stir in the bread crumbs, and cook until the crumbs have absorbed the butter and begin to separate and turn golden.

Cauliflower Relish

This tasty fresh vegetable condiment is a delightful side dish for grilled or broiled fish, and it keeps well in the refrigerator for several days. Though I call it a relish, I serve it much like a side salad of coleslaw.

1 large head or 2 small heads cauliflower
⅓ cup light olive oil
⅓ cup vegetable oil
1 large onion, cut into wedges
10 peeled cloves garlic
4 peeled and thinly sliced carrots
1 tsp whole peppercorns
1½ cups white vinegar
One 4-oz can chopped jalapeño peppers,
    drained (save the liquid)
1 heaping Tb salt
10 small bay leaves
½ cup peeled, seeded, and chopped red peppers
    or pimentos
¾ tsp thyme
¾ tsp oregano
¾ tsp marjoram

Cut the cauliflower into flowerets, peel the stem, and slice the stem into small pieces.

In a large, heavy saucepan or Dutch oven, heat the olive and vegetable oils, add the onion wedges, and cook, stirring, for 2 minutes. Add the garlic, carrots, and peppercorns, and cook for 5 minutes. Add the vinegar and simmer, covered, for 3 minutes.

Add 2 cups water and the liquid from the drained jalapeño peppers, cover, and bring to a boil. Add the salt and cauliflower, reduce the heat, and cook gently over medium heat, covered, for 6–10 minutes, or until the cauliflower is just tender but still crunchy. Add the bay leaves, jalapeño peppers, red peppers or pimentos, thyme, oregano, and marjoram, and simmer, covered, for 2 minutes. Remove from the heat, let cool to room temperature, cover, and refrigerate until ready to use.   MAKES ABOUT 8 CUPS

Clarified Butter

Clarified butter is the pure butter fat remaining after any milk proteins, salts, or water in the butter are removed. The milk proteins in butter will begin to brown and burn once the butter is heated past the boiling point of water. The simple process of clarifying butter leaves you with butter fat that is tolerant of the high temperatures used in many fish cookery recipes. Clarified butter keeps for weeks in the refrigerator.

To clarify butter: Cut the butter into small chunks and place it in a heavy-bottomed saucepan. Melt the butter over medium heat until it gently boils, but watch to make sure it doesn't boil over. Foam and bubbles will form on the surface to mark the escape of water and proteins. When the bubbles have just about subsided, the clarification is completed. What remains is a thick layer of clear pure butter fat (the clarified butter), and beneath it in the pan is a milky whitish layer of water and proteins. With a ladle, lift out just the absolutely clear liquid and place it in a storage jar; or, if you wish, strain the butter liquid through cheesecloth, leaving the milky residue in the bottom of the pan and then discarding it. Refrigerate the clarified butter. Although amounts may vary with the quality of the butter, 1 pound of butter should render about 1½ cups of clarified butter.

Compound Butters

Flavored butters make a delicious topping for grilled, broiled, and baked fish, since they both lubricate the fish and add an enhancing flavor. Compound butter is butter softened to room temperature—so that it can be easily mixed—and flavored with ingredients beaten into it; the butter is then chilled in a bowl or mold or in a roll for later use. The flavoring possibilities are almost limitless; several are presented below, but let your imagination be your guide. The citron butter and escargot butter are so versatile that I have given instructions for enough butter to make a roll. The remaining butters call for a smaller amount, but any of them can be doubled, tripled, or more. I use unsalted butter, but you can use salted butter, if you prefer.

To chill the butter in a mold: Line the mold with plastic wrap, allowing some extra wrap to hang over the sides of the mold. Fill the mold, pressing the butter down firmly, cover, and refrigerate it to chill. To unmold, lift the butter from the mold by pulling up the overhanging plastic wrap; turn the molded butter onto a plate and remove the wrap.

To make a compound butter roll: One-half pound of butter makes about a 6-inch roll; one pound of butter makes a 12-inch roll. Place the softened butter in a mixer and beat in whatever seasonings or herbs you prefer. Cut a sheet of aluminum foil that is about 6 inches longer than the roll you intend to make, and about 8 inches wide. Cut a piece of waxed paper the same size and lay them on a work surface together so that the waxed paper makes an inner lining for the aluminum foil, which will be the outside wrapping. With a spatula, shape the soft flavored butter into a long sausagelike roll about 1½ inches in diameter, and position the roll down the long side of the waxed-paper lining and about 2 inches in from one long edge; fold that closer edge of paper and foil up over the butter roll and continue to roll the butter in the paper and foil until you have used up the entire width of the wrapping. Then twist the ends of the paper and foil in opposite directions at the end of the cylindrical roll to tighten the wrapping; as the wrapping becomes taut from the twisting, the butter will be further shaped into a uniform roll. Refrigerate the roll to chill or place it in the freezer for later use. As soon as the flavored butter is firm again, it can be unwrapped and rounds sliced off to be placed on cooked fish.

ANCHOVY BUTTER

This butter, unchilled, makes great anchovy toasts. Spread the flavored, softened butter on triangles of pita bread and toast in the oven; serve with cocktails.

4–8 flat anchovies, to taste
¼ lb softened unsalted butter
1 tsp fresh lemon juice

In a small bowl, mash the anchovies to a paste. Add the butter and lemon juice, beat all together, cover, and chill.   MAKES ABOUT ½ CUP

❖Use 2 tablespoons processed anchovy paste in place of anchovies.
❖*Anchovy Butter Roll:* Double the ingredients and turn this into a chilled butter roll to slice and put on top of fish. Add 1–2 tablespoons chopped fresh parsley and/or chopped fresh shallots.

BLACK OLIVE AND CAPER BUTTER

¼ lb softened unsalted butter
2 Tb finely chopped black olives
1–2 Tb small or chopped capers

In a small bowl, beat the butter, olives, and capers together, cover, and chill.   MAKES ABOUT ½ CUP

❖*Hot Pepper Butter:* Replace the capers with finely diced hot peppers and drops of hot pepper sauce to taste.

CITRON BUTTER ROLL

½ lb softened unsalted butter
2 Tb fresh lemon juice
2 Tb fresh lime juice
Grated zest of 1 lemon
Grated zest of 3 limes

Place the butter in a bowl, add the remaining ingredients, beat well to incorporate the juices into the butter, and chill in the bowl or shape into a roll.
MAKES A 6-INCH ROLL

❖Add more grated zest.

ESCARGOT BUTTER ROLL

½ lb softened unsalted butter
2 finely chopped cloves garlic
2 Tb finely chopped fresh parsley
2 Tb finely chopped shallots or chives

Place the butter in a bowl, add the remaining ingredients, beat the mixture until well blended, and chill in the bowl or shape into a roll and chill.

MAKES A 6-INCH ROLL

❖*Chive or Scallion Butter Roll:* Omit the garlic and increase the chives or add scallions.
❖*Cilantro Butter Roll:* Replace the parsley with 2–3 tablespoons chopped cilantro. Replace the shallots with finely minced red peppers and a few drops of hot pepper sauce.
❖*Garlic Butter Roll:* Omit the shallots and add more garlic.
❖*Herb Butter Roll:* Chop a mixture of your favorite fresh herbs and add to the softened butter with the shallots.

GREEN PEPPERCORN BUTTER

¼ lb softened unsalted butter
1–2 Tb chopped green peppercorns
Freshly grated black pepper (optional)

Beat the butter and peppercorns together in a bowl, add grindings of black pepper, if you like, cover, and chill.

MAKES ABOUT ½ CUP

HORSERADISH BUTTER

¼ lb softened unsalted butter
2 Tb grated fresh horseradish, or bottled horseradish, squeezed dry
Freshly ground pepper

Beat the butter and horseradish together in a bowl, season to taste with freshly ground pepper, cover, and chill.

MAKES ABOUT ½ CUP

❖*Ginger Butter:* Use finely minced or grated fresh ginger instead of the horseradish.

SMOKED SALMON BUTTER

4 oz smoked salmon bits
¼ lb softened unsalted butter
1 tsp fresh lemon juice
2 tsp chopped fresh dill (optional)

In a bowl, pound the salmon into a purée. Add the butter and lemon juice, beat all together, add dill, if desired, cover, and chill.

MAKES ABOUT ½ CUP

SUN-DRIED TOMATO BUTTER

¼ cup softened unsalted butter
2 Tb puréed softened sun-dried tomatoes (see
    To soften sun-dried tomatoes, page 218)
Hot pepper sauce (optional)

Place the butter in a bowl, mix in the sun-dried tomatoes, add hot pepper sauce to taste, if desired, cover, and chill.

MAKES ABOUT ½ CUP

❖Use a combination of sun-dried tomatoes and tomato paste.
❖*Red Pepper Butter:* Use red pepper purée instead of sun-dried tomatoes.

Crème Fraîche

2 cups heavy cream
1 cup buttermilk

In a saucepan, stir together the cream and buttermilk, and heat over a low setting until the mixture is hot but not close to boiling, not more than 80 degrees by liquid thermometer. Pour the mixture into a container, partially cover, and let it sit at room temperature for 6–8 hours until it has thickened and tastes slightly acidic. Cover and refrigerate until ready to use; keeps up to 2 weeks covered and refrigerated.

MAKES 3 CUPS

Cucumber-Dill Sauce

At our house, grilled swordfish is almost always served with this refreshing sauce, and so are other grilled, broiled, and sautéed fish on frequent occasions.

 1 cup peeled, seeded, and finely diced cucumbers
 Salt
 1 cup sour cream or yogurt
 1 Tb chopped fresh dill
 Fresh lemon juice
 Freshly ground pepper

Place the diced cucumbers in a colander, sprinkle them lightly with salt, and let them drain for 30 minutes. Pat the cucumbers dry with paper towels and place them in a bowl. Add the sour cream or yogurt and the dill, fold together, and season to taste with lemon juice and salt and freshly ground pepper.   MAKES 2 CUPS

Easy Rice Pilaf

 2 Tb butter
 1 Tb vegetable oil
 ½ cup vermicelli or other thin pasta, broken
   into ½-inch pieces
 1 cup uncooked long-grain parboiled rice★
 2 cups liquid (chicken broth, shrimp broth, or a
   combination of broth and water)
 Salt and freshly ground pepper

★I like to use Uncle Ben's Converted Rice.

In a large saucepan, heat the butter and oil, stir in the pasta, and cook until the pasta is lightly browned. Stir in the rice and cook for about 1 minute, or until it is lightly colored. Add the liquid, stir once, cover, and bring to a boil. Reduce the heat and cook at a gentle boil until the liquid is absorbed, about 15–20 minutes. Season with salt and freshly ground pepper.
                               MAKES 3–3½ CUPS

Egg Sauce

The traditional egg sauce often served with fish is nothing more than a classic béchamel sauce with hard-boiled eggs folded in. You can make a fine sauce by sieving the yolks and slicing the whites, or slicing both yolks and whites, or, as I have done here, chopping them both. If you use this sauce to enrobe a poached fish—finnan haddie, for example—you might want to increase the amount to 3 hard-boiled eggs and cut them in wedges before folding them in.

 2½ Tb butter
 3 Tb flour
 2 cups hot milk
 2 chopped hard-boiled eggs
 Salt and freshly ground pepper
 Fresh lemon juice

In a 2-quart saucepan, melt the butter, add the flour, and whisk them together over low heat for 2 minutes. Remove the pan from the heat, add the milk, and whisk the mixture until it is smooth. Return the pan to the heat, bring the mixture to a boil, and cook gently, stirring continuously, for 4–5 minutes. Fold in the chopped eggs and season with salt, freshly ground pepper, and a few drops of lemon juice to taste.
                           MAKES ABOUT 2 CUPS

❖For a richer taste, use 1 cup fish broth and 1 cup milk, or use 1 cup light cream and 1 cup milk.

❖Flavor the sauce with 1 tablespoon dry sherry or cognac.

❖*Egg and Parsley Sauce:* Add 2–3 tablespoons finely chopped parsley.

❖*Egg and Dill Sauce:* Add 2–3 tablespoons finely chopped fresh dill.

❖*Egg and Cheese Sauce:* Stir ¼ cup finely grated fresh Parmesan cheese into the sauce before adding the eggs. Or fold in ¾ cup finely grated Swiss or Cheddar cheese.

❖*Egg and Mustard Sauce:* Add 1 or more tablespoons Dijon-style mustard.

❖*Egg and Caper Sauce:* Add 1–2 tablespoons chopped capers.

❖*Piquant Sauce:* Add 1 tablespoon each chopped onions, dill pickles, and parsley.

Fish Stock

This stock is an essential for fish cookery. Fish stock is the base of the best fish soups and stews, and a valuable ingredient in some sauces. An occasional fish store might sell fish stock, but it is hard to find in markets, and when I do see it, I am usually astonished at the price asked for a mere pint of stock. You can make it yourself for almost no cost at all! For convenience and cost effectiveness, I recommend making a large amount and freezing it in smaller units so that it is always readily available in your kitchen. Most good fish markets, with a little notice, will provide you with the fish frames that flavor the stock. A fish frame is the head, spine, and tail of the fish. Sometimes frames are available without the heads; that is acceptable, but the head with its clinging bits of meat gives additional flavor, so get frames with heads when you can. I prefer cod and haddock frames because they seem to produce the purest broth, but frames from any lean white-fleshed fish will do; do not use frames from an oily fish such as bluefish or mackerel. The fish frames should be just as fresh as you would want fillets of fish to be; do not accept any yellowing or smelly frames. The directions below call for 10 pounds of fish frames. That translates into 3 cod frames, with the heads on, from fish that are 24–30 inches long. The dry vermouth or dry white wine is optional, but I add it myself for the richer flavor it imparts to the stock.

    10 lb meaty fish frames
    1 peeled large onion
    4–5 stalks celery
    1 tsp thyme
    1 qt dry vermouth or white wine (optional)

Wash the frames very thoroughly, rinsing off any blood or bits of entrails that might be clinging to the frames. Remove the gills from any heads; gills give an off taste to the broth. Place all the ingredients in a large stockpot and add enough water to cover the fish frames by at least 2 inches. (It will take about 3½–4 quarts of liquid to cover 10 pounds of fish frames.) Bring the pot to a boil, skim off any foam, reduce the heat, and simmer for 30 minutes. (Unlike the preparation of a veal stock, for example, when it helps to simmer the bones for hours, fish stock isn't improved by cooking the frames longer than suggested.) Strain the mixture through a colander into another large pan, pressing the frames in the colander slightly to release any remaining juices from the frames. Boil the strained stock for 15 minutes more to reduce it slightly and intensify its flavor, if you wish. Let it cool, place it in storage containers, cover, and refrigerate or freeze.   MAKES 3½–4 QUARTS

❖To intensify fish stock, add either mussel broth or clam broth to the finished fish stock. Always alert diners that the fish stock contains shellfish broth in case anyone is allergic to shellfish.

❖The recipe can be halved, but if you are going to the trouble of making it, it is wise to make plenty for the freezer and to store it in small units in case you need only a little for a sauce or stew.

French Bread Croutons

French bread
Olive oil

Cut the bread into ½-inch-thick slices. Brush the slices on both sides with olive oil until well coated. Place the bread on a baking sheet and bake in a preheated 350-degree oven for 10–15 minutes or until golden brown.

❖*With Garlic:* Cut 2 peeled cloves garlic in half. Rub the oiled slices of bread with the cut side of the garlic and bake as above. For even more intense flavor, rub the slices with the garlic once more after browning the bread in the oven.

❖*With Cheese:* After the slices of oiled bread have been toasted, sprinkle them with freshly grated Parmesan cheese or other grated cheese and run them under a preheated broiler just until the cheese is lightly browned.

Hollandaise Sauce

I have seen very good cooks brought to their knees by a separating hollandaise sauce. We had more than a few nightmare evenings at the Straight Wharf Restaurant when the hollandaise got too hot and separated while there were perhaps twenty orders for poached salmon with hollandaise up on the board. Having acknowledged what a tricky sauce it can be, let me suggest a few ways to raise the chances of a successful sauce:

1. Have the egg yolks and butter at the same temperature when combined.
2. Don't rush; heat the egg yolks slowly and add the butter slowly.
3. Use the best-quality unsalted butter.
4. Do not overheat the completed hollandaise or it will separate.

Consistent beating during the gradual addition of the melted butter to the heated egg yolks is necessary to make a creamy sauce. A good balloon whisk attached to a strong arm will do the job, but I like to use a food processor or blender. If you are concerned about using raw eggs to make this sauce, try to find pasteurized eggs in liquid form; many supermarkets now carry different brands of them.

> ½ lb unsalted butter
> 3 egg yolks
> 1 Tb water
> Salt and freshly ground pepper
> 1–2 Tb fresh lemon juice
> Finely grated lemon zest

Melt the butter in a saucepan, then remove it from the heat; the butter should be warm but not boiling hot when added to the egg yolks. Place the egg yolks in the top of a double boiler over simmering water, add the tablespoon of water, and beat the egg yolks and water together until the egg yolks thicken.

(The thicker the egg yolks get, the thicker the final sauce will be. If you want a light hollandaise to coat a vegetable, beat the egg yolks only to a light cream consistency. If you want a thick hollandaise, one that you might then lighten with whipped cream, beat the egg yolks to a thick texture. The melted butter will thicken the sauce slightly more, but the basic consistency is established by the egg yolks.)

Once the egg yolks are at the desired consistency, remove them from the heat and scrape them, using a rubber spatula, into a food processor or blender. Turn on the motor and very slowly, drop by drop, add the warmed melted butter. As the sauce thickens, you can increase the rate at which you add the butter. Do not add the milky residue of the melted butter to the mixture. Season with salt and freshly ground pepper and with 1 or more tablespoons of lemon juice, to taste. Add the grated lemon zest, if desired. Hold the sauce in a double boiler over warm water until ready to use; do not hold it over very hot water or it will separate.   MAKES 1½–2 CUPS

❖Whisk the butter into the egg yolks by hand, using a balloon whisk.

❖If the hollandaise has not thickened, or if it separates, try this technique: in a clean mixing bowl, put 1 tablespoon hollandaise sauce and 1 tablespoon lemon juice. Beat them together, then gradually beat the remainder of the sauce back in, a spoonful at a time, waiting until each addition thickens before adding the next.

❖*Mousseline Sauce:* For every 1½ cups hollandaise sauce, whip ½ cup heavy cream. Fold the whipped cream into the hollandaise just before serving, to lighten the texture.

Horseradish Cream

> 1 cup heavy cream
> 2–3 Tb bottled horseradish, squeezed dry, or
>   ½–¾ cup grated fresh horseradish
> Salt and freshly ground pepper
> Fresh lemon juice

Whip the cream until it is stiff and fold the horseradish into it. Season with salt and freshly ground pepper and a dash of lemon juice. Chill for 10 minutes to mingle the flavors.   MAKES 1½ CUPS

❖Add 1 teaspoon, or more if desired, of Dijon-style mustard.

❖Substitute 1½–2 cups sour cream or yogurt for the sweet cream; whisk the sour cream or yogurt until smooth and fold in the horseradish as above, or combine half sour cream and half yogurt.

❖Combine equal amounts whipped sweet cream and sour cream, or whipped sweet cream and yogurt before adding the horseradish.

❖Fold in chopped fresh dill or other finely chopped fresh herbs.

Lemon Butter Sauce

It's a shame that butter isn't as conducive to health as many other foods because its flavor in cookery is almost beyond superlatives; this variation, made with fresh lemon juice, of a classic white butter sauce (see page 114), is good enough to make grown men weep over it. While it is wise to restrict consumption of fats, every once in a while one can splurge on a divine emulsion, perhaps keeping the serving small so that guilt feelings will be minimal. The secret to making a butter-based sauce is to use *chilled* unsalted butter and to beat it over *very low* heat in a heavy-bottomed, nonaluminum-lined saucepan; careful heat control is very important. Heavy cream, which is optional in this recipe, helps to stabilize the sauce, and I recommend using it if you are just learning how to make the sauce. The cream also reduces the acidic quality of the sauce, giving it a very pleasant taste; try both ways and see which you prefer. Recently it has become fashionable to serve red wine with fish, so you may want also to try the red wine variation.

⅓–½ cup fresh lemon juice
¼ cup heavy cream (optional)
¾ lb *chilled* unsalted butter, cut into ¼-inch
    pieces
Salt and freshly ground pepper
Finely grated lemon zest (optional)

Put the lemon juice into a heavy-bottomed, nonaluminum-lined saucepan and bring it to a boil. Cook until the reduced juice (about 2 tablespoons) just films the bottom of the pan. If you are using the cream, add it now and cook until it is reduced by half. Turn the heat to very low and, whisking constantly, slowly add the butter, piece by piece, incorporating each piece into the sauce before adding the next piece. The sauce will gradually thicken, become creamy, and turn a light golden color with the addition of the but-ter. Season with salt and freshly ground pepper, and stir in the lemon zest, if desired. Keep the sauce warm over water of the same temperature as the sauce until ready to serve. MAKES ABOUT 1½ CUPS

❖*Red Wine Butter Sauce:* Replace the lemon juice with ¾–1 cup very good dry red wine and add 3 tablespoons chopped shallots. Bring to a boil, reduce the mixture to 2 tablespoons, and continue as above.

Lemon-Half Garnish for Lobster

Cut a small portion off both ends of a whole lemon to make flat bases for a half lemon to sit on without rolling about. Thrust the tip of a sharp paring knife halfway through the midsection of the lemon. Cut around the midsection in a sawtooth pattern, making sure to return to the original cut, separating the lemon into halves. Place half a lemon, flat side down, between the lobster claws, and decorate it with a parsley sprig.

Lobster Sauce (Sauce Américaine)

This aromatic essence of lobster can enhance many dishes, ranging from a delicate sole mousse and a lobster-and-leek timbale to a poached fish and a cheese soufflé. It takes a bit of time to make, but the flavor is worth the time and effort. Substitute lobster bodies (lobsters minus tails and claws) for the whole lobsters, if you wish; order 3–4 pounds of lobster bodies from your fish market (see variation below).

Two 1–1¼-lb lobsters (preferably female)
2 Tb softened butter (optional)
2 Tb butter
1 Tb vegetable oil
½ cup chopped onions or leeks
½ cup chopped carrots
½ cup chopped celery
½ cup cognac
1 cup *Lobster Stock* (page 358) or *Fish Stock*
    (page 355), or unsalted chicken broth
1½ cups beef stock
1 cup dry vermouth or white wine

Lobster Sauce (continued)

1 cup peeled, seeded, and chopped tomatoes
⅓ cup tomato paste
1 Tb fresh tarragon or 1 tsp dried
1 crushed clove garlic
Salt and freshly ground pepper
½ tsp cayenne pepper
1½ Tb softened butter
1½ Tb flour

Prepare the lobsters as in *To cut an uncooked or partially cooked lobster in pieces* (page 186) or kill the lobsters as in *Fast-Boil Method* (page 185) and then cut up the lobsters. If you wish to use the tomalley and roe, if any, push them through a fine sieve and blend the sieved tomalley and roe with 2 tablespoons softened butter in a bowl (the butter is optional at this point). Cover and refrigerate. Bring the tomalley-and-roe butter to room temperature again before using it.

In a large, high-sided sauté pan, heat 2 tablespoons butter and the vegetable oil, add the lobster pieces, and cook until they are red on all sides, about 5–6 minutes. Add the onions or leeks, carrots, and celery, and cook, stirring, for 2–3 minutes more. Pour in 6 tablespoons of the cognac, ignite it, and shake the pan until the flames die down. Add the lobster stock or fish stock, beef stock, vermouth or white wine, tomatoes, tomato paste, tarragon, garlic, ¼ teaspoon salt, and cayenne pepper, cover, and cook gently for 30 minutes, stirring occasionally.

Pour the contents of the pan into a large sieve set over a saucepan. Separate the lobster pieces from the vegetables in the sieve and remove the lobster pieces to a platter to cool. Press the juices out of the vegetables in the sieve. (You should have 1½–2 cups enriched lobster stock.)

In a small bowl, blend 1½ tablespoons softened butter with the flour until smooth. Whisk the butter-and-flour mixture into the hot lobster stock and simmer, whisking, for 2–3 minutes to thicken the sauce. If you are using the softened tomalley-and-roe butter, whisk it into the sauce now. Sieve the sauce again, if desired.

Remove the lobster meat from the shells, cut the meat into small pieces, and add to the sauce. Reheat gently, season with salt and freshly ground pepper, and add 1–2 tablespoons cognac, if you wish.

MAKES ABOUT 2½ CUPS

❖ If you want to use the meat of the lobsters for another dish or reserve it for a salad, cook the lobsters first, reserve the meat, and use the shells and the tomalley and roe, if desired, for this recipe.

❖ Use 3–4 pounds of lobster bodies in place of whole lobsters. Remove and discard the stomach sacs and intestinal tracts. Remove and discard the tomalley and any roe, if you wish.

Lobster Stock

After you've cooked and served whole lobsters, save the shells and bodies; they make an absolutely delicious stock, which can be the base for the best soups, stews, and chowders. The stock can be clarified for an elegant consommé, or the stock can be tucked away in the freezer awaiting a later occasion, perhaps a wintry night, and a recipe that recalls the essence of the sea. Frozen shells and bodies can go directly from the freezer to stockpot when you find the right moment to make the stock.

HERB BOUQUET

1 bay leaf
6 sprigs parsley
1 tsp thyme
2 crushed cloves garlic
12 crushed peppercorns
Dried orange peel (optional)

2–3 lb claw, tail, and body lobster shells
1 chopped large onion
2 chopped leeks (optional)
4 chopped stalks celery
2 tomatoes, cut in half
¼ cup tomato paste
2 tsp salt
4 qt water
2 cups dry vermouth
Salt and freshly ground pepper

Place all the ingredients for the herb bouquet in a piece of washed cheesecloth and tie with a piece of kitchen twine. If you haven't done so already, remove and discard the stomach sacs and intestinal tracts from the lobster body shells. Remove and discard the tomalley and any roe, if you wish. Place all of the ingredients in a large stockpot and bring the mixture to a boil. Lower the heat and cook gently for 1 hour. Pour the mixture through a large sieve into another pan or strain it through cheesecloth, pressing the solids down to extract all of the juices. Taste and, if necessary, season with more salt and freshly ground pepper. Use as is for a soup base, or chill or freeze for later use as in *Lobster Consommé* (below).

MAKES ABOUT 3 QUARTS

❖To intensify the flavor of the stock, return the strained stock to the heat, bring to a gentle boil, and cook until the volume is reduced to 2 quarts.

❖For an enriched flavor, sauté the lobster shells and bodies, onion, leeks, celery, and 2 chopped carrots in light olive oil for 5 minutes. Remove the cooked ingredients to a stockpot, add the remaining ingredients, substituting 1 quart chicken stock for one of the quarts of water, and cook as above.

❖Use this stock as the cooking liquid in *Paella* (page 315), or concoct a "refrigerator" soup using the stock with pasta and various leftover vegetables, or reduce 1 cup of the stock to a glaze and use it as the base for a sauce.

❖*Lobster Consommé:* Prepare the lobster stock as above. Chill the strained stock, allowing any fat to rise to the surface. Skim off all of the fat on the surface, making sure the stock is thoroughly degreased before clarifying the stock to make consommé. Carefully ladle the stock into a saucepan, leaving behind in the storage container any sediment that settled out of the stock while it chilled.

CLARIFICATION INGREDIENTS (per quart of stock; multiply as necessary)

2 egg whites
¾ cup *chilled* stock
¼ cup minced leeks or onions
¼ cup minced parsley
1 tsp tarragon

In a large bowl, whisk the egg whites and ¾ cup lobster stock together. Add the remaining ingredients, stir all together, and set aside. Bring the lobster stock in the saucepan to a boil, then gradually, in a thin stream, whisk it into the bowl of egg-white mixture.

Pour the mixture back into the saucepan, return it to the heat, and bring it to a simmer over medium heat, whisking slowly all the while. When the stock reaches a simmer, stop stirring and cook very gently for 25 minutes; do not disturb any egg-white foam on the surface of the mixture.

Line a sieve with 3–4 layers of washed cheesecloth and place the sieve over a large, clean bowl. Gently ladle the stock and the egg-white foam into the cheesecloth. The egg whites will collect in the cheesecloth and the clarified stock (consommé) will strain through into the bowl.

MAKES ABOUT 3–3½ CUPS

❖Heat before serving, season with salt and freshly ground pepper, and, if desired, with 2 tablespoons cognac or Madeira.

❖Add thinly sliced medallions of cooked lobster to the consommé and sprinkle lobster roe on top.

❖Garnish with a julienne of lightly blanched vegetables, such as carrots, red peppers, leeks, or Swiss chard leaves.

❖Reduce 1 cup of consommé to a light syrup. Gradually beat in butter as in *White Butter Sauce* (page 114) to form a light butter sauce. Stir in lobster roe and spoon over warm lobster meat.

Mango and Cilantro Chutney

This uncooked but soft "chutney," which is more like a fresh relish or compote, is quickly made and a refreshing condiment with fish and shellfish. I like it with grilled shrimp. The recipe comes from the Seychelles islands and thence to an associate, Donna Dalton, who worked at the Straight Wharf Restaurant, and now from me to you.

3 ripe mangoes
½ cup diced red onions
½ cup chopped red peppers
¼ cup golden raisins (optional)
½ cup loosely packed cilantro leaves
Hot red pepper flakes
1–2 Tb red wine vinegar or balsamic vinegar
1–2 Tb fruity olive oil
Salt and freshly ground pepper

Mango and Cilantro Chutney (continued)

Peel the mangoes and dice the flesh. (Makes about 2 cups) In a large bowl, combine all the ingredients, using hot red pepper flakes to taste, and season them with salt and freshly ground pepper. Cover and refrigerate. It will keep well in the refrigerator for 2–3 days, but the chutney gets softer as it sits.

MAKES ABOUT 4 CUPS

❖ This recipe can easily be divided or multiplied.

Peanut Sauce

Peanut sauce is a traditional satay accompaniment (see *Shrimp Satay with a Pickled Cucumber Salad,* page 271) and a good dipping sauce for grilled and broiled fish. Indonesian cookbooks often call for ingredients that are not readily available in some parts of the country, but this simple version uses ingredients that everyone should be able to find without difficulty. If coconut milk is not available in cans in your market, you can substitute plain old water, adding 1 tablespoon of light brown sugar to the water to make up for the sweetness of the coconut milk.

1 Tb vegetable oil
½ cup finely chopped onions
2 tsp finely chopped fresh ginger
1 tsp finely chopped garlic
½ cup peanut butter
½ cup coconut milk
¾ cup water
1 Tb fresh lemon juice
1 Tb soy sauce
½ tsp cayenne pepper

In a small saucepan, heat the oil, add the onions, and cook, stirring, for 3–4 minutes to wilt the onions. Stir in the ginger and garlic, and cook for 30 seconds. Remove the pan from the heat, add all the remaining ingredients, and whisk until smooth. Return the pan to the heat, bring the mixture to a boil, reduce the heat, and cook at a very gentle boil just above a simmer, stirring frequently, for 10 minutes.   MAKES ABOUT 1½ CUPS

❖ Add more cayenne pepper to taste.

To Peel Peppers
and Roasted Red Pepper Purée

To peel peppers: Choose thick-fleshed peppers, if possible. Lay the peppers on their sides on a broiler pan and place under a preheated broiler. Cook for 3–4 minutes, or until their skins blister. Using tongs or a long fork, rotate the peppers slightly and broil again until the skins darken and blister; continue rotating and broiling until all sides are blistered. Remove the broiled peppers to a brown paper bag, close the bag, and let the peppers sit for 15–20 minutes while the heat in the bag loosens their skins. Remove the peppers from the bag. With a paring knife, slit open one side lengthwise, open the pepper up, and remove and discard the stem, seeds, and white membranes. Cut the pepper in halves or thirds and peel off the blistered skin with your fingers or the paring knife. Cut the peeled flesh into strips or pieces as desired.

1 pound peeled peppers yields 1–1¼ cups
    peeled flesh
2 pounds peeled peppers yield 2–2½ cups
    peeled flesh

Roasted Red Pepper Purée: Peel the peppers as above. Cut the peeled peppers into pieces, place in a food processor or blender, and process until the peppers have become a thick sauce or purée. It will keep, covered and refrigerated, for up to a week.

1 pound peeled peppers yields about 1 cup purée.

Rouille

Rouille is similar to the garlic mayonnaise known as *Aïoli* (page 349), but the addition of pimentos and hot pepper sauce gives rouille a rosy hue and a flavor with more zing. I have replaced the egg yolks and oil used in the classic recipe for rouille with store-bought mayonnaise to eliminate concern over using raw eggs in an uncooked recipe. (If you wish to make rouille the classic way, see the recipe in *The Victory Garden Cookbook* and substitute liquid pasteurized eggs if you are concerned about using raw eggs in an uncooked recipe.) The amount of garlic depends on your taste; add even more if you like its flavor as much as I do. A food processor makes quick work of this sauce, and you can make the sauce ahead and refrigerate it until ready to use.

1–2 Tb minced garlic, or more to taste
Salt and freshly ground pepper
½ cup fresh bread crumbs, lightly packed
⅓ cup chopped drained pimentos
2 Tb chopped fresh basil or 1 tsp dried (optional)
Hot pepper sauce
1 cup mayonnaise

Food Processor Method: Place the minced garlic on a work surface, sprinkle ¼ teaspoon salt on the garlic, and mash the garlic and salt together into a purée with the back of a heavy knife; the purée need not be perfectly smooth. Put the puréed garlic in the bowl of a food processor fitted with a steel blade, add the bread crumbs, pimentos, basil (if you are using it), and a few drops of hot pepper sauce, and process until the ingredients are well mixed, scraping down the sides of the bowl with a rubber spatula, if necessary. Add the mayonnaise and process again to blend well. Season as desired with salt and freshly ground pepper, and hot pepper sauce. MAKES ABOUT 1½ CUPS

Hand Method: Purée the garlic and salt, as above, and place the purée in a bowl. Add the bread crumbs, pimentos, basil (if you are using it), and a few drops of hot pepper sauce, and pound the mixture into a paste with a pestle; add the mayonnaise and blend all together. Season with salt, freshly ground pepper, and hot pepper sauce, as desired.

Salmon Stock

Salmon stock is a great base for sorrel sauce and other sauces; it's easy to make and easy to store in batches in the freezer. Make sure that the salmon frame is very fresh.

One 7–8-lb salmon frame (preferably with head on)

Break the salmon frame up into a few pieces for ease of handling. If you are cooking the head as well as the skeleton, cut out the gills. Wash the frame well, put the pieces in a large pot, and add 2 quarts water. Bring the water to a boil, skim off the foam, reduce the heat, and simmer for 20 minutes, skimming the foam again occasionally. Pour the stock into a large colander over another pot. Discard the frame left in the colander. Bring the strained stock back to a gentle boil and cook until the liquid reduces to 4 cups. Remove from the heat, let cool, and refrigerate or freeze. MAKES 4 CUPS

❖For added flavor, prepare the cooking water as you would a court bouillon, adding chopped celery, onions, peppercorns, bay leaf, and thyme. Strain the stock as above.

Shrimp Broth

Save shrimp shells in the freezer. When you have shells from three pounds of shrimp, you will have enough to flavor this broth.

2 Tb butter
1 cup chopped onions
1 cup chopped celery
1 chopped carrot (optional)
Shells from 3 lb (or more) shrimp
8 cups water, or a combination of water and chicken broth
2 Tb tomato paste
1 cup dry vermouth (optional)

In a large pot, heat the butter, add the onions, celery, and carrots, if you like (carrots will add some sweetness), and sauté gently for 2–3 minutes. Add the shrimp shells and sauté for 5 minutes. Add the water or broth, tomato paste, and vermouth, if desired. Stir the mixture, bring to a boil, reduce the heat, and simmer for 30 minutes. Remove from the heat and strain. When the broth has cooled to room temperature, cover it and refrigerate or freeze. MAKES ABOUT 6 CUPS

❖To intensify the flavor of the stock, reduce it by boiling.
❖Substitute olive oil for butter.

Spaetzle

Spaetzle is a German noodle traditionally served with meat dishes, but I think it goes just as well with fish. You can buy an inexpensive spaetzle maker; it looks like a large grater and is very simple to use. However, you can also make these noodles by pushing the dough through the holes of a large colander. They are fun to make. If you wish, you can make the noodles way ahead and keep them covered with water in the refrigerator. When you are ready to cook, drain them and either reheat by dropping them into boiling water or pat them dry and sauté them in butter. The recipe can be doubled or tripled.

2 cups flour
1 cup milk
8 egg yolks
3–4 Tb butter
Salt and freshly ground pepper

In a mixing bowl, combine the flour, milk, and egg yolks, and beat them together until the mixture is smooth. Let the dough rest for a few minutes.

Bring a large pot of water to a boil and push the dough, a bit at a time, through the spaetzle maker, or a colander, directly into the boiling water. When the spaetzle rise to the top (in just seconds), they are done. Lift the cooked noodles with a slotted spoon and drop them immediately into a bowl of ice water to stop the cooking action, then drain them well. (Refrigerate them, if you wish, covered with cold water, until ready for the final sauté.)

In a large sauté pan, heat the butter. Add the spaetzle and cook over medium-low heat, turning the noodles in the butter, for 3–5 minutes. Add more butter, if you wish. Season with salt and freshly ground pepper, and serve.   MAKES ABOUT 5 CUPS

❖ Flavor the dough with lemon juice or finely minced fresh herbs.

Tart Shell for a 10-Inch Tart, Partially or Completely Baked

2 cups all-purpose flour
¾ tsp salt
12 Tb *chilled* butter
2 Tb *chilled* vegetable shortening
¼–⅓ cup ice water

Mixer Method: Place the flour and salt in the bowl of an electric mixer. Cut the butter into small pieces and add to the bowl along with the shortening. Turn the beater on and off until the butter and shortening have broken down to the size of peas. Quickly add the ice water, bit by bit, and stop the minute the dough begins to mass on the blade. Place the dough on a lightly floured board and knead it with the heel of your palm a few times to work it. Shape the dough into a 5-inch circle, cover with waxed paper, and chill in the refrigerator for 2 hours before using.

Food Processor Method: Put the flour and salt into the bowl of a food processor. Cut the butter into small pieces and add along with the shortening. Turn the processor on and process for 2–3 seconds to break the butter into pea-size pieces. Add the ice water little by little and process in quick on–off pulses until the dough forms a mass on the blades (about 15 seconds of processing in all). Place the dough on a floured board and proceed as above.

To partially bake: Roll out the dough on a lightly floured board to a thickness of ³⁄₁₆ inch and to a diameter 2 inches larger than the diameter of the buttered pan you are using. Fit the dough into the pan, pressing the excess dough slightly down the inside of the pan to make the sides thicker. Decorate the edge and prick the bottom and sides of the dough with a fork. Refrigerate for 30 minutes. Butter one side of a sheet of aluminum foil slightly larger than the tart pan and place the foil, buttered side down, in the pie shell. Fill the foil-lined shell with dried beans or washed pebbles for weight to keep the bottom from puffing up or the sides from puffing in as the shell bakes. Bake in a preheated 425-degree oven for 8 minutes. Remove the tart shell from the oven, lift out the foil and the beans or pebbles, straighten up the sides of the shell if they have sagged, and prick the bottom of the dough again. Return the shell to the oven for 2–4 minutes or until just lightly browned. Remove and let cool on a rack for 15 minutes.

To bake shell completely: Bake as above. For the final bake, leave the shell in the oven an additional 6–8 minutes or until nicely browned.

Tartar Sauce

Since this is the most frequently used sauce with fish, it is worth giving it a fresh taste and avoiding the tired sauce served in some restaurants.

> 2 cups mayonnaise
> ¼ cup finely chopped dill pickles
> ⅓ cup finely chopped green peppers
> 2 Tb finely chopped scallions
> 2 Tb finely chopped parsley
> 1 Tb finely chopped capers (optional)
> 1–2 Tb fresh lemon juice
> Salt and freshly ground pepper

Put the mayonnaise in a bowl and add all of the chopped ingredients. Mix well and season with lemon juice and salt and freshly ground pepper. Cover and refrigerate.   MAKES 2½–3 CUPS

Tomato Pulp—Peeled and Seeded Tomatoes

Tomato pulp is the flesh remaining after tomatoes have been cored, peeled, and seeded. Bring a pot of water to a boil and have a large bowl of ice water standing to one side. With a sharp paring knife, cut a cone shape around the stem of each tomato and then remove and discard the core. Drop the tomatoes into the boiling water and let them cook just until the skin begins to split and pucker—about 10 seconds for garden-ripe tomatoes, seconds or minutes more for winter or firm tomatoes.

Remove the tomatoes with a slotted spoon and drop them immediately into the ice water to stop the cooking action. When the tomatoes are cool enough to handle, in just a few seconds, remove them from the

ice water and pull off the skins. Cut the tomatoes in half crosswise, parallel to their stem ends, and gently squeeze each half to force out the jellylike juice and the seeds. What remains is the "pulp" of the tomatoes.

Peeled, Seeded, and Chopped Tomatoes

When the pulp is chopped, it becomes the "peeled, seeded, and chopped tomatoes" so often referred to in this book. To chop the tomato pulp, place the flat side of each tomato down on a work surface. Slice vertically through the tomato, spacing the slices according to the size dice you want—½ inch apart, ¼ inch apart, etc. If the tomato half is very thick, hold your knife parallel to the work surface and slice horizontally across the tomato, keeping the same spacing. Finally, cut down across the vertical slices to cut the tomato into cubes or dice.

> 2 pounds ripe tomatoes yield approximately 3 cups peeled, seeded, and chopped tomatoes
> 3 pounds ripe tomatoes yield approximately 4 cups peeled, seeded, and chopped tomatoes

Tomato Fondue

Tomato fondue is not really a sauce, but rather heated bits of chopped ripe tomatoes enrobed in their own juices. It is essential to have garden-ripe tomatoes for a delicious fondue. If you don't have them, make *Fresh Tomato Sauce* (page 364), using part canned tomatoes. A plain tomato fondue, as well as its flavored variations, is a light and colorful accompaniment to poached, sautéed, and grilled fish dishes.

> 3 cups peeled, seeded, and chopped ripe tomatoes, in ½-inch dice
> 2 Tb butter
> ¼ cup minced shallots or onions (optional)
> Salt and freshly ground pepper

Place the chopped tomatoes in a sieve to drain off the excess liquid. In a sauté pan large enough to hold the

Tomato Fondue (continued)

tomatoes, heat the butter, add the shallots or onions (if you are using them), and sauté until they are just softened. Add the tomatoes, bring the mixture to a boil, and cook over medium-high heat for 4–5 minutes to evaporate the juices and lightly thicken the mixture. Season with salt and freshly ground pepper.

MAKES ABOUT 2½ CUPS

❖ Use olive oil instead of butter.

❖ Add minced garlic with the shallots.

❖ Add strips of herbs such as basil or sorrel, or chopped fresh herbs such as parsley, tarragon, or thyme.

❖ Add some of the fondue to *Lemon Butter Sauce* (page 357).

Tomato-Citrus Fondue

3 cups peeled, seeded, and chopped ripe tomatoes, in ½-inch dice
2 oranges
1 lemon
2 Tb butter
1 Tb chopped fresh parsley
Salt and freshly ground pepper

Place the diced tomatoes in a sieve to drain off excess liquid.

Finely grate the rind of 1 orange into a small bowl; squeeze the juice of that orange into the bowl. Finely grate 1 tablespoon lemon rind, and add it and the juice of the lemon to the orange rind and juice. Using the small side of a fruit zester (if you do not have a zester, grate the rind), cut the rind of the second orange into thin julienne strips and set the strips aside; reserve the flesh of this orange for another use.

In a saucepan large enough to hold the tomatoes, heat the butter, add the tomatoes and orange-lemon mixture, bring to a boil, and cook over medium-high heat for 5–6 minutes to boil down the liquids and thicken the sauce. Add the parsley and season with salt and freshly ground pepper. Stir in the reserved strips or grated rind of the second orange and serve.

MAKES 2–2½ CUPS

❖ Add other herbs.

❖ Enrich the fondue by beating in 1–2 additional tablespoons butter.

Fresh Tomato Sauce

When the garden is full of ripe tomatoes, it is such a simple thing to quickly make this delicious, slightly chunky sauce. You may well find yourself craving the same sauce in the dead of winter; combine half fresh tomatoes for texture and half canned tomatoes for color and flavor and you will have a reasonable alternative to the truly fresh sauce. By the way, in midsummer stock your freezer with a fresh tomato sauce. Make a large quantity of this sauce to freeze, or see *Fall Freezer Tomato Sauce,* in *The Victory Garden Cookbook,* page 323.

2 Tb light olive oil
½ cup chopped onions
1 tsp minced garlic (optional)
4 cups peeled, seeded, and chopped tomatoes
1 tsp fresh thyme
Salt and freshly ground pepper
1–2 Tb shredded fresh basil (optional)
Fresh lemon juice (optional)

In a 4-quart saucepan, heat the oil, add the onions, and cook until they are wilted, 4–5 minutes. Stir in the garlic (if you are using it) and add the tomatoes, thyme, and ¼ teaspoon salt. Bring the mixture to a boil, cover, reduce the heat, and cook gently for 5 minutes to release the juices of the tomatoes; then uncover the pan and boil gently, stirring occasionally, for about 15 minutes, or until the sauce has reduced and thickened. Stir in the basil (if you are using it) and season the sauce with salt and freshly ground pepper and a few drops of lemon juice, if desired.

MAKES 2½–3 CUPS

❖ Use more or less onions, or substitute a few tablespoons shallots.

❖ Add or substitute other fresh herbs.

❖ For a stronger flavor, add 1 tablespoon tomato paste.

Vinaigrette

I have met cooks who pride themselves on their vinaigrette made with one "secret" ingredient that purportedly makes the vinaigrette extraordinarily good. To me, the secret of a great vinaigrette is to use the very best-tasting oil and vinegar you can find—you hardly need anything else. A vinaigrette can be made with just those two ingredients, or you can add various flavorings—balsamic or other flavored vinegars, mustard, garlic, herbs, among others—depending on what you are dressing. Let the character of the recipe be your guide. I keep the vinaigrette for a salad of delicate young greens very simple, but add mashed garlic to a vinaigrette to dress a hearty lentil salad, or I replace the vinegar with fresh lemon juice when I am dressing asparagus or braised leeks. The options are many; here are the basics.

¼ tsp salt
½ tsp Dijon-style mustard
2 Tb red wine vinegar
9 Tb light olive oil
Salt and freshly ground pepper

In a small bowl, combine the ¼ teaspoon salt, mustard, and vinegar. In droplets at first, gradually beat in the oil to make a smooth emulsion. Season with salt and freshly ground pepper.   MAKES ABOUT ¾ CUP

❖Use a combination of very good light olive oil and excellent vegetable oil.

❖Replace a teaspoon or more of the vinegar with balsamic vinegar. Balsamic vinegar imparts a very distinctive flavor, so try it sparingly at first and add more as you wish.

❖Reduce or eliminate the mustard, or add more to taste.

❖To make a thicker emulsion, whisk in a beaten egg white or a tablespoon heavy cream before adding the oil.

❖*Garlic Vinaigrette:* Mash 1 teaspoon finely minced garlic with the salt to make a purée; proceed as above.

❖*Lemon Vinaigrette:* Replace the vinegar with fresh lemon juice. Add 1–2 teaspoons finely grated lemon zest, if desired. Reduce or eliminate the mustard, if you like.

❖*Herb Vinaigrette:* Add chopped chives, chopped shallots, chopped parsley, chopped cilantro, chopped tarragon, etc., to taste.

Safety Guidelines

What to Be Cautious About in Cooking and Eating Fish and Shellfish

I highly recommend *Fish: The Truth,* by Kenelm W. Coons. Ken, executive director of the New England Fisheries Development Association in Boston, has written a comprehensive overview of the fact and fiction regarding seafood safety. Ken notes that the 3.5 billion pounds of seafood marketed in the United States in a year would yield about 13 billion servings, and if one sets that kind of figure against known instances of illness from eating seafood, it turns out that one has a higher chance of being struck by lightning than of getting sick from seafood. Nevertheless, there are factors to be cautious about. Some of them are specific to a person's medical circumstances. When my daughter was pregnant, for example, her obstetrician recommended that she avoid certain fish such as swordfish that have a potential for carrying a high content of methyl mercury; all pregnant women and nursing mothers should exercise such caution. Anyone who has a medical condition that would make him or her susceptible to food-borne illness should watch his or her consumption of certain kinds of seafood. The "high-risk group" includes people with such ailments as liver disease, kidney disease, AIDS, alcoholism, immunodeficiency, cancer, diabetes, steroid dependency, and achlorhydria (a condition in which normal acidity of the stomach is reduced or absent). If you have any medical condition, consult your doctor about diet restrictions.

Here is a brief overview of some of the specific things to be aware of; it isn't as much fun to read as recipes, but I would rather people be safe than sorry. We should all take into account the allergic sensitivity some people have to seafood, particularly shellfish.

Molluscan Poisoning: Many of us love raw or barely cooked shellfish, such as clams, oysters, mussels and scallops, which get their food by circulating large quantities of seawater through their digestive systems; however, shellfish absorb bacteria, viruses, contaminants, and toxins in the water while they absorb nutrients. Scallops are less of a hazard because we often eat only the adductor muscle, but the roe and viscera of scallops would be as susceptible to contamination as other shellfish would be. Shellfish-growing areas are now controlled by government inspection, and the waters must conform to acceptable guidelines. Tagging is required so that the retailer knows—and therefore the customer can find out—where the shellfish came from. *Always* ask where shellfish you are purchasing came from. Be wary of shellfish sold by the casual fisherman. See the information boxes for individual kinds of shellfish in this book for more detailed purchasing advice.

One of the more severe forms of shellfish poisoning is *PSP,* or *paralytic shellfish poisoning.* We have all heard of "red tide," which is caused by rapidly multiplying microscopic dinoflagellates. These toxins, which are readily absorbed by shellfish, are not killed by cooking, freezing, or other processing. Symptoms appear quickly after eating PSP-contaminated seafood; they include numbness, weakness, vertigo, burning or tingling sensations, nausea, vomiting, diarrhea, and even convulsions. Because of the severity of the symptoms, there is a close watch for "red tide" in the shellfish industry.

Ciguatera Poisoning: Once, after a wonderful lunch of grilled kabobs of local fish on the island of Saint Martin, I had a mild case of ciguatera poisoning. A few hours after eating only a little of the contaminated fish, I experienced an attack of vertigo quite unlike anything I had ever felt before. The distress lasted only a few hours in my case, but symptoms can be more severe than mine and include gastric symptoms like diarrhea, abdominal pain, nausea, and vomiting, and neurological symptoms like vertigo, muscle cramps, and hot and cold flashes. The toxin for this illness is found in certain species of tropical and subtropical fish, including snapper, amberjack, grouper, barracuda, and other reef fish. Most cases are traceable to sport or local fishermen because commercial fishermen learn how to avoid areas where fish are known to carry this toxin. The fish get the toxin from what they eat, and they pass it along their food chain. The toxin is not eliminated by cooking, freezing, or other processing.

Scombroid Poisoning: Under certain conditions, especially storing fresh fish at too high temperatures, histidine in the flesh of the fish converts to histamine and can have toxic effects. Processing, cooking, and freezing do not eliminate the toxin. The fish most apt to be affected are mahi mahi, tuna, bonito, mackerel, and bluefish. Symptoms include severe abdominal distress, nausea, vomiting, diarrhea, a flushed appearance, and swelling or hives. Seek medical help if you suspect a case of scombroid poisoning. Many of the reported cases originate with sport fishing rather than commercial catch.

Chemical Contaminants: It was sobering when I first saw some of my beloved striped bass so contaminated with polychlorinated biphenyls, or PCBs, that their long, straight silver stripes had mutated into asymmetrical curves. PCBs are not the only concern; mercury and chemical pesticides have found their way into seafood to a worrisome degree. Some critics feel that the levels of these chemical contaminants set as permissible by the Food and Drug Administration are too high, and that anyone in a medically high risk group should be cautious about fish that might contain these contaminants. Contamination is most frequently found in freshwater lakes and streams and affects sport fishermen. Marine contamination effects are more noticeable as one moves up the food chain to larger fish such as tuna, swordfish, and sharks.

Bacterial Standards: A 1992 *Consumer Reports* analysis of some fish markets in the New York City area found an appalling amount of fish contaminated by poor handling being sold. Many in the seafood industry resented the report, fearing it would drive people away from consuming seafood, but I appreciated its publication. The biggest health problem with seafood in my experience doesn't lie with toxins or parasites or even with chemical pollution; it lies in bacterial contamination from unsanitary handling and improper refrigeration. I am appalled at some fish markets that I walk into and quickly out of again—but not before saying how shameful I found the odor and appearance of the seafood. If all consumers were assertive in this matter, fish marketing would improve very quickly.

Parasites: I still remember the first time I saw a fishworm. I was a novice fish cook, and this round orange worm spiraled out of a piece of flounder I had just unwrapped to cook at home. Horrified, I rushed back to the fish market and accused the dealer of selling me a piece of rotten fish. He seemed amused as he returned my purchase price, which only irritated me more. "All fish have worms," he said, but it was not until I began cutting and cooking fish on a daily basis that I learned he was more right than wrong. Unlike the toxins and contaminants discussed above in this section, parasites are killed by adequate cooking or freezing.

There are two basic groups of parasites found in the flesh of some fish caught in American waters: roundworms (nematodes) and tapeworms (cestodes). Let me stress that these parasites are not in the flesh of all fish, including the bottom-feeding fish. Whether a fish has parasites in its flesh or not depends largely on where the fish lives. The incidence of roundworms depends on local populations of seals and sea lions because the life cycle of the roundworms circles through these marine mammals. Adult worms produce eggs in the stomachs of the mammals, and when the eggs are excreted into the sea and hatch into larvae, small crustaceans eat many of them. Fish in turn eat the crustaceans, and when seals or sea lions eat the fish with parasites, the cycle is complete. Fishermen interrupt the cycle by catching some fish that have worms in their flesh. The older and larger the fish are, the more worms they are apt to have. Most fish fillets you buy at your local market have had any roundworms removed by "candling"; each fillet is passed over a translucent table with a light underneath which reveals any worms in the flesh, and they are removed. Two of the many species of roundworms in nature that are commonly found in our fish are known colloquially as codworms and herring worms. Codworms are 1–2 inches long and as thick as pencil lead. Their color varies from brown to orange to red-brown, and they are usually coiled but easily detectable. They can be found in many species of fish, including squid. Not all roundworms ingested lodge in the human body. Many pass through or are broken up in the process of digestion. They can, however, penetrate the lining of the stomach from 2–10 hours after they are eaten in inadequately cooked or raw fish and can cause gastric pain for as long as 2–3 weeks. Herring worms are smaller than codworms, about an inch long, white in color, with a fibrous feel to them. Their life cycle is similar to that of the codworm, and they exist in hundreds of species of fish, notably salmon and rockfish. Herring worms can penetrate the lining of the intestinal tract as well as the stomach, causing a severe distress of the gastrointestinal tract known as anisakiasis. The symptoms are nausea, vomiting, and sporadic stomach pain comparable to ulcer pain. The symptoms can begin from 1–12 hours after ingestion and can last as long as several months. Consequently, herring worms are a more serious threat to humans than codworms.

Tapeworms warrant more concern than most roundworms. Roundworms cannot survive indefinitely in the human body; they need to continue their life cycle elsewhere. But tapeworms can lodge in the intestinal tract and reproduce there. Freshwater fish are most affected by the tapeworms associated with parasitic infection. However, these tapeworms can also be found in anadromous fish, such as salmon, which live part of their lives in fresh water and part in salt water. Humans can harbor tapeworms without noticing any symptoms, but some sufferers report diarrhea, vomiting, fatigue, and cramps. A tapeworm resident in a human body for an extended period can cause anemia and deplete the body of important vitamins.

PREVENTIVE GUIDELINES FOR PARASITIC WORMS

Raw, Marinated, Cold Smoked or Salted Fish: Eating raw fish has escalated with the popularity of sushi and sashimi. When you are preparing—or eating—raw fish dishes such as sushi or sashimi, marinated fish dishes such as ceviche or gravlaks, or using cold smoked or salted fish that has spent any of its life in fresh water, be aware of the risks of tapeworm (and in the case of wild salmon, the additional risk of the nastier roundworm known as herring worm). Commer-

cial freezing temperatures of −40 degrees Fahrenheit kill any parasites within 15 hours, as do temperatures of −10 degrees Fahrenheit for 7 days. An FDA researcher, using a home freezer at a temperature of −4 degrees Fahrenheit, found that it took 5 days to kill roundworms in rockfish. To remove all doubt, buy only commercially frozen or previously frozen fish when preparing raw, marinated, cold smoked, or raw salted dishes.

Cooked Fish: It has become fashionable to serve fish rare, seared on the outside but still rare and uncooked inside. Fish flesh can certainly taste delicious cooked in this manner, but it leaves one susceptible to parasitic infection, especially from wild salmon and the other anadromous fish that divide their life cycles between fresh and salt waters. The temperature that kills any parasite is an internal temperature of 140 degrees Fahrenheit for cooked fish, and technically the fish should hold that temperature for 5 minutes. It should be cooked to the point where it is opaque throughout, and even at the center, the translucency of the raw flesh should be opaque.

Note: Parasitic infection is a threat mainly from fish caught in the wild. Farmed fish are generally raised in a controlled environment where they do not come in contact with the life cycle of parasitic worms.

ALLERGIC REACTIONS

As I have already mentioned in several places in this book, always advise your guests about what fish and shellfish you are serving—not just in preparations in which they might readily identify the seafood but, even more important, when the fish or shellfish is disguised in a mousse or sauce or soup. Many persons are allergic to different types of seafood, especially to shellfish, and need to know what's in a dish.

Let me conclude by saying that very few persons become ill from eating fish, and if you follow the suggestions above, you can practically eliminate the chance of parasitic infection. If you select fish markets wisely and become a knowledgeable purchaser of fish and shellfish, you can also minimize the risk of ingesting toxins and contaminants in fish flesh that would never be visible as parasites can be. Having taken due precaution, you can then enjoy cooking and eating seafood that is varied in taste, texture, and color, and versatile in its preparation—the perfect protein to accompany the best of nutritional vegetables. Utterly delicious.

Index

Afonseca, Acacio, 168
aïoli sauce
 basic recipe, 349
 warm, 146
aku, 293
albacore, 293
allergic reactions, 368
 to shrimp, 268
almonds
 cod with, 142
 lobster and chicken stew with,
  197
 scallops with, 253
amberjack fish salad, 95–6
anchovy(ies)
 briny sautéed eggplant with, 290
 butter, 3, 352
 chopped egg spread with, 7
 flounder baked with fennel and,
  175–6
 green bean and red onion salad
  with, 80
 and onion tart, 37–8
 oysters Rockefeller with, 37
 tapenade, 8–9
 toasts, 3–4
 tomato salad with, 93
 tuna and cauliflower salad with,
  110
appetizers
 cold, 9–28
  bluefish escabeche, 9–10
  celeriac "rémoulade," 21; with
   shrimp, 20–1
  fish terrine, 25–7
  gravlaks, 14, 17
  guacamole shrimp tostadas, 22

appetizers (*cont.*)
  lobster and avocado vinaigrette,
   12–13
  lobster with herb mayonnaise, 12
  lobster with chervil in lettuce,
   10–11
  marinated shrimp, 23–4
  marinated shrimp with onions
   and cilantro, 24
  marinated zucchini strips, 342–3
  melon with smoked salmon,
   ham, and lime, 17–18
  mussels vinaigrette, 13
  oysters with mignonette sauce,
   13–14; with raw bar relish,
   14
  poached scallops with celery,
   18–19
  raw shellfish table, 14
  scallops ceviche, 18–19
  shrimp cocktail, 21–2
  shrimp rémoulade, 21
  smoked fish, cucumber, and
   caviar canapés, 24–5
  smoked salmon with mustard-
   dill sauce, 18
  swordfish tonnato, 27
  tabbouleh, 28
  see also dips
 hot, 28–51
  artichokes with oregano and
   parsley, 28–9
  asparagus, roasted, 29–30
  asparagus with yogurt sauce, 30
  chili clams, 32–3
  codfish pancakes, 154
  deviled crabmeat, 167

appetizers (*cont.*)
  deviled seafood and artichoke
   ramekins, 44–5
  eggplant, grilled, with tapenade
   topping, 34
  fish cakes with tomato-basil
   butter sauce, 233
  leeks vinaigrette with Mediterranean topping, 34–5
  monkfish grilled on skewers,
   216
  mussels marinière, 35
  onion and anchovy tart, 37–8
  oysters Rockefeller, 35, 37
  pancakes, vegetable: corn, 41;
   leek and sorrel, 42–3;
   parsnip, 41–2; potato, 41
  quahogs stuffed with aromatic
   vegetables, 31–2
  scallops baked with shallots,
   39–40
  scallops broiled with bacon, 40
  seafood, grilled, with sweet-
   and-hot grape sauce, 43–4
  shrimp Samurai with sesame-
   stir-fried spinach, 46–7
  shrimp satay, 272
  shrimp skewers in cilantro-lime
   marinade, 47–8
  smoked cod ramekins, 30–1
  smoked fish fritters, 155
  smoked salmon and sorrel
   toasts, 38–9
  smoked salmon with vegetable
   pancakes, 40–3
  spring salad with warm shrimp,
   46

appetizers (*cont.*)
    squid, sautéed, 49
    steamed soft-shell clams, 33
    sunflower seed–crusted striped
        bass, 118
    Swiss chard and cheese squares,
        49–50
    swordfish Portugaise, 299
    tomato pie, 45–6
    white beans with shrimp and
        basil, 48–9
    zucchini Corfu, 50–1
    zucchini salmon with seafood
        mousse, 240
apple-and-squash purée, 247
applesauce, broiled mackerel with,
    208, 211
Arctic char, 112
    mixed fish grill with, 111–13
artichoke(s)
    basic recipe, 349–50
    bottoms, basic recipe, 350
    and deviled seafood ramekins,
        44–5
    hearts
        basic recipe, 350
        shrimp salad with, 104
    lobster with chicken and, 190–1
    mousse, salmon with, 242–3
    with oregano and parsley, 28–9
    and scallop fettuccine, 312–13
    stuffed with shrimp, 29
arugula salad
    with salmon, 103–4
    with scallops, 248
    with squid, 105
asparagus
    boiled, 260, 262
    Chinois, 319
    lobster salad with, 100
    roasted, 29–30
    salad, composed, 80
    and salmon, with pasta, 311–12
    soup, 53
    stir-fry of scallops, shrimp, and,
        257
    with yogurt sauce, 30
avocado
    crab Louis in, 98
    guacamole, 7
        shrimp tostadas, 22
    and lobster vinaigrette, 12–13

bacon
    bluefish fillets grilled with, 123–4
    chicory salad with, 85
    crab and broccoli quiche with, 166
    Italian, *see* pancetta

bacon (*cont.*)
    mesclun salad with, 88
    pasta with smoked bluefish and,
        303
    potato salad with, 90
    scallops broiled with, 40
    shad roe sautéed with, 262–3
    spinach salad with, 94
        with lettuce and smoked
            bluefish, 95
        spring salad with warm shrimp,
            46
bacterial standards, 367
bananas
    grilled, with parsnips, 330–1
    mahi mahi with drunken vegeta-
        bles and, 215–16
    sole pan-fried with, 168
Barrett, Judith, 314
basil
    pesto
        red snapper with, 310–11
        tomatoes with crabmeat and,
            97–8
    red pepper pesto pasta with,
        310–11
    roast lobster with, 199
        and tomatoes, 199–200
    -tomato butter sauce, 232
bass, 116–17
    broiled, 118–19
    buying, 117
    fried, on bed of tomato fondue,
        119–20
    grilled whole, with fennel, 119
    and lobster soup, 70–1
    poached, with white butter sauce
        and new potatoes, 114–15
    preparation, 117
    salad, with cucumber and dill, 96
    steamed, with scallions and ginger,
        113–14
    storage, 117
    sunflower seed–crusted, with
        spaghetti squash and herb
        beurre blanc, 115, 118
    types of, 116–17
    yields, 117
basting sauce, 123
    Oriental, 123
bean(s)
    black
        and radishes, 337
        soup, 53–4; with shrimp, 54
    chili, with shrimp, 280–1
    fava
        sautéed, 319–20
        succotash, 341–2

bean(s) (*cont.*)
    green, *see* green bean(s)
    lima, succotash, 341–2
    salad
        fish and, 94–5
        parsley and pinto beans, 89
    shell, succotash, 320
    white
        and cabbage soup, 56
        with shrimp and basil, 48–9
        Tuscan-style, 321
béchamel sauce, 350
beer
    clams steamed in, 33
    shrimp poached in, 22
Benson, Marilyn, 242
Berkowitz, Roger, 112
Berkowitz family, xii
beurre manié, 229–30
bigeye tuna, 293
bisque, lobster, 70–1
blackened fish, 140–1
blackfin tuna, 293
blue crabs, 160
bluefish, 125–6
    baked
        with fennel, 124, 126–7
        with peppers and onions,
            127
        with tapenade and crumb top-
            ping, 124
    broiled
        baby fillets, 122
        with mustard mayonnaise,
            122
        with soy marinade, 120–1
    buying, 125
    cooking methods, 126
    escabeche, 9–10
    grilled fillets
        with bacon, 123–4
        with basting sauce, 122–3
    pâté, 4–5
    preparation, 126
    salad, 94–5
    sautéed
        with lemon and capers, 128
        with piquant Spanish sauce,
            128–9
    smoked
        buying, 125
        with pasta, 303
        pâté, 4–5
        salad, 95
    yields, 126
bok choy and scallop soup, 75–6
bourride, 63–4
brandade, 5–6

bread crumbs, buttered, 351
broccoli
    and crab quiche, 165–6
    pasta with shrimp and, 313
    and sole paupiettes, 177
    stir-fry
        with garlic, 322–3
        with scallops and shrimp, 257
        with shrimp and garlic,
            270–1
        with shrimp and snow peas,
            269–70
broccoli de rabe
    braised, 323
    fish timbales on bed of, 153
    and potato soup, 54–5
    scallops and mushrooms baked on
        bed of, 259
    and sole paupiettes, 177
    tian, 344
broth
    clam, 32
    see also stock
Brussels sprouts
    purée of potatoes and, 321–2
    sautéed, 322
bulghur, tabbouleh, 28
Burke, Jim, 105
butter(s)
    anchovy, 3, 352
    beurre manié, 229–30
    chive, 353
    cilantro, 353
    citron, 352
    clarified, 351
    compound, basic recipe, 352
    escargot, 32–3
        basic recipe, 353
        shrimp baked with, 284–5
    garlic, 353
    green peppercorn, 353
    herb, 353
    horseradish, 353
    lemon, 120
        with capers, 120, 122
    olive and caper, 352
    red pepper, 353
    sauce
        ginger-lime, 220
        herb beurre blanc, 115, 118
        lemon, 357
        mustard-tarragon, 235
        tomato-basil, 232
        white, 114
    scallion, 353
    shellfish, 9
    smoked salmon, 353
    sun-dried tomato, 353

cabbage
    braised
        with collard greens, 323–4
        salmon with, 231
    Chinese
        and spinach salad, 81
        stir-fry, 324
    coleslaw, 82
    coleslaw salad, 102
        broiled salmon and, 102–3
    and crab pasta crêpes, 305–7
    and crab strudel, 307
    curried, 152
    grilled shrimp on bed of, 273–4
    leaf, lobster in, 194–6
    lobster and
        au gratin, 207
        pasta timbales, 309
    salmon with, 238
    and sole paupiettes, 177
    soup, 56
    sweet and sour, 322
    tian, 344
Caesar salad, 84–5
canapés, smoked fish, cucumber, and
    caviar, 24–5
caper(s)
    bluefish with lemon and,
        129–30
    butter
        lemon, 122
        olive, 352
    cod Messina-style with, 141–2
    crab cakes with, 164, 165
    crab Louis with, 98
    egg sauce with, 354
    flounder with, 168
    -and-herb vinaigrette, 111–13
    in Portugaise sauce, 298
    salmon paillardes with, 228
    scallops with, 253
    soft-shell crabs with, 159
    in smoked salmon with toasts,
        18
    sole topped with crabmeat and,
        174
    tapenade with, 8–9
    tapenade spread with, 124
    tapenade topping with, 34
    tomato fondue with, 164–5
Caratelli, Marie, 28, 305
caraway coleslaw, 82
Cardini, Caesar, 84
carp roe, 8
carrot(s)
    braised with celery, 325
    and kohlrabi julienne, 324–5
    lobster consommé with, 359

carrot(s) (*cont.*)
    logs, and sugar snap peas, 333
    pancakes, 42
    roasted "French fries," 332
    salad, julienned, 81–2
    stir-fry of scallops, shrimps, and,
        257
cataplana-style
    clams, 133–5
    mussels, 135
cauliflower
    relish, 351
    salad, with tuna, 109
    soup, 55
caviar
    canapés of cucumber, smoked fish,
        and, 24–5
    salmon, 225–6
    smoked salmon with, 18
    squash and chestnut soup with,
        62–3
celeriac
    "rémoulade," with shrimp,
        20–1
    roasted "French fries," 332
    split pea soup with, 60–1
celery
    braised
        with carrots, 325
        with cod and leeks, 149
    coleslaw with, 82
    flounder baked with anchovy and,
        175
    salad, with Parmesan cheese, 81
    scallops, poached, with, 18–19
    sole with potatoes and, 171
ceviche, 19–20
cheese
    baked, mesclun salad with, 87
    blue, spinach salad with, 94
    croutons with, 355
    and egg sauce, 354
    feta
        Greek salad with, 85–6
        shrimp baked with tomato con-
            casse and, 280
        sliced tomatoes with, 93
    finnan haddie with chilies and,
        156–7
    goat, warm tomato salad with,
        92–3
    Jarlsberg, crab and broccoli quiche
        with, 166
    mozzarella, sliced tomatoes with,
        93
    Parmesan, celery salad with, 81
    Saga Blue, green salad with, 86
    salsa dip with, 8

cheese (*cont.*)
　　Swiss
　　　　onion soup topped with, 60
　　　　scallops baked with mushrooms
　　　　　　and, 259
　　　　Swiss chard and, squares, 49–50
　　　　tomato pie with, 45–6
chemical contaminants, 367
cherrystone clams, 131
　　yields, 132
chestnut and butternut squash soup
　　　　with caviar, 62–3
chicken
　　and lobster
　　　　with artichokes, 190–1
　　　　stew, 196–7
　　paella, 315–17
　　shrimp with
　　　　creole, 284
　　　　gumbo, 283
　　vegetable chowder with shrimp
　　　　and, 77
chicory
　　salad, 85
　　tian, 344
Child, Julia, 16, 25, 215, 235–6
chili
　　clams, 32–3
　　shrimp, 280–1
chinook salmon, 224
chive butter, 353
chowder
　　clam
　　　　Manhattan, 64–5
　　　　New England, 65–7
　　corn
　　　　with salmon, 74
　　　　with yellow peppers, 56–7
　　fish
　　　　brandade topping for, 6
　　　　monkfish and eggplant, 215
　　　　New England, 67
　　scallop, 74–5
　　vegetable, with shrimp and
　　　　chicken, 77
　　see also soup
chum salmon, 225
chutney, mango and cilantro, 359–60
ciguatera poisoning, 367
cilantro
　　butter, 353
　　halibut baked with, 181
　　-lime marinade, 47–8
　　in macadamia pesto, 299
　　and mango chutney, 359–60
　　marinated shrimp with onions
　　　　and, 24
　　monkfish broiled with, 216

cilantro (*cont.*)
　　in pepper relish, 289
　　in raw bar relish Al Forno, 14
　　steamed sea bass with, 114
citrus
　　butter, 352
　　escabeche, 10
　　tomato fondue, 364
clam(s), 131–3
　　angel hair pasta with, 304
　　cataplana-style, 133–5
　　chili, 32–3
　　chowder
　　　　Manhattan, 64–5
　　　　New England, 65–7
　　clambake for fifty, 204–6
　　fried, 130, 133
　　hard-shell, 131–2
　　　　buying, 131
　　　　to open with heat, 132
　　　　preparation, 131
　　　　to shuck, 132
　　　　storage, 131
　　　　types of, 131
　　　　yields, 132
　　lobster Fra Diavolo with, 190
　　paella with, 317
　　quahogs stuffed with aromatic
　　　　vegetables, 31–2
　　sauce, white, 135–6
　　soft-shell, 132–3
　　　　fried, 130, 133
　　　　preparation, 132–3
　　　　raw, to shuck, 133
　　　　steamed, 33
　　　　storage, 132
　　　　yields, 133
　　spaghetti squash with, 304–5
　　swordfish roasted with cherry
　　　　tomatoes, olives, and, 296
clarifying of stock, 359
cocktail sauce, 21
cod, 137–9
　　baked, 149–50
　　　　Whale Rock Point, 150
　　braised, with leeks, 148–9
　　buying, 138
　　cakes, with tomato-basil butter
　　　　sauce, 231–3
　　chowder, with smoked cod and
　　　　parsnips, 69
　　hash, 143
　　Messina-style, 141–2
　　mousse, 152–3
　　poached
　　　　with aïoli sauce, 146–7
　　　　cold, 147
　　　　whole, 147

cod (*cont.*)
　　salt, 139
　　　　balls or cakes, 153–4
　　　　brandade, 5–6
　　　　gratin of onions, potatoes, and,
　　　　　　157
　　　　preparing, 139
　　　　salad, 96–7
　　sautéed, with eggplant and tomato
　　　　sauce, 140
　　smoked, 139
　　　　fritters, 154–5
　　　　ramekins, 30–1
　　soup
　　　　with coconut and cilantro, 68
　　　　with winter vegetables, 68–9
　　steaks, broiled, 181
　　tongues and cheeks sautéed,
　　　　142–3
　　yields, 139
　　see also haddock; scrod
Cohen, Helen, 342
Cohen, Kate Morash, 50
coho salmon, 224
Cole, John N., 116
coleslaw, 82
coleslaw salad, 102
　　with broiled salmon, 102–3
collard greens
　　braised, with cabbage, 323–4
　　grilled shrimp on bed of, 273–4
　　and lentil soup, 58
　　scallops and mushrooms baked on
　　　　bed of, 259
　　tian, 344
consommé, lobster, 359
Coons, Kenelm W., 367
Coquilles Saint-Jacques au gratin,
　　　　258–9
corn
　　chowder
　　　　with salmon, 74
　　　　with scallops, 75
　　　　with yellow peppers, 56–7
　　on the cob, boiled, 181–2
　　Mexican, 325
　　pancakes, 41
　　pudding, 325–6
　　radishes and black beans with,
　　　　337
　　salad, 82
　　sautéed, 325
　　succotash, 341–2
cornmeal
　　scallops fried with, 257
　　scrod sautéed in, 136, 140
coulibiac, 243–7
court bouillon, 219

crab(s), 160–3
  black bean soup with, 54
  and broccoli quiche, 165–6
  buying, 161–2
  and cabbage pasta crêpes, 305–7
  and cabbage strudel, 307
  cakes, 159, 164
    fresh fish and, 233
    with two tomato sauces, 164–5
  deviled, in scallop shells, 166–7
  dip, with cloves, 9
  gazpacho with, 69–70
  lobster stuffed with, 203
  preparation and cooking, 162–3
  salad
    Louis, 98
    with tomatoes and pesto cream,
      97–8
  shrimp stuffed with, 282
  soft-shell, 161–2
    cleaning, 163
    sautéed, 157–9; with garlic,
      159; with capers, 159
    and shrimp gumbo, 283
  sole topped with, 174–5, 178
  types of, 160–1
  yields, 163
crackers, dips for, 3–9
crayfish, 183–4
cream
  horseradish, 356–7
  sauce, 157.
    aromatic vegetable, 193–4
    rosemary, 179
crème fraîche
  basic recipe, 353
  shallot and dill sauce, 222
Creole sauce, 284
crêpes
  dilled, 201
  lobster, 200–2
  pasta, crabmeat, and cabbage,
    305–7
croutons
  basic recipe, 355
  garlic, 84
crudités, 3
  dips for, 4–9
Cuban black bean soup, 53–4
  with shrimp, 54
cucumber
  canapés of caviar, smoked fish,
    and, 24–5
  dilled peas and, 332
  -dill sauce
    basic recipe, 354
    Bess's, 236
  pasta with shrimp and, 313

cucumber (*cont.*)
  salad, 83
    pickled, 272
    with striped bass and dill, 96
    tomato and, 92
  salsa with, 8
  sautéed, 326
  -yogurt soup, 55
curry paste, 274
cusk, 137–9

dandelion green
  and lentil soup, 57–8
  salad, 94
David, Elizabeth, 8
dill
  chopped egg spread with, 7
  and cucumber and striped bass
    salad, 96
  -mustard sauce, 18
  sauce
    cucumber, 236, 354
    egg, 354
    with shallots and crème fraîche,
      222
dips, 3–9
  bluefish pâté, 5
  brandade, 5–6
  egg and fresh dill, 7
  eggplant, 6
    and red pepper, 6–7
  guacamole, 7
  olive salad, 50
  salsa, 7–8
  salsa and cheese, 8
  shrimp, 9
  smoked bluefish pâté, 4–5
  tamara, 8
  tapenade, 8–9
Dover sole, 169
  pan-fried with banana, 168
  see also flounder
dressing
  ginger, 105
  mustard–sour cream, 101
  mustard-tarragon, 104
  rémoulade, 101
  Russian, 98
  white pepper, 11
  see also vinaigrette
Dungeness crab, 161
  cakes, with two tomato sauces,
    164–5

egg(s)
  Benedict, fisherman's almost,
    241–2

egg(s) (*cont.*)
  poached
    on brandade-topped English
      muffin, 6
    codfish hash with, 143
    salmon hash with, 230
    smoked fish fritters with, 155
  sauce, 354
  spinach salad with, 46
    with lettuce and smoked
      bluefish, 95
  spread, with dill, 7
  stuffed with tapenade, 9
eggplant
  Corfu, 51
  dip, 6
    Mediterranean, 6–7
  grilled
    in mixed grill, 344–5
    with tapenade topping, 34
  and monkfish stew, 214–15
  Parmesan, 328–9
  ratatouille, 326–8
  salting, 34
  sautéed, 328; briny, 290
  and tomato sauce, cod sautéed
    with, 140
endive
  curly, salad, 85
  in salade Niçoise, 108
escabeche, bluefish, 9–10
escargot butter, 32–3
  basic recipe, 353
  chili clams with, 32–3
  shrimp baked with, 284–5
escarole and lentil soup, 58
espada, pan-fried, with bananas, 168

fava beans
  sautéed, 319–20
  succotash, 341–2
Felluga, Livio, 340
fennel
  bluefish baked with, 124, 126–7
  finnan haddie baked with, 156
  flounder baked with, 175–6
  gazpacho with, 70
  grilled whole bass with, 119
  lobster and, au gratin, 207
  and Parmesan salad, 81
  salt cod and onions gratin with, 157
fettuccine, scallop and artichoke,
  312–13
fiesta soup, 59–60
fig, melon with smoked salmon and,
  18
filo dough, in crab and cabbage
  strudel, 307

Fine, Sue, 23
finnan haddie, 138–9
  baked, 156
  and cheese squares, 51
  with chilies and cheese, 156–7
  kedgeree, 317
  Naomi's, 155–6
  pasta with, 305
first courses, *see* appetizers
fish
  basic information, xii–xvi
  buying, xiii–xiv
  and chips, 143–5
  chowder
    brandade topping for, 6
    New England, 67
  cooking time, xvi
  fillets, xiii–xiv
  frames, xiv
  frozen, xiv
  grilled skewers, 43–4
  and leeks, au gratin, 207
  and lobster crêpes, 202
  microwaving, xvi
  mixed grill, 111–13
  mousse, 25, 26
  pea soup with, 61
  poached, with white butter sauce
    and new potatoes, 114–15
  preparation, xiv–xvi
  safety guidelines, 366–8
  salad(s), 94–110
  and shrimp
    curry, 275
    tempura, 279
  smoked
    bluefish pâté, 4–5
    canapés of cucumber, caviar,
      and, 24–5
    and cheese squares, 51
    fisherman's eggs almost Bene-
      dict, 241–2
    melon with ham, lime, and,
      17–18
    ramekins, 30–1
    salmon toasts, with sorrel,
      38–9
  soup, 63–77
    bourride, 63–4
    garden vegetable, 62
    Straight Wharf, 76–7
    see also soup
  steaks, xiii–xiv
  stock, basic recipe, 355
  storage, xiv
  terrine, Straight Wharf, 25–7
  tonnato, 27

fish (*cont.*)
  whole, xiii
    roasted, 286
  see also specific species; seafood
Fisher, M. F. K., 15
flatfish, xiii, 169–71
  buying, 170
  cooking, 171
  preparation, 170–1
  storage, 170
  types of, 169–70
  yields, 171
  see also Dover sole; flounder; halibut
flounder, 169–71
  baked, with fennel and anchovy,
    175–6
  buying, 170
  cooking, 171
  with crabmeat topping, 174–5
  dugléré, 177–8
  fisherman's eggs almost Benedict
    with, 241–2
  Florentine, 178
  with herbs and tomato coulis,
    171–2
  in lettuce packets, with smoked
    salmon, 178–9
  with lobster or crab, 178
  meunière, 167–8
  with mushrooms, 178
  pan-fried, with banana, 168
  in parchment, 171–3
  and shrimp tempura, 279
  and spinach paupiettes, 176–7
  supper, with peas and potatoes,
    168, 171
  see also Dover sole
fritters, smoked haddock or cod,
    154–5

garlic
  angel hair pasta with clams, pars-
    ley, and, 304
  to blanch, 339
  broccoli and shrimp stir-fry,
    270–1
  butter, 353
  croutons, 84
    basic recipe, 355
  finnan haddie with, 155
  lentils with, 218
  marinade, for shrimp, 275
  potatoes with
    mashed, 335–6
    roast chunks, 337
    roast sliced, 336
  salsa with, 255

garlic (*cont.*)
  scallops with
    baked, 39–40
    sautéed, with parsley, 253
  sauce, *see* aïoli
  sea bass steamed with, 114
  shrimp sautéed with shallots and,
    271
  soft-shell crabs with, 359
  summer squash with, 339
  swordfish with, 289
  tomato fondue with, 364
  vinaigrette, 365
  white beans with, 321
gazpacho, with crabmeat, 69–70
Germon, George, 14
Gibbons, Euell, 249
Gifford, Dun, 122–3, 204, 257
Gifford, Gladys, 257
Gilpatrick, Pam, 12
ginger
  butter, 353
  dressing, 105
  -lime butter sauce, 220
  marinade, 114
gnocchi, squash, 340–1
Goodman, Deborah, 242
goosefish, *see* monkfish
Gore, Bruce, xii, xiv
grape sauce, sweet-and-hot, 43
gravlaks, 14, 17
  grilled, 17
Greek salad, 85–6
green bean(s)
  salad
    Niçoise, 107–8
    with red pepper and tuna, 108–9
    with seared red onion, 79–80
    with shrimp, 104–5
  with shallots
    and garlic, 320–1
    and lemon butter, 320
Grigson, Jane, 315
guacamole, 7
  shrimp tostadas, 22
gumbo, shrimp, 283

haddock, 137–9
  baked, with sesame sauce, 150
  blackened, 140–1
  dry-poached, with warm vinai-
    grette, 145–6
  grilled with herbs, 148
  lettuce-wrapped, 151–2
  smoked
    fritters, 154–5
    see also finnan haddie

haddock (*cont.*)
  yields, 139
  see also scrod
hake, 137–9
halibut, 169–71
  baked, with radishes and scallions,
    180–1
  broiled, 181
  buying, 170
  cakes, with tomato-basil butter
    sauce, 231–3
  cooking, 171
  grilled, with herb-and-caper
    vinaigrette, 111–13
  poached, with rosemary cream
    sauce, 179–80
  yields, 171
ham
  bluefish baked with, 126
    with potatoes and onions,
      127–8
  melon with smoked salmon, lime,
    and, 17–18
  pasta with smoked bluefish and,
    303
  and shrimp
    creole, 284
    gumbo, 283
  smoked cod ramekins with, 31
  smoked fish fritters with, 155
  see also prosciutto
Hamwey, Olga, 150
hash
  codfish, 143
  salmon, 230
herb(s), fresh
  beurre blanc, 115, 118
  bluefish salad with, 95
  broiled striped bass with, 119
  butter, 353
  -and-caper vinaigrette, 111–13
  cod fillets baked with, 150
  codfish hash with, 143
  crab cakes with, 165
  cucumbers with
    salad, 273
    soup, 55
  fish timbales with, 153
  flounder baked with fennel and,
    176
  haddock grilled with, 148
  horseradish cream with, 357
  in lobster stuffing, 203
  Manhattan clam chowder with, 65
  mayonnaise, 12
  new potatoes with, 334
  parsnip pancakes with, 42

herb(s) (*cont.*)
  potatoes with
    new, steamed, 334
    roast chunks, 337
    roast sliced, 336
    salad, 90
  risotto with, 315
  salmon paillards with, 227–8
  scallops with, 254
  scrod sautéed with, 137
  smoked fish fritters with, 154–5
  sole with, 173–4
    and mushrooms, 178
  tomato fondue with, 364
  tomato salad with, 93
    with lobster, 99
  vinaigrette, 365
herring salad, 99
Hersey, John, 125
hollandaise
  basic recipe, 356
  tomato, 242–3
homard, 183
honey-lime butter sauce, 221
Hopkins, Bess, 235
hors d'oeuvres, *see* appetizers
horseradish
  butter, 353
  codfish balls with, 154
  cream, 356–7
Howig, Ingrid Espelid, 222
Hyde, Joe, 13, 289, 295

Jerusalem artichoke pancakes, 42
Jonah crab, 160

Kafka, Barbara, xvi
kale
  and cheese squares, 50
  and lentil soup, 58
  scallops and mushrooms baked on
    bed of, 259
Kantor, Tom, 23
kedgeree, 317
Killeen, Johanne, 14
King, Shirley, xiii
king crab, 161
Knecht, Jerry, xii, 138
kohlrabi
  and carrots julienne, 324–5
  crab Louis with, 98
  scallops and bacon hors d'oeuvres
    with, 40
  smoked fish, and caviar canapés, 25

langostino, 266
Lapsang souchong salmon, 17

leeks
  braised
    cod with, 148–9
    haddock stuffed with, 152
    salmon and, 231
    with tomatoes, garlic, and
      olives, 329
  crabmeat and cabbage pasta crêpes
    with, 307
  finnan haddie baked with, 156
  flounder baked with potatoes and,
    176
  grilled, 329
  and lobster
    au gratin, 207
    pasta timbales, 308–9
  salt cod and potatoes gratin with,
    157
  scallops baked with, 255–6
  and sorrel pancakes, 42–3
  vinaigrette with a Mediterranean
    topping, 34–5
lemon
  butter, 120
    basic recipe, 352
    with capers, 122
    sauce, 35
  garnish for lobster, 357
  -tomato fondue, 364
  vinaigrette, 365
lentil(s)
  salad, 83–4
  salmon poached with, 217–19
  soup, with dandelion greens, 57–8
lettuce
  haddock fillets wrapped in, 151–2
  lobster in, 10–11
  salads
    Caesar, 84–5
    Greek, 85–6
    mesclun, 86–8
    with Saga Blue cheese, 86
    with spinach and smoked
      salmon, 95
  sole and smoked salmon in packets,
    178–9
lime
  butter, 352
    sauce, with ginger, 220
  marinade, for shrimp, 47–8
  melon with smoked salmon, ham,
    and, 17–18
littleneck clams, 131
  yields, 132
lobster(s), 183–8
  Américaine, 191–2
  with artichokes and chicken, 190–1

lobster(s) (*cont.*)
    and avocado vinaigrette, 12–13
    baked stuffed, 202–3
    bisque, 70–1
    boiled, 186
    broiled, 189
    buying, 184
    in cabbage leaf with sweet pepper
        sauce, 194–6
    with chervil in lettuce, 10–11
    cold, with tomatoes, 100–1
    color of, 184
    consommé, 359
    cooking methods for, 186–8
    crêpes, 200–2
    dip, with chives, 9
    Fra Diavolo, 189–90
    frozen cooked, 185
    gazpacho with, 70
    grilled, 188–9
    with herb mayonnaise, 12
    and leeks au gratin, 207
    lemon garnish for, 357
    molting, 184
    mousseline, with scallops, 260
    paella with, 317
    partially steamed and filled shells,
        197
    pasta with peppers and, 309–10
    pasta timbales of leeks, prosciutto,
        and, 308–9
    preparation of, 185–6
    in puff pastry, 192–3
    roast
        with salsa sauce, 198–9
        with tarragon and mousseline
            sauce, 199–200
    salad
        with cherry tomatoes, 99
        composed, 101
        old-fashioned, 99–100
    sauce, 357–8
    sautéed, with aromatic vegetable
        cream sauce, 193–4
    Savannah, 200
    and scallion stir-fry, 182
    and shrimp
        chili, 281
        gumbo, 283
    size of, 184
    sole with, 174, 178
    soup, with striped bass, 70–1
    steamed, 181–2, 186
        with Chinese seasonings,
            197–8
        no-mess, 198
    stew, 73–4
        with chicken, 196–7

lobster(s) (*cont.*)
    stock, 358–9
    storage of, 184–5
    stuffing in BIG shrimp, 281–2
    tetrazzini, 307–8
    types of, 183–4
    white beans with, 48
    yields, 188
lobsterette, 183
lox, 225

macadamia nuts
    parsnips with, 331
    pesto, 299
mackerel, 209–10
    broiled, with warm applesauce,
        208, 211
    buying, 210
    pan-roasted, with Moroccan spice
        tomato sauce, 207–8
    preparation, 210
    yields, 210
Mackie, Leslie, 231
mahi mahi, 216
    coriander-crusted, with drunken
        vegetables and banana,
        215–16
mako shark, 294
mango and cilantro chutney,
    359–60
Manhattan clam chowder, 64–5
marinade
    for fish, 111–12
        escabeche, 10
        monkfish, 214
    for grilled seafood, 43–4
    for shrimp, 269
        cilantro-lime, 47–8
        garlic-flavored, 275
        satay, 272
    soy, 120–1
        with sake, 295
marinara sauce, 306
Marotto, Ann, 45
Mason, Leah and Willie, 95
Mayer, Ben, 50
Mayer, Bob, 160
mayonnaise
    additions to, 101
    herb, 12
    tomato, 164
McGhee, Peter, 147
McSweeny, Michael, 215, 299
melon with smoked salmon,
    smoked ham, and lime,
    17–18
mesclun salad, 86–8
Messina-style cod, 141–2

Mexican corn, 325
mignonette sauce, 13–14
Miller, Arthur, 169
Miller, Judy, 159
molluscan poisoning, 366–7
monkfish, 213–14
    broiled, with muffuletta tomato
        sauce, 211–14
    buying, 213–14
    and eggplant stew, 214–15
    pea soup with, 61
    preparation, 214
    and shrimp
        chili, 281
        tempura, 279
    storage, 214
    yields, 214
Morash, Naomi, 155
Morash, Russell, 30, 234
mousse
    cod, 152–3
    fish, 25–6
    seafood, 238–40
    sole, 173–4
mousseline sauce, 356
muffuletta tomato sauce, 212
mushroom(s)
    deviled crabmeat-stuffed, 167
    finnan haddie baked with, 156
    flounder baked with, 176
    haddock stuffed with, 152
    and lobster tetrazzini, 307–8
    scallops with, 259–60
        mousseline, 260
        Provençal, 254
        scalloped, 258
    smoked cod ramekins with, 31
    sole with, 172, 178
    soup, 58–9
    swordfish with cream and, 296–8
mussels, 36–7
    buying, 36
    cataplana-style, 135
    lobster Fra Diavolo with, 190
    lobster and striped bass soup with,
        73
    marinière, 35
    paella, 315–17
    pasta with clams, garlic, parsley,
        and, 304
    preparation, 36–7
    and scallop stew, 75
    storage, 36
    vinaigrette, 13
    yields, 37
mustard
    crabmeat in scallop shells with,
        166

mustard (*cont.*)
  sauce
    dill, 18
    egg, 354
    seafood and artichoke ramekins
      in, 44–5
    tarragon butter sauce, 235
  –sour cream dressing, 101
  -tarragon dressing, 104
  vinaigrette, 87

Nettleton, Joyce, xvi
New England
  clam chowder, 65–7
  fish chowder, 67
Niçoise salad, 107–8
noodles, Chinese sesame, 276
Normandy-style scallops, 254
nuts, spinach, lettuce, and smoked
    bluefish salad with, 95

okra
  shrimp gumbo, 283
  and tomato stew, 330
olive(s)
  brandade with, 6
  butter, with capers, 352
  cod Messina-style with, 142
  leeks braised with tomatoes, garlic,
    and, 329
  in leeks vinaigrette with a
    Mediterranean topping, 34–5
  muffuletta tomato sauce with, 212
  in onion and anchovy tart, 37–8
  salad, 50
  shallot and red pepper topping,
    222
  swordfish and clams roasted with
    tomatoes and, 296
  tapenade, 8–9
  tapenade spread, 124
  tapenade topping, 34
onion(s)
  and anchovy tart, 37–8
  baked, 330
  balsamic, shad roe sautéed with,
    262–3
  bluefish baked with, 126
    and peppers, 127
    and potatoes, 127–8
  browned, mashed potatoes with,
    335–6
  corn sautéed with, 325
  finnan haddie with, 155
    baked, 156
  gratin of potatoes, salt cod, and,
    157
  and green bean salad, 79–80

onion(s) (*cont.*)
  and lobster pasta timbales, 309
  marinated shrimp with cilantro
    and, 24
  in mixed grill, 345
  soup, 60
orange-tomato
  fondue, 364
  sauce, 264
Oriental basting sauce, 123
oyster(s), 15–16
  buying, 15–16
  with mignonette sauce, 13
  Rockefeller, 35, 37
  to shuck, 16
  stew, 75
  storage, 16
  types of, 15
  yields, 16

paella, 315–17
pancakes
  carrot, 42
  codfish, 154
  corn, 41
  leek and sorrel, 42–3
  parsnip, 41–2
  potato, 41
  zucchini, 43
pancetta
  pasta and peas with, 311
  and scallop hors d'oeuvres, 40
  and shrimp skewers, 48
paralytic shellfish poisoning (PSP),
    366–7
parasites, 170, 367–8
parsley
  angel hair pasta with clams, garlic,
    and, 304
  salad
    with orzo, 88
    with pinto beans, 89
  sauce, 351
    egg, 354
  scallops with garlic and, 253
  steamed sea bass with, 114
parsnips
  cod and smoked cod chowder
    with, 69
  flounder baked with, 176
  grilled, with bananas, 330–1
  macadamia nut, 331
  pancakes, 41–2
  roasted "French fries," 332
  scallop chowder with, 75
pasta
  angel hair, with clams, garlic, and
    parsley, 304

pasta (*cont.*)
  crêpes, crabmeat and cabbage,
    305–7
  with finnan haddie, 305
  lobster Américaine with, 192
  and peas, with pancetta, prosciutto,
    parsley, and Parmesan, 311
  with peppers and lobster, 309–10
  red pepper pesto, 310–11
  salad(s)
    green bean and shrimp, 105
    parsley and orzo, 88
  salmon and asparagus with, 311–12
  with scallops
    and artichokes, 312–13
    and tomatoes, 314
  with shrimp and cucumbers,
    313–14
  smoked bluefish with, 303
  timbales, of lobster, leeks, and
    prosciutto, 308–9
  vegetable soup with, 62
    with shrimp and chicken, 77
  with white clam sauce, 136
pâté
  bluefish
    fresh, 5
    smoked, 4–5
  Straight Wharf fish terrine, 25–7
paupiettes, gray sole and spinach,
    176–7
pea(s)
  braised, with scallions, 332
  dilled, with cucumbers, 332
  pasta with shrimp and, 313
  Portuguese, 240
  salad, 88
  sole with potatoes and, 168, 171
  split pea soup, with celeriac, 60–1
  sugar snap
    to blanch, 332–3
    and carrot logs, 333
    and pasta, with pancetta, pro-
      sciutto, parsley, and Parme-
      san, 311
    roasted, 277
peanut sauce, 360
pecans, squash and chestnut soup
    with, 63
Pépin, Jacques, 230
peppercorn butter, 353
peppers
  hot
    butter, 352
    and cheese squares, 50
    chili clams with, 32–3
    finnan haddie with, 156–7
    pickled, 32–3

peppers (*cont.*)
    in raw bar relish Al Forno, 14
    relish, 289
    salsa, 7–8
    swordfish and clams roasted
        with, 298
    to peel, 360
    sweet
        bluefish baked with onions and,
            127
        bluefish escabeche with, 9–10
        butter, 353
        and cheese squares, 50
        cod and leeks braised with, 149
        coleslaw with, 82
        compote, salmon with, 228–9
        and corn chowder, 56–7
        corn sautéed with, 325
        crab Louis with, 98
        and cucumber salad, 83
        and eggplant dip, 6–7
        green bean and tuna salad with,
            108–9
        in mixed grill, 345
        pasta with lobster and, 309–10
        pasta with shrimp and, 313
        pesto, 310–11
        to prepare, 310
        purée, 360
        ratatouille, 326–8
        relish, 289
        salad, 88–9
        sauce, 195
        shallot, and olive topping, 222
        in Spanish sauce, 128
        spinach, lettuce, and bluefish
            salad with, 95
        and squash salad, 90–1
        stir-fry of scallops, shrimp, and,
            257
    see also pimento
pesto
    macadamia, 299
    red pepper, 310–11
    tomatoes with crabmeat and, 97–8
pie, tomato, 45–6
pie shell, 165
pilaf, rice, 354
pimento
    crab cakes with, 165
    deviled crabmeat with, 167
    shallot, and olive topping, 222
    smoked fish, and cucumber
        canapés, 25
pine nuts
    Chinese cabbage stir-fry with, 324
    cod with, 141–2
    toasting, 301

pink salmon, 225
pipérade, 127
piquant sauce, 354
pita bread anchovy toasts, 3–4
pizza, onion and anchovy, 38
plaice, 169
plum sauce, sweet-and-hot, 44
poisoning
    ciguatera, 367
    molluscan, 366–7
    paralytic shellfish, 366–7
    scombroid, 216, 294, 367
pollock, 137–9
porbeagle shark, 294
Porter, Gladys, 150
Portugaise sauce, 298
potato(es)
    bluefish baked with onions and,
        127–8
    clams cataplana-style with, 135
    cod and leeks baked with, 149
    creamed, 335
    crust, salmon with, 230–1
    flounder baked with leeks and, 176
    French fried, 144
    gratin of onions, salt cod, and, 157
    mashed, with garlic and brown
        onions, 335–6
    new
        boiled, 334
        hash brown, with garlic, pars-
            ley, and lemon, 336
        poached striped bass with,
            114–15
        "salt," 334
        steamed, 334
        tapenade topping for, 9
    pancakes, 41
    purée of Brussels sprouts and, 321–2
    roast
        chunks, 336–7
        sliced, 336
    salad
        grilled, 89
        with salt cod, 97
        vinaigrette, 90
    salmon on bed of, 234
    sole with peas and, 168, 171
    soup, with broccoli de rabe, 54–5
prawns, 266
prosciutto
    bluefish baked with, 128
    pasta and peas with, 311
    pasta timbales of leeks, lobster,
        and, 308–9
    salmon with, 236–8
    and scallop hors d'oeuvres, 40
    smoked cod ramekins with, 31

Prudhomme, Paul, 140
Puck, Wolfgang, 235
pudding, corn, 325–6
puff pastry
    lobster in, 192–3
    salmon and rice in (coulibiac),
        243–7
pumpkin soup, 59–60

quahogs
    stuffed with aromatic vegetables,
        31–2
    see also clam(s): hard-shell
quiche, crab and broccoli, 165–6

radishes
    halibut baked with scallions and,
        180–1
    parsley and orzo salad with, 88
    warm, and black beans, 337
raisins
    cod with, 141–2
    coleslaw with, 82
ratatouille, 326–8
raw bar relish Al Forno, 14
raw shellfish table, 14
red crab, 160–1
Reddington, Michael, 234
relish
    cauliflower, 351
    fresh pepper, 289
    raw bar, 14
rémoulade
    celeriac, with shrimp, 20–1
    classic, 101
ribollita, 56
rice
    coulibiac, 243–7
    kedgeree, 317
    lobster Américaine with, 192
    paella, 315–17
    pilaf, 354
    pumpkin soup with, 59
    salad, 88
    with shrimp
        gumbo, 283
        and tomatoes and squash,
            314–15
    tian, 344
risotto with shrimp, tomatoes, and
    squash, 314–15
rock crab, 160
rock lobster, 183–4
rosemary cream sauce, 179
rouille, 360–1
roundfish, xiii
    buying, xiii
    fillets, xiii–xiv

roundfish (*cont.*)
  frames, xiv
  to gut, xv
  to remove gills, fins, head, and tail,
    xv
  to scale, xiv–xv
  to skin, xv
  steaks, xiii–xiv
  storage, xiv
  whole, xiii
  see also specific species
Russian dressing, 98
rutabaga
  mashed, 337
  roasted "French fries," 332
  sautéed, 337

safety guidelines, 366–8
Safford, Holly, 22
salads
  asparagus, composed, 80
  bean, parsley and pinto beans, 89
  cabbage
    coleslaw, 82
    coleslaw salad, 102
  Caesar, 84–5
  carrots, julienned, 81–2
  celery and Parmesan, 81
  chicory, 85
  Chinese cabbage and spinach, 81
  corn, 82
  cucumber, pickled, 272
  fish, 94–110
    amberjack, 95–6
    with beans, 94–5
    with cauliflower, 109
    composed, 101
    with cucumber and dill, 96
    with green beans and red pep-
      pers, 108–9
    herring, 99
    Niçoise, 107–8
    salt cod, 96–7
    spinach, lettuce, and smoked
      fish, 95
  Greek, 85–6
  green, with Saga Blue cheese, 86
  green and white summer, 83
  green bean and seared red onion,
    79–80
  lentil, 83–4
  mesclun, 86–8
  olive, 50
  pasta, parsley and orzo, 88
  pea, 88
  potato
    grilled, 89
    vinaigrette, 90

salads (*cont.*)
  scallop, 19
    marinated, 20
  seared red pepper, 88–9
  spinach
    with cheese dressing, 94
    wilted, 94
  spring, with warm shrimp, 46
  squid, with arugula, 105
  summer squash, 91–2
  tomato, 92
    warm, with grilled bread and
      goat cheese, 92–3
  wild rice and scallion, 301
  zucchini and pepper, 90–1
salmon, 223–7
  with artichoke mousse and tomato
    hollandaise, 242–3
  braised, leeks and, 231
  broiled
    on bed of warm potatoes, 234
    with coleslaw salad, 102–3
    with mustard-tarragon butter
      sauce, 234–5
  buying, 226
  cakes, with tomato-basil butter
    sauce, 231–3
  caviar, 225–6
  chowder, with corn, 74
  coulibiac, 243–7
  fisherman's eggs almost Benedict,
    241–2
  gravlaks, 14, 17
  grilled
    and asparagus with pasta,
      311–12
    with herb-and-caper vinai-
      grette, 111–13
    with Portuguese peas, 240–1
  hash, 230
  Lapsang souchong, 17
  lox, 225
  mesclun salad with, 87
  paillards, with parsley, sage, rose-
    mary, and thyme, 227–8
  poached
    with lentils and sun-dried
      tomato sauce, 217–19
    and scallops with ginger-lime
      butter sauce, 220–1
    whole, 219–20
  with potato crust, 230–1
  preparation, 226–7
  roasted
    with cucumber-dill sauce,
      235–6
    with prosciutto, 236–8
    with sautéed cabbage, 238

salmon (*cont.*)
  salad
    sweet-and-tart, with arugula,
      103–4
    in tomato flower, 103
  sautéed
    butterflied, 222
    with sweet red pepper com-
      pote, 228–9
  smoked, 225
    butter, 353
    in lettuce packets with sole,
      178–9
    melon with ham, lime, and,
      17–18
    toasts: with mustard-dill sauce,
      18; with sorrel, 38–9
    with vegetable pancakes, 40
  with sorrel sauce, 229–30
  steamed, on a bed of winter veg-
    etables, 216–17
  stock, 361
  storage, 226
  with tomato fondue, 233–4
  types of, 224–5
  yields, 227
  zucchini, with seafood mousse,
    238–40
salsa, 7–8
  green tomato, 225
  warm, 198–9
salsify pancakes, 42
Sanford, Thekla and Richard, 9,
  10
Sarvis, Shirley, 10
satay, shrimp, 271–3
sauce
  aïoli, 349
    warm, 146
  Américaine, 357–8
  basting, for bluefish, 123
  béchamel, 350
  butter
    ginger-lime, 220
    herb beurre blanc, 115, 118
    lemon, 357
    mustard-tarragon, 235
    tomato-basil, 232
    white, 114
  clam, white, 135–6
  cocktail, 21
  cream, 157
    aromatic vegetable, 193–4
    rosemary, 179
  Creole, 284
  cucumber-dill, 354
  egg, 354
  grape, sweet-and-hot, 43

sauce (*cont.*)
  hollandaise
    basic recipe, 356
    tomato, 342–3
  lobster, 357–8
  mignonette, 13–14
  mousseline, 356
  mustard-dill, 18
  parsley, 351
  peanut, 360
  Portugaise, 298
  sesame, 150–1
  shallot, crème fraîche, and dill,
    222
  sorrel, 229
  sour cream, 25–6
  Spanish, 128
  sweet pepper, 195
  tartar, 363
  tomato, 152
    with eggplant, cod sautéed
      with, 140
    fresh, basic recipe, 364
    hollandaise, 242–3
    marinara, 306
    Moroccan spice, 208
    muffuletta, 212
    orange, 264
    sun-dried, 218
  tonnato, 27
  velouté, 350
  white, 350
  yogurt, 30
sausage
  clams cataplana-style with, 133–5
  dandelion and lentil soup with, 58
  paella, 315–17
  pasta with smoked bluefish and,
    303
  peas with, 241–2
  pea soup with fish and, 61
  quahogs stuffed with aromatic
    vegetables and, 32
  scallops grilled with, 255
  shrimp with
    creole, 284
    gumbo, 283
  smoked fish fritters with, 155
scallion(s)
  braised, with peas, 332
  butter, 353
  halibut baked with radishes and,
    180–1
  and lobster stir-fry, 182
  scallops and bacon hors d'oeuvres
    with, 40
  soy marinade with, 121
  and wild rice salad, 301

scallop(s), 249–52
  au gratin, 258–9
  baked
    with leeks, 255–6
    with shallots, 39–40
  and bok choy soup, 75–6
  bourride with, 64
  broiled, with bacon, 40
  buying, 251
  ceviche, 19–20
  chowder, 74–5
  fish timbales with, 153
  fried, 257
  grilled, with green tomato salsa,
    254–5
  lobster Fra Diavolo with, 190
  mousseline, 259–60
  and mussel stew, 75
  paella, 315–17
  pasta with
    and artichokes, fettuccine,
      312–13
    with tomatoes, 314
  poached, with celery, 18–19
    salmon and, with ginger-lime
      butter sauce, 220–1
  preparation, 252
  Provençal, 253–4
  salad
    with chicory, 85
    mesclun, 88
  sautéed
    with apple-squash purée,
      247–8
    meunière, 253
    with vermouth-cream sauce,
      254
  scalloped, 257–8
  and shrimp
    chili, 281
    curry, 275
  smoked, Chinese cabbage and
    spinach salad with, 81
  soffritto, 258
  stir-fry, with shrimp and zucchini,
    256–7
  storage, 251–2
  types of, 250
  yields, 252
scampi, 263–4, 266
  Maltese, 275–6
scombroid poisoning, 216, 294, 367
scrod
  pan-fried, in an egg coating, 136
  sautéed, in fresh bread crumbs,
    136, 140
  see also cod; haddock
sea bass, *see* bass

seafood
  deviled, and artichoke ramekins,
    44–5
  grilled skewers, with sweet-and-
    hot grape sauce, 43–4
  tabbouleh, 28
sesame
  noodles, 276
  sauce, 150–1
  seeds, to toast, 91
shad, 261–2
  baked, with boiled asparagus, 260,
    262
  buying, 261
  preparation, 262
  roe, 261, 262
    sautéed, with bacon and bal-
      samic onions, 262–3
  storage, 261–2
  yields, 262
shallot(s)
  in mignonette sauce, 14
  olive, and red pepper topping, 222
  roasted, 338
  sauce, 229
    crème fraîche and dill, 222
  scallops sautéed with, 248
  and shrimp curry, 274–5
  swordfish and clams roasted with,
    298
shark, 294–5
  grilled skewers, with sweet-and-
    hot grape sauce, 43–4
shellfish
  microwaving, xvi
  safety guidelines, 366–8
  storage, xiv
  table, raw, 14
  vegetable soup with, 62
  see also clam(s); crab(s); lobster(s);
    mussels; oyster(s); scallop(s);
    shrimp
shrimp, 265–8
  allergy to, 268
  artichokes stuffed with, 29
  baked
    with escargot butter, 284–5
    with scallops and mushrooms,
      259
    with tomato concasse, 280
    with vegetable-bread topping,
      279–80
  black bean soup with, 54
  broiled
    Thai, with roasted sugar snap
      peas and sesame Chinese
      noodles, 276–8
    with tomato-orange sauce, 264

shrimp (*cont.*)
broth, 361
buying, 266–7
celeriac "rémoulade" with, 20–1
chili, 280–1
cocktail, 21–2
corn and yellow pepper chowder with, 57
Creole, 283–4
curry, with shallots, 274–5
deviled, and artichoke ramekins, 44–5
dip, 9
fish timbales with, 153
gazpacho with, 70
grilled, on a bed of cabbage and collard greens, 273–4
guacamole tostadas, 22
gumbo, 283
lobster stuffed with, 203
with lobster stuffing, 281–2
marinated, 23–4
    with onions and cilantro, 24
paella, 315–17
and pancetta skewers, 48
pasta with cucumbers and, 313
preparation, 268
risotto with tomatoes, squash, and, 314–15
salad
    asparagus, 80
    Chinese cabbage and spinach, 81
    corn, 82
    green bean and red onion, 80
    with green beans, 104–5
    with mustard-tarragon dressing, 104
    spring, 46
Samurai, with sesame–stir-fried spinach, 46–7
satay, 271–3
sautéed, with shallots and vermouth, 271
scampi, 263–4
    Maltese, 275–6
skewers
    in cilantro-lime marinade, 47–8
    with sweet-and-hot grape sauce, 43–4
sole topped with, 174
stir-fry
    with broccoli and garlic, 270–1
    with broccoli and snow peas, 269–70
    with scallops and zucchini, 256–7
storage, 267–8

shrimp (*cont.*)
tempura, 278–9
vegetable chowder with chicken and, 77
white beans with basil and, 48–9
yields, 268
side-by-side soup, 57
skipjack tuna, 293
snapper, 287–8
braised, with West Indian garlic and thyme sauce, 285
buying, 287
preparation, 288
roasted, with Swiss chard, 285–6
storage, 287–8
yields, 288
snow crab, 161
sockeye salmon, 224–5
soft-shell clams, *see* clam(s): soft-shell
soft-shell crabs, 161–2
cleaning, 163
sautéed, 157–9
sole, *see* Dover sole; flounder
sorrel
and leek pancakes, 42–3
smoked salmon toasts with, 38–9
soup
asparagus, 53
black bean, 53–4
bourride, 63–4
broccoli de rabe and potato, 54–5
cabbage, 56
cauliflower, 55
cucumber-yogurt, 55
dandelion and lentil, 57–8
fish, 63–77
    bluefish and Chinese cabbage, 64
    bourride, 63–4
    cod, coconut and cilantro, 68
    cod and winter vegetables, 68–9
    garden vegetables, 62
    lobster and striped bass, 71–3
    Straight Wharf, 76–7
mushroom, 48–9
onion, 60
pumpkin, 59–60
scallop and bok choy, 75–6
side-by-side, 57
split pea, with celeriac, 60–1
squash and chestnut with caviar, 62–3
vegetable, 61–2
    with clams, 135
see also chowder
sour cream
and mustard dressing, 101
sauce, 25–6

Southern-style pan-fried scrod, 136, 140
soy marinade, 120–1
with sake, 295
spaetzle, 362
spaghetti squash
with clams, garlic, and parsley, 304–5
sunflower seed–crusted striped bass with, 115, 118
with white clam sauce, 135–6
Spanish sauce, 128
spinach
to blanch and chop, 338
and bluefish soup, 64
braised, 338–9
and cheese squares, 50
creamed, 338
fisherman's eggs almost Benedict with, 241–2
fish timbales on bed of, 153
haddock fillets stuffed with, 152
and lobster
    au gratin, 207
    pasta timbales, 309
oyster stew with, 75
salad, 88
    with cheese dressing, 94
    with Chinese cabbage and ginger, 81
    with lettuce and smoked bluefish, 95
    with warm salmon, 88
    with warm shrimp, 46–7
    wilted, 94
scallop and mussel stew with, 75
scallops baked on bed of, 260
    with mushrooms, 259
sesame–stir-fried, shrimp Samurai with, 46–7
and sole
    Florentine, 178
    paupiettes, 176–7
to wash, 338
wilted, with garlic and lemon, 338
spiny lobster, 183–4
spreads
chopped egg and dill, 7
see also dips
spring salad with warm shrimp, 46
squash
and apple purée, 247
flounder baked with, 176
"pillows," with fresh sage, 340–1
risotto with shrimp, tomatoes, and, 314–15
soup, with chestnuts and caviar, 62–3

squash (*cont.*)
  spaghetti, *see* spaghetti squash
  summer
    in mixed grill, 344–5
    pasta with shrimp and, 313
    roasted, 338
    salad, 91–2
    sautéed, 339–40
    see also zucchini
squid, 106–7
  buying, 106
  to clean, 107
  cooking methods, 107
  frozen, 106
  lobster Fra Diavolo with, 190
  paella with, 317
  pasta with clams, garlic, parsley, and, 304
  salad, warm with arugula, 105
  sautéed, 49
  and shrimp chili, 281
  storage, 107
  types of, 106
  yields, 107
steamers, *see* clam(s): soft-shell
steelhead, 225
stew
  cod and leek, 149
  lobster, 73–4
    and chicken, 196–7
  monkfish and eggplant, 214–15
  okra and tomato, 330
  oyster, 75
  scallop and mussel, 75
  shrimp gumbo, 283
stock
  fish, 355
  lobster, 358–9
  salmon, 361
  shrimp, 361
stone crab, 161
striped bass, *see* bass
strudel, crab and cabbage, 307
succotash
  fava or lima bean, 341–2
  shell bean, 320
Sweeney, Kep, 115
sweet potatoes, roasted slices, 342
Swiss chard
  and bluefish soup, 64
  and cheese squares, 49–50
  fish timbales on bed of, 153
  lobster consommé with, 359
  sautéed, 286
  scallops baked on bed of, 260
swordfish, 291–2
  broiled, with fresh pepper relish, 289

swordfish (*cont.*)
  buying, 291–2
  grilled
    with eggplant, 290, 295
    skewers, with sweet-and-hot grape sauce, 43–4
  with mushrooms and cream, 296–8
  with Portugaise sauce, 298–9
  preparation, 292
  roast, with clams, cherry tomatoes, and olives, 296
  sautéed, 286, 288–9
  storage, 292
  tonnato, with lemon thyme, 27
  yields, 292

tabbouleh, 28
tamara dip, 8
tapenade, 8–9
tapenade spread, 124
  bluefish baked with, 124
tapenade topping, 34
  grilled eggplant with, 34
tapeworms, 367–8
tarragon
  cream sauce, 180
  -mustard butter sauce, 235
  -mustard dressing, 104
tart
  onion and anchovy, 37–8
  shell, basic recipe, 362–3
tartar sauce, 363
tartoor, 150–1
Taylor, Rodman, 250–1
tea leaves, salmon marinated with, 17
tempura, 278–9
terrine, fish, 25–7
tetrazzini, lobster, 307–8
thresher shark, 294
timbales
  fish, with curried cabbage and tomato sauce, 152–3
  gray sole and spinach paupiettes, 176–7
  pasta, of lobster, leeks, and pro-sciutto, 308–9
toasts
  anchovy, 3–4
  brandade, 6
  with shellfish butter, 9
  with smoked salmon
    and mustard-dill sauce, 18
    and sorrel, 38–9
tomatillos, salsa with, 8
tomato(es)
  -basil butter sauce, 232
  broiled, with herb-crumb top-ping, 342

tomato(es) (*cont.*)
  concasse, shrimp baked with, 280
  escabeche with, 10
  fondue
    basic recipe, 363–4
    with capers, 164–5
    citrus, 364
    fried bass on bed of, 119–20
    salmon with, 233–4
  herb mayonnaise in, 12
  leeks braised with, 329
  lobster with, 191–2
    cold, 100–1
    roast, with basil, 199–200
  mayonnaise, 164
  and okra stew, 330
  pasta with
    and clams, garlic, and parsley, 304
    and scallops, 314
    and shrimp, 314
  peeled and seeded, 363
  pie, 45–6
  ratatouille, 326–8
  risotto with shrimp, squash, and, 314–15
  salad, 92
    cherry tomato and lobster, 99
    with crabmeat and pesto cream, 97–8
    green bean and red onion, 80
    salmon salad in tomato flower, 103
    warm, with grilled bread and goat cheese, 92–3
  salsa, 7–8
    green, 255
  sauce, 152
    bluefish sautéed with, 130
    with eggplant, cod sautéed with, 140
    fresh, basic recipe, 364
    hollandaise, 242–3
    lobster Fra Diavolo with, 190
    marinara, 306
    Moroccan spice, 208
    muffuletta, 212
    orange, 264
    sun-dried, 218
    swordfish and clams roasted with olives and, 296
  shrimp stuffed with, 282
  sole with
    coulis, 173–4
    and potatoes, 171
  stuffed with tapenade, 9

tomato(es) (*cont.*)
  sun-dried
    butter, 353
    scallops mousseline with, 260
tomcod, 138
tonnato, swordfish, 27
topneck clams, 131
  yields, 132
tostadas, guacamole shrimp, 22
trout, salmon, 225
tuna, 292–4
  buying, 293–4
  grilled
    with herb-and-caper vinai-
      grette, 111–13
    with macadamia pesto, 299
    with wild rice and scallion salad,
      300–1
  preparation, 294
  salad
    with cauliflower, 109
    with green beans and red pep-
      pers, 108–9
    Niçoise, 107–8
  storage, 294
  types of, 293
  yields, 294
turbot, 170
turkey, pumpkin soup with, 59

vegetable(s)
  aromatic
    cream sauce, 193–4
    quahogs stuffed with, 31–2
    scallops with, 258
    -bread topping, shrimp baked
      with, 279–80

vegetable(s) (*cont.*)
  chowder
    Manhattan clam, 65
    with shrimp and chicken, 77
  codfish balls with, 154
  codfish hash with, 144
  crêpes, 202
  drunken, mahi mahi with,
    215–16
  flounder baked with, 176
  leftover, cabbage soup with, 56
  lentils with, 218–19
  lobster consommé with, 359
  mixed grill, 344–5
  salads, *see* salads
  salmon steamed on bed of,
    216–17
  scallop and mussel stew with, 75
  shrimp stuffed with, 282
  soup, 61–2
    with clams cataplana-style, 135
    with fish, 63–77
    tempura, 278–9
  tian, 344
  see also specific vegetables
velouté sauce, 350
vinaigrette
  basic recipe, 365
  herb-and-caper, 111–13
  warm, fish with, 145–6
Voorhees, Eugenie, 314

Warner, William, 160
Wasserman, Norma, 314
water chestnut and bacon hors
  d'oeuvres, 40
watercress, salade Niçoise with, 108

Westphal, Helga, 99
White, Jasper, 112, 216
white butter sauce, 114
white pepper dressing, 11
white sauce, basic (béchamel), 350
whiting
  broiled, 149
  fried, 145
wild rice and scallion salad, 301
Williams, Claude, 285

Yakitori dipping sauce for lobster,
  198
yellowfin tuna, 293
yogurt
  -cucumber soup, 55
  sauce, 30

Zuccaro, Paul, xii
zucchini
  escabeche with, 10
  grilled, Corfu, 50–1
  marinated, 342–3
  in mixed grill, 344–5
  pancakes, 43
  pasta with shrimp and, 313
  ratatouille, 326–8
  salad
    with peppers, 90–1
    with summer squash, 91–2
  salmon, with seafood mousse,
    238–40
  sautéed, 344
  "scales," poached salmon with, 220
  stir-fry, with scallops and shrimp,
    256–7
  tian, 343–4

A NOTE ON THE TYPE

The text of this book was set on the Macintosh in Bembo, a facsimile of
a typeface cut by one of the most celebrated goldsmiths of his time,
Francesco Griffo, for Aldus Manutius, the Venetian printer, in 1495. The
face was named for Pietro Bembo, the author of the small treatise entitled
De Aetna in which it first appeared. Through the research of Stanley
Morison, it is now acknowledged that all old-face type designs up to the
time of William Caslon can be traced to the Bembo cut.

The present-day version of Bembo was introduced by the Monotype
Corporation, London, in 1929. Sturdy, well balanced, and finely propor-
tioned, Bembo is a face of rare beauty and great legibility in all of its sizes.

COLOR SEPARATIONS BY NORTH MARKET STREET GRAPHICS,
LANCASTER, PENNSYLVANIA

PRINTED AND BOUND BY R. R. DONNELLEY & SONS,
WILLARD, OHIO

DESIGNED BY BARBARA BALCH